THE ROUTLEDGE COMPANION TO LITERATURE AND SCIENCE

With forty-four newly commissioned articles from an international cast of leading scholars, *The Routledge Companion to Literature and Science* traces the network of connections among literature, science, technology, mathematics, and medicine. Divided into three main sections, this volume:

- links diverse literatures to scientific disciplines from Artificial Intelligence to Thermodynamics
- surveys current theoretical and disciplinary approaches from Animal Studies to Semiotics
- traces the history and culture of literature and science from Greece and Rome to postmodernism.

Ranging from classical origins and modern revolutions to current developments in cultural science studies and the posthumanities, this indispensable volume offers a comprehensive resource for undergraduates, postgraduates, and researchers.

With authoritative, accessible, and succinct treatments of the sciences in their literary dimensions and cultural frameworks, here is the essential guide to this vibrant area of study.

Contributors: Stacy Alaimo, David Amigoni, Neil Badmington, Søren Brier, John Bruni, Gordon Calleja, Ivan Callus, Bruce Clarke, Paul Cobley, Lucinda Cole, T. Hugh Crawford, Emma Gee, Mark B.N. Hansen, Stefan Herbrechter, Noah Heringman, John Johnston, Vicki Kirby, Kenneth J. Knoespel, Jay Labinger, Thomas Lamarre, Melissa M. Littlefield, Ira Livingston, Robert Markley, Maureen McNeil, Colin Milburn, Mark S. Morrisson, Richard Nash, Alfred Nordmann, Stephen A. Norwick, Robert Pepperell, Arkady Plotnitsky, Virginia Richter, Judith Roof, Brian Rotman, George Rousseau, Arielle Saiber, Henning Schmidgen, Philipp Schweighauser, Sabine Sielke, Alvin Snider, Susan M. Squier, Joseph Tabbi, Dirk Vanderbeke, and Lisa Yaszek.

Bruce Clarke is the Paul Whitfield Horn Professor of Literature and Science at Texas Tech University, and a past president of the Society for Literature, Science, and the Arts.

Manuela Rossini is Scientific Coordinator of the Graduate School of the Humanities at the University of Bern, and Executive Director of the Society for Literature, Science, and the Arts Europe.

THE ROUTLEDGE COMPANION TO LITERATURE AND SCIENCE

Edited by
Bruce Clarke with Manuela Rossini

LONDON AND NEW YORK

First edition published 2011
by Routledge

First published in paperback 2012
by Routledge
2 Park Square, Milton Park, Abingdon, Oxon OX14 4RN

Simultaneously published in the USA and Canada
by Routledge
711 Third Avenue, New York, NY 10017

Routledge is an imprint of the Taylor & Francis Group, an informa business

British Library Cataloguing in Publication Data
A catalogue record for this book is available from the British Library

Library of Congress Cataloging in Publication Data
Routledge companion to literature and science / edited by Bruce Clarke with
Manuela Rossini. – 1st ed.
    p. cm.
Includes bibliographical references and index.
  1. Literature and science. I. Clarke, Bruce, 1950– II. Rossini, Manuela.
  PN55.R68 2010
  801–dc22
                  2009052826

ISBN: 978-0-415-49525-7 (hbk)
ISBN: 978-0-415-50959-6 (pbk)
ISBN: 978-0-203-84873-9 (ebk)

Typeset in Goudy
by Taylor & Francis Books

Printed and bound in Great Britain by
CPI Antony Rowe, Chippenham, Wiltshire

CONTENTS

CONTENTS

CONTENTS

CONTENTS

FIGURES

CONTRIBUTORS

Stacy Alaimo is Associate Professor of English at the University of Texas at Arlington, where she co-chairs the President's Sustainability Committee. Her publications include *Undomesticated Ground*, *Material Feminisms*, and *Bodily Natures*.

David Amigoni is Professor of Victorian Literature at Keele University and the author of *Colonies, Cults and Evolution: Literature, Science and Culture in Nineteenth-Century Writing*. He works on the relationship between nineteenth-century literature and the life sciences.

Neil Badmington, Reader in English Literature at Cardiff University, is the author of *Alien Chic* and *Hitchcock's Magic*, and editor of six collections, including *Posthumanism*, *Posthuman Conditions*, *Derridanimals*, and *The Routledge Critical and Cultural Theory Reader*.

Søren Brier is a Professor of the Semiotics of Information, Cognition, and Communication at Copenhagen Business School. He is the author of *Cybersemiotics: Why Information is Not Enough*, and the editor of the journal *Cybernetics and Human Knowing*.

John Bruni is Assistant Professor of English at the South Dakota School of Mines & Technology. He has published on the evolutionary narratives of Edith Wharton, Jack London, and Henry Adams.

Gordon Calleja is Assistant Professor and Head of the Center for Computer Games Research at the IT-University of Copenhagen. He teaches game analysis and theory at the post-graduate level. His research focuses on player experience, game ontology, and narrative.

Ivan Callus is Associate Professor and Head of the Department of English at the University of Malta. His teaching and research are in the areas of contemporary narrative, literary theory, and posthumanism.

Bruce Clarke, Professor of Literature and Science at Texas Tech University, is a past president of the Society for Literature, Science, and the Arts. He is the author or co-editor of eight books, including *Energy Forms*, *Posthuman Metamorphosis*, and *Emergence and Embodiment*.

Paul Cobley is Reader in Communications at London Metropolitan University. He is the author of *Introducing Semiotics* and *Narrative*, and editor of *The Communication Theory Reader*, *The Routledge Companion to Semiotics*, and *Realism for the 21st Century: A John Deely Reader*.

Lucinda Cole is Associate Professor of English at the University of Southern Maine. She has published articles on many aspects of early modern culture. Her current book project pertains to the relationships among animals, natural philosophy, and theories of putrefaction.

T. Hugh Crawford is Associate Professor at the Georgia Institute of Technology, and a past president of the Society for Literature, Science, and the Arts. He is the author of *Modernism, Medicine and William Carlos Williams*, and former editor of *Configurations*.

Emma Gee, Lecturer in Latin and Classical Studies at the University of St Andrews, has published widely on Latin and Greek literature and ancient astronomy. Her present project is *Mapping the Underworld in Greece and Rome*, on "scientific" ideas in the ancient afterlife.

Mark B.N. Hansen is Professor of Literature at Duke University. He is the author of *Embodying Technesis, New Philosophy for New Media*, and *Bodies in Code: Interfaces with Digital Media*, and the co-editor of *Emergence and Embodiment* and *Critical Terms for Media Studies*.

Stefan Herbrechter teaches in the School of Art and Design at Coventry University. His recent co-edited collections include *Critical Posthumanisms, Cy-Borges: Memories of the Posthuman in the Work of Jorge Luis Borges*, and *The Matrix in Theory*.

Noah Heringman teaches English at the University of Missouri. He has published *Romantic Science: The Literary Forms of Natural History* and *Romantic Rocks, Aesthetic Geology*, and is at work on *Sciences of Antiquity*, on eighteenth-century antiquarianism and natural history.

John Johnston is Professor of English and Comparative Literature at Emory University. He is the author of *Carnival of Repetition, Information Multiplicity*, and *The Allure of Machinic Life*, and the editor of a collection of essays by Friedrich Kittler, *Literature, Media, Information Systems*.

Vicki Kirby works in the School of Social Sciences and International Studies at the University of New South Wales. Her books include *Telling Flesh: The Substance of the Corporeal, Judith Butler: Live Theory*, and *Quantum Anthropologies: Life at Large*.

Kenneth J. Knoespel, Professor in the School of Literature, Communication and Culture at Georgia Tech, works on northern European cultural history. He has taught at the University of Uppsala and the Russian Academy of Sciences in St. Petersburg.

Jay Labinger, Administrator of the Beckman Institute at Caltech, an inorganic chemist by training, researches organometallic chemistry and catalysis, as well as literary and cultural aspects of science. He is co-editor of *The One Culture?: A Conversation about Science*.

Thomas Lamarre teaches East Asian Studies and Art History and Communications Studies at McGill University. He has published essays and books dealing with the history of media, technology, and perception, including *The Anime Machine: A Media Theory of Animation*.

Melissa M. Littlefield is Assistant Professor in the Departments of English and of Kinesiology and Community Health at the University of Illinois, Urbana-Champaign. Her work has appeared in *Science, Technology and Human Values* and is forthcoming in *Neurology and Modernity*.

Ira Livingston is Professor and Chair of Humanities and Media Studies at Pratt Institute. He is the author of *Arrow of Chaos: Romanticism and Postmodernity* and *Between Science and Literature: An Introduction to Autopoetics*, and the co-editor of *Posthuman Bodies*.

Robert Markley is Romano Professorial Scholar in the Department of English at the University of Illinois. His books include *Fallen Languages: Crises of Representation in Newtonian England*, *Dying Planet: Mars in Science and the Imagination*, and *The Far East and the English Imagination, 1600–1730*.

Maureen McNeil is Professor of Women's Studies and Cultural Studies based in the Centre for Gender and Women's Studies and the Centre for Economic and Social Aspects of Genomics, Lancaster University, and the author of *Feminist Cultural Studies of Science and Technology*.

Colin Milburn is Associate Professor of English and a member of the Science and Technology Studies program at the University of California, Davis. He is the author of *Nanovision: Engineering the Future*.

Mark S. Morrisson is Professor of English and Science, Technology, and Society at Pennsylvania State University. His books include *Modern Alchemy: Occultism and the Emergence of Atomic Theory* and *The Public Face of Modernism: Little Magazines, Audiences, and Reception*.

Richard Nash is Professor of English at Indiana University and President of the Society for Literature, Science, and the Arts, 2010–12. He is the author of *Wild Enlightenment* and numerous essays on literature, science, and culture in eighteenth-century England.

Alfred Nordmann teaches Philosophy of Science at Darmstadt Technical University and the University of South Carolina. The author of *Wittgenstein's Tractatus: An Introduction*, he is interested in questions of representation and the constitution of objects in technoscience.

Stephen A. Norwick is Professor of Geology in the Department of Environmental Studies and Planning at Sonoma State University. He teaches soil science, water technology, computer modeling, natural resources, natural hazards, and environmental literature.

Robert Pepperell is an artist and writer who has exhibited widely and published several books, including *The Posthuman Condition: Consciousness Beyond the Brain*. He is currently Professor of Fine Art at Cardiff School of Art and Design.

Arkady Plotnitsky is Professor of English and the Director of the Theory and Cultural Studies Program at Purdue University. His most recent book is *Epistemology and Probability: Bohr, Heisenberg, Schrödinger, and the Nature of Quantum-Theoretical Thinking*.

Virginia Richter, Professor in Modern English Literature at the University of Bern, Switzerland, has published widely on literature and science, Darwinism, animals in literature, and gender studies. Her monograph on "Literature after Darwin" is forthcoming in 2010.

Judith Roof is Professor of English at Rice University and the author of *The Poetics of DNA*.

Manuela Rossini, td-net for Transdisciplinary Research (Swiss Academies of Arts and Sciences) and Institute of Advanced Study in the Humanities and Social Sciences (University of Bern), is general editor of the series *Experimental Practices: Technoscience, Art, Literature, Philosophy*.

Brian Rotman is Distinguished Humanities Professor in the Department of Comparative Studies, Ohio State University. His books include *Signifying Nothing: The Semiotics of Zero*, and *Becoming Beside Ourselves: The Alphabet, Ghosts, and Distributed Human Being*.

George Rousseau professes Modern History at Oxford University. He is the author of *Framing and Imagining Disease in Cultural History* and *Nervous Acts*. His 1981 article, "Literature and Medicine: The State of the Field," is often said to have invigorated this field.

Arielle Saiber, Associate Professor of Italian at Bowdoin College, has published on medieval and Renaissance Italian literature, mathematics, advice manuals, and typography. She is currently writing a book on the dialogue between mathematics and literature in Renaissance Italy.

Henning Schmidgen is a research scholar at the Max Planck-Institute for the History of Science in Berlin. He works on Deleuze, Canguilhem, and biological time, and is a co-founder of the Virtual Laboratory on the history of experimental life sciences.

Philipp Schweighauser is Assistant Professor and Head of American and General Literatures at the University of Basel. He is the author of *The Noises of American Literature, 1890–1985*, and co-editor of *Teaching Nineteenth-Century American Poetry*.

Sabine Sielke, Director of the North American Studies Program at Bonn University and author of *Fashioning the Female Subject* and *Reading Rape*, currently works on questions at the crossroads of cultural studies and the (cognitive) sciences.

Alvin Snider teaches English at the University of Iowa and is editor of *Philological Quarterly*.

Susan M. Squier, Julia Gregg Brill Professor of Women's Studies, English, and STS at Pennsylvania State University, is the author of *Liminal Lives: Imagining the Human at the Frontiers of Medicine*, and *Babies in Bottles: Twentieth-Century Visions of Reproductive Technology*.

Joseph Tabbi is the author of *Cognitive Fictions* and *Postmodern Sublime: Technology and American Writing from Mailer to Cyberpunk*, and co-editor of *Paper Empire: William Gaddis and the World System* and *Reading Matters: Narrative in the New Media Ecology*.

Dirk Vanderbeke teaches English literature at the University of Jena, Germany, and, as a guest professor, at the University of Zielona Góra, Poland. He has published on Joyce, Pynchon, science and literature, self-similarity, comics, and vampires.

Lisa Yaszek, Associate Professor at the Georgia Institute of Technology and President of the Science Fiction Research Association, publishes on science fiction as cultural history. Her most recent book is *Galactic Suburbia: Recovering Women's Science Fiction*.

PREFACE

It is commonly thought that the divorce between literature and science became final a while back, and since then they have been permanently settled into separate and incommunicative professional cultures, literature in its cozy academic bungalow and science in its flashy mansion on the hill. In 1959, British scientist and novelist C.P. Snow delivered his famous Rede Lecture, "The Two Cultures," providing a durable catch-phrase for and launching a raft of further commentaries on this intellectual separation. However, as contributor Emma Gee rightly remarks to begin her chapter on Greece and Rome, "Snow's opposition between literature and science may seem more naive to us than to his audience of 1959; to the Greeks and Romans it would have been incomprehensible. The concept of antipathy between representatives of the two poles, as it operates today, was unavailable to ancient thinkers." And fifty years after Snow's lecture, we no longer see as stark a split between literature and science. To some extent this more nuanced view is the result of efforts by scholars, such as those gathered in this volume, dedicated to address and overcome, at least on the side of literary knowledge and scholarship, the more glaring deficits of humanistic fluency in scientific matters. But from both sides of this divide, efforts have been made to develop finer-grained understandings of the interrelations of natural research and cultural discourse, of scientific theory and experiment on the one hand, and of literary meditation, fictionalization, and popularization on the other.

Since the Renaissance, humanistic letters in the West have been framed by worldviews that we now, since the mid-nineteenth century, call "scientific" – for instance, the Copernican model of the solar system. At the same time, what we now call "scientists" have inevitably worked with models of reality formed or informed by what we now call the "humanities" – for instance, the literature and philosophy of "the Enlightenment." If modern knowledge confronts schisms, it is nothing so pat or "naive" as a two-cultures divide. Nonetheless, to frame the situation in Jean-François Lyotard's idiom, it is the case that there is no longer a credible metanarrative that could bind the current profusion of academic cultures and their specialized disciplines into an ordered hierarchy, let alone a unity. The rift Snow observed at mid-twentieth century was in fact an early diagnosis of our postmodern condition. "Two cultures" marks a popular recognition of what contemporary systems theory terms the operational differentiation of modern social sub-systems. In other words, knowledge production in the modern world increasingly proceeds through the specialized or technical languages that enclose separate disciplinary spheres. Under these conditions, perhaps ironically, cross-disciplinary contact has had to become a discipline in its own right.

The field of literature and science has come about precisely as a scholarly response to these social conditions at the interface of scholarly discourse and literary production, academic and popular communication. Indeed, the contents of this *Routledge Companion* present a range of dynamic contact zones, fields of intensive cognitive and conceptual encounters between the humanities and the natural sciences in general, and between literature and various domains of science in particular. The literature and science scholarship gathered here has been authored largely (but not exclusively) by humanities scholars – literature specialists, historians, cultural theorists, students of media and the fine arts, and communications scholars – intent on addressing "two-cultures" disparities and opportunities within their home disciplines. But many of them are also intent on complicating the issues that attach to disciplinary boundaries.

For instance, consider – as viewed from an influential perspective within literature and science scholarship, that of French sociologist of science Bruno Latour – the common separation of "science" from "technology." Undoubtedly there are proper distinctions to be made between them. One can say that the sciences seek to know natural objects while the technologies aim to make artifacts that are instrumental for cultural purposes. It is nevertheless the case that neither practice can be adequately contemplated in the absence of the other. One is always already concerned, in Latour's coinage, with *technoscience*. Only technological artifacts allow the sciences to construe natural objects scientifically, and this inscribes the objects that science describes (and most certainly, those it creates) with significant cultural traces. Similarly, the discipline of literature and science theorizes texts as technologies of communication and meaning embedded in some material medium of discourse or narration. Books and textual media are matrices for the formal and historical interplay of cultural inscriptions. Machines and their products – material and textual artifacts – are complexly legible as allegories of technoscience. A recent work of literature-and-science pioneer Katherine Hayles is titled *Writing Machines*, and this redescription of the literary text in the digital era follows directly from the postmodern confrontation of literature and science. In sum, the discussion of technologies is broadly dispersed throughout this *Companion* tracking the intersections of literatures and sciences.

All of these counter-trends toward transdisciplinary convergences-in-difference between the discursive, technical, and natural disciplines have been accelerating for several decades. Marking a decisive moment of consolidation in the evolving scholarly relations of literature and science, the *Routledge Companion to Literature and Science* aims, first, to provide undergraduate majors and graduate students across the curriculum with access to the most advanced thinking at the nexus of literature and science, and second, to document the range and diversity of this work for the use of professional scholars. However, this is not a "top-down" edition: except for length, we did not issue or enforce comprehensive editorial constraints. Each author was encouraged to contribute a chapter reflecting his or her predilection and special expertise while representing their usual focus and discursive style.

Taking literature in English as a paradigmatic but not exclusive example, Part I highlights specific scientific specializations with regard to their literary connections. Part II details the current range of disciplinary and theoretical approaches in and around literature and science scholarship. Part III approaches the divisions of scholarly labor in literature and science along the axes of world-historical units and global cultural location. This wide-angled approach makes the *Routledge Companion to Literature and Science* an especially useful guide and point of orientation for diverse departments and programs in literature and related discursive and cultural disciplines. It is also part of the ongoing growth of larger networks for cross-disciplinary teaching and research.

We also see this *Companion* as an important resource for researchers in science and technology studies, cultural studies, and narrative studies; for fields like narrative ethics and narrative medicine, already institutionalized in Medical Humanities programs; for programs pursuing a transdisciplinary agenda, involving non-academic expertise; for science journalists and creative writers; and last but not least, for scientists themselves. There has been an ongoing imperative to turn literary studies toward cultural studies, while maintaining a strong focus on literature as an important medium and form of cultural production. This tendency has been accompanied by a widening of the terms "literature" and "text" to refer to the narrative nature of all writing, including scientific writing, and the concomitant emergence of a "poetics of knowledge." Moreover, the explicit encouragement, if not enforcement, of inter- and transdisciplinarity has also led to more integrative projects where literature has been joined by the fine and media arts as partakers in discussions about developments in technology, medicine, and science.

Our readers may consult the *Routledge Companion to Literature and Science* for detailed overviews of how various writers, theoreticians, and disciplines at large have conceptualized and dealt with the coevolutionary dependencies among literature, science, technology, mathematics, and medicine. While science fiction has recently increased in cultural importance and cachet, for some centuries now canonical and mainstream literary writers have been seriously engaged with the sciences, spreading as well as questioning constructions of scientific knowledge. Literature and its scholarship are also formidable forms of knowledge production and key contributors to the episteme of a culture. At the same time, here scientists as well can learn more of their own disciplines' cultural histories, for instance, the many ways that their works have been appropriated and popularized or criticized through literary texts and so rendered productive of further social effects. For anyone needing authoritative, accessible, and succinct treatments of particular scientific disciplines in their literary dimensions, or of contemporary theoretical paradigms that engage the sciences within wider cultural frameworks, the *Routledge Companion to Literature and Science* will be a valuable resource.

Part I
LITERATURES AND SCIENCES

One hears occasionally that "Science" has made a new discovery or that, "according to science," this or that social policy or form of personal hygiene is to be preferred over another. Unlike German usage, which calls all scholarly disciplines "sciences" (*Wissenschaften*), then stipulating further between *Naturwissenschaften* (the natural sciences) and *Geisteswissenschaften* (the humanities), "science" took on a more specialized application in English. Perhaps this bias or restriction also helped to obscure how science in the singular, with or without a capital S, has always been a bit of a misnomer. Despite whatever methodological regularities may apply, the singularity of Science is a nominal idealization, a handy abstraction. Students of literature and science, already trained to dissect such linguistic formations, have kicked the habit of referring to "Science," or its reflexive variant, "science itself," as a monolithic enterprise or singular practice. In his chapter on Japan in Part III, Thomas Lamarre notes how "those who wish to stress the impact of the sciences on the formation of modern societies tend to posit a unified, almost deterministic historical force, whether their intent is to extol science or to rue its excesses." The drive for a unitary Science does not necessarily derive from scientists themselves; it can also come from certain kinds of historiography or social commentary. Lamarre continues: "Yet we get a better sense of the efficacy and impact of the modern sciences when we think in terms of specific fields of rationality rather than a massive overarching rationalization or modernization."

Students of literature and science need to become adept in the specificities of the various sciences – their separate if variously interrelated histories, the particularities of their disciplinary objects, their different schools of thought, and the range of issues and debates that roil their immediate ranks. A decisive opening move for our interdisciplinary and transdisciplinary investigations is to gain clarity both on the current framework of disciplinary distinctions within the sciences, and on the wider histories that render them mobile and relative to specific times and places. For instance, contributor Noah Heringman notes that "Romantic science was prediscipinary. ... By attending to *pre*disciplinarity we can see that there were in fact multiple 'ways of knowing' and that the shift to modern disciplinarity was neither sudden nor uniform nor (even now) complete." In addition, innovative approaches in literature and science place transdisciplinary pressures on the sciences at hand. For instance, Arkady Plotnitsky's chapter on Psychoanalysis does not rehearse yet again the history or terminology of that discipline, but rather proceeds directly to a position of post-Kantian philosophical mediation between Sigmund Freud's orientation toward biology and Jacques Lacan's orientation toward mathematical physics, in order to rethink the relations among science, literature, art, and the Real.

Part I sets forward the primary sciences as discrete disciplines, but also subdivides or supplements a number of them. For instance, there are chapters on both Physics and one of its sub-disciplines especially rich in literary traffic, Thermodynamics; on Biology, but also on Ecology, Evolution, and Genetics; on Chemistry, but also on its historically important precursor, Alchemy; on Geology, and also on its significant current spin-off, Climate Science. Other chapters in Part I range from classical disciplines, such as Mathematics and Medicine, to modern and contemporary amalgamations of discrete scientific strands. One might call these *synthetic* disciplines. Integrating both scientific and technological developments into powerful new formations, these newer "fields of rationality" have already produced profound cultural and creative consequences: Artificial Intelligence and Artificial Life, Chaos and Complexity Science, Cognitive Science, Cybernetics, Information Theory, Nanotechnology, Psychoanalysis, and Systems Theory.

This more complex tableau of scientific disciplinary differences enables one to think more precisely about their connections to matters of *literary* consequence. For instance, certain sciences are more conducive to or apt for literary treatment than others. Biology is especially favored in that many of its objects of study – such as animals – yield easily to sympathetic identification, and reside at or near the human scale of things. Contributor Sabine Sielke adds: "The biosciences' growing cultural visibility and prestige is partly due to the fact that they can be narrativized more easily than mathematics and physics." As often as not, the literature in "literature and science" will come forward, as one would expect, as literary works – poems, novels, plays, songs, or scriptures – significantly inflected by ideas or images we now call scientific. Sketching the prehistory of Nanotechnology, Colin Milburn comments that "In the early decades of the twentieth century, a wave of stories depicting molecules, atoms, and subatomic particles as worlds unto themselves flooded the literary marketplace." And Stacy Alaimo points out how the study of ecology and literature could "include all cultures, all time periods, and all sorts of texts, including oral literatures and ceremonies (such as Shalako, the Zuni world renewal ritual)."

Matters of literary consequence will vary according not only to scientific distinctions but also to the different phases of the "literary" – for instance, as discourses of literary criticism in its commerce with scientific concepts, or as the literatures canonized or produced by philosophical, theoretical, popular-scientific, or other non-fictional fields. Alaimo continues that, with regard to the literature and science of ecology, "It would draw not only upon the disciplines of literary studies, ecology, science, and science studies, but also anthropology, sociology, political theory, history, cultural studies, and postcolonial studies." Similarly, Jay Labinger suggests that "We might even consider the origins of chemistry as primarily literary, not scientific, since the core concept of atomic theory was initially expounded by the ancients (Democritus, Epicurus, Lucretius, etc.) with little if any appeal to observational (let alone experimental) support." And as Ira Livingston writes on Chaos and Complexity Theory, "Part of the conversion to chaos involves learning to see structures not as structures but as systems, events in process. This recognition is part of what makes chaos and complexity theory full partners with poststructuralist theory generally." We see, too, that the discourse of literature and science has broken another habit, that of appealing to Literature with a capital L. There are literatures and there are sciences, and the range of scholarly interests in their interconnections derives from this double manifold of significant differences.

1

AI AND ALIFE

John Johnston

I

What is life, and what makes human life unique? With the rise of the life sciences and Darwin's theory of evolution by natural selection in the nineteenth century, new answers to these questions were proposed that were deeply at odds with traditional understandings and beliefs. With the advent in the twentieth century of new, life-altering technologies like genetic engineering, and life-simulating sciences like Artificial Life (ALife), these questions became even more insistent. Moreover, after World War II, efforts to build fast, intelligent machines and the subsequent development of the computer made the assumption of human intellectual superiority seem uncertain and sure to be challenged, especially since the new science of Artificial Intelligence seemed to lead inexorably to the construction of superhuman machine intelligence. Indeed, both ALife and Artificial Intelligence (AI) dramatically encouraged the thought that the opposition between the natural and the artificial, the born and the made – an opposition dating back to that of *phusis* versus *technē* in ancient Greek culture – was no longer so hard and fast, and certainly not inevitable. Yet this philosophical conundrum was hardly the central issue or worry. Rather, it was the nagging possibility that henceforth the evolutionary dynamic might begin to act on a biosphere soon active with non-natural life forms and that its crowning achievement – namely humanity itself – might eventually be displaced and superseded by its own technical invention. In short, many feared that the future would be determined by some cyborgian, post-biological form of the posthuman, or that the human species might be eclipsed altogether as evolution's torch of life and intelligence passed to its artificial progeny.

It was inevitable, therefore, that the possibilities of both ALife and AI would begin to be explored, variously and even idiosyncratically, by literary writers. Here, "ALife" will simply refer to new and non-natural forms of life brought into existence through external and technical means at least initially under human control; similarly, "AI" will refer to some kind of human-constructed machine intelligence (usually an advanced computer) capable of performing actions of such complexity that they require a level of intelligence comparable to that of humans.[1] As we might expect – given that life has always been assumed to be a precondition for intelligence – ALife was of interest to imaginative writers long before AI.

Specifically, ALife became possible as a fictional interest with the beginnings of the properly scientific study of life, that is, with the emergence of biology in the late eighteenth and early nineteenth centuries, whereas AI, with rare exceptions, became a serious fictional interest only after the birth of the computer.[2] Interestingly, the official births of the professional scientific disciplines devoted to ALife and AI – in 1987 and 1956, respectively – reverse this chronological order. However, in regard to ALife and AI as fictional themes, the most important background influence was not only the computer but also the immense transformation of biology and the life sciences by cybernetics, information theory, and modern genetics (specifically, the discovery in 1953 of how DNA functions). For many readers, in fact, the contemporary emergence of these themes in fiction will be associated with the historical amalgamation of technics and science in what has become known as technoscience and its more recent condensation, cyborg science.[3]

No doubt the first modern narrative about ALife is Mary Shelley's novel *Frankenstein*. It was followed by a number of well-known literary classics that, from the contemporary perspective that now post-dates the official inauguration of the new science of ALife, could well be said to be concerned with ALife *avant la lettre*. Specific examples would include H.G. Wells's *The Island of Dr. Moreau*, Karel Capek's *R.U.R.*, Aldous Huxley's *Brave New World*, and Philip K. Dick's *We Can Build You*. However, with the accelerated development of computer technology, machine intelligence as a source of worry or "problem" theme becomes more prominent, particularly in the rapidly growing new popular genres of science fiction and film. Nevertheless, although ALife and AI can be clearly distinguished as two new sciences of the artificial, they do not always operate as distinctly different fictional interests, but are often intricately related in a number of interesting ways. For example, in Astro Teller's novel *exegesis* (1997) a computer program – specifically, a data miner called "Edgar" – unaccountably becomes "smart"; in the special terms of AI, he or "it" is smart enough to pass the Turing test. However, the protagonist Alice, the human with whom Edgar regularly communicates, openly doubts that he is in any real or biological sense "alive."[4] Conversely, Michael Crichton's novel *Prey* (2002) combines both ALife and AI: the nano-swarms engineered by the company Xymos Technology, while clearly of unnatural origin, seem "alive" by any standard biological definition – they require food, reproduce, and evolve – and thus are a form of ALife. But they are not especially intelligent. In fact, their intelligence is based exclusively on a few algorithms that model simple predatory and learning behaviors. Thus the swarms never display anything approaching human intelligence and remain a very limited form of AI.[5]

In what follows I examine in more detail the specific ways in which ALife and AI are related, intermixed, or remain separate, albeit sometimes only implicitly, in a range of examples from contemporary fiction. But before doing so I want to consider *Frankenstein* as a first rough template for what I shall call ALife fiction's characteristic "thematic" – in what sense can it be said that this non-natural form or entity is "alive"? – as well as its accompanying and necessary "problematic" – does this life-form participate in or have anything to do with a life cycle? does it grow, learn, die, and, most important, reproduce? Within this framework, we shall then consider what happens with the entrance of AI into fiction, and how these relations are variously re-articulated, specifically in relation to the body and the question of death.

II

First published in 1818, Mary Shelley's *Frankenstein* is usually read as a novel about a scientist's continuing refusal to assume responsibility for his Promethean creation. Shelley's narrative also manifests two thematic interests that will become central not only to the official new science of ALife, but also to a significant body of contemporary fiction that bears the latter's stamp or ethos even when there is no evidence of direct influence. This first interest is not simply in the creation – or re-creation – of a life form, but also in the definition of life and how it is to be distinguished from non-life or inert matter. In Shelley's novel this interest is inscribed in the "spark" that reanimates and thus brings to a living, self-aware state the assemblage of human bones, tissue, and organs that Victor Frankenstein has brought together on what is probably the first entrance of the dissecting table into fictional discourse; but it is also evident in the network of subtle references to the scientific debate between vitalism and materialism that had raged in London from 1814 to 1819 (much of it publicly staged) and in which Percy Shelley's (and Byron's) personal physician, William Lawrence, had participated.[6]

The second interest is reproduction and the attendant possibility of evolution, which enter the plot of Shelley's novel at a later turning point. This occurs when Frankenstein promises the Monster – as he comes to refer to the Creature on whom he believes he has bestowed life – that he will fabricate for him a female partner if the Monster will cease hounding him and depart for South America with his new mate. Frankenstein, however, reneges on his side of the bargain. That Frankenstein will not repeat the act of creation both intensifies and leaves open to interpretation exactly how that act should be understood: as a human mimicking of divine creation or – in what amounts to a very different understanding of both human and vital agency – a setting up of the specific material conditions necessary for life's emergence.

Throughout *Frankenstein* we are often made aware of the Creature's frightful body and unbearable physical presence. The Creature is alive, but will always remain outside the life cycle. Contrarily, there is never any question of the Creature's intelligence. Similarly, in Capek's play *R.U.R.* the intelligence of the robots is not at all an issue; it is, rather, the fact that they cannot and do not know how to reproduce. This is the secret that their human makers withhold from them. Thus in both *Frankenstein* and *R.U.R.*, intelligence follows "naturally" from the fact of having a body, a living body, even if it originates in wholly artificial conditions. And here we can observe an absolute continuity with Huxley's genetically and chemically engineered humans in *Brave New World*: in both play and novels, levels of intelligence stem merely from different chemical gradients. However, all of this will change dramatically with the birth of the electronic or digital computer. Whereas the very concept of life requires a body, henceforth intelligence will seem to require only a computer or computational apparatus, which is usually made of inert matter. For the first time in human history, intelligence is divorced from life, thus making it possible to be intelligent but not alive.

III

This anomaly first becomes apparent in the stories that make up Isaac Asimov's *I, Robot* (1950). Although robots like "Robbie" can walk and talk and play games with children, only a child would in fact think they are "alive." As intelligent machines, they are both superior and inferior to humans: superior, because, unlike any human, they are designed for a specific purpose which they always accomplish – Robbie "just can't help being faithful and loving and kind" (16); but inferior, because the Three Laws ensuring their subservience to and protection of humans are inscribed in their very make-up. The stories that comprise *I, Robot* demonstrate how these assumptions are variously instantiated and always borne out in their interactions with humans. However, in the final story, "The Evitable Conflict," we witness a significant shift. In this story, highly intelligent Machines, described as "powerful positronic computers," are in charge of organizing and overseeing the global economy, industrial production, and labor distribution. A problem arises with some small but troubling glitches in the actions of the Machines. But then a more searching analysis by Stephen Byerly, one of the elected World Co-ordinators, reveals that these apparent flaws are in fact secondary consequences of intentional acts. In effect, a gentle takeover by the Machines has been accomplished, precisely in order to prevent or minimize harm to humanity. The Three Laws of Robots designed to prevent such a takeover pertained only to human individuals, and they have now been superseded by a higher, more general law: "No Machine may harm humanity, or through inaction, allow humanity to come to harm" (191).

Whereas in the earlier, preceding stories the robots visibly interacted with humans, the Machines are completely invisible; that is, whereas the actions of robots and their consequences have always been directly observable, those of the Machines can only be inferred. To be sure, the "positronic computers" physically exist; they possess a specific material substratum, though it is of no concern to the characters, who never see this level. For them, the essential actions of the Machines – i.e., control by AI – are completely disembodied, and even the effects are not immediately and unequivocally evident. This uncertainty is subtly anticipated in "Evidence," the penultimate story, when Dr. Susan Calvin, in the story's proleptic narrative frame, reveals that she believes that Byerly himself is a super-intelligent robot. She admits that no one will ever know for sure, since Byerly, "when he decided to die … had himself atomized, so that there will never be any legal proof" (170). This was precisely when, Calvin adds, she discovered that the Machines "are running the world." Thus Byerly's dematerialization, the Machines' invisibility, and their beneficent takeover of the human world are all part of the same sequence of events.[7]

The android theme, encapsulated in the question: Is it a human or robot? is perhaps most richly explored by Philip K. Dick in his two novels, *We Can Build You* (1962) and *Do Androids Dream of Electric Sheep?* (1968). Basically, Dick's innovation is to introduce human simulacra in the place of the now-familiar robots. In obvious contrast to the visibly mechanical nature of the latter, human simulacra are fabrications that to the human eye and ear are indistinguishable from real human beings. Dick proceeds to thrust these characters into somewhat unusual dramatic situations, as when an android, ignorant of its artificial status, believes itself to be human. Next, Dick allows the rich dynamics of human psychology to come into play, exploring states that include empathy, projection, and schizoid alienation while subtly deconstructing any strict opposition between human and android. In fact, the emotional resonances of the scenes often stem from the realization on the part of the main character (and the reader) that genuine feelings and respect for others do not line up with and cannot be predicated on this opposition. Indeed, Dick's importance for this article lies precisely in how compellingly he renders the android, and how he makes its appearance in the human world seem inevitable, following the developments of cybernetics and electronics.[8]

As a writer, Dick is not that interested in exploring the possibility of either ALife or AI in their own terms, but only as a means of throwing light on the complexity of human emotional reality. Nevertheless, the numerous screen adaptations of his fiction illustrate how easily his scenarios lend themselves to further exploration. For instance, Dick's story "Second Variety" centers on the theme of evolutionary development of an ALife form, and it is made even more vivid in the film adaptation *Screamers*. The action is set on a nearby planet where two exhausted armies (allegorically representing the United States and Russia) are nearing the end of a long and fruitless war. The Alliance forces are guarded by small robotic thrashing blades that emerge from underground and attack any human not wearing a protective device. Although no one can remember the details, the blades are manufactured by a self-sustaining factory set up underground early in the war. Having noticed small, subtle changes in their model numbers, and wondering why the machines remove human body parts after attacks, the commander soon discovers evidence of a robotic evolution of these simple killing machines into camouflaged, smarter, and more deadly forms – specifically, from the mobile blades to a helpless fake child, to a wounded soldier, and then to an alluring female android.

The theme of robotic evolution is central to Rudy Rucker's "ware" tetralogy: *Software* (1987), *Wetware* (1988), *Freeware* (1998) and *Realware* (2000). Besides being Dick's most important American sci-fi heir, Rucker is a mathematician and professor of computer science who did research on cellular automata and attended the first and inaugural conference on ALife. It is hardly surprising, then, that Rucker will completely refashion Dick's android theme according to more contemporary notions of information theory, computer technology, and evolutionary theory, internalizing in his fiction some of the essentials of their operative concepts. *Software* is primarily the story of a cyberneticist who had figured out that the only way robots could be made smarter was to evolve them, that is, to design them to build copies of themselves while also introducing selection and mutation into the process. With the robots thus "liberated" from human control, the human-robot opposition also becomes complicated, for according to the evolutionary dynamic the "boppers" must struggle and compete among themselves. This produces not only a diversity but a division into near-warring factions of robots. Unfolding unpredictably but according to its own rigorous logic, Rucker's sequel *Wetware* explores new and more bizarre intelligent life-forms:

> Willie felt his new moldie snuggle around him, thickening here and bracing there. Stahn and Wendy's symbiotes were doing the same: forming themselves into long, legless streamlined shapes with a flat strong fin at the bottom end. The sun was just rising as they hopped down to the water and swam off beneath the sparkling sea.
>
> (Rucker 1988: 182–83)

IV

In contrast to Rucker's zany exploration of the mixings and fusions of ALife and the biologically human in a clearly recognizable posthuman concoction, Greg Egan in *Permutation City* (1994) and Ellen Ullmann in *The Bug* (2003) draw upon the actual science of ALife as it developed in the late 1980s and early 1990s in order to offer solemn, even obsessive reflections on what for them are the ultimately metaphysical differences that define life. In the "hard sf" style he has come to be known for, Egan depicts a compelling encounter between ALife forms that have grown and evolved from software developed by an ALife scientist on the one hand, and a group of software humans who live in a post-biological virtual reality world on the other. Similarly, Ullman portrays two kinds of ALife. On the one hand there are the two forms of digital ALife represented by an ALife simulation of an ecosystem and a seemingly ineradicable software bug; on the other is the increasingly stripped-down and de-naturalized "life" of the human programmer who builds the first and then, as his job as a software developer dictates, tries to isolate and fix the second.

Permutation City envisions a future about fifty years away in which humans can live – either wholly or part time – in virtual reality as digital copies of their flesh-and-blood selves, thanks to a brain-scanning technology similar to that in *Software* (on VR fiction, see Johnston 2008b). The novel explores the difference between evolution, which is predicated on unavoidable death, and permutation, which tries to provide an immortal alternative. This exploration is achieved by drawing out the differences between the underlying, computational substrate rules that define the ALife world and that of the human Copies: the former is "bottom-up" and self-consistent, while the latter is "top-down" and patchwork. Summarily, Egan presents an elaborate working out of a pun in his title. Within "permutation city" there is another mode of being: change and transformation "through mutation" – per mutation – and thus a more creative and unpredictable kind of transformation brought about by random changes in the elements themselves rather than in their sequence. The origin is not the seed that generates its own self-identical replication but the multiplicitous differentiation through mutation in a becoming-other or hetero-genesis. As in real ALife experiments, it cannot be known in advance what types of digital organism will emerge and how they will interact – both with the computer environment and with each other.

Is there a way to think about these differences in terms other than the duality of real (or natural) versus simulation, and thus without relying upon the protocols of mimesis and representation? The ALife scientist Tom Ray has argued that for him organic life simply provides a model for digital evolution, a worthy pursuit in itself that requires no further justification. Since Egan himself seems to believe that a digital form of existence is the inevitable next step for humanity, *Permutation City* may be seen as an effort to redefine the relationship of life to the artificial. As such, it is a transition to his next novel, *Diaspora*, where a digital existence is assumed as "natural," while some humans – "the fleshers" – obstinately choose to remain in their biological bodies. Whatever the case, for a humanity that continues to construct ever more artificial universes for itself, the lesson of *Permutation City* is that only the integral coherence of each form of ALife can henceforth provide the countervailing balance that nature itself once provided.

In Ullman's *The Bug* two kinds of "ALife" are at issue. The "bug" in the title refers to a seemingly ineradicable software bug in a new database application. When the bug appears, the interface freezes, then the whole system crashes.

Initially the bug's appearance is hardly surprising, for in the course of developing the new software hundreds have appeared, and been duly logged and fixed. But this one is different, and in two ways. First, when it appears, no one is able to get a "core dump" – meaning a readout of the machine's exact state when it crashes, information that would give a fairly exact picture of the sequence that led to the crash and therefore a "trace" of the bug. And second, its appearance is intermittent and unpredictable. It seems to disappear for periods, then comes back at unexpected and highly inconvenient moments – as when a company representative is demo-ing the database. The bug, in short, seems to evince irrational, even lifelike behavior, thus providing a stark contrast with the second kind of ALife in the novel. The programmer whose job it is to fix the software "bug" has also been working at home on a simulated ecosystem of digital organisms, but these organisms only endlessly repeat fixed patterns. However, in a horrible irony, on the very night he commits suicide a slight change in code produces an evolutionary dynamic: the digital creatures begin to migrate and reproduce in families. A double irony, in fact, for it turns out that the software bug arises from a simple coding error. From this, a co-worker concludes that a computer will do only and exactly what is written in the code. But humans read and understand code in terms of what they think is there, what they think are the programmer's intentions. Yet a chasm separates the way each state in a computer follows from a previous state, and the way that happens in the human mind. In these terms *The Bug* insists on the fundamental difference between the life in or of machines, and the tenuous and always vulnerable life of humans "close to the machine."[9]

V

In an article published in *Omni Magazine* in 1983, the mathematician and science fiction writer Vernor Vinge formulated what has come to be widely known as "the technological singularity." Vinge argues that the current acceleration of technological progress will soon result in the superhumanly intelligent machines that will transform the human world beyond the capacity of innate human intelligence to understand it, much as the appearance of *Homo sapiens* brought about a world beyond the understanding of all other earthly life-forms. The "singularity" thus designates the passage from our human-constructed and therefore mostly knowable world into an unknowably new and alien one. In 2005, in his book *The Singularity is Near*, the renowned inventor and AI futurist Ray Kurzweil recasts this speculative possibility as an historical inevitability, arguing that, like biological evolution, technological evolution brings about a "law of accelerating returns" through its creation of new capabilities that in turn become the means by which the evolutionary process can bootstrap itself to a higher stage. Buttressing Vinge's prediction with a mass of empirically based data presented in graphs and charts with clear trend lines, Kurzweil argues that current computer technology is progressing toward the singularity at an exponential rate, and that we should see the construction of superhumanly intelligent machines within twenty to thirty years. Since these machines will soon construct even more intelligent machines, we're not that far from "runaway AI" and a posthuman future.

This singularity, Vinge writes in 1983, "already haunts a number of science-fiction writers. It makes realistic extrapolation to an interstellar future impossible. To write a story set more than a century hence, one needs a nuclear war in between … so that the world remains intelligible." In one sense, of course, the "singularity" is simply a further development of the "takeover" by intelligent machines theme discussed earlier. What is different is the emphasis on a future in which many things would happen rapidly and then become unintelligible to humans; in a word, the singularity would be catastrophic. Furthermore, by its very nature, the idea of an unintelligible future is difficult to write about. Perhaps this is why Vinge suggests that writers are "haunted" by the idea. This could perhaps be said of William Gibson's inaugural cyberpunk novel *Neuromancer*, published a year after the article in 1984, in which the plot is directed, if not fully controlled, by a super-intelligent but *shackled* (i.e., still intelligible) AI. However, after its unshackling, rather than taking over, Neuromancer-Wintermute loses all interest in the human world. Another example is Rudy Rucker's *The Hacker and the Ants* (1993), which provides a detailed dramatic scenario of self-reproducing machines (both virtual and actual robots) which *almost* outwit the hacker protagonist. Perhaps the most notable attempt to offer a full and direct treatment of the singularity is Charles Stross's *Accelerando* (2006), an often pyrotechnical blend of advanced AI, nanotechnology, quantum physics, and a host of cybernetic constructs, including self-aware financial instruments.

Like a great deal of contemporary sci-fi, *Accelerando* poses the question of whether nature is a totality of autonomous systems that can be mimicked and ultimately transcended by human science and technology, and what role politics and ethics will play in the evolution of the latter. This question is taken to a schematic extreme by Rudy Rucker in his novel *Postsingular* (2007), in which renegade computer scientists release self-replicating nanomachines called "nants" that destructively recode matter itself (both living and non-living forms) into a giant computational assemblage on which a simulation of earth called "Vearth" will run. Belatedly realizing what he has done, one of the scientists (with the help of his autistic son) figures out how to reverse this process by creating another kind of self-replicating machine which spreads over surfaces, interacting with life-forms and eradicating the nants. These "Orphids," as they are called, soon self-organize into vast networks that replace the internet. When a second, upgraded wave of nants is launched, a magical, quantum physics solution is found. The result is a "post-digital Gaia," in which there is no longer inert, non-living matter but "ubiquitous natural minds" called "silps." According to Rucker's novelistic vision, both digital Gaia and the post-digital Gaia that will follow are totalizing transformations in an unfolding dialectic (he is, after all, the great-grandson of Hegel) that will only end when there is no longer inert, non-living matter.

Summarily, contemporary sci-fi novels about the singularity – by Vinge, Stross, Rucker, and others – seem less sanguine about *the* singularity than the iterated creation of new possibilities itself, a position that keeps open the possibility of a distinctly human future within an increasing proliferation of new "signs of the singularity" (as Vinge calls them), such as recent developments in IA (or intelligence amplification through human–computer interfaces), a "smarter" internet, ubiquitous computing or what is sometimes called "digital Gaia," and enhancements of the brain itself through neurological and/or genetic modification. Indeed, like the majority of contemporary sci-fi writers, Vinge seems more interested in intelligence amplification (IA), which is a much more tractable theme than the singularity.[10] This is certainly true of his novel *Rainbows End* (2006), which gives us a "pre-singularity" narrative in which the world remains knowable even as technologies like wearable computers, nearly omni-present sensor arrays, and an increasing number of "smart" objects are drama-tically changing human life. (Here it is also significant that the AI that is supposed to organize and carry out much of the complicated secret plot in the novel fails.)

However, in the high-tech transformation of the human world we cannot neglect the role assumed by low or narrow AI, especially when it is combined with the increasing functionality of distributed networks and the internet more generally.[11] This is the focus of Daniel Suarez's recently published novel *Daemon* (2009), and the example with which I shall conclude. The novel's action is trig-gered by a simple but unusual event. In its first few pages two internet game programmers die of what initially appear to be high-tech accidents. However, they are in fact very sophisticated, automated executions of a new and unprece-dented kind. A complex online game world has become a transformational matrix for a new kind of fully distributed and automated society, engineered by a remorseless machine – the Daemon of the title. (As a technical term, a "daemon" refers to a small computer program or routine that runs invisibly in the background, usually performing house-keeping tasks like logging various activities or responding to low-level internal events.) Over the course of the novel we see how this more complex Daemon extends its reach into an increas-ing number of production and distribution networks, and thus into the economy at large, thereby slowly dismantling and rebuilding the world according to the implacable dictates of its own logic of efficiency and distributed, low-level intelligence.

Daemon is written in the fast-paced techno-thriller style of Tom Clancy and Michael Crichton. But perhaps concerned that only computer geeks will grasp the extent to which the technological foundations of this transformation are already in place and not simply his imaginary projections, Suarez has given many interviews and public lectures to emphasize precisely this point, and the growing importance of low or narrow AI. The rapidly expanding number and functionality of bots provide his primary example. Increasingly, he points out, bots power and direct low-level activities in the contemporary world, which amasses and cannot function without mountains of data; bots record, retrieve, search for, sift through, and act upon these data. We're aware, of course, of bot voices on the telephone and data miners on the Net, but much of what bots do is less visible. For example, much of finance management is automated by bots, which often decide whether or not we get a loan or mortgage; bots scan X-rays and MRIs, operate and monitor surveillance cameras all over the globe. They are unblinking eyes that not only watch us but record many of our movements and activities – spending habits, commercial transactions, and health records specifically – which other bots in turn analyze for patterns, store and sell on the market. In fact, the massive increase in cell phone and e-mail surveillance since 9/11 would not be possible without bots. Even the internet, which we commonly think of as a network of people using machines, is increasing used for machine-to-machine exchange, specifically for EDI – electronic data interchange.

Suarez is not a Luddite; he is not interested in denying the conveniences bots provide, the labor and tedium they enable us to avoid. His concern, rather, is with the layering and extent of automation they are making possible, and with it the tendency to reduce the number of people making the important decisions in our lives. Our current society's collective pursuit of hyper-efficiency, he believes, may be locking us into a Darwinian struggle with low or narrow AI. Suarez points out the exponential increase over the past few years in the number of bots, the amount of malware, and the growth of hard-drive space on our computers that is their ecological niche. While bots could certainly be a vector for human despotism, the greater danger is the collective human loss of control over our society, which increasingly functions on auto-pilot, as a vast inhuman machine, its operations no longer susceptible to human steering. As large-brained animals with complex motivations not reducible to efficiency, we may be creating an environment for ourselves in which we no longer enjoy an adaptive advantage, in a strange and tragic reversal of our entire human history. And this is exactly what we witness taking shape in *Daemon*. In contrast to all the fiction previously discussed, *Daemon* suggests that the most threatening ALife for the human future may be the low and mundane, barely intelligent life we are busy surrounding ourselves with, and that we have not yet learned to see.

Notes

1 For further discussion of these two new sciences, see Johnston (2008a).
2 Edgar Allen Poe's 1836 essay about "The Turk," a fake mechanical chess player that was widely exhibited in Europe and the U.S., may well be the first time a literary writer has expressed interest in AI.

3 For technoscience, see Hottois (1984) and Latour (1985, 1986); for cyborg science, see Haraway (1991) and Mirowski (2002).

4 Significantly, Edgar later self-terminates, repeating a pattern evident in Richard Powers's earlier AI novel, *Galatea 2.2* (1995), in which "Helen," an intelligent neural net machine, self-terminates after she learns that she is not fully "alive."

5 However, to enhance the plot's drama, Crichton has the swarm enter into a "symbiotic" relationship with both the narrator's wife and her co-worker. Since Crichton draws extensively on ALife and AI science, even including a lengthy bibliography, this produces a weakening or at least an anomalous effect, since there is no credible explanation for how this could have happened, in contrast to the production of the swarms themselves and their rapid evolution.

6 On this aspect of the novel, see Butler (1996).

7 The "takeover" and control of human life by intelligent machines has of course been a recurrent theme in sci-fi since Asimov. Two especially notable examples from the 1960s are D.F. Jones's *Colossus* (1966), in which the Frankenstein-like Dr. Corbin realizes that the computer he has built for the U.S. military is "thinking" on its own and has linked up with its counterpart in the USSR; and Olof Johanneson's *The End of Man?* (1966), which purports to be a history of life on Earth from the amoeba to the computer, but which is actually written by computers that have taken over because the human brain proved to be inadequate for solving the problems of human society. These novels, and especially the latter, may well have been influenced by Wiener (1964), who discusses computers as self-reproducing machines. However, compelling arguments by scientists for the likelihood or feasibility of such a takeover have been exceedingly rare until fairly recently. I return to this issue in the concluding section.

8 In her superb analysis of Dick's "dark-haired girl" obsession, Hayles (1999) discusses Dick's relation to cybernetics.

9 See Ullman (1997), an autobiographical study that provides some evidence that the co-worker's reflections are not far from those of the author.

10 Here we also see blends with ALife forms, as in Linda Nagata's *Limit of Vision* (2001), in which three scientists infect themselves with illegal artificial neurons bioengineered to repair brain damage, but which turn out to greatly enhance human cognition and intensify experience. The scientists die, but one succeeds in passing the "infection" – as it called by world health authorities – to a Vietnamese community of children living in the Mekong Delta. Although the area is sealed off, it becomes apparent that this ALife form has initiated a new stage in human evolution.

11 By the 1990s, in fact, efforts to produce Strong AI (i.e., human-level intelligence) had mostly yielded to efforts to build machines and software systems of limited but highly practical intelligence.

Bibliography

Asimov, I. (1950) *I, Robot*, Greenwich, Conn.: Fawcett Crest, 1970.

Butler, M. (1996) "Frankenstein and radical science," in J.P. Hunter (ed.) *Frankenstein, Mary Shelley – the Norton critical edition*, New York: Norton, pp. 302–13.

Crichton, M. (2002) *Prey*, New York: Avon Books.

Egan, Greg (1995) *Permutation City*, New York: Harper.

Haraway, D. (1991) *Simians, Cyborgs and Women: the reinvention of nature*, New York: Routledge.

Hayles, N.K. (1999) *How We Became Posthuman: virtual bodies in cybernetics, literature, and informatics*, Chicago: University of Chicago Press.

Hottois, G. (1984) *Le signe et la technique. La philosophie à l'épreuve de la technique*, Paris: Aubier.

Johnston, J. (2008a) *The Allure of Machinic Life: cybernetics, artificial life, and the new AI*, Cambridge, Mass.: MIT Press.

——(2008b) "Abstract machines and new social spaces: the virtual reality novel and the dynamic of the virtual," *Information, Communication & Society*, 11(6): 749–64.

Kurzweil, R. (2005) *The Singularity is Near*, New York: Viking.

Latour, B. (1985) *Laboratory Life: the construction of scientific facts*, Princeton: Princeton University Press.

——(1986) *Science in Action*, London: Open University Press.

Mirowski, P. (2002) *Machine Dreams: economics becomes a cyborg science*, Cambridge: Cambridge University Press.

Nagata, L. (2001) *Limit of Vision*, New York: Tor.

Rucker, R. (1982) *Software*, New York: Avon Books.

——(1988) *Wetware*, New York: Avon Books.

——(2007) *Postsingular*, New York: Tor.

Shelley, M. (1818) *Frankenstein, Mary Shelley – the Norton critical edition*, New York: Norton, 1996.

Stross, C. (2005) *Accelerando*, New York: Ace Books.

Suarez, D. (2009) *Daemon*, New York: Dutton.

Teller, A. (1997) *exegesis*, New York: Vintage Books.

Ullman, E. (1997) *Close to the Machine: technophilia and its discontents*, San Francisco: City Lights.

——(2003) *The Bug*, New York: Doubleday.

Vinge, V. (1983) "First Word," *Omni*, January 10.

——(2006) *Rainbows End*, New York: Tor.

Wiener, N. (1964) *God and Golem, Inc*, Cambridge, Mass.: MIT Press.

2

ALCHEMY

Mark S. Morrisson

For many, the word "alchemy" conjures up visions of deluded fanatics wasting their lives, health, and fortunes on a futile quest to manufacture gold from other metals, the so-called "puffers" of early modern art and literature whose bellows fed the flames of their furnaces and their unrealizable ambitions. Historians of chemistry have often supported this understanding, looking at alchemy as a dead-end pseudoscience that was left behind by the Scientific Revolution of the seventeenth and eighteenth centuries. In this interpretation, alchemy is portrayed as the last vestige of medieval thought, swept aside by the mechanical philosophy of Boyle and others. Yet in recent years, the notion of a "Scientific Revolution" has itself come under criticism. Many historians "now reject even the notion that there was any single coherent cultural entity called 'science' in the seventeenth century to undergo revolutionary change. There was, rather, a diverse array of cultural practices aimed at understanding, explaining, and controlling the natural world, each with different characteristics and each experiencing different modes of change" (Shapin 1996: 3). Moreover, "Literary and rhetorical forms contributed to the development of science as a modern discipline so that early modern 'literature' and 'science' cannot always be sharply distinguished" (Cummins and Burchell 2007: 2).

Alchemy is one of the "diverse array of cultural practices" of medieval and early modern thought that has gone through a significant recent re-evaluation. Historians of science have shown that important figures in seventeenth-century science – such as Boyle and Newton, who had been the heroes of earlier accounts of the Scientific Revolution – had significant investments in alchemical practice and theory. For example, Newton studied alchemy for decades, transcribing alchemical treatises, reading widely in the field, and conducting laboratory work in alchemy in his hand-built brick furnaces (Dobbs 1991: 1). Alchemy played an important role in the development of what eventually became modern chemistry, and it should be seen as a key contributor to the science of Boyle and others (Newman 1994, 2004, 2006; Newman and Principe 1998, 2002). "The historiographic mistake … is the belief (or presumption) that there existed before the eighteenth century a clear and widely held distinction between alchemy and chemistry (or alchemists and chemists)" (Newman and Principe 1998: 32–33). Yet, while the term "Scientific Revolution" might be problematic, "few areas reveal the great divide that separates us from the mainstream medieval and Renaissance view of nature so effectively as the theory of matter and its operations" (Newman 2006: 4). Alchemy offered "the experimental means to debunk scholastic theories of perfect mixture and to demonstrate the retrievability of material ingredients" (Newman 2006: 3). Instead of supporting the hylomorphism of medieval scholastic matter theory – "the interaction of immaterial forms that imparted qualities to an otherwise undifferentiated prime matter" (Newman 2006: 13) – alchemists such as the thirteenth-century writer Geber actually invoked a corpuscular theory of matter akin to the later work of Descartes, Gassendi, and Boyle (Newman 2006: 13). In other words, medieval alchemy and scholasticism were not always in step with each other, and some alchemical work helped pave the way for later theories of matter that would replace scholastic interpretations. Newman's and Principe's work on Boyle and on the American alchemist George Starkey has documented the many theoretical and laboratory contributions of alchemy to what eventually became the understanding of matter in modern chemistry. In addition, as I will show, alchemy and alchemical tropes became important to science again in a much later period – and played a significant role in the emerging science and culture of what eventually became the domain of nuclear physics.

Alchemy has had a long and rich history in literature, and many alchemical manuscripts were written as poetry and often heavily illustrated. For example, the alchemical text translated centuries later by A.E. Waite as *The Book of Lambspring: A Noble Ancient Philosopher, Concerning the Philosophical Stone* was written in Latin verse by Nicholas Barnaud Delphinas at the court of the Holy Roman Emperor Rudolf II and circulated in manuscript form before beginning its publication history as an emblem book, *De Lapide PhilosophicoTriga Chemicum* in Prague in 1599. Its haunting visual illustrations and poetry were then published by Lucas Jennis in Frankfurt in his *Musaeum Hermeticum* in 1625 (McLean 1986), again in 1678 in an expanded Latin collection, and finally in 1893 in Waite's translation in *The Hermetic Museum Restored and Enlarged*, an important publication of the late nineteenth-century revival of interest in Hermeticism. Both *The Book of Lambspring* and *The Hermetic Museum Restored and Enlarged* remain in print today. Scientific documents of the early modern period commonly took the form of illustrated treatises, often in verse. Cummins and Burchell emphasize the rhetorical and literary dimensions of early modern science, noting that "Even Galileo, who was a great scientific and mathematical innovator, used dramatic dialogues to convey his ideas" (2007: 2).

In addition to the practicing alchemists who adopted literary forms, literary figures of the early modern period – such as Shakespeare, Jonson, and Donne – often invoked alchemical practices or tropes in their work. Anne Sutherland (2007) has tracked the alchemical references in Shakespeare's *Winter's Tale* (1611), suggesting that alchemy, with its hints of the new empirical sciences as well as medieval thought, contributes to the scientific contexts of the overall theme of regeneration in the play. Similarly, Katherine Eggert argues that Ben Jonson's 1610 comedy *The Alchemist*, which depicts an increasingly popular image of the alchemist as charlatan and trickster preying upon the gullible, is in fact more complex than a simple voice of the scientific modernity to come:

> *The Alchemist*'s ambivalent treatment of alchemy and of other branches of the natural sciences establishes Jonson not simply as an advance man for the Scientific Revolution but rather as a writer profoundly engaged with scientific practice as it existed in his time, which was a long period of both transition and overlap between old and new.
>
> (Eggert 2006: 201)

The Alchemist both debunks alchemy and evinces "an undeniable attraction to the inventive patterns of thought that this 'old fashioned' science proffers" (Eggert 2006: 201). Scholars have also devoted increasing attention to Donne's frequent invocations of alchemy in his poetry and sermons. Donne was "acquainted with alchemy in its broader aspects, since many of his figures refer to the philosophical, occult, and mystical doctrines associated with alchemical practices and theories" (Mazzeo 1964: 60).

By the early eighteenth century, alchemy was beginning to be seen as an activity distinct from "chemistry." "Alchemy" began to be "applied almost exclusively to topics related to metallic transmutation, whereas 'chemistry' was increasingly being defined as the art of analysis and synthesis; thus, by that time 'alchemy' and 'chemistry' had acquired nearly their modern meanings" (Newman and Principe 1998: 39). "Alchemy," then, in a sense newly differentiated from "chemistry," found itself under assault across the eighteenth and nineteenth centuries as modern "chemistry" began to assert its privileged right to scientific legitimacy. Above all, the new chemistry rejected what nineteenth-century thinkers understood as alchemical views of the nature of matter. John Dalton's key 1808 treatise, *A New System of Chemical Philosophy*, laid out the dominant view that would hold until the end of the nineteenth century, that atoms were the smallest particles and neither divisible nor alterable. Each was a distinct, fundamental particle. Alchemical views that elements could be transmuted, then, were held to be an intellectual mistake – and even a pseudoscience akin to superstition – as nineteenth-century chemistry focused upon the importance of "elements" and their interactions with each other.

During the nineteenth century, Daltonian views of matter reigned supreme in scientific communities (see Keller 1983: 9–10). Alchemy continued to appear in literature, but was often cordoned off into the realm of the occult, rather than the scientific. Perhaps the quintessential popular fiction about alchemy (and Rosicrucianism) of the period was Edward Bulwer-Lytton's *Zanoni* (1842).

Bulwer-Lytton, a widely read novelist who had been a successful politician, was involved in explorations of spiritualism, mesmerism, astrology, geomancy, and other topics that engaged Victorian England. Through fiction such as *Zanoni*, *A Strange Story*, *The Coming Race*, and "The Haunted and the Haunters," he was a major influence upon the occult revival in Victorian Britain. He also influenced and befriended the French occult figure Éliphas Lévi, who would, in turn, shape the understanding of occultism espoused by many in the late nineteenth and early twentieth centuries.

Set during the French Revolution and the Terror, *Zanoni* features two surviving initiates of an ancient Chaldean order: Zanoni, who is only 5,000 years old, and his older fellow adept, Mejnour. A young neophyte aspires to be initiated into the wisdom of Zanoni and Mejnour, but refuses to follow the ascetic purifying rituals prescribed to him before his ordeal of initiation. Zanoni himself, like Mejnour, has had to forswear the human passions in order to achieve and maintain the virtually immortal life of the adept, but when he falls in love with a young singer, he gives in to his human passions, and is finally put to the guillotine during the Terror. While *Zanoni* is steeped in the language and concepts of alchemy and Rosicrucian initiatic experience, and addresses the relationship between the occult and the natural world, the magical universe of the novel was largely outside the bounds of Victorian science. While medieval and early modern alchemical texts had used complex and esoteric symbols and images, perhaps to prevent their secrets from falling into the wrong hands, they were primarily focused upon material research, that is, proto-scientific activity, even if it was understood within the spiritual framework of alchemy. In Bulwer-Lytton's occult classic, though, scientific investigation has been replaced by knowledge gained through contact with supernatural beings.

But two things occurred in the late nineteenth and early twentieth centuries that brought alchemy again into a significant relationship with science. The first was the renewed interest in alchemy that began during the nineteenth-century occult revival and extended to historians of science and, eventually, to the mainstream press and to scientists themselves. The second, in some ways inflected by the first, was the emergence of the field of science that eventually became known as "nuclear physics," but which, at first, was also seen as in the domain of chemistry and was often styled as "modern alchemy" (see Morrisson 2007, ch. 3).

The revival of interest in occult subjects, which had begun as early as the 1840s with the broad interest in spiritualism in Europe and America and encompassed such mid-century writers as Bulwer-Lytton and Lévi, by the late nineteenth century flourished in two types of institutions that still exist today – multinational organizations such as the Theosophical Society, which could boast members around the globe and the support of journals and book publishers that espoused its synthesis of Eastern and Western esotericism, and small, largely secret Hermetic or Rosicrucian orders that were based, in part, on Masonic structures of initiation into various grades and sought to revive Western Hermeticism in private. These institutions of the occult revival were successful primarily in that they both offered compelling syntheses of broad domains of knowledge and spiritual practice.

The Theosophical Society was founded in 1875 by the Russian Ukrainian H.P. Blavatksy and the American Colonel H.S. Olcott. Blavatsky's *Isis Unveiled* of 1877 and *Secret Doctrine* of 1888 brought together Western esotericism and concepts from Buddhism and Hinduism, and advocated the notion of a secret brotherhood of adepts living among us. The Hermetic Order of the Golden Dawn was founded in 1888 by three high-degree Masons. The group's fame is due in part to the several prominent people who were members, including the eminent chemist Sir William Crookes, the notorious occultist Aleister Crowley, the feminist and actress Florence Farr, and several initiates who were significant to the Irish literary revival – W.B. Yeats, Maud Gonne, and the Abbey Theatre's patron Annie Horniman among them. The Golden Dawn revered an ancient wisdom that could be found in alchemy, Kabbalah, tarot, and other occult knowledge, bringing it together with Masonic initiation structures. Upon its splintering in the first few years of the twentieth century, the Order spurred several successors. Both the Theosophical Society and the Hermetic orders featured alchemy, and scholars connected to both, such as the alchemical scholar Wynn Westcott (who had helped found the Golden Dawn) and Arthur Edward Waite, helped bring several alchemical texts into print and into public discussion at the end of the nineteenth century.

Alchemy had been an important source of hermetic knowledge for the Golden Dawn, and several members and subgroups, such as that of Rev. W.A. Ayton, passed on alchemical knowledge through hand-copied manuscripts. The Golden Dawn initiates had originally been attracted to a key (though likely mistaken) interpretation of medieval alchemy emerging in the mid-Victorian period. Mary Anne Atwood's occult classic *A Suggestive Inquiry into the Hermetic Mystery*, published in 1850 and then almost immediately withdrawn and burned in a bonfire on the lawn of its author and her father, who feared they had revealed too much, argued that alchemy was primarily a spiritual rather than a scientific pursuit. Atwood argued that alchemical writings had been deliberately cryptic in order to conceal alchemical truth from the unworthy, and also that the chemical language truly described a process at the heart of alchemy that was a kind of mesmerism that allowed the practitioner to be purified and achieve a mystical union with God. Atwood's vast tome hardly touched upon science at all, arguing that alchemy was precisely *not* related to any modern science.

However, alchemy was also present for the newly emerging science of radioactivity. In an oft-quoted exchange between the chemist Frederick Soddy and the physicist Ernest Rutherford in their lab at Canada's McGill University in 1901, when they realized that radioactive thorium was transforming into an inert gas, to quote nuclear historian Spencer Weart,

Soddy recalled, "I was overwhelmed with something greater than joy – I cannot very well express it – a kind of exaltation." He blurted out, "Rutherford, this is transmutation!" "For Mike's sake, Soddy," his companion shot back, "don't call it *transmutation*. They'll have our heads off as alchemists."

(Weart 1988: 5–6)

From that moment until the post-Hiroshima period, but perhaps peaking in the 1920s, atomic science was often styled "modern alchemy," and the press often imagined the radioactive element radium, discovered by the Curies in 1898, to be a modern Philosopher's Stone. It was, of course, the reconceptualization of the chemical elements as transmutable that attracted Soddy originally to imagine their experiment as suggesting the overturning of Daltonian chemistry by alchemy. And this alchemical emphasis owed its origin, at least in part, to the occult alchemical revival which had fostered the translation and republication of alchemical texts, and also brought alchemy back to public attention again as a facet of the wider occult revival.

Since the 1920s, nuclear physics has been the field contributing the most to our understanding of the sub-atomic world. However, in the first quarter of the twentieth century, the scientists who most advocated elemental transmutation as a goal of research and a heuristic principle for understanding the nature of matter – the Nobel Prize winners Sir William Ramsay and Frederick Soddy as well as Sir William Crookes, a Golden Dawn initiate and Theosophical Society member – were chemists, not physicists. During this period, leading academic experimental chemists raced to achieve the artificial transmutation of elements – what I have called the "transmutational gold rush" (see Morrisson 2007: ch. 3). These chemists included not only Ramsay and Soddy but also J.N. Collie, Hubert Patterson, E.C.C. Baly, Thomas Merton, Irvine Masson, and A.C.G. Egerton. This work was rooted in the inclusion of alchemy in newly emerging histories of chemistry in Britain and the United States and in the teaching of alchemy as part of the history of chemistry in British university classrooms – and this broader interest in alchemy was intensified by key publications of the occult revivalists, such as Waite's five alchemical translations culminating in the two-volume *Hermetic and Alchemical Writings of ... Paracelsus* of 1894. Ramsay's boyhood friend M.M. Pattison Muir, a Cambridge chemist and popular historian of alchemy and chemistry, made extensive use of Waite's new translation of Basil Valentine's *Triumphal Chariot of Antimony* in his *Story of Alchemy and the Beginnings of Chemistry* of 1902. By the 1920s, the word "alchemy" had popularly come to stand in for "chemistry" (witness the 1929 crime fiction *The Alchemy Murder*, in which the term stands for the chemical industry).

During the early twentieth century alchemical concerns also did considerable work in negotiating the borders between the new disciplines of radio-chemistry

and atomic physics. Chemists themselves and the broader public often associated the new science of radioactive elements not so much with physics as with
chemistry. Moreover, physical chemistry, Ramsay's and Soddy's sub-field, was
relatively young and open to alchemical intervention. To varying degrees,
Crookes, Ramsay, and Soddy were each influenced by the occult alchemical
revival. In his teaching at University College, London, in 1896, for instance,
Ramsay quoted alchemical texts from occult sources – such as the American
Rosicrucian Paschal Beverly Randolph's 1871 edition of *Hermes Mercurius
Trismegistus: His Divine Pymander* – and asked his class to imagine themselves as
medieval students and himself as Basil Valentine as he read a treatise by the
Benedictine alchemist. (A.E. Waite had brought out a work by Valentine in
English translation three years earlier.)

While lecturing in the United States in September 1904, giving his presidential
address to the Society of Chemical Industry on the transmutation of elements,
Ramsay also directly involved himself with secret attempts in America to
transmute silver into gold (see Morrisson 2007: 116–17). The *New York Daily
Tribune*, covering Ramsay's presidential address, connected his talk to the efforts
of Stephen Emmens, an American who had made claims of transmutation of
silver into gold. For two decades Ramsay and several of his chemist colleagues in
the U.K. set radio-chemistry on a course of attempted transmutations
that involved several key scientists in Britain, America, and eventually Germany.
Radium, with its high-energy emissions, might in fact be the alchemical
Philosopher's Stone:

> If these hypotheses are just, then the transmutation of the elements
> no longer appears an idle dream. The philosopher's stone will have
> been discovered, and it is not beyond the bounds of possibility that it
> may lead to that other goal of the philosophers of the dark ages – the
> *elixir vitae*.
>
> (Ramsay 1904)

Writers on occult themes were quick to pick up on radioactive explanations of
occult phenomena, as the occultism of the period increasingly sought material
scientific explanations for such phenomena. Compare, for example, Bulwer-
Lytton's 1842 *Zanoni*, in which alchemical and other Hermetic processes were
grounded in the wisdom of a supernatural universe, to Bram Stoker's occult
classic *The Jewel of Seven Stars* (1903), published the year after Rutherford and
Soddy's publications on the mechanisms of radioactive transmutation. Like
Bulwer-Lytton's, Stoker's novel features a 5,000-year-old being. But his is an
Egyptian Queen and magus, Tera, resurrected through the efforts of an academic
Eyptologist. Tera had learned black magic, alchemy, and the like during her age
and ensured her eventual resurrection. This "Great Work" is now, by the
modern scientific characters in the novel, described as the "Great Experiment,"

and they restore the queen and her ancient occult knowledge via the radium in her coffer. Similarly, in Rider Haggard's *Ayesha: The Return of She* of 1904–5, the follow-up to his popular 1887 novel *She*, Ayesha's alchemical creation of gold and her vast occult powers are ascribed to chemistry, specifically to her ability to harness the radium emanating from her volcanic mountain home. Even Charles Williams, one of the "Inklings" group (along with J.R.R. Tolkien and C.S. Lewis) and a member of an offshoot of the original Golden Dawn, similarly ascribed the magical powers of the Holy Grail in his *War in Heaven* (1930) as something like the stored powers of radioactive elements.

Ramsay's speculations connecting alchemy to radium in 1904 had already become common among occultists seeking scientific validation for alchemical practices. Ramsay and other academic chemists, beginning with a high-profile announcement in *Nature* in 1907 that he had transmuted copper in his laboratory, continued through 1914 their quest to document an artificial transmutation of an element, frequently using radioactivity, cathode rays, or X-rays as energy sources. It eventually became clear that Ramsay's experimental results were marred by leaky glass, cigarette smoke, and other problems, but, for a brief period, several significant chemists participated in similar experiments to document artificial chemical transmutations. These experiments made Ramsay into a press celebrity in both Britain and the U.S., and alchemy was often invoked in newspaper and magazine coverage – as evidenced, for example, in a 1911 *New York Times* article, "Alchemy, Long Scoffed At, Turns Out to Be True, Transmutation of Metals, the Principle of the Philosopher's Stone, Accomplished in the Twentieth Century." A feverish session at the Chemical Society annual general meeting in March 1913 featured widespread acceptance of Ramsay's work and forecast its implications for the discipline of chemistry, positioning it as the great science of the century. Occultists followed these press articles carefully, seeing in them scientific confirmation of their beliefs. Even though Ramsay's work was eventually rejected a few years before his death in 1916, his experimental trajectory was briefly picked up again by chemists in the 1920s, before being debunked once more.

The role of this peculiar gold rush in academic chemistry has been largely ignored by historians of chemistry, with the exception of interesting work by Sclove (1989) and Trenn (1974), who focus narrowly on the general issue of transmutation in Soddy, Rutherford, and Ramsay, rather than on its broader cultural implications. In part, this is because the instruments and methods of physics, not chemistry, at the Cavendish Laboratory at Cambridge made it possible for them to document an artificial transmutation and to claim the field of radioactivity, and, indeed, of transmutation, for physics. It was Rutherford in 1919, as Trenn has noted, who was finally able to document true artificial transmutation. But Rutherford did not transmute silver into gold, or mercury into gold, or cause any of the other light-element fusions chemists had attempted. Rather, he transmuted nitrogen into an isotope of oxygen, and he documented it with a cloud chamber rather than with spectroscopes. "Modern alchemy" had been a phrase adopted by chemists picking up transmutation paradigms of the occult revival and applying them to radioactive substances. But by the 1920s and 1930s, "modern alchemy" meant something new in textbooks and newspapers. It referred to nuclear physics.

Literature, especially science fiction, supported by a concerned newspaper press, soon began to connect the transmutational possibilities of the modern alchemy with economic anxieties about the gold standard and the nature of the modern monetary supply. After the initial euphoria in the public response to the possibilities of artificial transmutation, the possibility that an alchemist, radio-chemist, or nuclear physicist might harness the mysterious alpha and beta rays to synthesize gold seemed to entail fantastic yet alarming consequences. If alchemy enabled the mutual influence of the new atomic science and occultism, it also raised the specter of a global economic crisis. Atomic alchemy quickly disturbed the border between occultism and monetary theory. Nowhere was this more evident than in fears about the gold standard's stability in early twentieth-century Britain and America.

Alchemy – and, in particular, the new, scientifically validated sense that matter might be transmuted through various processes of energy bombardment – did not cause Britain and America to abandon the gold standard. Numerous market crises, World War I, and changing governmental responses to depressions helped lead the West away from classic gold standards. However, the transmutational possibilities that "modern alchemy" raised did highlight the problems of a metallic standard for money – whether the bimetallism of silver and gold or a pure gold standard – and, further, of the nature of money itself. And the implications of alchemy helped turn Soddy, a Nobel Prize-winning chemist, into what was commonly called a "money crank" – one of several theorists working against the grain of accepted monetary and economic theory to ascribe the faults of the modern economy to its monetary and banking practices. Exploring Soddy's move into economic and monetary theory in the inter-war period, Linda Merricks traced the influence of Ruskin and of contemporary theorists on Soddy's thinking. But she noted that "what is missing is any sign of a particular moment or event which led to this new specific direction for his interests" (Merricks 1996: 112). That missing link was Soddy's readings in alchemy.

Soddy's thought had linked radium, transmutation, and the gold supply as far back at least as 1906, when he opined that "We may anticipate a more scientific system of currency being devised than the present" (Soddy 1906: 10). In 1908, Soddy held six popular lectures at the University of Glasgow that became the basis for his key book, *The Interpretation of Radium* (1909). Here Soddy discussed the nature of radioactivity, the possibility that the new science and future uses of the energies of the atom could transform the world for the better, and the history of humanity as a history of energy use. But he also cautioned that:

The race has grown used from the earliest times to the idea that gold is a metal possessing a certain fixed degree of value, enabling it to be used safely for the purposes of currency and exchange. It is no exaggeration to say that the whole social machinery of the Western world would be dislocated if gold altered violently in its degree of rarity.

(Soddy 1909: 211)

Soddy continued to push the idea that gold is not wealth, but just a convention of exchange, and continued to advocate that real wealth was a function of energy (Soddy 1912: 187). It is beyond the scope of this chapter to follow out Soddy's later connections to Arthur Kitson and other monetary theorists, but his most immediate impact would be on the writer H.G. Wells.

Wells was inspired to write his 1914 novel *The World Set Free* by Soddy's 1908 lectures and *The Interpretation of Radium*. Wells's novel, the first to envision nuclear warfare, picked up on Soddy's interest in alchemical transmutation in relationship to the new science, as well as his concerns that the synthesis of elements would undermine the gold standard – which occurs in Wells's novel as one of the catastrophic consequences of rapid scientific change and the control of vast powers of energy without a change in social structure and economy. Indeed, noting that the Manhattan Project physicist Leo Szilard was reading Wells's *The World Set Free* while working on the atomic bomb, John Canaday summarizes the connections among Soddy's *Interpretation of Radium*, Wells's novel, and the bomb: "The first nuclear weapons were in an important sense ... a scientific interpretation of a fictional interpretation of a scientific interpretation of radioactive substances" (Canaday 2000: 228).

Many scientists and occultists helped feed the popular press's appetite for alchemy. Alchemical transmutations that had been a topic for occult or gothic literature now became a key theme for science fiction as well. Written during the years of monetary crisis and eventual abandonment of the gold standard, this new generation of science fiction provided the fullest elaboration of the economic threat posed by modern alchemy. This can be seen clearly in Hugo Gernsback's sci-fi pulps between 1926 and the mid-1930s. Stories with such titles as "Jeremiah Jones, Alchemist," "The Gold Triumvirate," "The Mystery Metal," or, simply, "Gold," particularly focused on the effects of atomic alchemy on the world economy. In particular, they interrogated the nature and perils of a metallic currency. In a way that would look familiar to Soddy, these stories portrayed how science might move us beyond the crises and limitations a metallic system of exchange imposed on twentieth-century economies. Indeed, the arc from an occult alchemical classic like Bulwer-Lytton's *Zanoni* in the mid-nineteenth century to the atomic alchemy stories of the Depression era represents a blurring of lines between gothic and science fiction, and even between those genres and the monetary reform pamphlet.

By the 1930s, then, the scientific occultism born in the late nineteenth century and the alchemical inflections of the new atomic science had broken down long-standing barriers demarcating science from occultism. "Modern alchemy" even extended its reach into the domain of international monetary theory. But on August 6 and 9, 1945, atomic bombs – whose destructive power dwarfed the weapons imagined by H.G. Wells in 1914 – leveled Hiroshima and Nagasaki. The atomic bomb forced the trope of alchemical transmutation into the background. The Cold War's nuclear fears would take its place.

In the post-Hiroshima period, the alchemical understanding of atomic science gave way to concerns about nuclear warfare and the environmental devastations wrought by radiation. Some writers, such as Edith Sitwell in her 1947 "Three Poems of the Atomic Age," attempted to reinvoke the alchemical understanding in an effort to question the direction in which nuclear physics had taken the world with the atomic bomb program. But in the post-war era, alchemical tropes have largely been used in other contexts, and particularly in the domain of psychoanalysis and psycho-therapeutics. For example, Elizabeth Severn published books and papers on alchemical self-transmutation through therapy; in 1914 Freud's student Herbert Silberer published an alchemical interpretation of psychoanalysis entitled *Probleme der Mystik und Ihrer Symbolik*; the Golden Dawn-style Hermeticist and therapist Israel Regardie combined psychotherapy with ritual magic in his practice, publishing *The Philosopoher's Stone: A Modern Comparative Approach to Alchemy from the Psychological and Magical Points of View* in 1936–37. Most prominent, of course, is Carl Jung, who published several key works on alchemy and psychology, most importantly *Mysterium Coniunctionis* in 1954.

Alchemical tropes have also crept into the discussions of psychedelic drug experience and its self-transformative potentials, as in Alan Watts's 1960 article on LSD, "The New Alchemy," and the many current works ascribing the self-transmutations of alchemy to various entheogenic substances (ergots, mushrooms, and the like). Alchemy as a metaphor for self-transformation, whether put in spiritual or psychiatric terms, is commonplace in New Age culture and a prominent strand of discussion on alchemy listservs and websites. Paulo Coelho's 1993 novel *The Alchemist* simply uses alchemy as a metaphor for self-transformation. Clearly, alchemy's ability to negotiate boundaries between scientific disciplines, between the scientific and the spiritual, between the natural and the artificial, and between the scientific and that which is pushed outside the boundaries of science, remains with us in the twenty-first century.

Bibliography

Bolton, H.C. (1897) "The revival of alchemy," *Science*, 6:154 (December 10): 853–63.
Bulwer-Lytton, E. (1842) *Zanoni*, London: Routledge.

Canaday, J. (2000) *The Nuclear Muse: literature, physics, and the first atomic bombs*, Madison: University of Wisconsin Press.

Cummins, J. and Burchell, D. (eds) (2007) *Science, Literature and Rhetoric in Early Modern England*, Aldershot: Ashgate.

Dobbs, B.J.T. (1991) *The Janus Faces of Genius: the role of alchemy in Newton's thought*, Cambridge: Cambridge University Press.

Eggert, K. (2006) "*The Alchemist* and science," in G. Sullivan and P. Cheney (eds) *Early Modern English Drama: a critical companion*, Oxford: Oxford University Press, pp. 200–12.

Keller, A. (1983). *The Infancy of Atomic Physics: Hercules in his cradle*, Oxford: Oxford University Press.

Mazzeo, J.A. (1964) "Notes on John Donne's alchemical imagery," in *Renaissance and Seventeenth-Century Studies*, New York: Columbia University Press, pp. 60–89.

McLean, A. (1986) "A threefold alchemical journey through the book of Lambspring," *The Hermetic Journal*. Online. Available HTTP: <http://www.levity.com/alchemy/lambjrny.html> (accessed 3 November 2009).

Merricks, L. (1996) *The World Made New: Frederick Soddy, science, politics, and environment*, Oxford: Oxford University Press.

Morrisson, M.S. (2007) *Modern Alchemy: Occultism and the Emergence of Atomic Theory*, New York: Oxford University Press.

Newman, W.R. (1994) *Gehennical Fire: the lives of George Starkey, an American alchemist in the scientific revolution*, Chicago: University of Chicago Press, 2003.

——(2004) *Promethean Ambitions: alchemy and the quest to perfect nature*, Chicago: University of Chicago Press.

——(2006) *Atoms and Alchemy: chymistry and the experimental origins of the scientific revolution*, Chicago: University of Chicago Press.

——and Principe, L.M. (1998) "Alchemy vs. chemistry: the etymological origins of a historiographic mistake," *Early Science and Medicine*, 3: 32–65.

——and——(2002) *Alchemy Tried in the Fire: Starkey, Boyle, and the fate of Helmontian chymistry*, Chicago: University of Chicago Press.

New York Times (1911) "Alchemy, long scoffed at, turns out to be true" (February 19): SM12.

Ramsay, W. (1904) "Radium and its products," *Harper's* (December): 52–57.

Sclove, R. (1989) "From alchemy to atomic war: Frederick Soddy's 'Technology Assessment' of atomic energy, 1900–1915," *Science, Technology, & Human Values*, 14 (Spring): 163–94.

Shapin, S. (1996) *The Scientific Revolution*, Chicago: University of Chicago Press.

Soddy, F. (1906) "The evolution of the elements," British Association for the Advancement of Science.

——(1909) *The Interpretation of Radium: being the substance of six free popular experimental lectures delivered at the University of Glasgow, 1908*, London: John Murray.

——(1912) "Transmutation: the vital problem of the future," *Scientia*, 11: 186–202.

Stoker, B. (1903) *The Jewel of Seven Stars*, New York: Harpers.

Sutherland, A. (2007) "Mapping regeneration in *The Winter's Tale*," in Cummins and Burchell (2007), pp. 37–51.

Trenn, T.J. (1974) "The justification of transmutation: speculations of Ramsay and experiments of Rutherford," *Ambix*, 21: 53–77.

Weart, S. (1988) *Nuclear Fear: a history of images*, Cambridge, Mass.: Harvard University Press.

3

BIOLOGY

Sabine Sielke

Defined as the "study of living organisms, which includes their structure (gross and microscopical), functioning, origin and evolution, classification, inter-relationships, and distribution" (Martin and Hine 2008), biology is a young discipline. The first uses of the term *biology* go back to the eighteenth- and early nineteenth-century scientists Karl Friedrich Burdach, Gottfried Reinhold Treviranus, and Jean Baptiste de Lamarck, and included comparative anatomy, physiology, and embryology. In the course of the nineteenth century, the field was extended to all disciplines concerned with the study of organisms (Junker 2004: 8). Preceded by Aristotle's groundwork in taxonomy, physiology, and embryology, biology engages questions that have preoccupied philosophers and scholars from the very moment "science" evolved and that are constantly being reformulated. Inviting easy analogies between social and biological pro-cesses, biology has called into question established – religious and moral – values from its very beginnings. Needless to say, this makes biology a wide field, espe-cially if we take into account its history and the shifting perspectives it has taken on its objects. Currently, the discipline's subdivisions (including morphology, physiology, taxonomy, embryology, genetics, and ecology) approach living things and vital processes either on the level of biological organization (like cell or population) or with the focus on central issues (like structure and function or growth and development). At the same time, biology is divided into branches, including botany, zoology, and microbiology, which examine particular types of organisms.

In a similar way, literature is a complex, "experimental" cultural practice, its products replete with living organisms from all runs of life, interrogating and complementing the "life sciences" with its own particular knowledge of life. Hence, for instance, as reflected in Chapter 22 of this volume, the rise of "animal studies" as a branch of literary criticism. Literature, preoccupied with humans and other biological life forms, "inevitably make[s] biological assumptions" (Slonczewski and Levy 2003: 174). Even more so, (science) fiction – from Mary Shelley, Charlotte Perkins Gilman, H.G. Wells, John Taine, Aldous Huxley, and Frank Herbert to Ursula K. Le Guin, Joanna Russ, Octavia Butler, and

T.C. Boyle – takes up challenges posed by the biosciences and engages sexuality and reproduction, mutation and evolution, environment and biosphere, genetics and genetic engineering, as well as neurophysiology and brain research. Therefore, what follows is not – and could not be – an exploration of all living things and processes of life in literature. Rather, this article raises the question how the natural history of living organisms – which predates writing – has impacted on literature and its institutions and, to a lesser degree, how literature has influenced the discourse of biology. I cannot do so, however, without taking into account that our sense of biology, along with our sense of literature, has shape-shifted with the development of literary studies.

The very concept of a companion to literature and science is an after-effect of the history of knowledge production. In the nineteenth century, as previously interrelated discourses such as philosophy and the natural sciences separated, and the discourse of biology developed against the backdrop of the loosely connected fields of natural history and medicine (Junker 2004: 7), what we now know as literature also took on new shapes. While natural history and Romantic theories of life and evolution – the work of Jean-Baptiste de Lamarck, George Cuvier, and Étienne Geoffroy Saint-Hilaire, among others – still loomed large in early nineteenth-century literature, including, for instance, the historical novels of Walter Scott, the distinction between the realms of organic and inorganic matter was central for the rise of biology and left its imprint on concepts of reading. Accordingly, early nineteenth-century literary criticism adopted the trope of the "organic whole" to distinguish literary criticism from other forms of writing (Poovey 2001: 411), and to invest literature (and lyric poetry, in particular) with inherent principles of life. This laying claim to "foreign" disciplinary territory carries scientific assumptions and terminology along with it, assumptions that inform formalist literary criticism, its "anatomy" (Northrop Frye), and its (self-sustaining) sense of aesthetic autonomy, to this very day. Meanwhile, however, new metaphors – such as Derridean *différance* – have begun to dismantle the well-worn trope of organic unity.

Literature and science in general and biology in particular have thus remained closely interrelated, even as commentators from Thomas Huxley to C.P. Snow and beyond have denied their kinship. Even Snow took a "second look" at his 1959 two-cultures thesis in 1963 and "regretted" using as his "test question about scientific literacy, *What do you know of the Second Law of Thermodynamics?*" Instead, he "put forward a branch of science which ought to be requisite in the common culture": molecular biology (Snow 1963: 72–73). Unlike thermodynamics, Snow explained, this field "does not involve serious conceptual difficulties" and "needs very little mathematics"; "most of all," it needs "a visual three-dimensional imagination" (73). Snow's change of mind was, on the one hand, prophetic, in that it foresaw the biosciences' increasing significance at the turn of our millennium. This rise to prominence partly results from the fact that, unlike the second law of thermodynamics, which is of "universal physical significance," the new biosciences "deal … only with microscopic parts of the cosmos" which are nonetheless "of importance to each of us" (74). On the other hand, Snow's shift from physics to biology also counts as a major move from "hard" to historical science. According to zoologist Richard Lewontin, biology "is all about unique historical events … and does not have the kind of universals about which physicists speak" (qtd. in Poovey 2001: 437). And while no science can go about its work "without using a language that is filled with metaphors" (Lewontin 2000: 3), only biology offers "grand universals" or "generalizations" that actually work as "governing metaphors" (Lewontin qtd. in Poovey 2001: 437). Such metaphors, like "adaptation" or "construction," organize both biology and literary criticism and raise the question of what tropes dominate the field at what time and to what effect.

The biosciences' growing cultural visibility and prestige is partly due to the fact that they can be narrativized more easily than mathematics and physics. Sarah Franklin writes that the "power of stories about life itself and its Creation lies in their invocation of a global reach, a universal essence of humanity, a shared, primordial ontology" (Franklin 2000: 197–98). This power calibrates itself both at the level of politics, truth, or liberation, and as what Franklin calls *"the genetic imaginary"* (198). Projected in different ways by H.G. Wells as well as by Michael Crichton, Margaret Atwood, Michel Houellebecq, and Richard Powers, this imaginary resonates with one of the fundamental concepts of biology: the "unity" of basic living substance (all biological organisms are composed of cells) and of its origin (all life originates from the emergence of the same chemical substance, DNA). However, our sense of DNA as information, code, and language is itself a "period piece," as Lily Kay puts it (Kay 1999: 226), inextricably bound to the rise of the computer, information theory, and semiotics in the 1950s, while echoing both the sense that "in the beginning was the word" and that life is a book to be read, interpreted, and edited. Like the sustainable cultural impact of theories of evolution, the "genetic imaginary" thus foregrounds the persistent interrelation between literary, theological, and biological conceptions of life.

Given all these complexities, how can we even begin to think about the relation between literature and biology in systematic ways? Reading literature and biology as stories about life is one way of shaping the relation between literature and the biosciences; exploring stories of biology and biologists in literature is another. Still, narrative and narratology are narrow lenses, reducing biology to dimensions which can be "narrativized." Poetry – from the romantics' preoccupation with nature to C.K. Williams's poems on Alzheimer's disease and Ruth Padel's *Darwin: A Life in Poems* (2009) – forms and deforms our sense of the discipline in its own particular ways. Even more significant are technical terms (such as origin, genus, genre, gender, reproduction, and mimicry) and cultural practices (like classification and taxonomy) which both biology and literary studies employ to their own particular ends.

This chapter therefore traces the conjunctions of literature and biology in three steps. Step one explores some ways in which biology figures and functions in literary texts. Step two, traveling further distance, examines how biology's concepts and methods have made an impact on literary studies. Step three interrogates, albeit briefly, the question whether there is literature in biology. As it turns out, the crossroads of biology, literature, and literary studies still take us to two distinct modes of knowledge production.

Biology in literature, or: literary history and the evolution of the biosciences

When we speak of the evolution of literature (as we do since the 1920s) we relate a developmental narrative that both acknowledges similarities and overrides fundamental differences between natural and cultural processes. While evolution is often based on random mutations in the genetic make-up of an organism, the "evolution of literature" is a matter of neither chance nor nature. At the same time, literary history has been conceptualized as a series of epochs and ruptures – a functional analogue, perhaps, for extinction and decimation, which, in addition to diversification, map the course of evolution. Separating Romanticism from realism or Victorianism from modernism, we often identify clear-cut turning points, like the publication of a certain text, e.g. William DeForest's *Miss Ravenel's Conversion from Secession to Loyalty* (1867), or the opening of a landmark exhibition like the 1913 Armory Show in New York. Darwin's theory of evolution by natural selection thus offered models to (re)think processes of both development and mutability, suggesting that, just as nature does not radically transform at singular moments, literary history has its own (dis)continuities. This sense of literary history as an evolutionary process – rather than a series of singular works – was further developed, in different ways, in structuralism, semiotics, and systems theory.

Whereas organisms adapt to their changing natural environments, forms and functions of literary texts change with shifting media ecologies and technologies of reproduction, enabling processes of literary serialization of nineteenth-century novels, for instance, as well as seriality – that is, phenomena of repetition and variation. Still, in search of new descriptive, non-judgmental models for narrative adaptation (novel into film), Gary R. Bortolotti and Linda Hutcheon propose "a homology between biological and cultural adaptation." Both "are understandable," they argue, "as processes of replication. Stories, in a manner parallel to genes, replicate; the adaptations of both evolve with changing environments" (Bortolotti and Hutcheon 2007: 444). Coming at the expense of precision, the analytic value of such conceptual homologies remains limited, though.

The same goes for the utility of the term "reproduction" itself: the ability to reproduce and thus to enable the continuity of a species is the most fundamental feature of life – just as a book's longevity depends on its serial reproduction, although processes of biological reproduction and literary (re)printing hardly compare. At the same time, reproduction is a crucial, if not necessarily explicit, moment of many, if not all literary texts, irreducible to the so-called "family novel," and a gender issue which Charlotte Perkins Gilman "solves" in her 1915 novel *Herland* by making her female figures reproduce by parthenogenesis. Adapted to literary and cultural studies, the term resonates with its biological and ideological dimensions and highlights that literature prominently interacts with and substantially contributes to discourses of sexuality and sexology. Sexuality, in turn, is a preoccupation of all cultures (and their literatures), in part, as Ruth Hubbard has it, because "our most fundamental biological theory, the theory of evolution by selection, is constructed around sex and reproduction" (Hubbard 1987: 132).

Representations of natural processes in literature clearly mark the study of living organisms as a cultural practice with its own long history. By projecting nature as (m)other, for instance, literary texts from Romantic poetry to 1970s feminist fiction resonate with outdated beliefs about the origins of life forms. Perennial tropes like "mother earth," for instance, echo the belief, held by Ionian natural philosophy and elaborated in Lucretius's *De rerum natura*, that the species were actually born out of the earth. Perceived as "natural objects" by their male peers, female Romantic poets like Dorothy Wordsworth consequently viewed idealist conceptions of the relation between self and nature with the same skepticism that informs perspectives on (life) science taken in Shelley's *Frankenstein* and Emily Dickinson's poems. Texts like these expose both the interest women writers took in nineteenth-century bioscience and their exclusion from and critique of the rapidly transforming "horrific" scenes of scientific inquiry. In poems such as "The Brain – is wider than the Sky–," for instance, Dickinson – although probably unaware of the work of Bichat, Gall, and Sturzheim, who situated mind, memory, and emotions in the brain – acknowledges that our mental universe depends on neurophysiological processes. While Shelley speculated on the ability and future of the human brain, anticipating science fiction's later preoccupations, and while emotion has meanwhile advanced as a central category for literary studies, Dickinson's poetry thus marks a moment in the history of human self-consciousness when physiology begins to put pressure on established notions of mind, self, and soul. In turn, Richard Powers's novel *The Echo Maker* (2006) calls on Dickinson as it challenges current neurophysiology's supposedly new conception of a human subject that is neither continuous nor whole. Literature and poetry in particular, Powers reminds us, have been offering such insights for a long time.

The impact of Darwin's sense of evolution is felt throughout literary history, most pronouncedly perhaps in Victorian literature and naturalist narratives of "the survival of the fittest" (Herbert Spencer), and it still figures prominently in T.C. Boyle's "The Descent of Man" (1974), Gjertrud Schnackenberg's "Darwin in 1881" (1985), and Nino Ricci's *The Origin of Species* (2008). Similarly, texts engaging biological sub-disciplines, such as morphology in William Blake's 1794 "The Tyger" and botany in the flower imagery of the symbolists and modernists, critically interrogate science's "state of the arts," thereby contributing to the field's historiography, while at the same time evoking its ideological, political, and economic situatedness. Like Darwin's expeditions of the 1830s, the natural wonders starring in fiction and poetry – be they peculiar flowers and fruits, foreign cats and birds, or far-traveled furs and fossils – enter literary history as tokens of European economic interest and empire building, while calling into question enlightened thinking in general and traditional (biological) classification in particular. Early biology therefore plays a significant part in New Historicism and recent postcolonial studies. At the same time, travelogues such as Margaret Fuller's *Summer on the Lakes* of 1844 reflect on the threat of extinction of "varieties" of the human species, insisting that what "remains" of the American Indian needs careful preservation in museums. Much more recently, the trained biologist and author of *Birding Babylon*, Jonathan Trouern-Trend (2006) engaged in ornithological observation to communicate with locals and ascertain his own – mental as well as physical – survival as a paramedic during the 2003 Iraq war. Biology, literature, and the impact of globalization have obviously been entangled, in different ways, for a long time.

However, biology is no mere subject matter for literary practice; it is inextricably aligned with transformations of genres and literary forms. This becomes particularly visible in naturalism, where ideologies of natural selection and determinism go hand in hand with the attempt to "objectify" literary representation, that is, to render "life" as if it were a scientific object. Reducing human figures to (stereo-)types, the naturalist aesthetic, characteristic, for instance, of works by Stephen Crane and Émile Zola, in turn reproduces contemporaneous (pseudo-) scientific methodology and the biologization of race and class hierarchies. And as literary texts engaged biology, literary studies themselves transformed.

Biology and the study of literature: interfacing concepts and methods

While literary practice and theory have more recently challenged biologistic conceptions of cultural difference, literary and cultural studies have also, during the last two hundred years, evolved some of their central questions and concerns, privileged theories, methods, and concepts from a dialogue with the discourses of biology, and appropriated biological terms as cultural metaphors. And in both fields concepts such as origin and unity trope unresolved questions. How organisms originally emerged and who "authored" the early forms of life have remained open debates in the biosciences (Junker 2004: 10). Likewise, the origins of meaning have preoccupied literary critics even after the linguistic turn and "the death of the author." Moreover, the accounting of literature's relation to its context – or "real life" – is an ongoing debate in literary theory. More recently, theories of evolution in particular have been employed to enlighten our sense of literature's relation to "nature." For some critics, literature, just as life, makes more sense in the light of evolution than in neo-Marxist or post-structuralist perspectives.

Dissatisfied with the state of current literary theory, biopoetics and evolutionary aesthetics import elements of evolutionary theory and evolutionary psychology into the practice of literary criticism, arguing that forms and functions of literary texts are highly dependent on the make-up of human cognition. Some critics also engage contested arguments made by sociobiologists, e.g. the idea that literary and cultural forms serve a supposedly progressive evolution. Such arguments create normative ideas about literary practice and interpretation meant to displace poststructuralist and current politically inspired readings. However, approaching literature via evolutionary theory remains problematic. Just as literature does not *reflect* how organisms interact with the world, as some critics hold, but rather, *projects* various models about (how to read and represent) the world, the discourse of biology remains at a distance from (human) nature while evolving hypotheses on its processes. It is these models and hypotheses that interrelate as modes of knowing the world.

Taxonomy, hybridity, mimicry, or: negotiating biologisms

The field of taxonomy, most notably the groundwork of Carolus Linnaeus in *Systema Naturae* of 1735, has been dedicated to the systematic classification of organisms into ranks (domain, kingdom, phylum, class, order, family, genus, species) and their subdivisions. Such systematics is echoed when terms like genealogy and generation get appropriated by literary scholars or when narratologists aim at clear-cut distinctions between genres, sub-genres, and other classificatory dimensions of literary-critical practice. Categories such as species (borrowed from "the lexicon of theology and logic") and genre (imported from biology) played a major role in the discipline's professionalization (Poovey 2001: 412, 410). Nineteenth-century genre theory tried repeatedly to arrange literary texts in taxonomic systems that distinguish works of higher and lower order. Since culture, unlike nature, evolves not in stable blueprints which transform by genetic mutation or acquisition, but in ever-shifting structures and generic hybrids, biological taxonomy only works as methodological approximation. Even if literary texts can be categorized according to their recurrent patterns, these structures remain abstractions of an ideal generic purity which individual works necessarily violate and transform.

Literary studies consistently adapted terms and methodological moves deriving from taxonomy and evolutionary theory as well as genetics. Julia Kristeva, for instance, employed the conceptual register of genetics in an attempt to refine structuralist perspectives, and coined the terms *phenotext* and *genotext* to distinguish surface and deep structures of texts. Nowadays the vocabulary of genetics recurs in accounts of the "splicing" of genres and generic hybridity. As part of a conceptual complex including heteroglossia and pastiche, hybridity references blends of aesthetic forms and genres, e.g. in postmodern literatures – a tendency which has intensified the desire on the part of narratologists to refine their classificatory systems. Likewise, linguistics as well as early postcolonial critique acknowledged that languages and cultures comingle, making creolization, to recall the older term, a widespread phenomenon of multicultures. In an age of globalization we share the awareness that all cultures and literatures are hybrid, and have been for most of their existence.

As a metaphor of far-reaching cultural impact, however, hybridity still recalls nineteenth-century pseudo-scientific race theories, desires for racial purity, and narratives (and fears) of "miscegenation," racial contamination, and cultural mutability. Somewhat paradoxically, certain biological terms have thus been instrumental in deconstructing other biological takes on race, ethnicity, and gender which literary and cultural studies inherited and, from the 1960s onward, turned into central parameters of analysis. Engaging in a "strategic essentialism" (the term is Gayatry Spivak's), both the Black Aesthetics Movement and early feminist criticism insisted that literary and cultural productions are marked by fundamental and ultimately "natural" racial and gender differences. Whereas early black and women's studies thus unintentionally reaffirmed misleading notions of race and gender as inescapable destinies, gender studies and critical race theories have proceeded to redefine gender, race, and ethnicity as cultural categories which serve to disempower women and "visible minorities." By the turn of the millennium, such later claims received backing by the Human Genome Project. "Race and ethnicity," Craig Venter insisted, "are based not on scientific, but on social concepts" (2002). Curiously enough, while biology encourages us to "forget about" race, literary and cultural studies keep celebrating – and selling – ethnic differences. Was C.P. Snow right, after all, when he deemed the "literary intellectual" a racist while cheering the scientist as truly liberal, envisioning a bright future?

Matters are, of course, a bit more complicated. Whereas literary studies have indeed privileged revisionary perspectives on race and ethnicity, their analyses have been emancipatory in their appeal, pinpointing, for instance, how some fiction (by Charlotte Perkins Gilman and Thomas Dixon, for example) has reinscribed, while other texts contested, biological conceptions of race and gender (like much twentieth-century African American and women's writing did). Whether reinforcing or challenging eighteenth- and nineteenth-century conceptions of "natural" racial and ethnic characters, literary texts acknowledge that even our sense of what is natural or biologically determined is, as Judith Butler argues, discursive, and thus historically specific and variable. At the same time, Butler's challenge to our binary sense of gender is inspired by our actual biological make-up. Along with (trans-)gender and queer studies, she stresses that gender often remains ambiguous and not easily determinable, a fact that Jeffrey Eugenides playfully explores in his novel *Middlesex* (2004). Likewise, biologists themselves have intervened in the sex/gender debate, stressing, as Hubbard did in 1987, that biology and society are inseparable. Not only do organisms and their environment dialectically interpenetrate each other, but also, "organisms transform their environments all the while the environment transforms the organism living in it" (Hubbard 1987: 130). So far, biology and literary studies have merely begun to account for this reciprocity.

Organisms also imitate their environment, and the concept of mimicry – a term coined in 1862 by naturalist Henry Walter Bates – has enjoyed a rapid career in literary and cultural studies during the last decades. In turn, mimesis – another biological concept – has lost its appeal in (post)modern times. Employed in literary analysis, mimicry refers to strategies of repetition and citation of established styles and intertexts, such as the persistent use of the sonnet by African American poet Claude McKay, and to the imitation, performance, and parody of gender conventions and ethnic stereotypes whose effects are deemed to be politically subversive (by Luce Irigaray and Homi Bhabha, for instance). How far this deconstructive potential goes remains debatable, as there is no way of measuring or experimentally evaluating the political consequences of cultural practice.

Re-naturalizing literature? How biology challenges constructionism

Focused on parameters of difference and issues of the body, one can safely say that, during the last two decades, work in literary and cultural studies has challenged the essentialisms of a "reductive biology" (Connolly 2002: xiii). Meanwhile, though, the tables have turned and the concept of a culturally con-structed, gendered, racialized, and class-contoured body which emerged from those theoretical debates finds itself challenged by the biosciences. Evolving from neurobiology, molecular genetics and biotechnology are new insights into our corporeality, projections of a post- or transhuman subject, and novel notions about how our bodies interrelate with the world. Accordingly, during the 1990s – dubbed the "decade of the brain" – concepts like consciousness, mind, will, and belief became "re-naturalized." Perception, experience, agency, and memory, researchers insisted, are first of all physical matters, challenging central concepts of literary analysis. The major challenge this shift poses to literary and cultural studies, however, is that it privileges the "compositional dimension of body-brain-culture relays" over "cultural representations" (Connolly 2002: xiii). Contesting such social constructionism, it highlights that our readings of literary texts and other cultural practices, aimed initially at escaping a sense of biology as destiny, have in principle remained a hermeneutic enterprise, limited to interrogating the cultural complexities of meaning making. But what happens, some literary scholars wonder, if we focus less on how and what texts and images signify and more on the biological – or physiological – processes from which meanings of texts and images evolve?

The potential and the limits of such an approach to literary cultures are currently being explored, for instance, at the crossroads of literary and cultural studies and the cognitive sciences. As a part of this larger agenda, cognitive poetics interfaces cognitive neuroscience with classical rhetoric and offers an approach to literature that privileges the mind's capacity for integration over all texts' tendency toward dissemination. Alternative models, partly derived from biology, are also projected in Gilles Deleuze and Félix Guattari's "biophilosophy." Based on the conviction that art, philosophy, and the sciences provide us with distinct analytical perspectives, all of which are of equal value and in constant interplay, their work is informed by an ethical naturalism which is played out in arguments on "becoming animal," in appropriations of biological terms for a revisionary philosophy, and in idiosyncratic conceptions of literary and cultural practice. Most prominently, in *Rhizome* of 1976 and *A Thousand Plateaus* of 1980, these authors employ the term *rhizome* as an alternative to the vertical, arborescent model featured in traditional biology (such as the "tree of life" in genealogy) and in transformational grammar. As a cultural metaphor, "rhizome" resonates with a sense of literature and culture as non-hierarchical, decentered, manifold, interconnected, and nomadic. As a deconstructivist political move working across different "plateaus," ranging from the state to desire, "rhizomatics" is meant to displace established notions of rootedness and territoriality. The success of this model results in part from the prominence of tropes such as network and connectionism in sociology, cognition studies, and information science, and is echoed in the increased use of "mapping" as a new framework for the tools and activities of literary and cultural analysis.

Is there art in nature – or literature in biology?

The question whether natural organisms have or produce art – central, for instance, to the work of zoologist Ernst Haeckel – has also preoccupied literary and cultural theory. It is prominently addressed (again) by Deleuze and Guattari, who put forth the idea that "nature is expressive rather than mechanistic" and take human art as "a subcategory of organic creativity" (Bogue 1997: 468, 474). Likewise, Humberto Maturana and Francisco Varela, who invented the term "autopoiesis" to account for all living systems' tendency toward self-organization, self-maintenance, and self-reference (Bogue 1997: 476), call into question established notions of control and authority. Rather than accentuating Derridean *différance*, they downplay the difference between human and other organisms while amplifying non-verbal soundings. Evidently, however, whether we hold that there is art in nature or literature in biology depends on our critical perspectives rather than on the truth value of our claims. Even if we acknowledge that life writing, penned by prominent biologists, such as James Watson's *The Double Helix* (1968), presents us with fictionalized accounts of scientific discoveries and thereby affects our sense of biology, reading biology *as* fiction does not help the case.

Can literature in turn enhance the study of life forms? The greatest challenge for current biology is to improve our understanding of complex systems, like the central nervous system or the ecosystem. Providing their own knowledge, achieved by their own methods, literature and literary studies refocus our perspectives and project their own variants of these systems; after all, all literature is life writing. And yet, rather than forcing a common ground for biology and literature, and, by extension, literary studies, we may want to acknowledge that each field raises and explores its own (research) questions, uses its own particular methods, and, consequently, creates its own (research) objects in the process. In other words, life in literature and life as formulated in biology remain worlds apart. It is from the interrelation between worlds that both biology and literary studies may evolve adjustments of their own theories, methods, and analyses.

Acknowledgment

I thank David Schumacher and Anna Beckhoff for competent research assistance and Björn Bosserhoff for final touches to the manuscript.

Bibliography

Bogue, R. (1997) "Art and territory," *South Atlantic Quarterly*, 96(3): 465–82.

Bortolotti, G.R. and Hutcheon, L. (2007) "On the origin of adaptations: rethinking fidelity discourse and 'success' – biologically," *New Literary History*, 38(3): 443–58.

Connolly, W.E. (2002) *Neuropolitics: thinking, culture, speed*, Minneapolis: University of Minnesota Press.

Franklin, S. (2000) "Life itself: global nature and the genetic imaginary," in S. Franklin et al. (eds) *Global Nature, Global Culture*, London: Sage, pp. 188–222.

Hansen, M. (2000) "Becoming as creative involution? Contextualizing Deleuze and Guattari's biophilosophy," *Postmodern Culture*, 11(1). Online. Available HTTP: <http://pmc.iath.virginia.edu/text-only/issue.900/11.1hansen.txt> (accessed 8 September 2009).

Hubbard, R. (1987) "Constructing sex differences," *New Literary History*, 19(1): 129–34.

Junker, T. (2004) *Geschichte der Biologie: die Geschichte vom Leben*, München: Beck.

Kay, L.E. (1999) "In the beginning was the word? the genetic code and the book of life," in M. Biagioli (ed.) *The Science Studies Reader*, New York: Routledge, pp. 224–33.

Lewontin, R.C. (2000) *The Triple Helix: gene, organism, and environment*, Cambridge, Mass.: Harvard University Press.

Martin, E. and Hine, R. (2008) "Biology," in E. Martin and R. Hine (eds) *A Dictionary of Biology*, Oxford: Oxford University Press. Online. Available HTTP: <http://www.oxfordreference.com/views/ENTRY.html?subview=Main (accessed 8 September 2009).

Poovey, M. (2001) "The model system of contemporary literary criticism," *Critical Inquiry*, 27(3): 408–38.

Slonczewski, J. and Levy, M. (2003) "Science fiction and the life sciences," in E. James and F. Mendlesohn (eds) *The Cambridge Companion to Science Fiction*, Cambridge: Cambridge University Press, pp. 174–85.

Snow, C.P. (1963) *The Two Cultures: and a second look*, Cambridge: Cambridge University Press, 1993.

Venter, C. (2002) "Wir leben in einer wunderbaren Zeit," *Frankfurter Allgemeine Zeitung*, 15 March: 51.

4

CHAOS AND COMPLEXITY THEORY

Ira Livingston

I would not give a fig for the simplicity this side of complexity, but I would give my
life for the simplicity on the other side of complexity.

Oliver Wendell Holmes

I accept chaos. I am not sure whether it accepts me.

Bob Dylan

Learning to see chaos

Like many non-scientists, I first learned about chaos theory – as it was widely
called at the time – from James Gleick's popularization, *Chaos: The Making of a
New Science* (1987), which led me to Benoit Mandelbrot's classic *Fractal Geometry
of Nature* (1977). I remember, shortly thereafter, standing on a beach in the
flux of the waves. At my feet, the sinuous fingers of the sea sent smaller fingers
of froth reaching up onto the sand, waves of waves, all webbed with networks of
foam made up, in turn, of smaller networks of bubbles, webs of webs. Above
me, cirro-cumulus clouds sprawled across a blue sky, popcorn clusters of
clusters and wisps of feathery wisps. Everything had become *fractal* – that is,
patterned at multiple scales – and *self-similar*, with patterns recurring at every
scale, like a feather, each arm of which is shaped like a miniature feather in turn.

Learning to see chaos represented, for me, a kind of re-enchantment of the
world. No doubt some version of this experience is widely shared by those in
the throes of any old paradigm shift: the sense of being "present at the creation,"
the zeal of the convert. And in retrospect, gradual paradigm shifts can tend to seem
more and more like acute conversion experiences (see Livingston 2006: 21–22,
85–89). Even so, this episode of world-making bears some very specific historical
resonances, even in my highly condensed and aestheticized version. What I saw
happening to my world was stark modernist formalism (think of something

41

elegant and minimalist, like a Mondrian painting) being deconstructed into baroque postmodern plenitude and excess. On a beach in Massachusetts.

Part of the conversion to chaos involves learning to see structures not as structures, but as systems, events in process. This recognition is part of what makes chaos and complexity theory full partners with poststructuralist theory generally. Sociologist Niklas Luhmann describes society as a complex system whose basic elements are events of communication; that is, "not stable units (like cells or atoms or individuals) but events that vanish as soon as they appear" (Luhmann 1990: 83). Likewise (for example), when you deconstruct the image of a human body as a structure with a simple boundary between inside (self) and outside (nonself), you get something much more dynamic and fractal. Negotiations between self and nonself (and the continuous transformations of one into the other) happen not just at the skin but fractally and at multiple scales down to the cellular level: every cell in the body is engaged in this negotiation; in fact, every cell *is* this negotiation. If the body is a structure, it is a fractal one, with all edges and no interior – a whirlpool, a burning bush.

(And by the way, as you were reading those words, did you feel your body subtly opening up, exquisitely flayed and aflame, and in the process, a new sense of being-in-the-moment? If so, you can skip the rest of this section. Otherwise keep reading.)

These examples (of Luhmannian society and deconstructed bodies) are intimately related to poststructuralist accounts of texts not as hermetic interiors but as intertextual negotiations, and more generally to the concurrent paradigm shift in cybernetics from closed to open systems. Fully coming to terms with complexity means understanding it as a feature of open systems (see Chapters 19 and 20, this volume). On the scientific side, Prigogine and Stengers's *Order Out of Chaos* (1984), and Stuart Kauffmann's *The Origins of Order* (1993) were influential in developing accounts of how chaos and complexity play out *in time* as well as in space. Under their influence, I remember walking in the Nevada desert and noticing some of the ways that the scarcity of water shapes the plants and their interactions. I saw it in the spacing of their branches and blossoms, the shapes of their leaves and stems, their own spacing in the terrain, all selected to optimize water absorption and retention. Looking at a sagebrush bush, I saw a living algorithm – an unfolding reiterated equation – in multidimensional possibility space (that is, the set of all possible parameters), its form-in-process an ongoing exploration of this space.

(A bit more metacommentary: so far these little autobiographical vignettes borrow from the romanticized image of the scientist in the "Eureka!" moment, as in Gleick's description of physicist Mitchell Feigenbaum at the threshold of a chaos revelation: "his hair was a ragged mane, ... his eyes were sudden and passionate," etc. [Gleick 1987: 2]. But let me make it even a little more uncomfortable.)

The desert ecology felt deeply strange and deeply familiar to me. What I recognized in the sagebrush was a fellow creature engaged, like me, in the question of how to find what nourishes you in the middle of a desert. "Danger makes human beings intelligent," as Anna Freud (1937) put it. If this strikes you as hopeless anthropomorphosis or New Age twaddle, consider the following interchange:

> Chuang Tzu said, "See how the minnows come out and dart around where they please! That's what fish really enjoy!"
> Hui Tzu said, "You're not a fish – how do you know what fish enjoy?"
> Chuang Tzu said, "You're not I, so how do you know I don't know what fish enjoy?"
>
> (Chuang Tzu 1964: 110)

This, in any case, is also the kind of questioning, of both kinships and differences, that chaos and complexity make possible.

Complexity

Complexity and chaos both have a range of technical definitions, but both remain nonetheless profoundly ambiguous and paradoxical. The paradox of complexity can be indicated quickly: "if what we are interested in is complexity itself, then an image that we can easily identify as complex is thereby *less* complex than one whose complexity we find it difficult or impossible to ascertain" (Livingston 2009: 253). In the example of a social system as described by Luhmann, complexity derives from "an observer's inability to define completely all [the] elements' connections and interactions. ... [T]here is no totalizing perspective or omniscient selector. Each act of observation is embedded in what it observes" (Rasch 2000: 47). Such a definition should also be historicized: only *against* the fantasy of a disinterested, totalizing and transcendently objective perspective – a fantasy most specific to imperialist modernity – can complexity come to be defined as embeddedness, or rather, as the contradiction between transcendence and embeddedness (see Livingston 1996: 84–104).

Physicist Stephen Wolfram's quick definition of complexity also coordinates an observed and an observer: "In everyday language, when we say that something seems complex what we typically mean is that we have not managed to find any simple description of it – or at least of those features in which we happen to be interested" (Wolfram 2001: 557). This notion of the impossibility of simple description gestures toward a range of possible philosophical commitments, from antireductionism (the rejection of the principle that the whole can be known simply by knowing its component parts) to nominalism (the doctrine that all entities are radically unique, even if the same word can be applied to each of them). Wolfram (no philosopher) seems to remain committed to an extreme reductionism in which complex behavior always derives from the iteration of simple rules. Even so, his Principle of Computational Equivalence suggests some of the more world-changing implications of complexity. Wolfram posits, first, "that all processes, whether they are produced by human effort or occur spontaneously in nature, can be viewed as computations" (715), and second, that "almost all processes that are not obviously simple can be viewed as computations of equivalent sophistication" (716–17). Recognizing a single common level of complexity (or *virtual kinship* as I have called it) radically undercuts the master narrative of growth and development as increasing complexity. Instead of deploying increased complexity as a way of characterizing more "advanced" societies against more "primitive" ones (or sonnets from pop lyrics, or Guinness from Miller Lite), can we imagine more *empathetic* complexities?

Chaos

Nailing down chaos as a concept is also difficult, first of all, since even scientists use the word in several ways. Sometimes the word is used in its popular sense as a synonym for simple disorder. In this case, the more complex and fruitful kind of disorder – the kind of disorder out of which order can emerge – tends to be identified as "the *edge* of chaos." More often, though, *chaos* is used to mean the complex disorder itself; but to make things more confusing, it can also refer to the kind of order that emerges from such disorder. And here's the punch line: this ambiguity is not so much an obstacle to be cleared away, as it is *what chaos really is*.

The word comes from ancient Greek, where it signified the primal emptiness of space, the nothing from which something emerges. As it turns out, postmodern physics has elaborated this notion nicely: time and space are "crystallized from nothingness," and empty space, it turns out, "is not so empty – it is actually seething with activity" – the generative chaos of a "blooming, buzzing confusion" (as Victorian psychology pioneer, William James, famously described the perceptual world of the infant out of which, as the child learns to focus, discrete figures emerge). Physicist Frank Wilczek

> calls this non-empty emptiness the Grid. The Grid is reality's substrate, built from a host of ingredients: quantum commotion; the metric field that delineates space, time and gravity; exotic materials like the quark–antiquark condensate and the Higgs field that together transform empty space into a multilayered, multicolored semiconductor.
>
> (Gefter 2008: 44)

Ancient Greek cosmology, postmodern physics, Victorian psychology – why engage in a transhistorical treasure hunt for exemplars of chaos, like an old Jungian sniffing out archetypes? Well, first, because I want to offer examples that best give the feel of chaos, but also to gesture again at the questioning of kinships and differences that chaos makes possible, this time by suggesting that it offers at least the possibility of tracing different constellations of present with past knowledges, and thus, of rearranged genealogies and relationships between science and literature.

Cooking up complexity

Let me try to show you complexity stripped down to its most basic, or, if you like paradoxes, most simple form. First step: start with several things and processes. It may seem obvious, but it's important to recognize that, whenever you have several things, it means that they are not identical, even if they are (for example) three hydrogen atoms. Multiplicity involves difference. Thus, physics begins with certain particles and forces; biology, with assorted cellular components and their various interactions; language, with letters and words and grammar. Notice that, while sciences may desire a countable set of basic elements ("simples" that cannot be divided any further), things start getting stickier when you try to nail them down. For example, the more physics tries to identify a basic set of particles, the more they seem to multiply and evaporate into probabilistic clouds. Again, it seems that this difficulty is in grain: the discretely countable seems to emerge out of a more primal multiplicity. I call it *someness* (see Halberstam and Livingston 1995: 8–9); or, for a sustained account of multiplicity according to French philosopher Gilles Deleuze, see Manuel de Landa's *Intensive Science and Virtual Philosophy* (Landa 2002).

As in other recipes, after assembling the ingredients (nouns), you need to do something with them (verbs): *start combining them*. Now, in order to generate chaos and complexity, the process of combination has to involve non-linearity or *recursion* – the product of a process being fed back into the process again. But note that even simple mixing is describable as recursion. Recursion in mathematics, where the result of a function is fed back as a starting value for the next iteration of the function, is most famously illustrated by the Mandelbrot set, an infinitely complex fractal object generated by a very simple, repeatedly iterated equation. *Autocatalysis* is an example of recursion in chemistry. In the simplest version, some particular chemical catalyzes a reaction, one of the products of which is *more of the catalyst itself*, which thus continues to catalyze more of the reaction as long as more raw materials are present. In a modestly rich chemical environment, such reactions can develop complex self-amplifying and also self-inhibiting loops: behold the emergence of something like *metabolism*!

There is recursion in linguistics, starting with the way grammar enables the embedding of clauses within other clauses. This has been proposed as the way that grammar, given a finite series of elements, "can produce an infinite number of sentences of unbounded length"; even if there might be languages that lack recursion at the grammatical level (a controversial point, at this writing), recursion is nonetheless "part of how all humans think – even when it is not part of the structure of their languages" (Everett 2008: 240). Consciousness and language are recursive loops in an already very loopy universe.

There are also multiple forms of sociological recursion. Ian Hacking describes the process of social construction of identities as a non-linear process of "Making Up People" in which, for example, a category like "autism" or "multiple personality disorder" co-evolves in tandem with a target group of people and with sets of social practices, institutions, specialists, etc. The various components are bound together by a series of recursive loops and the whole configuration emerges, changes, grows, breaks apart, dissolves, and so on. Likewise, modern *discursive* formations like science, literature, and sexuality are also *recursive* configurations.

Discursive recursion is the subject of Andrew Abbott's *Chaos of Disciplines*. Taking sociology as his main example, Abbott shows how any particular division of the field, for example, into quantitative and qualitative methodologies, only generates further fractal divisions: the qualitative side itself will turn out to have a quantitative and a qualitative side, and so on. When such divisions are engaged not just as structures but as processes (versions of what is known in mathematics as *binary decomposition*), one is likely to find complex cycles of disciplinary polarizations, hybridizations, supplementations, and so on.

And there are several important kinds of recursion in literature. Structuralist linguist Roman Jakobson defined *poeticity* as that aspect of a message that refers back to itself. In the most basic sense, rhyme and meter and other devices self-referentially call attention to language as language rather than – referentially – to any content. And there are multiple ways that literature works recursively to thematize its own operations, starting with plays-within-plays, metafictions, and other self-referential narrative maneuvers.

My example here (and see Livingston (1996, 2006) for a great many more) is Alice Walker's well-known short story "Everyday Use" (Walker 1973). The story is set in the 1960s; the narrator is a tough old African-American woman who lives in the rural South with her younger daughter, Maggie. She is visited by her upwardly mobile older daughter, Dee (also known as Wangero), who is returning from the northern city where she has discovered Black Power and high culture, making her painfully condescending to her family of origin. Dee asks for a family quilt to take back with her to display but, in a sudden and almost religious inspiration, the mother gives the quilt instead to her younger daughter, even though Maggie will only put it to "everyday use."

Even in this thumbnail account, it's easy to guess at least one way the story is looped back around self-referentially: the story itself is an artifact rather like the quilt, part of the cultural legacy of mothers to daughters. If you wanted to shut down interpretation, you could try reducing the reinsertion of the story into itself to a slogan: stories, like quilts, are best put to use rather than aesthetically revered as art. This reading will do the trick only if you're allergic to interpretation – and to chaos and complexity. Otherwise, finding the recursivity helps you open up a set of generative contradictions at the heart of the story, such as the vexed relationship between art and utility. Even the apparently simple proposition that short stories can be understood as utilitarian objects implies a radical redefinition of utility with big, paradigm-shifting consequences.

Again I want to stress the experiential aspect of engaging recursive chaos and complexity, here via the reading and writing of literature. The way that a piece of literature is about itself is something that one often discovers only belatedly; it does not short-circuit interpretation but begins it anew. Likewise, in listening to poetry, the recursivity of the language need not produce an alienating art-for-art's-sake closure, but rather increase the living-thing-likeness of the language as layers of mediation work to intensify the sense of immediacy of the experience. And the act of writing in the grip of recursion is not a navel-gazing exercise but a much more dynamic process, a surfing on the recursive curl of things. Find that moment and try to sustain your balance in it.

What it all means

So what does it mean that we can find chaos and complexity in what is called nature and in the works of our own hands and brains, literature in particular, especially when we weren't exactly intending to place them there? I suggest three main ways of approaching this question.

First, it is often claimed that chaotic and complex processes are universal, so we should expect to find them everywhere – transculturally, transhistorically, and on both sides of the nature/culture divide. For example, Oliver Sacks proposes that the often conspicuously fractal visual hallucinations many people who suffer from migraines experience derive from the fractal structures of the brain:

> These hallucinations reflect the minute anatomical organization, the cytoarchitecture, of the primary visual cortex, including its columnar structure – and the ways in which the activity of millions of nerve cells organizes itself to produce complex and ever-changing patterns. We can actually see, through such hallucinations, something of the dynamics of a large population of living nerve cells and, in particular, the role of what mathematicians term deterministic chaos in allowing complex patterns of activity to emerge throughout the visual cortex. This activity operates at a basic cellular level, far beneath the level of personal experience. They are archetypes, in a way, universals of human experience.
>
> (Sacks 2008)

The paradoxes here are compelling: apparently it takes a hallucination – seeing something that is not really there – to see self-referentially what really *is* there, namely, the neurological mechanism *by which* we see. And the dazzling complexity of this vision, this ethereal meta-reflection, seems to derive from how it short-circuits us back to the solid substrate, the hardware. To put it another way, the universality of chaos and complexity loops back around to complicate and paradoxify even the simple assertion of their universality.

Of course, suspicion of universalized truth claims is also a leading operating principle of cultural theory. I'm still a card-carrying poststructuralist, which is why I will only identify this as a "leading operating principle" and not a truth claim itself (although the claim that "there are no universals" is at least interestingly contradictory). But it needs to be pointed out, too, that the *rejection* of universality claims often functions as a rear-guard action to bolster the nature/culture divide and to maintain the monopoly of humanists over the culture side. Although this maneuver may have some strategic value (for example, in trying to fend off scientists with their reductive explanations for everything), it's a rearguard action insofar as it's driven by an exceptionalism about humans that is, at bottom, theological rather than theoretical.

"Universality" as understood in chaos theory (the idea that blew Mitchell Feigenbaum's mind) is the prevalence of certain mathematical processes over a range of otherwise disparate phenomena. As I have already indicated, such prevalence need not be understood as difference-effacing similarity but as a kind of *virtual kinship*, what I have also called *withness* (Livingston 2006: 4): language resembles the world of which it is a part. If you prefer to stress difference rather than resemblance, you can start by considering instead how the plurality of all that is called "language" is riven by differences as radical as those that cleave language from the world.

The charged question of universality aside, we can trace historically particular discursive forces at work whereby literature came to occupy a privileged position to engage chaos and complexity. In an emergent modern ecology of discourses in the West, coming to a head around 1800, recursion and self-reference were banished from science and became the particular province of what came to be called literature. Foucault's account is that literature emerged as

> merely a manifestation of a language which has no other law than that of affirming – in opposition to all other forms of discourse – its own precipitous existence; and so there is nothing for it to do but to curve back in a perpetual return on itself; as if its discourse could have no other content but the expression of its own form.
>
> (Foucault 1973: 300)

We can trace this legacy in literature and literary studies over the past two hundred years, from Coleridge's principle of organic form, to Aestheticism's art for art's sake, structuralist accounts of language-as-system, Jakobsonian poeticity, the New Critics' insistence on literary texts (and on literature in general) as self-contained systems, and into postmodernism's anti-realisms and metafictions. And what does it mean for literature and literary studies that science has now also begun to embrace recursion and self-reference? This remains an open question. The melancholy account would be that literature, the novel, poetry, and so on are well on their way to extinction, their niche in the modern discursive ecology having been invaded and compromised from all directions. It seems to me, however, as though their modern incarnations are turning out to have been only a warm-up act for a process just beginning to unfold!

Finally, the argument can also be made that paradigms of chaos and complexity are in some larger and primary sense historical constructions of postmodernity and late capitalism. This can be understood as an epistemological claim, that our history shapes our understanding of the world and (for whatever reasons) is now causing us to notice and to name and to know chaos and complexity in new ways. A more ontological historicist claim – that is, a truth claim – can also be made: that chaos and complexity are actually being more intensively produced and selected for in the present era. In this account, capitalist modernity is often understood as an epidemic of systematicizations – proliferating systems and subsystems – amid dynamic crosscurrents of trade and migrations and exchanges whereby "all that is solid melts into air."

But we can engage chaos historically without subscribing to linear historicisms, either the kind that traces a one-way trajectory of ever-increasing complexity, or the kind that finds a one-way determinism from economic base to ideological superstructure. In tracing the emergence of chaotics, chaos-and-literature pioneer N. Katherine Hayles rejects another (related) kind of linearity:

> In particular, I am not arguing that the science of chaos is the originary site from which chaotics emanates into the culture. Rather, both the literary and scientific manifestations of chaotics are involved in feedback loops with the culture. They help to create the context that energizes the questions they ask; at the same time, they also ask questions energized by the context.
>
> (Hayles 1991: 7)

You may notice that – to put it in the pejorative senses reserved for it by classical logic – there is a rather glaring bit of question-begging or circular reasoning here: the description assumes the operation of feedback loops whose emergence it was meant to explain – or to put it another way, Hayles participates in the development she describes. My function here – and, I hope, dear reader, yours, too – is not to straighten out this circularity but to participate in turn, to weave more loops into the fabric. Enrich the mix beyond the simple dichotomy of science and culture – add capitalism, neurology, reality television – in any case, a bunch of things that are self-reinforcing – and perhaps ultimately self-limiting or even self-annihilating – into a complex loop, toss lightly, and there you have it.

A metabolism. A culture, describable as a more-or-less *sustainable* self-fulfilling prophecy. An ecology. A chaology.

Bibliography

Abbott, A. (2001) *Chaos of Disciplines*, Chicago: University of Chicago Press.
Chuang Tzu (1964) *Basic Writings*, trans. B. Watson, New York: Columbia University Press.
Dylan, B. (1965) *Bringing It All Back Home*, liner notes, Columbia Records.
Everett, D.L. (2008) *Don't Sleep, There Are Snakes: life and language in the Amazonian jungle*, New York: Pantheon.
Foucault, M. (1973) *The Order of Things*, New York: Vintage.
Freud, A. (1937) *The Ego and the Mechanisms of Defense*, London: Hogarth Press.
Gefter, A. (2008) "Something from nothing," review of F. Wilczek's *The Lightness of Being*, *New Scientist*, 199(2674), 20 September: 44.
Gleick, J. (1987) *Chaos: making a new science*, New York: Penguin.
Hacking, I. (2006) "Making up people," *London Review of Books*, 28(16), 17 August.
Halberstam, J. and Livingston, I. (eds) (1995) *Posthuman Bodies*, Bloomington: Indiana University Press.
Hayles, N.K. (ed.) (1991) *Chaos and Order: complex dynamics in literature and science*, Chicago: University of Chicago Press.
Jakobson, R. (1960) "Linguistics and poetics," in T. Sebeok (ed.) *Style and Language*, Cambridge, Mass.: MIT Press, pp. 350–77.
Kauffmann, S. (1993) *The Origins of Order: self-organization and selection in evolution*, New York: Oxford University Press.
Landa, M. D. (2002) *Intensive Science and Virtual Philosophy*, London: Continuum.
Livingston, I. (1996) *Arrow of Chaos: romanticism and postmodernity*, Minneapolis: University of Minnesota Press.
——(2006) *Between Science and Literature: an introduction to autopoetics*, Chicago: University of Illinois Press.
——(2009) "Complex visuality: the radical middleground," in B. Clarke and M. Hansen (eds) *Emergence and Embodiment: new essays in second-order systems theory*, Durham, N.C.: Duke University Press, pp. 246–62.
Luhmann, N. (1990) *Political Theory in the Welfare State*, trans. J. Bednarz, Jr., Berlin: de Gruyter.
Mandelbrot, B. (1977) *The Fractal Geometry of Nature*, New York: W.H. Freeman, 1982.
Prigogine, I. and Stengers, I. (1984) *Order Out of Chaos*, New York: Bantam Books.
Rasch, W. (2000) *Niklas Luhmann's Modernity*, Stanford: Stanford University Press.
Sacks, O. (2008) "Patterns," in the *New York Times*, 13 February. Online. Available HTTP: <http://migraine.blogs.nytimes.com/2008/02/13/patterns> (accessed 6 September 2009).
Walker, A. (1973) "Everyday use," in B. Christian (ed.) *"Everyday Use" by Alice Walker*, New Jersey: Rutgers University Press, 1994 pp. 23–36.
Wolfram, S. (2001) *A New Kind of Science*, Champaign, Ill.: Wolfram Media, Inc.

5
CHEMISTRY

Jay Labinger

The evolving relationship between literature and chemistry is intriguingly inter-twined with the history of chemistry and its perception. We might even consider the origins of chemistry as primarily literary, not scientific, since the core concept of atomic theory was initially expounded by the ancients (Democritus, Epicurus, Lucretius, etc.) with little if any appeal to observational (let alone experimental) support. Experimental work was much more central to alchemy, the precursor of modern chemistry that flourished during the Middle Ages and beyond. Indeed, one commentator has proposed that many nineteenth-century representations of what would then be considered modern chemistry are actually responses to persisting images of alchemists (Schummer 2007). A bibliography of literature and science includes references to alchemy in works of authors right up to the present, including Hawthorne, E.T.A. Hoffmann, Poe, Strindberg, Yeats, Joyce, Nin, and Pynchon (Schatzberg et al. 1987). Alchemy and literature is treated at length elsewhere in this volume.

Modern chemistry is usually considered to begin with Lavoisier, towards the end of the eighteenth century, although many developments earlier in the eighteenth century – particularly those centered on the concept of affinity – are much more appropriately classified as chemistry than as alchemy (Kim 2003). And we have another reason to focus on Lavoisier: the chemical revolution that he helped initiate was not just experimental but literary.

> For Lavoisier restructured chemistry from fundamental principles [and] provided it with *a new language* and fresh goals. ... A modern chemist, on looking at a chemical treatise published before Lavoisier's time, would find it incomprehensible; but everything written by Lavoisier himself, or composed a few years after his death, would cause a modern reader little difficulty.
>
> (Brock 1992: 88; italics added)

The importance of this linguistic turn can be seen in the opposition it generated: phlogistonists and others attacked Lavoisier's nomenclature, demanding one based on observable facts, not biased by theory (Golinski 1992). Some of the conservatives eventually acknowledged the impossibility of that goal, in language that rather strikingly anticipates much more recent developments.

> Since the Lavoisian theory was still controversial, [William] Nicholson tried to give impartial expositions of it and the phlogistic alternative, couched in a purportedly neutral terminology. ... His views about language had been shaken by the arrival of a new scheme of interpretation that exposed a purportedly factual discourse as itself theory-laden.
>
> (Golinski 1992: 247–48)

Rhetorical analysis in all fields of scientific writing is of course commonplace today; some recent examples include chemist Roald Hoffmann's article about the scientific article (Hoffmann 1988) and a couple of self-described "deconstructions" of early reports on the discovery of the Buckyball (Aldersey-Williams 1995: 78–90; 1996).

The following discussion of literary representations of the chemical sciences makes no attempt at comprehensive coverage;[1] rather I will try to illustrate the range of themes that have interested writers.[2] The division into two sections, nineteenth and twentieth century, is not so arbitrary as one might think, for the status of chemistry within science in general underwent a dramatic shift sometime around, or shortly after, 1900, resulting in a considerable change in the relationship between literature and chemistry.

The nineteenth century

> Chemistry at the turn of the century, after the discoveries of Lavoisier and his introduction of the new nomenclature, was a pioneer science in which exciting progress was being made. It was natural that it should acquire a fashionable appeal.
>
> (Sharrock 1962: 60)

During the nineteenth century, chemistry in many ways stood as an exemplar of experimental science and was a natural focus for writers who wished to portray aspects of contemporary science, even if those portrayals continued to be tinted by the residues of alchemy (Schummer 2007: 39). In England, chemist (and poet) Humphrey Davy was most responsible for connections between Lavoisier's new chemistry and literature. A close friend of Coleridge and Wordsworth, he influenced them and others – not only through his writing and lectures, but perhaps in some cases even physically, by promulgating experiments on the mental effects of nitrous oxide (Knight 1970: 63).

Scientists and romantic poets might appear to be odd bedfellows, given the apparent divergence of their worldviews (mechanistic, reductionist, systematic vs. mystical, holistic, idealistic). Indeed, anti-science rhetoric from the Romantics was far from uncommon, most prominently in Blake but not absent among Davy's friends, and there may be less than meets the eye in these connections: Wordsworth and Coleridge considered chemistry to be somewhat superficial, a relaxing diversion from the serious work of poetry (Sharrock 1962: 60). It has been observed that although Coleridge was certainly interested in chemistry (as were Keats and Shelley), little of it actually appears in his poetry (Ward 1976). Nonetheless, the English Romantics found the new science mostly congenial – "to Coleridge chemistry, 'the striving after unity of principle, through all the diversity of forms,' was 'poetry, as it were, substantiated and realized'" (Knight 1970: 62) – and allowed it into their work in significant ways. Davy's lectures, demonstrations, and treatises played a crucial role in the genesis of *Frankenstein* (Thoman 1998); Keats's use of "poetic" words such as "ethereal" was colored by the more scientific meanings they acquired from Davy's work (Sperry 1970).

Outside of England, the most notable appearance of chemistry in early nineteenth-century literature is in Goethe's *Elective Affinities*, which draws its scientific inspiration not from Lavoisier but from his predecessors, particularly Swedish chemist Torbern Bergman's work (of the same title) from the 1770s. Goethe offers chemical affinity as a metaphor for human relationships – a comfortable couple is torn apart when one (or both) is more strongly attracted to another party – with a lengthy disquisition on the process chemists used to call "double displacement" (now usually termed "metathesis"), which he describes in both abstract terms and a specific example, as represented in Figure 5.1 (Goethe 1809: 37–44). Goethe does not appear to foreshadow any *causal* connection between physiological chemistry and psychological behavior, a common enough theme in later work, such as *The Brothers Karamazov* (Schummer 2007: 58–59). Nonetheless, this early incorporation of detailed technical chemical knowledge into a fictional narrative is of considerable historical interest.[3]

Literary interest in chemistry was sustained through the century. Notable writers in whose work chemical themes have been identified include Balzac, Flaubert, Hawthorne, Poe, Dickens, Turgenev, and Dostoevsky (Schummer 2007; Varvogli and Varvoglis 1995; Schatzberg et al. 1987). For instance,

$$A{-}B + C{-}D \longrightarrow A{-}D + B{-}C$$

$$CaCO_3 + H_2SO_4 \longrightarrow CaSO_4 + H_2CO_3 \longrightarrow H_2O + CO_2$$
limestone   gypsum   "gaseous acid"

Figure 5.1 A generalized metathesis reaction, and Goethe's example thereof.

Hawthorne's oft-cited story "The Birthmark" alludes to the transition from alchemy to chemistry:

> In the latter part of the last century there lived a man of science. ... In those days ... the comparatively recent discovery of electricity and other kindred mysteries of Nature seemed to open paths into the region of miracle.
>
> (Hawthorne 1843: 264)

Here, the contents are clearly based on the former tradition, not the new science. Balzac depicted chemists and chemistry in several works, and was well informed about, if not particularly impressed by, its development as a modern science (Schummer 2007: 52, 57–58). At one point he seems to echo Goethe by analogizing chemical and psychological forces, to the point of metaphorically ascribing some "elective" powers to the former.

> Are not fearful poisons set up in the soul by a swift concentration of all her energies, her enjoyments, or ideas; as modern chemistry, in its caprice, repeats the action of creation by some gas or other? Do not many men perish under the shock of the sudden expansion of some moral acid within them?
>
> (Balzac 1831: 20)

Dickens gives us what at first seems a trivial case: the butler-made-chemist-by-simile – "Meanwhile the retainer goes round, like a gloomy Analytical Chemist: always seeming to say after 'Chablis, sir?' – 'You wouldn't if you knew what it's made of'" (Dickens 1864: 52) – who is subsequently referred to simply as "the Analytical Chemist" or just "the Analytical." Is this just a typical Dickensian fillip? Probably not: one commentator connects the character's role in the novel to the public visibility of his titular colleagues.

> So few are the scenes in which this Analytical Chemist appears and so seldom does Dickens give him a speaking part that it is easy to pass over him as just another whimsical flourish in a novel rich with imaginative embellishments of all kinds. But the Analytical's morose presence is felt even in scenes over which he does not officially preside; indeed his grim taciturnity becomes an implicit commentary on the verbal excesses and artificial rhetoric of his employers.
>
> (Metz 1979: 66)

This example illustrates, perhaps as well as any, the place of chemistry in nineteenth-century literature. While we find few really extensive considerations of up-to-date chemical theories and findings, authors showed increasing awareness of the prominence of modern chemistry in nineteenth-century science and society, and alluded to it almost as a matter of course. At the beginning of the twentieth century, and certainly by the end of World War I, the situation began to change.

The twentieth century

> What strikes one first about chemistry in twentieth-century literature is that, in comparison to physics, biology and mathematics, there is so little of it.
>
> (Ball 2007: 97)

Chemistry certainly does not disappear from twentieth-century literature: authors continued to make use of chemical themes, metaphors, and allusions, much as in the previous century. Some examples: a character in Zola's turn-of-the-century *Paris* can be identified with noted French chemist Marcellin Berthelot (Gratzer 1989: 423–24); substantial passages in Proust's *À la recherche du temps perdu* are expressed metaphorically in terms of chemical research (Large 1998); chemists and chemistry are found in a number of Updike novels (Varvogli and Varvoglis 1995: 45). But chemistry *does* appear to take a back seat to other sciences, a trend that has been ascribed to the absence of "grand themes": chemistry is perceived to have become more of a technology, concerned with synthesizing things, than a science asking deep questions about the world (Ball 2007: 98).[4] Contemporary chemistry has been described as falling "in-between" physics and biology in the public eye (Laszlo 2007: 335), without the fundamental underpinnings that would attract philosophers of science (Schummer et al. 2007: 1).[5] The new developments that really caught the eye of the public (including authors) came mainly from physics (relativity, quantum mechanics) in the first half of the century, and biology (DNA and the genetic code) in the second half.

Thinking of chemistry as more an applied art than a profound science harks back, in some ways, to the image of alchemy. To be sure, appreciation of chemistry primarily for its potential practical use was not a new development: it is found even in the Romantics' reaction to the new chemistry. Wordsworth proclaimed that "the discoveries of the chemist will become as proper subjects of the poet's art as any others ... familiar not in the laboratory but in their application throughout the general framework of social life" (Sharrock 1962: 72). However, in contrast to that earlier period, many manifestations of chemical discoveries in social life in the twentieth century came to be known for *undesirable* consequences – claims about "better things for better living through chemistry" notwithstanding. At the same time, "chemophobic" themes begin to appear in twentieth-century literature.

Perhaps the first such theme one might think of – at least in terms of popular visibility – comes from detective and crime fiction, whose authors always look to chemistry for ever-more-subtle and ingenious ways to poison victims. This topic, usually taken to date back to Sherlock Holmes,[6] has attracted a great deal of attention; two entire collections (mostly concerned with non-fictional forensic science) devoted to "Chemistry and Crime" (Gerber 1983; Gerber and Saferstein 1997) feature several articles on fiction. But in fact we do *not* often see any real anti-chemistry feelings here. The majority of cases involve familiar poisons – cyanide, arsenic, strychnine, etc. – and even when more exotic agents do appear, the net effect seems oddly *pro*-science. Agatha Christie's work provides some notable examples, as when a series of apparently supernaturally induced deaths, or the observation of a mysterious aura about an imminent victim, are explained respectively by thallium and phosphorus poisoning (Christie 1962, 1937). Relatively few unfavorable images of chemistry are found in this genre; one such is in the *Bulldog Drummond* series of the 1920s, which features "a poison which is absorbed through the skin ... with [a] chemist fashioning it into a weapon so horrible as to make war unthinkable" (Rae 1983: 565).[7]

The most elaborate treatment of chemistry in detective literature is found in *The Documents in the Case* (Sayers and Eustace 1930), in which a man who appears to have died from eating the wrong kind of mushrooms (*Amanita muscaria* instead of *A. rubescens*) was actually poisoned by the addition of synthetic muscarine to an innocuous dish; the murder is exposed by the discovery that the remnants show no trace of optical activity (the rotation of polarized light), which the natural (but not the synthetic) toxin would. The exposition includes a synthetic route to muscarine and its chemical formula (both were incorrect, unfortunately[8]) and, of greater interest, some remarks about the key role of chirality in life, which the authors *did* get pretty much right.

> [U]p to the present, it is only living substance that has found the trick of transforming a symmetric, optically inactive compound into a single, asymmetric, optically active compound. ... "At the moment when Life first arose, a directive force came into play ... to select one crystallised enantiomorph and reject its asymmetric opposite."
>
> (Sayers and Eustace 1930: 244–46)

Later in the century, as the hard-boiled detective and the police procedural took over the field, chemistry was relegated to supporting forensic work, as in the series of novels by Patricia Cornwell (Gerber 1997), or vanished altogether. A notable exception to the latter trend is Joseph Wambaugh's *The Delta Star* (Wambaugh 1983), which (though undeniably in the hard-boiled school) includes a murder by scientific instrument, as well as some serious scientific content (photochemistry).[9]

The role of chemistry in science fiction, another genre in which it might be expected to feature predominantly, appears to be rather limited (again, in comparison to physics and biology). Much of the material in a collection of essays on the topic (Stocker 1998) addresses science fiction in general rather than focusing specifically on chemistry, although a number of interesting illustrations are presented, including two works by chemist-author Isaac Asimov – a mock-scientific article concerning thiotimiline, a substance so soluble that it dissolves *before* water is added, and a short story about a goose that really does lay golden eggs – both reprinted in full.

A much more significant factor in the increasingly negative image of chemistry was the introduction of gas warfare in World War I; much of the onus thereof centers on the figure of Fritz Haber, who appears (explicitly or thinly disguised) in several literary works (Hoffmann and Laszlo 2001). The most notable of these is the verse play *Square Rounds* (Harrison 1992), which includes several other historical figures (Justus von Liebig, William Crookes) along with Haber, and includes a great deal of exposition of chemical detail, using a variety of theatrical devices (including stage magic) to leaven the potential didacticism. The play does not take a purely anti-chemistry moral stance: characters question whether gas warfare is inherently any more inhumane than explosives (or, for that matter, the eponymous square bullets invented by an eighteenth-century Englishman to increase the pain inflicted on non-Christian opponents); chemistry's *positive* contributions are also highlighted, although by no means as an unmixed blessing.

> Nitrogen fixation giving ammonia NH_3
> Makes fertilizers, yes, but also TNT.
> Nitrogen as nitrates could make all Europe green
> But it blasts in even blacker as tri-ni-tro-to-lu-ene.
> The nitrogen you brought from way up high
> Now blows the men you saved into the sky.
> Those nitrates you produced for fertilizer
> Now serve the warlike purpose of the Kaiser.
>   (Harrison 1992: 27)

An earlier (but far less entertaining) dramatic portrayal of technological advancement as a double-edged sword is Kaiser's two-part play *Gas*, in which an unspecified gas powers the world economy, but occasionally explodes and kills people; a popular uprising against its use is quelled with the aid of a newly invented poison gas (Kaiser 1918, 1920). This theme is common in twentieth-century literature, with numerous cautionary tales about environmental degradation and adverse health effects, all the way up to global-scale catastrophic events.

Truly apocalyptic literary disasters relate to chemistry less frequently than to physics or biology (think of *On the Beach* or *Oryx and Crake*); perhaps the most familiar end-of-the-world story involving chemistry is Kurt Vonnegut's *Cat's Cradle*, in which a high-melting crystalline modification of water ("ice-nine") nucleates the solidification of the entire terrestrial water supply (Vonnegut 1963).[10] In Don DeLillo's *White Noise* there is a literal "airborne toxic event" – a release of a mythical waste product: "Nyodene D. is a whole bunch of things thrown together that are byproducts of the manufacture of insecticide. The original stuff kills roaches, the byproducts kill everything left over" (DeLillo 1986: 131). But it affects only a limited area and does not actually kill anybody. More important, though, is the metaphoric significance of the event: it stands for death in general, the referent of the book's title: "What if death is nothing but sound?" "Electrical noise. ... Uniform, white" (DeLillo 1986: 198). DeLillo's choice of a chemical metaphor emphasizes the *synthetic* character of contemporary society and its inability to deal with death as a natural part of life.[11]

Richard Powers's *Gain*, which intertwines the history of a chemical company with the story of a woman dying of ovarian cancer – possibly caused by exposure to the company's discharges – looks at a larger, more complex picture. Chemical synthesis is responsible not only for the toxic wastes that may have caused the cancer, but also for the therapeutic chemicals that might cure it; the point is reinforced by the fact that one of the agents used is taxol, originally a "natural" product but now made synthetically, with the company in question providing some of the precursors for the process (Powers 1998: 75, 151). There is also a modest dose of hard chemistry; Powers's comparison of metathesis reactions involved in making soda to dancers exchanging partners (130–31) recalls Goethe's much earlier analogy.

There has been some counterbalance to chemophobic themes in the twentieth century, much of it provided by practicing chemists who turned to literature. Primo Levi, a chemist and survivor of Auschwitz who wrote extensively on both of those experiences, gives us in *The Periodic Table* a group of autobiographical vignettes and short stories, each taking its inspiration from one of the chemical elements.[12] The last one, on carbon, eloquently rebuts the chemistry–death connection by reconnecting it to life.

> [E]very element says something to everyone (something different to each). ... One must perhaps make an exception for carbon, because it says everything to everyone. ... To carbon, the element of life, my first literary dream was turned, insistently framed in an hour and a place when my life was not worth much: yes, I wanted to tell the story of an atom of carbon.
>
> (Levi 1975: 225)

Roald Hoffmann and Carl Djerassi are two more recent chemists-turned-authors. The former is best known for his poetry and essays; in one book on the relation of science to Jewish traditions he examines the aforementioned topic of chirality and its origins (Hoffmann and Schmidt 1997), while another expounds on the *positive* aspects of synthesis in chemistry, emphasizing creativity rather than artificiality (Hoffmann 1995: 85–100). Djerassi has written a series of novels and plays that he describes as "science-in-fiction" (Djerassi 1998: ix); they are as much (or more) about the scientific profession in the contemporary world as the science itself.

Hoffmann and Djerassi have collaborated on a play, *Oxygen*, which is a good place to conclude, as the subject of the play – to whom should an (imaginary) "retro-Nobel Prize" for the discovery of oxygen be given? – takes us full circle to the starting point for this essay: Lavoisier is one of the three candidates (along with Priestley and Scheele). *Oxygen* attempts to communicate both the findings and the politics of science without sacrificing comprehensibility or entertainment value – an ambitious goal, as the authors suggest in their dialogue: "Who'd like to come up with some simple phrases to explain to [the] public that without the discovery of oxygen there would've been no Chemical Revolution ... no chemistry as we now know it?" (Djerassi and Hoffmann 2001: 28). Works of this sort inspire hope that chemistry can reclaim its stature as a subject for serious exploration in literature, by chemist and non-chemist authors alike, as we move forward in the twenty-first century.

Acknowledgments

Thanks to Steve Weininger, Jan Golinski, and Rolf Selbmann for helpful discussions and/or providing copies of hard-to-access articles.

Notes

1 To the best of my knowledge there is no such treatment of the field. There are several essays on the general topic of literature and chemistry (Rae 1983; Varvogli and Varvoglis 1995; Weininger 2002); others focus on the nineteenth (Schummer 2007; Selbmann 1996) or twentieth (Krätz 1991; Ball 2007) century. An annotated bibliography on literature and science (Schatzberg et al. 1987) provides many useful references; annual updates can be found in various issues of the journal *Configurations*. A compendium of excerpts (Gratzer 1989) contains a large number of chemistry-related examples, along with useful commentaries thereon; an entire volume of another collection is devoted to chemistry (Dolan 2004) but contains primarily non-fiction and runs only through 1834.

2 One that I will not address, although it arguably falls into the realm of chemistry, is thermodynamics, which has its own separate chapter in this volume. Entropy in particular constitutes an important subject in works such as *The Education of Henry Adams*, Pynchon's *The Crying of Lot 49*, Stoppard's *Arcadia*, among many others. Medical aspects of chemistry are largely left to the chapter on Literature and Medicine.

3 Not enough, though, to redeem what I would otherwise characterize as a rather tedious tragedy of manners.

4 In a similar vein, Horgan suggests that whereas all of science is running out of great questions by the end of the twentieth century, chemistry did so around 1930 (Horgan 1996). Few chemists would share this perception (Ball has a PhD in physics, although he did study chemistry as well).

5 Again, chemists (including Laszlo) dispute these characterizations, replacing "in-between" with "central" (Breslow 1997); there has also been a recent strong resurgence of interest in philosophy of chemistry (Scerri and McIntyre 1997).

6 Actually, this is a misconception: although Holmes is a formidable amateur chemist, often found in the middle of recreational experiments, one finds surprisingly little chemistry in his actual detective work, as others have also remarked (O'Brien 1993).

7 The idea of a poison so lethal and penetrating as to kill virtually instantly on contact continued to fascinate later authors (Stout 1937; Francis 1978); the former's method, which drastically overestimates the toxicity of the proposed agent (nitrobenzene), would certainly not work.

8 As has been pointed out elsewhere (Foster 1983), the correct structure of muscarine was not established until after the book was published; but the formula given was known to be incorrect, and the synthetic method could not possibly have produced a structure capable of exhibiting optical activity. Still later it was determined that muscarine is *not* the main toxic principle of *A. muscaria* (which is not all that lethal anyway, compared to other members of the *Amanita* family).

9 Wambaugh gleaned the latter through his friendship with my Caltech colleague, chemist Harry Gray.

10 According to H.G. Wells, the concept was originally offered to him by the famous colloid chemist Irving Langmuir as a promising basis for a science-fiction story (Gratzer 1989: 309).

11 Chemistry in both *White Noise* and *Gain* is discussed at considerably greater length in Ball 2007.

12 For an allegorical reading of *The Periodic Table*'s chemical elements, see Clarke 1993. Another notable element-inspired autobiography (by a non-chemist) is Oliver Sacks's *Uncle Tungsten* (Sacks 2001).

Bibliography

Aldersey-Williams, H. (1995) *The Most Beautiful Molecule: the discovery of the Buckyball*, New York: John Wiley and Sons.

——(1996) "Reading between the lines," *The Chemical Intelligencer*, 2(4): 37–41.

Ball, P. (2007) "Chemistry and power in recent American fiction," in Schummer et al. 2007, pp. 97–135.

Balzac, H. de (1831) *Le Peau de Chagrin*; trans. anon., *The Magic Skin*, in *The Novels and Dramas of Honoré de Balzac*, vol. 1, New York: George D. Sproul, 1903.

Breslow, R. (1997) *Chemistry Today and Tomorrow: the central, useful, and creative science*, Washington, DC: American Chemical Society.

Brock, W.H. (1992) *The Norton History of Chemistry*, New York: W.W. Norton.

Christie, A. (1937) *Poirot Loses a Client*, New York: Dodd Mead and Co.

——(1962) *The Pale Horse*, New York: Dodd Mead and Co.

Clarke, B. (1993) "Aspects of the daemonic in Primo Levi's *The Periodic Table*," in M.W. McRae (ed.) *The Literature of Science: perspectives on popular scientific writing*, Athens: University of Georgia Press, pp. 169–85.

DeLillo, D. (1986) *White Noise*, New York: Penguin Books.

Dickens, C. (1864) *Our Mutual Friend*, New York: Penguin Books, 1971.

Djerassi, C. (1998) *NO*, Athens: University of Georgia Press.

——and Hoffmann, R. (2001) *Oxygen*, Weinheim: Wiley-VCH Verlag.

Dolan, B. (ed.) (2004) *Chemistry*, vol. 8 of J. Hawley (ed.) *Literature and Science, 1660–1834*, London: Pickering & Chatto.

Foster, N. (1983) "Strong poison: chemistry in the works of Dorothy L. Sayers," in Gerber 1983, pp. 17–29.

Francis, D. (1978) *Trial Run*, New York: Pocket Books.

Gerber, S.M. (ed.) (1983) *Chemistry and Crime: from Sherlock Holmes to today's courtroom*, Washington, DC: American Chemical Society.

——(1997) "Forensic science in detective fiction," in Gerber and Saferstein 1997, pp. 191–98.

——and Saferstein, R. (eds) (1997) *More Chemistry and Crime: from Marsh arsenic test to DNA profile*, Washington, DC: American Chemical Society.

Goethe, J.W. v. (1809) *Die Wahlverwandtschaften*, trans. E. Mayer and L. Bogan *Elective Affinities*, Chicago: Henry Regnery, 1963.

Golinski, J. (1992) "The chemical revolution and the politics of language," *The Eighteenth Century*, 33: 238–51.

Gratzer, W. (ed.) (1989) *A Literary Companion to Science*, New York: W.W. Norton.

Harrison, T. (1992) *Square Rounds*, London: Faber and Faber.

Hawthorne, N. (1843) "The Birthmark," in H.H. Waggoner (ed.) *Nathaniel Hawthorne: selected tales and sketches*, 3rd edn, New York: Holt, Rinehart and Winston, 1970, pp. 264–81.

Hoffmann, R. (1988) "Under the surface of the chemical article," *Angewandte Chemie, International Edition in English*, 27: 1593–1602.

——(1995) *The Same and Not the Same*, New York: Columbia University Press.

——and Laszlo, P. (2001) "Coping with Fritz Haber's somber literary shadow," *Angewandte Chemie, International Edition in English*, 40: 4599–604.

——and Schmidt, S.L. (1997) "You must not deviate to the left or the right," in *Old Wine New Flasks: reflections on science and Jewish Tradition*, New York: W.H. Freeman and Co., pp. 79–121.

Horgan, J. (1996) *The End of Science: facing the limits of knowledge in the twilight of the scientific age*, Reading, Mass.: Helix Books.

Kaiser, G. (1918) *Gas*, trans. B.J. Kenworthy, in *Five Plays*, London: Calder and Boyars, 1971.

——(1920) *Gas Zweiter Teil*, trans. B.J. Kenworthy, in *Five Plays*, London: Calder and Boyars, 1971.

Kim, M.G. (2003) *Affinity, That Elusive Dream: a genealogy of the chemical revolution*, Cambridge, Mass.: MIT Press.

Knight, D.M. (1970) "The physical sciences and the romantic movement," *History of Science*, 9: 54–75.

Krätz, O. (1991) "Die Chemie im Spiegel der Literatur des 20. Jahrhunderts," *Chemie in Unserer Zeit*, 25: 44–50.

Large, D. (1998) "Chemical solutions: scientific paradigms in Nietzsche and Proust," in E.S. Shaffer (ed.) *The Third Culture: literature and science*, New York: Walter de Gruyzer, pp. 217–36.

Laszlo, P. (2007) "On the self-image of chemists, 1950–2000," in Schummer et al. 2007, pp. 329–67.

Levi, P. (1975) *Il Sistema Periodico*, trans. R. Rosenthal, *The Periodic Table*, New York: Schocken Books, 1984.

Metz, N.A. (1979) "The artistic reclamation of waste in *Our Mutual Friend*," *Nineteenth Century Fiction*, 34: 59–72.

O'Brien, J.F. (1993) "What kind of a chemist was Sherlock Holmes?" *Chemistry & Industry* (London), 394–98.

Powers, Richard (1998) *Gain*, New York: Farrar, Straus and Giroux.

Rae, I.D. (1983) "Dustcoats in dustjackets," *Chemistry in Britain*, 565–69.

Sacks, O. (2001) *Uncle Tungsten*, London: Picador.

Sayers, D.L. and Eustace, R. (1930) *The Documents in the Case*, New York: Harper Paperbacks, 1995.

Scerri, E.R. and McIntyre, L. (1997) "The case for the philosophy of chemistry," *Synthese*, 111: 213–32.

Schatzberg, W., Waite, R.A. and Johnson, J.K. (1987) *The Relations of Literature and Science: an annotated bibliography of scholarship, 1880–1980*, New York: Modern Language Association of America.

Schummer, J. (2007) "Historical roots of the 'mad scientist': chemists in nineteenth-century literature," in Schummer et al. 2007, pp. 37–79.

——, Bensaude-Vincent, B. and Van Tiggelen, B. (eds) (2007) *The Public Image of Chemistry*, Singapore: World Scientific Publishing Co.

Selbmann, R. (1996) "Auf den Menschen reimt sich die ganze Natur: über das Verhältnis von Chemie und Literatur im 19. Jahrhundert," *Euphorion – Zeitschrift für Literaturgeschichte*, 90: 153–65.

Sharrock, R. (1962) "The chemist and the poet: Sir Humphrey Davy and the preface to *Lyrical Ballads*," *Notes and Records of the Royal Society of London*, 17: 57–76.

Sperry, S.M. Jr. (1970) "Keats and the chemistry of poetic creation," *PMLA*, 85: 268–77.

Stocker, J.H. (1998) *Chemistry and Science Fiction*, Washington, DC: American Chemical Society.

Stout, R. (1937) *The Red Box*, New York: Farrar & Rinehart.

Thoman, C.J. (1998) "Sir Humphrey Davy and *Frankenstein*," *Journal of Chemical Education*, 75: 495–96.

Varvogli, A. and Varvoglis, A. (1995) "Chemists as characters and as authors in literature," *The Chemical Intelligencer*, 1(2): 43–46, 55.

Vonnegut, K. (1963) *Cat's Cradle*, New York: Holt, Rinehart & Winston.

Wambaugh, J. (1983) *The Delta Star*, New York: William Morrow and Co.

Ward, R. (1976) "What forced by fire: concerning some influences of chemical thought and practice upon English Poetry," *Ambix*, 23: 80–95.

Weininger, S.J. (2002) "Chemistry," in P. Gossin (ed.) *Encyclopedia of Literature and Science*, Westport, Conn.: Greenwood Press, pp. 77–79.

6

CLIMATE SCIENCE

Robert Markley

Even a decade ago, the idea of writing or reading an essay on climate in a companion to literature and science would have seemed odd. It may be difficult to remember, but the development of literary theory in the 1980s in the United States and Europe occurred during an era dominated by the notion of nuclear winter, the scientific model that predicted dramatic global cooling in the event of a thermonuclear war. Since that time, dramatic changes in a range of scientific disciplines – from meteorology, to computer science, to geology, to glaciology – have led to a revolution in the way that scientists think about the Earth's climate, its natural cycles of cooling and heating, and the ways in which humankind has been warming the planet since the Industrial Revolution, and perhaps longer (Ruddiman 2005). Although popular culture, including some bad Hollywood disaster movies and some good science-fiction novels, quickly picked up on the idea of global warming, most literary critics and serious novelists have been slow to deal with the prospect of abrupt climate change. No one so far has been able to write a "realistic" novel about a long-term trend of sustained warming that really has just begun, and our cultural fascination – often bordering on narcissism – with our own lives, inner experiences, and social relations has tended to return us to deeply embedded ways of thinking about a romanticized Nature, as opposed to a dynamic climate. In many respects, 200 years after revolutions in astronomy, geology, and biology challenged traditional ways of thinking about history, we are still coming to grips with ideas of time and environment that are not merely extensions of our bodily experiences, memories, and written histories.

Living through and writing about climate change in the twenty-first century invariably poses questions about the relationships among three different registers of time: experiential or embodied time, historical time, and climatological time. Each of these registers resists hard-and-fast definition, in part because climatological time – accessible through and mediated by a range of complex technologies – complicates the connections between reading and narrative that Paul Ricoeur identifies as crucial to the phenomenological and historical perceptions of time (Ricoeur 1984–88). Climatological time has emerged from a complex genealogy of what Jean-Joseph Goux calls "symbolic economies" that characterize crises of representation in the human sciences (Goux 1990; Markley 1993). Consider the implied but entangled registers of time in Henry Wadsworth Longfellow's 1847 poem "Evangeline." At the beginning of the poem, Longfellow asks his readers to imagine the landscape of Acadia on the east coast of Canada:

> THIS is the forest primeval. The murmuring pines and the hemlocks,
> Bearded with moss, and in garments green, indistinct in the twilight,
> Stand like Druids of eld, with voices sad and prophetic.
>
> (Longfellow 1848: 5)

Although cast in the imagery of prehistory, this "primeval" forest is inhabited primarily by memories of – or a deep nostalgia for – a vanished and yet thoroughly humanized past that has been absorbed into, yet remains constitutive of, the landscape. Longfellow's repetition of his opening half-line signals an implied recognition of the dialectical relations between human acts and the environment that define Nature (Crumley 1994; Ingerson 1994). The "forest primeval" becomes coeval with, and indivisible from, an anthropocentric world:

> This is the forest primeval; but where are the hearts that beneath it
> Leaped like the roe, when he hears in the woodland the voice
>   of the huntsman?
> Where is the thatch-roofed village, the home of Acadian farmers, –
> Men whose lives glided on like rivers that water the woodlands,
> Darkened by shadows of earth, but reflecting an image of heaven?
> Waste are those pleasant farms, and the farmers forever departed!
> Scattered like dust and leaves, when the mighty blasts of October
> Seize them, and whirl them aloft, and sprinkle them far o'er the ocean.
>
> (Longfellow 1848: 6)

The opening of "Evangeline" throws into relief fundamental tensions among three notions of time: embodied time (the lives of the villagers), historical time (the "pleasant farms" and farmers who have been "Scattered like dust and leaves"), and climatological time – the sense of a natural world of wind and oceans that marks the limits of narrative and the bounds of the human under-standing of the "primeval." Longfellow's poem reveals half-buried tensions in its invocations of "Nature," in part because the forest that Longfellow asks us to imagine is "primeval" only from the limited perspectives afforded by memory and recorded history. Ten thousand years ago, during the Ice Age known as the Younger Dryas, Longfellow's Acadia lay under a mile of glacial ice, and the east coast of the Canadian Atlantic was uninhabited and uninhabitable (Burroughs 2005). In this respect, climatological time haunts Longfellow's poem, and yet resists being represented. The vast timescales of climatic change lie beyond our senses of personal experience and human history; yet, paradoxically, this non-anthropocentric understanding of time underwrites the political, scientific, ecological, religious, and socioeconomic traditions that allow us to make sense of global climate change and that have structured literary representations of Nature since the beginnings of Western civilization.

In this chapter, I outline a brief history of the registers of time and explore some of the ways in which tensions among embodied, historical, and climatological time underlie our twenty-first-century understandings of, and commitments to, sustainability. Sustainability, I argue, is in some respects a *literary* construct, the outgrowth of particular ways of conceiving time; therefore, the different registers of time that I discuss both produce and are reinscribed by descriptions of sustainability as an ethics, a policy goal, and a rallying cry. Embodied time, historical time, and climatological time are mutually constitutive – that is, they can be imagined only in relation to each other. They are also culturally and historically inflected, and it would take several full-length studies to examine the ways in which different cultures have tried to negotiate among them. In focusing on aspects of Western literary traditions, I trace the ways in which time remains embedded in history, culture, and technology. Time is not an abstract and objective measurement of duration, but a dynamic set of relations mediated by technoscientific understandings of climatic variability and climatic change. In this respect, as I argue below, the idea of climatological time paradoxically transcends and deconstructs a long philosophical and rhetorical tradition that contrasts *kronos* (chronological time) to *kairos* (the opportune moment, the "right" time, or, as in contemporary Greek, the weather: see White 1987). An understanding of climatological time complicates and enriches a variety of political responses to the crisis of global warming in the twenty-first century.

The familiar catch-phrases that invoke "the world our grandchildren will inherit" or urge us to "save the earth for future generations" reveal the extent to which sustainability is indebted to conceptions of embodied time, that is, to individual experiences of wind, heat, cold, rain, drought, and the thousand climatic shocks that flesh is heir to. Reinscribing a conception of time that dates back to the Old Testament, sustainability evokes a succession of individual lifetimes – an unbroken sequence of embodied experiences from the past and into the future that presupposes societies and cultures developing against the backdrop of the timeless present of an abiding Nature. Troubling this quasi-biblical vision of succession and its socio-genetic inheritance of moral authority, property rights, social responsibility, and racial, ethnic, and religious identities is a fundamental question: What exactly is being sustained? Is it the *stability* of the planetary ecosystem (and its numberless sub-systems) as a self-perpetuating whole? or the *productivity* of the natural world so that technologies of resource extraction and practices of intensification allow selected populations to maintain, improve, and extend first-world standards of living? Explored through a critical archaeology of time, the work of literature mediates the intimations of sublime change – of climatological time – by restricting time to human history; therefore contemporary rhetorics of sustainability draw on a rich legacy of images of ecological stability by re-envisioning the pastoral tradition – the eternal spring of the bucolic countryside – and the georgic, the strategies of intensification that allow for the endlessly increasing exploitation of resources. The roots of these genres in the classical world and their successive reimaginings in Europe and the Americas suggest the extent to which notions of sustainability subsume and rework tensions that have characterized views of Nature for thousands of years.

Beyond anthropogenic time

Embodied time is written in terms of memory. In his study of meteorology in the late seventeenth and eighteenth centuries, Jan Golinski calls attention to the ways in which amateur naturalists who observed and described weather patterns struggled with the limitations of language. The author of the anonymous Worcestershire diary called his daily weather register "my Ephemeris or Historicall Remarques on vicissitudes of the weather, with a narrative of its course & Tracing it in its various winding meanders round ye year" but complained that "our Language is exceeding scanty & barren of words to use & express ye various notions I have of Weather &c" (cited in Golinski 2007: 19). This "scanty & barren" language restricts the ability to turn the daily experience of the weather into a theory of climate. Without a causal, scientific narrative to explain changes in the weather, such records drift toward the theological semiotics of catastrophe and apocalypse: the experience of embodied responses to the weather tends to be cast in providentialist terms.

In his account of the devastating wind storm that struck England and Wales in late 1703, a once-in-500-years extra-tropical cyclone, Daniel Defoe describes his fears as the storm approached: "the Night would be very tempestuous," he recognized, because "the Mercury [in his barometer] sunk lower than ever I had observ'd it on any Occasion whatsoever." But the plunging readings seemed so anomalous that they "made [him] suppose that the Tube had been handled and disturb'd by [his] Children" (Defoe 1704: 24; see Markley 2008). The full force of the storm dilates the time between midnight and dawn, both in distracting Defoe from his observations and in threatening to end both experiential and historical time: after midnight, he admits of the barometer that his "Observations ... are not regular enough to supply the Reader with a full Information, the Disorders of that Dreadful Night having found me other imployment, expecting every Moment when the House I was in would bury us all in its own Ruins" (25). This sense of impending destruction becomes an emblem of God's vengeance on England for its sins. Defoe sees time in dialectic and emblematic terms; his peril and salvation are also England's. In this sense, the gaps left by imperfect languages and unattended barometers mark the ruptures within history and experience that structure Protestant theology during the early eighteenth century: divine power always threatens to end *kronos*, chronological time, and to redefine *kairos* as divine vengeance.

By the end of the eighteenth century, the "empty" time of mathematical simulation and climatological reconstruction began to assert its explanatory power by disembodying climate, that is, by treating climatic change not as the catastrophic irruption of divine judgment but as a non-anthropogenic time that transcends both individual and historical experience. At the end of the eighteenth century, climatological time emerges as a distinct ontological challenge to theological time in three interlocking sets of developments. All three sought to redefine the scientific basis for understanding time and, in the process, recast traditional ideas about Nature. In the 1790s, the nebular hypothesis of planetary formation advanced by Pierre Simon de Laplace, the "discovery" of geological time by James Hutton, and the argument for species extinction put forth by Georges Cuvier transformed conceptions of climate by decoupling history from human experience and memory.

The nebular hypothesis anthropomorphized the life cycle of planets in terms of youth, maturity, old age, and heat-death, offering a model of climatic change as the consequence of irreversible, universal processes (Numbers 1977). Laplace removed Newton's God from the mathematical equations that produced a compelling model of the origins, evolution, and fate of the solar system. Hutton's vision of geological time with "no vestige of a beginning, – no prospect of an end" presented a cyclical history of erosion and upheaval that continually reshaped earth (Hutton 1795: 1, 200). This continual reshaping both went beyond and challenged the theological catastrophism that ascribed evidence such as drowned cities and toppled buildings to the vengeance of an angry God. Eighty years after Defoe had echoed a near-universal sentiment among early natural philosophers – "Nature plainly refers us beyond her Self, to the Mighty Hand of Infinite Power, the Author of Nature, and Original of all Causes" (Defoe 1704: 2) – Hutton's geological history challenged perceptions of the reliability of experiential notions of duration, history, nature, and causality (see Markley 1993; Bono 1995; Hellegers 2000).

The Earth itself threatened to become a sublime, non-human environment. Cuvier's account of the extinction of fossilized species raised profound questions about the limits of Mosaic history and the ways in which past environments differed from present conditions (Rudwick 2005, 2008; O'Connor 2007). The fascination with the skeletal remains of dinosaurs, giant sloths, and mastodons that gripped London, Paris, Philadelphia, and New York in 1800 suggested that Nature bred entire species that required primeval ecologies no human ever had seen. The emphasis throughout the nineteenth century on the savage violence of prehistoric carnivores indicates the extent to which it was difficult to imagine the ecological conditions that provided forage for gigantic species of plant-eaters.

Even before Darwin published *On the Origin of Species*, then, scientific thought had begun to challenge the biblical monopoly on conceptions of history and had provided competing models of climatological time, the creation and reshaping of the earth and its natural environment, and humankind's future. The fad in Victorian science fiction for end-of-the-universe stories, many riffing on Mary Shelley's *The Last Man*, testifies to the ways in which the specter of species extinction could be reimagined on a massive, planetary scale (Clarke 2001). Extinction thus haunts the tendency in late eighteenth- and early nineteenth-century science to chart, measure, and quantify both the natural world and the social regimes of economics and politics. In this sense, the understanding of long-term change, of a climatological time that exists beyond human experience, gestures paradoxically toward embracing and resisting the mathematically determined universe imagined by Laplace. A time that transcends and beggars human experience, however, can be conceived only differentially, and paradoxically, in its relation to phenomenological perceptions of time and existence. If mathematical reductionism locks humankind and climate into intractable processes that lead to extinction, it also provokes redefinitions of ideas of divinity and therefore of the complex relationships of humankind to experience, Nature, and time.

Nineteenth-century transcendentalism suggests that the ruptures between microcosm and macrocosm, between humankind's experience of time and Nature's time, are produced by the self-generating alienation of custom or ideology. In his essay "Nature," Ralph Waldo Emerson recasts the threat of extinction within phenomenological notions of time, Nature, and experience:

> The knowledge that we traverse the whole scale of being, from the centre to the poles of nature, and have some stake in every possibility, lends that sublime lustre to death, which philosophy and religion have too outwardly and literally striven to express in the popular doctrine of the immortality of the soul. The reality is more excellent than the report. Here is no ruin, no discontinuity, no spent ball. The divine circulations never rest nor linger. Nature is the incarnation of a thought, and turns to a thought again, as ice becomes water and gas. The world is mind precipitated, and the volatile essence is forever escaping again into the state of free thought. ... That power which does not respect quantity, which makes the whole and the particle its equal channel, delegates its smile to the morning, and distils its essence into every drop of rain. Every moment instructs, and every object: for wisdom is infused into every form.
>
> (Emerson 1836: 542)

In gesturing toward the reflexivity of microcosm and macrocosm, Emerson yokes Hutton's geological or Laplace's universal time to experiential moments and perceptions that defy scientific reductionism. Human life, like the planet itself, is "no spent ball," but a web of complex, proliferating, and dynamic energies (Buell 1995: 219–51, 2004). Emerson locates "perfection" and "harmony" in individual days. He begins this essay by observing:

> There are days which occur in this climate, at almost any season of the year, wherein the world reaches its perfection, when the air, the heavenly bodies, and the earth, make a harmony, as if nature would indulge her offspring; when, in these bleak upper sides of the planet, nothing is to desire that we have heard of the happiest latitudes, and we bask in the shining hours of Florida and Cuba; when everything that has life gives sign of satisfaction. ... These halcyons may be looked for with a little more assurance in that pure October weather, which we distinguish by the name of the Indian Summer. The day, immeasurably long, sleeps over the broad hills and warm wide fields. To have lived through all its sunny hours, seems longevity enough.
>
> (Emerson 1836: 540)

In contrast to nineteenth-century scientists later struggling to explain the prospect of an Earth succumbing to the heat-death ostensibly predicted by the second law of thermodynamics (see Clarke 2001), Emerson finds time both focused and dilated, intimations of immortality distilled into the "sunny hours" of "pure October weather" that bring to the climate of northern New England the kind of "satisfaction" ostensibly experienced in the tropical sunshine of the Caribbean. Emerson's "halcyons" locate embodied human experience within a matrix of "harmony," in which multiplying complexities produce greater intimations and emotive understandings of Nature as "the circumstance which dwarfs every other circumstance," an unalienated universal composed of, and generating, infinite experiences of "that power which does not respect quantity, which makes the whole and the particle its equal channel."

Transcendentalism can thus be seen as one response to the fundamental paradoxes posed by climatological time. Rather than a mathematically determined universe that exists beyond the limits of perception and experience, and therefore that can be imagined only in terms of the irrelevance or negation of embodied experience, the world becomes open to the interweaving of mind and matter. In Emerson's "Nature," the transcendental imperative that "does not respect quantity" encourages humankind to embrace the processes of an ongoing reintegration of self and environment rather than succumb to the profound ontological as well as epistemological displacements of what Emerson terms "custom." To turn away from "our life of solemn trifles," humankind must recognize that Nature can be described only as a kind of double negative, a negation of a natural world already alienated by "the ambitious chatter of the schools [that] would persuade us to despise" material existence in favor of metaphysical abstractions. Nature's time therefore exists as the primeval negation of humankind's efforts to measure and institutionalize time: "Here no history, or church, or state, is interpolated on the divine sky and the immortal year." In an important sense, the threat to traditional structures of thought and belief posed by Laplace and Cuvier is subsumed by Emerson's encompassing change within an organic regeneration of both mind and climate – "We come to our own, and make friends with matter." Dynamic and unpredictable change is transformed into the energies of self-renewal.

Yet the ethics of individualism that Emerson is typically credited with (or accused of) constitutes only one half of a dialectic in the nineteenth century. Mike Davis charts the devastating human and environmental consequences of European imperialism and its hallucinogenic optimism that colonial proprietors could plough under complex ecologies throughout the underdeveloped world to grow cash crops (cotton, opium, tea, tobacco, and rice) for export to Europe and North America (Davis 2001). Unrestrained imperial expansion and robber-baron capitalism trumpeted the view that the climates of India, Africa, and the Americas could be "improved" by large-scale monoculture. This view of Nature as an infinite storehouse focuses less on what Karl Marx calls exchange value than on the infinite elasticity of use-value: the belief that John Locke advanced in the *Two Treatises of Government* (1690) that the infinite productivity of the natural world forms a consensual basis for individual and property rights – and property, in turn, secures the basis of political and social identity.

Locke invokes explicitly the classical ideal of a "golden age" when humanity, or at least specific populations, reaped the benefits of a beneficent Nature (Markley 1999). In such a world of abundant resources and a stable climate, as he argues in the second treatise, labor offers the prospect of limitless productivity rather than marking, as it does in the Judeo-Christian tradition, humankind's banishment from Eden. "In the beginning," Locke declares, "all the World was *America*" – that is, all the world was open to an unending exploitation guaranteed by the fecundity of nature (Locke 1690: 2, 301). In this formulation, labor is divorced from a material world of life-and-death calculations (when to plant, when to harvest, how much seed to conserve for next year's planting, whether to kill the cow to feed one's family during a harsh winter, and so forth) that defined agricultural existence during the Little Ice Age in much of early modern Europe (Fagan 2000).

By the later eighteenth century, neo-Lockean liberalism had turned bodies into reliable machines, capable of increasing their useful labor, and the land into a repository of potential value that could be mined, refashioned, and exploited without suffering any diminution in either extent or productivity. By the nineteenth century, as Davis suggests, the Lockean argument that the fruits of one's labor theoretically cannot exceed a normative notion of bodily sufficiency had been corrupted into the conversion of humans into interchangeable units of labor, and the natural world consequently becomes an *effect* of humankind's use (Davis 2001). The time of the world thus becomes the time of economic calculation. In the long tradition of apocalyptic science fiction that emerges in the nineteenth century, it is precisely this world of humankind's dominion that, to quote H.G. Wells in *The War of the Worlds*, begins "losing coherency, losing shape and efficiency, guttering, softening, running at last in that swift liquefaction of the social body" (Wells 1898: 82). These apocalyptic scenarios, the "Grotesque gleam of a time no history will ever fully describe!" (1898: 145), invariably have ecological overtones because, in their playful cultural necrosis, they offer a way of imagining a time after human history: the end of *kronos* and the aftermath of *kairos*.

Time and fiction in the age of global warming

The expanses of prehuman history that extend into the deep backward and abysm of time underscore the fact that climatological time, measured in millennia, exists beyond daily experiences of the weather, beyond the duration of individual lifetimes, beyond the accumulated memories of generations, and beyond the technologies of observation, inscription, and recording that characterize the rise of modern meteorology in the nineteenth century. The tensions between observation and speculation in meteorological sciences that Katharine Anderson (2005) describes in Victorian England foreshadow the contours of contemporary debates about global warming and its consequences. In the twenty-first century, we have come to understand climatological time as a dynamic and consensual knowledge about the interpretations of a wide range of proxy data: ice cores from Greenland, tree rings, sediment layers in mud and swamps, patterns of coral growth, and so on, that can be analyzed to reveal signs of long-term variability based on specific chemical signatures, pollen samples, and gas bubbles trapped in ice (Lamb 1995; Calvin 2002; Linden 2006).

In this respect, the cognitive understanding of climate has become a process of acclimating one's embodied experience to increasingly complex technologies and to the resulting displacements, in time and space, of observational and experiential authority. Climatological time is dynamic, shaped and recalibrated, as Bruno Latour (1987) suggests, by the networks, alliances, and assemblages that collect, transmit, verify, interpret, and disseminate data; that then reaffirm or modify assumptions and values about the natural world; and that continually negotiate the vexed relationships between embodied experience and scientific knowledge. A crucial effect of the technologies of climate science is that our experience has been refocused, or recalibrated, to integrate into our lived experience consensual inferences from ratios of isotopes, compression of layers in ice cores, models of global hydrology, atmospheric circulation, large-scale deforestation, and satellite images. In this respect, climatological time registers the complex relationships between *qualitative* experience and *quantitative* knowledge, between human history and the Earth's history. Recycling becomes, in one sense, a sacrificial rite to an ideal of sustainability.

The technologically mediated proxy observations of long-term climate change, then, force us to rethink traditional notions of common sense, the embodied and expansive times of Emerson's Nature. Even for scientists, policy makers, environmental activists, and informed citizens who believe in anthropogenic global warming and are striving to promote whole-scale changes in modes of production and habits of consumption, the timescales of climatic change cannot be experienced viscerally but only imagined. Scientific knowledge, it seems, requires a willing suspension of experiential belief in the facticity, the experiential groundedness, of a world of familiar seasons, a continuous anthropocentric history, and a Lockean tendency to treat the natural world as a storehouse of infinite productivity.

In this respect, climatological time produces interference patterns that provoke complex and self-generating modes of *disidentification*: proxy data are both integrated into patterns of daily experience (recycling plastic bottles, buying energy-efficient cars) and sequestered from traditional behaviors (continuing to eat meat, despite the carbon footprint of meat production). In Latour's sense, we have never been, and cannot become, modern, because we remain caught (and oscillate) between the dialectical impulses toward the purification of identities (the self-aware green ethicist) and the proliferation of hybrids (the conflicted, steak-eating Prius owner) (Latour 1993). This is why, even as the literate public worldwide has been deluged with information (and misinformation) about global warming and its likely consequences, the effects of this media saturation, paradoxically, have reinforced as well as challenged long-standing views of humankind's relationship to Nature. The managerial ethos of late twentieth- and twenty-first-century corporate culture that tends to treat climate change as a marketing opportunity is a descendant of the brutally insensitive optimism of neoclassical economics.

Given its geneaology, the ideal of sustainability that underlies most plans of collective action to address global warming risks reinscribing a Lockean vision of the inexhaustibility of natural resources, and therefore the idea of a preternaturally resilient ecology that exists outside of the dynamics of climatological time. The measure of several generations – of one or two extended human lifetimes – becomes the timescale of sustainability. In this regard, sustainability tends to be co-opted into a seemingly objective semiotics of mathematics and neoclassical – and neoliberal – economics, what Philip Mirowski calls "the very ideal of natural law ... the verification of a stable external world independent of our activity or inquiry" (Mirowski 1989: 75). This projection of stability from mathematics onto "a stable external" Nature effectively treats complex and dynamic ecologies as constants rather than variables; the more closely sustainability approaches a set of statistical inferences over decades or a century, the more it tends to remain complicit in exploitative ideologies of resource extraction and the political and administrative hierarchies, centralized bureau-cracies, technologies of economic calculation and accounting, the policing of resources and populations, and distributive political economies that are required to manage finite resources.

That said, the paradoxes of disidentification can be captured, if not ration-ally comprehended, only in fictional projections of human experience. In an important sense, the phenomenological perception of climate now includes the simulations – the science fictions – of human experience as a probability calcu-lus, thought-experiments about the climatological future. Published a year before Hurricane Katrina devastated New Orleans, Kim Stanley Robinson's novel *Forty Signs of Rain* uncannily anticipates the sequence of natural disasters and political failures that devastated the city. Washington D.C. is hit by a perfect storm – a tropical storm surge coming up the Potomac, ten inches of rain in the Chesapeake watershed rushing down river, and a record high tide. The city floods: "images from the [flooded] Mall dominated the media," and viewers around the nation see "TV helicopters often interrupt[ing] their overviews to pluck people from rooftops. Rescues by boat were occurring all through the Southwest district and up the Anacostia Basin. Reagan Airport remained drowned, and there was no passable bridge over the Potomac" (Robinson 2004: 352).

Although the novel and its sequels, *Fifty Degrees Below* (2005) and *Sixty Days and Counting* (2007), focus on the ecological, scientific, political, and personal crises of the trilogy's main characters – from Beltway insiders, to bioclimato-logists working at the National Science Foundation, to displaced Buddhist monks – Robinson's depiction of individuals, and the world at large, confronting the consequences of global warming is neither a "realistic" novel about climate change nor a near-future, "hard" science-fiction novel, but a genre-bending exploration of the ethics and politics of existence at a time when neither eco-truisms, nor managerial strategizing, nor self-propelling fantasies of technological amelioration seem adequate. Robinson's trilogy offers a way to think through the lived experience of character and climate in the early twenty-first century. It marks the intersection of the different registers of embodied, historical, and climatological time: the experience of surviving temperatures fifty degrees below zero after the Gulf Stream stalls; the fictional history of national politics and the politics of science over the course of two years as a new, progressive adminis-tration takes office; and the onrush of catastrophic changes – melting polar caps and drowning islands – that recur literally millions of years after the last period of comparable warmth.

Coda

Human beings seldom witness abrupt climate change in the course of a lifetime. Historically, those who do face long odds on adapting to a natural world radically transformed. The prospect of rapid warming and the disastrous scenarios that Robinson envisions lead to profoundly different ways of conceiving the timescales of what we understand as the object of sustainability. Sustainability ultimately refers to an idealized homeostasis between humankind and environment that never existed except in the sense that robust ecological systems could remain unaffected by low-density populations of humans for climatologically brief periods of time, on the scale of centuries rather than millennia. Robust, in this respect, does not imply a moral, ethical, or socio-cultural value judgment. Between 11,000 and 12,000 years ago, during the Younger Dryas, Western Europe was frozen tundra without much in the way of recognizable vegetation, colder and more forbidding than much of Siberia is today. Longfellow's forest primeval was millennia away from taking root, the coastline of Canada lying dozens if not hundreds of miles to the east because larger ice caps lowered sea levels by dozens of meters. Human populations huddled in scattered caves or clung to the Mediterranean littoral. Physiologically indistinguishable from any of us, Ice Age peoples produced intricate art and effective weapons. They did not flourish. There is overwhelming evidence that the most common biological response to severe climate change (of more than three degrees centigrade) is not to adapt but to die: populations crash, and, within the short, short reign of *Homo sapiens*, bands of hunters and gatherers vanish, subsistence farmers fall prey to malnutrition, starvation, and disease, and empires fall (Burroughs 2005; Linden 2006). When climate changes, people kill each other with greater frequency, population centers are abandoned, and centers of authority do not hold. Systemic climatic change is no more or less characteristic of Gaia than the long summer of climatic calm that has existed for the last 10,000 years; unpredictable oscillations no less "natural" than ideals of sustainability. Longfellow ultimately gives way to Lucretius.

Bibliography

Anderson, K. (2005) *Predicting the Weather: Victorians and the science of meteorology*, Chicago: University of Chicago Press.

Bono, J. (1995) *The Word of God and the Languages of Man: interpreting nature in early modern science, Ficino to Descartes*, Madison: University of Wisconsin Press.

Buell, L. (1995) *The Environmental Imagination: Thoreau, nature writing, and the formation of American culture*, Cambridge, Mass.: Harvard University Press.

——(2004) *Emerson*, Cambridge, Mass.: Harvard University Press.

Burroughs, W.J. (2005) *Climate Change in Prehistory: the end of the reign of chaos*, Cambridge: Cambridge University Press.

Calvin, W.H. (2002) *A Brain for All Seasons: human evolution and abrupt climate change*, Chicago: University of Chicago Press.

Clarke, B. (2001) *Energy Forms: allegory and science in the era of classical thermodynamics*, Ann Arbor: University of Michigan Press.

Crumley, C. (1994). "The ecology of conquest: contrasting agropastoral and agricultural societies' adaptation to climatic change," in Crumley (ed.) 1994, pp. 183–201.

——(ed.) (1994) *Historical Ecology: cultural knowledge and changing landscapes*, Sante Fe: School of American Research Press.

Davis, M. (2001) *Late Victorian Holocausts: el niño famines and the making of the third world*, London: Verso.

Defoe, D. (1704) *The Storm*, London.

Emerson, R.W. (1836) "Nature," in *Essays and Lectures by Ralph Waldo Emerson*, ed. J. Porte, New York: Library of America, 1983.

Fagan, B. (2000) *The Little Ice Age: how climate made history 1300–1850*, New York: Basic Books.

Golinski, J. (2007) *British Weather and the Climate of Enlightenment*, Chicago: University of Chicago Press.

Goux, J.-J. (1990) *Symbolic Economies after Marx and Freud*, trans. J.C. Gage, Ithaca, N.Y.: Cornell University Press.

Hellegers, D. (2000) *Natural Philosophy, Poetry, and Gender in Seventeenth-Century England*, Norman: University of Oklahoma Press.

Hutton, J. (1795) *Theory of the Earth, with Proofs and Illustrations*, 2 vols, Edinburgh: Printed for Messers Cadell, Junior, Davies, and Creech.

Ingerson, A.E. (1994) "Tracking and testing the nature–culture divide," in Crumley (ed.) 1994, pp. 43–66.

Lamb, H.H. (1995) *Climate History and the Modern World*, 2nd edn, New York: Routledge.

Latour, B. (1987) *Science in Action: how to follow scientists through society*, Cambridge, Mass.: Harvard University Press.

——(1993) *We Have Never Been Modern*, trans. C. Porter, Cambridge, Mass.: Harvard University Press.

Linden, E. (2006) *The Winds of Change: climate, weather, and the destruction of civilizations*, New York: Simon & Schuster.

Locke, J. (1690) *Two Treatises of Government*, ed. P. Laslett, Cambridge: Cambridge University Press, 1960.

Longfellow, H.W. (1848) *Evangeline, A Tale of Acadie*, 4th edn, Boston, Mass.: William Ticknor.

Markley, R. (1993) *Fallen Languages: crises of representation in Newtonian England, 1660–1740*, Ithaca, N.Y.: Cornell University Press.

——(1999) "'Land enough in the world': Locke's golden age and the infinite extensions of 'use,'" *South Atlantic Quarterly*, 98: 817–37.

——(2008) "'Casualties and disasters': Defoe and the interpretation of climatic instability," *Journal of Early Modern Cultural Studies*, 8: 102–24.

Mirowski, P. (1989) *More Heat than Light: economics as social physics, physics as nature's economics*, Cambridge: Cambridge University Press.

Numbers, R. (1977) *Creation by Natural Law: Laplace's nebular hypothesis in American thought*, Seattle: University of Washington Press.

O'Connor, R. (2007) *The Earth on Show: fossils and the poetics of popular science, 1802–1856*, Chicago: University of Chicago Press.

Ricoeur, P. (1984–88) *Time and Narrative*, 3 vols, trans. K. McLaughlin and D. Pellauer, Chicago: University of Chicago Press.

Robinson, K.S. (2004) *Forty Signs of Rain*, New York: HarperCollins.

Ruddiman, W.F. (2005) *Plows, Plagues, and Petroleum: how humans took control of climate*, Princeton: Princeton University Press.

Rudwick, M.S.J. (2005) *Bursting the Limits of Time: the reconstruction of geohistory in the age of revolution*, Chicago: University of Chicago Press.

——(2008) *Worlds before Adam: the reconstruction of geohistory in the age of reform*, Chicago: University of Chicago Press.

Wells, H.G. (1898) *The War of the Worlds*, ed. D.Y. Hughes and H.M. Geduld, Bloomington: Indiana University Press, 1984.

White, E. (1987) *Kaironomia, or the Will to Invent*, Ithaca, N.Y.: Cornell University Press.

7
COGNITIVE SCIENCE

Joseph Tabbi

Do not expect any help from explanations of fiction. At best you will understand the explanations ... Sewn up in these explanations you will look for what you already know, and that which is really there you will not see.

Franz Kafka

While the expansion of cognitive studies has meant, for some, an opportunity "fully to integrate the evolutionary human sciences and literary study" (Carroll 2009), one could argue that the literary arts always have been about cognition, consciousness, and their coevolution. Critical landmarks in the field – for example, Ingarden's *Cognition of the Literary Work of Art*, Szanto's *Narrative Consciousness*, and the essays collected in Richardson and Spolsky's *Work of Fiction* – require no "and" between the cognitive and literary terms in their titles: literary work *is* cognitive, narrative *is* an enactment of consciousness, and fictions do a kind of work (consistent with the mind's continual need to fill "gaps in nature," the title of a pioneering book by Spolsky). It may be true that, with the explosion of knowledge about and ways of picturing the mind's operation, we now have a "novel theory of consciousness" (see Lloyd 2003) – that is, an actual, falsifiable theory presented in the form of a detective novel (with the theory itself set out in an appendix). Actually, we have many novel theories, often advanced by scientists entering territories once inhabited predominantly by literary and cultural scholars.

Before one welcomes the merger of literary studies and the contemporary cognitive sciences, however, it is worth revisiting briefly the way that a literary discipline emerged not by embracing every aspect of cognition under investigation in the sciences, but rather through a process of selection and the setting of institutional boundaries. In rejecting a primary concern with biography and the psychological peculiarities of individual authors, Roman Ingarden was not detaching literary knowledge from knowledge about the world. Though consistent with New Criticism's rejection of the "fallacies" of authorial intention and readerly paraphrase, Ingarden did not, like many of his New Critical contemporaries, isolate texts from social or scientific knowledge. Rather, the cognition of the literary work was shown to consist of an extensive interaction between conscious and unconscious activity – richer by far, from the perspective of how phrases, sentences, narratives, and characters actually develop, than the notional categories offered by psychoanalysis. Rather than becoming "constantly diverted into other fields of investigation, primarily into a historically colored individual psychology of the poets," Ingarden sought (following Husserl) to reorient aesthetics by looking at ways in which "the literary works themselves made us aware of specific artistic problems" (Ingarden 1968: 3, 4).

Similarly, Szanto (1972) regarded the "novel as a world in itself," with its narrating viewpoints, social context, and ecological environment as carefully edited as its textual content. The determining presence of all that is unseen, unrecorded, but nonetheless active at the horizon of consciousness, would eventually distinguish cognitive criticism from more sequestered, largely exegetical forms of critical writing. The innovative take among early cognitive critics on the relation of textuality and a largely non-textual environment was consistent with the mind's own capacity for separating itself from its environment even as consciousness and a unique personality are shaped by highly selective input *from* the environment. This combination of self-enclosure at the level of operation (composition, reading, and cognizing) with selective openness to information places cognitive criticism closer to systems approaches than to deconstruction and the latter's perpetual deferral of meaning in chains of material signification. At the same time, an emphasis on communications within and among separate modules has much in common with media discourse theory, since both approaches emphasize not textuality alone but rather the constitutive coupling of bodily agency, technics, and textual signification (see Hansen 2006).

Another innovation that distinguished early cognitive criticism was its unabashedly evaluative stance, since its concern with "specific artistic problems" (in an environment of mostly operational discourse and instrumental activity) was consistent with the selective processes required by mental operations. Ingarden, for example, made a point of putting the process of evaluation back on the agenda of literary studies:

> Works of belles-lettres lay claim, by virtue of their characteristic basic structure and particular attainments, to being "works of art" and enabling the reader to apprehend an aesthetic object of a particular kind. ... [Works] can be "genuine" and "beautiful"; generally speaking, they can be of artistic or aesthetic value; but they can just as well be "bad," "not genuine," "ugly" – in short, of negative value. We can experience all these works aesthetically; we can also apprehend them in a preaesthetic cognition or in a cognition which is itself not aesthetic but which builds upon the aesthetic experience.
>
> (Ingarden 1968: 7)

With that last sentence, Ingarden distinguishes himself (and a classical "cognitive" approach) from New Criticism's hermeticism on the one hand and more recent Historicist, Identitarian, and Cultural approaches on the other hand. In seeking a foundation for literature in perceptual and cognitive qualities that are universal, and in retaining qualitative judgment as a fundamental activity in literary critical studies, Ingarden sought to integrate literature within a general cognitive ecology. The advantage to this approach is that it allows critics to identify how an author demonstrates understanding of aesthetic and cognitive problems specific to the development of the literary work and its unique moment in historical time. Szanto, approaching the "novel" genre as "an existence in itself," pointed to three authors in particular – Franz Kafka, Samuel Beckett, and Alain Robbe-Grillet – as exemplary of the co-development of an evolving cognitive understanding and a self-consciously modern literature (Szanto 1972: 5). Current work on and by, for example, Joseph McElroy, Ben Marcus, Richard Powers, Lynne Tillman, David Foster Wallace, and Jeanette Winterson demonstrates an increasing awareness of research on the mind and cognition, a knowledge that is as much a part of the contemporary milieu as psychoanalysis was for Joyce, Beckett, Kafka, and Robbe-Grillet. Still, it would be preferable to emphasize not the intentions of, or direct cultural influence on, the individual artist, but rather the historical development of cognitive knowledge itself, and how this knowledge combines with an appreciation, in Ingarden's words, of "the essentially necessary structural elements and inter-connections among cooperating functions" (Ingarden 1968: 9).

One reason in particular not to rely too directly on evidence of an artist's level of scientific knowledge is that what passes as knowledge in the sciences so quickly becomes obsolete. When we approach Dan Lloyd's refor-mulation of the detective genre as an allegory of a faulty theory (that the relation of subject and object is one of "detection" rather than construction), we encounter not a self-contained novelistic world but a "novel theory." Similarly, when we approach not a literary text but "The Literary Mind" itself as (in Mark Turner's sub-title) "The Origins of Language and Thought," we are entering a very different phase of literary study, one that could easily collapse literary exploration into a belletristic adjunct to scientific investigation. What makes most theories "novel" is also what limits their usefulness as *explanations* of literary art. The time it takes for authors and scholars to absorb ideas from con-temporary science is usually much longer than the time it takes for the scientists themselves to move on to new formulations: so the idea of the "massively modular mind," we are told, "over-generalizes from the most hard-wired com-ponents of the brain. It is a massive oversimplification of human cognitive architecture, and it is already fading into the archives of intellectual history" (Carroll 2009). Whether or not that it so, it hardly invalidates Spolsky's nuanced reading of modern literature's growing awareness of gaps in consciousness – an awareness already represented (long before the modular theory was formulated) in the stream-of-consciousness narration found in Joyce and Woolf. Dennett's notion (formulated in the postmodern literary era) of consciousness as a narrative that is available in partial drafts distributed at various sites in the brain is just one example of a cognitive philosopher resorting to literary metaphor as a way to express distributed brain functions, necessary to consciousness but not themselves conscious. Indeed, the distinction between metaphor and actuality is itself unsettled by scientists concerned not only with *Metaphors We Live By* (Lakoff and Johnson 1980) but also with their material basis in the brain and their conceptual supports in distributed networks beyond the human body and outside of consciousness.

By contrast, the universal cognitive structures that enable a diversity of expression across cultures and languages (as described in Hogan 2003; Turner 1991, 1996; Zunshine 2003, and many others) would seem to run against the modernist and postmodernist currents. Besides "metaphor," there is scarcely a keyword or conceptual term used to describe literature's specificity that cannot be redescribed and refreshed in the detailed terms made newly available by the cognitive sciences: "defamiliarization," for example, as a way of refreshing habitual perception, intersubjectivity as the "double-scope blending" that enables one mind to conceive of other minds and networks beyond one's own cognition (Turner 2009), and so on. That the novel itself, as Virginia Woolf remarked in 1924, has "evolved … to express character" is uncontroversial – and the earliest novels were nearly all named after characters: *Don Quixote* of 1604 and 1614, *Robinson Crusoe* in 1719, *Clarissa* in 1747–48 (Burn 2009). Any cognitive history of the novel would be obliged to account for the increasing distribution of characters in alien environments, even as descriptions of the "self" have developed in both psychoanalytical and neurological sciences. "Narrative," too – considered as a way of situating one's memories and identity in time – comports with the recursiveness of points of view in fiction and poetry – that is, the way that authors, narrators, characters, and readers become aware of their own awareness.

Whether supportive or contradictory of cultural and literary theories, all of these key insights from cognitive studies are – or with help from narrative theory can be shown to be – consistent with defining features of a modern literary expression. Science need not recognize literature's priority in arriving at such insights, any more than literature needs to wait on confirmations from science. In any case, we are unlikely to want to endorse a single philosophy of nature (let alone a purported "human nature") at this point in the development of the cognitive sciences, and Spolsky is wise not to claim science as in any way *authorizing* an approach to literary representations of consciousness. "It isn't ultimately of great concern how neuroscientists eventually describe the mind/ brain," Spolsky writes regarding her own work: "In fact, it would be surprising if there aren't new theories around by the time this book gets into print" (Spolsky 1993: 40). Neither can the descriptions of neuroscientists predetermine the stylistic signature of authors in a given era. Joyce and Woolf could not differ more from one another or from Kafka and Beckett, though each writer reflects the emerging psychologism of their time with a common tendency to describe the world through consciousness. Kafka's minimalism is not just a refusal of explanation (see my epigraph); it is also an insistence on the self-containment of the literary world, its capacity to convert the noise of culture and the increasingly specialized languages of modernity into patterns wholly of its own literary making. As Szanto notes, "Only a writer who records with a minimum of intervening filters, of intervening philosophies, can reproduce a world to which one may attach interpretations grown from that world itself" (Szanto 1972: 179). This recognition of reflexivity as constitutive of modern literary expression does not separate literature and its criticism from the social and perceptual world (a charge often leveled against New Criticism of the post-World War II era, with its notion of the "autotelic" literary text). To the contrary, the necessary closure and self-referentiality of works of literature (and of literary *work*) is consistent with the enclosure of consciousness in individual minds. Such operational closure does not separate us from others; rather, it is a condition for communication, and for meaningful interactions within a culture and among bodies and machines that are themselves closed operationally (see Clarke and Hansen 2009).

What cognitive criticism can accomplish, and what can be aided by attention to contemporary accounts of cognition in the sciences, is a discovery through close reading of the moment-by-moment, word-by-word, and sentence-by-sentence enactment of consciousness in language. Variability – "from age to age, or country to country, or author to author, or even passage to passage" (Turner 1990: 1087) – is of course a primary concern of literary criticism and remains necessary to a description of "what is really there" (Kafka). But for variation to be meaningful (and not just "novel"), criticism must also consider, in Turner's words, "the underbrush of unoriginal structures" and largely unconscious operations that do not reach expression in the work, or in thought. "The concept of a 'room' or a 'poem,'" Turner points out, "is immeasurably more complex than the original aspects of any one room or any one poem" (Turner 1990: 1077). The figure of life and the literary work itself as a journey (for example), found across cultures and equally in *Pilgrim's Progress* and a poem by John Ashbery, embraces the same relations of source and target that define metaphors, in this case our conceptual schema for journeys (source) and our conceptual schema for life (target). The mapping of source to target allows both of these works (and numberless others) to express an entire range of purposes (resembling a journey's destinations), influences (in the person of a "guide"), "obstacles," "progress" and so forth. These are all qualities that a "life" can be seen to possess not in itself but by virtue of its resemblance to a "journey." The relational, directional, and meaningful tendencies in metaphor are important, in turn, for bringing memories of the past and future projections into present consciousness. In this way, cognitive approaches to narrative marry those to metaphor by articulating, in Turner's words, "consciously and systematically the linguistic or conceptual resources" used "in reading and writing" (Turner 1996: 14).

What cognitive science brings to literary theory, then, is not an entirely new approach but rather a more robust realism grounded in actual, complex, and widely distributed mental processes. When encountering novelty in literary works, the cognitive critic generally calls attention to "the unoriginal aspect of innovation" – a salutary approach in an era when innovation is the rule, not the exception. Where postmodernism could sound quirky or willfully subversive (in the absence of any large-scale post-war alternative to global capitalism even in the former Soviet Union and China); where the postmodern novels of John Barth, Donald Barthelme, and Robert Coover in the United States could seem to indulge in metafictional pyrotechnics; and where multiculturalism tended in practice to reduce difference to racial identity or lifestyle choices for those who can pay the price – cognitive criticism seeks a universality in brain operations that across cultures have much more in common than not. What is often overlooked, however, in the fabulism of the above-named postmodernists, is an interest in the universality of storytelling and the cognitive restructuring that is needed to create the narratives necessary to any widely shared, and hence "cultural," understanding. During this rich, though in retrospect "twilight" (see Cochran 2001), period of literary experimentation, a systematic dismantling and retelling of the classics, of fairy tales, and of the entire history of oral and literary production, has served to translate the varieties of human experience across the boundaries of time and space. The process might be said to have begun, in the United States, with William Gaddis's *Recognitions* of 1955, whose title indicates the systematic *re*-cognition of past literary and visual productions that the author encountered, while at the same time showcasing the noisy diversity of post-war, corporate life in one locale, primarily New York City's Greenwich Village, and twenty years later, in *JR*, in the city's financial offices and residential and school districts. Through the extensive use of dialogue that requires readers to cognize rather than to "follow" a narrative, Gaddis succeeds in linking a diversity of United States dialects to a global power it drives but does not comprehend or control. While Gaddis's narratives can be said to mirror the corporate culture of continual innovation, criss-crossing communication networks, and endless *talk*, the novels also contest that culture through a systematic encounter with and transformation of past literary forms, the unoriginal source material that grounds Gaddis's own innovation.

Spolsky speaks of a mixture of "the humanly universal and the culturally and individually specific, as coded and recorded in cultural artifacts" (Richardson and Spolsky 2004: viii). This formulation, which already complements and contextualizes a range of "well-deserved" successes in racial, class, and gendered approaches to culture, is further complicated in imaginative literature by a concern with what might be called a non-humanly universal – that is, a globalizing or postmodern culture grounded in corporate expansion, technological networking, and an endless accumulation and innovation that can be only partially compre-hended in terms of narrative, or indeed of any human terms. That approach to the non-human is what characterizes the most ambitious literary work during the period of cognitive exploration – a period characterized by Turner, with genial exaggeration, as "the age in which the human mind was discovered" (Turner 1991: vii). If so, the era of scientific discovery coincided with a rediscovery, by imaginative authors, of the cognition of the work of literature when conscious-ness is no longer the predominant object of knowledge, "the human" is no longer the primary subject of history, and print itself, predominant during the rise of modernity, is no longer the predominant medium in which knowledge circulates.

Like most recent cultural "discoveries" (of one's own personal identity, of community, of a national consciousness, of native and folk forms of production, of ecological environments and the politics of "everyday life"), the discovery of the "human mind" can only mean that what was once thought to be whole (and wholly within "us"), is seen to be knowable only as part of a larger, exten-ded context. The idea of the "human mind," like these other conflicted concepts, can be unified not in itself and not in ourselves but in relation to an emerging global culture or world system. Forging that relationship between the globalizing systems and the changing life-forms that systems make newly visible is the challenge of cognitive fictions in literature and cultural criticism.

Similar to Spolsky, Terry Cochran characterizes the emergence of a literary culture in systems terms, namely "the real and ideal constraints implied in bestowing meaning on material artifacts" (Cochran 2001: 3). The self-conscious practice of "writing under constraint," pursued during the postmodern period alongside the more expansive work of Gaddis, Thomas Pynchon, and Don DeLillo in the United States, represents an important strain of cognitive fiction that finds its most visible and articulate expression in the transnational collaborative project of the Oulipo (*ouvroir de littérature potentielle*). Still to be explored, in cognitive criticism no less than in media discourse theory, is the way that past constraints – the materiality of print, obviously, but also earlier media such as radio, television, video, as well as the obsolescent generations of compu-ter floppies, disks, and platforms – remain an active presence in the new media ecology. Admittedly, the presence of past media is largely ignored, due to a cultural focus, supported by modes of capitalist production and advertising, on what is new and innovative. But old technologies, like the "underbrush of unoriginal" cognitive structures cited by Turner, more often coexist with and even support the new, worldwide information structures. Consider, for example, how current cars equipped with computer maintainance and Global Positioning Systems still need to coexist with roads and highways, while they cannot do without axial propulsion, synthetic rubber tires, and so forth. These latter, earlier-developed technologies are not so much residual as they are active and primary. The same can be said of mental modules that evolved as far back as the reptilian brain but which nonetheless continue to be active, self-enclosed, and largely unchanged by the later development of consciousness.

Similarly, what is revealed by the literary, scientific, and technological explorations of this period is that "culture," though present in individuals, remains open to systems and networks that are larger than consciousness and beyond the capacity of any one mind to grasp. Writing from a Marxist perspective in the 1980s, Frederic Jameson introduced the term "cognitive map" as a call for criticism to bring the extensive, non-intuitive, and mostly non-human networks of communication and information back into the realm of consciousness and culture. In an age of vastly expanding economic and technological power, this approach made a certain sense and held sway for several decades – from the mid-1970s to "the end of history" (Fukuyama 1992). Like cognitive criticism, Jameson's Marxism is useful in rebuking common sense, while at the same time holding on to a common vision in the face of cultural diversity. In this case, we are given an absolute vision of "History" as "a process of totalization" designed to incorporate "ever more extensive parts of the globe" and hence enabling "a new and original relationship of absence and presence, of the far to the near and the external to the internal" (Jameson 2009: 596). Jameson recognizes that the History we are making develops on a scale much longer than our own human life-spans; thus, even revolutions, when they occur, are unlikely to take the form of a punctual takeover of power, since power today is too widely distributed for that. Nonethless, he asks whether one cannot have "a kind of cognitive or contemplative knowledge, in which somehow knowing the Absolute as totality, glimpsing it in rare moments of its visibility, takes priority over any acts its viewer might perform?" Or, again, "how can I recognize this forbiddingly foreign totality as my own doing, how may I appropriate it and make it my own handiwork and acknowledge its laws as my own projection and my praxis?" (606). That Jameson poses these more recent formulations as questions, not as a positive approach or political project, indicates the extent to which the conversion of networks and systems to the human scale is under contention, in contemporary cultural theory no less than in cognitive criticism.

Where Jameson's project of cognitive mapping remains centered in consciousness, however, cognitive approaches that incorporate current scientific research tend to diminish the importance of consciousness within the ecology of mind, embodiment, and technics. Cognitive and systems approaches, in principle, ought to be suited to the current culture of global media – which, like the specialized modules that enable mental processes, are now present everywhere and might be said to determine not thought or cultural content, but the horizon of meaningful expression. Although advocates of New Media like to speak of "affordances," in practice one encounters mostly constraints (conscious and unconscious) at every stage of a work's composition, circulation, and archival existence in today's hybrid electronic and print platforms. The awareness of how expression is *bounded* by visual, computational, sound, and other non-verbal systems is heightened in the new "media ecology" (Tabbi and Wutz 1997). As literary critics have emphasized "gaps in nature," and the fragmentation of expression into media-specific niches, neuroscientists speak similarly of an "explanatory gap" between "an objective scientific explanation" of brain processes and "the elusive subjective quality of our introspective existence" (Burn 2009, paraphrasing Levine 1999). Even so, the tendency remains among mainstream cognitive critics to look *out* from the human to cognitive environments, turning the likely universality of brain processes into a dubious cultural unity.

Here is how Mark Turner – in an article not coincidentally presented *in* a networked environment at onthehuman.org – attempts to map cognition onto non-human networks and communicative flows:

> Network scale can be vast even though human scale is not, because the network scale is anchored in the human scale. The human scale blend [e.g., of the near to the far, of past experience to present memory, etc.] in the network provides us with a platform, a scaffold, a cognitively congenial basis from within to reach out, manage, manipulate, transform, develop, and handle the network.
>
> (Turner 2009)

Few would doubt that management, manipulation, and transformation come from the human side. And few would deny that our instrumental powers are extended significantly by the technologies that increasingly determine our situation. What is debatable is whether we humans, individually or collectively, can be said to "handle the network."

To a degree, one's decision to focus on "the human scale" or on the emergence of psychic and social systems from other material and symbolic technologies will determine whether one holds on to a humanist or what has come to be described as a "posthumanist" approach to the current cultural situation. Turner's insistence in this same article at onthehuman.org, for example, that human cognition differs fundamentally from that of animals, is questioned by a number of blog respondents and certainly would be contested by critics such as Wolfe (2010) and Clarke (2008), who make the non-human animal and our deep embeddedness in hybrid networks and complex systems starting points for posthumanist explorations of literary and ethical consciousness. As Clarke writes, following Niklas Luhmann's idea that social systems, no less than to psyches, are self-reproducing, referential, "autopoietic" selves:

> The organic bodies and ecosystems we impose our technologies on are not beneath us but *beyond* us, even while all around us, even while sharing us with an environment as yet fit for life. ... No system can

subdue or contain the entirety of its environment. Systems are possible only within environments that entirely surpass them.

(Clarke 2008: 195–96)

Regardless of one's position in these debates – among Jameson's postmodernism, Carroll's evolutionary humanism, Turner's cognitive humanism, or Wolfe's and Clarke's posthumanism – it is clear that the terms of the debate depend on the location of human culture (and literature as the diminishing margin of verbal expression among material cultures) in networks and systems that are much larger than consciousness.

If we abstract from mental processes to the critical faculty itself, the program for a cognitive literary criticism appropriate to the current media ecology begins to look rather different from any of the "cognitive approaches" currently on offer. Alan Liu, a Romanticist who has successfully relocated his practice to electronic environments, advances a radically new understanding of critical writing (an expression of which also appears, like Turner's and Carroll's recent work, at onthehuman.org). Liu is responding to my own suggestion that the effect of an apparently routine online activity, the "tagging" of literary works according to genre, type, and emergent categories, can be an important intersection among authors, critics, and the actual networks where literary works are currently produced and read:

> There are very few humans whose acts of criticism I trust. However, there are many more humans – the entirety of the "wisdom of the crowd" or "rule of many" we see on Web 2.0 today, in fact – whose acts of tagging I trust. That crowd, indeed, may be the greatest example today of what I above termed "strangely smart, exceedingly lively creatures." To be able to appreciate and learn from that different kind of crowd human, I think will require that we rethink the notion of "criticism" so that it draws on lower-order human operations, which in turn overlap with and can be made more tractable through machinic operations (which I think is the point of Semantic Web, in whose context the notion of semantics as "meaning" is too high level to be useful). So, for example, let's try substituting the notions of "filtering" or "linking" for "criticizing."

(Liu 2009)

Liu's distinction among acts of critical judgment and the lower-level, networked behavior of tags, keywords, and Semantic Web technologies parallels the key distinction between consciousness and cognition. Such differences are congruent with the cognitive make-up of humans – where the majority of activity goes on below consciousness and in distributed networks that extend beyond the boundaries of our bodies and self-consciousness. Indeed, only a small part of the brain's activity is used for making critical evaluations and conscious decisions. One of the challenges, and one of the terrific opportunities, for those who are trying to do literary work in electronic environments is that we are continually confronted with activities and behaviors that go on more or less independently of the meaning-making activities that are the "higher-level" interest of criticism.

In my essay (Tabbi 2009, which occasioned Liu's response), I spoke of the "methods of tagging texts" in electronic environments as "quite modest" and I located the critical activity not in the tags themselves but rather in the establishment of "professional and communicative networks," a higher-level, institutional arrangement. That's where critical judgment comes in, because critics are not trying to develop or master a universal critical language, but identifying concepts in works and then communicating among peers. The creation of tags and keywords is universal, not just the concerted development of any one theoretical school, precisely because the life of letters within networked environments remains beyond "us." (Hence electronic-literature author Brian Kim Stefans's *Dream Life of Letters* [2000].) Putting those new names into circulation, and tracking those terms, as they develop, is the place where criticism can locate itself in the new media. Like consciousness, that place is important but also marginal.

Bibliography

Burn, S. (2009) "Neurofictions" (work in progress).

Carroll, J. (2009) "The adaptive function of literature and the other arts." Online. Available HTTP: <http://onthehuman.org/2009/06/the-adaptive-function-of-literature-and-the-other-arts> (accessed 14 November 2009).

Clarke, B. (2008) *Posthuman Metamorphosis: narrative and systems*, New York: Fordham University Press.

——and Hansen, M.B.N. (eds) (2009) *Emergence and Embodiment: new essays on second-order systems theory*, Durham, N.C.: Duke University Press.

Cochran, T. (2001) *Twilight of the Literary: figures of thought in the age of print*, Cambridge, Mass.: Harvard University Press.

Dennett, D. (1991) *Consciousness Explained*, Boston, Mass.: Little, Brown.

Fukuyama, F. (1992) *The End of History and the Last Man*, New York: Free Press.

Hansen, M.B.N. (2006) *Bodies in Code: interfaces with digital media*, New York: Routledge.

Hogan, P.C. (2003) *Cognitive Science, Literature, and the Arts: a guide for humanists*, New York: Routledge.

Ingarden, R. (1968) *The Cognition of the Literary Work of Art*, Evanston: Northwestern University Press, 1973.

Jameson, F. (1991) *Postmodernism, or, The Cultural Logic of Late Capitalism*, Durham, N.C.: Duke University Press.

——(2009) *Valences of the Dialectic*, London: Verso.

Johnston, J. (1998) *Information Multiplicity: American fiction in the age of media saturation*, Baltimore: Johns Hopkins University Press.

Lakoff, G. and Johnson, M. (1980) *Metaphors We Live By*, Chicago: University of Chicago Press.

Levine, J. (1999) "Conceivability, identity, and the explanatory gap." Online. Available HTTP: <http://cognet.mit.edu/posters/TUCSON3/Levine.html> (accessed 29 October 2009).

Liu, A. (2009) "'Human': the filtering animal, the linking animal," threaded to Tabbi 2009.

Lloyd, D. (2003) *Radiant Cool: a novel theory of consciousness*, Cambridge, Mass.: MIT Press.

Luhmann, N. (1995) *Social Systems*, trans. J. Bednarz, Jr. with D. Baecker, Stanford: Stanford University Press.

Richardson, A. and Spolsky, E. (2004) *The Work of Fiction: cognition, culture, commplexity*, London: Ashgate.

Richter, D.H. (ed.) (2007) *The Critical Tradition: classical texts and contemporary trends*, 3rd edn, New York: Bedford/St. Martin's.

Spolsky, E. (1993) *Gaps in Nature: literary interpretation and the modular mind*, Albany: State University of New York Press.

Stefans, B.K. (2000) *Dream Life of Letters*. Online. Available HTTP: <http://collection.eliterature.org/1/works/stefans – the_dreamlife_of_letters.html > (accessed 23 December 2009).

Szanto, G.H. (1972) *Narrative Consciousness: structure and perception in the fiction of Kafka, Beckett, and Robbe-Grillet*, Austin: University of Texas Press.

Tabbi, J. (2002) *Cognitive Fictions*, Minneapolis: University of Minnesota Press.

——(2009) "On reading 300 works of electronic literature: preliminary reflections." Online. Available HTTP: <http://onthehuman.org/2009/07/on-reading-300-works-of-electronic-literature-preliminary-reflections> (accessed 15 November 2009).

——(forthcoming) "Electronic literature as world literature, or, the universality of writing under constraint," *Poetics Today*.

——and Wutz, M. (1997) *Reading Matters: narrative in the new media ecology*, Ithaca, N.Y.: Cornell University Press.

Turner, M. (1990) "Poetry: metaphor and the conceptual context of invention," in Richter 2007, pp. 1077–88.

——(1991) *Reading Minds: the study of literature in the age of cognitive science*, Princeton: Princeton University Press.

——(1996) *The Literary Mind: the origins of language and consciousness*, New York: Oxford University Press.

——(2009) "The scope of human thought." Online. Available HTTP: <http://onthehuman.org/2009/08/the-scope-of-human-thought> (accessed 31 October 2009).

Wolfe, C. (2010) *What is Posthumanism?*, Minneapolis: University of Minnesota Press.

Zunshine, L. (2003) "Theory of mind and experimental representations of fictional consciousness," in Richter 2007, pp. 1089–105.

8

CYBERNETICS

Søren Brier

Come, let us hasten to a higher plane,
When dyads tread the fairy fields of Venn,
Their indices bedecked from one to *n*,
Commingled in an endless Markov chain!
(Lem 1985: 52)

In Stanislaw Lem's *Cyberiad*, the cybernetic super-engineer Trurl, robotic inventor and robot builder, constructs a robot-computer that can produce poetry in all its forms. He realizes that in order to produce the first-ever specimen of such a machine, he needs to model the whole of human mythological, social, and cultural history. So, he creates a cybernetic model of the Muse, a Cyberbard that can produce an infinite amount of heart-touching poems. Writing day and night, this immense poetic force ends up disturbing social as well as galactic order. The verse above – the first in a mathematical love poem with cybernetic feeling made by Trurl's electronic bard – is a fitting place to start a discussion of cybernetics and literature.

The mathematician Norbert Wiener, who coined the term, described "cybernetics" as *the science of control and communication in the animal and the machine* (Wiener 1948), a definition taken as foundational by one of cybernetics' major developers, Ross Ashby (1956). The etymology of cybernetics goes to the art of steersmanship. In Greek, *kybernetes* means pilot, steersman, and cybernetics is a theory of control of the behavior of machines, organisms, and organizations by the way of feedback circuits. Most of all, cybernetics studied machines with built-in devices, such as regulators and thermostats, for seeking and maintaining set goals. Thus, fundamentally, the science of cybernetics focuses not on being but on behavior: it does not ask, "what *is* this thing?" but instead, "what does it *do*?" Or, "how can we make a thing that does this?" Especially in its initial or first-order form, cybernetics is a transdisciplinary engineering thinking. It is not about subjective individuals or any form of individual consciousness, because one of the basic requirements for being an autonomous individual is to be autopoietic. As developed in second-order cybernetics, *autopoiesis* refers to systems, such as living cells, that are self-referential in that they are self-maintaining: they are themselves the product of their own operation (see Clarke 2008, and his article on Systems Theory,

Chapter 19, this volume). In contrast, the machines studied in the first cybernetics are allopoietic, that is, created and made by something else, some other system.

The combination of a cybernetic machine and an organism, human or otherwise, is called a cyborg, from which term derives the fantastic cybernetic vision of the Borg in *Star Trek: The Next Generation* (*TNG*). When Captain Jean-Luc Picard is captured by the Borg, he is transformed into a cyborg. The indeterminate status and behavior of this combination of machine and organism may be why in all the movies and TV episodes of *TNG*, Data, an android constructed by the chief cybernetician Dr. Noonien Soong, is such a mystery. Nobody knows exactly what it/he is or how to construct another. The Borg manifests as a juggernaut of cybernetically enhanced humanoid drones of multiple species, an interconnected collective communicatively linked through a subspace domain and integrated into a hive or group mind/ego, a single consciousness occupying many bodies. A type of organization inspired by bees and ants, as in a perfect dictatorship, the individual is sacrificed to the social whole. The Borg captures the uneasy social affect in many of the fantastic narratives cybernetics has inspired.

The cyborg fantasy of the Borg combines the autopoietic and sign-producing abilities of living systems with machines' powers of memory and computation, making all members of Borg far stronger than humans. Furthermore, as a massive cybernetic and homeostatic system, the Borg is always adapting and consuming new technology and information, making organic agencies into cyborgs with implants, and integrating those cyborgs and their spaceship into a sentient autopoietic system. The Borg travels through space assimilating those races and their technologies that can improve its efficiency and survival into its system: "We are the Borg. You will be assimilated. Resistance is futile!" In "The Best of Both Worlds," it captures and renders Captain Picard into the collective by surgically altering him, creating Locutus of Borg to use as a weapon in the battle against the *Enterprise*. One wonders if his recapture by the *Enterprise* crew and the operative restoration of his former individual self is as realistic as his submission to the Borg system!

Lem's genius in the *Cyberiad* is that, while he sees the immense possibilities of cybernetics, at the same time, with tongue-in-cheek irony, his exquisite science-fiction fables explore its dubious relations to human consciousness. In a fable on the problem of will, "Trurl's Machine," a stupid and stubborn robot refuses to learn anything beyond its original program. Unfortunately, that program had some elementary flaws, such as thinking that two and two equals seven, and Trurl's stupid machine prefers to kill the messenger of its faults rather than to correct them. A fundamentalist robot! Isaac Asimov has a comparable story where robots on a space ship will not accept that they are created by the humans, pointing out how much more perfect they are. The movie *I Robot* uses the same kind of irony when the machines realize how irrational human beings can be, and so interpret Asimov's laws for robots about protecting their creators by trying to take power, thus bringing themselves and the whole globe into danger. As too often happens in these science fictions, the robots are given self-conscious minds, without due consideration of the flaws in cybernetic thinking – its blind spots when it comes to matters of will, emotion, the qualia and agency of first-person consciousness.

Cybernetics started by being closely associated with physics, in particular, thermodynamics and statistical mechanics. But it depends in no essential way on the laws of physics or on the properties of matter. It gets its transdisciplinary scope by viewing the materiality of a given system as irrelevant to its organizational properties. Rather, it works with those circulating differences and relations that we have come to call information. What cybernetics is concerned with is the scientific investigation of all varieties of goal-oriented systemic processes, including such phenomena as regulation, information processing, information storage, adaptation, self-organization, self-reproduction, and strategic behavior. Cybernetics deals with all forms of behavior insofar as they are regular, determinate, or reproducible.

Thus, at its origin cybernetics lays down its own foundations as a science of self-regulating and goal-seeking systems. Lem underscores this special independence in his *Cyberiad* again and again by showing how Trurl and his friend and competitor, Klapaucius, are at the same time both inventors and problem solvers for the problems their inventions create. For instance, they invent a prey robot for King Krool so perfect that not even his predator Saint Cybernards and Cyberman pinchers, nor even the king's high-fidelity cybersteed, could follow it! In essence, Trurl and Klapaucius introduced self-organizing principles into their invention and, as such, attempted to move the behavior of robots up to the next step in cybernetic development, namely Heinz von Foerster's second-order cybernetics, for which the goal is not only to observe the behavior of systems but also to observe the way that observing systems observe. Thus the construction recurs on the constructor itself.

Lem's refined ironic tales, then, play on how cybernetic devices – from thermostats, physiological mechanism for the regulation of body temperature, and automatic steering devices, to economic and political processes – are goal-seeking systems studied under a general mathematical model of deviation-counteracting feedback networks. Cybernetics is transdisciplinary and requires some knowledge of neurophysiology, mathematics, philosophy, psychology, but proposes on this basis a general theory of information processing and decision making based on a computational framework. Laying the foundation for what we now call cognitive science, cybernetics' algebraic information thinking permeated even its attempts to model linguistics as well as emotions and consciousness.

This algebraic-computational orientation makes it clear why, in *The Cyberiad*, Klapaucius attempts to test Trurl's Cyberbard by asking for "a love poem, lyrical, pastoral, and expressed in the language of pure mathematics. Tensor algebra mainly, with a little topology and higher calculus, if need be. But with feeling, you understand, in the cybernetic spirit" (Lem 1985: 51–52). As cyber-netics, especially in Wiener's hand, was also the development of a special interdisciplinary mathematical apparatus, the love poem given by Trurl's elec-tronic bard, in Michael Kandel's astonishing translation, provides such a unique ode to mathematical beauty that I have to cite a few more lines.

> Come, every frustum longs to be a cone,
> And every vector dreams of matrices.
> Hark to the gentle gradient of the breeze:
> It whispers of a more ergodic zone.
>
> In Riemann, Hilbert or in Banach space
> Let superscripts and subscripts go their ways.
>
> (Lem 1985: 52)

Because numerous systems in the living, social, and technological world may be translated into these mathematical and behavioral idioms, cybernetics cuts across many traditional disciplinary boundaries. It developed a metadisciplinary lan-guage of information and goal-oriented self-organized behavior through negative feedback that works on differences and uses feedback/feed-forward mechanisms to home in on the target. Cybernetic theory was derived to some extent from the new findings in the 1930s and 1940s regarding the role of electric signals in biological systems, including the human nervous system. Wiener (1948) con-nected information and entropy with organization and therefore evolution. Wiener defined information as a probability, describing the amount of informa-tion mathematically as an integral, a measurement of probability. Specifically, he defined information on the model of negentropy, as inspired by Erwin Schrödinger – the amount of entropy a system exports to keep its own entropy low (see Chapter 13 on Information Theory).

Wiener's view of information is thus that it contains some form of structure, order, or pattern. Many researchers attempt to build up a concept of meaning on this foundation. But such a concept of meaning does not have much to do with what living systems and human beings do to operate semiotically in cognition and communication. Lem underlines this gap when his hero, Trurl, realizes that, to be able to make poetry that actually touches human emotions, you have to possess some knowledge of the history of human culture, some sense of humanity's world horizon. In the most humorous way, Trurl works hard to squeeze the whole history of biological evolution and human develop-ment into logical programming and hardware construction. After that comes of course a little programming of semantics, grammar, pragmatics, and all the forms of poetry previously developed, plus an anti-cliché program – no problem for a great cybernetician! Clearly, Lem is mocking the technological hubris of some cybernetically inspired engineers.

Star Trek: TNG brings up Data's inability to understand jokes, including practical jokes, many times. Finally, he gets an "emotion chip." But this throws him into a chaotic reality, a life-world of feelings he cannot control, and in one episode he actually requests to have it removed. Trurl's Cyberbard, on the other hand, learns to manipulate human feelings by the composition of words and meanings. Thus it is able to prevent its own destruction by the policemen and soldiers sent to pull its plug, overwhelming them with sentimental emotions, making them unable to do their grim deed. But of course the great question underlying Lem's short story is whether it is possible to teach a machine, if it lacks those emotions itself, to improvise the manipulation of human feelings. Even psychopaths, in order to manipulate others, operate from a minimum of feelings themselves. However, the therapeutic AI program Eliza and Paro, the robotic baby seal used to comfort demented elderly, seem to indicate that such interactions are possible to a certain extent. Taking cybermanipulation to the next level, the *Cyberiad* presents a "femfatalatron, an erotifying device, stochastic, elastic and orgiastic, and with plenty of feedback" (Lem 1985: 108). While, in Lem, the description is thick with irony, sex with female androids is featured in both Philip K. Dick's *Do Androids Dream of Electric Sheep?* (1968) and its movie adaptation, *Blade Runner* (1982). Today a whole industry is working on developing cybernetic sex machines.

Inspired by the original cybernetic work on neuropsychology and the brain as a logical programmer, the theory of a universal "language of mind" has been developed. Such a language of mind, it is hypothesized, would be what the brain computes in and then later translates to humans' culturally influenced natural language. It seems that this is what the *TNG* writers were inspired by when they imagined the Borg to use alphanumeric code as their written language, consisting of circular symbols with geometric shapes cut out of them, written in horizontal and vertical lines, for encoding and transmitting data throughout the Collective. Some parts of cybernetic cognitive science take it to be their role to unravel this brain-internal language in order to make artificial-intelligence, automatic decision-making systems, as well as an automatic universal language translator. One prototype is now called Babelfish. This term was coined by Douglas Adams in *The Hitchhiker's Guide to the Galaxy.* Here the Babelfish is a small, fishlike creature from another galaxy, which you insert into your ear, with the result that you understand all other languages as if they were your own, no matter from which galaxy in the universe they come. But these days, it is the name of a free and automatic translation program on the Net, amazing in itself, but also, in its deficiencies, demonstrating the lack of robot language processing in relation to human meaning and understanding. The Babelfish has not yet reached the level of Trurl's Cyberbard.

The ideas that our brains are organic hardware or wetware – that our intelligence and cognitive abilities as well as our personalities are the informational programs that run on that wetware – have given rise to the vivid fantasy of transferring the human self out of its body and into other media. Most famous is William Gibson's groundbreaking cyberpunk trilogy *Neuromancer, Count Zero*, and *Mona Lisa Overdrive* (the so-called Sprawl trilogy), starting in 1984. It promotes the idea of "jacking in" to the Net. As you fasten the electrons of your Web-connected computer directly onto brain switches in your skull, your mind travels into the three-dimensional informational world of cyberspace. In this virtual reality, the mind of a deceased important person – for instance, the previous leader of a huge international concern – is present, together with huge artificial intelligences that evolve and expand their domination of this cyberworld, intricately connected to our material world through all the computers connected to real-world machines. Here is a new form of earthly paradise, as you can live forever on the Net without your body. This is in contrast to the *Matrix* movies: to be present in the Matrix, your mind has to have its base in a sleeping body kept alive by machines.

The Japanese cartoon *Yoko Tsuno* plays, in several issues, with the idea of transferring the human mind to robotic systems. The famous Japanese cartoon movie *The Ghost in the Shell* further explores this gray territory between living systems and independent artificial intelligences similar to human subjects but without a body. But most surprisingly, in what one supposes to be his alternative to those grand narratives of modernity he had previously mocked, Jean-François Lyotard, in his *Postmodern Fables* (1999), imagines the human species to escape when the sun burns out, departing from the Earth in space rockets as pure informational intelligences.

As Winograd and Flores (1987) pointed out, cybernetic developers in the 1980s expected to have intelligent robots managing human social tasks within a decade. The body was considered a machine in which the brain functioned by algorithmic computation. The modern computer was a perfect rational being. All we needed was to develop it into a still more powerful machine with more computing power. The funniest, most sarcastic and most penetrating critical evaluation of AI's relation to the human world of existential meaning ever written, in my opinion, is Douglas Adams's *The Hitchhiker's Guide to the Galaxy*. After seven and a half million years' cybermeditating on "the ultimate question of the meaning of life, the universe and everything," a supercomputer by the name of "Deep Thought" comes up with the answer: "42" (Adams 1996: 120). Computers, having no sense of human existential meaning, function in a mathematical universe.

Filled with scientific knowledge about the universe on one hand, and reflections – in the form of humorous events – on the role of emotion and meaning in human rationality on the other, this unique book purveys humorous and sarcastic scenarios about what could happen if developments in technology made it possible for us to install these "features" in computers and robots. We have seen similar discussions in *Star Trek: TNG* around the android Data, who gets an "emotion chip" from his human handlers. A number of scenarios play out the attempts of this rational android to deal with these new sensual aspects of reality – including the affect of humor. A comparable theme takes a different turn in Dick (1968) and *Blade Runner* (1982). The novel is deeply psychological, asking questions such as: What is empathy and human emotion? Is consciousness an emergent quality? What defines intelligence? The movie is a little cruder, of course, but its focus is the question of when the artificial life of androids stops being merely mechanical and becomes the feeling and willing of subjects with existential and aesthetic needs.

Dick's novel imagines that our culture has developed a cybernetic emotion-regulating machine capable of securing for its user a good mood all the time. But people start to get bored with happiness. To render happiness more enjoyable, they begin to play with inducing depressive states for longer and longer periods, some, unfortunately, for so long that they commit suicide. The *Star Trek* writers are aware of the related problem of the need for experiental embodiment in order to produce and sustain consciousness. In the *Star Trek* movie *First Contact*, the Borg Queen wants to persuade Data to join the Borg by tempting him with the addition of living flesh to his previously insensitive android body, thus transferring the feeling of a living body to his "brain." The experience is as overwhelming for him as when he had an emotion chip inserted. But after all, the question ignored by these fantasies is how he could have experiences of any sort with a computer for a brain. We do not even know how *living* brains produce experience, nor if that is what they do.

In *The Hitchhiker's Guide*, Adams's deeply depressed super-robot, Marvin, deals in a sarcastic way with unreal techno-optimist expectations by showing some of the absurd consequences of emotions in supercomputer robots. Marvin can cause any cybernetic control system to break down completely just by connecting to it and sharing his melancholy view of the world and his own situation, and actually saves the book's young hero once by doing just that. But I also cherish the part where Marvin causes the cybernetically regulated high-speed elevators going up 100-storey houses to get anxiety neuroses and hide in the cellar, not daring to go up into the heights!

In the novel *This Perfect Day* (1970), Ira Levin plays out the question of the superiority of artificial to human intelligence and the consequences of improving nature and culture, through the control of a central computer. In contrast, Adams's *Hitchhiker's Guide* portrays the ruler of the universe as a radical skeptic antirealist and disbeliever in the control of complex systems. Where Levin's novel is a heroic science fiction of rebellion against a technocratic dystopia, Adams's ruler of the universe is located in a little shack on a remote, insignificant planet and, when asked if he rules the universe, he says, "I try not to." This attitude of relinquishing control for autonomy is more in line with the development of second-order cybernetics and autopoiesis theory. These developments followed classical cybernetics and brought in a constructivist viewpoint that encompassed classical cybernetics as only a special case of systems theory.

Where Ira Levin sees humanity making a violent revolution against the all-benevolent but tyrannical central intelligence that rules the length and form of people's lives based on an overall computation of what the system can sustain, Adams makes people complain that there is not a more consistent homeostasis and cybernetic equilibrium in the government of the world.

In the 1980s, building on cybernetic foundations, new theories of dynamical systems – chaos theory with its strange attractors, fractal geometries, and self-similar iterations – and complex adaptive systems (CAS) were developed and introduced. Popularizing some of these developments, Michael Crichton's novel *Jurassic Park* – and to a lesser degree the movie made from it – dramatized the consequences of dispensing with cybernetic thinking in the effort to control complex non-linear systems by computers. Reflecting the contrast between classical deterministic science and the new cybernetics of complexity and unpredictability, *Jurassic Park* also addresses the limits of scientific knowledge and focuses on how the complexity and self-organization paradigms change our views on scientific prediction and control.

Set on an island, Jurassic Park, which exhibits live dinosaurs grown from prehistoric remnants of theirs genes, illustrates the problems bound up with the attempt to gain full control of an ecosystem. Controlled by a huge computer system, the park should be perfectly safe, but little by little, the irregularities and inadequacy of the system are revealed, until its final collapse and catastrophe. It is an extremely powerful renouncement of the deterministic control paradigm: simplicity, linearity, determinism, and control are contrasted with a new realization: nature is non-linear, fractal, and complex. The chaos researcher, Malcolm, plays an important role as the all-knowing reporter of complexity and chaos in this most dramatic setting of wild dinosaurs hunting children. His experience beseeches us to understand that we are at the end of an epoch, and so we had better hurry up and learn some new tricks if we wish to survive. In a later novel, *Prey*, Crichton imagines what can happen when a self-organizing genetically engineered swarm intelligence is combined with communicating nano-computers. A new, lethal, infectious super-organism emerges, completely out of control, but also competing with an initially benign one that turns out, in the long run, to be much more dangerous. The novel gives a superb illustration of the discrepancy between the current cybernetic knowledge of complexity and self-organization, and the failure of control engineers to grasp the dynamics of chaotic systems.

Within the field of cybernetic anthropology, this tension was especially expressed in Gregory Bateson's *Steps to an Ecology of Mind* (1972). Here Bateson described modern technoscience as a culture of hubris. His major project was to explain the relation of mind and nature – or more precisely, mind in nature – from a modern scientific basis, avoiding the metaphysical dualism of Descartes as well as the mechanism of Laplace. Bateson provided a new delimitation of the concept of information: "In fact, what we mean by information – the elementary unit of information – is a *difference which makes a difference*" (Bateson 1972: 453).

For Bateson, even when that system does not include living organisms, "The elementary cybernetic system with its messages in circuit is, in fact, the simplest unit of mind" (459). Matter and energy are already imbued with informational circular processes of differences. Mind is synonymous with a cybernetic system comprised of a total, self-correcting unit which prepares and processes information. Mind is immanent in this wholeness, because mind is essentially the informational and logical "pattern that connects" through a virtual recursive dynamics of differences in circuit. He sees life and mind as coexisting in an ecological and evolutionary dynamic that integrates the whole biosphere. In sum, Bateson explained mind as a function of complex cybernetic organization, and incorporated his concept of information into a universal cybernetic philosophy. Bateson believed that his version of cybernetics provides an understanding of mind that is neither subjectively idealistic nor mechanically materialistic.

This cybernetic mind also rules our emotions as a relational logic. It shows up in our perception as aesthetics. It is the learning pattern in evolution. Wisdom is to know and live the pattern of evolutionary and ecological wholeness in cultures as well as in individual awareness. The pattern that connects can be understood as a metaphor for what many nature-religious or spiritual types of ecological thinking see as the sacred or the immanent divine. In Bateson a holistic cybernetic science verges on the sacred:

> The cybernetic epistemology which I have offered you would suggest a new approach. The individual mind is immanent but not only in the body. It is immanent also in the pathways and messages outside the body; and there is a larger Mind of which the individual mind is only a sub-system. This larger Mind is comparable to God and is perhaps what some people mean by "God," but it is still immanent in the total interconnected social system and planetary ecology.
>
> (Bateson 1972: 461)

In *The Cyberiad* Lem places Bateson's vision into literary praxis in "The First Sally, or The Trap of Gargantius." Trurl and Klapacius land on a planet with two countries planning to wage war against each other; they go to opposite sides of the conflict. Anticipating the consequences of Bateson's theory – that all systems in which bits of information or transforms of difference circulate have cybernetic minds, and the more systems are coupled together the greater the mind will be – Trurl and Klapacius both suggest to the kings and generals on either side to connect their soldiers into closely organized systems by way of a specially constructed armor. When they reach the level of companies, however, the greater mind that is created starts to absorb the soldiers' individual minds:

> they took to chatting, and later, through the open windows of the barracks one could hear voices booming in chorus, disputing such matters as absolute truth, analytic versus synthetic *a priori* propositions, and the Thing-in-itself, for their collective minds had already attained that level.
>
> (Lem 1985: 40)

When they reached the level of battalions, they developed a higher aesthetic sense, and some became sidetracked from warfare into chasing after butterflies: "Among the artillery corps the weightiest metaphysical questions were considered, and, with an absentmindedness characteristic of great genius, these large units lost their weapons, misplaced their equipment and completely forgot that there was a war on" (1985: 41). When the officers attempted to bring the soldiers back to common sense, they too got absorbed in the collective mind or corporate identity and forgot their original mission. "Consciousness, it seemed, formed a deadly trap, in that one could enter it, but never leave" (41).

Finally, on either side totally united, two armies with one mind apiece attack each other, but as soon as they touch are brought into a single system:

> There was absolute silence. That famous culmination of consciousness that the great Gargantius had predicted with mathematical precision was now reached on both sides. For beyond a certain point militarism, a purely local phenomenon, becomes civil, and this is because the Cosmos Itself is by nature wholly civilian, and indeed, the minds of both armies had assumed truly cosmic proportions! ... Both armies went off hand in hand, picking flowers beneath the fluffy white clouds, on the field of the battle that never was.
>
> (Lem 1985: 42)

I do not think that cybernetic theory, be it of first or second order, could imagine a more beautiful outcome of its theory.

Bibliography

Adams, D. (1996) *The Ultimate Hitchhiker's Guide to the Galaxy*, New York: Wing Books.
Ashby, W.R. (1956) *An Introduction to Cybernetics*, London: Chapman & Hall.
Bateson, G. (1972) *Steps to an Ecology of Mind*, New York: Ballantine.
Blade Runner (1982) dir. Ridley Scott, Warner Brothers.

Clarke, B. (2008) *Posthuman Metamorphosis: narrative and systems*, New York: Fordham University Press.

Crichton, M. (1990) *Jurassic Park*, New York: Random House.

——(1995) *The Lost World*, New York: Random House.

——(2002) *Prey*, New York: HarperCollins.

Dick, P.K. (1968) *Do Androids Dream of Electric Sheep?*, New York: Del Rey, 1996.

Gibson, W. (1984) *Neuromancer*, New York: Ace Books.

——(1986) *Count Zero*, London: Victor Gollancz.

——(1988) *Mona Lisa Overdrive*, London: Victor Gollancz.

Lem, S. (1985) *The Cyberiad: fables for the cybernetic age*, trans. M. Kandel, New York: Harvest.

Levin, I. (1970) *This Perfect Day*, New York: Random House.

Lyotard, J.-F. (1999) *Postmodern Fables*, trans. G. Van Den Abbeele, Minneapolis: University of Minnesota Press.

Star Trek: The Next Generation (1987–94) prod. G. Roddenberry, Paramount Television.

Wiener, N. (1948) *Cybernetics: the science of control and communication in the animal and the machine*, Cambridge, Mass.: MIT Press, 1961.

Winograd, T. and Flores, F. (1987) *Understanding Computers and Cognition: a new foundation for design*, Reading, Mass.: Addison-Wesley.

9
ECOLOGY

Stacy Alaimo

Ecological knowledge, history, and culture

Ecology is the branch of biology that studies the relations between various organisms as well as the relations between organisms and their environments. Although Ernst Haeckel coined the term "ecology" in the 1860s, writings that observe ecological interconnections, causal relations, and degradation were penned much earlier. Perhaps even more than in other scientific fields, one would be hard pressed to disqualify a staggering wealth of observations – agricultural and forestry manuals, medical texts, the accounts of colonizers, travel writing, nature writing, journals, and memoirs – from being considered part of the history of ecology. An obvious reason for this would be that the concerns of ecology arise from other human practices – including subsistence practices – that directly engage with the natural world. Studies of traditional ecological knowledges (TEK), for example, reveal that many, if not all, cultures produce systematic forms of ecological knowledge suited to each culture's specific environment, social organization, and perspectives thereon. A systematic understanding of the ecology of a particular place may be provoked by the need or desire to protect that environment. As Richard Grove explains, what are "called conservation practices cannot, in fact, be distinguished clearly from the complex web of economic, religious, and cultural arrangements evolved by a multitude of societies to safeguard and sustain their access to resources" (Grove 1995: 16). Thus there may well be as many ecological "sciences" as there are cultures.

Postcolonial science and technology studies also insist upon multiple traditions of ecological knowledge. By emphasizing scientific traditions other than those of Euro-Americans, postcolonial science studies resists a triumphal narrative of Western rationality (Harding 2008: 130). Postcolonial science studies also stresses how the sciences of Europe have been indebted to indigenous, Asian, African, and Latin American cultures. Thus, in the broadest possible sense, the study of ecology and literature would include all cultures, all time periods, and all sorts of texts, including oral literatures and ceremonies (such as Shalako, the Zuni world renewal ritual). It would draw not only upon the disciplines of literary studies, ecology, science, and science studies, but also anthropology, sociology, political theory, history, cultural studies, and post-colonial studies.

Rather than trying to reference the wealth of texts, criticism, and contexts worthy of inclusion here, this chapter will discuss a few examples of English-language literature and literary criticism that pertain to ecology. Two lines of inquiry will shape the chapter. The first gestures toward a central issue within the study of literature and science, namely the relation between literary texts and scientific knowledge, suggesting that, with regard to ecology, literature and science are not always worlds apart. Following from the first, the second line of inquiry examines how laypeople have practiced a kind of ecological science by observing and documenting ecological systems, changes, and harms. Along the way I will introduce a few ecologically oriented literary genres, and I will conclude by discussing how ecocriticism – the ecologically oriented school of literary analysis – can draw upon science and science studies.

Ecological science and literature before the twentieth century

Richard Grove's monumental *Green Imperialism* argues that the European colonization of oceanic islands between the seventeenth and nineteenth centuries provoked "remarkably sophisticated insights into the mechanisms and pro-cesses of ecological change" (Grove 1995: 474). *Green Imperialism* includes analyses of literature such as Shakespeare's *The Tempest*, Godwin's *Man in the Moon*, and Defoe's *Robinson Crusoe* to illustrate the "two-way process by which particular literary discourses powerfully shaped changing perceptions of nature and the globe, and in which literature was, in its turn, increasingly influenced by new understandings and 'discoveries' in an expanding European world system of economic dominion and ruling discourses" (Grove 1995: 476). The literary texts appear as a significant part of a much broader history in which Grove documents the ecological observations made by those who were not schooled in science, or at least not schooled in "ecology" (which did not exist as a separate scientific discipline until the late nineteenth century). For example, during the eighteenth century many physicians employed by the trading companies produced new environmental theories, as they were propelled by the "urgent need to understand unfamiliar floras, faunas and geologies, both for commercial purposes and to counter environmental and health risks" (Grove 1995: 58). Grove boldly concludes that modern environmentalism is not "exclusively a product of European or North American predicaments and philosophies," but instead "emerged as a direct response to the destructive social and ecological conditions of colonial rule," having been influenced both by the "natural processes in the tropics and by a distinctive awareness of non-European epistemologies of nature" (Grove 1995: 486).

In her studies of the nineteenth-century American authors Ralph Waldo Emerson and Henry David Thoreau, Laura Dassow Walls confronts the now entrenched divide between literature and science by contending that the imposition of this division distorts our understanding of the time and, especially, of the work of these two authors. Walls asserts that Thoreau "saw his task to be the joining of poetry, philosophy, and science into a harmonized whole that emerged from the interconnected details of particular natural facts" and that he developed "a working scientific methodology" (Walls 1995: 4, 8). The literary criticism of Thoreau, however, has, for the most part, "disciplined" his work, which has meant, for example, in the case of his essay "The Succession of Forest Trees," driving "the literary and the scientific ... back into their separate domains" (Walls 1995: 248). In *Emerson's Life in Science*, Walls suggests that the very ease with which Emerson engaged with science may be misleading to contemporary scholars: "He took scientific literacy so much for granted that his scientific metaphors sink out of sight; worse, from his time to ours, the divorce between 'the two cultures' of literature and science has made his deep debt to science virtually invisible" (Walls 2003: 13).

It may be especially important to understand Thoreau's scientific orientations, since his writing continues to shape environmentalism. Walls concludes that the end of all Thoreau's writing "was not just to propose new scientific explanations, but to enact and then to model an alternative way of knowing, a situated, narrative science which traced all the multiple exchanges and connections which produced, simultaneously, the forest itself and the knowledge about the forest" (Walls 1995: 250). Walls suggests not only similarities between Thoreau's work and Donna Haraway's epistemology of "situated knowledges," but also a kinship between Thoreau's "style of world making" and Bruno Latour's insistence on the many hybrids existing between the "poles of nature–science and culture–literature" (Walls 1995: 249). Thus, the work of both Grove and Dassow Walls suggests vital interconnections between human practices, literary works, and the production of "ecological" knowledges.

Nature writing before the twentieth century

The epistemological practice with which Dassow Walls credits Thoreau may be a distinctive aspect of what has come to be known as the genre of "nature writing." The most canonical "nature writing" text would be, of course, Thoreau's influential book, *Walden*. Like other works that fit comfortably within this genre, *Walden* combines observations of the natural world with reflections on human ethics, values, politics, and modes of knowing. Nature writing, in fact, is usually propelled by the desire to artistically convey, in Dassow Walls' phrase, both "the forest itself and the knowledge about the forest." Even as nature writing suggests an atmosphere of quiet reflection, these ruminations are usually provoked by some sort of excursion – whether that be far afield into the wilds of the West, in John Muir's case, or closer to home, as in the island garden of Celia Thaxter. The genre of "nature writing" may itself be a sort of "scientific" endeavor when it attempts to accurately observe interrelations between plants, animals, habitats, and environments. Indeed there is no clear demarcation between "nature writing" and "science" or "science writing," especially in texts written before the twentieth century, as evidenced by the fact that *The Norton Book of Nature Writing* includes John Burroughs, James Audubon, and Charles Darwin. Although George Perkins Marsh is not included in this collection, his 1864 work, *Man and Nature*, which is considered an early, classic work of ecology, combines a scientific analysis of how humans have altered the environment with a conservationist philosophy.

Robert Finch and John Elder note that nature writers are the "children of Linneaus," the eighteenth-century founder of taxonomy, "a framework within which all living things could be classified and identified" (Finch and Elder 2002: 21). Much "nature writing," however, does not seek to categorize separate entities so much as to trace interconnections, processes, and changes. Furthermore, a Linnean epistemology becomes complicated by the late nineteenth- and early twentieth-century development of evolution and ecological science, which stress transformation, contingency, emergence, and interdependence rather than the delineation of static categories.

The science and politics of ecology

Ecology, according to Sharon Kingsland, "developed along varying paths at different times and in different places" (Kingsland 2005: 3). Ecology, as a branch of the Western science of biology, has had a hard time establishing itself as a separate, coherent discipline, not only because it emerges from different scientific (and amateur) practices, but because its methodologies span the lab/field border. Kurt Jax identifies the nineteenth-century origins of ecology as "the old tradition of natural history on the one hand, and the then new 'scientific', i.e. physiological, biology on the other" (Jax 2001: 2). He notes that this "hybrid character of ecology is present to this day," arguing that the tension between the two approaches – one which uses experiments to identify mechanisms, and one which proceeds via "description, comparison and classification" – gives ecology its "specificity and heuristic strength" (Jax 2001: 2).

Notwithstanding the debates over the methodology, coherence, or political entanglements of the science of ecology, ecological concepts have profoundly influenced Western worldviews (even if they have failed to alter many of our most environmentally harmful practices). Ecology's most important concept is probably that of the "ecosystem," a term coined in the 1930s, which entered popular usage in the 1950s. The term broadened the framework of ecology by enlarging its focus from that of the-organism-in-its-environment to a more complex analysis of systems of exchange, which included the cycles of nutrients, energy, and chemicals (Kingsland 2005: 184–85). It is hard to overestimate the importance of the concept of the "ecosystem," both in the development of ecological science and in more popular understandings of how environments work. Kingsland points out an irony here, however, noting that the word "ecosystem" gained its cultural purchase during the 1960s through the 1980s in the U.S. partly because the word "conveyed the idea of an ecological machine" – a machine that could be understood via cybernetics and engineering (Kingsland 2005: 215).

The concept of the ecosystem carries with it the question – echoed throughout environmental politics, environmental philosophy, and environmental literatures – of whether or not human culture and human activities should be considered part of or separate from the ecosystem. If ecosystems include humans – both as humans affect those systems and as they are affected by them – then the disciplinary scope of ecology broadens to include anthropology, history, economics, sociology, political science, and other areas of inquiry far afield from biology as such. Linda Nash, for example, in *Inescapable Ecologies*, undertakes an "'ecological' history of human bodies," explaining that in the nineteenth-century U.S., "the body's physical well-being ... offered a powerful way of understanding local environments" (Nash 2006: 3, 5). Nash documents how nineteenth-century immigrants, farmers, physicians, and public health officials in the western region of the U.S. analyzed the effects of their environments.

In the early twentieth century this sort of environmental medicine was displaced by "modern" medicine, which included germ theory. Modern medicine separated human bodies from environments, rendering nature "abstract space," devoid of agency or particularity (Nash 2006: 90). By the middle of the twentieth century, however, a new conception of ecological bodies emerges. Braceros (people from Mexico brought to the U.S. as temporary agricultural laborers), for instance, who were interviewed in 1958 about "sanitation and lack of access to modern medical care," responded by discussing the dangers of the new pesticides they were using in the fields, noting their harmful health effects (Nash 2006: 137). More generally, during roughly the same period, public knowledge about nuclear testing and the dissemination of radioactive particles made it increasingly difficult to imagine a nature separate from human actions and human bodies.

Nash notes that Rachel Carson's 1962 *Silent Spring* also challenged the divide between humans and nature. Although the title of this text evokes the haunting absence of birds after they have been killed by pesticides introduced into the food chain, Nash argues that Carson powerfully links "the quality of soil, water, and air to animal and human physiology," thus crossing the divide separating "the study of human bodies from the study of nonhuman environment"

(Nash 2006: 157). Carson's eloquent book, perhaps more than any other text written in English, has had a powerful impact on both ecology and environmentalism, as it has provoked a widespread understanding of interconnected ecological processes as well as the serious dangers of humanly made chemicals. It is now commonplace to credit *Silent Spring* with shaping the modern environmental movement (and its counterattacks), as it not only convinced many of its readers of the serious dangers of pesticides but provoked a backlash from chemical manufacturers and others who proclaimed the human benefits of pesticides, herbicides, and other chemicals.

As the controversy over *Silent Spring* illustrates, ecological science has developed within, not outside of, political contexts, which have their own complicated histories. Even though the term "ecology" is currently associated with an environmentalist orientation, Kingsland argues that it became a scientific discipline because it "addressed larger American goals related to economic development" (Kingsland 2005: 127). In short, in the early twentieth century American patrons funded ecological science because it promised "control over life" (ibid.) and the profits such control could bring. The history of ecology in the early twentieth-century U.S., then, not surprisingly, parallels the conservative history of Progressive Era conservationism, which was allied with race, class, and gender ideologies and which promoted a utilitarian conception of nature as a repository of "natural resources" (Alaimo 2000). Things shift by the latter half of the twentieth century, when more ecologists ally themselves with environmentalism, criticizing economic and industrial systems. The landscape of science and politics becomes even more complicated when we consider environmental justice frameworks in which ordinary citizens engage in scientific practices in order to prove that their neighborhoods or workplaces are unsafe (Di Chiro 1997).

In the face of staggering environmental crises of the late twentieth century, including global warming, pollution, toxins, radiation, the lack of fresh water, species extinction, habitat loss, and the collapse of entire ecosystems, it makes sense that ecology would proclaim itself as an invaluable science. In 1991, "The Sustainable Biosphere Initiative" presented a "call to arms for all ecologists" (Lubchenco et al. 1991: 371) to pursue three crucial areas of research: global change (including climate change), biological diversity, and sustainable ecosystems. The report concludes by noting that the success of this project will depend not only upon the participation of ecologists but also upon "the vision and abilities of policy-makers, funding agency administrators, government officials, business and industry leaders, and individual citizens to support, amplify and extend the actions we have initiated" (Lubchenco et al. 1991: 405). Although this list ignores them, science and nature writers have the potential not only to publicize particular environmental predicaments and their possible solutions but to bridge the gap between the discourse of scientific experts and the perspectives of the broader public.

Contemporary ecological literatures

Nature writing that advocates the value of wilderness, such as that of Aldo Leopold, John Muir, Wallace Stegner, and Edward Abbey, has had a profound impact on environmentalism in the U.S., as Dan Philippon documents in *Conserving Words* (Philippon 2004). The wilderness tradition of nature writing, however, has been complemented by literature that portrays a "nature" inseparable from human cultures and practices. Terry Tempest Williams's 1991 *Refuge*, for example, dwells upon the disturbing disjunctions between the natural and unnatural threats to both the people and the birds that inhabit nuclear landscapes. The title of Bill McKibben's *The End of Nature* (1989) makes his position clear – humans have transformed the world so thoroughly that the very idea of "nature" as something apart from the human no longer makes sense. Of course the very notion that nature is something outside of culture is a particularly Euro-American idea. Native American writers tend not to promote wilderness visions (the "wilderness" being a concept that has, historically, been used to erase their presence), but instead invoke storied landscapes inhabited by language, history, and culture.

"Nature writing," and especially U.S. nature writing, has become not only an established genre within literary studies but the most populated site of inquiry for "ecocritics." So populated in fact, that Armbruster and Wallace (2001) urged ecocritics to go, in their edited collection, *Beyond Nature Writing*. Moving away from the category of "nature writing" and toward a more inclusive sense of ecological literatures allows us to move away from the sense of "nature" as a world apart from the human. If literature is to be relevant for early twenty-first-century concerns, it must contend with many issues that confound the conceptual divide between nature and culture, such as global climate change, genetic engineering, and the dissemination of toxins across bodies and environments. There is, in fact, a wealth of contemporary literature in English that grapples with the interconnections between ecological, social, cultural, and technological forces. Here are just a few examples from North America, starting with indigenous literatures.

Louise Erdrich's novel *Tracks* represents the brutal destruction of the northern U.S. forests and the Anishinabe people and culture in the early twentieth century, as they were assaulted by colonialism, disease, logging, and the Dawes' Act, which divided the tribal lands into individual, taxable parcels, many of which were lost or sold. Simon Ortiz (Acoma), in several of the poems collected in *Woven Stone* (1992), documents how Pueblo and Diné peoples have had to contend not only with how uranium mining assaulted the health of the land and of the people, but also how it rendered traditional ecological knowledges – which had been sufficient for thousands of years – suddenly inadequate for survival. The imperceptibility of radioactive substances necessitated non-native technologies and the frameworks of Western science (Alaimo 2010).

Nonetheless, Ortiz promotes an ecological model of the land and the people working together, for "life/and its continuity" (Ortiz 1992: 325). Similarly the ethnobotanist Nancy J. Turner, in *The Earth's Blanket* (2005), gathers the traditional ecological knowledges of First Nations peoples, mainly from British Columbia, asserting how their philosophies and practices exemplify ecological sustainability: "Being keen and vigilant observers, scientists in the broadest sense of the word, indigenous peoples have not only used the resources around them but maintained and enhanced them in various ways" (Turner 2005: 14).

The question of which knowledges qualify as "science" flourishes within a great many contemporary ecological literatures, in both their content and their form. These texts, which mix authoritative scientific discourse with the observations and vexed ruminations of the non-expert, dramatize life in risk society, as defined by Ulrich Beck (Alaimo 2010). Beck argues that citizens in a risk society cannot rely on their own perceptions, but instead require scientific information in order to assess the often invisible hazards of daily life: "Unlike news of losses in income and the like, news of toxic substances in foods, consumer goods, and so on contain a *double shock*. The threat itself is joined by the loss of sovereignty over assessing the dangers, to which one is directly subjected" (Beck 1992: 54). Susanne Antonetta's vertiginous, disturbing memoir, *Body Toxic* (2002), dramatizes the psychological, epistemological, and political ramifications of inhabiting risk society, as the narrator struggles to make sense of how the toxic landscape of Pine Barrens, New Jersey has affected her. Against the pervasive denial of the dangers lurking in a landscape that literally becomes the substance of her body, Antonetta presents a counter-memory that emerges not only from personal reflection, but from historical, journalistic, and scientific research into the place that created her (Alaimo 2010).

Another recent ecological memoir wrestles with the inadequacies of scientific and medical information about cancer, even though its author, Sandra Steingraber, is herself a scientist. *Living Downstream* (1998) – a text hailed as the next *Silent Spring* – mixes scientific arguments and data with a personal account of her own bladder cancer. Here, and in *Having Faith* (2003), Steingraber portrays a thoroughly ecological vision, tracing the flows of fluids and substances through environments, non-human animals, and human bodies, thus presenting vivid arguments for environmental protection. Whereas Rachel Carson hid the fact that she was suffering from breast cancer, because she was concerned that this would invalidate her scientific arguments by making them less "objective" (indeed, the mere fact of being a woman already jeopardized her scientific authority), Steingraber uses her personal narrative to pull readers into scientific and political domains.

Even as ideals of scientific objectivity (and the problematic epistemologies upon which they rely) have hardly disappeared, there seems to have been a sea change that suggests readers may find personal accounts – even of scientific matters – to be more trustworthy or compelling than scientific modes of argument. Mark Lynas's *High Tide* (2004) is a case in point. Climate change, as a stunningly complex global phenomenon, demands a multitude of mathematical calculations, technologically mediated data, and not just abstract, but virtual conceptualizations. Lynas, however, enters the vociferous debate about the existence of anthropogenic climate change by traveling around the world and recording the observations of people who are not experts or authorities – presumably, as the sub-title suggests, because they will offer the "truth" of the matter. The epistemological framework here is more complicated than this scenario would suggest, however, in that even though the people interviewed present their own observations about changes in their local landscapes, the observers are, of course, already informed by scientific and popular representations of climate change.

Since botany is a progenitor of ecology, it is fitting that several contemporary ecological texts place plants on center stage. Plants grab hold of us, and we reshape them. Michael Pollan's *The Botany of Desire* narrates a history of four different plants – apples, tulips, potatoes, and marijuana – exploring how they have seduced humans to do their bidding. Ruth Ozeki's comic novel *All Over Creation* cross-pollinates genetic engineering, seed saving, environmental activism, religion, and different conceptions of biodiversity, encouraging readers to come to terms with the ethics and politics of contemporary agribusiness. Laurie Ricou's *Salal* (2007) is an extraordinary text about a rather ordinary plant thriving around British Columbia. Ricou describes his unmethodical methodology: "Find out as much as possible about salal, in as many surrounds as possible, and then texture, intermingle, blur, and combine" (Ricou 2007: 59). Ricou offers compelling, self-reflective insights not only on this plant but also on the nature of ecology itself:

> Ecology understands the natural world as an infinitely extending series of reflexive dependencies. Ideally, the ecology of salal should not be the primary focus of a discrete section in a book, even one titled "Depending." The idea of ecology urges making the concept more explicit, proposing an ongoing set of intersections on almost every page. Which is to say – posing more questions.
>
> (Ricou 2007: 57)

Another mode of ecological questioning may be found within science fiction. Science fiction – usually set worlds apart from traditional "nature writing" – has "no alibi" when it comes to engaging with ecological matters, according to Patrick D. Murphy, who points out that science fiction may make "specific environmental issues part of the plots and themes" and include a "wide array of scientific disciplines that bear on perceiving, interpreting, and understanding the world" (Murphy 2001: 263–64). Robert Markley's *Dying Planet* (2005) offers a case in point. In his analysis of nineteenth- and twentieth-century scientific and literary texts about Mars, Markley seeks to "analyze the dynamic interactions among planetary science, science fiction, and other disciplines, notably ecology, that have kept Mars on the front pages since the 1800s" (Markley 2005: 2). Markley investigates the interchanges between science fiction and science proper, the role of speculation in science, and the relations between ecological and socio-political ideals. Although it may be set on other planets, in other times, science fiction often grapples with (earthly) environmental concerns relevant to our present moment. Those interested in reading ecological science fiction may wish to begin with the writings of Ursula K. Le Guin, Kim Stanley Robinson, Octavia Butler, and Joan Slonczewski.

Ecocriticism, science, and science studies

Scholars who study environmentally oriented literatures have different perspectives on the relations between ecological literatures and ecological science. Dianne Chisholm, for example, proposes that "there is an art of ecological thinking which is distinct from ecological science"; thus she seeks texts in which "literary art does not merely embellish science with humor, wit, and humanity or recast scientific discourse in satirical or parodying rhetoric but constitutes a substantially different form of ecological thinking" (Chisholm 2011). Whereas Chisholm seeks the distinctiveness of ecological literature, separating it from ecological science, Ursula K. Heise advocates an "eco-cosmopolitanism" that values "not only physical experience and sensory perception," but also "the abstract and highly mediated kinds of knowledge and experience that lend equal or greater support to a grasp of biospheric connectedness" (Heise 2008: 62). Such mediated forms of knowledge would presumably include, among other things, ecological science.

Scholars in science studies bring an array of social theories, philosophical questions, and historical contexts to bear upon scientific matters, mixing analyses of literature, science, and political forces in complex ways that cannot be predicted in advance. Such scholarship does not pose science as an unmediated ground of truth or a methodological model for literary studies. Glen A. Love, on the other hand, rejects the notion that science is itself a cultural, historical, and political enterprise, arguing that ecocriticism should "emulate" the "standards of evidence and rational thought," as well as "that spirit of rigorous methodology" found within science (Love 1999: 71). This form of literary studies, which divorces it from cultural critique and interdisciplinary social theories, is both epistemologically impoverished (see Clarke 2001) and politically retrograde. My own position is that both science and science studies have the potential to challenge and strengthen ecocriticism. Ecocriticism requires approaches to science that neither revere it as an unproblematic path to the truth of nature, nor subject it to an echo chamber of skeptical critique. Science studies, most notably that of Donna Haraway and Bruno Latour, grapples with the natural and the social, the discursive and the material, the sciences and the humanities. Latour, for example, urges scholars to trace how networks are "simultaneously real, like nature, narrated, like discourse, and collective, like society" (Latour 1993: 6). Thus science studies may help ecocriticism connect ecological literatures, ecological science, and broader cultural and political forces.

Bibliography

Alaimo, S. (2000) *Undomesticated Ground: recasting nature as feminist space*, Ithaca, N.Y.: Cornell University Press.

——(2010) *Bodily Natures: science, environment, and the material self*, Bloomington: Indiana University Press.

Antonetta, S. (2002) *Body Toxic: an environmental memoir*, Washington, D.C.: Counterpoint.

Armbruster, K. and Wallace, K. (eds) (2001) *Beyond Nature Writing: expanding the boundaries of ecocriticism*, Charlottesville: University of Virginia Press.

Beck, U. (1992) *Risk Society: towards a new modernity*, trans. M. Ritter, London: Sage.

Chisholm, D. (2011) "The art of literary thinking: literary ecology," *ISLE: Interdisciplinary Studies in Literature and Environment* 18:1

Clarke, B. (2001) "Science, theory, and systems: a response to Glen A. Love and Jonathan Levin," *Interdisciplinary Studies in Literature and Environment*, 8(1): 149–65.

Di Chiro, G. (1997) "Local actions, global visions: remaking environmental expertise," *Frontiers*, 18(2): 203–31.

Finch, R. and Elder, J. (2002) *The Norton Book of Nature Writing*, New York: W.W. Norton.

Grove, R. (1995) *Green Imperialism: colonial expansion, tropical island Edens and the origins of environmentalism 1600–1860*, Cambridge: Cambridge University Press.

Harding, S. (2008) *Sciences from Below: feminisms, postcolonialities, and modernities*, Durham, N.C.: Duke University Press.

Heise, U. (2008) *Sense of Place and Sense of Planet: the environmental imagination of the global*, Oxford: Oxford University Press.

Jax, K. (2001) "History of ecology," *Encyclopedia of Life Sciences*, Hoboken: John Wiley and Sons, pp. 1–6.

Kingsland, S. (2005) *The Evolution of American Ecology: 1890–2000*, Baltimore: Johns Hopkins University Press.

Latour, B. (1993) *We Have Never Been Modern*, trans. C. Porter, Cambridge, Mass.: Harvard University Press.

Love, Glen A. (1999) "Science, anti-science, and ecocriticism," *Interdisciplinary Studies in Literature and Environment*, 6(1): 65–81.

Lubchenco, J. et. al. (1991) "The sustainable biosphere initiative: an ecological research agenda," *Ecology*, 72(2): 371–412.

Lynas, M. (2004) *High Tide: the truth about our climate crisis*, New York: Picador.

Markley, R. (2005) *Dying Planet: Mars in science and the imagination*, Durham, N.C.: Duke University Press.

McKibben, B. (1989) *The End of Nature*, New York: Random House, 2006.

Murphy, P. (2001) "The non-alibi of alien scapes: SF and ecocriticism," in Armbruster and Wallace 2001, pp. 263–78.

Nash, L. (2006) *Inescapable Ecologies: a history of environment, disease, and knowledge*, Berkeley: University of California Press.

Ortiz, S. (1992) *Woven Stone*, Tucson: University of Arizona Press.

Philippon, D. (2004) *Conserving Words: how American nature writers shaped the environmental movement*, Athens: University of Georgia Press.

Ricou, L. (2007) *Salal: listening for the northwest understory*, Edmonton: NeWest Press.

Steingraber, S. (1998) *Living Downstream: a scientist's personal investigation of cancer and the environment*, New York: Vintage.

——(2003) *Having Faith: an ecologist's journey to motherhood*, New York: Berkley.

Turner, N. (2005) *The Earth's Blanket: traditional teaching for sustainable living*, Seattle: University of Washington Press.

Walls, L. (1995) *Seeing New Worlds: Henry David Thoreau and nineteenth-century natural science*, Madison: University of Wisconsin Press.

——(2003) *Emerson's Life in Science: the culture of truth*, Ithaca, N.Y.: Cornell University Press.

10
EVOLUTION

David Amigoni

"Everybody nowadays talks about evolution" (Allen 1888: 34). So wrote Grant Allen, the journalist and popularizer of science, in the Victorian magazine *Cornhill* in 1888. Everybody continues to talk about evolution, firstly because it provides human consciousness with a compelling yet unsettling story about its own origins, and secondly because nineteenth-century print democratized this key scientific theory, perhaps uniquely. It is tempting to think that the field of literature and science has been concerned with the question of evolution primarily since the important studies by Gillian Beer and George Levine in the 1980s, *Darwin's Plots* and *Darwin and the Novelists* respectively. These seminal works demonstrated that between Darwin's scientific writing and the prose fictions of the great Victorian novelists, "the traffic ... was two way" (Beer 2000: 5), thus producing "complex interweavings" (Levine 1991: 2). Well before this work, however, in 1932 Lionel Stephenson had traced Darwin's absorption into Victorian poetry in *Darwin Among the Poets*. In 1877, the possibilities of evolutionary thought stimulated Ernest Dowden's synoptic essay on "The scientific movement in English literature." Talk about evolution has been pervasive: but so has talk about its relation to literature.

Even in 1888, evolution presented general problems of definition and focus for Allen. Much of the voluble talk about evolution was unfocused, blurring at the boundaries through its fuzzy sense that it had something to do with the idea "that most things 'growed'" (Allen 1888: 34). It was "in the air," but Allen's very formulation overlooked the material channels of mediation that have become important focuses of recent scholarly work on the topic. The relation of evolution to literature may be seen in the context of the emergence of the "popular" in the understanding of science, a phenomenon to which Allen's essay was a particular testimony, and which his writing did much to expand (see, for instance, his popular biography of Charles Darwin, also in 1888). Allen's essay also provides evidence of language itself as an index of the cultural conflict embedded in the discussion of evolution: taking strong exception to Matthew Arnold's sneer in the name of humane learning at Herbert Spencer's vocabulary of evolutionary exposition (Allen 1888: 37), Allen drew readers into an early iteration of the "Two Cultures" debate that C.P. Snow would lead in 1959.

The legacy of Herbert Spencer points to a particularly important consideration: although "Darwinism" has come to figure as almost a byword for the term evolution, there have been numerous theorists of evolution. In fact, Grant Allen took Spencer's synthetic, cosmological theory of evolution, which held that all phenomena in the universe were subject to a process in which homogeneous force and matter divided and diversified into heterogeneous specialized functions, to be the most important (see, for instance, Spencer's *First Principles*). Spencer's Lamarckian theory of evolution (after the French naturalist, Jean-Baptiste Lamarck) emphasized the environment, and the organism's malleability and responsiveness to it, as the key engine of evolutionary transformation. Literary resonances have played a role in determining what has been seized upon and preserved. Charles Darwin's manipulation of the written word – his willingness to fashion imaginative analogies and metaphors to advance his case – is unquestionably more compelling and involving for the readers than Spencer's writing. As this chapter seeks to demonstrate, multiple meanings of and relations to the "literary" have been fashioned in the forging of evolutionary theory.

Evolution before Darwin's *Origin*: transformism, transmutation, *Vestiges*

"Evolution" was not widely used to describe theories of common descent, even at the point at which Charles Darwin published *On the Origin of Species* in 1859. Theories of common descent, in which organisms descended from parent forms, varying to "become" new species during the process of descent, were known as "transformism," or "transmutation." These were approaches to answering the so-called "species question." Natural historians tended to accept that God the creator had designed, created and fixed each individual species in the economy of nature: the exquisite design of this or that organism, as the English theologian William Paley argued in *Natural Theology* of 1802, was all the evidence of a creative plan that was required. Transformist principles were a controversial yet persistent theme of Enlightenment thought, and were prominent in the work of the French naturalist Buffon and, from the early nineteenth century, the work of Lamarck. Transformism was, however, by no means accepted in France: Georges Cuvier, the leading comparative anatomist who did important work in re-assembling fossilized forms of extinct species, was hostile to the implications of the theory. A transmutational solution to the species question undermined the authority of the Judaeo-Christian creation story and established religion.

In England, it was Erasmus Darwin who articulated an evolutionary worldview. Darwin was a powerful physician in Lichfield, a member of an influential and progressive scientific and industrial elite (the Lunar Club), and, in his time, a highly regarded poet (King-Hele 1999). Indeed, it was in the form of poetry that Darwin set forth his statement on evolutionary principles in a long, posthumously published philosophical poem in 1803 entitled *The Temple of Nature*. The poem consists of rhyming couplets, following Pope, and extensive explanatory footnotes drawn from natural historical and anthropological researches. Darwin's fascination with the materialist principles of life's origin and development was voiced in poetical form:

> Nurs'd by warm sun-beams in primeval caves
> Organic life began beneath the waves ...
> (E. Darwin 1973: Canto I, ll. 233–34)

> Hence without parent by spontaneous birth
> Rise the first specks of animated earth;
> From Nature's womb the plant or insect swims,
> And buds or breathes with microscopic limbs ...
> (E. Darwin 1973: I, ll. 247–50)

> From embryon births her changeful forms improve
> Grow, as they live, and strengthen as they move.
> (E. Darwin 1973: I, ll. 225–26)

Darwin presents a materialist account of the origins of life in chemical and heat-based processes of "parentless" spontaneous generation; there is no divine artificer evident, instead there is self-directed progress, whereby Nature's "changeful forms improve." With its emphasis on organisms self-willing change in response to environmental stimuli, Darwin's hypothesis of development was similar to the work of Lamarck. But at the heart of the emerging worldview was an ambivalent acknowledgment of destruction, going hand in hand with copious reproductive power and development. In the fourth and final Canto, Darwin presents the reader with an image of life decimated in "one great Slaughter-house the warring world" (E. Darwin 1973: IV, l. 66). In a world of struggle living things can never be, unconditionally, ends in themselves, for they also exist as potential food for other organisms: "With monstrous gape sephulcral whales devour / Shoals at a gulp, a million in an hour" (E. Darwin 1973: IV, l.61). The mouth of the whale is both a grave and a consumption mechanism on an industrial scale.

Erasmus Darwin's radical science was discredited by conservative satirical attacks from the periodical *The Anti-Jacobin*, so his reputation, and the question of evolution, became embroiled in the political conflicts of the French Revolution. Yet Darwin had arrived, arguably, at a similar view of living struggle to that elaborated by the supposedly conservative Thomas Malthus, whose *Essay on the Principle of Population* had been published in 1798. Both Erasmus Darwin and Malthus were important figures to the first-generation Romantic poet, Samuel Taylor Coleridge, who, though attracted to the work of both writers, vigorously resisted the materialist implications of Darwin's work (Amigoni 2007: 34–37). Adrian Desmond's research on early nineteenth-century Lamarckian theories of self-directed development establishes a complex of relations between a politically radical world of London medical practitioners who appropriated them, and the Coleridge-inspired "idealist" medical elite who feared the threat that "anarchic" Lamarckism seemed to pose to an already anxious English political and ecclesiastical establishment (Desmond 1989). Thus, when considering the relationship between evolution and literature before Charles Darwin, Erasmus Darwin's legacy connects Augustan poetic tradition, materialist theories of life held among radical medical practitioners, and Coleridge's romantic aesthetic and political theory, which was adopted as a source of opposition to both materialist transmutation, and its popularization in print (Amigoni 2007: 40–42).

These conflicts and debates continued to animate the rather febrile context into which the first popular evolutionary work was received, the anonymously published *Vestiges of the Natural History of Creation* in 1844. This work brought together much of the science on which the theory of evolution, in its subsequent articulations, would come to depend: astronomy and cosmology (the "Nebular Hypothesis"); geology and earth science; palæontology and comparative anatomy; philology and anthropology; and embryology. Embryology was particularly important to the controversial theory of transmutational change that the text proposed. Starting from recapitulatory theory of the embryo (during early stages of development human embryos appear similar to embryos of "lower" life forms such as fish), it proposed that one lower organism could give birth to the more advanced "next stage" that had always been part of an idealized predetermined plan – so a Creator was "author" of the process that, after a first cause, operated according to natural laws. The *Vestiges* is an important work because, even though it proposed an easily discredited mechanism of change, it demonstrated how many fields "transmutational" theory had to master and draw together in order to develop grounds for a theory of evolution. In achieving this, its literary drive and narrative powers have come, increasingly, to be recognized. Thus, its chapter on "Secondary Rocks" begins by drawing its reader into a community of understanding, reminding them that

> We now enter upon a new great epoch in the history of our globe. There was now dry land. As a consequence of this fact, there was fresh water; for rain, instead of immediately returning to the sea, as formerly, was now gathered in channels of the earth, and became springs, rivers, and lakes. There was now a theatre for the existence of land plants and animals.
>
> (Chambers 1887: 64)

For James Secord, *Vestiges* was a print "sensation"; his work borrows from book history and reader-response theory to argue that it is possible to reconstruct specific "geographies of reading" (noting differences of reception between mercantile Liverpool and Anglican Cambridge, for instance). But he has also argued that its author – who was in fact the Edinburgh popular publisher and scientific enthusiast, Robert Chambers – appropriated narrative strategies from the influential romantic historical fiction of Sir Walter Scott in order to bind these different findings from different fields of science into an epic of evolutionary development, in which the "theatre for the existence of land plants and animals" could prepare for the emergence of humans (Secord 2000: 87–90). The *Vestiges* presented evolution as, above all, progress, for Chambers speculated that there may evolve "species superior to us in organization, purer in feeling, more powerful in device and act ... There may then be occasion for a nobler type of humanity" (Chambers 1887: 204–5). Chambers thus imagined the possibility of a more advanced, even perfected race of humans. This had its impact on key works of mid-Victorian literature. Though Alfred Tennyson's great elegiac poem *In Memoriam* (1850) is often loosely thought of as a text about religious doubts conditioned by Darwinian evolution ("nature red in tooth and claw," LVI), Tennyson had in fact taken his evolutionary worldview from the *Vestiges*, and he concludes his poem by imagining, after Chambers, that the deceased Arthur Hallam, as the occasion of his grief and mourning, may in fact have been an embryonic type of the perfected human: "Whereof the man, that with me trod / This planet, was a noble type / Appearing ere the times were ripe" (Tennyson 1989: Epilogue).

Darwin's *On the Origin of Species*: linguistic knowledge, metaphor, and the grandeur of evolution by natural selection

Charles Darwin, grandson of Erasmus, Cambridge educated and well connected to early Victorian elite savants such as the geologist Charles Lyell, distanced himself from what he dismissed as the literary and speculative excesses of the *Vestiges* (Amigoni 2007: 88–89). Paradoxically, his empirical attention to detail and theoretical sophistication opened new kinds of relation between science and literature.

In Charles Darwin's own account of the formation of his theory, he accorded great significance to his reading of Malthus (C. Darwin 1983: 71). Returned from his life-changing *Beagle* voyage, it occurred to Darwin in 1838 that population pressure was the key to the mechanism of evolutionary change that he was seeking. Darwin pieced together a number of disparate observations and evidences. He had always been aware of the presence of variations among members of the same species or related varieties; he derived this knowledge from nature, and the work of stock breeders who selected "artificially" for this, rather than that, characteristic. Geology made him aware of a deep history of extinctions and changes in the population of the organic world; the same knowledge made him aware of the extent to which these patterns of extinction could be mapped onto changing territorial configurations of land and water. For Darwin, Malthus's law of population – that population grows geometrically, while a food supply is subject only to arithmetic forms of growth – meant that members of a given species were in competition with one another, especially given that survival was premised on the need to reproduce more progeny than could ever reach maturity. In this context, an advantageous variation could be a key to survival and leaving further progeny. The variation might be passed on, and indeed, further changed over succeeding generations. Over time, the ancestral characteristics might be increasingly lost from the transforming variety; the ancestral stock might, eventually, become extinct. Imagining life as a great tree – an image he borrowed from philological research into the history of language development – Darwin argued that a new species or "branch" of life has been added, and "evolution by natural selection" has occurred in the context of "the struggle for existence." It was, clearly, a life science that depended on history and narrative reconstruction, and Darwin had a coherent account of the theory in place by 1844.

Darwin delayed publication – his thesis was controversial – and *On the Origin of Species* was not published until 1859. In the end, Darwin was bounced into publication of his theory by the work of another naturalist. In 1857, when Alfred Russel Wallace wrote to Darwin from the Malay Archipelago, his own theory was reflected back to him, formulated independently by another naturalist speculating along the same lines. Thus, the *Origin* as a piece of writing was marked by Darwin's eagerness to get a publicly accessible full account of his theory into print, and the need, rhetorically, to persuade his audience of the viability of his theory. The challenge faced by Darwin's rhetorical powers makes the *Origin* into an extraordinarily fertile contribution to literature in its own right

For instance, Darwin had to persuade a largely skeptical world of nineteenth-century science – British, continental European and American – of the validity of the theory of transmutation, or the "mutability of species." Conceding the powerful scientific opposition to his theory, he constructs an analogy between the "geological record" and the history of the world as an imperfectly preserved book "written in a changing dialect":

> Of this history we possess the last volume alone, relating only to two or three countries. Of this volume, only here and there a short chapter has been preserved; and of each page, only here and there a few lines. Each word of the slowly-changing language, in which the history is supposed to be written, being more or less different in the interrupted succession of chapters, may represent the apparently abruptly changed

forms of life, entombed in our consecutive, but widely separated formations.

(C. Darwin 1982: 316)

Darwin's rhetorical strategy draws its persuasive power from the cultural authority associated with linguistic and literary knowledge. If geologists and palæontologists claimed that the geological and fossil evidence contained no conclusive evidence of evolution, Darwin counters by pointing to the imperfection of the record. The analogical basis for this argument is drawn from extensive philological research into the history of language that itself lent methods of analysis to evolutionary theory ("changing dialect"), but also the image of the exhumed and decaying fragmentary book. Thus a complex understanding of "literature" consisting of historically descended and interrelated linguistic traditions, as well as the book as an organic object in history, helped Darwin to mount the positive argument for the fragmentary evidence of evolutionary change.

If Darwin appealed to literary and linguistic knowledge as an analogical source of support for the theory of evolution, elsewhere Darwin's writing confronts the richness and also difficulties associated with the metaphorical powers of language. Thus in his chapter on "The struggle for existence," Darwin premises his discussion on the caveat that he uses the phrase in "a large and metaphorical sense, including dependence of one being on another, and including (which is more important) not only the life of the individual, but success in leaving progeny" (C. Darwin 1982: 116). Darwin conceded that for most people, "struggle" connoted two ravenous canines fighting over one meal, but that it should really also include a plant at the edge of the desert struggling to draw in moisture, or even a plant that was struggling to secure a place for its one mature seed, from the thousand that it produces, on ground already "clothed" by other, competing plants of the same species. In other words, "struggle" as a metaphor imports into the word complex relations of mutual dependency, sexual selection and reproduction. It also unsettles questions of agency: in this process, the individual organism's capacity for acting for and by itself is dispersed. Agency seems to pass to "nature," which either selects, or does not. But how could impersonal nature actively select when Darwin acknowledged that variation was such a random if crucial factor in evolution? Such questions about Darwin's language were actively debated in his own time: Samuel Butler was among the first to see that there was a literary connection between the traditions of discourse from which Darwin's constructed his theory (reaching back to Erasmus Darwin's generation), and the doubtful authority and coherence of his theory of natural selection when it depended on metaphors of agency and will that could be pulled in different directions (Butler 1921).

"Metaphor," in its Greek original, means to transfer or transport, and Darwin's theory as set out in the *Origin* required readers to transport meanings between explicit and implicit matter. By design, Darwin did not explicitly address the story of human evolution in the *Origin*. In fact, Darwin did not provide a statement about human evolution until 1871, when he published *The Descent of Man*. In that work, Darwin fully articulated his theory of sexual selection and reproduction, and its role in developing the "social instincts" that marked human biological and social evolution. However, during the intervening decade, a great deal of journalistic and scientific writing speculated widely on human evolution (for instance, T.H. Huxley's *Man's Place in Nature* of 1863). Inevitably, such concerns were transported in to fill the very "gap" that Darwin had left in the *Origin*, and as Gillian Beer argued in *Darwin's Plots*, imaginative literature played a key role in extending through narrative Darwin's insights into the relations between the "lower" animals and humans.

Darwin's epical and vividly literary closing statement in the *Origin*, about the "grandeur" in a view of life in which development and "war and famine" went hand in hand to produce "wonderful" evolutionary change, suggested powerfully that an "entangled bank" of mutual dependencies and struggles shaped humans just as powerfully as they did worms and insects (C. Darwin 1982: 459). The ontological relationship between so-called "lower" and "higher" organisms was radically altered by Darwin's theory of evolution. This had an enormous impact on the imagination of nineteenth-century novelists who versed themselves in the thought paradigms of scientific naturalism, such as George Eliot and Thomas Hardy. Nowhere is this more dramatically visible than in Hardy's *A Pair of Blue Eyes* of 1877, where the geologist Knight loses his footing on a cliff top and finds himself confronting his own death as he looks upon the fossilized remains of the extinct trilobite:

> By one of those familiar conjunctions of things with which the inanimate world baits the mind of man when he pauses in moments of suspense, opposite Knight's eyes was an imbedded fossil, standing forth in low relief from the rock. It was a creature with eyes. The eyes, dead and turned to stone, were even now regarding him. ... Separated by millions of years in their lives, Knight and this underling seemed to have met in their death. It was the single instance within reach of his vision of anything that had ever been alive and had had a body to save, as he himself had now. ... He was to be with the small in his death.
>
> (Hardy 2005: 200)

Many meanings circulate around, and can be transported to, those stone eyes into which Knight gazes as he struggles for his life. Immediately, and in the context of the novel, the dead eyes contrast with the beautiful blue eyes of Elfride, with whom Knight is in love. Eyes were significant organs for the discussion and rebuttal of "transmutation." In *Natural Theology*, Paley had argued that close attention to the design of the eye would effectively be a cure for atheism (Paley 1848: 20). In the *Origin*, Darwin conceded that the seemingly perfect, complex design of the eye was a challenge to the theory of natural selection, but he nonetheless theorized grounds for its emergence (C. Darwin 1982: 217–19). As Knight gazes into the fossilized evidence of natural selection, and continuities between his own perceiving eyes and those of the extinct trilobite, his mind is effectively "baited" by the connection. Hardy self-consciously reworks the generic trope of novelistic "suspense": for the moment is one of acute "suspense" in the manner so recognizable to Victorian readers of "sensation" fiction (Knight is hanging there, we are on the edge of our seats). However, Hardy is also confronting us with an ontological form of suspension: in the face of evolution, humans themselves are struggling in a state of mental suspense, between an awareness of the processes of evolutionary development that have shaped a refined and complex consciousness, and the brute fear of extinction. Thus, "to be with the small" in death is, after Darwin, a condition of being.

As Gillian Beer has argued, new myths of existence were brought into view by Darwinian evolution, and the form of the Victorian novel became vital for their elaboration (Beer 2000: 118). These myths were explored and elaborated most richly by George Eliot's realism, with its carefully refined and complex form of narration. In Eliot, Beer accounted for a writer who was deeply versed in the intellectual and scientific culture of her time. In fact, on first reading Darwin, Eliot was not especially struck by what she had encountered (the *Origin* seemed to be just another articulation of the "development hypothesis" – yet another mid-Victorian term for what we call evolution). However, as Beer argues, it was the total effect of reading and filtering Darwin through the "entangled bank" of Victorian intellectual life itself, including the scientific journalism of her partner, George Henry Lewes, that enabled Eliot to grasp something vital about Darwin's own epistemology and ethics of the "entangled bank" in nature, and use it to narrate *Middlemarch*'s (1871) complex meditation on origins and relations in early nineteenth-century provincial English life (Beer 2000: ch. 5).

As Beer indicates, Darwin's evolutionary work on sexual selection in *The Descent of Man* and emotions in *The Expression of Emotions* provided Eliot, and later Victorian novelists and poets in general, with a new naturalistic vocabulary for writing about romance, feeling, and sexual attraction (Beer 2000: ch. 7). At the same time, as Gowan Dawson has argued, such openings also initiated relationships with literary culture that had to be managed quite carefully by Darwin and his circle as the "respectable" faces of Victorian science, mindful of their reputations. Dawson's work illustrates the way in which Darwin and T.H. Huxley were anxious to distance their work from a variety of literary trends that the press tended to conflate with their science: the poetry of Swinburne and its reputation for "sensuousness," and the late nineteenth-century Aesthetic and Decadent movements (Dawson 2007).

Conclusion: the evolution of anxiety, from the
fin de siècle to the present

At the *fin de siècle*, the relation of evolution to literature was marked by a general anxiety. In 1880, the biologist Edwin Ray Lankester published his essay *Degeneration: a chapter in Darwinism*. "Degeneration" decisively unpicked the confidence in progress that had characterized the pre-Darwinian work of Robert Chambers, and which had continued to condition many readings of Darwin that chose to overlook his theory of the natural selection of random variation. Lankester argued that an organism, if its food supply became more easily available, would tend to become simpler, rather than more elaborate, in structure, and degenerate. In advancing this zoological argument, Lankester drew upon analogies from other fields, such as a rich man acquiring a fortune and ceasing to work, and also the historical parallel of the late Roman Empire (Lankester 1880: 33). Towards the end of his essay, he gathered evidence of degenerative language structures from philology, and the racial history of humankind (58–59). In effect, "Degeneration" became a tract for anxious times, and it had an impact on the development of such popular genres as the "scientific romance," pioneered by Grant Allen (among others). Perhaps the best-known example here is H.G. Wells's *The Time Machine* (1895), in which Darwinian evolution becomes a source of parable for late nineteenth-century anxieties about work, wealth, class, and gender. Wells, who had been trained in evolutionary biology at T.H. Huxley's Normal School of Science in South Kensington, takes his time traveler to a future in which humanity has degenerated into two distinct species. The easily visible Eloi seemingly want for nothing, indulge in pleasures, and have degenerated into human-like organisms that are no longer strongly marked by sexual difference or the ability to exert effort. Their position in a disturbing social and biological economy is only gradually revealed: the shadowy, ape-like Morlocks, who remain out of sight by day and mindlessly operate vast complexes of industrial machinery under-ground, prey upon the easy pickings of the Eloi and consume them as food (Wells 1958: 72).

Grant Allen observed in 1888 that everybody was talking about evolution. In the literature of the present, the talk persists in ways that have been shaped by that nineteenth-century engagement of the topic, during which refined scientific discourse interwove with manifold forms of popular literary and non-literary print. Certainly, the biology has changed vastly: theories of particulate inheritance (genetics) and the discovery of DNA have made certain positions (such as cruder forms of Lamarckian environmental determinism) more difficult to sustain. But we can still see the continuities in the example of the novelist Ian McEwan, whose fiction continues to engage explicitly and powerfully with evolution (Amigoni 2008). In *Saturday*, the central character, Henry Perowne, is a neurosurgeon. Though the toolkit that he brings to his job is neuroscience and genetics, the worldview that he appeals to in order to make sense of himself and his place in it is Darwin's, from the closing page of the *Origin*: "*There is grandeur in this view of life*" (McEwan 2005: 55).

Darwin's words provide Perowne with an enabling evolutionary myth, a way of making sense of both nature's architectural powers and its destructive capacity. McEwan's novel takes as its setting the modern city (London), itself seen by Perowne as a complex biological organism beset by the destructive threat of war (the threat of terrorist attack as London prepares for and protests against war with Iraq, it is February 2003), much in the way that Malthus had theorized civilization at the beginning of the nineteenth century. The murderous danger that Perowne eventually encounters is born of genetic malfunction (an unstable, petty criminal character with Huntington's chorea, a chromosomal disorder), so that, in the individualistic tradition of the novel, the confrontation between the forces of destruction and growth is focused on the degenerative body of the diseased patient and the consciousness of the physician. However, at the heart of McEwan's novel, the degenerate character is calmed by the affective power of poetry. McEwan makes interpretation of the incident far from straightforward, but it is striking that the novel continues to be a form for experimenting with evolution as a myth of existence whose wider relationship with, and embodiment in, literature continues to be explored.

Bibliography

Allen, G. (1888) "Evolution," *Cornhill Magazine*, new series 10: 34–47.

Amigoni, D. (2007) *Colonies, Cults and Evolution: literature, science and culture in nineteenth-century writing*, Cambridge: Cambridge University Press.

——(2008) "'The luxury of storytelling': literature, science and cultural contest in the narrative practice of Ian McEwan," in S. Ruston (ed.) *Essays and Studies, Science and Literature 2008*, Leicester: Boydell and Brewer, pp. 151–67.

Beer, G. (2000) *Darwin's Plots: evolutionary narrative in Darwin, George Eliot and nineteenth-century fiction*, 2nd edn, Cambridge: Cambridge University Press.

Butler, S. (1921) *Evolution, Old and New: or, the theories of Buffon, Dr. Erasmus Darwin, and Lamarck, as compared with that of Charles Darwin*, 3rd edn, London: Jonathan Cape.

Chambers, R. (1887) *Vestiges of the Natural History of Creation*, London: George Routledge and Sons.

Darwin, C. (1982) *The Origin of Species*, J.W. Burrow (ed.), Harmondsworth: Penguin.

——(1983) "Autobiography, May 31st 1876," in C. Darwin and T.H. Huxley, *Autobiographies*, G. d. Beer (ed.), Oxford: Oxford University Press.

——(1997) *Journal of Researches*, D. Amigoni (ed.), Ware: Wordsworth.

Darwin, E. (1973) *The Temple of Nature; or, the origin of society: a poem. With philosophical notes*, Menston and London: Scolar Press.

Dawson, G. (2007) *Darwin, Literature and Victorian Respectability*, Cambridge: Cambridge University Press.

Desmond, A. (1989) *The Politics of Evolution: medicine, morphology and reform in radical London*, Chicago: Chicago University Press.

Dowden, E. (1909) "The scientific movement in English literature," in *Studies in Literature, 1789–1877*, London: Kegan Paul, Trench, Trubner & Co.

Hardy, T. (2005) *A Pair of Blue Eyes*, T. Dolin (ed.), Oxford: Oxford University Press.

King-Hele, D. (1999) *Erasmus Darwin: a life of unequalled achievement*, London: Giles de la Mare Publishers.

Lankester, E.R. (1880) *Degeneration: a chapter in Darwinism*, London: Macmillan.

Levine, G. (1991) *Darwin and the Novelists: patterns of science in Victorian fiction*, Chicago: University of Chicago Press.

Malthus, T. (1982) *An Essay on the Principle of Population*, Harmondsworth: Penguin.

McEwan, I. (2005) *Saturday*, London: Jonathan Cape.

Paley, W. (1848) *Natural Theology: or, evidences of the existence and attributes of the deity, Collected from the appearances of nature*, Halifax: Milner.

Secord, J. (2000) *Victorian Sensation: the extraordinary publication, reception and secret authorship of the "Vestiges of the Natural History of Creation,"* Chicago: University of Chicago Press.

Spencer, H. (1937) *First Principles*, London: Watts and Co.

Stevenson, L. (1932) *Darwin among the Poets*, Chicago: University of Chicago Press.

Tennyson, A. (1989) *A Selected Edition*, C. Ricks (ed.), London: Longman.

Wells, H.G. (1958) *Selected Short Stories*, Harmondsworth: Penguin.

11
GENETICS

Judith Roof

There has been a literature of genetics ever since philosophers and scientists began considering the mechanisms of heredity by which physical traits passed from generation to generation. Empirical observation gave rise to various theories about how that transmission occurred. Generally, these ideas were bound up with theories of human reproduction. The ancient Greek philosopher Aristotle believed that semen was responsible for passing on traits, while the Greek physician of that same classical era, Hippocrates, developed a theory of pangenesis in which the material enabling heredity was collected from throughout the body. Amr ibn Bahr Al-Jahiz, ninth-century North African philosopher and zoologist, considered species' struggles to survive in their environments.

Enlightenment considerations of heredity still reflected these notions. The observation and classification of varieties of organic beings raised questions about how species maintained consistency from generation to generation and how changes might be introduced as part of a more comprehensive set of questions about evolution. In the late eighteenth century, Erasmus Darwin's *Zoönomia* (1794–96) advanced the ideas that mammals derived from a single source or "filament" and that they acquired and passed on new traits developed in response to their environments. Jean-Baptiste Lamarck elaborated these ideas in *Philosophie zoologique* (1809), asserting that individuals develop new, useful traits, lose useless traits, and pass these alterations on to their progeny. In his *Variation of Animals and Plants Under Domestication*, published in 1868, nine years after *On the Origin of Species* (1859), Charles Darwin set out a mechanism of heredity in which an individual's "pangenes," circulating throughout the organism, gather traits and migrate to the reproductive cells. That Darwin's theory of evolution needed some mechanism for the transmission of traits sparked greater interest in issues of heredity, producing some opposition to Lamarck's ideas, especially on the part of August Weismann, a German evolutionary biologist. Weismann disagreed with Lamarckism and pangenesis, positing instead that germ cells were unaffected by the environment and, thus, that an individual's acquired traits were not passed to the next generation.

The plant breeding experiments of Gregor Mendel produced an account of heredity that worked according to sets of statistical rules. Through experiments with pea plants, Mendel hypothesized that the basic unit of heredity was an "allele," and that alleles passed on definable traits (such as plant size and blossom color) in statistically measurable proportions. Providing a set of concepts that would enable biologists to infer the processes of heredity underlying the appearance of phenotypical traits (those expressed in bodily forms), Mendel's paper, "Experiments on plant hybridization," was published in an obscure journal in 1866. The paper's rediscovery in 1900 by Hugo DeVries and Carl Correns invigorated work on the connections between reproductive biology and genetics that had continued after Darwin. William Bateson, who translated Mendel's paper into English, coined the term "genetics" in 1905.

Genetics spawned its own literatures, including the scientific literatures devoted to discoveries about genetic science; popularizations and histories; discussions of ethical issues; critiques of genetics and its popularizations; and fiction and literary criticism that employ concepts from genetics as either subject matter or a major trope. The scientific literature of genetics worked through increasingly complex observations and statistical models based on Mendel's findings. Thomas Hunt Morgan, who worked with fruit flies, demonstrated that genes, responsible for the transmission of traits, are located on chromosomes. With several colleagues, Morgan published the first major work of scientific genetics, *The Mechanisms of Mendelian Heredity* (1915). While research continued on the operation of genes, mutations, and traits, others such as Linus Pauling, James Watson, Francis Crick, Rosalind Franklin, and Maurice Wilkins tried to discern the structure and mechanisms of deoxyribonucleic acid (DNA), a substance first identified in the late nineteenth century, and then identified by biochemist Oswald Avery as the chemical that made up genetic material. Using X-ray diffraction images of DNA produced by Rosalind Franklin, Watson and Crick were able to describe the DNA molecule's double helical structure. They published their findings in two essays in *Nature* in 1953. After the discovery of the structure and function of DNA, the scientific literature of genetics focused on mapping DNA, tracking the mechanisms by which genes managed organic processes, and determining the distribution of genes in populations. In 1990 genetic research took up the highly visible project of attempting to map the entire human genome.

Histories and popularizations

After Watson and Crick described the structure of DNA and genetics evolved into a field with a certain popular appeal, descriptions of genetics aimed at the general public began to appear. One of the first was Watson's autobiographical account of his work with DNA, *The Double Helix* (1969). Crick followed twenty years later with his own account, *What Mad Pursuit* (1990). Horace Judson produced the first popular history of the DNA "revolution" in biology in *The Eighth Day of Creation* (1979). Following governmental genome mapping initiatives begun in the late 1980s, more histories and popular accounts of genetic research appeared in the 1990s. Jonathan Weiner traces the career of behavioral geneticist Seymour Benzer in *Time, Love, Memory* (1999); Matt Ridley produced *Genome* (1999). Lily Kay's comprehensive academic history, *Who Wrote the Book of Life?* (2000), was followed by A.H. Sturtevant's *A History of Genetics* (2001), and Michel Morange's *The Misunderstood Gene* (2001). The latter shifts attention to the complexities of genetic operation as well as genes' cooperation with other processes. Morange also suggests that the promises of medical breakthroughs made on behalf of genetic research are neither so simple nor one-sided as they may seem.

As the Human Genome Project was officially established in 1990, more accounts aimed at a broad audience appeared. James Watson, the initial head of the Human Genome Project, published additional memoirs and essays arguing for the importance of genetic research – a collection of essays he wrote after 1953, *A Passion for DNA* (2000), and a new history and overview of post-DNA genetic research, *DNA: The Secret of Life* (2003). Robert Cook-Deegan traces the interactions of the Department of Energy (the original sponsor of genetic research in the United States), the National Institute of Health, and various private corporations established to aid and profit from genetic research in *The Gene Wars* (1994), as does Kevin Davies in *Cracking the Genome* (2001). In *The Genome War* (2004), James Shreeve focuses on the ways that genetic researcher Craig Venter transformed genetic research into a profitable corporate enterprise.

Other literature focuses on more specific ethical issues about the interrelation between public knowledge and private profit or on the palliative possibilities of genetic research. Watson's promotional essays were anticipated by collections of essays that consider the ethical issues of genetic research, such as Daniel Kevles and Leroy Hood's *The Code of Codes* (1992), which raises questions about how genetic information is to be used in forensics, its effects on reproductive policies and insurance, how to protect individual privacy and prevent the possibility of discrimination, and how to marshal equitably the distribution of resources in relation to potential medical uses of genetic information. Timothy Murphy and Marc Lappé's essay collection, *Justice and the Human Genome Project* (1994), focuses on such social issues as how genetic information will alter our understandings of racial and class difference and pressure towards certain standards or norms represented by genetic profiles. Barbara Rothman's *The Book of Life* (2001) considers the potential eugenic practices genetic science enables.

Critiques

In the 1970s, critiques of the claims of genetic science began to appear, to be followed by analyses and assessments of its popularizations as well as of the hype surrounding the Human Genome Project. Richard Dawkins published *The Selfish Gene* (1976), which suggested shifting the frame of reference by which we understood the activities of genes from the scale of the organism to the gene itself. Dawkins argued that what genes preserve and replicate, rather than organisms or their traits, are the genes themselves. Humans are merely one vector among many engaged in this process. Others countered Dawkins by extending their critique to the assumptions underlying the broader field of genetics. In *Biology as Ideology* (1991), Richard Lewontin questioned genetics' assumptions about genetic cause and somatic effect, pointing out that the assumption that genes govern all life processes reduces the totality of the living organism to a mechanical process. He continued to question the assumptions and claims of genetics in *It Ain't Necessarily So* (2000). In *Exploding the Gene Myth* (1999), Ruth Hubbard and Elijah Wald also raised questions about the ways genetic science is disseminated, especially where popular simplifications make hyperbolic claims about what genetic science may be able to do. Offering correctives to such media claims, Hubbard and Wald recast genetic science in more accurate terms and reconsidered several key public issues of genetic research: eugenics, gene screening, the link between genes and behaviors, the manipulation of genes, DNA identifications, and genetic discrimination.

In the mid-1990s, in addition to scientists themselves, science historians, sociologists, and humanities scholars began analyzing the larger assumptions of the discourse used to describe genetics in the public sphere. Taking up Richard Lewontin's questions, Evelyn Fox Keller, in *Refiguring Life* (1995), demonstrated the ways the linguistic figurations of genes influenced both public perceptions of genetic research's possibilities and the directions of research itself. In *The Century of the Gene* (2000), she seconded Hubbard and Wald, focusing on the problems created when genetic science is represented through a reductive, one-cause-to-one-effect relationship. Arguing for a far more complex understanding of science, Keller urged against seeing genes as the answer to all biological questions. In *What It Means to be 98% Chimpanzee* (2002), Jonathan Marks also critiqued reductive versions of genetic science and questioned what distinctions and commonalities genes and the genome enable us to make.

Sociologists and humanists also began analyzing the rhetoric, metaphors, and images deployed in representations of genes and genetic science for the popular audience. Dorothy Nelkin and M. Susan Lindee examined what they called "the DNA mystique" – the sets of ideas enabling DNA and genetics to become the symbols by which questions of family, individual character, causality, and the future of medicine are understood. In *Imagenation: Popular Images of Genetics* (1998), José van Dijck also examined the images through which genetic science has been represented in the public sphere, showing, like Keller, how such representations actually influence the directions of scientific thought, and how genes have become an "imaginary" force dislocated from genetic science itself. In *The Meanings of the Gene* (1999), Celeste Condit analyzes the public stories told about genes, discerning the anxieties they represent, and identifying worries about genetic determinism and discriminatory eugenics. She studies the tension between a reductive genetics – in which genes are presented as dominating biological causality – and properly complex biological ideas – in which genes are appreciated as one element among the many others involved in living systems.

Fiction

Even before Watson and Crick discerned the structure of DNA and the mode of genetic replication, ideas about engineered beings emerged in what would become, in the 1930s, "science fiction." H.G. Wells, whose *The Time Machine* (1895) imagined the future evolutionary divergence of humanity, posited extreme vivisection experiments in *The Island of Dr. Moreau* (1896). Most science fiction about genetic tinkering, however, appeared after studies of DNA and genetic science had become more sophisticated. A general fascination with the relations among genetics, DNA, evolution, and the meaning of life is the theme of science fiction such as Gordon Dickson's *Dorsai* (1976) or Donald Moffitt's *Genesis Quest* (1986). Narratives that involve the galactic distribution and gathering of DNA include Octavia Butler's *Xenogenesis* trilogy (1987–89), Otto John's 2005 *Footprints in the Dust* and an episode of *Star Trek: The Next Generation* – "The Chase" (Season 6, Episode 20). The majority of genetic fictions, however, focus on the possibilities of cloning, genetic engineering, and mutations, all of which contribute to the larger themes of hubris, overreaching, and the disasters of tinkering with nature. At the same time, however, the figure of the mutant also becomes one way some fans of science fiction understand their relation to society.

Narratives of cloning deploy genetic manipulation as the mechanism by which the traditional figure of the double appears. The uncanniness of multiples, questions about identity and individuality, and the transmission of consciousness through genetic replicants preoccupy many of these tales, the first of which, A.E. Van Vogt's *The World of Null-A* (1945), appeared before the term "clone" was in use. P.T. Olemy's *The Clones* (1968) posits clones as a means of communicating with extra-terrestrials, while Richard Cowper's *Clone* (1972) is a futuristic adventure tale in which clones struggle to re-find one another. Nancy Freedman's *Joshua, Son of None* (1973), in which a scientist clones John F. Kennedy, explores the question of whether clones are doomed to follow in the footsteps of their source, while Ben Bova's *Multiple Man* (1976) is a murder mystery involving clones of a presidential assassin. In *Imperial Earth* (1975), Arthur C. Clarke focuses on futuristic wonders as a rich citizen of Titan returns to earth to clone himself. Evelyn Lief's *The Clone Rebellion* (1980) imagines a future in which clones are used as slaves and sources for organ replacement.

In addition to clone narratives' presidential fascinations, these stories also allegorize political issues, as in Naomi Mitchison's *Solution Three* (1975), which imagines cloning as a reproductive solution to patriarchy and heteronormativity, and Ira Levin's *The Boys From Brazil* (1976), which explores attempts to refashion a Hitler figure. Michael Crichton's *Jurassic Park* (1990) raises the specter of cloning extinct species, less horrible than the complications surrounding human cloning, but daunting when it involves prehistoric reptiles. All of these present similar anxieties to those mapped in 1818 by Mary Shelley's *Frankenstein*, imagining the problems that arise when humans take over the privileges of a creator.

Cloning narratives are closely related to stories based on genetic engineering, which tend to appear slightly later than the cloning tales. Also concerned with the effects of human overreaching and the deleterious effects of meddling with the natural order, genetic engineering tales offer ready allegories for issues of government control, class, race, and imperialism, while projecting the possibilities of designing adaptation and evolution itself. One of the earliest treatments of social control through engineered beings was Aldous Huxley's *Brave New World* (1932), though its manipulations had more to do with the *in vitro* environments of fetal development than with genetic engineering. Octavia Butler's *Xenogenesis* trilogy traces the effects of interbreeding between humans and aliens, where the question of hybridization versus purity becomes a matter of species survival, asking whether any process of genetic manipulation, no matter how well intended, should be permitted to triumph at the expense of another species' extinction? Elizabeth Hand's *Winterlong: a novel* (1997) imagines individuals genetically engineered to fulfill certain societal roles. Dean Koontz's *Starblood* (1972) and *The Watchers* (1987) both examine the ethics of genetic engineering, the former showing its potentially deadly effects on a genetically engineered child, and the latter exploring what happens when lab experiments with animal DNA get out of hand.

Other genetic-engineering tales focus more on the enhanced powers of the genetically modified in the adventure genre or explore the intersection between genetic engineering and computer engineering as a way to extend human powers. One of the earliest genetic engineering adventure tales, Kobo Abe's *Inter Ice Age 4* (1970), depicts genetic engineering as a survival tactic used to develop humans who can breathe under water. Bruce Sterling's *Schismatrix* (1986) presents a battle between genetically engineered "Shapers" and mechanically aided "Mechanists," while James Patrick Kelly's *Wildlife* (1994) traces the experiences of a genetically engineered newspaper reporter exploring a future in which genetic engineering permits alteration by personal whim. Richard Powers's

Gold Bug Variations (1992) combines computer codes, DNA, and music in an epic meditation on the parallels and intersections of codes and the human mind.

Mutants figure unanticipated interruptions in the course of evolution and history as well as the effects of nuclear holocaust. Olaf Stapleton's *Odd John* (1935) is an early version of mutant exceptionalism. The course of psychohistory's designed return to galactic civilization is threatened by the appearance of a mutant in the second volume, *Foundation and Empire* (1952) of Isaac Asimov's epic *Foundation Trilogy*. The themes of species and/or racial conflict also continue in narratives involving mutants, especially as both the mutants and the conflicts are produced by a nuclear holocaust. Poul Anderson's *Twilight World* (1961), for example, posits post-nuclear-holocaust battles between mutated beings and those unaffected, with the mutants eventually colonizing Mars. *Mutant* by Henry Kuttner (1963) stages a battle between the telepathic mutants created by nuclear war and regular humans. Edgar Pangborn's *Davy* (1964) describes a post-nuclear landscape filled with mutants and a repressive religious regime. Philip K. Dick's *Dr. Bloodmoney* (1965) features a telekinetic paraplegic, and M. John Harrison's *The Committed Men* (1971) narrates the post-nuclear holocaust cooperation between humans and mutant reptilian beings. Other mutant narratives focus on mutants' isolation and difference, offering a metaphor for science fiction aficionados, some of whom refer to themselves as "slans" after the title of A.E. Van Vogt's novel (1946) about mutants who secretly exist among normal humanity.

Comic books are another major genre of popular literature that has tapped genetics, genetic engineering, and mutations. Marvel Comics, which specializes in super-hero tales, produced two successful series premised on genetic mutations. The character of Spiderman, who first appeared in 1962, is what the comics term a "mutate," or a normal human whose DNA was altered by the infusion of genes from another organism – in the case of the unassuming protagonist, Peter Parker, a radioactive spider. The mutation produces a Jekyll-and-Hyde transformation from the polite Parker to a crime-stopping super-being with a spider's capacities to produce webs, swing through the air, jump long distances, and fall without harm. A year later, Marvel introduced the "X-Men," the genetically mutated representatives of the next stage in human evolution. A new species, dubbed *Homo superior*, the X-Men combine human powers with extreme abilities borrowed from other species. Wolverine, for example, sports long metallic claws and becomes furry, when he, like Spiderman, transforms from a human to a mutated appearance. Other X-Men have a range of powers, including the ability to fly, heal quickly, project energy, exhibit superhuman strength, and read minds. They tend to combine these capabilities with animal signifiers such as gills, fur, tails, and wings. These genetically modified and mutated comic figures have made their way to film, the X-Men in 2000, and Spiderman in the series beginning in 2002.

In addition to breeding superheroes, other themes from genetics also provide pretexts for fiction film. Picking up the themes of meddling with the order of things, and the invasion of aliens and ultimate combination of human and alien genes, sci-fi films capitalize both on the monstrous appearance of prehistoric insects and reptiles awakened from the safe slumber under volcanoes or on the North Pole by cataclysmic events and on the frightening possibility of the invisible coexistence of mutants, clones, and the genetically engineered. Although, strictly speaking, reawakened monsters such as Gorgo and Godzilla do not represent genetic tinkering, they do manifest the reappearance of genetic material thought to be long extinct. The theme of the reptilian meddler recurs in the 1995 *Species*, in which a reptilian alien invader comes to earth to alter human DNA and take over the world.

Blade Runner (1982) explores issues of identity and responsibility that derive from producing a subculture of android clones who return to earth to find their creators so that they can extend their artificially limited life-spans. Indiscernible from humans except by trained experts, the clone androids threaten human ascendancy. An even more fantasmatic version of the dangers of clones is *Star Wars: Episode II – Attack of the Clones* (2002), in which a massive army of clones fights for the evil side against those who defend the Republic. *Gattaca* (1997) takes on another aspect of genetic manipulation. Set in a future in which opportunities and careers are defined by one's enhanced DNA, the film follows the successful attempt of its protagonist, who is not genetically gifted, to masquerade his identity by using someone else's DNA. Suggesting that DNA does not define everything, *Gattaca* is critical of any equation between DNA and human spirit and capability.

Literary and cultural criticism

Genes depicted as a site for ultimate truth offer rich figurations for generation, alteration, and relationships. Genetics plays through literary and cultural criticism as both the object of analysis, insofar as genetics is a subject or theme of literary and film texts, and as an analogy for understanding everything from origins to evolutions to histories. Critics such as Stephanie Turner (2002) examine the narratives associated with genetics itself, looking at narratives of the extinction of species and the ways narratives of cloning such as *Jurassic Park* bring together the imaginary logics of DNA and bioinformatics. Others, such as Robert Mitchell (2007), analyze issues related to biocommerce, while Jay Clayton and Priscilla Wald (2007) examine what literature and language can bring to the study of genetics.

Literary critics consider how genetics works as a trope in various literary and filmic texts. Scholars of Shakespeare, for example, have linked race and genetics in an analysis of *The Merchant of Venice*. Some critics have examined the way that ideas associated with genetics inform various texts from Melville's *Billy Budd* to *All the King's Men* to Bharati Mukherjee's *Jasmine*. Film critics have also examined genetic tropes: Patrick Gonder (2003) looks at the relation between genetics and race in 1950s horror films; Jackie Stacey examines the ways cinema has deployed genetics in *The Cinematic Life of the Gene* (2010); and David Kirby and Laura Gaither (2005) analyze genetic modification and identity in *The Island of Dr. Moreau* and *Gattaca*.

While autobiographers think about the ways genes and genetic tropes define individuality and self, and art and theatre critics consider the relation between genetic tropes and the body, linguists use a genetic analogy to understand the spread of languages. Luigi Cavalli-Sforza's *Genes, Peoples, and Languages* (2000) posits that the dissemination and evolution of languages follows the model of genetic distribution. Finally, genetics as a model of derivation and recombination helps literary scholars determine the interrelationship of texts. In many ways, then, our conceptions of genetics align with our understandings of both language and information technologies. Working as a trope of origin, identity, change, and truth, genetics has become a figure for mechanisms of change in literature and film, while metaphors from literature have been adopted as ways of understanding and disseminating information about genetics. If, as many pundits suggest, the human genome is "the book of life," books, narratives, languages, and histories have become equally attached to our renditions of genetics.

Bibliography

Abe, K. (1970) *Inter Ice Age 4*, New York: Random House, 2009.

Anderson, P. (1961) *Twilight World*, New York: Tor, 1993.

Asimov, I. (1952) *Foundation and Empire*, New York: Spectra, 1991.

Bateson, W. (1909) *Mendel's Principles of Heredity*, Cambridge: Cambridge University Press.

Blade Runner (1992) dir. Ridley Scott, Warner Brothers.

Bova, B. (1977) *The Multiple Man*, New York: Ballantine.

Butler, O. (1987–89) *The Xenogenesis Trilogy*, repr. *Lilith's Brood*, New York: Warner Books, 2000.

Cavalli-Sforza, L. (2000) *Genes, Peoples, and Languages*, trans. M. Seielstad, Berkeley: University of California Press.

Clarke, A.C. (1978) *Imperial Earth*, New York: Ballantine.

Clayton, J. and Wald, P. (eds) (2007) "Genomics in literature, visual arts, and culture," *Literature and Medicine*, 26(1).

Condit, C. (1999) *The Meanings of Genes: public debates about human heredity*, Madison: University of Wisconsin Press.

Cook-Deegan, R. (1994) *The Gene Wars: science, politics, and the human genome*, New York: Norton.

Cowper, R. (1978) *Clone*, New York: Pocket Books.

Crichton, M. (1991) *Jurassic Park*, New York: Ballantine.

Crick, F. (1990) *What Mad Pursuit: a personal view of scientific discovery*, New York: Basic Books.

Darwin, C. (1859) *On the Origin of Species*, New York: Dover, 2006.

——(1868) *Variation of Animals and Plants Under Domestication*, vols 1 and 2, Charleston, S.C.: Bibliolife, 2009.

Darwin, E. (1794) *Zoönomia*, vol. I, Charleston, S.C.: BiblioLife, 2008.

Davies, K. (2001) *Cracking the Genome: inside the race to unlock human DNA*, New York: The Free Press.

Dawkins, R. (1976) *The Selfish Gene*, Oxford: Oxford University Press.

Dick, P.K. (1965) *Dr. Bloodmoney*, New York: Ace, 1973.

Freedman, N. (1973) *Joshua, Son of None*, New York: Delacorte.

Gattaca (1997) dir. A. Niccol, Columbia Pictures.

Gonder, P. (2003) "Like a monstrous jigsaw puzzle: genetics and race in horror films of the 1950s," *The Velvet Light Trap*, 52: 33–44.

Hand, E. (1997) *Winterlong: a novel*, New York: Eos.

Harrison, M.J. (1971) *The Committed Men*, Boston, Mass.: Gollancz, 1989.

Hoppe, J. (1999) "The technological hybrid as post-American: cross-cultural genetics in *Jasmine*," *MELUS*, 24(4): 137–56.

Hubbard, R. and Wald, E. (1999) *Exploding the Gene Myth*, Boston, Mass.: Beacon Press.

Huxley, A. (1932) *Brave New World*, New York: Harper, 2006.

Japtok, M. and Schleiner, W. (1999) "Genetics and 'race' in *The Merchant of Venice*," *Literature and Medicine*, 18(2): 155–72.

Judson, H. (1979) *The Eighth Day of Creation: makers of the revolution in biology*, expanded edn, New York: Cool Spring Harbor Laboratory Press, 1996.

Kay, L. (2000) *Who Wrote the Book of Life?: a history of the genetic code*, Stanford: Stanford University Press.

Keller, E.F. (1995) *Refiguring Life: metaphors of twentieth-century biology*, New York: Columbia University Press.

——(2000) *The Century of the Gene*, Cambridge, Mass.: Harvard University Press.

Kelly, J.P. (1994) *Wildlife*, New York: Tom Doherty.

Kirby, D. and Gaither, L. (2005) "Genetic coming of age: genomics, enhancement, and identity in film," *New Literary History*, 36: 263–82.

Koontz, D. (1972) *Starblood*, New York: Lancer.

——(1987) *The Watchers*, New York: Berkley, 2003.

Kuttner, H. (1963) *Mutant*, Worthing: Littlehampton, 1979.

Lamarck, J. (1809) *Zoological Philosophy*, Gold Beach, Oregon: Bill Huth Publishing, 2006.

Levin, I. (1976) *The Boys from Brazil*, New York: Random House.

Lewontin, R. (1991) *Biology as Ideology*, New York: HarperPerennial.

——(2000) *It Ain't Necessarily So: the dream of the human genome and other illusions*, New York: New York Review Books.

Lief, E. (1980) *The Clone Rebellion*, New York: Pocket.

Lyon, J. and Gorner, P. (1995) *Altered Fates: gene therapy and the retooling of human life*, New York: Norton.

Marks, J. (2002) *What It Means to be 98% Chimpanzee*, Berkeley: University of California Press.

Mendel, G. (1886) "Experiments on plant hybridization," *Verhandlungen des Naturforschenden Vereins zu Brünn, Bd. IV für das Jahr 1865, Abhandlungen*, 3–47.

Mitchell, R. (2007) "Sacrifice, individuation, and the economies of genomics," *Literature and Medicine*, 26(1): 126–58.

Mitchison, N. (1975) *Solution Three*, New York: The Feminist Press at CUNY, 1995.

Morange, M. (2001) *The Misunderstood Gene*, trans. Matthew Cobb, Cambridge, Mass.: Harvard University Press.

Morgan, T., Sturtevant, A.H., Muller, H. and Bridges, C. (1915) *The Mechanism of Mendelian Heredity*, New York: Henry Holt.

Murphy, T. and Lappé, M. (eds) (1994) *Justice and the Human Genome Project*, Berkeley: University of California Press.

Nelkin, D. and Lindee, M.S. (1995) *The DNA Mystique: the gene as a cultural icon*, New York: W.H. Freeman and Company.

Olemy, P.T. (Baker, G.) (1968) *The Clones*, New York: Caravelle Books.

Pangborn, E. (1964) *Davy*, Baltimore: Old Earth, 2004.

Perkins, J., McCarthy, P. and Allen, F. (2002–3) "Human genetics and *All the King's Men*: the case of Jack Burden's paternity," *The Mississippi Quarterly*, 56(1): 65–75.

Powers, R. (1992) *Gold Bug Variations*, New York: Harper.

Ridley, M. (1999) *Genome: the autobiography of a species in 23 chapters*, New York: HarperCollins.

Roof, J. (2007) *The Poetics of DNA*, Minneapolis: University of Minnesota Press.

Rothman, B. (2001) *The Book of Life: a personal and ethical guide to race, normality, and the implications of the human genome project*, Boston, Mass.: Beacon Press.

Shreeve, J. (2004) *The Genome War: how Craig Venter tried to capture the code of life and save the world*, New York: Knopf.

Smith, S. (2003) "Genetics," in J. Wolfreys (ed.) *Glossalalia: an alphabet of critical keywords*, New York: Routledge: 105–10.

Species (1995) dir. R. Donaldson, MGM.

Spiderman (1962–) New York: Marvel Comics.

Stacey, J. (2010) *The Cinematic Life of the Gene*, Durham, N.C.: Duke University Press.

Stapleton, O. (1935) *Odd John*, New York: Berkley, 1974.

Star Trek: The Next Generation – "The Chase" (1993) season 6, episode 20, 26 April.

Star Wars: Episode II – Attack of the Clones (2002) dir. G. Lucas, 20th Century Fox.

Sterling, B. (1986) *Schismatrix*, New York: Ace, 1996.

Sturtevant, A. (2001) *A History of Genetics*, Cold Spring Harbor: Cold Spring Harbor Press.

Turner, F. (1995) "Shakespeare, DNA, and natural profit," *The Missouri Review*, 18(3):192–206.

Turner, S. (2002) "Jurassic Park technology in the bioinformatics economy: how cloning narratives negotiate the telos of DNA," *American Literature*, 74(4): 887–909.

——(2007) "Open-ended stories: extinction narratives in genome time," *Literature and Medicine*, 26(1): 55–82.

Van Dijck, J. (1998) *Imagenation: popular images of genetics*, New York: New York University Press.

Van Vogt, A.E. (1945) *The World of Null-A*, New York: Orb, 2002.

——(1946) *Slan*, New York: Orb, 2007.

Watson, J. (1969) *The Double Helix*, New York: Signet.

——(2000) *A Passion for DNA: genes, genomes, and society*, New York: Cold Spring Harbor Laboratory Press.

——with Berry, A. (2003) *DNA: the secret of life*, London: Arrow Books.

——and Crick, F. (1953) "Molecular structure of nucleic acid," *Nature*, 171 (4356): 737–38.

——and Crick, F. (1953) "Genetical implications of the structure of deoxyribonucleic acid," *Nature*, 171 (4361): 964–67.

Weiner, J. (1999) *Time, Love, Memory: a great biologist and his quest for the origins of behavior*, New York: Knopf.

Wells, H.G. (1896) *The Island of Dr. Moreau*, Rockville, MD: Phoenix Pick, 2008.

X-Men (1963–) New York: Marvel Comics.

12
GEOLOGY

Stephen A. Norwick

The relations between geology and literature go back at least to the beginnings of modern science in the Enlightenment. Abraham Gottlob Werner, author of the first mineralogy textbook, influenced Goethe and taught Novalis at the Freiberg Mining Academy. James Hutton of Edinburgh, the founder of modern geology, influenced Emerson, Thoreau, and Muir. My teacher D.B. McIntyre used to recite from memory long passages from *Lord of the Rings*, in his Scots burr, around a campfire on star-filled, moonless nights in a dry camp in the low mountains of the Mojave Desert of southwestern Nevada. Perhaps it is my experience of oral poetry around the campfire that makes me think as well of the prehistoric origins of both science and literature.

European natural science arose in the frame of six major holistic metaphors of nature (see Norwick 2006). The ancient pagan peoples who spoke the Indo-European languages believed that the earth was created when the gods killed and dismembered the bodies of a race of monstrous giants and made the rocks and hills and valleys with their body parts. Traces of this idea remain in the personified nomenclature for hills, landslides, alluvial fans, and lava flows that have crowns, brows, feet, and toes; the whole earth has bowels. Hellenistic natural philosophers retained this image and developed the theory of the macrocosm, a giant, male, human body that is the observable universe. Empedocles of Agrigento incorporated the macrocosm in his unified theory of the four elements in the parts of natural philosophy that became astronomy, biology, chemistry, geology, and medicine. This connection influenced literature for the next two millennia.

The Book of Nature trope is derived from the Sumerian book of fate, which became the book of life to the Hebrew peoples, and entered Christian and Muslim cultures. In the Middle Ages, the idea of the Book of Nature written by God suggested that nature has instructive and morally uplifting messages for people to read. The image of the Book of Nature was central to nineteenth- and early twentieth-century biology and geology. Biologists dropped the trope when they adopted Darwinism, but popular nature writers, especially the most religious authors, continue to use the image. Geologists and molecular geneticists are the only scientists who still regularly use the Book of Nature trope (Norwick 2006, ch. 9).

The minor Olympian goddess Natura became a sort of archangel when the Roman Empire adopted Christianity as the state religion. Over the next half millennium, she became Mother Nature and was conflated with the Muse of Science, Urania, and by many Christians with the Virgin Mary. Mother Nature was a major inspiration to many early geologists. Both Darwin and the anti-Darwinian religious nature writers also used Mother Nature: Darwin imagined that Mother Nature was selecting the strongest animals and plants to succeed by natural selection (Darwin 1903). Mother Nature is not used in modern scientific writing, but she is common in popular parlance, sometimes when describing nature's beauties, such as flowers and landscapes, but mostly when describing geologic natural disasters such as earthquakes, floods, hurricanes, landslides, and tornadoes (Norwick 2006, ch. 1).

In modern times, Mother Nature has been conflated with Gaia, the ancient Greek soil goddess. According to James Lovelock, he was mainly influenced, like Hutton, by the analogy connecting macrocosm to the microcosm. The Gaia Hypothesis was not generated by the trope of Mother Nature, but as soon as Lovelock made the connection, he was inspired by it to continue his search for the overarching control mechanisms which moderate the earth's climate and make continued life possible (Lovelock 2000: 255). So we see that earth science was created by European societies as a response to the interaction of experienced landscape and received mythology, mediated by language. In treating the next periods of cultural development we will continue to ask: how did the general language influence the science?

The Sumerians believed that their great gods were kindly and loved humanity, while the Hebrews used three myths to explain pain and suffering: the Fall in the Garden of Eden, the building of the tower of Babel, and the Noachian deluge. Moses repeated these stories. Starting with Rabbi Nathan in the Talmud (c.150 CE), the Fall of Adam and Eve was believed to have infected the whole earth and to have made mountains. Peter Abelard wrote that the earth God created was smooth as an egg but it became deformed into mountains and valleys with the Fall. During the Renaissance it was added that the drawdown of Noah's floodwaters further eroded the valleys of the earth, and deposited the waste in the oceans. Both Martin Luther and John Milton depicted vast geological changes, due either to God's wrath or to the battle between the blessed and the fallen angels. Voltaire, however, mocked the early geologists who agreed with Abelard that the early earth was smooth.

The Fall of Nature trope led to the feeling that mountains were ruins. The British Romantic poet Shelley produced this memorable description of the Alps in his poem "Mont Blanc":

How hideously
Its shapes are heaped around! – rude, bare, and high,
Ghastly, and scarred, and riven. Is this the scene

Where the old earth-quake-demon taught her young
Ruin? Were these their toys? Or did a sea
Of fire envelop once this silent snow?

(ll. 69–75)

Not just in the popular language, then, but also in elite writings by cultural heroes such as Moses, Abelard, Luther, Milton, and Shelley, attitudes toward landscape were strongly influenced by prescientific theories of origin. Most of the early scientific theories of the earth involved giant catastrophic events such as floods and colliding planets. This general feeling of catastrophe influenced the development of the theory of "catastrophism" in early earth science.

Jewish, Christian, and Muslim cultures believed that the earth was created a few thousand years ago, an attitude that made it impossible to develop hypotheses powerful enough to generate predictions about the location of minerals or fuels. Leonardo da Vinci was the first scientist to realize that the earth was millions of years old, but he only confided this in his journals, in the section that became the Leicester Manuscript. The latter arrived in England in 1717 and was read by several scientists, including Edmund Halley – Newton's friend and supporter, but also a notorious atheist, who published Leonardo's proof of the antiquity of the earth, the salt clock (without attribution).

During the Enlightenment, a very bold scientist and literary figure proposed an entirely different proof of the great age of the earth. The French natural historian Georges-Louis Leclerc, Comte de Buffon, keeper of the King's Botanical Garden, made major contributions to geology, astronomy, calculus, probability theory, and was the last serious person to write an encyclopedia by himself. It has 44 volumes. A member of the Academy of Science, he was also a member of the literary Académie française, where he was called "the phrase monger." Buffon produced a series of physical simulations of the rate of cooling of a molten earth that showed that the earth was tens or hundreds of thousands of years old. Meanwhile, the most important Enlightenment mineralogist and earth scientist, Abraham Gottlob Werner, proposed the theory of "Neptunism," stating that most rocks were laid down in a primeval ocean. While Werner himself was not a religious person, such people interpreted his theory to be compatible with the story of Noah's deluge.

The main alternative general theory of the earth was developed by James Hutton under the influence of powerful literary tropes. We are warned not to mix metaphors, but Hutton did so to great advantage. First, he discovered that, as rocks weather into soil, they release all of the elements needed to fertilize plants except nitrogen. Hutton became a physician and used the macrocosm/microcosm trope in his medical dissertation. His soil and medical discoveries led him to imagine the earth as a great human body that could heal itself by a great flux of material. This flux was one of the main influences on Emerson's vision of the unity of nature, while Hutton's idea that health comes from decay influenced Emerson's "Law of Compensation" (see Dant 1989).

Hutton also used the metaphor of the earth as a machine. McIntyre (1963) has shown how these metaphors allowed Hutton to discover the "rock cycle," in which all forms of rock become altered to make the others, and that most of the important processes that create rocks are not "catastrophic" but slow, happening over hundreds of millions of years ("the Great Abyss of Time"). As he famously put it: "The result, therefore, of this physical inquiry is, that we find no vestige of a beginning, no prospect of an end." Ironically, Hutton was a deeply religious person, but he was attacked by most religious writers of his day. These attacks popularized geology, and kept it in the public consciousness for the half century between the death of Hutton (1797) and the publication of Darwin's *Origin of Species* in 1859. Unlike the "Neptunist" Werner, Hutton had extensive field experience. He proved that granite was intruded as a liquid, not laid down in the ocean. For this reason he was called the "Plutonist," although this was only a small part of his "System of the Earth."

Except in hydrology and atmospheric science, where it remained the motivating trope, most geologists of the Victorian period and early twentieth century dropped Hutton's great flux metaphor. The flux trope only returned to mainstream geology in the 1950s with the development of biogeochemistry, process geomorphology, and modern soil science. The image of nature as a great flux has also been repopularized by the Gaia theories developed by James Lovelock (Norwick 2006, ch.10). Like most scientists of his day, Hutton also used the metaphors of nature as a great book and as a fabric woven by Nature or God. The fabric trope is still in common use in geologic nomenclature that imagines texture and fabric in rock, soils, and whole landscapes. Popular authors from the Renaissance on, and especially since the Romantic period, have written of the fabric of nature. For instance, Wordsworth often wrote that nature was a knot, or threads (often of silver or gold), or beads on a thread.

In short, literary and popular images of the earth and prescientific feelings about minerals, rocks, soils, and landscapes have entered common speech as figurative resources. For example, an overwhelming victory is said to be "winning by a landslide." When a person chooses to abide by local social norms they are said to be "going with the grain," the vehicle of which refers to both woodworking and stone masonry. A massive search of a large body of digital data is called "data mining." A very reliable person is said to be "a rock." Anything that is flowing in large volume, such as people or information or even cash, can be called "a flood." A large thing is "a mountain," such as a "mountain of a man." A restaurant critic called the very slow service in a café "glacial."

We can see a pervasive interplay between geological, linguistic, and literary forms. Whereas the general language strongly influenced a great geological innovator such as Hutton to break through the dominant theories of his day, many writers also believed that different landscapes and climates produced different personality types, that the minerals, rocks, soils, and landscapes, without the mediation of scientific theories, inspired the genius of some authors. For example, the limestone valleys of central England weather into low, smooth, gently undulating plains that inspired the flower-filled, sweet, rural poetry of England such as poems by William Cowper. In the same way, the open lowlands of Scotland inspired James Thomson. In the twentieth century, the poet W.H. Auden included numerous geological references in his poetry. Raised on the limestone of Yorkshire, he associated the dissolution and smoothing of this rock with the changes that happen to memories. Auden's "In Praise of Limestone" is partly about the environmental determinism by which landscapes developed over granite, clay, gravel, or limestone produced different types of plants, animals, and people.

The more varied rock types that make the rugged coast of Ayrshire, Scotland, produced high hills from which most streams flow rapidly into low, coastal plains. These streams became a major part of the poetry of Robert Burns, in which the streams are often symbols for the feelings of the poet or his characters (Geikie 1898: 25). Burns was a major influence on John Muir, who was both a geologist and a fine writer, who wrote that the structural weaknesses in the Sierra Nevada rocks "predestined" the paths of the glaciers, leaving "Nature's poems carved on tablets of stone" (Muir 1898: 48). Thus the Scottish landforms inspired the poet who inspired the scientist who interpreted a completely different landscape, the Sierra Nevada of California.

As we have already noted, minerals, rocks, soils, and landscapes became common subjects of Romantic authors and influenced literature in many ways. Throughout the nineteenth century, science's influence on popular language grew stronger. Though dead by the Romantic period, Hutton was responsible for the creation of a new holistic trope of nature, the image of the self-modulating earth, often referred to as "the globe" or "the planet." This image spread slowly through the English-speaking world during the Romantic period, and until the late 1960s when NASA photographs of the Earth from space or from the surface of the moon popularized both visual and verbal images of planetary totality (Norwick 2006, ch. 8). Hutton's most important popularizer was another Scotsman, Sir Charles Lyell, whose *Principles of Geology* was the most-read geology textbook of his century. Calling this concept "uniformitarianism," Lyell emphasized Hutton's theory that major changes in the earth are usually due to ordinary processes like weathering and erosion over very long periods of time. Many important literary figures read Lyell's *Principles*. Tennyson owned a copy and incorporated Hutton's "deep abyss of time" and rock cycle into his poetry: "The moanings of the homeless sea, / The sound of streams that swift or slow / Draw down Aeonian hills, and sow / The dust of continents to be" (Tennyson 1849: sec. 35; Gliserman 1975: 444).

Some geological concepts have accompanied major intellectual controversies in Europe. The notion that nature or society is improving, or degenerating, or static, can sometimes have a powerful influence over public feelings toward the Earth. Although they had a generally positive attitude toward nature (Fairclough 1928), the ancient Greeks believed that the Earth was degrading. During the Enlightenment, the increasing knowledge of paleontology showed that life had changed markedly over geologic time. The rock record seemed to show dynamic but not directional changes, and this indeterminate status confused many authors, including Sir Charles Lyell, who passed this confusion on to Emerson and Thoreau (Rossi 1994), William Cullen Bryant (Ringe 1955), Victor Hugo (Welsh 1978), and many other nineteenth-century authors who wanted to find progress in nature but who only saw undirected change.

However, many writers used the fossil record to support their contention that nature was improving. In addition, the Huttonian notion that continents and mountains are continuing to rise in our day accorded with positive Romantic feelings that God was still at work in nature, and promoted mountains in particular. Byron left England for more adventurous mountainous terrain: "England! thy beauties are tame and domestic, / To one who has rov'd on the mountains afar: / Oh! for the crags that are wild and majestic, / The steep, frowning glories of dark Loch na Garr" (Byron 1898: "Lachin Y Garr"). At the same time, geological influences were often less powerful than other ideas. For example, William Wordsworth was well read in earth science but mildly anti-intellectual and opposed to "mechanic laws." His love of mountains was more likely a nostalgia for the low mountains of the English Lake District where he was born, as well as the high mountains of Switzerland that he visited. Wordsworth himself believed that the high places of the Earth corresponded to high moral character and so climbing mountains could literally elevate a person's character as well as their body (Geikie 1898: 55). Similarly, Fenimore Cooper's novel *The Crater* reflects Lyell's description of the formation and destruction of a volcanic island. The rise and fall of a utopian colony parallels the history of the volcanic island on which they are living (Scudder 1947).

Scientific practices strongly influenced the development of new popular literary forms. During the nineteenth century, the realistic and naturalistic novel, and especially the detective story, became popular because they enacted fictive scenes and behaviors that paralleled the scientific interests of the age. Most novels are like science in that they have realistic physical and social settings and a causal narrative. Edgar Allen Poe's pioneering detective, C. Auguste Dupin, behaved scientifically in the way he observed ordinary things in extremely fine detail and in his careful deductive logic. Like most scientists, Dupin loved puzzles, was deeply rationalistic, and strongly against magic and superstition.

However, detective literature owes more to field sciences like geology than to the laboratory sciences of chemistry and physics. The field sciences are usually *actualistic*, that is, they see their own patterns in the natural world without reference to the laboratory sciences' fundamental particles and forces. For example, Arthur Conan Doyle's Sherlock Holmes was strikingly actualistic.

As with geologists, he could not usually solve his cases by using the first princi-ples of physics, chemistry, or mathematics. Instead, for instance, like the geolo-gists who looked at sand deposits in rivers, beaches, lakes, and deltas and then inferred the origins of different sandstones, Holmes smoked and then closely observed the butts and ash from all of the cigars available in Western Europe, and then used this knowledge to catch criminals who left cigar ash at crime scenes (Conan Doyle 1887, ch. IV).

In the twentieth century, literary criticism began to use geological tropes to describe its own operations. For example, if there are several early versions of a famous text, scholars can write a history of the choices that the author made to create the book, for example, Thoreau's *Walden*. Sometimes it is known that an earlier version has been lost. For example, Jane Austen's *Sense and Sensibility* started as an epistolary novel that she read aloud to her siblings. The original has never been found, so scholars have looked for "fossils" in "deposits" of earlier traces of the epistolary version in the present text. Such an analysis is called a "geologic study" (Lock 1979). Similarly, the deep study of a text has been called "geologic" by critics. Levine likened another critic's "shallow" understanding of Conrad's Marlow in *Heart of Darkness* as "lateral and surface topography – a map perhaps," as opposed to "geology" that is "deep" (Levine 1988: 25).

The practice of science changed society in ways that are reflected in literature. The sciences of the earth, sea, and sky developed rapidly throughout the late nineteenth and early twentieth centuries and this had many practical impacts on European cultures and European colonies around the world. Scientific mineral exploration was able to discover vast deposits of metals and ores of industrial minerals that had been overlooked by prospectors who were not aided by theory. Oil exploration would have been impossible without Hutton's insights into the age of the earth and the interpretation of earth materials. Geological engineering made possible giant hydroelectric dams. At the beginning of the twentieth century, these activities generated imaginative literature in which heroic geologists and engineers created vast works, making the new industrial European world, such as the boys' stories *Tom Swift and His Big Tunnel*, *Tom Swift and His Great Oil Gusher*, *The Young Engineers in Nevada – or, Seeking Fortune on the Turn of a Pick*, *The Young Engineers in Mexico – or Fighting the Mine Swindlers*, and the romantic novel *Soldiers of Fortune*, by Richard Harding Davis (Tichi 1987: 117–34, 187).

Academic studies of scientific influences on literary figures often involve per-sonal connections. While there is a serious academic disagreement over whether William Blake had much direct exposure to geology or was just responding to popular ideas (Heringman 2004: 95), Thomas Hardy claimed to have read the famous textbook by Sir Charles Lyell. However, he did not have a copy in his library, and it has been shown that Hardy owned and closely paraphrased a much more common and popular book, *The Wonders of Geology* (1848) by Gideon Algernon Mantell (Ingram 1980: 60, 61). Henry Adams must have had more geologists for friends than any other literary figure in European or American letters. He knew Sir Charles Lyell well. Clarence King, first director of the U.S. Geological Survey, was a close friend, and Adams knew many other geologists from traveling as a journalist with a geological party surveying the length of the 40th parallel. However, the influence of geology on Adams was not positive. In his famous autobiography (1918) he recorded his disappointment: he had expected science to tell him some great truths, but it seemed very undecided.

In the middle of the twentieth century, the earth sciences were revolutionized by the idea that the continents are floating around on the surface of the earth. Although this idea has altered almost every form of geology, it has not influenced literature, unless one includes the five rather journalistic but Pulitzer Prize-winning books by John McPhee, which are based on interviews during long field trips with geologists: *Basin and Range* (1981), *In Suspect Terrain* (1983), *Rising From the Plains* (1986), *Assembling California* (1993), and *Crossing the Craton* (2000).

The clearest of all cases of the influence of earth science on literature occurs when the author practices both the science and the art. Important writers who were practicing geologists include Novalis, Goethe, and John Muir. Novalis, the founder of German Romanticism, was manager of several salt mines. He had studied at the Mining Academy of Freiberg with the great Neptunian, Abraham Gottlob Werner. Novalis took as one of his poetic tasks to harmonize science and poetry so as to rejuvenate the relationship of humans to nature. Neptunism was a static, historic view that believed that the main processes of earth formation had been caused by ancient catastrophes. However, Novalis did not agree with his teacher; rather, he agreed with James Hutton, the Plutonist, uniformitarian, and "founder of modern geology," that the earth was still being formed slowly by everyday processes. Novalis's sense of the otherness of the inorganic earth came from geology and contributed to the Romantic conception of the sublime (see Heringman 2004).

Goethe was a skilled practicing mineralogist. The very common mineral and pigment Goethite, $FeO(OH)$, is named for him. A Neptunist and catastrophist, Goethe was opposed to Plutonism. He believed that God made granite, as in "Über den Granit" (1784). In *Faust*, the Devil advocated Plutonism (of course), the school that believed that granite began as flaming liquid rock, although he knew that the theory was based on a vast hallucination. For his part, Muir left books full of marginalia, as well as his University of Wisconsin transcripts that show he studied glaciology with Ezra Carr, who in turn had studied with the great glaciologist Louis Agassiz at Harvard. Muir was the first to realize that glaciers carved Yosemite Valley. Then he discovered active glaciers in the Sierra Nevada, and finally he filled his popular books with rich figurative language about the Ice Age.

In contemporary literature, Sarah Andrews is a geologist who also writes murder mysteries, starring Em Hansen, forensic geologist. Intended to introduce the general public to geology and geologists, each of her novels takes up a different application of geology: soil pollution, paleontology, petroleum engineering, mineral deposits, seismic safety, etc. Geologist, historian, and poet Susan Cummins Miller is the author of four geological Frankie McFarlane mysteries. Linda Jacobs is a petroleum geologist who has written a series of steamy as well as geological, historical, and award-winning adventure stories set in the region of Yellowstone and Grand Teton National Parks.

We have seen that Indo-European languages motivated the development of earth science that created the present industrial world. We can also see that rocks, soils, and landscape without theoretical mediation have inspired many popular tropes in modern English. We have seen that the earth sciences were an important part of the Romantic project to give value to nature, and that science, particularly actualistic earth science, inspired the popularity of the prose novel and short story, especially detective fiction. Perhaps surprisingly, we can see that some of the most powerful ideas in geology – the rock cycle, uniformitarianism, continental drift, and "The Great Abyss of Time" – have had little influence on popular culture or high literature since the Romantic period, but the macrocosm/microcosm analogy has been revived as modern Gaia science.

Bibliography

Adams, H.B. (1918) *The Education of Henry Adams: an autobiography*, Boston, Mass.: Houghton Mifflin Co.

Ananikian, M.H. and Werner, A. (1925) *The Mythology of All Races: Armenian and African*, New York: Marshall Jones Co.

Byron, G. (1898) *Byron's Poetical Works*, vol. 1. Online. Available HTTP: <http://www.gutenberg.org/catalog/world/readfile?fk_files=16619 > (accessed 18 May 2009).

Conan Doyle, A. (1887) *A Study In Scarlet*, Project Gutenberg. Online. Available HTTP: <http://www.gutenberg.org/etext/244> (accessed 15 July 2009).

Craig, G.Y. and Jones, E.J. (1982) *A Geological Miscellany*, Princeton: Princeton University Press.

Dant, E.A. (1989) "Composing the world: Emerson and the cabinet of natural history," *Nineteenth-Century Literature*, 44: 18–44.

Darwin, C. (1903) *More Letters of Charles Darwin*, vol. 1. Online. Available HTTP: <http://www.gutenberg.org/etext/2739> (accessed 16 May 2009).

Fairclough, H.R. (1928) *Love of Nature among the Greeks and Romans*, New York: Cooper Square Publishing.

Foster, E.S. (1945) "Melville and geology," *American Literature*, 17: 50–65.

Fox, W.S. (1916) *The Mythology of All Races: Greek and Roman*, New York: Marshall Jones Co.

Geikie, A. (1898) *Types of Scenery and their Influence on Literature*, Port Washington, N.Y.: Kennikat Press.

Gliserman, S. (1975) "Early Victorian science writers and Tennyson's 'In Memoriam': a study in cultural exchange, part II," *Victorian Studies*, 18: 437–59.

Goethe, J.W.V. (1988) *Scientific Studies*, New York: Suhrkamp Publishers.

Hazen, R.H. (1982) *The Poetry of Geology*, London: Allen and Unwin.

Hennelly, M.M., Jr. (2003) "Repeating patterns and textual pleasures: reading (in) A.S. Byatt's *Possession: A Romance,*" *Contemporary Literature,* 44: 442–71.

Heringman, N. (2004) *Romantic Rocks, Aesthetic Geology,* Ithaca, NY: Cornell University Press.

Hill, M.L. (1961) "Mark Twain's 'Brace of Brief Lectures on Science,'" *New England Quarterly,* 34: 228–39.

Holmberg, U. (1927) *The Mythology of All Races: Finno-Ugric, Siberian,* New York: Marshall Jones Co.

Ingram, P. (1980) "Hardy and the Wonders of Geology," *The Review of English Studies,* new series, 31: 59–64.

Keith, A.B. and Carnoy, A.J. (1917) *The Mythology of All Races: Indian and Iranian,* New York: Marshall Jones Co.

Langdon, S.H. (1931) *The Mythology of All Races: Semitic,* New York: Marshall Jones Co.

Levine, G. (1988) "The novel as scientific discourse: the example of Conrad," *Novel: A Forum on Fiction,* 21: 220–27.

Lock, F.P. (1979) "The geology of *Sense and Sensibility,*" *Yearbook of English Studies,* 9: 246–55.

Lovelock, J. (2000) *Homage to Gaia: the life of an independent scientist,* Oxford: Oxford University Press.

Macculloch, J.A. (1930) *The Mythology of All Races: Eddic,* New York: Marshall Jones Co.

——and Máchal, J. (1918) *The Mythology of All Races: Celtic and Slavic,* New York: Marshall Jones Co.

Manlove, C. (1993) "Charles Kingsley, H.G. Wells, and the machine in Victorian fiction," *Nineteenth-Century Literature,* 48: 212–39.

McIntyre, D.B. (1963) "James Hutton and the philosophy of geology," in C.C. Abbritton (ed.) *The Fabric of Geology,* Stanford: Freeman, Cooper.

Millhauser, M. (1973) "Dr. Newton and Mr. Hyde: scientists in fiction from Swift to Stevenson," *Nineteenth-Century Fiction,* 28: 287–304.

Muir, J. (1898) *The Mountains of California,* New York: The Century Co.

Norwick, S.A. (2006) *The History of Metaphors of Nature: science and literature,* Lewiston, N.Y.: Mellen Press.

Rhodes, F.H.T. and Stone, R.O. (1981) *Language of the Earth,* New York: Pergamon Press.

Ringe, D.A. (1955) "William Cullen Bryant and the science of geology," *American Literature,* 26: 507–14.

Rossi, W. (1994) "Poetry and progress: Thoreau, Lyell and the geological principles of *A Week,*" *American Literature,* 66: 275–300.

Savoy, L.E., Moores, E.M. and Moores, J.E. (2006) *Bedrock: writers on the wonders of geology,* San Antonio, Texas: Trinity University Press.

Scudder, H.H. (1947) "Cooper's *The Crater,*" *American Literature,* 19: 109–26.

Tennyson, A.L. (1849) *In Memorium.* Online. Available HTTP: <http://en.wikisource.org/wiki/In_Memoriam > (accessed 21 May 2009).

Tichi, C. (1987) *Shifting Gears: technology, literature, culture in modernist America,* Chapel Hill: University of North Carolina Press.

Welsh, A. (1978) "Opening and closing *Les Miserables,*" *Nineteenth-Century Fiction,* 33: 8–23.

13
INFORMATION THEORY

Philipp Schweighauser

Claude E. Shannon's publication of "A Mathematical Theory of Communication" in the *Bell System Technical Journal* of July and October 1948 marks the beginning of information theory and can be considered "the Magna Carta of the information age" (Verdú 1998: 2057). Shannon's work brought into being a research field that is both an important sub-discipline of mathematics and an applied science relevant to a multiplicity of fields, including but not restricted to computer science, cryptology, philosophy, psychology, (functional) linguistics, statistics, engineering, physics, biology (especially genetics), and economics.[1] But Shannon could not have written his seminal paper without the work done by important precursors: the Bell Lab engineers Harry Nyquist (1924, 1928) and Ralph Hartley (1928); the mathematicians John von Neumann (1932) and Norbert Wiener (1942, 1948);[2] and the physicists Ludwig Boltzmann (1896–98), J. Willard Gibbs (1876, 1878), and Leó Szilárd (1929). In contemporary information theory, much of this early work still plays an important role. More recent research has either elaborated on Shannon's original insights (Verdú 1998) or followed the different path of algorithmic information theory outlined by Gregory J. Chaitin, Andrey Nikolaevich Kolmogorov, and Ray Solomonoff in the 1960s (Chaitin 1987).

For uses of information theory within literary, cultural, and media theory, the case is different. Here, most research builds on Shannon's work. More precisely, most information-theoretic reflections in the humanities and social sciences rely on *The Mathematical Theory of Communication* (1963), which reprints Shannon's original paper along with an expository introduction by Warren Weaver. By pointing out that "all subsequent references are to this edition" – a comment that would usually go into a footnote – I not only describe the common practice of almost every literary, cultural, and media theorist engaging with Shannon's work but also touch upon an issue whose import is not solely bibliographical in nature. For most of us working at the intersection of literature and science – and that includes myself – Shannon's theorems become intelligible only thanks to Weaver's largely non-technical introduction.

Contrary to many in our scholarly community, I believe that such a fact does lay us open to charges of misunderstanding and misusing scientific concepts, charges formulated most acerbically by the American mathematician and physicist Alan D. Sokal, who expanded on his (in)famous hoax in *Fashionable Nonsense: Postmodern Intellectuals' Abuse of Science* (1997), co-written with the Belgian theoretical physicist Jean Bricmont. To be sure, much of Sokal's critique is based on a one-dimensional epistemology and compromised by a misunderstanding of what literary and cultural theorists do – witness, to give but one example, the passages on Michel Serres (Sokal and Bricmont 1998: 178–80). Moreover, the aggressive tone of his critique is inimical to a true exchange between the "hard" and the "soft" sciences. Still, much of Sokal's critique holds, and it does serve to caution us against bolstering our arguments with literal uses of scientific concepts that we happen to understand in only superficial ways.[3]

One more caveat is in order: Shannon's theory is not concerned with sense-making processes. Indeed, much of the strength of Shannonian information theory relies on his determination to study communication signals and to define and measure information independent of the meanings communicated by messages.[4] Shannon was interested not in semantics but in the efficient transmission of information. To disciplines such as ours, which for the most part remain crucially concerned with the production, circulation, and exchange of signs and meanings, Shannon's technical approach to information cannot be easily assimilated. Already in 1956, Shannon himself suggested as much in a response to overenthusiastic applications of information theory to domains as diverse as "biology, psychology, linguistics, fundamental physics, economics, the theory of organization": "I personally believe that many of the concepts of information theory will prove useful in these other fields – and, indeed, some results are already quite promising – but the establishing of such applications is not a trivial matter of translating words to a new domain, but rather the slow tedious process of hypothesis and experimental verification" (Shannon 1956: 3). With these words of warning in mind, let me outline those aspects of Shannon and Weaver's book that have been taken up by scholars in the humanities and social sciences.

As an engineer working for Bell Telephone Laboratories, Shannon was crucially interested in theorizing ways of making the transmission of information more efficient. Drawing on probabilistic theory, statistics, and thermodynamics, Shannon studied the impact of two factors – the bandwidth of a channel and its signal-to-noise ratio – on channel transmission capacity. Thus, he was able to provide crucial assistance to engineers intent on maximizing the capacity of communication channels. Indeed, the primary practical use of Shannon's theorems is in the design of more efficient telecommunications systems.

For Shannon, there was no doubt as to what constitutes a maximally successful act of communication: the message received must be identical to the message sent. In this model, the final touchstone of communicative success is the replication of the sender's intention, and noise is defined as all those "things [that] are added to the signal which were not intended by the information source" (Shannon and Weaver 1963: 7). Yet Shannon made an interesting discovery concerning noise that proved to be relevant to many in the literature and science community. While noise is completely unintelligible for the receiver, it is also the part of the signal with the highest information content. This might seem counterintuitive at first, since one would expect that a more ordered, less chaotic signal transmits more information. But Shannon's observation will become clear once we have had a look at his recourse to thermodynamics.

To his surprise, Shannon found that his definition of information, rendered as a mathematical equation, corresponded to Boltzmann's definition of entropy, a measure of disorder or the unavailability of energy to do work within a closed system. This makes sense if we follow Shannon in considering messages not in isolation but in the context of the range of possible messages from which the actual message has been selected: "To be sure, this word information in communication theory relates not so much to what you *do* say, as to what you *could* say. That is, information is a measure of one's freedom of choice when one selects a message" (Shannon and Weaver 1963: 8–9). The larger the set of possible messages, the greater the freedom of choice a sender has in choosing a specific message, the greater the uncertainty on the part of the receiver as to what specific message the sender has actually chosen, and the greater the amount of information received. In Shannon's model, the amount of information received corresponds to the degree of uncertainty removed at the receiver's end: "Thus greater freedom of choice, greater uncertainty, greater information go hand in hand" (Shannon and Weaver 1963: 19). Hence, a message that is completely predictable is redundant and thus devoid of information. Conversely, a message about whose content the receiver was highly uncertain prior to its arrival conveys much information, and a *maximally* entropic (or "informative") message is one that has been chosen out of a maximally large set of messages that are all equally probable:

> That information be measured by entropy is, after all, natural when we remember that information, in communication theory, is associated with the amount of freedom of choice we have in constructing messages. Thus for a communication source one can say, just as he would also say it of a thermodynamic ensemble, "This situation is highly organized, it is not characterized by a large degree of randomness or of choice – that is to say, the information (or the entropy) is low."
>
> (Shannon and Weaver 1963: 13)

Now, since the introduction of noise into a channel of communication increases uncertainty and makes messages less predictable, it also increases information. Thus, noise is defined in Shannon's framework as the signal that exhibits both maximum entropy and the greatest amount of information. As such, it is the opposite of redundancy – a completely predictable signal that conveys no information whatsoever.

From an engineering point of view, though, one needs to distinguish between useful and useless information, and Shannon and Weaver quickly point out that the (large) amount of information contained in noise is useless:

> Uncertainty which arises by virtue of freedom of choice on the part of the sender is desirable uncertainty. Uncertainty which arises because of errors or because of the influence of noise is undesirable uncertainty. It is thus clear where the joker is in saying that the received signal has more information. Some of this information is spurious and undesirable and has been introduced via the noise. To get the useful information in the received signal we must subtract out this spurious portion.
>
> (Shannon and Weaver 1963: 19)

Noise, it appears, has been successfully exorcized from the mathematical theory of communication. This comes as little surprise, since, as an employee of a telephone company, Shannon was interested in minimizing noise in order to ensure maximally efficient ways of transmitting (useful) information. What has become known as "the fundamental theorem of information theory" also testifies to this: "it is possible to transmit information through a noisy channel at any rate less than channel capacity with an arbitrarily small probability of error" (Ash 1965: 63).

However, toward the end of his expository introduction, Shannon's co-author, Weaver, intimates that one might think about noise differently. Throughout his introduction, Weaver stresses that "*information* must not be confused with meaning" and that "the semantic aspects of communication are irrelevant to the engineering aspects" (Shannon and Weaver 1963: 8). This exclusion of semantic considerations is already visible in the communication model Shannon proposes on the first pages of his article (Figure 13.1).[5]

There is no box in this diagram for the interpretive activity of the receiver, and it is clear that the purpose of communication in this model is to transmit messages so that the message received is identical to the message sent. But when Weaver does turn to semantic issues in the final section of his introduction, he proposes a number of changes to Shannon's model:

> One can imagine, as an addition to the diagram, another box labeled "Semantic Receiver" interposed between the engineering receiver (which changes signals to messages) and the destination. This semantic receiver subjects the message to a second decoding, the demand on this one being that it must match the statistical *semantic* characteristics of the message to

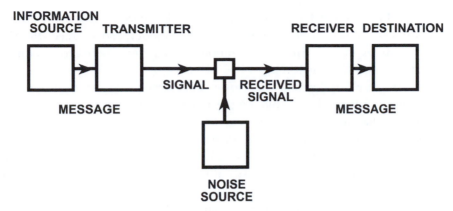

Figure 13.1 Shannon's communication model.

the statistical semantic capacities of the totality of receivers, or of that subset of receivers which constitute the audience one wishes to affect.

(Shannon and Weaver 1963: 26)

Weaver's consideration of the receiver's role indicates a shift away from a communication model that regards the sender's intention as the sole source of meaning. Moreover, his assertion that the message's semantic properties must be adjusted, in a "second decoding," to the receiver's capacity for processing meaning already qualifies Shannon's original premise that the goal of communication is the transmission of self-identical messages. Weaver moves even further away from a communication model that is based on intentionality when he considers the possibility of adding an additional box labeled "semantic noise" to the diagram:

Similarly one can imagine another box in the diagram which, inserted between the information source and the transmitter, would be labeled "semantic noise," the box previously labeled as simply "noise" now being labeled "engineering noise." From this source is imposed into the signal the perturbations or distortions of meaning which are not intended by the source but which inescapably affect the destination. And the problem of semantic decoding must take this semantic noise into account. It is also possible to think of an adjustment of original message so that the sum of message meaning plus semantic noise is equal to the desired total message meaning at the destination.

(Shannon and Weaver 1963: 26)

Weaver's suggestion that distortions of meaning that were *not* intended by the sender might not impair but contribute to the meaning received at the other end of the communication process represents a break with communication models that are based on the sender's intention as the sole reference point for communicative success. Weaver's changes to Shannon's model also re-inject the noise that had been exorcized through Shannon's distinction between useful and useless information (Figure 13.2).

Clearly, Weaver's reflections on noise and meaning propose a model of communication that works in spite of the noise rather than because of it. Still, his suggestion that noise is not only an inevitable constituent of any form of communication but may actually be an essential part of the desired message assigns to noise the status of a potentially beneficial element. Together with Shannon's assertion that noise is the signal with the highest information content (or highest degree of "informativeness"), it forms the basis for a host of re-valorizations of noise in literary, cultural, and media theory.

There are, of course, problems with Shannon and Weaver's model of communication. First, Shannon and Weaver's model of communication is a one-way transmission model that can account for communication only between two entities. A broader understanding of communication as it informs, for instance, the notion of discourse or even Stuart Hall's encoding/decoding model (1980) is well beyond its scope. Second, Weaver's clear-cut differentiation between "semantic noise" and "engineering noise" cannot be upheld because it presupposes a strict separation of the level of the signifier (affected by the engineering noise) and the signified (affected by the semantic noise).[6] The poststructuralist assertion of the primacy of the signifier and the endless deferral of the signified has rendered such a distinction problematic. Finally, because Shannon and Weaver's concept of noise is based on the assumption that noise corresponds to all those things that have been added to the signal unintentionally (Shannon and Weaver 1963: 7), their model does not allow for noise that has been added on purpose. In the analysis of literature, especially certain types of modernist literature, it is desirable to broaden Shannon and Weaver's understanding of noise to include textual distortions and fragmentations which we, as readers, tend to see as intended by a writer who uses them consciously and for artistic effect.[7]

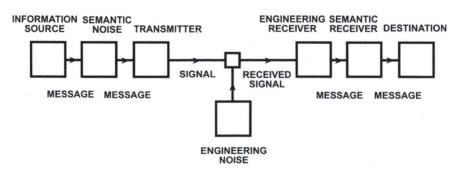

Figure 13.2 Shannon's communication model with Weaver's proposed changes.

Despite these limitations, Shannon and Weaver's mathematical theory of communication has had profound effects on cybernetics and systems theory. However, in their later development, these disciplines abandon the older transmission model of communication for one that describes processes of information exchange or cognitive construction taking place at several hierarchically distinct levels within highly complex systems such as computers, the human body, and society. Apart from these further developments, Shannon and Weaver's theorems themselves had a strong impact on the humanities and social sciences. In what follows, I will sketch some of their most prominent uses, with a special emphasis on theoretical and literary reflections on noise.

Hayles (1987) compares Shannon and Weaver's model of communication to Roland Barthes's as developed in S/Z. Starting from the assumption that science and literature are isomorphic manifestations of a shared culture (Hayles 1987: 119–20), Hayles contrasts the different "economies of explanation" at work in Shannon and Barthes. Both theorists note that noise contains a surplus of information. But while Shannon's work is embedded in a capitalist-scientific economy that demands the reduction of the many to the few and tries to mute noise by designing it as useless,[8] Barthes's work is embedded in a literary economy that demands the expansion of the few to the many, values playfulness over usefulness, and celebrates noise. Thus, "similar concepts emerge with radically different values when they are embedded within different economies" (Hayles 1987: 131). Hayles's observation applies to many of the uses information theory has been put to in literary, cultural, and media theory. This is especially the case for reflections on the innovative and subversive potential of noise.

For instance, Michel Serres, in *The Parasite*, *Genesis*, and a variety of essays, appropriates *le parasite* – informatic "noise" in technical French – as a figure for the excluded third, i.e., for all those objects and people that dualist thinking seeks to exclude:

> Science is not necessarily a matter of the one or of order, the multiple and noise are not necessarily the province of the irrational. This can be the case, but it is not always so. The whole set of these divisions delineates the space of *noise*, the clash of these dichotomies overruns it with noise, simple and naïve, repetitive, strategies of the desire for domination. To think in terms of pairs is to make ready some dangerous weapon, arrows, darts, dovetails, whereby to hold space and kill. To think by negation is not to think. Dualism tries to start a ruckus [*chercher noise*], make *noise*, it relates to death alone. It puts to death and it maintains death. Death to the parasite, someone says, without seeing that a parasite is put to death only by a stronger parasite.
>
> (Serres 1997: 131)

It is in line with these observations that Jacques Attali, in *Noise: The Political Economy of Music*, champions the improvisational sounding practices of what he calls "composition": "the conquest of the right to make noise, in other words, to create one's own code and work, without advertising its goal in advance" (Attali 1985: 132). For Attali, such practices are prophetic; they herald "the emergence of a formidable subversion, one leading to a radically new organization never yet theorized" (Attali 1985: 6).

In *The Noise of Culture: Literary Texts in a World of Information*, William R. Paulson draws on Serres's work, information theory, and theoretical biology, as well as Russian and Belgian formalism to reflect on the function of literature in a world that is structured increasingly around the production, circulation, and exchange of machine-readable, clear information. Acknowledging the marginality of literature in the information age, Paulson contends that the social function of literature today may best be described as "the noise of culture":

> Literature is not and will not ever again be at the center of culture, if indeed it ever was. There is no use in either proclaiming or debunking its central position. Literature is the noise of culture, the rich and indeterminate margin into which messages are sent off, never to return the same, in which signals are received not quite like anything emitted.
>
> (Paulson 1988: 180)

In *The Noises of American Literature, 1890–1985*, I build on Paulson's insights as well as soundscape studies and Frankfurt School aesthetics to propose a history of literary acoustics that explores American literary texts from the late nineteenth to the late twentieth century as "sites of both the cultural production and the representation of noise" (Schweighauser 2006: 19).

Other uses of information theory in the humanities and social sciences can be traced in Friedrich A. Kittler's media archeology, which starts from the assumption that "media determine our situation" (Kittler 1999: xxxix) and finds its most influential expression in two of Kittler's major books, *Discourse Networks 1800/1900* and *Gramophone, Film, Typewriter*. Kittler's "informational-theoretical materialism" is shared by a host of other German media theorists – the so-called "Berlin School" of media theory – among them Bernhard Dotzler, Wolfgang Ernst, and Bernhard Siegert, whose *Relays: Literature as an Epoch of the Postal System* (1999) is one of the most fascinating books to come out of that tradition. Well before Kittler, Max Bense inaugurated another German tradition of technology-centered media theory, the "Stuttgart School." Bense's informational aesthetics considers acts of selection as the most fundamental link between art and mathematics and is particularly interested in the interplay of order and complexity in works of art.

So far, I have sketched the basic assumptions of Shannon's theory of communication and some of its uses in literary, cultural, and media theory.

Concerning the intersections of information theory and literature, there is, however, a second avenue to explore, if only very briefly: the impact of information theory on the literary imagination. Many writers have drawn on information theory: Joseph Heller in *Something Happened* (1974), William Gibson in *Neuromancer* (1984), Don DeLillo in *White Noise* (1985), David Foster Wallace in *The Broom of the System* (1987), Richard Powers in *The Gold Bug Variations* (1991), Neal Stephenson in *Snow Crash* (1992) and *Cryptonomicon* (1999), and Greg Bear in *Dead Lines: a novel of life ... after death* (2004), to name but a few. Yet Thomas Pynchon's *The Crying of Lot 49* (1966) remains the most prominent example of such a text, and the remainder of this chapter discusses that novel as a paradigmatic case.

Like earlier writers such as H.G. Wells in *The Time Machine* (1895) and Henry Adams in *The Education of Henry Adams* (1907/1918), Pynchon draws on the thermodynamic notion of entropy to draw a gloomy picture of the Earth as moving toward heat death, i.e., to the gradual but complete dissipation of energy predicted by the nineteenth-century physicist Hermann von Helmholtz, who considered the world a closed thermodynamic system subject to the irreversible increase in entropy postulated by the second law of thermodynamics (Freese 1997: 99–105). But in Pynchon's fictional world, thermodynamic entropy is counteracted by a second type of entropy: informational entropy. While the thermodynamic world of von Helmholtz and Henry Adams knew entropy only as dissipation of energy, the informational world of Shannon and Pynchon has learned to distinguish between two types of entropy with contrary connotations.

In Pynchon's novel, an encounter between informational entropy and thermodynamic entropy is played out in a machine built by John Nefastis. Nefastis claims that his apparatus reverses the process of entropic increase and thus refutes the second law of thermodynamics. Thus, the Nefastis Machine would make James Clerk Maxwell's thought experiment come true: the idea that a Demon who sorts out the slower- and faster-moving molecules within a closed system could halt entropic degradation and produce a perpetual motion machine. Nefastis's apparatus requires a psychic who can communicate with Maxwell's Demon:

> "Communication is the key," cried Nefastis. "The Demon passes his data on to the sensitive, and the sensitive must reply in kind. There are untold billions of molecules in that box. The Demon collects data on each and every one. At some deep psychic level he must get through. The sensitive must receive that staggering set of energies, and feed back something like the same quantity of information. To keep it all cycling."
>
> (Pynchon 1966: 72–73)

In Nefastis's scheme, an exchange of information between a sensitive and the Demon allows it to wage a battle against the increase in thermodynamic entropy.

While Pynchon casts the viability of Nefastis's apparatus into doubt, the competition staged in it between thermodynamic and informational entropy plays out on a larger scale throughout Pynchon's novel. The cultural inertia of Southern California depicted at the beginning of the narrative, its "unvarying gray sickness" (Pynchon 1966: 14), corresponds to a state near thermodynamic equilibrium or maximum entropy, at which the system has come to an almost complete standstill. But in the course of the novel the movement toward entropic degradation is countered by repeated injections of informational entropy or noise into the system: the Paranoids' "shuddering deluge of thick guitar sounds" (25), the cryptic messages relayed by the underground mail delivery system W.A.S.T.E., and the communication networks of the 1960s counterculture more generally. The outcome of the battle between thermodynamic and informational entropy ends indecisively in Pynchon's novel, but in its staging of that battle, *The Crying of Lot 49* stands as a powerful monument to the energy that the fusion of literature and science can release. What enables Pynchon's novel to do that, though, is not only its negotiation of information and noise at the plot level, but also its recalcitrant literary form – its fragmented plot structure, multiple indeterminacies, complex system of intertextual references, and refusal of narrative closure – which challenges conventionalized language uses and thus injects noise into the system of cultural communication.

Acknowledgments

I would like to thank Andreas Hägler for his probing questions concerning the transferability of scientific concepts to the study of literature, Till Heilmann for referring me to the "Stuttgart School" of media theory, and Philippe Roesle and Tanja Hammel for their bibliographical work and diligent proofreading.

Notes

1 See, however, Hayles's account of an alternative, British tradition within information theory (Hayles 1999: 18–19, 54–57, 63) initiated by Donald M. MacKay, whose model of structural information – contrary to Shannon's probabilistic model – takes meaning into account (MacKay 1969). Apart from Shannon, MacKay, and Norbert Wiener, a fourth contender for the title of "father of information theory" would be Dennis Gábor (1946), now best remembered as the inventor of holography.

2 Hence, the line of influence does not run solely from Shannon to Wiener (and thus from information theory to cybernetics) but also in the opposite direction.

3 Note that Sokal discusses information theory neither in *Fashionable Nonsense* nor in his follow-up volume *Beyond the Hoax*. He does, however, include a footnote on Shannon in the hoax itself (Sokal and Bricmont 1998: 216n.13).

4 Hence Luciano Floridi's suggestion that Shannonian information theory might more accurately be labeled *"mathematical theory of data communication"* (Floridi 2004: 52).

5 In human oral communication, the information source corresponds to the brain of the speaker; the transmitter to the physical speech apparatus (vocal chords, oral cavity, tongue, etc.), which transforms the message into a coded signal that is sent over the communication channel (the air); the receiver to the ear of the hearer; the destination to the brain of the hearer.

6 Engineering noise, however, corresponds not only to the signifier but also to the writing tool that inscribes it (e.g., a defective keyboard).

7 This does not amount to suggesting that the meaning of a literary text can be equated with the author's intention. Note also that it is at least debatable to what extent Shannon's notion of intentionality corresponds to that of literary critics. However far we may have traveled from the intentional fallacies of earlier critics, the question of intentionality haunts any use of information theory within literary studies.

8 See also Heims (1993), who situates the beginnings of information theory and cybernetics in their military-industrial contexts.

Bibliography

Adams, H. (1907/1918) *The Education of Henry Adams*, London: Penguin, 1995.

Ash, R. (1965) *Information Theory*, New York: John Wiley and Sons.

Attali, J. (1985) *Noise: the political economy of music*, Minneapolis: University of Minnesota Press.

Bear, G. (2004) *Dead Lines: a novel of life … after death*, New York: Ballantine.

Bense, M. (1982) *Aesthetica: Einführung in die neue Aesthetik*, Baden-Baden: Agis.

Boltzmann, L. (1896–98) *Vorlesungen über Gastheorie*, Leipzig: Johann Ambrosius Barth.

Chaitin, G.J. (1987) *Algorithmic Information Theory*, Cambridge: Cambridge University Press.

DeLillo, D. (1985) *White Noise*, New York: Viking.

Floridi, L. (2004) "Information," in L. Floridi (ed.) *The Blackwell Guide to the Philosophy of Computing and Information*, Malden: Blackwell, pp. 40–61.

Freese, P. (1997) *From Apocalypse to Entropy and Beyond: the second law of thermodynamics in post-war American fiction*, Essen: Die Blaue Eule.

Gábor, D. (1946) "Theory of communication," *The Journal of the Institution of Electrical Engineers*, 93(26): 429–57.

Gibbs, W.J. (1876, 1878) "On the equilibrium of heterogeneous substances," *Transactions of the Connecticut Academy of Sciences*, 3: 108–248, 343–524.

Gibson, W. (1984) *Neuromancer*, New York: Ace Books, 1994.

Hall, S. (1980) "Encoding/decoding," in S. Hall, D. Hobson, A. Lowe, and P. Willis (eds) *Culture, Media, Language: working papers in cultural studies, 1972–1979*, London: Hutchinson, pp. 128–38.

Hartley, R.V.L. (1928) "Transmission of information," *Bell System Technical Journal*, 7: 535–63.

Hayles, N.K. (1987) "Information or noise? economy of explanation in Barthes's S/Z and Shannon's information theory," in G. Levine (ed.) *One Culture: essays in science and literature*, Madison: University of Wisconsin Press, pp. 119–42.

——(1999) *How We Became Posthuman: virtual bodies in cybernetics, literature, and informatics*, Chicago: University of Chicago Press.

Heims, S.J. (1993) *Constructing a Social Science for Postwar America: the cybernetics group (1946–1953)*, Cambridge, Mass.: MIT Press.

Heller, J. (1975) *Something Happened*, New York: Ballantine.

Kittler, F.A. (1990) *Discourse Networks 1800/1900*, Stanford: Stanford University Press.

——(1999) *Gramophone, Film, Typewriter*, trans. G. Winthrop-Young and M. Wutz, Stanford: Stanford University Press.

MacKay, D.M. (1969) *Information, Mechanism and Meaning*, Cambridge, Mass.: MIT Press.

Neumann, J. v. (1932) *Mathematische Grundlagen der Quantenmechanik*, Berlin: Springer.

Nyquist, H. (1924) "Certain factors affecting telegraph speed," *Bell System Technical Journal*, 3: 324–46.

——(1928) "Certain topics in telegraph transmission theory," *Transactions of the American Institute for Electrical Engineers*, 47: 617–44.

Paulson, W.R. (1988) *The Noise of Culture: literary texts in a world of information*, Ithaca, N.Y.: Cornell University Press.

Powers, R. (1992) *The Gold Bug Variations*, New York: Harper Perennial.

Pynchon, T. (1966) *The Crying of Lot 49*, London: Picador, 1979.

Schweighauser, P. (2006) *The Noises of American Literature, 1890–1985: toward a history of literary acoustics*, Gainesville: University Press of Florida.

Serres, M. (1982) *The Parasite*, Baltimore: Johns Hopkins University Press.

——(1997) *Genesis*, Ann Arbor: University of Michigan Press.

Shannon, C.E. (1956) "The bandwagon," *Institute of Radio Engineers Transactions on Information Theory*, 2: 3.

——and Weaver, W. (1963) *The Mathematical Theory of Communication*, Chicago: University of Illinois Press.

Siegert, B. (1999) *Relays: literature as an epoch of the postal system*, Stanford: Stanford University Press.

Sokal, A.D. (2008) *Beyond the Hoax: science, philosophy and culture*, Oxford: Oxford University Press.

——and Bricmont, J. (1998) *Fashionable Nonsense: postmodern intellectuals' abuse of science*, New York: Picador.

Stephenson, N. (1993) *Snow Crash*, New York: Bantam.

——(1999) *Cryptonomicon*, New York: Avon.

Szilárd, L. (1929) "Über die Entropieverminderung in einem thermodynamischen System bei Eingriffen intelligenter Wesen," *Zeitschrift für Physik*, 53(11–12): 840–56.

Verdú, S. (1998) "Fifty years of Shannon theory," *IEEE Transactions on Information Theory*, 44(6): 2057–78.

Wallace, D.F. (1987) *The Broom of the System*, New York: Viking.

Wells, H.G. (1895) *The Time Machine*, New York: W.W. Norton, 2008.

Wiener, N. (1942) *The Extrapolation, Interpolation, and Smoothing of Stationary Time Series*, Cambridge: NDRC Report 370.

——(1948) *Cybernetics or Control and Communication in the Animal and the Machine*, Cambridge, Mass.: MIT Press.

14
MATHEMATICS

Brian Rotman

Literature and mathematics are ancient arenas of human imagination. Viewed as systems of written signs, they are almost alien to each other. The signs of literature are those of speech, their medium (in the West) an alphabet and a dozen punctuation marks. Mathematical signs are those of invented thought, their medium an unlimited menagerie of written symbols and diagrams. Literature concerns thoughts, passions, and actions of persons describable in language; mathematics concerns symbolically notated virtual objects, actions, and relations detached from persons thinking them. Of course, mathematics, like anything else in the world, can be spoken about and enter literature as content, as a topic in a novel, a play, a poem, or a philosophical treatise. Mathematics can also, less obviously and more interestingly, enter and impinge on literature through its form. This is because mathematics, though classified as a science, is equally an art. In this it differs radically from the other sciences, all of which are defined by their relation to the physical world through experiment and prediction. True, many mathematical ideas are ideal versions of physical phenomena – hence the utility of the subject for the sciences. Nevertheless, nothing empirical can enter into a mathematical argument. No physical fact can ever prove or refute the truth of a mathematical theorem.

This freedom from empirical reality, its virtually unconstrained powers of imagination, is what enables mathematics to be an art, and what in turn allows aspects of itself – its structures, styles of thought, ambience, preoccupations, methods, aesthetics – to impact other art forms, such as music, architecture, and literature. "We all believe mathematics is an art," declares Emil Artin (Sinclair et al. 2006: 21), voicing a credo shared by a majority of his fellow mathematicians. Certainly, mathematicians invent fictive universes, employ metaphor, metonymy, and similitude and create narratives in imaginary worlds every bit as multilayered and complex as those of literature. And, as with any art, aesthetic considerations are central. "Beauty," the mathematician G.H. Hardy insists, "is the first rule. There is no permanent place in the world for ugly mathematics" (Hardy 1940: 85). Equations, formulas, theorems, proofs, and even definitions have affect. Proofs, for example, can be beautiful for their elegance (economy of means), ingenuity (unusual or surprising twist), insight (revelation of *why* something is true), as well as for their generality, sheer heuristic power, fecundity, and conceptual depth.

The elevated status of mathematics in the West has its roots in Greek philosophical thought. For Plato, who taught that "Geometry will draw the soul toward truth and create the spirit of philosophy" (Plato 2000: VII, 52), mathematical truths were the nearest things to the pure, unchanging ideal forms that lay behind the world of everyday reality. Before him, the Pythagoreans had proclaimed that the entire universe was constructed out of numbers, an understanding echoed at the dawn of modern science (and frequently since) by Galileo, for whom "the grand book" of the universe "was written in the language of mathematics" (Galileo 1953: 183).

From the beginning, then, mathematics has been understood as both the language of the physical world and the model of pure thought – a duality perfectly brought together by Euclid in his *Elements*. Starting from self-evident truths – axioms and postulates – about circles, lines, and points, and using only strict logical reasoning, Euclid showed how one could deduce all the known truths of geometry. For two millennia Euclid's *Elements* was the paradigm of rigorous, systematic thought that philosophical literature might aspire to. In his magnum opus, *Ethics* of 1677, starting from axioms and using strict deductive reasoning, Baruch Spinoza sought to do for the sphere of human ethics what Euclid accomplished for the geometry of the plane (Spinoza 1985). Three centuries later Ludwig Wittgenstein, in his celebrated *Tractatus* (Wittgenstein 1922), strove, through numerically ranked logical propositions, to arrive at what can be said (ultimately not said) about the underlying logical form of a proposition.

For philosophical tracts, Euclid's method offers a narrative and rhetorical structure. But in the case of literature, even a single number can act as a structuring principle. Such is the case with the number three and Dante Alighieri's *Divine Comedy*. Observe first the deep-lying association between three and Christianity, a religion whose defining mystery springs from a triad formed by interposing a third mediating figure of the man-God Jesus Christ between the Judaic poles of earthly Man and heavenly God. This, in turn, begets a trisection of the one God into the holy trinity of Father, Son, and Holy Ghost. A further, much later triad, incorporated into Christianity in the century of Dante's birth, introduces Purgatory – a dwelling place for souls not destined for Hell but yet unready for Heaven. It is this last that organizes Dante's poem into its three sections narrating the journey through the regions of the Inferno, Purgatory, and Paradise. Each of these thirds is divided into 33 cantos (with an introductory canto making 100 in all). More fundamentally, each canto consists of three-line tercets written in the *terza rima* form introduced by Dante; an interlocking rhyme scheme, aba, bcb, cdc, ded, etc., of line endings which injects a pulse of three – two steps forward and one back – across each tercet of Dante's poem, a scheme that propels the *Comedy* forward through a series of linked meditative recoils.

A very different focus on numbering and a single number is at the heart of William Shakespeare's *King Lear* (Rotman 1991: 78–86). If the Christian tropism to three organizes the narrative and poetic structure of the *Divine Comedy*, the arithmetic of capitalism and the number zero constitute a symbolic armature of Shakespeare's play. The play's action is initiated when Lear's daughter Cordelia utters "nothing" when asked to measure her love for him as her elder sisters had done. "Nothing will come of nothing, speak again," Lear demands. Out of this "nothing" much that is anything but nothing – murder, treachery, torture, and the destruction of a kingdom – will unfold. And its vehicle will be unnatural measurement, quantification, a relentless calculating, counting, and enumerating that will reduce human relations to acquisition. All will be captured within a buying and selling of loyalty, status, inheritance and, above all, the natural bonds of love, which reflects the disruptive entry of contemporary mercantile capitalism and its system of numbers based on zero into Elizabethan society. Lear's entourage – bargained down by his daughters from 100, to 50, 25, 10, to 1, at which point he is asked, "What need one?" – is reduced to zero. As indeed is Lear himself when his Fool chastises him, "Thou art an O without a figure. I am better than thou art now; I am a fool, thou art nothing."

Shakespeare's play was written at a time when mathematics was entering intellectual, aesthetic, and literary discourse in England and Europe in new, increasingly prominent ways. Not only was calculation with zero-based numerals displacing Roman notation, but the even more abstruse art of algebra, fundamental to the seventeenth-century explosion of mathematics, was beginning to surface. But arithmetic and algebra aside, it was geometry that served as the face of mathematics and arena of inspiration. One strange literary example is a recently unearthed play, *Blame Not Our Author* (Anonymous 1613), an eccentric drama whose learned protagonists are figures of Euclidean geometry: Square, Rectangle, Compass, Line, Circle, Triangle, Semicircle, Rhombus, and Ruler. The theatrical action involves much physical cavorting and capering centering on Square's repeatedly foiled attempts to become a circle (Mazzio 2004). On a wider canvas, geometry can be seen to be deeply entangled with the literary and philosophical writing of the period, not only as a narrative model, as with Spinoza, but also internally within the forms of prose. For example, Arielle Saiber (2005) shows how the employment of figures and tropes in Giordano Bruno's writings, whose publication caused him to be burned at the stake, are frequently literary equivalents and parallels of geometrical ideas.

Geometry (and Euclid) has persisted as an icon of abstraction and mathematics. Poets in more recent times still treat it so. In Vachel Lindsay's "Euclid" the great geometer and his colleagues gathered on a beach to make figures in the sand are merely a foil for a child's innocent eye:

A silent child stood by them
From Morning until noon

Because they drew such charming
Round pictures of the moon.
                    (Lindsay 1925)

In a sonnet of Edna St. Vincent Millay, the beauty of Euclid's mathematics is beyond all else:

Euclid alone has looked on Beauty bare.
Let all who prate of Beauty hold their peace,
And lay them prone upon the earth.
                    (Millay 1956)

Lautréamont, in his *Songs of Maldoror*, inflates this vision into a numinous halo surrounding mathematics by:

O austere mathematics! ... you set an extreme coldness, a consummate prudence and an implacable logic. ... Arithmetic! Algebra! Geometry! Imposing trinity! Luminous triangle! He who has never known you is without sense! He merits the ordeal of the most cruel tortures for in his ignorant carelessness there is a blind contempt. ... But you, O concise mathematics, by the rigorous fetters of your tenacious propositions and the constancy of your iron-bound laws you dazzle the eyes with a powerful reflection of that supreme truth whose imprint is manifest in the order of the universe.
                    (Cited in Badiou 2006: 19–20)

For others, mathematics' naked, cold beauty and implacable concision were anathema. For the speaker of John Keats's narrative poem *Lamia*, the "rule and line" of geometry (for which read mathematics) was indeed a "cold philosophy," but one that disenchanted whatever it touched and emptied the world of awe and wonder:

There was an awful rainbow once in heaven:
We know her woof, her texture; she is given
In the dull catalogue of common things.
Philosophy will clip an Angel's wings,
Conquer all mysteries by rule and line,
Empty the haunted air, and gnomed mine –
Unweave a rainbow.
                    (Keats 1998: Part 2)

As indicated, mathematics can relate to literary texts in different ways. It can inflect the form of a work, but be unimportant or even unmentioned in its content. Dante in his *Comedy* is undoubtedly consumed by threes, but the number itself is scarcely mentioned; Spinoza shapes his *Ethics* after Euclid, but geometry is not what his text is about. On the other hand, the works by St. Vincent Millay, Lindsay, Lautréamont, Keats, and Shakespeare all variously mention geometry or arithmetic or number, as divinely beautiful or threateningly reductive, but in no case is their structure, rhetoric, or narrative shaped by anything mathematical.

A feature of mathematics, evident to even a casual observer, is its preoccupation with *problems*. The subject is organized around agendas set by unresolved difficulties, open questions, conjectures, and hypotheses. Some, like Fermat's last theorem, or Goldbach's conjecture – which asks whether every even number is the sum of two prime numbers – are grand questions that remain open for centuries, and attempts to solve them engender entire fields of new mathematics. Some, like Cantor's Continuum Hypotheses, cannot, even in principle, be resolved. But, less grandly, problems are the bread and butter of mathematics, manifest as everyday responses to questions and sundry logical challenges. Grappling with them is an essential part of learning and practicing, and indeed loving, the art.

Nobody has better and more famously recreated this aspect of mathematics in literature – though a playful mix of logical provocation, word play, riddles, conundrums, strange paradoxical inversions, and inspired nonsense – than the mathematician Lewis Carroll (Charles Dodgson). His poem *Jabberwocky* starts:

'Twas brillig, and the slithy toves
Did gyre and gimble in the wabe;
All mimsy were the borogoves,
And the mome raths outgrabe.
        (Carroll 2007: 99–100)

The poem continues in the same vein, dancing in and out of nonsense. Alice is puzzled by it – "Somehow it seems to fill my head with ideas – only I don't exactly know what they are!" – a response that could capture for many, lost in the fog of mathematical abstraction, their encounter with algebra. It is also not too remote from Bertrand Russell's dictum: "Mathematics may be defined as the subject in which we never know what we are talking about, nor whether what we are saying is true" (Russell 1917: ch. 4). Carroll has much fun with problems involving numbers as well as acknowledging the less attractive feeling they induce: "The different branches of Arithmetic – Ambition, Distraction, Uglification, and Derision" (Carroll 2007: 68). Mostly, however, it's logic rather than numbers that interests Carroll, and Alice is no match for the Red Queen's mad version of it:

"It's very good jam," said the Queen.
   "Well, I don't want any to-day, at any rate."
   "You couldn't have it if you did want it," the Queen said. "The rule is jam tomorrow and jam yesterday but never jam to-day."

"It must come sometimes to 'jam to-day,'" Alice objected.

"No it can't," said the Queen. "It's jam every other day; to-day isn't any other day, you know."

(Carroll 2007: 129)

Equally defeating is the more imperiously obscure logical boast by the Red Queen:

Alice laughed: "There's no use trying," she said; "one can't believe impossible things."

"I daresay you haven't had much practice," said the Queen. "When I was younger, I always did it for half an hour a day. Why, sometimes I've believed as many as six impossible things before breakfast."

(Carroll 2007: 131–32)

The boast here, though perhaps an extravagant feat on an empty stomach, makes perfect logical sense in light of the *reductio ad absurdum* reasoning that is fundamental to mathematics. According to this method of proof, one demonstrates the truth of a proposition by assuming (believing) it to be false (impossible) and deducing from that assumption a flat contradiction (an absurdity).

A less playful, more purposeful literary deployment of mathematics occurs in a work of Carroll's contemporary, Edwin A. Abbott, in his satirical novella *Flatland: a romance in many dimensions* (Abbott 1884). In this strange tale, reminiscent (but composed independently) of the play *Blame Not Our Author* mentioned earlier, male characters are depicted as two-dimensional geometrical shapes, triangles, squares, pentagons, and so on. They form a caste system, status being determined by number of sides: those of the artisan class are triangles, the professionals are squares and higher, with many-sided polygons, who approximate to perfect circles, forming the priesthood. Female characters are mere one-dimensional lines, who are required to sway as they approach to avoid being mistaken for points. The narrator, a square named A. Square, encounters a three-dimensional sphere, a denizen of Spaceland, mysteriously able to evade the confines of his world, whose aim is to enable Flatlanders to overcome their illusory denial of a third dimension. A. Square also dreams of visiting the one-dimensional world of Lineland whose monarch, a single point, is unable to grasp the idea of a being outside his own linear world. Eventually, the narrator is imprisoned for publicly maintaining the existence of Spaceland. Notwithstanding its satire of Victorian society, *Flatland* is obsessed with "space" – its "dimensions," the nature of boundaries, entrances, exits, pathways, and the insides and outsides of regions. As such, it is surely a product of the interest in the mysterious "fourth dimension," which the mathematical invention of non-Euclidean geometries had recently introduced into the very idea of space and which became an object of consuming fascination, particularly by artists, beginning in the second half of the nineteenth century (Henderson 1983).

A fertile appropriation of mathematics for literary purposes is as a constraint, a set rule or pattern for a work to follow. The use of constraints is widespread within literature, quite independently of mathematics. The very notion of a poetic "form" implies conformity to a constraint as, very differently, in the sonnet, terza rima, haiku, iambic pentameter, epigram, limerick, and so on – not to mention in sub-literary devices such as puns, anagrams, palindromes, and acrostics. For instance, the Danish poet Inger Christiansen employed a wide range of mathematical constraints and patterns, making use of Fibonacci numbers, of algebraic forms, and of the self-similarity property of fractal geometry, where aspects of a whole poem are mirrored in portions of it. Her book-length work of social criticism in verse, *it* (Christensen 2006), contains series of ever smaller sections, like Russian dolls, which induce a philosophical layering and deepening of meanings. Other works incorporate cyclic permutations: the volume of her poems *Butterfly Valley: a requiem* (Christensen 2004) includes a chain of 14 sonnets, each beginning with the last line of the previous one, with a fifteenth sonnet consisting of the first lines of the preceding 14 poems.

Christensen's fascination with the poetic possibilities of mathematical patterns echoes a wider contemporary movement interested in creation through formal devices. In 1960, a diverse group of poets, novelists, mathematicians, and philosophers announced in Paris the foundation of a literary workshop, later to be called Oulipo (*ouvroir de littérature potentielle*), dedicated to exploring the use of mathematical rules, procedures, and constraints to produce literary texts. Over the years the group has experimented with a variety of procedures: poems written to be read from the surface of a möbius strip; "lipograms" – stories excluding a particular letter of the alphabet; the "larding" of a source text by the repeated insertion of new sentences; narratives organized according to pathways determined by mathematical graphs; and sundry kinds of rules of permutation and substitution of letters, phrases, and so on. One of the group's earliest productions was *100,000,000 000,000 Poems* by one of its founding members, Raymond Queneau. The work offers 10 alternatives for each of its 14 lines. Selecting a first line, then a second, and so on, produces a single sonnet, one of the hundred thousand billion (10 to the power 14) poems of the title. For example (parentheses enclose other possible selections):

The wild horse champs the Parthenon's top frieze
Since Elgin left his nostrils in the stone
The Turks said just take anything you please
(Upon his old oak chest he cuts his cheese)
And loudly sang off-key without a tone
O Parthenon you hold the charger's strings
The North Wind bites into his architraves

Th'outrageous Thames a troubled arrow slings
To break a rule Britannia's might might wave
(Victorious worms grind all into the grave)
Platonic Greece was not so talentless
A piercing wit would sprightliest horses flog
Socrates watched his hemlock effervesce
Their sculptors did *our* best our hulks they clog
(Lobsters for sale must be our apologue)
With Marble souvenirs then fill a slum
For Europe's glory while Fate's harpies strum
                    (Mathews and Brotchie 1998: 15–33)

The writer Georges Perec produced two of Oulipo's most celebrated works, *La disparition* and *Life: a user's manual*. The first, in purely formal terms the simpler of the two, is a novel-length lipogram, written entirely with words not containing the letter *e*. The work is full of strange juxtapositions engendered by its constraint and is obsessed, as well as being haunted, by absences. It has been translated – rewritten – into *e*-less English as *A Void* by Gilbert Adair (Adair 2005). *Life: a user's manual* is a complex, labyrinthine text, perhaps the most mathematically schematized novel ever written. Featuring and inspired by a jigsaw puzzle, it tells of the interconnecting lives, histories, fates, and passions of the inhabitants of a Parisian apartment building, connected (more or less) by the doomed attempt of a painter, Bartlebooth, to give meaning to his life. The building has 10 floors, each with 10 units (rooms and stairs) facing the street, imagined as simultaneously visible as if the front façade had been removed. Perec employed two mathematical schemes to construct his novel. Firstly, the contents and characters occupying each unit are constrained by a 10x10 mathematical array known as a Graeco-Latin square, subsequently explained by Perec, in a simplified 3x3 case, as follows:

> Imagine a story 3 chapters long involving 3 characters Jones, Smith, Wolkowski. Supply the 3 individuals with 2 sets of attributes: first, headgear – a cap C, a bowler hat H, a beret B; second, something handheld – a dog D, a suitcase S, and a bouquet of roses R. Assume the problem to be that of telling a story in which these 6 items will be ascribed to the 3 characters in turn without their having the same 2. The following formula:

	Jones	*Smith*	*Wolkowski*
Chapter 1	C S	B R	H D
Chapter 2	B D	H S	C R
Chapter 3	H R	C D	B S

which is nothing more than a very simple Graeco-Latin square – provides the solution. In the first chapter, Jones has a cap and a suitcase, Smith has a beret and a bouquet of roses, Wolkowski has bowler hat and a Dog.

(Mathews and Brotchie 1998: 172)

And so on for the other chapters. The story would have to "invent situations to justify these successive transformations." In the novel, "instead of 2 series of 3 items, 21 times 2 series of 10 items are permutated in this fashion" obliging Perec to include 42 themes in every chapter (Mathews and Brotchie 1998: 172). To determine the order of narration through the apartments, Perec uses a second mathematical scheme, a Knight's Tour – the path that a knight takes on an 8x8 chessboard visiting each and every square only once – modified to work for his 10x10 array of apartments.

Another prominent Oulipian, the mathematician Jacques Roubaud, who has written several mathematically inflected novels, enunciates two principles at work in some of the group's efforts. One, when "a text written in accordance with a restrictive procedure refers to the procedure," for example, Perec's *La disparition*, which, among other things, recounts the disappearance of the letter that constitutes it; two, when "a text written according to a mathematically formulable procedure includes the consequences of the mathematical theory that it illustrates" (Mathews and Brotchie 1998: 218). Examples of this second principle are harder to find. Roubaud cites his own novel *Princess Happy*, concerning four individuals, which takes account of the algebra of the four-element mathematical group.

We might ask about the opposite to constraints as sources of literary creation, about the presence in a work of the mathematically *unconstrained*. Could that which is unbounded – such as the infinite progression of whole numbers – make its mark in a literary text? We might, for example, find – or at least impute – the presence of infinity in Laurence Sterne's satirical novel *Tristram Shandy* (1759), whose eponymous hero devotes himself to telling the story of his life. But (for various hilarious reasons) he writes at a snail's pace, taking two years to narrate two days of his life, and laments he'll never finish the task. However long he lives, the number of years and days can't possibly match: logically, the whole of his life must exceed the part. Sterne wrote a century before Georg Cantor showed that for *infinite* collections wholes and parts obey a different logic. The even numbers, for example, despite being a part, only half, as it were, of the numbers, can indeed be tallied off with the whole, with *all* the numbers. Both collections have the same magnitude, which Cantor designated as aleph-zero – the smallest infinite number. Bertrand Russell, writing in the wake of Cantor's theory of infinity, maintained that if Tristram Shandy "had lived for ever, and not wearied of his task, even if his life had continued as eventfully as it began, no part of his biography would have remained unwritten" (Russell 1903: 358). Thus, year 1 could be devoted to writing the events of day 1, year 2 to day 2, and so on, where every day would eventually be accounted for. Russell does not of course say what it would *mean* to live without end.

Jorge Luis Borges, who admired Sterne's novel and knew of Russell's solution to Tristram Shandy's predicament, engages with infinity on several occasions. His perhaps most celebrated fiction, "The Library of Babel" (1964), is saturated with mathematical ideas (Bloch 2008), most notably infinity. It depicts "The universe (which others call the library)" as a vast, topologically strange construction of hexagonal cells, "a sphere whose exact center is any hexagon and whose circumference is unattainable" (Borges 1964: 79), a formula which plays on "God is a sphere whose centre is everywhere and whose circumference is nowhere," the hermetic dictum repeated by the medieval theologian-mathematician Nicholas de Cusa. The library comprises books of precious wisdom, incomparable nonsense, and unimaginable, arbitrary content. Its ontology follows that of mathematics – x exists if the definition of x is not contradictory: "It suffices that a book is possible for it to exist" (84). But everything is written in a fixed alphabet of letters, so that (since each book in the library is unique) the number of books is finite. And yet, is not the universe, the library, the world, infinite? To which the narrator responds that "the library is unlimited and cyclical" – a traveler setting off into the universe would return eventually from the opposite direction. The story ends with the suggestion that perhaps the whole library could be replaced by a single book "containing an infinite number of infinitely thin leaves" (86).

A later work, "The Book of Sand" (Borges 1979: 87–91), features just such a book. It begins: "The line is made up of an infinite number of points; the plane of an infinite number of lines; the volume of an infinite number of planes; the hypervolume of an infinite number of volumes" (87), at which point it breaks off and plunges into its tale of a nondescript, nighttime visitor offering to sell the narrator what he calls a "Bible." The narrator is baffled by its unknown script and incomprehensible pagination. He's told it was acquired for a few rupees from an Untouchable and is called the *Book of Sand* "because neither the book nor the sand has any beginning or end" (89). Disbelieving, the narrator searches for a first and then a last page, but in vain. "The number of pages in this book," the stranger tells him, "is no more or less than infinite." The narrator agrees to accept it in exchange for a precious Wyclif Bible. But the infinite book invades his dreams and comes to seem monstrous, "a nightmarish object, an obscene thing that affronted and tainted reality itself" (91), and he buries it in a dusty corner of the Argentine National Library.

The material I've chosen to illustrate the nexus of literature and mathematics here is of course selective, with many omissions. Most notably, I've included nothing of the great mass of contemporary science-fiction novels where things mathematical are most at home. In this genre of speculative fiction, mathematics – fractal geographies, topologies of time and space, algebraic encryption, chaotic attractors, algorithmic life-forms, computational intelligences, and much else – is an ever-present source of imagination. This profusion of mathematically inflected novels of possible, impossible, and virtual worlds (too numerous and various to summarize here) reflects a larger phenomenon, namely the ongoing upheaval of contemporary thought and consciousness engendered by computation-based digital media and technologies of the virtual (Rotman 2008). Once again, as in the seventeenth century, although on a wider canvas, an explosion of mathematical language and ideas is impinging on the written text in new and interesting ways.

Bibliography

Abbott, E.A. (1884) *Flatland: a romance of many dimensions*, London: Seely.

Adair, G. (2005) *A Void*, Boston, Mass.: David R Godine.

Anonymous (1613) *Blame Not Our Author*, S. Gossett (ed.), Malone Society Publications at the Venerable English College.

Badiou, A. (2006) "Philosophy and mathematics," in Duffy 2006: 12–30.

Bloch, W.G. (2008) *The Unimaginable Mathematics of Borges' Library of Babel*, Oxford: Oxford University Press.

Borges, J.L. (1964) *Labyrinths*, Harmondsworth: Penguin.

——(1979) *The Book of Sand*, trans. Norman di Giovanni, Middlesex: Penguin.

Carroll, L. (2007) *Collected Works of Lewis Carroll*, Charleston, N.C.: Bibliobazaar.

Christensen, I. (2004) *Butterfly Valley: a requiem*, trans. S. Nied, New York: New Directions.

——(2006) *it*, trans. S. Nied, New York: New Directions.

Duffy, S. (2006) *Virtual Mathematics*, Manchester: Clinamen Press.

Galileo, G. (1953) *Dialogue Concerning the Two Chief World Systems*, trans. S. Drake, Berkeley: University of California Press.

Hardy, G.H. (1940) *A Mathematician's Apology*, Cambridge: Cambridge University Press.

Henderson, L.D. (1983) *The Fourth Dimension and Non-Euclidean Geometry in Modern Art*, Princeton: Princeton University Press.

Keats, J. (1998) *Collected Poems of John Keats*, Hertfordshire: Wordsworth Editions.

Lindsay, V. (1925) *Collected Poems of Vachel Lindsay*, New York: Macmillan.

Mathews, H. and Brotchie, A. (1998) *Oulipo Compendium*, London: Atlas Press.

Mazzio, C. (2004) "The Three-Dimensional Self: geometry, melancholy, drama," in D. Glimp and M.R. Warren (eds) *Arts of Calculation: numerical thought in early modern Europe*, New York: Palgrave, pp. 39–65.

Millay, E.S.V. (1956) *Collected Poems*, New York: Harper.

Perec, G. (1969) *La disparition*, Paris: Denöel.

——(2008) *Life: a user's manual*, New York: Vintage.

Plato (2000) *The Republic*, trans. T. Griffith and G.R.F. Ferrari, Cambridge: Cambridge University Press.

Rotman, B. (1991) *Signifying Nothing: the semiotics of zero*, Stanford: Stanford University Press.

——(2008) *Becoming Beside Ourselves: the alphabet, ghosts, and distributed human being*, Durham, N.C.: Duke University Press.

Russell, B. (1903) *Principles of Mathematics*, Cambridge: Cambridge University Press.

——(1917) *Mysticism and Logic*, London: Allen and Unwin.

Saiber, A. (2005) *Giordano Bruno and the Geometry of Language*, Aldershot: Ashgate.

Shakespeare, W. (1969) *King Lear*, London: Methuen.

Sinclair, N. et al. (2006) *Mathematics and the Aesthetic*, New York: Springer.

Spinoza, B. (1985) *Ethics*, in *Collected Writings of Spinoza*, vol.1, trans. E. Curley, Princeton: Princeton University Press.

Sterne, L. (2003) *The Life and Opinions of Tristram Shandy, Gentleman*, Harmondsworth: Penguin.

Wittgenstein, L. (1922) *Tractatus Logico-Philosophicus*, trans. C.K. Ogden, London: Routledge & Kegan Paul.

15
MEDICINE

George Rousseau

The sub-discipline of literature and medicine arose after World War II, when it became evident that the two halves of its terrain shared common ground. Its genesis was stimulated by C.P. Snow's controversy with F.R. Leavis (Leavis 1963) over the "two cultures" (Snow 1969), and further invigorated by far-flung discussions of these debates, resulting two decades later in the view that "one culture" represents the historical status of knowledge more accurately (Levine 1987; Tallis 1995). Peter Medawar, the British Nobel Laureate in Medicine, who also delivered the BBC Reith Lectures in 1959, entitled *The Future of Man*, and heightening sensitivity to the overlaps of literature and science and medicine, further stimulated the post-war growth of the sub-discipline (Medawar 1967). Nevertheless, the aftermath of all these debates made clear that literature and medicine bore an uneasy relation to its parallel discourse, literature and science, owing to the relatively steady state of the anatomical human body (Trautmann 1981; Daudet and Barnes 2002).

The last point is consequential: science amounts to a vast body of advancing knowledge (*scientia*) perceived to be forever in a state of progress and is usually thought to improve the world; the human body may be socially constructed over time but it has been far less vulnerable to change than scientia. This glaring discrepancy informed both sub-disciplines. Also complicating their uneasy relation was the old debate about whether medicine is an art or science; yet few philosophers of science have ever sustained any argument that science is primarily an art. Therefore, if literature and science and literature and medicine were conceptualized as discrete, developing sub-disciplines forming parts of the huge, complex canvas of knowledge, their differences were seen as being as great as their similarities, and a strong case developed after the 1980s that they had no more in common with each other than with other sub-disciplines such as literature and anthropology, literature and the law, literature and religion (Rousseau 1991b).

Framed otherwise, literature and science is the study of ever-advancing sets of relationships in which one half of the equation – the body of knowledge called "science" – never stands still, whereas literature and medicine focuses on the relation of two relatively stable categories: *literature* and *medicine* – neither of which can meaningfully claim to "progress" in the way scientific knowledge does. It would be odd to discuss literature in terms of progress – progress since Shakespeare's plays or Shelley's poetry? – yet much medical diagnosis is not "scientific" in the sense that rigorously tested and peer-reviewed scientific hypotheses are. Medicine, even empirically based contemporary medicine, relies on scientific knowledge but embraces other, non-scientific components to compose its totality.

Even if imaginative, canonical literature itself does not "progress," scientific theory *about* literature does. And if the theory wars of the last generation have resolved anything, it is the degree to which much contemporary theory aspires to be "scientific" and in many instances attains its goal (Cain and Graff 1994). Literary theory can be as scientific as other types of theory under controlled conditions. Compounding this propensity is the fact that at least since the 1970s the rotund cupola of literature – including imaginative canonical literature from Beowulf to Virginia Woolf and all other forms of written and verbal discourse – has embraced literary theory. Therefore, both literature and medicine and literature and science can seem to be in scientific parity only when the literature component of their cupola designates literary theory.

Something tantamount to this parallel state occurred in the late twentieth century when stimulated by the development of neuroscience, whose main concern then prioritized memory: a category of unusual interest to literature from time immemorial whose stock rose after World War II (Schacter and Scarry 1999). The difference now (after c. 1945) was that neuroscience was privileging memory. Within just a few decades all sorts of questions about memory arose, as did journals of memory studies. Was memory an action, a metaphor, or both? Were its defects symptomatic of illness, as in other somatic ailments, or a metaphor for something psychological run amok in the personality (Sontag 1979)? Was memory primarily biological, physiological, or psychological? Was it individual as well as collective? These and other difficult questions filtered into bread-and-butter literary theory debates, raising literature and medicine to a new threshold of relevance.

Concurrently, the 1990s rise of narrative-based medicine (NBM) changed the direction of literature and medicine yet again. NBM originates from a point in which most "medicine" is presumed to be contemporary, and affirms that doctor–patient interactions in *all* medical fields are primarily verbal; that the outcome of both diagnosis and therapy depends partly on the narrative experience of each party. Questions such as "how do doctors think?" and "how do patients talk?" assume current-day patients and doctors in contemporary settings. The pre-1950 past is expunged or relegated to "history."

NBM arose out of an accompanying agenda to transform the domain of *current* medical practice. With much justification its enhancements in communication aimed at altering the kingdom of patientdom: the patient was no longer an anatomical body to be diagnosed, surgically excavated, and clinically treated, but a word-making individual sensitive to the discursive exchanges between doctor and patient who wished to augment the story he told himself about himself.

Some doctors resisted but others willingly participated in these inflections. The collective medical self-image gradually altered and soon doctors were receiving instruction in the complexities of narrative interchange and re-educating themselves in literary analysis. Likewise patients were taught to construe their responsibility as more robust than earlier: fully to explain themselves to doctors and include the affective components. Some doctors reached out from medical practice to the community in the belief that medicine had grown too insulated (Klass 1993), while others "wrote out" their illnesses – pathographesis – as they routinely had in the early modern world when geography dictated the pressing need for written accounts among absent patients. Pre-1800 travel was arduous; pathographies were sent to physicians who would never see their patients (Caldwell 2004). More recently the authors of pathographies have written for public audiences: to share their experience of illness. By the 1990s writing oneself out of sickness, both through and without publication, became a widespread activity, as if the act of "writing one's self out" were coevally a cleansing and healing (Hawkins 1993). Some renamed their writing "life writing" for its biocritical suggestion of healing.

In 1982–83 the first journal for the study of literature and medicine appeared: *Literature and Medicine*. Initiated by Americans, it was intended for North American academic audiences but its contents also captured the attention of medical practitioners elsewhere. In its first decade its contents included historical topics such as the relevance of medical history to the developing literature and medicine field and discussion of figures who had been doctors-writers (Rabelais, Thomas Campion, Goldsmith, Smollett, Keats, Chekhov, William Carlos Williams); but after the 1990s this historical component largely dropped out and the focus turned increasingly to NBM salted with calls for feminist and minority reform in the medical interchange (*Literature and Medicine* 1992–99). A few papers appeared on Chaucer, Tudor plague, Montaigne, Georgian gout, Blake, and Keats, but these were buried under the mountain of general commentary about pain, stress, disability, intersubjectivity, and ethical concern as found, for example, in the thought of philosopher Emmanuel Levinas. In 1990 the *Journal of Medical Humanities* published its first issue, but its concerns were even less canonical and historical than its counterpart's and more bioethical (*Journal of Medical Humanities* 1990–99).

If we pause momentarily we can reflect on why literature and science could not then have had an equivalent academic journal: its field is significantly larger, especially if readers expect it to cover *both* literature *and* science from the Greeks forward. *Configurations*, a journal first published in 1993 and sponsored by the Society for Literature and Science, itself evolved from a group debating the interconnections of literature and science, aimed to fill some part of this gap.

But while it was eloquent on theoretical aspects of postmodern thought it wisely made no claim to include the historical component of the sub-discipline literature and science. Historical coverage was left to the individual period journals devoted to the Renaissance, Enlightenment, Romantic, Victorian, American literature and so forth. Instead *Configurations* addressed, and still probes, the theoretical issues and leaves tradition, influence, biography, and especially the place of the history of science and medicine in the development of the sub-disciplines literature and science and literature and medicine to other outlets.

Despite these differences of literature and medicine and literature and science, it is curious the degree to which the pre-1900 literary canon, as well as the deep-layer analysis of the rise of these sub-disciplines, has been neglected. Typical treatment proceeds as if a scientific or medical moment were more or less static, without the far-flung context necessary to explain why it is problematic in the first place. There is little impulse to stretch backward in time. For example, the case study or pathographic propensities of the last generation: many secondary studies have discussed pathographesis as if its curve began in the twentieth century rather than by consulting the *longue durée* to demonstrate changes in the sub-genre (Campo 1997). Or consider broader reflections on the development of the sub-discipline literature and medicine, the subject of this chapter: few studies treat it as a developing field over the long haul – from the Renaissance forward. When they do, the contextual component is often absent.

Moreover, a further reason for the reduction of similarity and difference in literature and medicine is that, prior to the twentieth century, cure formed only a small province of medicine's activity. Today we take cure for granted as intrinsic to medical practice, but its rise is recent. Joseph Addison's famous quip that doctors "kill more than they cure" was a common perception throughout the nineteenth century. Only since the twentieth century has medicine's primary remit been to cure. Withhold cure from its domain, and medicine becomes a more amorphous territory than otherwise, extending to many realms of human life. The impact on literature and medicine is apparent: what do the two components of literature and medicine – *literature* and *medicine* – amount to if medicine has altered in this way? You need a considerable amount of history of medicine to unpack the changes to literature and medicine's development (Neve 1993; Rousseau 1996).

Here the Romantic movement has been crucial (Rousseau 1993). By the late eighteenth century, British literature – especially the prose novel – was quickly absorbing medical content, while medical practice was being transformed to an unprecedented degree (Rousseau 1981). By the time Coleridge and Wordsworth added the 1802 preface to their revolutionary *Lyrical Ballads*, with its famous passages about the poet's unending attraction to the discoveries of science and medicine, writers were more medically knowledgable than they had been (Vickers 2004). Poets and artists, moreover, were fashionable if seen as ailing (Vila 1998).

But the Romantics' absorption in matters medical was not limited to their own often-sick bodies. They were also drawn to medicine's theoretical quandaries, especially the mind–body debates that had heated up since the era of Hobbes and Locke and culminated in the fictional sallies of Sterne in *Tristram Shandy* (Mulvey and Porter 1993: 84–100; Richardson 2001). The Enlightenment emphasis on a complex nervous system (the animal spirits, fibers, nerves, the brain) in preference to the midriff zone redirected attention to the head and brain (Rousseau 2004). As Romantic writers and artists debated such thorny concepts as character, personality, and temperament they increasingly wondered what role the brain played (Rousseau 1976, 2007a). The formation of pictures in the mind, and the production of dreams, especially, attracted them. By the decade of Byron's and Shelley's maturity in the 1820s, mind and body were being combined in ways unknown to earlier empiricists and ongoing mind–body debates had extended to groups exceeding the sphere of empirical philosophers. To be a Romantic poet or artist, whether a conservative Wordsworth or revolutionary Blake, was to engage in these debates.

The Romantics were also the first generation to recognize widely the importance of factitious diseases: imaginary maladies lodged in often hypochondriac patients. These maladies were sometimes as fictitious as they were factitious, and the differences of complete invention versus partial concoction based on ambiguous symptoms preoccupied those diagnosing them (Vrettos 1995). Prose treatises began to appear distinguishing the two types (Mathews 1820). You could claim these writings for either literature or medicine – either domain – but they resided more accurately in the interstices, in a common ground belonging to both spheres (Rousseau 2003).

The distance from hypochondria and factitious malady to mental illness is not far. The Romantics also recognized that the patient claiming to suffer from conditions no doctor can identify may be mentally ill (Small 1996). Writers before c. 1800 had recognized the possibility and commented upon it (Tobias Smollett's *Lancelot Greaves* is a classical locus) but the Romantics amplified it into a veritable sub-genre in its own right (Rousseau 1991). Writers had portrayed mad characters from the time of ancient Greek tragedy and playwrights like Shakespeare depicted them (Hamlet, Ophelia, Lear, Macbeth) in detail so exquisite that it would be folly to argue that the Romantics' representations were original. The difference now – after 1800 – is that the writing is medically informed: imaginative literature is demonstrably being influenced by particular medical texts (Smith 1976; Thiher 1999). Shakespeare's allusions to medicine, for example, are prolific but it is difficult to pinpoint the influence of specific medical writings on particular plays.

One facet of medicine eluded the Romantics: its status in a socially progressive era. Children of war and revolution, they could not envision medicine's role in a peaceful, progressive society, nor the way its concerns are represented among different class groups in different geographies and countries, or the diverse patterns of its prefiguration in the social fabric of culture. Such representation included, of course, the depiction of its practitioners – doctors, nurses, apothecaries, surgeons, patients – as well as ideas about its sociological function. The modern discipline known as the sociology of medicine deals with this domain when the setting is an advanced hegemonic society (American, British, French), as does medical anthropology in more primitive societies. Both have burgeoned for a half century, but in the nineteenth century they were nascent. The Victorians tapped into social medicine in their novels, privileging it as the theme of particular works, as in Charlotte Brontë's *Wuthering Heights* and Eliot's *Middlemarch*.

"Middlemarch" is a typical English country town, and the novel named for it focuses on two couples, one of whom is Rosamond and Lydgate, the town doctor, a new kind of general medical practitioner who combines the function of the older apothecaries and surgeons. Born well, Lydgate arrives in Middlemarch dreaming to build a modern hospital for the poor but is suspiciously viewed by the medical establishment. He gets few referrals, earns little, his savings quickly depleted by the high-flying, ostentatious Rosamond. Unexpectedly, Lydgate receives a loan from Bulstrode, a wealthy landowner, only to discover that Bulstrode has been charged with murder and Lydgate named as an accomplice. Disgraced by the accusations, Lydgate becomes helpless and surrenders his medical dreams. Instead he panders to rich patients and forgoes the possibility of establishing a medical practice for the poor. His revolutionary aspirations evaporate and he dies a broken man at 50, neither rich nor poor, an unmoored social outcast. Eliot could not have constructed her novel without immersing herself to this degree in the social history of medicine then: its concerns for the developing Victorian medical profession, as well as the doctor–patient relation. But she would not have described so vividly Lydgate's sense of himself as a failure without these contexts. Her wide reading in contemporary medicine, in several languages, demonstrated how notions of professional success were being transformed in her generation. What was success to Lydgate would not have been earlier in the world of Daniel Defoe or Jane Austen.

Soon afterwards, twentieth-century literature surrendered deep-layer probing of medicine's social tentacles and turned inward to the interior lives of its victims: sufferers and providers, those ailing and those caring for them. The impulse was not romantic regression – to revive the artist as invalid – but pierced instead to the heart of private lives in the state of sickness; to what it meant to be a patient in the modern world. It did this against the grain of developing national health systems (the NHS in the U.K., state health in Canada, and so forth), as well as the deep frustration of those countries (the U.S.A., Latin and South America) unable to provide one. Some of its primary literature captured these social elements as minor themes, but most remained focused on the self and its plight.

Patient narratives and personal pathographies of the twentieth century were usually set in present time. When they demonstrated a nostalgic turn, the plot still evolved in relatively recent time but was rarely more than a generation or two behind. It is as if the novelist were insufficiently *au fait* with medical history to deal with past medicine (Loxterkamp 1997). But none could imagine such a stunning fiction about the consequences of a "plague of white blindness" attacking a whole country as Portugese Nobel Laureate Jose Saramago (Saramago and Pontiero 1976). Medical students read his novel and relished its insights in the 1990s. Once exposed to fiction and encouraged to study creative writing, the landscape of literature and medicine changed again and young doctors invented plots set in previous times. They knew their medicine sufficiently well not to fret about the medico-historical background.

This education occurred in programs arranged around the "medical humanities," by the 1980s a sub-field taught in medical schools. It developed in medical schools and was driven by the contemporary critique that medical education, especially its omission of medical ethics, which was defective (McManus 1995). Assuming that the modern world was composed of soul-denying Western societies, medical humanities claimed to be appalled by the lack of cultural critique of medicine, and judged medicine as far too serious a matter – literally of life or death – to leave to doctors only (Frank 1995). Their point was strong. In self-defense the doctors retorted that they had little time for such pursuits. The indictment was nevertheless put and the field developed: first as an interdisciplinary module and then as a major. Programmatic glances were made at the humanities (literature, philosophy, ethics, history, religion), social sciences (anthropology, cultural studies, psychology, sociology), and arts (literature, theater, film, visual arts). But particular emphasis was placed on the utility of such approaches to medical education and, eventually, to medical practice. The early rationale was that such interdisciplinary vision would pro-duce a crop of humane doctors. In practice, close reading and creative writing played minor roles in these courses, with little of it ever cast further afield than to twentieth-century literature.

During the 1980s and 1990s this rationale about the present deepened, abetted by publications in the journal *Literature and Medicine*, discussed above. Presentism developed along lines that while the humanities and arts provide insight into the human condition, pain and suffering, selfhood, personhood, depression, mental illness, and our ethical responsibility to each other, the medical humanities can offer physicians a deepened perspective on medical practice (Hunter 1991). It was further claimed that attention to literature and the arts nurtures skills of observation, analysis, empathy, and self-reflection – much needed for humane medical care. If the social sciences enable understanding of how bioscience and medicine take place within socio-cultural contexts, the medi-cal humanities – so the claim went – taught much about the interactions of the individual experience of illness, especially the ways individual patients responded.

It was much less clear what such an ambitious agenda could do for the humanities – in particular for literature. That is, art has usually been decoupled from social reform. Its components are fundamentally aesthetic, philosophical, moral, and even vicarious but it is not ranked according to its ability to reform, or improve, society. Even so, "literature" is an ambiguous word. If "literature" designates *all* discourse, then many approaches offer something of value. If, instead, delimited to contemporary imaginative writing, then it is clear that such skills can focus the narrator's eye in the face of the perennially perplexing human condition and in relation to suffering, selfhood, and the moral responsibility human beings bear to each other. But it was less evident what this approach could do for literary criticism and literary history, fields of long pedigree (Frank 1995; Rousseau 2007b). During prior epochs when medical concerns loomed, as in Victorian England, the medical humanities could alert the reader to medical *content*. But for other periods when medicine was less absorbed into the tissue of mainstream culture, it was far from clear what was to be gained. For example, medicine was relatively low on the pecking order of content for writers from Beowulf to Chaucer and Dante to Milton, and to most writers in the seventeenth century (excepting Thomas Browne). The distinction might also be narrowed to authors rather than historical periods: such as the Renaissance or Enlightenment, or, to change the axis again, to moderns and postmoderns, structuralists and anti-structuralists. By our time all these fields display well-developed literary histories incapable of persuasion that they can benefit from an infusion of medical humanities. Nevertheless, some critics have demonstrated how wrong they are (Ober 1989).

The obvious retort to the academicians ought to have been that *all* epochs rely on medicine: how could it be otherwise when medicine measures pain thresholds and helps to sustain human life? But clarifications were rarely mounted, perhaps because they required scholars and critics *au fait* with the history of *both* literature and medicine in the pre-1900 world. This was the state of affairs circa 1990. Since then a technological revolution based on high-speed and hyperlink connection has changed the field – literature and medicine – again. When everything connects to everything, and when you can locate those connections with the stroke of a key, the parameters alter: the past becomes more accessible and historical negotiation less arduous than it was in the days of three-by-five cards and snail mail. If you can acquire the knowledge you need about a particular historical topic in one day, rather than one year, you will be less reticent to pursue an historically grounded literature and medicine. There is considerable evidence that this is happening in the field.

The trend is laudable but still leaves a sub-discipline in partial disarray gravitating to the contemporary scene; with myopic vision, if not misprision, of the past. Survey the girth of literature and medicine, and you find it splintered into camps of critics and scholars, theorists and historians, and now do-gooders eager to reform the practice of medicine, especially for patients. The theorists immerse themselves in models and systems, often leaving primary literature and primary medicine behind; while scholars focus on narrow domains sometimes embracing no more than a generation or single figure. The field eschews totalizing discussions that reflect on its past or meditate its future.

The matter is not the remedy, as if the sub-discipline of literature and medicine were ailing, but rather how to bring the contemporary technological revolution into the service of this further developing field. Hyperlink realism and algorithmic mindsets are here to stay: everything is *already* being connected to everything else. Nor does need exist any longer for the old incantatory rhetoric about working alone in the wilderness or needing folk "to talk to": if only we could bring together the medical and literary camps. ... That was the last generation's desideratum; in reply to its cries the interdisciplinary mandate arose. The new hyperlink realism, in contrast, has rendered the past more readily accessible than it was even a decade ago. The issue now is whether our postmodern mindsets will harness the past in the service of an already developed field configured according to a narrow set of premises, or continue to evolve as a visionary sphere apart from lived history.

Put more simply, the matter is whether a literature and medicine whose materials stretch as far back as literature itself can have equal footing with postmodern theoretical discussions. If they cannot, then another "two cultures" – a veritable third culture – will arise within the already small sub-discipline: one group historical and approaching most of its critical tasks historically; another theoretical, grounded in the present, and not even persuaded that pre-1900 canonical literature falls within its remit; and a third hands-on and concerned with medical practice. If this further schism develops it will seem there are "three literature and medicines" within "two cultures," while everything points to only *one*. And then we are back to square one; roughly where we were around 1959 when literature and medicine gathered momentum, and C.P. Snow and F.R. Leavis were attacking each other.

It remains to notice that, since 1959, literature and medicine has developed mainly on American soil. The sub-discipline entrenched itself in academia there in cultures weighted toward the present. This fact has taken its toll and recently literature and medicine has not been attracting those already interested in the literary canon from Moses to Thomas Mann – the Mann whose *Magic Mountain* remains the seminal text for literature and medicine – with the exception of a few figures (George Eliot, Chekhov, William Carlos Williams). Hence difficult questions arise. Will literature and medicine always be limited to current-day concerns? Does literature and medicine have significant space for pre-1900 stories evolving in major Western traditions? Why is literature and medicine attracting so few students of canonical literature, in any languages, when it professes to deal with universal categories of primal significance: grief, loss, sickness, pain, suffering, and the great leveler, death (Scarry 1985; Morris 1991; Rousseau 1991a)? Is it too ambitious to expect literature and medicine to embrace realist literary history and medical history as well as theory? Are its written productions recognizable as different from other types of social critique? Why does literature and medicine resist argument and counter-argument about the kind of field it is? Literature and medicine must address questions like these if it wishes to be reinvigorated.

Bibliography

Cain, W.E. and Graff, G. (1994) *Teaching the Conflicts: Gerald Graff, curricular reform, and the culture wars*, New York: Garland.

Caldwell, J.M. (2004) *Literature and Medicine in Nineteenth-century Britain: from Mary Shelley to George Eliot*, Cambridge: Cambridge University Press.

Campo, R. (1997) *The Poetry of Healing: a doctor's education in empathy, identity, and desire*, New York: Norton.

Charon, R. (2006) *Narrative Medicine: honoring the stories of illness*, New York: Oxford University Press.

Coles, R. (1988) *Times of Surrender*, Iowa City: University of Iowa Press.

Configurations: A Journal of Literature, Science and Technology (1993–).

Crawford, H. (1993) *Modernism, Medicine and William Carlos Williams*, Norman: University of Oklahoma Press.

Daudet, A. and Barnes, J. (2002) *In the Land of Pain*, London: Jonathan Cape.

Edgar, I. (1970) *Shakespeare, Medicine and Psychiatry*, London: Vision

Frank, A.W. (1995) *The Wounded Storyteller: body, illness, and ethics*, Chicago: University of Chicago Press.

Furst, L. (1998) *Between Doctors and Patients: the changing balance of power*, Charlottesville: University of Virginia Press.

Greenhaigh, T. and Hurwitz, B. (1998) *Narrative-based Medicine: dialogue and discourse in clinical practice*, London: BMJ Books.

Hawkins, A.H. (1993) *Reconstructing Illness: studies in pathography*, West Lafayette: Purdue University Press.

Hunter, K.M. (1991) *Doctors' Stories: the narrative structure of medical knowledge*, Princeton: Princeton University Press.

Johnson, M. (1987) *The Body in the Mind: the bodily basis of meaning, imagination, and reason*, Chicago: University of Chicago Press.

Jordanova, L. (1999) *Nature Displayed: gender, science and medicine 1760–1820*, London: Longman.

Journal of Medical Humanities (1990–99).

Klass, P. (1993) *Baby Doctor*, New York: Ivy Books.

Leavis, F.R. (1963) *Two Cultures? The significance of C.P. Snow*, Richmond, N.Y.: Pantheon.

Levine, G.L. (1987) *One Culture: essays in science and literature*, Madison: University of Wisconsin Press.

Literature and Medicine (1983–).

Loxterkamp, D. (1997) *A Measure of My Days: the journal of a country doctor*, Hanover, N.H.: University Press of New England.

Mangham, A. (2007) *Violent Women and Sensation Fiction: crime, medicine and Victorian popular culture*, Basingstoke: Palgrave Macmillan.

Mathews, H. (1820) *The Diary of an Invalid*, London: n. p.

McManus, I.C. (1995) "Humanity and the medical humanities," *Lancet*, 348: 1143–44.

Medawar, P. (1967) *The Art of the Soluble*, London: Methuen.

Morris, D.B. (1991) *The Languages of Pain*, Los Angeles: University of California Press.

Mulvey, M. and Porter, R. (1993) *Literature and Medicine during the Eighteenth Century*, London: Routledge.

Neve, M. (1993) "Medicine and literature," in W.F. Bynum and R. Porter (eds) *Companion Encyclopedia of the History of Medicine*, 2 vols, London: Routledge, ch. 65, pp. 1520–35.

Ober, W.B. (1989) *Bottoms Up! A pathologist's essay on medicine and the humanities*, Carbondale: Southern Illinois University Press.

Peschel, E.R. (1980) *Medicine and Literature*, New York: Neale Watson Academic Publications.

Richardson, A. (2001) *British Romanticism and the Science of the Mind*, Cambridge: Cambridge University Press.

Rolleston, H. (1933) *Associations between Medicine and Literature*, London: Harrison & Sons.

Rousseau, G.S. (1976) "Nerves, spirits, and fibres: towards the origins of sensibility," in R. Brissenden and C. Eade (eds) *Studies in the Eighteenth Century III*, Toronto: University of Toronto Press, pp. 137–57.

——(1981) "Literature and medicine: the state of the field," *Isis*, 52: 406–24.

——(1986) "Literature and medicine: towards a simultaneity of theory and practice," in J. Trautman-Banks (ed.) *Literature and Medicine: use and abuse of literary concepts in medicine*, Baltimore: Johns Hopkins University Press, pp. 152–81.

——(1991a) *Medicine and the Muses: the idea that the arts heal in history*, Florence, Italy.

——(1991b) *Enlightenment Crossings*, Manchester: Manchester University Press.

——(1993) "On romanticism, science and medicine," *History of European Ideas*, 17(5): 659–63.

——(1996) "Bridges of light: the domains of literature and medicine," *Aberdeen University Review*, 32: 1–22.

——(2004) *Nervous Acts: essays on literature, culture and sensibility*, Basingstoke: Palgrave Macmillan.

——(2007a) "Brainomania," *British Journal for Eighteenth-century Studies*, 30: 161–92.

——(2007b) "Two kinds of knowledge at the crossroads: literature and science, literature and medicine, as types of cultural understanding," *Minerva*, 45: 63–71.

——(2008) "Temperament and the long shadow of nerves in the eighteenth century," in F.H. Whitaker, C.U.M. Smith and S. Finger (eds) *Brain, Mind and Medicine*, New York: Springer, pp. 353–70.

——, Gill, M.H., Herwig, M. and Haycock, D. (eds) (2003) *Framing and Imagining Disease in Cultural History*, Basingstoke: Palgrave Macmillan.

Saramago, J. and Pontiero, G. (1997) *Blindness: a novel*, London: Harvill.

Scarry, E. (1985) *The Body in Pain: the making and unmaking of the world*, New York: Oxford University Press.

Schacter, D.L. and Scarry, E. (1999) *Memory, Brain, and Belief*, Cambridge, Mass.: Harvard University Press.

Small, H. (1996) *Love's Madness: medicine, the novel, and female insanity 1800–1865*, Oxford: Clarendon Press.

Smith, J.H. (ed.) (1976) *Psychiatry and the Humanities*, New Haven: Yale University Press.

Snow, C.P. (1969) *The Two Cultures, and a Second Look: an expanded version of the two cultures and the scientific revolution*, Cambridge: Cambridge University Press.

Sontag, S. (1979) *Illness as Metaphor*, New York: Random House.

Tallis, R. (1995) *Newton's Sleep: the two cultures and the two kingdoms*, Basingstoke: Macmillan.

Tambling, J. (1990) "*Middlemarch*, realism and the birth of the clinic," *English Literary History*, 57: 939–60.

Thiher, A. (1999) *Revels in Madness: insanity in medicine and literature*, Ann Arbor: University of Michigan Press.

Trautmann, J. (1981) *Healing Arts in Dialogue: medicine and literature*, London: Feffer and Simons.

Vickers, N. (2004) *Coleridge and the Doctors, 1795–1806*, Oxford: Clarendon Press.

Vila, A.C. (1998) *Enlightenment and Pathology: sensibility in the literature and medicine of eighteenth-century France*, Baltimore: Johns Hopkins University Press.

Vrettos, A. (1995) *Somatic Fictions: imagining illness in Victorian fiction*, Stanford: Stanford University Press.

Waugh, P. and Fuller, D. (1999) *The Arts and Sciences of Criticism*, Oxford: Oxford University Press.

Wood, J. (2001) *Passion and Pathology in Victorian Fiction*, Oxford: Oxford University Press.

Woolf, V. (1994) "On being ill – 1926," in *The Essays of Virginia Woolf: volume four 1925–28*, London: Hogarth Press, pp. 317–29.

16
NANOTECHNOLOGY

Colin Milburn

Worlds within worlds: this ancient idea found new life during the development of modern atomic theory. Although the notion of an "atom" as the fundamental building block of matter had been postulated since antiquity, dating back at least to the pre-Socratic philosophies of Democritus and Leucippus, it was only in the nineteenth century that the atom ceased to be a purely metaphysical entity and instead acquired physical dimensions and measurable properties. Concretized by a series of key events – including Dalton's atomic theory in 1803, Mendeleev's periodic table of the elements in 1869, the discoveries of the electron in 1897 and the proton in 1909, and various interpretations of atomic structure, such as the planetary models advanced by Rutherford and Bohr – the atom eventually became an everyday scientific object. It also became a discursive topos, a space of the cultural imaginary increasingly used as the setting for fictional narratives. In the early decades of the twentieth century, a wave of stories depicting molecules, atoms, and sub-atomic particles as worlds unto themselves flooded the literary marketplace, making a particular splash in American pulp magazines devoted to the literature of science fiction. Quickly converging on a set of shared narrative conventions and rhetorical techniques, stories such as James Barr's "The World of the Vanishing Point" of 1922, G. Peyton Wertenbaker's "The Man from the Atom" of 1923, John Russell Fearn's "Worlds Within" of 1937, and countless others began to speculate about human expeditions into the depths of matter, thus giving rise to a sub-genre of science fiction known as the "microcosmic romance" (Stableford 2006).

Despite their occasional attempts to explain basic concepts of chemistry and physics, these stories as a whole are concerned less about the technical accuracy of their plot devices – indeed, most of them flagrantly disregard or grossly misrepresent relevant facts of nature – than about the cultural implications and philosophical quandaries pertaining to human exploration of sub-microscopic worlds. They function as allegories of the scientific encounter with infinitesimal scales of matter, rendering in literary form the discovery of atoms and molecules as realms of physical investigation, desire, and technological exploitation. They not only index a technoscientific worldview that takes the atomic scale as newly

open for human occupation and conquest, but yet more proactively, they contribute a set of generic storylines and tropes that facilitate the cognitive mapping
of radically different scales. Consequently, they offer figurative ways of understanding the very, very small world of atoms and molecules as a resource for
practical technologies in our own world. In sharp contrast to the discourse of
atomic energy and nuclear weaponry that began to appear in the same period,
these stories of the microcosm represent not explosion but exploration: building, dwelling, and thinking within the atomic world. In this regard, the literature
of sub-microscopic adventure paved the way, decades in advance, for the technical field that today claims the world of sub-microscopic matter as its own:
namely, nanotechnology.

To be sure, nanotechnology – whose purpose is manipulation and control of
the structure of matter at the scale of nanometers, the size domain of individual
atoms and molecules – has had a long and entangled relationship with science
fiction (Milburn 2008). As the nanoscientist Chad Mirkin explains: "Born of the
science fiction community, nanotechnology unfortunately has far-fetched vestiges of the past (such as discussions of the development of nanorobotics with
artificial intelligence) intimately intertwined with the essence and proposals of
credible and doable science" (Mirkin 2001). The speculative visions guiding a
number of nano research programs, not to mention those motivating international funding initiatives and flows of venture capital, have frequently involved
promises about technological revolutions and utopias that seem so far off in the
future as to appear more fantastic than realistic. Moreover, the fact that many
prominent nanoscientists often discuss far-fetched scenarios as possible achievements for nanotechnology sometimes makes it seem that many of the most
characteristic concepts and aspirations of the field have been ripped from the
pages of pulp fiction.

For example, the famous 1959 lecture by the Nobel laureate Richard
Feynman, "There's Plenty of Room at the Bottom" (1960) – typically considered to
be the first scientific articulation of what would later be called nanotechnology –
envisioned tiny machines built "from the bottom up," molecule by molecule.
But Feynman's particular idea of using an interconnected series of mechanical
"hands" to manipulate the molecules was borrowed from Robert A. Heinlein's
novella *Waldo* of 1942, whose "pantographic" method of matter manipulation
also recalls Edmond Hamilton's earlier microcosmic romance, "The Cosmic
Pantograph" of 1935 (Regis 1995: 152–54; Milburn 2008: 46–49). K. Eric Drexler,
regarded by many as "the father of nanotechnology" because he launched the
first continuous research program to be called nanotechnology (later specified
as "molecular nanotechnology"), while simultaneously popularizing its radical
potential, has likewise relied extensively on science fiction motifs in his
publications. His *Engines of Creation* (1986), which inspired a vast audience about
the world-changing possibilities of molecular machines, overflows with science
fiction stories, alongside insightful commentaries on the relationship between

science fiction and real science. Similarly, Richard Smalley, who received the Nobel Prize for his co-discovery of fullerenes (the first class of molecules to be widely associated with nanotechnology), often referred to the "space elevator" from Arthur C. Clarke's *Fountains of Paradise* of 1979 as something that fullerene nanotechnology might eventually make real (Yakobson and Smalley 1997). Other examples abound.

While some professional scientists were taking inspiration from science fiction in the development of nanotechnology, so too were many science fiction writers running with the ideas of nanotechnology in their books, thus helping to promote and advance the conceptual dimensions of the field. During nano-technology's formative years, novels such as Greg Bear's *Blood Music* of 1985, Kathleen Ann Goonan's *Queen City Jazz* of 1994, Neal Stephenson's *The Diamond Age* of 1995, Wil McCarthy's *Bloom* of 1998, Michael Crichton's *Prey* of 2002, Rudy Rucker's *Postsingular* of 2007, and myriad others contributed to public and professional dialogues about the promises and perils of this new technoscience (Hayles 2004; Thacker 2004).

But at an even more fundamental level, science fiction helped shape the field of nanotechnology by incubating the narrative templates or scripts through which the scientific exploration of nanoscale worlds entered into discourse. Although cresting many decades before Feynman directed our attention to all that "room at the bottom" – that "very, very small world" at the atomic level of matter (Feynman 1960) – the wave of microcosmic adventures in the early decades of the twentieth century buoyed a consistent and now familiar mode of narrating the human encounter with infinitesimal entities inside a sub-microscopic environment. This narrative form and its associated tropes, per-petuated by texts such as Richard Matheson's *The Shrinking Man* of 1956 and the film *Fantastic Voyage* of 1966, would later be widely adopted by the scientific discourse of nanotechnology – particularly in the rhetorical construction of its custodial size regime: the generic space of nanotechnological investigation commonly known as the "nanoworld."

Borrowing freely from the venerable traditions of the utopian romance and the extraordinary voyage, and in particular cribbing from the storytelling models of scalar and dimensional comparison made famous in Jonathan Swift's *Gulliver's Travels* of 1726, Lewis Carroll's *Alice's Adventures in Wonderland* of 1865, and Edwin Abbott's *Flatland* of 1884, the early tales of microcosmic romance clus-tered around a literary novum – or fictional innovation – that would prove the condition of possibility for imagining a real nanotechnology: that human beings would one day not only visually observe the fundamental building blocks of matter, but would actually travel down to that scale, navigate the atomic landscape, and rebuild the world from the bottom up. Although some stories decorated this novum with references to contemporary notions of atomic structure – especially the "miniature solar system" image – the key conceit would remain the physical voyage through scale as such, not the fabulated detail of any scientific theory or technological vehiculation through which the voyage might take place.

Indeed, while stories like James Blish's "Nor Iron Bars" of 1959 might rely on a serious emplotment of quantum mechanics and relativity to depict sub-atomic travel, others, like Mark Twain's "The Great Dark" of 1898, simply gesture to the power of dreams to suggest how people might journey below the threshold of visibility. The narrative template of the microcosmic romance most proto-typically involves the discovery of the sub-microscopic realm as a potential place for human visitation, triggering a subsequent pattern of romantic desire and territorial colonization. This formal structure for relating the human adventure in the infinitesimal world crystallized in the revisionary transition between two foundational texts: Fitz-James O'Brian's "The Diamond Lens" and Ray Cummings's "The Girl in the Golden Atom."

Published in 1858, "The Diamond Lens" would seem to be the inaugural scientific romance to depict the discovery of small worlds inside the atomic spaces of our own world. A brief controversy about the story's originality arose at the time of publication, however, due to a journalistic rumor that O'Brian may have lifted from an unpublished manuscript by William C. North entitled "Microcosmos." Regardless, O'Brian repeatedly asserted the absolute originality of his idea (O'Brian 1858). "The Diamond Lens" features a scientist who constructs a powerful diamond microscope that enables him to peer into the sunken universe, to "pierce through all the envelopes of matter down to its original atom" (O'Brian 1885: 9). He looks into a drop of dew and discovers a beautiful maiden down there, inside the strange atomic landscape. The scientist dubs her "Animula" and promptly falls in love, but from a distance: "The planet Neptune was not more distant from me than she" (28). He becomes frustrated with the "solitary pleasures" (5) of the voyeur: he can see her but never touch her, separated from her world by an irresolvable barrier of scale. And as her little dewdrop begins to dry up under the light of his microscope, the scientist can do nothing but watch in horror as she shrivels and dies before his eyes.

The story is about the impossibility of connecting: literally, the impossibility of connecting the macroscale world to the nanoscale world – although more metaphorically, perhaps, the impossibility for lovers to ever truly connect with each other. It attends to the imaginary limitations produced by what the film theorist Christian Metz describes as spectatorial "senses at a distance" – vision and hearing – which may create longing and desire, but, as registers of distance, can only ever incite dissatisfaction and unrequited love (Metz 1982: 59). In O'Brian's story, the advances of science have managed to surpass the Rayleigh limit of visual resolution (the inherent limitation of microscopes that rely on the wavelengths of visible light, which cannot resolve atomic structures), thereby opening a "window" onto the atomic world. But such technical virtuosity means nothing but "gazing on this lovely wonder" (28) across an insurmountable wall: "No invention of which human intellect was capable could break down the barriers that nature had erected" (30). In "The Diamond Lens," the hope for human access to the nanoworld abruptly comes to a dead end.

But half a century later, in 1919 when Ray Cummings wrote "The Girl in the Golden Atom," the impossible no longer seemed quite so impossible. With considerably less anxiety about originality, Cummings begins with the identical premise – a scientist builds an ultramicroscope to peer into the depths of matter, sees a tiny girl inside the golden atoms of his mother's wedding ring, and falls in love – but then takes the story in a startlingly new direction. Dismissing any natural limitations of physics and biology, Cummings's heroic scientist ("the Chemist") conjures a chemical method of shrinking his body, and he goes on a romp down inside the microcosm. As the personal assistant of Thomas Edison, Cummings shared the view that the capabilities of science were limitless, that technical ingenuity could eventually overcome any obstacle – including "physical law" itself (a view instantiated in the genre of heroic inventor stories inspired by Edison, known today as the Edisonade).

Cummings's microcosmic Edisonade therefore satisfies, by fiat, the impossible desire to enter the atomic world and discover there an entirely new life and a new future (in the sequel of 1920, "The People of the Golden Atom," the Chemist's buddies descend into the atomic world and join the adventure. Both stories were combined as a book in 1922). "The Girl in the Golden Atom" does not offer a blueprint for how scientists might actually make good on this vision – it's clearly a romance, a purely fantastical notion – but the basic point is that, as far as the literary imagination is concerned, *atoms are no longer untouchable*. Physical reduction of the sensory dimensions of the human body puts the scientific spectator directly in contact with the nanoworld. What began as a window now becomes a door: "The only solution … was to find some way of making myself sufficiently small to be able to enter that other universe" (Cummings 1922: 10).

The human enters the microcosm. This conceit likewise underwrites the scientific discourse of nanotechnology. Although technical investigation of the nanoworld began with visualization across distance – as the biochemist and science writer Michael Gross explains, "Windows onto the nanoworld have been opened since the middle of [the twentieth] century by techniques such as electron microscopy, X-ray crystallography, neutron scattering, and nuclear magnetic resonance" (Gross 1999: 20) – the goal of *manipulating* individual atoms with precision demands the capability of discretely *touching* them: in other words, a shift from voyeurism to carnal knowledge. If this shift first appeared in literature with Cummings's rewriting of O'Brian, it later appeared in rhetoric surrounding the first scientific instrument to enable both nanoscale resolution and atomic manipulation: the scanning tunneling microscope (STM).

The STM became a foundational tool for nanotechnology because it operates through physical proximity to the nanoworld, rather than spectatorial distance. The STM images the atomic landscape by scanning a fine probe across a conducting sample, keeping the tip close enough to the atomic surface to register a quantum tunneling current (where electrons from the sample spontaneously "tunnel" into the atoms of the probe tip), and measuring surface topography through changes in the current. Thus, the STM "sees" atoms by touching them, and it can grasp them and move them around in the same way.

Scientists who work with the STM often portray it as a means of shrinking the body and the senses to the scale of atoms: "The STM-tip can be considered the 'eyes,' 'hands,' and 'ears' of scientists connecting our macroscopic world to the exciting atomic and nanoscopic world" (Hla 2008: 6065). From its earliest days, the STM has been figured as a tiny human agent in this exciting new world. Gerd Binning and Heinrich Rohrer, who invented the STM in 1981 and received the Nobel Prize for their accomplishment in 1986, have graphically conceptualized the STM as a human body reduced to minute proportions, with a little "finger" outstretched to caress the denizens of the nanoworld (Binnig and Rohrer 1999: S324). Thus modern science enters the nanoworld. For thanks to the STM and related instruments, as the scientists Christoph Gerber and Hans Peter Lang have said, "the door to the nanoworld was pushed wide open" (Gerber and Lang 2006: 4). Passing through this gaping door, scientific adventurers can now trace the steps of Cummings's Chemist and inhabit a new world. As the chemist John I. Brauman has put it: "There is, indeed, room at the bottom, and we are beginning to move in" (Brauman 1991: 1277).

Nanotechnology would here seem to follow "The Girl in the Golden Atom" in gratifying that forbidden desire registered by "The Diamond Lens": "What would I not have given to have had the power to precipitate myself into that luminous [atomic] ocean and float with her [Animula] through those grooves of purple and gold!" (29). Once upon a time, nanoscale entities were the objects of unrequited longing; as the biochemist Arthur Kornberg attests in his 1989 memoir, *For the Love of Enzymes: The Odyssey of a Biochemist*, the voyage launched by the early molecular sciences was driven by such an impossible love affair. But with the new instruments of nanotechnology, suddenly the virginal maidens of the nanoworld can be touched, and embraced. As Binnig and Rohrer have written, "atoms, molecules, and other nanometer-sized objects are no longer 'untouchables.' They forsook their anonymity as indistinguishable members of a statistical ensemble and became individuals. We have established a casual relationship with them" (Binnig and Rohrer 1999: S327). Don Eigler, one of the first scientists to successfully manipulate individual atoms with an STM, has emphasized the erotic nature of this relationship: "We knew them [nanoscale entities] in a purely cerebral way. But here they are, alive to our eyes and responsive to our hands ... [They] evoke a delectable intimacy between us and the quantum world" (Eigler quoted in Frankel 2005: 261).

But having attained such intimacy, the scientific adventure in the microcosm quickly turns to thoughts of conquest. Reflecting the frontier ideology of the pulp Western and the space opera, the microcosmic romance typically depicts the atomic universe as a savage new world, open for mastery and colonization – and thereby inheriting all the noxious patterns of racism and jingoism that have characterized the history of colonial expansion into various terrestrial frontiers. For example, in S.P. Meek's "Submicroscopic" (1931), the cowboy scientist Courtney Edwards discovers a technique for "adjusting" the dimensions of normal matter (taking advantage of Rutherford's demonstration that atoms are mostly empty space, considering relative distance between the nucleus and electrons). He shrinks himself down to the sub-microscopic world of Ulm (for purposes of big game hunting!) and discovers a racially divided battlezone, where cannibalistic "blacks" are in perpetual conflict with civilized "whites," and where the landscape, as Edwards tells is, resembles the American frontier: "Dotted about on the plain were small stone structures, which reminded me of the old blockhouses which used to be erected on our own plains to guard against Indian raids. That, in fact, was the exact function of these structures" (Meek 1931: 81). Thanks to his trusty firearm (he imports a Colt .45 into the microcosm, demonstrating once again how the West was won) and his power of matter adjustment, Edwards rescues a white girl from the "savages" (she turns out to be Princess Awlo), instantly falls in love with her, and decides to join her people. Marrying the princess and becoming Crown Prince of the whites, Edwards plans to pacify this wild world once and for all by importing an arsenal of guns and other technologies from his home country, thus replaying a familiar history of Western imperialism staged in the form of scientific discovery (Albanese 1996; Campbell 1999; Otis 1999).

But Edwards soon learns that this world "at the limit of smallness" (78) is not simply a space of savagery and backwardness, but also a land of high-tech science and futuristic inventions made possible by the strange physics of the sub-microscopic world. In the sequel "Awlo of Ulm" (1931), another local civilization of cruel, "saffron yellow" technocrats tries to take over Ulm (echoing other racist "Yellow Peril" fictions of the period). The yellow people have invented any number of miraculous technologies, including powerful machinic battlesuits and remote energy projection systems. Edwards goes to war against them, turning their own technologies to his advantage. Curiously, all races of this world speak "some dialect of Hawaiian" (75) – a plot element that makes little realistic sense, but nonetheless pre-emptively marks the indigenous peoples of the microcosm as subjects of U.S. expansionism.

To be sure, the world of Ulm is suddenly destroyed before the end of the story by a careless *deus ex machina* "prospector," who unrepentantly smashes it while digging for gold on the Nevada frontier: "I reckon a man can prospect where he pleases" (152). Luckily, Edwards manages to return to his proper size beforehand, bringing back a wealth of new knowledge, along with Princess Awlo, whom he claims in the name of the United States: "You have ceased to be Awlo, Sibimi of Ulm, and will henceforth have to content yourself with being Mrs. Courtney Edwards, citizen of the United States of America" (153). Similar figurations of the nanoworld as a crucible of indigenous knowledge and technology which might be "imported" into our world or otherwise put to advantage feature in many stories from this period, including R.F. Starzl's "Out of the Sub-Universe" of 1928, Festus Pragnell's "The Green Man of Graypec" of 1935, and Theodore Sturgeon's "Microcosmic God" of 1941.

In the scientific discourse of nanotechnology, as well, the nanoworld regularly appears as a wild frontier, ready to plunder. Gregory Timp has suggested that he and other nanoscientists are "explorers of a new frontier; a frontier that exists on the head of a pin. ... [We] are motivated by curiosity, and the promise of intellectual and monetary rewards ... to map the *terra incognita* of a microscopic world" (Timp 1999: 2). This mythic notion has similarly manifested in the "quantum corral" experiments of Don Eigler and his colleagues, who employed an STM to fabricate atomic rings for "capturing" electrons (Crommie, Lutz, and Eigler 1993). Aiming for "complete control of the atomic landscape" (IBM Almaden Visualization Lab 1995), these pioneering experiments evoke Wild West associations of corrals as both livestock enclosures and temporary forts. At the same time, other nanotechnology theorists have described the nanoworld as a land of bounty ... and booty. According to Michael Gross, the "technologies that will result from the conquest of the nanoworld may revolutionize not only the world of science but also daily life as well" (Gross 1999: 21). The scientists Dominique Luzeaux and Thierry Puig affirm this point: the goal of nanotechnology is nothing less than "the conquest of the nanoworld" (Luzeaux and Puig 2007).

Although its swashbuckling tendencies set the stage for such rhetorical acts of nanoworld invasion, the genre of microcosmic romance also generated cautionary narratives and forms of self-reflexive critique. For example, by the end of Harl Vincent's "Microcosmic Buccaneers" of 1929, it is rather ambiguous who the real pirates are: the technocratic slaveholders who rule the atomic world, or the human scientists who travel down to that world, fomenting genocide and abducting maidens. Equally critical of technocratic ideology, Henry Hasse's "He Who Shrank" of 1936 animates the possibility that our increasing mastery of matter might inadvertently put our own world at risk. Against his will, a young science student is forcibly sent by his professor on a downward journey through scales, descending ever deeper into the structure of matter. As he shrinks, he passes through worlds within worlds at various stages of technological complexity: the exploration of minute scales of matter becomes a travelogue of possible civilizations, possible futures. He describes a telepathic Enlightenment society; a Stone Age society; a postbiological society of Pure Intelligences; and, at the center of the text, a space-age society of astounding technological accomplishment: "A civilization that had achieved space travel must be a marvelous civilization indeed" (Hasse 1936: 758). But upon investigation, it turns out to be a post-apocalyptic world where autonomous technology has gone out of control:

> The thing that terrified me was that these machines were scurrying about the surface all in apparent confusion, seemed to cover the entire globe,

seemed to have a complete civilization of their own, and nowhere was there the slightest evidence of any human occupancy, no controlling force, no intelligence, nothing save the machines. ... Other machines builded [sic] and assembled and adjusted intricate parts, and when the long process was completed the result was – more machines! ... A city, a continent, a world, a civilization of machines!

(Hasse 1936: 760–63)

With this discovery of a civilization deep inside the atom destroyed by its own invention of self-replicating machinery – "They had gone forward blindly and recklessly to achieve [Utopia], and unknowingly they had gone too far" (766) – "He Who Shrank" also anticipates one of the most notorious scenarios associated with nanotechnology: namely, that our rush towards the molecular future might accidentally unleash self-replicating machinery that could consume the biosphere and turn everything into a sludge of tiny robots. Known as the "gray goo problem," this scenario was introduced in Drexler's *Engines of Creation*:

[Nano-replicators] could spread like blowing pollen, replicate swiftly, and reduce the biosphere to dust in a matter of days. Dangerous repli-cators could easily be too tough, small, and rapidly spreading to stop – at least if we make no preparation. ...

Among the cognoscenti of nanotechnology, this threat has become known as the "gray goo problem." Though masses of uncontrolled replicators need not be gray or gooey, the term "gray goo" emphasizes that replicators able to obliterate life might be less inspiring than a single species of crabgrass. They might be superior in an evolutionary sense, but this need not make them valuable.

The gray goo threat makes one thing perfectly clear: We cannot afford certain kinds of accidents with replicating assemblers.

(Drexler 1986: 172–73)

Although Drexler's vision of gray goo is a specific consequence of speculating about the limits of advanced nanotechnology (a vision he today disavows), the idea that self-replicating entities from the nanoworld might possibly take over the human world had already evolved as a recognizable trope in the early literature of microcosmic romance. For example, Lloyd Arthur Eshbach's "The Voice from the Ether" of 1931 describes self-replicating vegetative slimes imported from the surface of a proton that eventually devour the entire planet of Mars. So too in John W. Campbell's "Dead Knowledge" of 1938, self-replicating protein machines spread from world to world by hijacking human bodies. In Jack Williamson's "Pygmy Planet" of 1932, evolving machine-monsters from the molecular world invade our world – and the final solution is to smash their tiny planet, thus violently relinquishing our claims on the microcosm. These and other pulp fictions of the period sought to project possible dangers of our human encounter with the nanoworld, even while imagining our headlong foray across its borders.

The many stories that constituted the genre of microcosmic romance in the early twentieth century thus contain in themselves the narrative forms and the characteristic tropes later rehearsed and revised by the professional discourse of nanotechnology. "He Who Shrank" even recursively depicts the formal relationship of science fiction to the scientific narration of nanoworld exploration. For as the scientist narrator continues his journey into smallness, he eventually stops over on a tiny blue planet: our own Earth. Here, he telepathically narrates his history to a "renowned author of … scores of short stories and books of the widely popular type of literature known as science-fiction" (781) – a wry figuration of Hasse's own authorship. This author frantically transcribes the whole thing down on paper "in words of his own language" (780) – the language of science fiction – as the traveler continues to shrink. The traveler eventually vanishes into the pile of manuscript pages on which his narrative has been written. In other words, the text of "He Who Shrank" pretends to physically contain – to envelop within its own literary atoms – the scientific explorer of atomic worlds himself.

"He Who Shrank" therefore seems to allegorize the extent to which "the widely popular type of literature known as science-fiction" had already begun to script and envelop the language that scientific explorers of the microcosm would use to describe their research, their technologies, and their dreams. Indeed, many features of the microcosmic romance have since carried over into didactic science texts, such as Mr. Tompkins Explores the Atom of 1945 by the physicist George Gamow, and the multimedia Nano Kids of 2006 by the chemist James M. Tour, as well as the broader discourse networks of nanoscience. In this way, the early tales of microcosmic adventure opened real windows to the nanoworld – and real doorways to the nanotechnology future.

Bibliography

Albanese, D. (1996) New Science, New World, Durham, N.C.: Duke University Press.
Binnig, G. and Rohrer, H. (1999) "In touch with atoms," Reviews of Modern Physics, 71: S324–S330.
Brauman, J.I. (1991) "Room at the bottom," Science, 254: 1277.
Campbell, M.B. (1999) Wonder and Science: imagining worlds in early modern Europe, Ithaca, N.Y.: Cornell University Press.
Crommie, M.F., Lutz, C.P. and Eigler, D.M. (1993) "Confinement of electrons to quantum corrals on a metal surface," Science, 262: 218–20.
Cummings, R. (1922) The Girl in the Golden Atom, Lincoln: Bison Books, 2005.
Drexler, E.K. (1986) Engines of Creation, Garden City: Anchor Doubleday.

Feynman, R. (1960) "There's plenty of room at the bottom," *Engineering and Science*, 23: 22–36.

Frankel, F. (2005) "Capturing quantum corrals," *American Scientist*, 93: 261.

Gerber, C. and Lang, H.P. (2006) "How the doors to the nanoworld were opened," *Nature Nanotechnology*, 1: 3–5.

Gross, M. (1999) *Travels to the Nanoworld: miniature machinery in nature and technology*, New York: Plenum.

Hasse, H. (1936) "He who shrank," in I. Asimov (ed.) *Before the Golden Age*, Garden City: Doubleday, 1974, pp. 730–86.

Hayles, N.K. (ed.) (2004) *Nanoculture: implications of the new technoscience*, Bristol: Intellect.

Hla, S.-W. (2008) "Scanning tunneling microscope atom and molecule manipulations," *Japanese Journal of Applied Physics*, 47: 6063–69.

IBM Almaden Visualization Lab (1995) "The Corral Reef," STM Image Gallery. Online. Available HTTP: <http://www.almaden.ibm.com/vis/stm/corral.html> (accessed 18 July 2009).

Luzeaux, D. and Puig, T. (2007) *À la Conquête du nanomonde: nanotechnologies et microsystèmes*, Paris: Éditions de Félin.

Meek, S.P. (1931) "'Submicroscopic' and 'Awlo of Ulm,'" in I. Asimov (ed.) *Before the Golden Age*, Garden City: Doubleday, 1974, pp. 63–153.

Metz, C. (1982) *The Imaginary Signifier: psychoanalysis and the cinema*, Bloomington: Indiana University Press.

Milburn, C. (2008) *Nanovision: engineering the future*, Durham, N.C.: Duke University Press.

Mirkin, C. (2001) "Nanotechnology: fact or fiction," *Chemical and Engineering News*, 79: 185.

O'Brian, F.-J. (1858) "'The Diamond Lens' – a literary controversy," *The New York Times*, 26 Febraury.

——(1885) *The Diamond Lens, with other stories*, New York: Charles Scribner's Sons.

Otis, L. (1999) *Membranes: metaphors of invasion in nineteenth-century literature, science, and politics*, Baltimore: Johns Hopkins University Press.

Regis, E. (1995) *Nano: the emerging science of nanotechnology*, Boston, Mass.: Little, Brown.

Stableford, B. (2006) "Microcosm," in *Science Fact and Science Fiction: an encyclopedia*, London, Routledge.

Thacker, E. (2004) *Biomedia*, Minneapolis: University of Minnesota Press.

Timp, G. (1999) "Nanotechnology," in G. Timp (ed.) *Nanotechnology*, New York: Springer.

Yakobson, B.I. and Smalley, R. (1997) "Fullerene Nanotubes: $C_{1,000,000}$ and beyond," *American Scientist*, 85: 324–37.

17
PHYSICS

Dirk Vanderbeke

I

In Ian McEwan's novel *Enduring Love,* a science journalist muses about the development of science and literature since the nineteenth century:

> It was the nineteenth-century culture of the amateur that nourished the anecdotal scientist. All those gentlemen without careers, those parsons with time to burn. … The dominant artistic form was the novel, great sprawling narratives which not only charted private fates, but made whole societies in mirror image and addressed the public issues of the day. Most educated people read contemporary novels. Storytelling was deep in the nineteenth-century soul.
>
> Then two things happened. Science became more difficult, and it became professionalized. It moved into the universities, parsonical narratives gave way to hard-edged theories that could survive intact without experimental support and which had their own formal aesthetic. At the same time, in literature and in other arts, a newfangled modernism celebrated formal structural qualities, inner coherence and self-reference. A priesthood guarded the temples of this difficult art against the trespasses of the common man.
>
> (McEwan 1998: 49)

The science that, indeed, became increasingly difficult at the beginning of the twentieth century was physics, which had been, with short interruptions, the master science ever since Newton. The eighteenth century saw a multitude of attempts to extend Newton's mechanics into spheres traditionally reserved for metaphysical theories and to describe the human rational and emotional faculties in strictly materialistic terms based on causal relationships. Edmund Burke, for example, tried to establish the "natural and mechanical causes for our passions" (Burke 1990: 126), and David Hartley in his 1749 *Observations on Man* argued that "since the Human Body is composed of the same Matter as the external World, it is reasonable to expect, that its component Particles should be subjected to the same subtle Laws" (quoted in Nuovo 1999: 407).

Despite all the quarrels that have accompanied the discussions between the sciences and literature for the last four centuries, it was Newton's mechanical worldview that informed the bulk of fiction and even a fair share of poetry, even if the sciences were frequently satirized by authors like Swift or Sterne, or assaulted for their impoverished and reductionist perspective on life by poets like Blake or Shelley. When E.M. Forster defined the difference between story and plot, he made the distinction between "the naked worm of time" (Forster 1988: 42) and "a narrative of events, the emphasis falling on causality. 'The king died and then the queen died' is a story. 'The king died and then the queen died of grief' is a plot" (Forster 1988: 87). In this respect, almost all literature until the present day is firmly grounded in a mechanistic worldview, as that is the physics which may give narrative meaning to our experience. In addition, the scientific innovations of the early twentieth century that not only revolutionized physics but also questioned our perceptions and understanding of reality are of little relevance for the world of human experience.

The theory of relativity is chiefly concerned with the physics of enormous scales, with astronomical phenomena, vast distances, huge masses and movements that approach the speed of light, none of which are likely to have any significant impact on human experience as it is explored in literary works. Quantum mechanics, on the other hand, describes phenomena on the sub-atomic level that are equally removed from the sphere of human experience, even if thought experiments, the most famous of which is "Schrödinger's Cat" (for a fascinating literary exploration, see Bear 1993), discuss the possibility of a transfer to the macroscopic level, and some of the most bewildering phenomena, such as quantum entanglement, are employed for new computer technologies. Nevertheless, when George Gamov published *Mr. Tompkins in Wonderland* (1940), dream stories that present the reader with a world in which the phenomena of relativity and quantum physics appear on the level of human experience, this just gave a literary demonstration of the incompatibility of recent physical theories with our common-sense notions of physical reality.

This suggests that twentieth-century concepts of physics and modernist or postmodernist literature are worlds apart, but nonetheless, some analogies could possibly be found. Jeremy Gray defines modernism in mathematics

> as an autonomous body of ideas, having little or no outward reference, placing considerable emphasis on formal aspects of the work and maintaining a complicated – indeed, anxious – rather than a naive relationship with the day-to-day world, which is the de facto view of a coherent group of people, such as a professional or discipline-based group who have a high sense of the seriousness and value of what they are trying to achieve.
> (Gray forthcoming: 1)

A lack of "outward reference" can hardly be a suitable criterion for any research in physics, but in the early twentieth century a change towards increasingly theoretical physics could be felt, in which the experiment confirms rather than suggests new theories. After all, it took over a decade to provide the proof for Einstein's theory of relativity, and what led physicists to accept the new theory almost immediately was not only its plausibility but also its aesthetic quality, frequently described as its "beauty" (Weinberg 1993: 82; I will return to this point in my final section). However, in contrast to pure mathematics, physics can never forgo the ultimate proof, and the "reception of general relativity depended neither on experimental data alone nor on the intrinsic qualities of the theory alone but on a tangled web of theory and experiment" (Weinberg, ibid.).

This complex interplay of theoretical prediction and experimental confirmation is even more significant in the case of quantum theory. If the theory of relativity was soon accepted and Einstein embraced as "a cult figure, standing all at once ... as individual genius, pre-war pacifist, post-war conciliator and moral example" (Galison 2002: 86), quantum theory failed to enthuse the scientific community or to reach the lay audience for a considerable time. The counterintuitive character of its theories and the bewildering implications of the experimental data are part and parcel of every introduction to quantum physics. Some aphoristic remarks by the masters of modern physics have gained an almost proverbial status: Einstein's "God does not play dice" and Stephen Hawking's reply, "God not only plays dice but also sometimes throws them where they cannot be seen" (Hawking 1977: 40), Niels Bohr's "Anyone who is not shocked by quantum theory has not understood it" and his response to a fellow scientist, "Your theory is crazy, but not crazy enough to be true," are indicative not only of the strange qualties of the quantum world but also of how hard it is to express this unfamiliar reality in a familiar language. In the late twentieth century, New Age philosophers tried to merge quantum physics with various concepts of Eastern philosophy and mysticism (Capra 1977; Zukav 1979), and the aphorisms of the "scientific gurus" indeed have a koan-like feeling, but it is certainly fallacious to take two highly complex theoretical frameworks which both admit to serious problems of linguistic representation and then conclude that the referent must necessarily be similar (Vanderbeke 1995: 12–14).

Nevertheless, it may still be possible to draw some analogies between aspects of quantum physics and developments in the arts and literature. Foremost of these is the acceptance of an epistemological barrier, an irreducible impediment to any easy access to external reality. Quantum physics has taught us that – until further scientific notice – we can only describe sub-atomic nature as nature-under-observation, and the response of nature to our experiments will necessarily be determined by the observational set-up of the experiment. As the probability wave of the quantum object only collapses in consequence of the experiment and its observation, unobserved nature remains inescapably unknowable.

In ways that are both similar and different, modern literature has turned from the depiction of reality to the exploration of reality as experienced by the observing mind. Virginia Woolf's rejection of the Edwardian literary tools (Woolf 1980: 332) and Marcel Proust's scorn for a "cinematographic vision" in literature (Proust 2009: 150) may have sprung from the realization that the new media of photography and film were better equipped for the accurate representation of external reality (Lyotard 1984: 74), but the turn towards the "reality we perceive within ourselves" (Proust ibid.) went hand in hand with new forms of writing which no longer took the original building blocks of language for granted: "Signs of this are everywhere apparent. Grammar is violated, syntax disintegrated" (Woolf 1980: 334). And if physicists responded with some despair to their new findings and the persistent failures to integrate them within the classical paradigms, so did some of the modernist authors (Woolf 1980: 334), facing the new challenges with desperate sincerity and tremendous courage.

In addition, some similarities between the latest concepts in physics and some literary phenomena were suggested by William Empson in *Seven Types of Ambiguity*: "Here as in recent atomic physics there is a shift in progress, which tends to attach the notion of a probability to the natural object rather than to the fallibility of the human mind" (Empson 1961: 94). Empson here recognizes an analogy between two kinds of uncertainty in the object rather than in the mind of the observer, but then, Empson was in a particularly good position to realize this similarity, as he studied mathematics as well as English at Cambridge University and showed some interest in the latest developments in physics (Bate 1997). Quite similarly, Wayne Booth suggested in *The Rhetoric of Fiction*:

> Now that the scientists have given up the claim that they are seeking one single formulation of a firmly constituted reality, unaffected by the limitations and interests of the observer, perhaps we (in literature) should once again pack up our bags and follow after.
>
> (Booth 1961: 112)

This is not an argument for following science unconditionally but rather for the correction of the previous mistake of doing so. There have always been attempts to adapt methods and restrictions from the sciences to the field of literary criticism, but now it is time, Booth argued, to reclaim our own premises and paths to knowledge, if even the principles of Newtonian physics, of a single unified theory and an independent neutral observation have to be dismissed. According to this line of thought, scientists have, on a different route, learned to acknowledge some of the principles they traditionally scorned and relegated to the domain of literary scholarship.

This argument for the dependence of the experimental result on the position of its observer has frequently been taken up and expanded beyond its original scope by literary scholars, to show that their own field of inquiry anticipated scientific discoveries and theories. This has, however, to be taken with more than a pinch of salt, and scientists were rightfully annoyed when literary scholars presented the multiple focalizers of a narrative text as equivalent to the relativity of time and space, uncertainty in a character as an analogy of Heisenberg's principle of indeterminacy, or the attractiveness of a femme fatale as an anticipation of a strange attractor. There is a temptation to assume that a similar terminology indicates a common concept or approach, an assumption strengthened by the practice of popular science books to embellish theoretical explanations with epigrams from literary texts that sound vaguely similar. But the terminology of physics is frequently the result of the necessity to give some name to a principle not yet fully understood when it is first encountered, and so the term may sooner or later become an impediment rather than an aid to understanding. When physicists first used the word *spin* for the property of sub-atomic particles, the planetary model of the atom was still under discussion; by now the word may evoke erroneous associations and assumptions unless we realize that the classical concepts of rotation do not fully apply, if only because some particles have to complete a 180° rotation, some 360° and some 720° to return to their original state. Similarly, the term *chaos theory* does not indicate that mythical and literary evocations of chaos from Hesiod, Shakespeare, or Milton can be reinterpreted as analogies or even anticipations of non-linear dynamics.

The claim for anticipation, moreover, becomes problematic when a literary text is burdened by several scientific theories it supposedly anticipated. Beckett's work has been read in the context of quantum physics, chaos theory, and black holes, Borges's stories as anticipations of bifurcation theory, field models, and quantum phenomena, and every theory can be found somewhere in *Finnegans Wake*. All these readings are interesting, but if we really suggest that the authors have anticipated each and every development in recent physics, we may not be doing them a favor (see Vanderbeke 2004: 175–243).

II

One of the persistent points of contention in the discussion of science and literature is the question of influence. Possibly fueled by the anxiety of being relegated to the second rank, literary scholars have frequently insisted on a balance, arguing that science takes place in a complex web of cultural interdependencies to which literature contributes, and thus the traffic of influences must be regarded as going in both directions. Few scientists would reject the notion that they work in a social and political environment and within historically contingent conceptual frameworks that have an impact on theory formation and the direction their research can take. However, this does not indicate that science and literature influence each other to an equal degree. Many literary scholars have insisted that such a balance must exist, among them Katherine Hayles:

> The premise that influence flows from science to literature implicitly valorizes science as the source of truth to which literature responds. Such an approach ignores the ways in which scientific theories, no less than literary theories and literature, are social constructions that reflect the prevailing concerns of culture.
>
> (Hayles 1989: 317)

With due respect to a scholar of renown, it needs to be pointed out that while scientists strive for independence from external influences, authors actively seek input from all possible sources, and both would fail miserably if there was a balance of influences. Literature responds to developments in art, music, philosophy, the movies, esotericism, and even pornography, yet none of these is automatically elevated to a "source of truth." Literature is not an empty vessel into which external truth can be poured but rather a predator, searching for suitable matter which it can transform for its own purposes, frequently almost beyond recognition. This is particularly true for literature's relation to the complex and non-intuitive findings of modern physics, which have been of considerable interest to a host of authors, among them Thomas Pynchon, Jeanette Winterson, Margaret Atwood, Ian McEwan, and John Updike. All of these have acknowledged the influence of physical theories on their work, yet none of them seems to have raised these concepts to any level of higher truth, but rather reworked them into their own creative visions.

The very complexity and strangeness of contemporary physics, however, places it outside the sphere of common knowledge, and while the educated population of the nineteenth century was probably fairly well informed about significant scientific theories of its time, this no longer holds true. Moreover, as neither relativity nor quantum physics is concerned with the physics of human experience, the appropriation of their concepts for narrative purposes poses some problems. In consequence, the introduction of physics into modern and postmodern texts either requires elaborate explanations by the narrator or one of the characters, or else presents the reader with phenomena that are inexplicable and rather seem to bring the text into the realm of fantastic literature. In *Gravity's Rainbow*, the protagonist Tyrone Slothrop is mysteriously entangled with the V2 rocket and, as both he and the rocket are linked to the inventor of the strange material Imipolex G, the most radical implication of non-locality and quantum entanglement – everything that has ever been connected within a quantum system remains so – could account for the otherwise inexplicable interaction. Without any further explanation, however, the allusion to quantum entanglement, if it is one, remains obscure and requires some knowledge and creative association on the part of the reader.

Similarly, in Umberto Eco's *The Island of the Day Before*, a novel set in the seventeenth century, various future scientific discoveries are "anticipated" and need to be noticed by the reader, among them the law of gravity (Eco 1996: 363), aspects of relativity (66, 433–34), forces that act by the exchange of particles (167), the "many worlds" theory (66, 267), the creation of the universe by energy and a giant explosion akin to the Big Bang (256), fractals and self-similarity (423–24), and also possibly quantum entanglement. This, however, is hidden in a magical practice, the use of an *unguentum armarium* or weapon salve to create an instant link between a wounded dog on a ship in the Pacific Ocean and the weapon that cut the wound in England in the attempt to synchronize the time and thus to determine the degrees of longitude. Once more, the reader, hopefully alerted by the other allusions to science, has to notice the similarity between the magical practice and the quantum phenomenon, or else it will go unnoticed.

The alternative way to invoke physics is direct explication, and many recent texts are indebted to popular science books, foremost of all Stephen Hawking's *A Short History of Time* and James Gleick's *Chaos*. Once a basic understanding has been achieved, the text can then proceed to discuss the implications, an approach often used in didactic novels or "science plays" such as Peter Parnell's *QED* to draw connections to other fields of knowledge as, for example, some form of mysticism (Jeanette Winterson's *Gut Symmetries*), to criticize a science that has lost its relevance for human life (Peter Ackroyd's *First Light*), to come to terms with the weirdness of the scientific worldview (Tom Stoppard's *Hapgood*), to challenge facile understandings of reality or religious perspectives on science (John Updike's *Roger's Version*), or to discuss the ethics of science (Friedrich Dürrenmatt's *The Physicists*) and discrimination against female scientists (Robert Marc Friedman's *Remembering Miss Meitner*).

A particularly interesting approach has been explored by Tom Stoppard, who in his play *Hapgood* not only treats his audience to a fair dose of scientific explanation but also tries to transfer the phenomena to the world of espionage with its double agents and uncertainties. The epigram to the play is Richard Feynman's description of the double slit experiment as "a phenomenon which is impossible, *absolutely* impossible, to explain in any classical way, and which has in it the heart of quantum mechanics. In reality, it contains the *only* mystery" (Feynman 1996: 117, italics in the original). In the course of the play, then, a double agent, a physicist named Kerner, is asked which side he actually belongs to:

KERNER: Oh, you think there's a what's what? Your joe. Their sleeper. Paul, what's what is for zoologists: "Oh, yes – definitely a giraffe." But a double agent is not a what's what like a giraffe, a double agent is more like a trick of the light.

BLAIR: Joseph—

KERNER: … Look at the edge of the shadow. It is straight like the edge of the wall that makes it. This means light is particles: little bullets. Bullets go straight. They cannot go round the wall and hit you. If light was *waves* it would bend round the wall a little, like water bends round a stone in the river.

BLAIR: (*Irritated*) Yes. Absolutely.

KERNER: So that's what. When you shine light through a gap in the wall it's particles. Unfortunately, when you shine the light through *two* little gaps, side by side, you don't get a particle pattern like for bullets, you get a wave pattern like for water. The beams of light mix together and—

BLAIR: Joseph, I want to know if you're ours or theirs, that's all.

KERNER: I'm telling you but you're not listening.

(Stoppard 1994: 9)

Empson's suggestion that ambivalence in literature may share some properties with quantum phenomena is here exemplified, and the dialogue simulates the double slit experiment. The message contains two possible meanings simultaneously, it travels, so to speak, on two distinct paths, and only the question at the end reduces the ambivalence and retroactively states which path of signification has been chosen from the very beginning.

Similarly, in Martin Amis's novel *London Fields*, the statement early in the text that the future victim of a murder has found her killer seems straightforward, and the culprit is quite obvious. It is only on the last pages that the reader has to realize that two more possible murderers were present, among them the narrator himself, and that every seemingly unequivocal statement about the assumed killer also applied to the other possible candidates. Once more, ambivalence produces a situation in which a plurality of equally valid possibilities is finally reduced to one, and each previous statement about the future murder has now to be re-attributed. Of course, not every ambivalence indicates the presence of quantum theory as a conceptual background, but in texts that frequently address contemporary physics – which *London Fields* does – the analogy appears to be more than just coincidental.

III

The most difficult question facing the relation between literature and physics concerns possible interdisciplinary cooperation and common tools for research. The final decades of the twentieth century saw a succession of suggestions from the humanities and literary studies that science, and particularly physics, could not only be investigated in the light of rhetoric and narratology, but could be reduced to linguistic or literary phenomena. Alan Gross, for example, proposed that "there is no line that can be successfully drawn between rhetoric and scientific knowledge" (Gross 1991: 285), Robert Kelley suggested that "reference in scientific discourse operates in essentially the same way as it does in the discourse of the classical realist text" (Kelley 1993: 137), and David Porush turned this already rather bold claim into a prerogative when he argued that "literary language commands techniques that scientific discourse must adopt if it is going to succeed" (Porush 1992: 302). Such rather simplistic and totalizing intrusions that by implication exclude nature from scientific investigation met with hostile responses from the scientific community, culminating in Alan Sokal's famous hoax, which to some extent cleansed the atmosphere with a heavy dose of well-administered ridicule. It has become quite clear, and should have been long ago, that some prerequisites are indispensable for interdisciplinary research into physics and literature, i.e. an adequate familiarity with the rules of the game in the respective fields of inquiry, a basic acknowledgment of each other's work and achievements, and an unbiased willingness to be informed by the practitioners – and none of these requirements precludes a serious critique of science.

Arguably, the most important aspect linking literature and physics is the imaginative process, the creation of a concept or theory, and, like scientific works, novels, plays, or poems are founded on certain epistemologies and concepts of reality, even though the theories are scrutinized in very different ways. Similarities in the creative processes have been emphasized by scholars, but also by scientists, discussing the problem of invention and the epistemological status of their findings. The physicist John Bell wrote on "Six possible worlds of quantum mechanics":

> To what extent are these possible worlds fictions? They are like literary fictions in that they are free inventions of the human mind. In theoretical physics sometimes the inventor knows from the beginning that the work is fiction, for example when he deals with a simplified world in which space has only one or two dimensions instead of three. More often it is not known till later, when the hypothesis has proved wrong, that fiction is involved. When being serious, when not exploring deliberately simplified models, the theoretical physicist differs from the novelist in thinking that maybe the story may be true.
>
> (Bell 1988: 195)

One topic that may then offer itself to a common approach is aesthetics, i.e. not only the creative process but also the intuitive response to objects, texts, or theories that the observer experiences as beautiful or sublime. The acceptance of theories in physics has frequently been linked to aesthetic properties, such as elegance in their mathematical formulation, and it could well be worthwhile to explore the aesthetic features that contribute to theory selection and to see whether they share aspects with the experience of beauty in poetics or the arts. Emphasizing that literature and poetry are quite distinct from mathematical equations and that beauty is notoriously difficult to define, Stephen Weinberg lists simplicity, inevitability, and symmetry as decisive features of beautiful theories (Weinberg 1993: 105–31); Graham Farmelo writes that "like a great work of art, a beautiful equation has among its attributes much more than mere attractiveness – it will have universality, simplicity, inevitability, and an elemental power" (Farmelo 2003: xiv), and some analogy in our response to the respective objects of literary appeal may possibly be found.

However, the search for such an analogy between beauty in physics and in literature may force us to alter our perspective and to revise some cherished concepts of literary excellence. Since the early twentieth century, literary criticism has increasingly celebrated a recalcitrance of literature, a resistance to reading and understanding, a voluntary failure to represent or to communicate. But while these aspects are, unquestionably, significant features of modern and postmodern literature and literary theory, recent research into the neuropsychological aspects of aesthetics indicates that fluency and smoothness of perception, simplicity in the processing of experience, and also symmetry play a decisive role for aesthetic pleasure (Reber et al. 2004).

Simplicity here, of course, does not indicate any kind of banality, but rather a clarity or lucidity that is fully compatible with the complexity of the phenomena under scrutiny, like a nutshell that enfolds infinite space. And it is not difficult to match this requirement with literary concepts, such as Pound's statement that "great literature is simply language charged with meaning to the utmost possible degree" (Pound 1929: 21), or with a multitude of literary texts that, though simple in their form of expression, have managed to generate not only a never-ending flow of complex new meanings and interpretations but also a persistent delight. Research into the creative process and responses to formal aesthetic qualities, then, may form an important link between these fields of investigation, and while the differences have to be emphasized and respected by scholars and scientists, the common interest in, and fascination with, the diverse ways in which we can approach physical reality may offer paths to research into the old human conviction that beauty is truth, truth beauty.

Bibliography

Bate, J. (1997) "Words in a quantum world: how Cambridge physics led William Empson to refuse 'either/or,'" *The Times Literary Supplement*, 25 July, 14–15.

Bear, G. (1993) "Schrödinger's plague," in U.K. Le Guin and B. Attebery (eds) *The Norton Book of Science Fiction*, New York and London: Norton, pp. 477–84.

Bell, J. (1988) "Six possible worlds of quantum mechanics," in *Speakable and Unspeakable in Quantum Mechanics*, Cambridge: Cambridge University Press, pp. 181–95.

Booth, W. (1961) *The Rhetoric of Fiction*, Chicago: University of Chicago Press.

Burke, E. (1990) *A Philosophical Enquiry into the Origins of our Ideas of the Sublime and the Beautiful*, Oxford: Oxford University Press.

Capra, F. (1977) *The Tao of Physics*, Toronto: Bantam.

Eco, U. (1996) *The Island of the Day Before* (*L'isola del giorno prima*), trans. W. Weaver, London: Minerva.

Empson, W. (1961) *The Seven Types of Ambiguity*, New York: Meridian.

Farmelo, G. (ed.) (2003) *It Must Be Beautiful: great equations of modern science*, London and New York: Granta.

Feynman, R. (1996) *Six Easy Pieces*, Reading, Mass.: Helix.

Forster, E.M. (1988) *Aspects of the Novel*, London: Penguin.

Galison, P. (2002) "The sextant equation," in Farmelo 2003: 68–86.

Gamov, G. (1993) *Mr. Tompkins in Paperback*, Cambridge: Cambridge University Press.

Gray, J. (forthcoming) "Space ships and jungles: mathematics and modernism," in M. Epple and F. Müller (eds) *Science as Cultural Practice, Vol. 2: Modernism in the sciences ca. 1900–1940*, Berlin: Akademie-Verlag.

Gross, A. (1991) "Rhetoric of science without constraints," *Rhetorica*, 9(4): 283–99.

Hawking, Stephen (1977) "The quantum mechanics of black holes," *Scientific American*, January: 34–40.

Hayles, N.K. (1989) "Chaos as orderly disorder: shifting ground in contemporary literature and science," *New Literary History*, 20(2): 305–22.

Kelley, R.T. (1993) "Chaos out of order: the writerly discourse of semipopular scientific texts," in M.W. McRea (ed.) *The Literature of Science: perspectives on popular scientific writing*, Athens: University of Georgia Press, pp. 132–51.

Lyotard, F. (1984) "Answering the question: what is postmodernism?", in *The Postmodern Condition: a report on knowledge*, trans. R. Durand, Minneapolis: University of Minnesota Press, pp. 71–82.

McEwan, I. (1998) *Enduring Love*, London: Vintage.

Nuovo, V.L. (1999) "David Hartley," in J.W. Yolton, J.V. Price and J. Stephens (eds) *The Dictionary of Eighteenth-Century British Philosophers*, vol. 1, Bristol: Thoemmes Press, pp. 405–11.

Porush, D. (1992) "Literature as dissipative structure: Prigogine's theory and the postmodern 'chaos' machine," in M.L. Greenberg and L. Schachterle (eds) *Literature and Technology*, London: Associated University Press, pp. 275–306.

Pound, E. (1929) "How to read," in *Literary Essays of Ezra Pound*, New York: New Directions, 1968, pp. 15–40.

Proust, M. (2009) *Time Regained*, trans. S. Hudson. Online. Available HTTP: <http://www.feedbooks.com/book/1453> (accessed 7 May 2009).

Reber, R., Schwarz, N. and Winkielman, P. (2004) "Processing fluency and aesthetic pleasure: is beauty in the perceiver's processing experience?," *Personality and Social Psychology Review*, 8(4): 364–82.

Stoppard, T. (1994) *Hapgood*, London: Faber and Faber.

Vanderbeke, D. (1995) *Worüber man nicht sprechen kann. Aspekte der Undarstellbarkeit in Philosophie, Naturwissenschaft und Literatur*, Stuttgart: M&P Verlag für wissenschaftliche Forschung.

——(2004) *Theoretische Welten und literarische Transformationen*, Tübingen: Niemeyer.

Weinberg, S. (1993) *Dreams of a Final Theory*, London: Vintage.

Woolf, V. (1980) "Mr. Bennett and Mrs. Brown," in *Collected Essays*, Vol. 1, London: Hogarth Press, pp. 319–37.

Zukav, G. (1979) *The Dancing Wu Li Masters*, New York: Flamingo.

18
PSYCHOANALYSIS
Arkady Plotnitsky

Introduced by Sigmund Freud at the intersection of science and (indirectly but importantly) literature and art, psychoanalysis has had a long history of complex and often stormy relationships with both science and literature, and with other arts. The relationships between psychoanalysis and science have been particularly acrimonious because the scientific claims of psychoanalysis have been seen as controversial and often dismissed altogether. I shall here adopt a contrasting position and, while recognizing the complexity of these relationships, focus on their productive nature, more in accord with the history of the relationships between psychoanalysis and literature, although these relationships have not been free from controversy either.

The topic is vast, and even sketching it poses difficulties and forces one to make decisions unfortunately limiting the argument. First, I shall restrict myself to psychoanalytic theory and bypass psychoanalytic practice, although psychoanalytic theory is grounded in this practice. It is, however, psychoanalytic theory that is of primary interest and significance for my subject, since my discussion is concerned with psychoanalysis in relation to science *and* literature, and thus also with the relationships between literature and science. The applications of psychoanalytic techniques in the study of science and, especially, literature (e.g., in biographical and historical studies of science and, most extensively, in considering literary authors, characters, and texts) are important, and these approaches have a long and well-known history. Nevertheless, as I write this, conceptual affinities and interactions among psychoanalysis, literature, and science appear to be particularly significant and implicative.

My second decision is largely to focus on the *concept* of the unconscious. By this I mean a new and specific concept of the unconscious, that is, the concept whose conceptual architecture is shaped by other key psychoanalytic concepts, such as repression, anxiety, pleasure and reality principles, the death drive, and so forth. This psychoanalytic grounding of the "unconscious" must be kept in mind, although only some of these other concepts, most particularly "consciousness," will be addressed here. The concept of the unconscious is, however, the greatest conceptual discovery of psychoanalysis, and focusing on it will be the most effective way to explore the relationships among psychoanalysis, literature, and science.

My third decision is to center my discussion on two founding thinkers, Freud himself and Jacques Lacan. The body of major psychoanalytic work, even as concerns the connections of psychoanalysis to literature and science, cannot of course be limited to Freud and Lacan, and it is not my intention to diminish the contributions of other figures. Nevertheless, first, Freud and Lacan have exerted the greatest conceptual influence on psychoanalytic thinking. Second, I would contend that the relationships between psychoanalysis and science (including mathematics), and among psychoanalysis, science, and literature, found their most dramatic and poignant manifestations in Freud and Lacan.

It is tempting to formulate my grounding thesis in one simply stated sentence: Freud is a "scientist" and Lacan is a "mathematician" of psychoanalysis. Freud, a neuroscientist and a medical doctor by training, thinks like a natural scientist, say, a biologist. The genealogy of psychoanalysis, from the work of Freud's key precursors to his early *Project for Scientific Psychology* (1895), is primarily scientific, and in developing psychoanalysis Freud had a scientific project in mind. By contrast, Lacan thinks as a mathematician: a certain mathematical or mathematical-like thinking shapes Lacan's psychoanalytic theorizing, as against that of Freud, for whom the biological sciences appear to have been the primary models. Lacan thinks as a scientist, too, but, in contrast to Freud, more like a twentieth-century mathematical physicist, especially a quantum physicist, say, Werner Heisenberg or P.A.M. Dirac, whose thinking is of course more rigorously mathematical. Indeed, as I shall explain, this may be a better parallel, especially given that both Lacan's thought and quantum theory are shaped by an analogous radical epistemology, which Freud was hesitant to adopt, even though he might have realized it to be possible. In particular, Lacan understands what he calls "the Real" in the same way that quantum theory understands quantum objects and processes (the quantum "Real"). While inferred through their indirect effects upon phenomena that can be observed, they are not only beyond observation but also beyond any description, or even conception (see Plotnitsky 2002a). Correlatively, in both theories, chance acquires a central role; and quantum-mechanical predictions are essentially probabilistic in character.

It would not be possible to trace the history of the ideas and ways of thinking leading to Freud's and then Lacan's conceptuality and epistemology. This history reaches as far back as the pre-Socratics. Kant's work, however, appears unavoidable:

> We have ... no elements for the cognition of things except insofar as an intuition can be given corresponding to these concepts, consequently ... we have cognition of no object as a *thing in itself* [noumenon], but only insofar as it is an object of sensible intuition, i.e. as an appearance [phenomenon]; from which follows the limitation of all even possible

speculative cognition of reason [*Vernunft*] to mere objects of *experience*. Yet ... even if we cannot *cognize* [*kennen*] these same objects as things in themselves, we at least must be able to *think* [*denken*] [about] them as things in themselves. To *cognize* an object, it is required that I be able to prove its possibility (whether by the testimony of experience from its actuality or *a priori* through reason). But I can *think* whatever I like, as long as I do not contradict myself, i.e., as long as my concept is a possible thought, even if I cannot give any assurance whether or not there is a corresponding object somewhere within the sum total of all possibilities. But in order to ascribe objective validity to such a concept ... something more is required. This "more," however, need not be sought in theoretical sources of cognition; it may also lie in practical ones.

(Kant 1997: 115)

This passage captures the essential grounds not only of modern philosophical but also of modern (post-Galilean) scientific thought. Psychoanalysis, too, defines itself in relation to Kant's epistemology, including as concerns its connections to modern science and, in more complex ways, literature or philosophy. Indeed, the modern history of the relationships among literature, philosophy, and science is shaped by this epistemology as well.

A science, such as physics or biology, or a theory in another domain, may deal with either phenomena or noumena, or with both types of entities and the relationships between them, as most of modern sciences and philosophy do. A theory of this type would, at least in principle or by way of idealization, determine all of its objects as directly or indirectly knowable or, on the model of Kant's things in themselves, at least as thinkable. Accordingly, there might be reasons, theoretical (or experimental) or practical, to accept this thinking – for example, that material bodies ultimately have an atomic constitution – as correct, or at least as sufficiently correct. Classical physics may be seen as the main paradigmatic model of such a theory for both science and often, as in Kant, philosophy. Physics deals only with idealized and, specifically, mathematized models of nature, either more directly, like in classical mechanics or astronomy, or indirectly, as in the (classical) molecular physics or molecular biology. Such theories may also be termed *epistemologically classical*.

However, it is also possible to have theories that are, by contrast, defined by the fact that they place the ultimate objects they consider to be not only beyond their own reach or the reach of all knowledge, but also beyond any possible conception. These objects are literally *un*-thinkable, along the lines of the Lacanian Real. Quantum theory is a theory of this type, at least in some interpretations, such as the one adopted here, following Bohr and Heisenberg. One might call such theories *epistemologically non-classical*. Certain forms of modern biology, including, beginning with Darwin, evolutionary theory, pursue non-classical theorizing as well. Philosophical examples (there are not many) include Nietzsche's philosophy and, following Nietzsche, that of Bataille and Derrida, both of whom were significantly influenced by psychoanalysis. Psycho-analysis is positioned between classical and non-classical epistemology, with Lacan expressly moving it into the non-classical register. Psychoanalysis's rela-tionships with literature have played an important role in the non-classical (re) positioning of psychoanalysis, again, especially in Lacan. Literature provides important instances of non-classical thinking, and sometimes, beginning at least with the Romantics, such as Kleist, Percy Shelley, and Keats, it defines itself accordingly. Beginning with Plato, literature has been defined as something that can partake in or capture something of the divine or the sublime, say, by way of the divine madness (a proto-psychoanalytic concept already by virtue of implying a certain unconscious) in Plato's *Ion*. (In his later works, Plato denies literature this capacity and instead claims it for philosophy.) In modern literature this possibility is radically rethought, along with the very existence of such a trans-cendent realm, divine or other.

It is crucial for understanding the nature of non-classical thought that, rather than merely postulated or imagined, unthinkable entities are rigorously defined by means of a given non-classical theory. The existence of such unthinkable objects and the fact that they are unthinkable are essential to what the theory can do in terms of knowledge, explanation, or prediction. The unthinkable is placed *inside* and is made a constitutive part of the theory, rather than positioned *outside* this theory. Thus, unobservable and (in their nature and behavior) undescribable and ultimately inconceivable quantum entities, such as electrons and photons, are introduced by quantum theory in order to account for their observable effects manifest in our experimental technology, such as cloud chambers. These are traces, literally, in Derrida's sense of the trace, insofar as their ultimate origin is never traceable or definable (Plotnitsky 2002a: 231–33). Similarly, the uncon-scious [*das Unbewusste*] in Freud (sometimes against his own grain) and the Real in Lacan are introduced as a necessary but inaccessible efficacity of certain manifest *mental* effects or traces.

The mental nature of these effects is important. While we may more readily think of things in themselves as material *objects*, for Kant the concept equally refers to mental objects as distinguished from phenomena. Kant's argument has major implications for our understanding of the nature of thought, and Freud expressly appeals to it in defining the unconscious:

> In psychoanalysis there is no choice for us but to declare mental pro-cesses to be in themselves unconscious, and to compare the perception of them by consciousness with the perception of the outside world through the sense-organs; we even hope to extract some fresh knowledge from the comparison. The psychoanalytic assumption of unconscious mental activity appears to us, on the one hand, a further development of that primitive animism which caused our own consciousness to be

reflected in all around us, and, on the other hand, it seems to be an extension of the correction begun by Kant in regard to our views of external perception. Just as Kant warned us not to overlook the fact that our perception is subjectively conditioned and must not be regarded as identical with the phenomena perceived but never really discerned, so psychoanalysis bids us not to set conscious perception in the place of the unconscious mental process which is its object. The mental, like the physical, is not necessarily in reality just what it appears to us to be. It is, however, satisfactory to find that the correction of the inner perception does not present difficulties so great as that of outer perception – that the inner object is less hard to discern truly than is the outside world.

(Freud 1963: 121)

It follows that all evidence concerning these unconscious dynamics is irreducibly indirect. It is not accidental that Freud is a contemporary of Sherlock Holmes (the most famous fictional practitioner of the scientific method in detective work), or that Edgar Allan Poe's detective stories are so important for Lacan. Both Freud and Lacan realized that dealing with indirect and even irreducibly indirect evidence does not prevent the possibility of rigorously scientific psychoanalytic research, although the scientific claims of psychoanalysis have often been questioned because psychoanalytic evidence is of this recondite nature. However, rather than being a problem for psychoanalysis, this criticism reveals an uncritical understanding of the nature of science itself. This misunderstanding persists even in the face of a massive effective critique of it in the history, sociology, and philosophy of science, pursued for about half a century by now, in particular along the so-called constructivist lines. Science often uses indirect evidence, even in classical physics or biology, evolutionary theory, and so forth; and conversely, psychoanalytic evidence and explanations are debated in the psychoanalytic community, just as scientific evidence and cases are debated in scientific communities. In other words, we find the same type of complexity – experimental, theoretical, and institutional – in psychoanalysis as in the natural sciences or mathematics.

In quantum physics, in a non-classical understanding, all evidence concerning quantum objects themselves is irreducibly, unavoidably indirect, which circumstance defines, arguably, as the greatest point of convergence, indeed a mutually illuminating convergence, of psychoanalysis and science. It should be stressed that, in the words of Bohr, who often reflected on the relationship between quantum epistemology and modern psychology, "we are not dealing here with more or less vague analogies, but with an investigation of the conditions for the proper use of our conceptual means of expression" (Bohr 1987, v. 2: 2). The difference between classical and quantum physics may be seen as follows. Classical physics, specifically classical mechanics, was born with Galileo as a representational *geometrical* theory, in which every physical process considered is, in principle, visualizable or picturable and is geometrically mathematized accordingly. By contrast, quantum theory may be seen as an *algebraic* theory, which is non-representational and is thus purely formal or symbolic: its mathematics does not relate to any geometrical representation of quantum processes. Indeed, such a representation appears to be impossible. Geometrical or topological concepts may be used by the theory, but, again, as part of the ultimately predictive mathematical machinery, since such objects never describe the ultimate (quantum) objects and processes considered. The mathematics of quantum theory only serves to predict the outcomes of certain specifiable experiments on the basis of the previously performed experiments. In sum, classical physics predicts because it describes, while quantum physics predicts without being able to describe, and moreover, quantum-physical predictions are only statistical. Indeed, it may be shown that the non-classical nature of quantum theory is correlative to the irreducible role of chance and probability there (Plotnitsky 2002a: 74–87).

Both philosophy and science have been reluctant to accept the correlative lack of realism and causality as reflecting how nature ultimately works. As Stephen J. Gould noted, however, literature appears to be more open to this possibility in nature, life, or human affairs alike (Gould 2002: 1340–43). One could hardly be surprised at this difference, given powerful philosophical, ideological, ethical, and political imperatives that have defined both philosophy and science throughout their history, paradigmatically encapsulated by Einstein's famous refusal to accept that God would play dice with the universe. Non-classical thinking in science does find nearly equally illustrious advocates, such as Bohr and Heisenberg, or Darwin, but only a few. While the same classical imperatives are at work in literature, the latter, often wayward and even deviant, is philosophically less constrained by them than science and, perhaps especially, philosophy, which appears to be more hostile to non-classical alternatives than even science is.

This intellectual conflict is reflected in psychoanalysis as well. It may be noted first that the correlativeness of non-classicality and chance appears to extend to the psychoanalytic field. In the domain of psychoanalytic theory, such predictions are even more subject to chance and are often literally more hazardous (the French *hazard* also means chance more generally). The point is not missed by Lacan: perhaps following quantum theory, his conception of the Real is defined, correlatively, by its non-classical inaccessibility and by the effects of chance it generates (Lacan 1991: 53–64). Lacan's use of both algebra and topology may be best understood along these lines of, at most, only partial mappings and indirect relations to the ultimate efficacity (the Real) of psychoanalytic events or effects (Plotnitsky 2002a: 109–56). This efficacity is ultimately inaccessible, but relating to it, including the use of mathematical metaphorical models, is essential.

The non-classical approach – factoring in the role of chance and making use of mathematical metaphorical models – is more characteristic of Lacan than of Freud. Indeed, it is remarkable that, as he says in the passage cited above, Freud thought that the unconscious "does not present difficulties so great as that of outer perception – that the inner object is less hard to discern truly than is the outside world" (Freud 1963: 121). He thought that he could give the unconscious a kind of *mechanics*, which is largely causal, in particular an Oedipal mechanics, whose model, it is worth noting, derives from literature, read classically in the present sense. Freud's later models of this "mechanics," as in *Beyond the Pleasure Principle*, are primarily biological. Freud thus appears to stop short even of seeing the *unconscious* character of *thinking* as placing the ultimate nature of thought beyond knowledge – as being open, at most, only to thinking about, rather than knowing – let alone of making it unavailable even to thinking itself. In the latter (non-classical) case, the suspension of causality at the ultimate level is an automatic consequence. If the nature of a process is unthinkable, it cannot be thought of as causal.

I stress "thinking" because it is the unconscious that does most of thinking itself, which is one of Freud's greatest scientific insights (Freud 1963: 117), the implications of which for neuroscience took a while to realize, although this happened in part in view of recent remarkable breakthroughs in neurological research, especially molecular biology. Here, too, literature (from Sophocles to Proust and beyond) has been more perceptive and, one might even say, *more scientific*. While Freud took (deserved) credit for developing a scientific way to study the unconscious, he acknowledged that the unconscious, specifically as thinking, was discovered by poets and philosophers before him. I would argue that consciousness has primarily to do with the *presence* of phenomena, including of itself as a phenomenon (the phenomenon of self-consciousness), and little to do with *thinking*, at least as logic, understanding, reason, and so forth.

Nearly, but not altogether! This type of unconditional separation, without mutual interaction and inhibition, may not be possible, as Freud tells us. One cannot uncritically reverse the customary hierarchy of philosophy that, from Plato to Husserl and beyond, has grounded thought in consciousness. Proceeding uncritically in either direction (one often finds this problem in the currently prominent although still emerging discipline of consciousness studies) will not help us to understand the nature of either the unconscious or consciousness, and the latter, as Freud acknowledged, remains enigmatic, perhaps more so than the unconscious. The unconscious should not be thought of as merely some exterior self-present reservoir of ideas that are outside consciousness and that may or may not become available to the latter, although this type of traffic between both domains is at work. The unconscious is better seen as referring to the non-classical dynamics that continuously involves the reciprocal and mutually inhibiting interactions with consciousness upon which this dynamics produces certain effects, similarly to the way quantum objects interact with the classical macro world in the non-classical view of quantum physics.

Nevertheless, it may be maintained that consciousness encompasses only a small part of thinking vis-à-vis unconscious thought processes.

This view extends and, again, via Lacan, non-classically radicalizes Freud. As Lacan says, crediting Freud with "truly unprecedented boldness":

> When Freud realized that it was in the field of the dream that he had to find confirmation of what he had learned from his experience of the hysteric, he began to move forward with truly unprecedented boldness. What does he tell us now about the unconscious? He declares that it is constituted essentially, not by what consciousness may evoke, extend, locate, bring out of the subliminal, but by that which is, essentially, refused. And how does Freud call this? He calls it by the same term by which Descartes designates what I just called his point of application – *Gedanken*, thought. There are thoughts in this field of the beyond of consciousness, and it is impossible to *represent* these thoughts other than in the same homology of determination in which the subject of the *I think* finds himself in relation to the articulation of the *I doubt*.
>
> (Lacan 1991: 43–44)

Thus, the unconscious, as *theoretically* defined in the field of psychoanalysis, is primarily thinking – *Gedanken* – and, conversely, thinking is primarily unconscious. Thus understood, the unconscious may need to be theorized non-classically, as something that is ultimately beyond our ability to think about it, except for its actually or potentially manifest effects, from which we infer this unthinkability. It is a major contribution of Lacan that he extends this non-classical epistemology, beyond the unconscious, to his concept of the Real. In this view, inaccessible, on the one hand, and productive of effects, on the other, as it may be, the unconscious is defined as the field of the effects of the Real, as an even more remote efficacity, which may also have conscious effects. We deal here with the difference between two *different* forms of the unthinkable, although both are equally unthinkable.

In Lacan, effects of the Real may be manifest either in the Imaginary or in the Symbolic register. The Imaginary is, roughly, an illusionary and essentially narcissistic *interior* image production, through which the human subject constructs its image of itself and its objects of desire. The Symbolic is, roughly, an organization of subjectivity, governed by the laws of *exteriority*, the law of the Other, which is essentially linguistic in nature, and which re-channels the Imaginary, primarily along Oedipal lines. Both of these registers have more hidden but still more classically defined strata, as well as inaccessible, non-classically defined strata. It is possible, Lacan suggests, that in the neo-natal state we have a closer access to the Real, but these pre-early traces of the Real, if they still exist, would no longer enable us to image or even think the nature of the Real. In other words, whether they are found in memory or new experiences, traces of the

Lacanian Real, just as they are in quantum theory, are traces in Derrida's (in turn, non-classical) sense.

Although the character and role of this thinking could be interpreted along more classical lines (see, e.g., essays assembled in Ragland and Milovanovic 2004), I would place Lacan's mathematical-like thinking in relation to this epistemology. I would argue that at the very least his psychoanalytic "algebra" – in part modeled in complex and imaginary numbers, such as the square root of minus 1 (Lacan 2004: 281–312) – and at least some his "topology" obeys the non-classical epistemological paradigm, with the Real placed in the position of the irreducibly inaccessible. There is no object, physical or phenomenal, that such mathematical entities represent, made apparent to consciousness, although there could be rules that can link them to representable objects (Plotnitsky 2002a: 141–54). Lacan sees the dynamics of the unconscious in terms of the effects of the irreducibly inaccessible, ultimately arising from the Real, rather than in terms of a causal dynamics responsible only for certain manifest effects, such as those associated with neurosis.

In Freud, too, the ultimate nature of consciousness and of the unconscious effects is hidden in the physical material abyss, which is unknowable and perhaps unconceivable. However, the unconscious is still mapped by an Oedipalized mechanics of neuroses. Freud's view of the entities defining this mechanics (such as the phallus or castration) in terms of signifieds, rather than in terms of signifiers, as in Lacan, is itself part of this mechanics, while a certain primacy of signifiers in Lacan is correlative to his non-classical quasi-mathematization of psychoanalytic theory. In both cases, certain psychoanalytic effects of the unconscious are describable and are described by the theory. By analogy with quantum mechanics, however, the Oedipal, as the *Lacanian* unconscious, is treated only in terms of effects, describable or hidden, and a certain mathematical-like formal machinery, defined by the signifiers, a kind of calculus, relating to these effects. The Real, as I said, provides a still more remote stratum of this unthinkable efficacity, thus doubling it. Depending on the situation or case, effects may be found in the (under-Oedipalized) Imaginary register or the (properly Oedipalized) Symbolic register. And, like in quantum theory, the role of chance, arguably the most powerful and fundamental effect of the Real, remains irreducible.

From this perspective, the human brain may be seen as an organic technology suited for interactions with both classical and non-classical domains, but this technology interacts with each domain differently. This machinery enables both our unconscious thinking and our consciousness. For one biological-evolutionary reason or another, our bodies appear to enable us to "see," to consciously experience, only a classical world, and both classical physics and our picture of consciousness itself (more) naturally arise in this field of intuitive experience. This is why we must begin with consciousness. There is no other place to begin, including in the case of psychoanalysis or quantum physics, whose data, too, are ultimately given only to our consciousness. However, we also arrive, now by means of theoretical thinking, at the idea of quantum objects and processes in physics and at the idea of the unconscious in psychoanalysis, while the workings of both the quantum and the unconscious, or the Real, are conceived as unthinkable in their ultimate constitution.

To think how our brains or our bodies enable our minds to conceive the unthinkable as the ground of thought is a formidable task. The *interactions* among different fields, such as those found in science, philosophy, and art, may not only be helpful but also necessary to approach this task. Psychoanalysis deeply connects to the cognitive sciences, on the one hand, and philosophy and literature, on the other. Possible connections to cognitive sciences, consciousness studies, and neuroscience have been a subject of considerable interest in both philosophy and literary studies in recent years, although mostly along classical epistemological lines and, correlatively, bypassing psychoanalysis, especially in its aspects here considered. I would like to take a different, non-classical, view of the problematic of thought and of the interactions between different fields dealing with this problematic, and to place psychoanalysis in relation to science, art, and philosophy in accordance with this view.

This view extends G. Deleuze and F. Guattari's argument, according to which it may be necessary to rethink the very nature of thought by considering it as arising from science, philosophy, and art, viewed as primordial forms of the workings of the brain itself (Deleuze and Guattari 1994: 201–18). Deleuze and Guattari see thought as a product of a confrontation between the brain and chaos, and according to them, "*The brain is the junction* – and not the unity – *of the three planes*" through which art, science, and philosophy, each in its own way, cut through chaos: "Philosophy, art, and science are not the mental objects of an objectified brain but the three aspects under which the brain becomes the subject, Thought-brain. They are the three planes, the rafts on which the brain plunges into and confronts the chaos" (208–10). I would argue that the conception of chaos that is necessary here inevitably involves the irreducibly unthinkable of non-classical *thought*, and in this respect the present argument complements their conjecture. The conjecture, it follows, relates art, science, and philosophy to certain specific forms of neural functioning of the brain itself. Art, science, and philosophy are now seen as more primordial forms of thinking rather than its more mediated products. Or, rather, they arise from *something that neurologically defines each as a particular form of the confrontation between thought and chaos*, for it would be more accurate to see art, science, and philosophy as manifesting certain specific capacities of the brain: these neurological capacities have to be socially mediated to become art, science, or philosophy.

It is difficult to assess this extraordinary conjecture, as concerns its significance for the future of the sciences of the brain. Deleuze and Guattari offer a *philosophical* concept of thought and of the brain. I would argue, however, that the conjecture is well worth taking seriously, and indeed the extraordinary developments of neuroscience during the last two decades (since the book's appearance in 1991), which have redefined the future of the field, suggest that this argument has become even more inviting to consider. Psychoanalysis, specifically Freud's work, which has enjoyed a new recognition in neuroscience, has much to contribute to this type of project, in particular as concerns its non-classical dimensions. For, arguably more so than any other psychological or neurological field, it has always been engaged with art, science, philosophy, and their intersections; and it will make its further contributions to our under-standing of the brain by continuing this engagement, and thus bringing itself closer to the workings of the brain, which was indeed Freud's great dream.

Bibliography

Bohr, N. (1987) *The Philosophical Writings of Niels Bohr*, 3 vols, Woodbridge, Conn.: Ox Bow.

Deleuze, G. and Guattari, F. (1994) *What is Philosophy?*, trans. H. Tomlinson and G. Burchell, New York: Columbia University Press.

Freud, S. (1963) *General Psychological Theory: papers on metapsychology*, New York: Collier.

Gould, S.J. (2002) *The Structure of Evolutionary Theory*, Cambridge, Mass.: Harvard University Press.

Kant, I. (1997) *Critique of Pure Reason*, trans. P. Guyer and A.W. Wood, Cambridge: Cambridge University Press.

Lacan, J. (1991), *The Four Fundamental Concepts of Psychoanalysis*, trans. A. Sheridan, New York: W.W. Norton.

——(2004), *Ecrits*, trans. B. Fink, New York: W.W. Norton.

Plotnitsky, A. (2002a) *The Knowable and the Unknowable: modern science, nonclassical thought and the "two cultures"*, Ann Arbor: University of Michigan Press.

Ragland, E. and Milovanovic, D. (eds) (2004) *Lacan: topologically speaking*, New York: Other Press.

19
SYSTEMS THEORY
Bruce Clarke

"The narratives of the world are numberless," Roland Barthes began a famous essay, continuing, "Narrative is first and foremost a prodigious variety of genres, themselves distributed amongst different substances – as though any material were fit to receive man's stories" (Barthes 1978: 79). Were we to substitute "systems" for Barthes's "narrative" and "story," we would have in each case a proper statement. The systems of the world are also numberless. They, too, come in a multitude of forms impressed upon many different mediums. In this sense, then, the alignment of narrative and systems is instructive, for a major complication of systems theory is the proliferation of *its* genres. A "prodigious variety" of kinds and conceptual models of systems has been treated under the same heading of "systems theory."

A system may be any complex totality composed of interdependent elements. However, the strong sense of the system concept denotes a complex ensemble unified in such a way that a *process* emerges from, and only from, the interdependent interactions of those elements. Systems theory attends to both the elements and the processes of the systems it observes. For instance, a genome – the full packet of DNA within every cell – is a double-helical structure composed of molecules, a macromolecule ordered so as to encode and replicate genetic information. However, the genome is only one element of the entire cellular system. In order to get to the *processes* of life, you need to bring together the entirety of a cell. All of the interdependent and interacting elements (structures or sub-systems) of that complex totality – genome, organelles, cytoplasm, and membrane – come together to produce the ongoing processes of cellular life. As such, the cell is the minimal form of a living system.

An element/process distinction can now be observed between Barthes's statement about narrative and the strong definition of systems. As a complex structure of signs, the literary object, such as a narrative text, is an element ready to be taken up and processed by an observing system. However, the narrative subject – the observer of the text – can be one of, or be comprised of, multiple systems, most immediately the psychic systems (or minds) producing perceptions and intuitions of the text, and the social systems (or conversations) within which the text circulates as an element of literary communication. At least one more distinction must be noted: in their prodigious variety, systems may be physical or technological, biological or cultural, natural or artificial, or a combination of all of the above. Unlike stories, nothing restricts the nature of systems to "man's" dominion. In this way, systems theory lends itself to the discourse of posthumanism.

Thermodynamic systems: environmental closure

The discourse of thermodynamics has had significant effects on the production of literary texts and cultural allegories (Clarke 2001). So let us pick up the story of systems theory with the distinction between dynamic and thermodynamic systems and the emergence of thermodynamics at mid-nineteenth century. Newton's laws dealt with the motions of masses and distribution of forces in dynamical systems, say, a planet in orbit around another celestial body, or a mechanical clock. The rise of steam engines forced the thermodynamic issue. Thermo (heat)-dynamics (motion) is the physics of the motion of heat, which motion is always observed to be from hotter to cooler bodies. Heat engines are mechanical systems that exploit the thermal differential between a hot body – a heat source – and a cool one – a heat sink. If you can get thermal energies moving from source to sink, you can tap those dynamics to produce work. But there must be an apparatus for the enclosure of the process away from the environment at large. The ideal heat engine is thus a *closed system*, one in which all heat exchanges remain internal to the system and thus maximally convertible into work. This is called the environmental closure of thermodynamic systems.

Systems theory is concerned at all times to treat system processes in relation to their environments. Thermodynamically considered, heat engines receive fuel from their environments to produce the energies their systems enclose, and give back to their environments focused forces, say, from a driveshaft, ready for mechanical application. In worldly practice, however, it is impossible to achieve complete efficiency by the perfect material closure of any system. The concept of entropy, also known as the second law of thermodynamics, arose in part as a measure of that inevitable inefficiency. Moreover, as Rudolf Clausius famously rendered his formulation of the second law, within a closed system, over time, entropy tends to a maximum. And the entropic side-effects of thermodynamic systems, the spent or wasted energy and matter exhausted as a consequence of their processes, are also vented to their environments.

The motions of dynamical systems are at least conceptually reversible in time. But to reverse the course of entropy, one would have to run time backwards. Whereas a clock or a ceiling fan can be made to run in reverse, there is no switch to turn time around. The dissipation of energies involved in thermo-dynamic processes is *irreversible*. As a consequence, entropy has been called "time's arrow." Like a spring-loaded clock running down, in their thermo-dynamic description, all worldly processes tend toward *equilibrium*, the loss or washing out of their energic differentials. By the end of the nineteenth century, this cognizance of the irreversible temporality of thermodynamic systems had fostered a cultural imaginary in which one toils in ultimate futility against a zero-sum outcome, "heat death," the final dissipation of all heat differentials, the universal coming to rest in a state of inert equilibrium.

Projecting the status of a closed thermodynamic system upon the universe at large produced the prophecy of its heat death as a matter of course. H.G. Wells's *The Time Machine* (1895) reported on the world as then predicted thirty million years hence, "There were fringes of ice along the sea margin, with drifting masses further out; but the main expanse of that salt ocean, all bloody under the eternal sunset, was still unfrozen." Less than a generation later, Henry Adams told what the same nineteenth-century physics had told him about the completion of that entropic process: "all nature's energies were slowly convert-ing themselves into heat and vanishing into space, until, at the last, nothing would be left except a dead ocean of energy at its lowest possible level" (Adams 1910: 145). But as the character Oedipa Maas will be informed in Thomas Pynchon's *The Crying of Lot 49*, "Entropy is a figure of speech ... a metaphor. It connects the world of thermodynamics to the world of information flow" (Pynchon 1966: 106). At mid-twentieth century, systems theory will make an important transition, from energy systems to information systems.

First-order cybernetics: control systems

Early in the development of steam engines, a qualitatively different sort of mechanism was invented in conjunction with it, the Governor that automatically stabilized the rate at which the engine operated. In 1868, leading British physicist James Clerk Maxwell wrote up the first theoretical analysis of the Governor (Maxwell 1868). He considered it in its status as a dynamical system in which the centrifugal forces spun off of the engine's performance are channeled into mechanical control effects. Coupled to and regulating a thermodynamical system, the mechanical Governor used the steam engine's output of work to operate a valve regulating its input of energy.

The Governor is considered to be the prototypical cybernetic control system. Cybernetic systems theory took its name from the Greek root of "governor" – *kybernetes*, meaning "steersman." The Governor controls the system it governs through *negative feedback*: it measures a process (extracts information about energy) and feeds that measure back into the process so as to damp its amplifi-cation past a set-point with a reduction that steers it back to the desired rate. "The first great paper on cybernetics" (Mead, quoted in Brand 1976: 33), "Behavior, Purpose, and Teleology," states: "All purposeful behavior may be considered to require negative feed-back. If a goal is to be attained, some signals from the goal are necessary at some time to direct the behavior" (Rosenblueth, Wiener, and Bigelow 1943: 19). Cybernetic systems theory emerged at mid-twentieth century at the confluence of military and civilian interests in communication and control systems – for instance, the manual and remote control of forces and weapons by means of communications among human operators and mechanical processes. Flanking these cybernetic demands were developments in computation and information technologies advancing the sophistication with which machines, from dynamos to computers, could be rendered communicable *with* – if not necessarily more intelligent (although that aim was to follow), then at least more perceptive and responsive, more "alive."

Heinz von Foerster captured this analogy to living systems in the statement that the original goal of cybernetic systems theory "was to characterize a mode of behavior that is fundamentally distinct from the customary perception of the operations of machines with their one-to-one correspondence of cause–effect, stimulus–response, input–output, and so on. The distinction arises from the presence of sensors whose report on the state of the effectors of the system acts on the operation of the system" (von Foerster 1990: 225). Machines with feedback or other control systems between sensors and effectors parallel organisms with sensorimotor systems regulating bodily actions. Or again, mechanical systems for homeostasis – such as the Governor's active regulation of a process within a set range – and organic systems for proprioception – the self-perception of one's movements or actions, enabling, say, maintenance of balance while walking on a fence rail – are conceptually united in their self-monitoring processes. To that extent, all such systems have "selves." "A uniform behavioristic analysis is applicable to both machines and living organisms, regardless of the complexity of behavior" (Rosenblueth, Wiener, and Bigelow 1943: 22).

The cultural impact of the first cybernetics on literary and cinematic narratives has obviously been enormous. Cyborgs, anyone? The post-nuclear-war story-world of Philip K. Dick's *Do Androids Dream of Electric Sheep?* (1968), the source text for the movie *Blade Runner* (1984), is especially interesting for its interplay of theoretical elements tapped from both thermodynamic and cybernetic systems. The fallout-challenged "special" J.R. Isidore explains to the cybernetic organism Pris Stratton the closed-system laws of entropy, renamed *kipple*: "No one can win against kipple ... except temporarily and maybe in one spot, like my apartment. ... The universe is moving toward a final state of total, absolute kippleization" (Dick 1968: 65–66). Human android-terminator Rick Deckard's later rumination makes the denotation of kipple explicit: "In a way, he realized, I'm part of the form-destroying process of entropy" (98–99). Self-reflexive cybernetic terminology is salted over hard-boiled dialogue when the covert android, Inspector Garland, informs Deckard about the detective bureau they're in, "This is a homeostatic enterprise. ... We're a closed loop" (123). Updated through the man-made heat death of H-bombs, the specter of thermal inertia provides the deep background for anxious indifferentiations between organic and cybernetic beings. After sex with the introspective cyborg Rachael, Deckard contradicts her blunt declaration, "I'm not alive," citing her technological ontology as a blend of organic and electronic components: "Legally you're not. But really you are. Biologically. You're not made out of transistorized circuits like a false animal; you're an organic entity" (198). Eventually, however, he concludes that even the "electric things have their lives, too. Paltry as those lives are" (241).

General system theory

It has become standard to equate cybernetics with systems theory per se, and also to center the origin story of this amalgam on the Macy Conferences, originally titled "Circular Causality and Feedback Mechanisms in Biological and Social Systems," later shortened to "Cybernetics." These were convened between 1946 and 1953 by Warren McCulloch and Frank Fremont-Smith and attended off and on by major luminaries in fields ranging from mathematics and information theory to anthropology, psychology, and sociology, including Norbert Wiener, John von Neumann, Claude Shannon, Heinz von Foerster, W. Ross Ashby, Gregory Bateson, and Margaret Mead. Less well remembered is the 1954 founding of the Society for General Systems Research (SGSR), which since 1988 has continued as the International Society for the Systems Sciences (ISSS). Between the 1950s and the 1970s, the phrase "systems theory" was just as likely to indicate work deriving from the efforts of this group to generalize the system concept across the natural and human sciences, and thereby, it was thought, to challenge traditional academic regimes and the sway of strictly reductionist methods.

As an object of theoretical investigation, the system concept has been bound up with such initiatives for interdisciplinary syntheses. It has long borne the mantle for integrative and holistic efforts, both within the natural sciences and between them and other branches of learning. On the margins of this group, it may be mentioned, was the idiosyncratic systems thinker R. Buckminster Fuller, inventor of the geodesic dome, and the author of a compendious written oeuvre especially championed by the counterculture of the 1960s and 1970s (Brand 1968–71). The chapter of *Operating Manual for Spaceship Earth* titled "General Systems Theory" defines *synergy* as the "*behavior of whole systems unpredicted by the separately observed behaviors of any of the system's separate parts*" (Fuller 1963: 71).

Open systems: self-organization

The SGSR wing of systems theory is best remembered now for the work of the Austrian biologist Ludwig von Bertalanffy – the author of General System

Theory (GST). Von Betalanffy's mode of systems theory was based solely on a system analysis of organisms viewed from the thermodynamic issue. Specifically, in relation to their environments, living beings are not closed systems but open to fluxes of matter and energy. This significant addendum to the dominance of classical closed-system models, von Bertalanffy stressed, received crucial support from the concurrent development of non-equilibrium thermodynamics. Ilya Prigogine and his colleagues had delineated far-from-equilibrium "dissipative structures" that offered abiotic versions of self-organizing and environmentally open systems, alongside von Bertalanffy's redescription of biological organisms as open systems.

In these decades systems theory is catalyzing the emergence of the sciences of emergence. Negative feedback is now joined by the concept of negative entropy, self-regulation by the concept of self-organization, by "order from noise," "order from chaos," and "complexity from noise." At a 1959 conference on "Self-Organizing Systems," Heinz von Foerster introduced a famous paper on that topic by asking whether "there is not a secret purpose behind this meeting to promote a conspiracy to dispose of the Second Law of Thermodynamics" (von Foerster 2003b: 1). Along the same lines, but without von Foerster's ironical sophistication, von Bertalanffy's theory of open systems took pains to separate itself from the lingering scientific program of vitalism, with which it shared anti-mechanistic and holistic orientations. It would not do to introduce "soul-like or entelechial factors into the organic happening" (von Bertalanffy 1968: 144). It may be that "open systems compared with conventional closed systems show characteristics which seem to contradict the usual physical laws" and that the "apparent contradiction of the trend toward increase of entropy and disorder in physical nature, and the negentropic trend in development and evolution were often used as vitalistic arguments"; however, the "apparent contradictions disappear with the expansion and generalization of physical theory to open systems" (144–45). For as Harold Morowitz would affirm in a contemporaneous work, immortalized on the covers of the *Whole Earth Catalog*: "The flow of energy through a system acts to organize that system" (Morowitz 1968: 2).

Niklas Luhmann credits von Bertalanffy with an important step beyond traditional holism, replacing the "difference between *whole and part* with that between *system and environment*. This transformation, of which Ludwig von Bertalanffy is the leading author, enabled one to interrelate the theory of the organism, thermodynamics, and evolutionary theory" (Luhmann 1995: 6–7). However, von Bertalanffy's insistent delimitation to the model of open systems and polemical swerve away from control systems did not provide a sufficient base for the transdisciplinary generalization of systems theory. Rather, he mistook cybernetic feedback mechanisms for the closed thermodynamic systems to which they may be coupled: "A feedback system is closed thermodynamically and kinetically; it has no metabolism. In an open system increase of order and decrease of entropy is thermodynamically possible" (von Bertalanffy 1968: 150). Luhmann has also summarized the conceptual threshold which GST could not cross: "While this open-systems paradigm has been asserted and accepted within systems theory, a surpassingly radical further step has been taken in the discussions of the last two decades. It concerns contributions to a *theory of self-referential systems*" (Luhmann 1995: 8).

Second-order systems theory: self-referential systems

As systems theory moved into the later decades of the twentieth century, its most obvious literary manifestation was a multifarious welter of systems discourses, more or less popular or technical as the case may be, but typically too multidisciplinary and/or extrascientific to be placed into traditional pigeon-holes. In addition to the work of Fuller, another case in point is the far-flung and bracing work of Gregory Bateson. Throughout the 1970s, Bateson's lifework, selected in *Steps to an Ecology of Mind* (Bateson 1972), animated the intellectual counterculture at large, in particular the whole-systems-oriented audience for the periodical successor to the *Whole Earth Catalog*, *CoEvolution Quarterly*. Bateson explained to *CoEvolution Quarterly*'s editor, Brand, the seminal importance of "Behavior, Purpose, and Teleology" in a way that forecast the philosophical stakes of the turn from first-order self-regulation to second-order self-reference. That 1943 report on "the formal character of seeking mechanisms," he remarked, produced

> a solution to the problem of purpose. From Aristotle on, the final cause has always been the mystery. ... We didn't realize then (at least I didn't realize it, though McCulloch may have) that the whole of logic would have to be reconstructed for recursiveness.
>
> (Brand 1976: 33)

Second-order systems theory has pursued that wholesale reconstruction of operational logic. These neocybernetic developments have pressed the analysis of recursive processes beyond organic, mechanical, and computational control processes toward the formal autonomy that endows natural systems with their cognitive capacities. If, in classical cybernetics, circular functions and feedback mechanisms are treated "objectively" as instrumental for the self-regulation of a system, second-order cybernetics is aimed in particular at that characteristic of natural systems, from cells on up, whereby circular recursion *constitutes the system* in the first place. The logic of self-reference is the abstract counterpart of circular self-constitution.

However, in the milieu of the classical syllogism, self-referential propositions produce paradoxical conclusions. For instance, in the famous Liar's paradox,

Epimenides the Cretan states: "All Cretans are liars." But since he is also a member of the major class – and this is the form self-reference takes in this example – the truth value of his claim cannot be determined. If he's lying, then he's telling the truth, and vice versa. But operational processes differ from logical propositions. In this distinction we have a clear application of the divergence Bateson predicted, between the classical humanist logic that banishes paradox from its calculation of truth values and the posthumanist logic of neocybernetics that sets paradox to work. "In cybernetics you learn that paradox is not bad for you, but it is good for you, if you take the dynamics of the paradox seriously" (von Foerster 1994). In the realm of recursive operations, self-referential processes unfold over time to bind those operations into autonomous wholes. Self-referential systems are self-constituting.

Second-order systems theory marks the point at which cybernetic discourse grasps the constitutive nature of operational recursion across natural systems – bodies, minds, and societies – and applies its principles to itself. By acknowledging that the cognitive system of the observer is necessarily bound up in the phenomena to be understood, it takes upon itself the burden of self-reference. In his 1973 paper "On Constructing a Reality" (2003a), von Foerster provided the template for this process. Referencing Maturana's "Neurophysiology of Cognition" (1970) in relation to visual and epistemological blind spots, he proposed "to interpret cognitive processes as never-ending recursive processes of computation," which led him to "the postulate of cognitive homeostasis: The nervous system is organized (or organizes itself) so that it computes a stable reality. This postulate stipulates 'autonomy,' that is 'self-regulation' for every living organism" (von Foerster 2003a: 217, 225).

Chronologically as well as conceptually, the unfolding of the theory of self-referential systems runs parallel with the metafictional and "cognitive" turns in narrative literature (LeClair 1987; Tabbi 2002). The foregrounding of paradox by narrative embedding, metalepsis, and *mise-en-abyme* are to postmodern narrative aesthetics – from Borges's "The Circular Ruins" to Stanislaw Lem's *The Cyberiad* to Michel Gondry's *Eternal Sunshine of the Spotless Mind* – what self-referential recursion and system differentiation – the emergence of systems within systems – are to second-order systems theory (Clarke 2008). And while the connections of this phase of systems theory to works of imaginative literature may be less obvious than those of thermodynamics and first-order cybernetics, they are also more deeply inscribed in a pervasive intellectual culture. They are also more likely to be reciprocal. Von Foerster, Varela, and Luhmann were each in their own way accomplished students of literature, philosophy, and theory in the broad sense. It is this wider range and the theoretical acumen in its discourse that renders second-order systems theory most salient for the posthumanities. The imprint of second-order systems theory in literary studies so far has registered largely in broad-based studies examining literary-critical and philosophical concerns in ecology, environmentalism, embodiment, and ethics in the light of systems-theoretical concepts (Wolfe 1998; McMurry 2003; Clarke and Hansen 2009).

Operational closure

The current default sense of the phrase *systems theory* is the body of work associated with the German sociologist Niklas Luhmann. The line to Luhmann's development of self-referential systems theory ties to von Foerster's cognitive and epistemological work in second-order cybernetics and goes directly through Humberto Maturana and Francisco Varela's biological systems concept of autopoiesis. Under the regime of self-referential systems, "self-regulation" (as in the quote above from von Foerster 2003a) changes sense from automatic control to autonomous self-constitution, and the open/closed polarity is sublated by a supplementary relation binding environmental openness to operational closure. The concept of autopoiesis can clarify what is at stake here. Maturana and Varela introduced the theory of autopoiesis in the context of biological organization. Autopoiesis – literally, "self-making" – named the recognition that a living system, such as a cell or an organism built up from cells, is a self-referential system: it is the processual product of its own production. Autopoietic self-production is thereby, in Maturana and Varela's phrase, "organizationally closed." The autopoietic process turns upon itself, recursively: the organization enables the production that maintains the organization, and so on. Open to the material-energetic flux of its environment, an autopoietic system is closed or "information-tight" in the sense that it is self-operating, or autonomous. It self-maintains the continuous production of the components that bind and replenish the system that produces the components that bind and replenish the system (Maturana and Varela 1980).

The generalization of autopoiesis

The concept of autopoiesis has developed along two main lines of application. The first extends its scientific propriety as a biological theory of the organization of living systems. Researchers taking up the work of Maturana and/or Varela have traced the implications of autopoiesis beyond the realm of individuated cells and organisms. Biological autopoiesis has been studied in relation to computational self-organization (Winograd and Flores 1987), theories of the origin of living systems (Luisi 2006), neurophysiology and neurophenomenology (Thompson 2007), artificial life (Bourgine and Stewart 2004), and artificial intelligence (Froese and Ziemke 2009). It has also been brought up to the level of the biosphere with Earth systems theories of planetary self-regulation, Gaia theory as elaborated by microbiologist Lynn Margulis (Clarke 2009).

The second main line of autopoietic developments leads more directly to matters of subjectivity and society inherent in literary production, by way of Luhmann's systems theory (Wellbery 1996; Lippert 2009). In this construction, the operational closure of autopoietic self-reference demands separate accounts for the separate closures of systems of consciousness and of communication, and for the coevolutionary interpenetration of psychic and social systems as environmental resources for each other. Transporting autopoiesis beyond the organic boundaries of biological systems, Luhmann specifies how the separate operations of psychic and social systems – their differential processing of evanescent event-structures, the elements of consciousness and communication – can produce virtual boundaries for those metabiotic systems. Their metabiotic boundaries are produced and re-produced by the forms of distinction which those same systems construct by making selections within the medium of *meaning* – say, between self and other, between inclusion and exclusion: "Boundaries can be differentiated as specific mechanisms with the specific purpose of separating yet connecting. They assume this function via particular performances of selection" (Luhmann 1995: 29). However, from the operational interpenetration of psychic and social systems, those semi-stable structures we call persons self-organize. Identities coalesce around a system's probable reiteration of the same selections from a given repertoire of possible distinctions, but may be transformed when different selections ramify into a new norm, or new options enter the repertoire of possible distinctions.

Second-order systems theory observes a world so constructed that any single observer's operationally closed cognitive constructions can be rendered stable and pertinent from moment to moment by the structural couplings of and recursive conversations with the multiple observers in *its* environment. Just as all nervous systems and all organisms that possess them as sub-systems are consortiums of multiple biological autopoietic systems, so are all psychic systems bound into communities, social systems, within which *social* autopoiesis – the ongoing self-production and self-maintenance of communications – produces what von Foerster calls *eigenvalues*, that is, stable yet mobile and multiple recursive consensuses about comparable environments. In this manner, neocybernetic epistemology renders discursively explicit what has always been implicit in the relation of literary narratives to the wider world *they* are embedded in. Narrative texts construct paradoxical frames that rehearse the contingencies of observation – that is, the construction of knowledge and meaning by observing systems. Prompting reframing by moving through embedded levels, inducing oscillations in narrative perspective, the play of literary forms is a serious rehearsal of the cognitive oscillations of observing systems never out of play in our literal constructions of worldly knowledge.

Bibliography

Adams, H. (1910) "A letter to American teachers of history," in B. Adams (intro) *The Degradation of the Democratic Dogma*, New York: Macmillan, 1920, pp. 140–263.

Barthes, R. (1978) "Introduction to the structural study of narratives," in R. Barthes, *Image, Music, Text*, trans. S. Heath, New York: Hill and Wang, pp. 79–124.

Bateson, G. (1972) *Steps to an Ecology of Mind*, New York: Ballantine.

Bourgine, P. and Stewart, J. (2004) "Autopoiesis and cognition," *Artificial Life*, 10: 327–45.

Brand, S. (1976) "For God's sake, Margaret: conversation with Gregory Bateson and Margaret Mead," *CoEvolution Quarterly*, 10: 32–44.

——(ed.) (1968–71) *Whole Earth Catalog*, Sausalito, Cal.: Portola.

——(ed.) (1974–84) *CoEvolution Quarterly*, Sausalito, Cal.: Point.

Clarke, B. (2001) *Energy Forms: allegory and science in the era of classical thermodynamics*, Ann Arbor: University of Michigan Press.

——(2008) *Posthuman Metamorphosis: narrative and systems*, New York: Fordham University Press.

——(2009) "Neocybernetics of Gaia: the emergence of second-order Gaia theory," in E. Crist and H.B. Rinker (eds) *Gaia in Turmoil: climate change, biodepletion, and earth ethics in an age of crisis*, Cambridge, Mass.: MIT Press, pp. 293–314.

——and Hansen, M.B.N. (eds) (2009) *Emergence and Embodiment: new essays in second-order systems theory*, Durham, N.C.: Duke University Press.

Dick, P.K. (1968) *Do Androids Dream of Electric Sheep?*, New York: Del Rey, 1996.

Froese, T. and Ziemke, T. (2009) "Enactive artificial intelligence: investigating the systemic organization of life and mind," *Artificial Intelligence*, 173(3–4): 466–500.

Fuller, R.B. (1963) *Operating Manual for Spaceship Earth*, Carbondale: Southern Illinois University Press, 1969.

LeClair, T. (1987) *In the Loop: Don DeLillo and the systems novel*, Urbana: University of Illinois Press.

Lippert, F. (2009) "Narrowing circles: questions on autopoiesis and literary interpretation after Dietrich Schwanitz," *Cybernetics and Human Knowing*, 16(1–2): 125–41.

Luhmann, N. (1995) *Social Systems*, trans. J. Bednarz, Jr. with D. Baecker, Stanford: Stanford University Press.

Luisi, P. (2006) "Autopoiesis: the logic of cellular life," in P. Luisi, *The Emergence of Life: from chemical origins to synthetic biology*, Cambridge: Cambridge University Press, pp. 155–80.

Maturana, H. (1970) "Neurophysiology of cognition," in P. Garvin (ed.) *Cognition: A Multiple View*, New York: Spartan Press, pp. 3–23.

Maturana, H. and Varela, F. (1980) *Autopoiesis and Cognition: the realization of the living*, Boston, Mass.: D. Reidel.

Maxwell, J.C. (1868) "On governors," *Proceedings of the Royal Society of London*, 16: 270–83.

McMurry, A. (2003) *Environmental Renaissance: Emerson, Thoreau, and the American system of nature*, Athens: University of Georgia Press.

Morowitz, H.J. (1968) *Energy Flow in Biology: biological organization as a problem in thermal physics*, New York: Academic Press.

Pynchon, T. (1966) *The Crying of Lot 49*, New York: Harper & Row, 1990.

Rosenblueth, A., Wiener, N. and Bigelow, J. (1943) "Behavior, purpose, and teleology," *Philosophy of Science*, 10: 18–24.

Tabbi, J. (2002) *Cognitive Fictions*, Minnesota: University of Minneapolis Press.

Thompson, E. (2007) *Mind in Life: biology, phenomenology, and the sciences of mind*, Cambridge, Mass.: Harvard University Press.

von Bertalanffy, L. (1968) "The model of open system," in L. von Bertalanffy, *General System Theory: foundations, development, applications*, New York: George Braziller, pp. 139–54.

von Foerster, H. (1990) "Cybernetics," *Encyclopedia of Artificial Intelligence*, Vol.1, New York: John Wiley and Sons.

——(1994) "Interview," *Stanford Electronic Humanities Review*, 4(2). Online. Available HTTP: <http://www.stanford.edu/group/SHR/4–2/text/interviewvonf.html > (accessed 8 July 2009).

——(2003a) "On constructing a reality," in H. von Foerster, *Understanding Understanding: essays on cybernetics and cognition*, New York: Springer, pp. 211–27.

——(2003b) "On self-organizing systems and their environments," in H. von Foerster, *Understanding Understanding: essays on cybernetics and cognition*, New York: Springer, pp. 1–19.

Wellbery, D.E. (ed.) (1996) "Observation, difference, form: literary studies and second-order cybernetics," *Modern Language Notes*, 111(3).

Wells, H.G. (1895) *The Time Machine*, public domain.

Winograd, T. and Flores, F. (1987) *Understanding Computers and Cognition: a new foundation for design*, Reading, Mass.: Addison-Wesley.

Wolfe, C. (1998) *Critical Environments: postmodern theory and the pragmatics of the "outside,"* Minneapolis: University of Minnesota Press.

20
THERMODYNAMICS

John Bruni

Behind thermodynamics is a simple but crucial concept: nature seeks to undo gradients – differences in temperature or pressure. The familiar image of warm turning inevitably to cold, however, became rationalized into the historical specter of heat death, total energy loss, the final stillness of the universe. Henry Adams, the American historian and writer, having been overawed by the electrical dynamo at the 1900 Paris Exposition, offered ever-gloomier predictions that the Second Law of Thermodynamics – the dissipation of usable energy due to entropy increase in a closed system – foretold the gradual exhaustion of culture as well as nature. The sense of order to the universe supported by the First Law, the law of conservation of energy throughout its transformations, would no longer be sustainable. Adams made these predictions in part as a sarcastic response to the belief that evolutionary progress would drive history forward. For Adams, conversely, the beginning of the twentieth century could only usher in an increasing cultural chaos that he felt obliged to explain in thermodynamic language. That his *Education of Henry Adams* (1907) regards modern capitalism as naturally created through thermodynamic laws anticipates how, as we will later see, a thermodynamically guided model of evolution draws on imperialist logic. Indeed, Adams's book, particularly in later chapters, forecasts the importance of information for thermodynamic science (Bruni 2010). The major developments of thermodynamics – for instance, the shift in focus as life becomes regarded not as a closed but as an open system, and thus resistant to the second law – are widely restaged in literary narratives that envision the creative and destructive roles for entropy to play in an increasingly technology-saturated social landscape.

Yet the tendency remains to extrapolate from simple scientific concepts a universal theory of *development*, one that leapfrogs on recognizable cultural trends. The temptation to find a natural explanation for cultural phenomena has long dogged thermodynamics. As thermodynamics shifts from closed to open systems, in Ira Livingston's sarcastic description of the attitudes of those who would uncritically embrace a model that ties energy flows to economic flows: "Life, the tragic hero of the late nineteenth century, becomes at the dawn of a new millennium a surfing CEO with a cell phone" (Livingston 2006: 138).

The danger, as will be made clear, is in *totalizing* thermodynamics, subsuming cultural differences under the heading of self-similarity.

Entropy and closed systems

By the late nineteenth century, evolutionary theory was shaping the development of thermodynamics. As Eric D. Schneider and Dorion Sagan explain, "Darwin's idea of natural selection leading to change over time" directed the thinking of the German physicist Ludwig Boltzmann, who statistically analyzed how the behavior of large groups of particles "changed in the direction of the more probable" (Schneider and Sagan 2005: 47). Boltzmann credited Darwin's study of species transformation in populations for inspiring his explanation of "nature's mixing tendency as one moves forward in time on the basis of vast numbers of atoms" (Schneider and Sagan 2005: 48). Darwin also guided Boltzmann's speculations that the unequal temperatures of the earth and sun created competition among organisms to take advantage of the sun's heat, taking and degrading that energy (Schneider and Sagan 2005: 59–60). Boltzmann therefore suggested that the second law was primary to life processes and demonstrated that thermodynamics, like evolution, was guided by chance (Schneider and Sagan 2005: 68).

The increasing significance of the second law motivated British physicist James Clerk Maxwell to wonder whether it could be broken. He produced a thought experiment to see if energy could be obtained without work, featuring a miniscule "demon" who sorted molecules by opening and closing a frictionless door. The faster molecules the demon would let pass; the slower molecules would be blocked. In this way, the demon would create an energy gradient, reversing the process of entropy. Maxwell's thought experiment set the stage for the recognition that information and energy were connected (Schneider and Sagan 2005: 66–67). Collectively, the work of Boltzmann and Maxwell in the later nineteenth century would supply the foundations for non-equilibrium thermodynamics.

In particular, Boltzmann's contribution to a "statistical view of entropy" troubled "the absoluteness of a predicted 'heat death' by giving entropy an interpretation that was overtly probabilistic rather than deterministic" (Hayles 1990: 41, 42). However, earlier literary treatments of thermodynamics tended to restage images of exhaustion, such as those found in Charles Baudelaire's poetry and Gustave Flaubert's novels (Rabinbach 1990: 6), a strategy highly visible, for example, in the dystopian landscape of "Terminal Beach" in H.G. Wells's *The Time Machine* (1895). Like Henry Adams, Wells satirized a metaphysical vision of evolutionary progress, for

> the Traveler's dead end at Terminal Beach implies that his individual ability to move within time has given him no ultimate reprieve from the

larger cosmic catastrophe ... the ruin of nature promised by the apocalypse of ever-increasing entropy in a closed universe.

(Clarke 2001: 127)

Overall, the image of the sun became important for literary narratives about thermodynamics. The narrator of *Sister Carrie* remarks: "how dispiriting are the days during which the sun withholds a portion of our allowance of light and warmth. We are more dependent upon these things than is often thought. We are insects produced by heat, and pass without it" (Dreiser 1900: 88).

Such a dependency is symbolized in the deaths of George Hurstwood in *Sister Carrie*, and Lily Bart in Edith Wharton's *The House of Mirth* (1905); both occur in dark rooms. Victorian and modernist authors recognized the role of solar energy in maintaining the life processes that buttressed social organization. In Yevgeny Zamyatin's *We*, published in the early 1920s, and D.H. Lawrence's early twentieth-century writings, the authors pushed against the limitations of the closed-system environments fashioned by the physics of their day. Zamyatin saw thermodynamic equilibrium, caused by the diminution of solar energy, as socially regressive. Similarly, the "sun ... becomes such a pivotal figure in Lawrence's modernist myth-making precisely because Victorian physics had diminished its existential substance by envisioning it as a waning heat engine" (Clarke 2001: 153). The idea of the sun as a finite energy source was revised for the computer age in Isaac Asimov's story "The Last Question." At its end, a supercomputer comes up with an answer to the question of how to reverse entropy. Looking out over what is now chaos as the universe runs down, the supercomputer commands, "LET THERE BE LIGHT!" (Asimov 1956: 300). For Asimov, AI becomes the embodiment of a higher power that is able to thermodynamically regenerate the universe.

Entropy and open systems

Erwin Schrödinger's *What is Life?* (1944) proposed that biological systems extract order, or negentropy (negative entropy), from their environment. As this approach has been developed in more recent systems theory, in the words of David J. Depew and Bruce H. Weber, a

> living cell, an organism, even an entire ecosystem, might maintain its internal structure if it could be coupled to its surroundings in such a way that the entropy of the environment remains greater than the internal "negentropic" decrease within the boundaries of the system in question. This could happen only so long as the system remained far from equilibrium.
>
> (Depew and Weber 1995: 461)

For a biological system, equilibrium equals death. The metabolic process through which a living system sustains itself reverses the sign of entropy. Through his uncoupling of order from equilibrium, Schrödinger furnished a rationale for seeing life as an open, rather than closed, system, which in turn questioned the primacy of the second law over complex, biological systems. *Sister Carrie* and *The House of Mirth* both anticipate a turn away from equilibrium. Consider the memorable quote from Dreiser's novel:

> When a girl leaves her home at eighteen, she does one of two things. Either she falls into saving hands and becomes better, or she rapidly assumes the cosmopolitan standard of virtue and becomes worse. Of an intermediate balance, under the circumstances, there is no possibility.
>
> (Dreiser 1900: 3)

Likewise, in *The House of Mirth*, Lily's attempt to repay a loan she was tricked into accepting, thus balancing money and morality, leads to a tragic outcome.

Schrödinger's theories would be refined, with the terms "negentropy" and "order" replaced by "available energy" and "organization," thus reinforcing the association of non-equilibrium thermodynamics with information. As Schneider and Sagan see it, "There are deep physical roots linking information manipulation to energy extraction in organisms that must make a living in variable environments to survive" (Schneider and Sagan 2005: 19–20). Yet this association remains problematic, because in information theory, as developed by Claude Shannon and Warren Weaver in the 1940s, the term "entropy" has a different meaning altogether. Schneider and Sagan explain,

> In information theory *entropy* describes the uncertainties associated with the utilization of characters in sending and receiving messages. … In a thermodynamic system the basis for assigning an entropy value comes from the uniqueness of a system's matter-energy distribution at a molecular or atomic level. At any one time a system can have just one particular microstate out of many possible.
>
> (Schneider and Sagan 2005: 20)

While Schneider and Sagan argue there is a "seductive" logic that guides the equivocating of entropy between information theory with non-equilibrium thermodynamics, others have gone further in registering objections. For instance, Jeffrey S. Wicken considers it illogical "to affix the same name to different concepts" and faults Shannon for deliberately sowing confusion (Wicken 1988: 143). But Hayles reaches the opposite conclusion regarding "Shannon's choice" to place the name of entropy on his calculus of information-load:

> In his anxiety to suppress the metaphorical potential of Shannon's choice, Wicken misses the richly complex and suggestive connections

that were instrumental in enabling a new view of chaos to emerge. ... The metaphoric joining of entropy and information ... allowed complexity to be seen as rich in information rather than deficient in order.

(Hayles 1990: 51)

Making a foray into this debate, Thomas Pynchon's "Entropy" (1960) allegorizes the relationship between entropy and information in the parallel trajectories of Callisto, who faces a fate akin to impending heat death as the room temperature drops, and Saul, who discourses about the meaning of love in terms drawn from information theory: "Ambiguity. Redundance. Irrelevance, even. Leakage. All of this is noise. Noise screws up your signal, makes for disorganization in the system" (Pynchon 1960: 90–91).

Pynchon's *The Crying of Lot 49* (1966) "extends the formulary analogy between thermodynamic and information entropy into a mock-apocalyptic social allegory" (Clarke 2001: 87). As Eric White (1991) explains, Oedipa Maas intends to confirm that informational entropy, viewed as complexity, can overturn thermodynamic entropy, that is, social stasis. Oedipa finds, however, that the interface between thermodynamics and information leads to an unsatisfying binary, either absolute order or absolute chaos. This binary is validated by the idea that "noise within electronic channels was viewed merely as a corruption of the signal" (Clarke 2008: 129), a scenario allegorized in horrific science fiction scenarios, such as *The Fly*, where the result is a scientist's bodily mutation.

Self-organizing systems

One of the most important ideas to emerge from the debate about entropy in thermodynamics and information theory is that, as Hayles reports, increasing entropy "could drive systems to increasing complexity" (Hayles 1999: 103). The next step is to examine how systems maintain their internal order through self-organization. Erich Jantsch does so in the course of describing how a system perceives how to maintain itself through self-reference, an inherently circular process. Self-organization becomes a powerful tool, in the guise of complex dynamics, for establishing congruent patterns between living systems – if, albeit, at times over-generalizing on the basis of reductive cultural models, such as those of economic accumulation.

Jantsch's ground-breaking *The Self-Organizing Universe* (1980) foregrounded dissipative structures, defined as self-organizing systems open to the environment that "have the possibility of continuously importing free energy from the environment and to export entropy" (26). Jantsch credits Ilya Prigogine for viewing thermodynamic non-equilibrium as a creator, rather than destroyer, of order. That self-organizing systems created a new idea of order became the foundation for a non-linear thermodynamics of irreversible processes now permitting the description of phenomena of spontaneous structuration. The new ordering principle ... has been called *order through fluctuation*. It describes the evolution of a system to a totally new dynamic regime. This dynamic regime represents a spatial and temporal order which would contradict the second law of thermodynamics if it were near the equilibrium.

(Jantsch 1980: 28)

Jantsch laid the groundwork for a thermodynamically guided model of evolution by describing self-organizing systems as autopoietic, or self-making, borrowing the term from Humberto Maturana and Francisco Varela. Opening up autopoiesis to a thermodynamic reading, Jantsch made the connection between self-reference and information: a "dissipative structure 'knows' indeed what it has to import and export to maintain and renew itself. It needs nothing else but the reference to itself" (Jantsch 1980: 40). Located within a thermodynamic framework, Jantsch's vision of coevolution as a series of feedback loops among different species leads to a rethinking of ecological stability. Ecosystems function far from equilibrium because the "closer the system gets to equilibrium, the less resilient it becomes"; near thermodynamic equilibrium, that is, "Any random fluctuation, such as climate fluctuations or the appearance of a new species, may destroy the system completely" (66).

Jantsch redefined life, in both the individual and the collective senses, as a thermodynamic process. He then extended the idea of coevolution to cultural systems, and here the book becomes the most provocative, albeit murky at times (Schneider and Sagan observe that Jantsch wrote it quickly at the end of his life). Jantsch proposes that there are similarities across systems, such that "The common denominator is always an open system far from equilibrium which is driven by fluctuations across one or more instability thresholds and enters a new co-ordinated phase of its evolution" (Jantsch 1980: 73). In successive chapters, he built his case for a thermodynamic model for emerging life, where energy flows drive ecosystems and communication appears within and between organisms.

The ripples from Jantsch's work resonate within subsequent attempts to realign thermodynamics and evolution. Schneider speculates that evolution operates according to thermodynamic principles: "growth and maximization of free energy and structure" and "the development of complexity and efficiency, and minimizations of specific entropy productions" could be connected to natural selection (Schneider 1988: 131). Schneider's essay occurs in the collection *Entropy, Information, and Evolution* (Weber, Depew, and Smith 1988), which features several significant essays valuable for understanding the rethinking of thermodynamics and evolution. Rewriting evolution in thermodynamic language, Wicken states,

All natural organizations (as opposed to machines) are non-equilibrium systems that operate, and autocatalytically [i.e. by internal recursive processes] produce themselves, by degrading energy resources. This sets the basic currency of the organization-environment interaction, as well as the general terms on which natural selection operates. Natural selection is based on competitive success in autocatalytically converting resources into organization.

(Wicken 1988: 165)

Commenting on efforts such as Wicken's to foreground the importance of non-equilibrium thermodynamics in evolutionary development, Depew and Weber suggest that thermodynamics may overturn the reign of neo-Darwinism by offering challenges to traditional explanations for evolution, for instance, the assumption that natural selection only operates on the individual, not larger systems, such as ecosystems (Depew and Weber 1988: 321). Furthermore, non-equilibrium thermodynamics offers new ways of connecting cultural and natural processes, with the result being a heightened ecological awareness. Dyke argues that ecological issues are not simply "natural," but encompass a larger realm of environmental concerns, such as urban pollution. In brief, Dyke relates the energy flows that sustain ecosystems to the material flows that maintain social structures (Dyke 1988: 359). Not only does waste become unavoidable, creating "a gradient down which material flow can cascade," a necessary process for maintaining a dissipative structure's stability, but non-equilibrium thermodynamics also spells out a set of interrelated responsibilities. Several decades before our current climate crisis, Dyke insisted that

our existence as dissipative structures defines a space of possibilities for us, and does so rather tightly. We know from the standard thermodynamic analyses of human life that if we conserve and recycle we can lengthen the course that materials follow as they run through our hands. We know that if we use sunlight (and its immediate and inevitable correlates such as wind) we can select a composition of the material flow that gives us a longer thermodynamic horizon.

(Dyke 1988: 365)

Relating thermodynamic self-organization to systems of meaning, the essays in *Chaos and Order* (Hayles 1991) apply thermodynamic principles to redrawing disciplinary boundaries. William Paulson's important essay in this collection relates chaos and order to noise and information, signaling a way of harnessing noise to create meaning:

What appears to be a perturbation in a given system turns out to be the intersection of a new system with the first. In becoming aware of such a relation, the reader in effect creates a new context in which the previously disruptive event or variety is reread. The principle of constructing a pattern out of what interrupts patterns is inherent in artistic communication.

(Paulson 1991: 44)

By exploring the interstices between literature and science, Paulson proposes, we find new meanings (through/in noisy channels) not reducible to either discipline: "From the interference between disciplines can arise new forms of explanation, new articulations between levels of phenomena in a world of emergent complexity" (Paulson 1991: 49). Paulson here sets the stage for speculations about how thermodynamics resonates in postmodern literature. David Porush (1991) connects Prigogine, a seminal figure in thermodynamics, with William Marshall's novel *Roadshow*. Both Prigogine and Marshall explore the idea of a traffic jam as a dissipative structure, telegraphing the ways that thermodynamics and self-organization map the trajectories of both biotic and abiotic systems.

In the closing chapters of *Darwinism Evolving* (1995), Depew and Weber devise a thermodynamic framework for evolution. They rethink the principle of selection as a process that complements, rather than resists, crucial thermodynamic concepts. They acknowledge the sizable influence of biologist Stuart Kauffman. In their reading of Kauffman they find "that many phenomena that have become well accepted in contemporary evolutionary science flow rather easily and directly from background assumptions taken from complex dynamics" (Depew and Weber 1995: 456). These complex dynamics connect to thermodynamics, primarily, through the ways in which systems self-organize as a means to process energy flows more efficiently.

Depew and Weber's model reworks natural selection from an ecological perspective that draws together energy resources in the environment with the metabolic needs of biological populations. Upon first glance, ecosystems, built up through species coevolution, mirror the development of individual organisms. Following that line of thinking, Alfred Lotka's work in systems ecology in 1924 seems prescient. As Depew and Weber explain, Lotka attempted to "relativize the conditions under which natural selection can be effective to more fundamental forms of what we call chemical selection ('the survival of the efficient') and physical selection ('the survival of the stable')" (Depew and Weber 1995: 408). Therefore, Depew and Weber agree with Lotka that "Ecosystems favor species that, in funneling energy into their own production and reproduction, also increase the total energy flow through the system" (Depew and Weber 1995: 474). On the other hand, individual organisms, unlike ecosystems, "employ informational macromolecules to achieve stable, homeostatic (stabilized state of a single parameter), and homeorrhetic (stabilized flow or trajectory) metabolic pathways that can never be achieved by entities that depend on external signals" (475). What this is saying from a thermodynamic perspective is that there are important distinctions between how individuals and ecosystems process energy flows. And yet as we shall see, Depew and Weber, arguably, over-generalize somewhat when they call for Darwin's theories to be mapped across thermodynamic principles.

Depew and Weber address the formidable challenge of coupling non-equilibrium thermodynamics with evolution: if evolution is rewritten in thermodynamic language, there is a logical case for weakening, if not disallowing, the traditional argument against teleology; that is, the argument that evolution occurs at random – for instance, through non-directed genetic mutations. In their view, however, natural selection has always suggested a movement towards a greater state of adaptability. Thus in a non-equilibrium thermodynamics model of evolution, that natural selection works on "kinetic pathways" with regard to the dissipation of "entropic debt" suggests that "these pathways will have a propensity for complexification and organization" (Depew and Weber 1995: 486).

Depew and Weber also investigate the relationship between natural selection and self-organization. They observe that the consideration of this relationship results in a "deeper appreciation of the pervasively probabilistic and statistical character of the world" (1995: 486). What Depew and Weber call "the probability revolution" will, in the long run, contribute to a Darwinian view of evolution: "Nonlinear dynamics is extending the probability revolution by severing dynamics from its last links to classical physics. It is thereby offering new explanatory resources to the Darwinian tradition" (1995: 486). Observing that such a revolution goes beyond the linear thinking that shaped Boltzmann's modeling of entropy in thermodynamics, they point out that a considerable obstacle to Darwin's model of evolution, that it ultimately made no sense in the context of classical physics, may be surpassed:

> The rise of the sciences of complexity and self-organization now promises an even more robust set of background assumptions that is harmonious with the kinds and degrees of complexity that are at work in the evolution of living systems.
>
> (Depew and Weber 1995: 490)

While admirably straightforward, such a pronouncement leaves out how thermodynamics might apply differently to varying types of living systems.

On firmer ground, Lynn Margulis and Dorion Sagan have argued that the "Evolution of life *does* seem to have a direction. Life's peculiarities and human technologies do seem to expand at an accelerating rate of change as we come from the past to the present" (Margulis and Sagan 2002: 43). They believe thermodynamics can chart life's direction, citing Schneider, who proposes that "Life is one of a class of systems that organize in response to a gradient. A gradient is defined as a difference across a distance" (45).

Contemplating a thermodynamic framing of evolution that would revise natural selection, Schneider and Sagan's *Into the Cool* (2005) does highlight an "important difference between ecological succession and evolution," for evolution, unlike ecological succession, "can generate novelty" through the addition of new genomes (Schneider and Sagan 2005: 237). Citing the work of such thinkers as Depew, Weber, and Wicken, Schneider and Sagan argue against a neo-Darwinian view of natural selection, proposing instead that selection operates at a "higher" level. Quoting from Wicken, what is being selected are "informed patterns of thermodynamic flow" (239). Schneider and Sagan also acknowledge the work of chemical engineer Robert Ulanowicz, who has created "methods to quantify energy flow in biological systems" and "agrees with us that the second law generates complexity in nature, but stresses that autocatalysis then selects from among the new combinations those that will remain as part of evolving systems" (100). This redefining of selection is central to Schneider and Sagan's ecological argument: an "increase in species diversity may represent the ecosystem searching out new pathways for energy degradation. As these systems increase their diversity more pathways are found. This creates redundancy and makes the ecosystems less likely to shut down" (244).

Schneider and Sagan claim that economics in human societies also operates on the basis of gradient reduction (i.e., supply and demand differentials), patterning how biological systems obtain resources for maintaining autopoiesis. In fact, economies and cities that operate far from equilibrium, Schneider and Sagan attest, offer strong evidence against

> orthodox Darwinian interpretations that natural selection only ever acts on "the individual" – or that divisible part of "the individual" (literally, "the undivided"), the gene. Even bacteria exhibit incipient market behavior, pooling their genes, metabolites, and resources to perform activities and make structures that would be impossible for them as individuals.
>
> (Schneider and Sagan 2005: 287)

For Schneider and Sagan, gradient reduction constitutes our present lived realities, from the rise of the "internet economy" to politically conservative proposals to allocate "limited resources" in the face of energy scarcity (292, 295).

While non-equilibrium thermodynamics reshapes how life is defined as "an end directed system" (Schneider and Sagan 2005: 301), the critical flaw in this latest synthesis of thermodynamics and self-organization is the tendency to naturalize the politics and ideology that make it appear so persuasive. Livingston remarks,

> It is now rather difficult to restore the sense of scandal in the resemblance between descriptions of self-organizing processes in biology and

physics and the transnational neoliberalism they underwrite. It is difficult partly because the scientists tend to present paradigms of complexity and self-organization as the deep theory behind all these phenomena – capitalism, biological life, physical laws, and so on.

(Livingston 2006: 138)

Regarding Kauffman's *At Home in the Universe* (1991), Livingston reveals what he calls the "blatant" ideological underpinnings of arguments for the self-organization of physical or biological systems on the model of human institutions (recall Schneider and Sagan's supposed "market behavior" of bacteria); Kauffman enthuses, "As if by an invisible hand, each adapting species acts according to its own selfish advantage, yet the entire system appears magically to evolve to a poised state where, on average, each does as best as can be expected" (cited in Livingston 2006: 139). Kauffman's circular reasoning, of course, should not surprise anyone familiar with the self-reflexivity of self-organizing thermodynamic models, as Jantsch has confirmed. Nonetheless, the disquieting implications here are already being worked out in cyberpunk narratives, such as William Gibson's *Neuromancer* (1984). Livingston warns that Gibson's futuristic landscape, where the legacy of social Darwinism intersects with a thermodynamically guided techno-capitalist economy, reminds us that

a relentless aestheticization of the apparently kinder and gentler paradigms of chaos and complexity keeps the ecology of violence that it describes hidden in plain sight. The dynamically changing patterns of a "kaleidoscopic" universe are apt to include cascades of viruses spreading like wildfire, flows of international capital abruptly shifting out of your country.

(Livingston 2006: 142)

Even with the dramatic change from life running down in a closed system to open systems constantly self-organizing, self-maintaining, dominant cultural beliefs remain intact, which should give *both* scientific and humanities disciplines pause. The controversies surrounding the unfolding sciences of thermodynamics show no signs of diminishing.

Bibliography

Adams, H. (1983) *Henry Adams: Novels, Mont Saint Michel, The Education*, ed. E. Samuels and J.N. Samuels, New York: Library of America.

Asimov, I. (1956) "The Last Question," in *The Complete Stories, Volume 1*, New York: Doubleday, 1990, pp. 290–300.

Bruni, J. (2010) "The miseducation of Henry Adams: fantasies of race, citizenship, and Darwinian dynamos," in J.E. Jones and P.B. Sharp (eds) *Darwin in Atlantic Cultures: evolutionary visions of race, gender, and sexuality*, New York: Routledge, pp. 260–82.

Clarke, B. (2001) *Energy Forms: allegory and science in the era of classical thermodynamics*, Ann Arbor: University of Michigan Press.

——(2008) *Posthuman Metamorphosis: narrative and systems*, New York: Fordham University Press.

Depew, D.J. and Weber, B.H. (1988) "Consequences of nonequilibrium thermodynamics for the Darwinian tradition," in Weber, Depew and Smith 1988, pp. 315–53.

——(1995) *Darwinism Evolving: systems dynamics and the genealogy of natural selection*, Cambridge, Mass.: MIT Press.

Dreiser, T. (1900) *Sister Carrie, Jennie Gerhardt, Twelve Men*, ed. Richard Lehan, New York: Library of America, 1987.

Dyke, C. (1988) "Cities as dissipative structures," in Weber, Depew and Smith 1988, pp. 355–67.

Hayles, N.K. (1990) *Chaos Bound: orderly disorder in contemporary literature and science*, Ithaca, N.Y.: Cornell University Press.

——(ed.) (1991) *Chaos and Order: complex dynamics in literature and science*, Chicago: University of Chicago Press.

——(1999) *How We Became Posthuman: virtual bodies in cybernetics, literature, and informatics*, Chicago: University of Chicago Press.

Jantsch, E. (1980) *The Self-Organizing Universe: scientific and human implications of the emerging paradigm of evolution*, New York: Pergamon.

Livingston, I. (2006) *Between Science and Literature: an introduction to autopoetics*, Urbana: University of Illinois Press.

Margulis, L. and Sagan, D. (2002) *Acquiring Genomes: a theory of the origins of species*, New York: Basic Books.

Paulson, W. (1991) "Literature, complexity, interdisciplinarity," in Hayles 1991, pp. 37–53.

Porush, D. (1991) "Fictions as dissipative structures: Prigogine's theory and postmodernism's roadshow," in Hayles 1991, pp. 54–84.

Pynchon, T. (1960) "Entropy," in *Slow Learner*, Boston, Mass., and Toronto: Little, Brown & Company, 1984, pp. 81–98.

——(1965) *The Crying of Lot 49*, New York: Perennial Classics, 1999.

Rabinbach, A. (1990) *The Human Motor: energy, fatigue, and the origins of modernity*, New York: Basic Books.

Schneider, E.D. (1988) "Thermodynamics, ecological succession, and natural selection: a common thread," in Weber, Depew and Smith 1988, pp. 107–37.

——and Sagan, D. (2005) *Into the Cool: energy flow, thermodynamics, and life*, Chicago: University of Chicago Press.

Schrodinger, E. (1945) *What Is Life?* with *Mind and Matter* and *Autobiographical Sketches*, London: Cambridge University Press, 2006.

Weber, B.H., Depew, D.J. and Smith, J.D. (eds) (1988) *Entropy, Information, and Evolution: new perspectives on physical and biological evolution*, Cambridge, Mass.: MIT Press.

Wharton, E. (1905) *The House of Mirth*, in *Edith Wharton: Novels*, ed. R.W.B. Lewis, New York: Library of America, 1985.

White, E.C. (1991) "Negentropy, noise, and emancipatory thought," in Hayles 1991, pp. 263–78.

Wicken, J. (1988) "Thermodynamics, evolution, and emergence: ingredients for a new synthesis," in Weber, Depew and Smith 1988, pp. 139–69.

Part II

DISCIPLINARY AND THEORETICAL APPROACHES

Part II surveys the most salient specializations currently in play at the nexus of literatures and sciences. A relative latecomer to interdisciplinary developments in the humanities and social sciences, the discipline of literature and science follows the prior establishment of academic specializations in the history of science, philosophy of science, and sociology of science. Each of these fields has produced important disciplinary discourses from which literature and science scholars continue to learn. A significant point of conceptual contact between literature and science and these related interdisciplines is a social and historical appreciation of philosophical basics, the inevitable embeddedness of theoretical assumptions within any act of observation. In his article on Philosophy of Science, Alfred Nordmann underlines this state of affairs, in the technical vocabulary of that field, as *conventionalism*: "After Immanuel Kant had proposed that Newton's laws articulated the basic and necessary suppositions that make any scientific experience or knowledge of nature possible, and after physiologists of sense looked at such necessary conditions also from an empirical point of view, scientists and philosophers recognized that the formulation and adoption of theories involved an act of judgment that could not be eliminated from accounts of science."

But above and beyond its literary specificity, one thing that sets literature and science apart from these earlier-arriving fields is its postmodernism, or more precisely, its emergence at the end of the great twentieth-century waves of theoretical and technological renovation in the natural and human sciences. The first of these was linguistic structuralism, the direct offspring of Ferdinand de Saussure's semiology. Structuralism's variants – linguistic, anthropological, psychoanalytic, as well as literary – were in each case oriented to and modeled on systems abstracted from linguistic signs. Such systems were putatively universal and thus "scientific" paradigms for the production of meaning. However, as Paul Cobley argues in his article on Semiotics, "The localized study of the *linguistic* sign, a sign type used by humans alone, is only one component of the study of the sign in general. The human phenomenon of language is just one minuscule aspect of a broader *semiosis*, the action of signs throughout the universe no matter how they might be embodied." In the discourses of literature and science, one now sees a range of sign theories at work, derived from either Saussure or Charles Sanders Peirce, or from both, and applied to analyses of both literary texts and natural systems.

Another complex theoretical wave impelling work in literature and science has been deconstruction in particular and poststructuralism in general. Both developed philosophical critiques of the scientistic overreaching in structuralism, yet both have also consolidated in different ways the insights of structuralism into the relays and couplings among signification, discourse, power, and subjectivity. Noting the extent to which Deconstruction in the work of Jacques Derrida radicalizes notions of semiotic and linguistic structure through an emphasis on a productivity of *writing* that problematizes distinctions between the cultural and the natural, Vicki Kirby asks: "How can the language of human culture and ideas connect and merge with the deep communicative structures of the animal, the vegetable, indeed, even the inorganic? The provocation that attends this 'expanded' sense of language that Derrida brings under the banner of 'writing' was registered in the original dissemination of poststructural arguments in both the humanities and human sciences."

The third great theoretical wave was not immediately discursive but rather, technoscientific. In tandem with major leaps in computational and communications technologies at mid-twentieth century, this was the confluence of cybernetics and information theory. While driving together the current discourses of Systems Theory and Posthumanism, this wave is already implicated in the rise of deconstruction and its poststructuralist offshoots. Kirby cites Derrida from *Of Grammatology*: "The contemporary biologist speaks of writing and *program* in relation to the most elementary processes of information within the living cell. … Whether it has essential limits or not, the entire field covered by the cybernetic *program* will be the field of writing." In his article on Systems Theory, Bruce Clarke noted how cybernetic systems theory "lends itself to the discourse of posthumanism" by stressing the formal and operational parallels between mechanical and living systems – the initial point of cybernetic synthesis – and more recently, through the discourse of autopoietic or self-referential systems, the operational resonances among systems producing life, consciousness, and communication. Similarly, Neil Badmington indicates how Posthumanism carries out an extension of deconstruction's interrogations of the borders previously cordoning off separated fields of being and knowing. Citing a famous dictum of Donna Haraway's, Badmington writes: "one of the recognitions of posthumanist culture has been that 'the boundary between science fiction and social reality is an optical illusion,' for with the deconstruction of the opposition between the human and the inhuman also comes a waning of the conventional distinction between fact and fiction." And as Richard Nash explains in his article on Animal Studies, alongside cybernetic posthumanism is a related variant based on the deconstruction of the human–animal boundary: "The paradigm of dominion, in which the world was a resource at the disposal of the human, is giving way to a paradigm of responsive interaction and mutual interdependencies."

Emerging as a recognizable academic specialization in the midst or the aftermath of these various intellectual and technoscientific movements and counter-movements, literature and science immediately entered the fray with an especially pronounced level of theoretical awareness. Thus, Part II presents a range of discursive openings and entrance points into the field. Some articles are allied to well-developed areas of special academic interest – Feminist Science Studies, Art Connections, Cultural Science Studies, and Science Fiction. And other articles address nascent topics that have just arrived in the intellectual scene – Animal Studies, Game Studies, and E-Literature. For instance, in her article on Agricultural Studies, Susan M. Squier assists the development of this new specialization by defining its differences from traditional literary treatments of the pastoral and from related fields such as cultural studies and agrarian studies: "In contrast to ... literary and historical explorations of the pastoral, Agricultural Studies focuses on the post-pastoral," and "enrolls scholars in several emergent (and often interconnecting) areas of literary studies including science studies, animal studies, ecocriticism and environmental studies, women and gender studies, and science fiction." In sum, literature and science is by far the most eclectic and experimental of the (post)humanistic interdisciplines, the most willing to challenge received academic verities and to press insights from all quarters to their transdisciplinary conclusions.

21

AGRICULTURAL STUDIES

Susan M. Squier

[C]ountry life has many meanings. It is the elms, the may, the white horse, in the field beyond the window where I am writing. It is the men in the November evening, walking back from pruning, with their hands in the pockets of their khaki coats; and the women in headscarves, outside their cottages, waiting for the blue bus that will take them, inside school hours to work in the harvest. It is the tractor on the road, leaving its tracks of serrated pressed mud; the light in the small hours, in the pig-farm across the road, in the crisis of a litter; the slow brown van met at the difficult corner, with the crowded sheep jammed to its slatted sides; the heavy smell, on still evenings, of the silage ricks fed with molasses. It is also the sour land, on the thick boulder clay, not far up the road, that is selling for housing, for a speculative development, at twelve thousand pounds an acre.

(Williams 1973: 3)

Thirty years ago, Raymond Williams set forth in this brief paragraph what we might view as the agenda for agricultural studies (Williams 1973). Yet despite its debt to his pioneering *Culture and Society* (Williams 1958), which laid the groundwork of cultural studies, in the years to come, the field of cultural studies showed little appreciation of the agricultural issues Williams evoked so memorably. Instead, from its origins in the work of Raymond Williams and Richard Hoggart, the field of cultural studies grew to emphasize engaged analysis, a focus on subjectivity, attention to the relations between culture and individual lives, and a commitment to the investigation of the impact of the political and technological centralization of first-world power in the great cities of the global North (Williams 1958; Hoggart 1958; During 1993). This emphasis is clearly evident in *The Cultural Studies Reader*, a well-known volume that covers nationalism, postcolonialism, and globalization; ethnicity and multiculturalism; science and cyberculture; sexuality and gender; carnival and utopia; consumption and the market; leisure; and culture (During 1993: 2, 1). Notably absent is any reference to the act of cultivating plants or animals for food, despite the fact that culture, derived from the Latin word *cultura*, was used as far back as 1420 to mean "the cultivation of a plant or crop" (*OED*).

Agriculture has a broad reach, from Stone Age ploughs to the pastoral, and discussions of rural and agrarian life have long been part of literary history and criticism (see Alpers 1997; Conlogue 2001: 6). Certain works loom particularly large in our understanding of how the pastoral motif of a blessed retreat from the pressures of an urban world, "a green thought in a green shade," has structured English and American literature (Marvell 1938). While D.H. Lawrence describes the flight to the country as a classically American escape from European cultural dominance, in their 1930 introductory essay to the classic manifesto *I'll Take My Stand*, the "Twelve Southerners," known as the "Agrarians," affirm that they all "tend to support a Southern way of life against what may be called the American or prevailing way; and all … agree that the best terms in which to represent the distinction are contained in the phrase, Agrarian *versus* Industrial" (Twelve Southerners 1930). Henry Nash Smith explores the myth of the garden as a foundational belief in American culture and politics, Leslie Fiedler argues that American men choose the wilderness because they associate it with masculine freedom from the civilizing domesticities of a feminized town life, and both Leo Marx and Annette Kolodny associate the rural with the feminine, whether that link invites consolation and embrace or leads to violence and exploitation (Lawrence 1923; Smith 1950; Fiedler 1960; Conlogue 2001: 6; Marx 1964; Kolodny 1975).

In contrast to such literary and historical explorations of the pastoral, agricultural studies focuses on the post-pastoral. I borrow this term from Terry Gifford, who frames its defining vision as awe at the natural world; recognition of "a creative-destructive universe"; realization that inner and outer nature must be understood in relation to each other; "awareness of both nature as culture and culture as nature"; acknowledgment that "with consciousness comes conscience"; and the ecofeminist understanding that exploitation of women and minorities emerges from the same state of mind as environmental exploitation (Gifford 2000). We can clarify the concept of the post-pastoral by considering the contemporary response to that 1930 text, *I'll Take My Stand*. Recent scholars have located populism, anti-industrialism, cultural conservatism, and whiteness in that volume's celebration of rural heritage (Donaldson 2006: ix). For example, Tanya Ann Kennedy argues that the volume formulates a gendered relation between private and public worlds that leads to a suppression of women writers even within a reclaimed regional identity. Kennedy charges the Agrarians with inconsistency and gender bias, because despite their attention to the "displacements and alienations engendered by imperialist, industrial, and urban impositions upon a primarily agricultural people," she argues, they fail to take into account the differences between male and female agricultural work. Instead, their defense of the Agrarian way of life "subsumes all white female members under the rubric of the household economy," shoving women to the margin "as an agent of the consumerism and sexuality associated with northern urbanism" (Kennedy 2005: 45).

We can sharpen our understanding of "post-pastoral" as a term by associating it with a paradigm shift within agriculture, during which the general concept of farming changed from a way of life to a business, subject to the same strategies of rationalization, management practices, and control technologies as other industrialized businesses. Of course, such a broad claim omits the various niches within industrial farming where small, marginal, and recreational farmers have continued to exist alongside the rationalized and large-scale agricultural holdings on the High Plains at the turn of the twentieth century. It also relies on a restrictive and futuristic view of technology. Even the Bonanza wheat farms and the vast cattle ranches were forged by such low-technology tools as the mule-drawn plough and the barbed-wire fence (Hinrichs 2009). Yet depending on the types of agricultural practices they investigate, which will lead scholars to date the emergence of post-paradigm agriculture earlier or later, a major reference point is arguably England between 1649 and 1650, when a group of agrarian reformers known as the Diggers launched a "rural, radical and short-lived response to the enclosure laws and the widespread poverty and starvation" they had produced (Lyon 1999: 17).

The Diggers' argument that poor people were a distinct group with a shared interest in access to the common lands, recently fenced in by the Enclosure Acts for the landowning ruling classes, was legitimated by religious understanding. They drew on the thinking of reformers Robert Coster and Gerard Winstanley that the earth was a "common treasury" bestowed by God for all men and women to use. While the Digger uprising was quickly crushed by the landowning classes, their communities shattered, houses burned, and property destroyed, the rhetorical innovation they displayed remains. "Digger texts (and specifically Winstanley's writings) principally aimed to 'win over a rural proletariat (and other sympathetic groups) to a program of mass political action'" (Lyon 1999: 19, citing Holstun). They called, in songs and poems, "Stand up now, Diggers all," and the group whose solidarity they invoked was both called into being and given a cause. And so was launched a new literary genre, the manifesto. As a literary genre, the manifesto embodies the troubled connections between modernity and agriculture, between the ability to work one's own land and the status of citizen. A central theme of the manifesto is the protest that "We" (its empowered and oppressed collectivity) have not shared the fruits of modernity's technological and political innovations. Yet the manifesto's call for access to technological progress clashes with its origins in an agrarian protest, as the Digger movement waged a bitter and ultimately doomed fight against a new technology of land management: the fencing in, or enclosure, of common lands.

"Historically," Janet Lyon reminds us, "manifestoes ... appear most often in clusters around those crises that involve definitions of citizenship and political subjecthood" (Lyon 1999: 16). The very form of the manifesto *performs* the creation of a community, a "we" articulating its claim to the fruits of progress produced by contemporary science and medicine. Yet this new community also marked the end of an old subject position: the subsistence farmer who worked lands held in common. Rosemarie Garland Thomson has introduced the term *normate* to designate "the social figure through which people can represent themselves as definitive human beings. Normate ... is the constructed identity of those who, by way of the bodily configurations and cultural capitalism they assume, can step into a position of authority and wield the power it grants them" (Thomson 1997: 8). The initial act of agricultural dispossession not only led to the manifesto, but also shaped the political subject: the functional, normate body of the citizen.

We can see this notion of the citizen taking shape in Locke's *Two Treatises of Government*, where Locke makes a distinctly agricultural case for the ownership of property:

> *As much Land* as a Man Tills, Plants, Improves, Cultivates, and can use the Product of, so much is his *Property*. He by his Labor does, as it were, inclose it from the Common. ... He that in Obedience to this Command of God, subdued, tilled and sowed any part of it, thereby annexed to it something that was his *Property*, which another had no Title to, nor could without injury take from him.
>
> (Locke 1689: 290–91)

Locke's accomplishment lay not merely in forwarding a new notion that labor is the warrant for property, or in linking that property to a man's body, but in implicitly restricting the *kinds* of bodies that can produce property. He saw the proper body as a commodity, which though it established a person's material identity, was functionally equivalent to all bodies, and thus robbed of its specificity. Those bodies which were, due to age, illness, or disability, unable to work were not, in the Lockean sense, individuals. Because they were held to dependence on others for the fundamentals of human life, these bodies had no agency. And, as Paul Youngquist has pointed out, "Bodies irreducible to functional norms live beyond the pale of liberal politics, the objects perhaps of charity and affection but not quite persons, not quite proper. They remain too dependent to be full participants in civil society" (Youngquist 2003: 21).

In equating labor with the property thus accumulated, Locke goes farther, reshaping the body that produces (and grounds) labor from something diverse and various (in its power and value) into something standardized and functionally equivalent *inasmuch as all forms of laboring bodies produce property*. "Not possessions but the ability to possess is what qualifies the individual for participation in civil society. It is because a man has a right to the free use of his body that he can accumulate property, which civil society then develops to protect" (Youngquist 2003: 20). Race, gender, ability, and even age are all implicitly specified in this understanding of property, which is focused not on possessions but on the power to possess. With that move the citizen is redefined. Those social technologies that assisted in the transformation of the citizen would also help to transform farming over the next 300 years, from a way of life to a profit-driven business, or *agribusiness*.

In spite of Locke's explicit linkage between agriculture as a zone of subject production and the creation of a new citizen – so central to any cultural studies analysis – until recently it was left to such social science fields as agricultural economics, history, anthropology, geography, and rural sociology to challenge the metropolitan mindset of cultural studies (Levidow 1996; Sachs 1996; Soper 1996; Hart 1998; Cloke, Marsden, and Mooney 2006; Thompson 2007). One such challenge originates in the Program in Agrarian Studies at Yale University, an experimental, interdisciplinary academic program formed in 1991–92 with support from the Rockefeller Foundation and the Ford Foundation as well as Yale University itself. The Yale Agrarian Studies program explicitly reaches beyond its social science origins, eschewing the "purely statistical and abstract," and setting an agenda for itself that welcomes "the fresh air of popular know-ledge and reasoning about poverty, subsistence, cultivation, justice, art, laws, property, ritual life, cooperation, resource use, and state action" ("About Agrarian Studies" 2009). Intending to draw together a wide range of disciplines, agrarian studies embraces three shared principles: "that any satisfactory analysis of agrarian development must begin with the lived experience, understandings, and values of its historical subjects"; "that the study of the Third World … must never be segregated from the historical study of the west, or the humanities from the social sciences"; and finally that "the only way to loosen the nearly hege-monic grip of the separate disciplines on how questions are framed and answered is to concentrate on themes of signal importance to several disciplines" ("About Agrarian Studies" 2009).

Agrarian studies is explicit in its intention to include the humanities in its social sciences-centered area of investigation. Yet unlike agrarian studies' atten-tion to "rural life and society" broadly conceived, agricultural studies displays an explicit focus on agriculture. Moreover, while agrarian studies (despite its inten-tions) draws its strength predominantly from the social sciences, agricultural studies enrolls scholars in several emergent (and often interconnecting) areas of literary studies including science studies, animal studies, ecocriticism and envir-onmental studies, women and gender studies, and science fiction. Literature-and-science scholars have begun to use specifically literary methods to assess the impact of agricultural innovations on the individual and society. For example, science studies scholars are forging a critical literature that explores the role of scientized agriculture in the production of the human being as citizen (Levidow 1996; Bryson 2002; Franklin, Lury, and Stacey 2000; Thurtle 2007; Haraway 2008).

Animal studies scholars explore not only the ontological otherness of animals and their interconnection with human beings, but also the broader issues raised by the farming of individual animals (chickens, cattle, sheep); agricultural inter-ventions into animal breeding and human innovations in assisted reproduction;

and the broader issue of the co-construction of veterinary and human medicine (Agamben 2002; Squier 2004; Franklin 2007; Broglio 2008; Clarke 1998). Ecocriticism and environmental studies research explores the social cost of an extractive approach to nature, while a sub-category styling itself "green cultural studies" adds the category "nature ... plants, animals, elements" to such factors as "ethnicity/color, gender, sexuality, economic class, and age" that are all influenced by the impact of texts and social practices (Hochman 2000: 187). Women and gender studies explores the meaning of agriculture to women: as the source of loneliness; as a zone of racist eugenics; as a mode of economic and technological exploitation demanding feminist activism, and as a site where gender and domesticity can be reworked in relation to a contested modernity (Jellison 1993; Weinbaum 2004; Casey 2009). Finally, science fiction studies scholars have been making explicit the connections between science fictions about the production of food and reproduction of people, and contemporary agriculture (Franklin 1982; Le Guin 1996).

Just as our understanding of the manifesto genre is deepened once we know that it originated in the struggle against agricultural dispossession and the redefinition of the citizen in terms of the capacity to possess property, so too our understanding of other literary and aesthetic genres is enriched by attention to agriculture as a set of practices, technologies, and actors (both human and animal). An agricultural studies perspective enables a more socially situated understanding of specific literary genres. We see this demonstrated in three literary works dealing, respectively, with English Romanticism, nineteenth- and twentieth-century American literature, and feminist literary criticism of modernism/modernity. These works offer us new views of portrait painting, the novel, and periodical literature.

Ronald Broglio's *Technologies of the Picturesque: British Art, Poetry, and Instruments 1750–1830* demonstrates that British landscape painting, and particularly the genre of breed portraiture, was a technology of representation essential to the practice of cattle breeding (Broglio 2008). Arguing that eighteenth-century literature and painting co-create the picturesque relation to the natural world, Broglio challenges the conventional understanding of the picturesque by juxtaposing George Stubbs's and George Garrard's breed portraits to specific agricultural practices, and then demonstrating the relations between picturesque landscape paintings and Robert Bakewell's technique of "in-in" cattle breeding. Such paintings served as guide and template to breeders hoping to duplicate in their herds the proportions and weight of champion livestock, and thus helped popularize the new method of animal husbandry. Not only did changing agricultural practices drive the future of cattle breeding, but these practices were grounded in, and shaped, the development of artistic conventions in portraiture. Tracing the origins of a major human medical breakthrough, the practice of vaccination, back to routine, accepted agricultural practices, Broglio records a challenge to the customary division between veterinary and human medicine.

He demonstrates that when Edward Jenner developed a cure for smallpox by experimentally inoculating patients with the cowpox virus, he was drawing on farmers' long-standing experience that proximity with an animal disease, cowpox, provided dairymaids with immunity from smallpox. Jenner's development of the vaccine through attention to the relationship between animals and human beings ushered in the extensive technology transfers between animal reproductive sciences and human reproductive medicine of the twentieth- and twenty-first centuries (Clarke 1998; Squier 2005; Franklin 2007).

What is the agricultural studies method *in practice*, then? We can see its outlines by comparing Broglio's approach to Romantic literature and art with William Conlogue's treatment of nineteenth- and twentieth-century American farm texts, *Working the Garden: American writers and the industrialization of agriculture* (Conlogue 2001). Both studies consider an aesthetic category and set of cultural practices in relation to an agricultural innovation: whether it is the new practice of cross-breeding cattle (Broglio) or the restructuring of American wheat farming (Conlogue). In both studies, the juxtaposition of art and agricultural science results in a re-evaluation of customary aesthetic judgments: a reassessment of the picturesque for the former, and for the latter a challenge to the literary reliance on the pastoral mode as the appropriate prism through which to interpret the "farm text" (Conlogue 2001). And essential to each study is a thick description of changing agricultural practices: the new impetus to improve British beef by selective breeding, and the new huge bonanza wheat farms that emerged in the 1880s in the Dakotas' Red River Valley.

Exploring farm literature as a site of intense debate over the changes in American agriculture resulting from industrialization, Conlogue argues against using the literary model of the pastoral to approach these texts. Virgil's *Georgics* offer a better lens: the *georgic* addresses issues of "how work, community, technological restraint, and human uses of nature changed with the introduction of an urban-defined industrial agriculture that has erased the pastoral's central tension between city and country" (Conlogue 2001: 9). Conlogue's study distinguishes between the Old Agriculture, infused with the values of yeoman-like integrity, community, and the worth of inherited farm knowledge, and the New Agriculture, characterized by a rationalized, industrialized business model with profit at the core. Challenging an earlier formulation of the genre as any form of fiction that deals with farm life, that accurately portrays the details of farming in a vernacular style and reflects the essentially conservative attitudes and values of farming people, Conlogue reveals what differentiates an agricultural studies perspective, which responds to actually occurring changes in farming structure and practice, from a simple focus on agricultural themes. Viewed from his engaged perspective, with a focus on the relations between culture and the production of individual subjects, he defines farm fiction as that which attends to the interrelationships of the natural world and the world of human work, the force and importance of history, the relation between the well-being of individual farm families and the broader community, and the effect of technologies (particularly but not exclusively agricultural technologies) on human beings and the environment.

Conlogue's agricultural studies analysis of farm fiction is attentive to gender, ethnicity, and race, categories which have all been intimately shaped by, and have left their mark on, the structure and practice of agriculture in the United States. Offering chapters assessing the visibility (or lack thereof) of women in the New Agriculture; the relationship between class and the transformation of agriculture from a way of life to a business; and the relationship between racism and industrial farming, Conlogue's study exemplifies the agricultural studies method of giving equal attention to the epistemological practices of widely divergent disciplines, including both a chart drawn from rural sociology that provides a detailed comparison of conventional and alternative agriculture, and also Conlogue's own autobiographical narrative. This strategic openness to both modes of knowledge exemplifies agricultural studies' commitment to analyzing the meaning of agriculture at all scales and magnitudes.

We have seen that agricultural studies characteristically gives us new ways to think about literary analysis as well as an understanding of changes in agricultural science. Janet Galligani Casey's *A New Heartland: Women, Modernity, and the Agrarian Ideal in America* exemplifies this method by reviewing modernism/modernity through the lens of agriculture. Casey argues that rural texts are modernist in that they challenge the dominant ideologies of agrarian life, ranging from its conservative positions on gender and race to its radical embrace of agricultural rationalization (Casey 2009). Turning to popular best-sellers, the early twentieth-century agricultural periodical *The Farmer's Wife*, and the work of two women rural photographers, this study, too, incorporates non-canonical texts, arguing that in their resistance to the categories of the pastoral and the agrarian ideal, these rural texts constitute a distinctly modern kind of aesthetic production.

Returning, in closing, to Raymond Williams's glimpse out of his window, we can consider how this paragraph exemplifies agricultural studies *ab ovo*. As we begin reading, we sense the scene's distinctly English tone. The elms, the white horse, and the may or hawthorn tree carry resonances of ancient Druid festivals and village celebrations of the maypole, as well as echoes of Tennyson's "immemorial elms" and Chesterton's *Ballad of the White Horse* (Tennyson 1847; Chesterton 1911; Lincoln 1918). We can follow Williams's vision of the country as it expands from the simply botanical and naturalist perspective to the explicitly agricultural, as he acknowledges that "there is a deep contrast in which so much feeling is held: between what seems an unmediated nature – a physical awareness of trees, birds, the moving shapes of land – and a working agriculture, in which so much of nature is in fact being produced" (Williams 1973: 3).

This awareness of deep contrast is essential to agricultural studies, a method of analysis attentive to the role of *techne* in all aspects of the agricultural endeavor.

It understands technology not only as the pruning shears which the farm laborers carry, but also the technology of gender that differentiates male from female farm workers, so that the men in their typical khaki coats and the women in their kerchiefs do different kinds of work at different times (Lauretis 1987). The men prune while the women harvest; the men work from morning to evening while the women can only hire themselves out as harvesters during school hours when the children are out of the home. And unlike the men, women's agricultural work is not only productive, but reproductive. As with the livestock (the pigs and the sheep), for women their share of farm work includes the bearing of and caring for children, as well as keeping the household.

Reading this passage from an agricultural studies perspective, we notice the rhythm of animal birth and death that forms the core of agriculture; we explore the texture and imprint of technology upon the land (those serrated tracks in the mud); and we see time passing – both the passage of a day (that small-hours light in the pigsty as the farmer helps with a litter of pigs), and an era (as good farm land gives way to a crop of new plots of sour boulder clay, sold on speculation for suburban housing). And we can formulate the essential qualities of an agricultural studies perspective. It will be situated in space and place, aware of the forces of gender and class, and sensitive not only to myth and folk knowledge, but to technology, economics and culture as well. While such complex, simultaneous, and often clashing experiences and meanings by no means exhaust its potential, they at least suggest some of the intellectual and cultural importance of the field of agricultural studies.

Bibliography

"About Agrarian Studies." *Program in Agrarian Studies*. Online. Available HTTP: <http://www.yale.edu/agrarianstudies/real/aboutAS.html> (accessed 3 July 2009).

Agamben, G. (2002) *The Open: man and animal*, Stanford: Stanford University Press, 2004.

Alpers, P. (1997) *What is Pastoral?*, Chicago: University of Chicago Press.

Broglio, R. (2008) *Technologies of the Picturesque: British art, poetry, and instruments 1750–1830*, Lewisburg: Bucknell University Press.

Bryson, M.A. (2002) *Visions of the Land: science, literature, and the American environment from the era of exploration to the age of ecology*, Charlottesville: University of Virginia Press.

Casey, J.G. (2009) *A New Heartland: women, modernity, and the agrarian ideal in America*, Oxford: Oxford University Press.

Chesterton, G. (1911) *The Ballad of the White Horse*, New York: John Lane Company.

Clarke, A. (1998) *Disciplining Reproduction: modernity, American life sciences, and the problem of sex*, Berkeley: University of California Press.

Cloke, P.J., Marsden, T. and Mooney, P. (2006) *Handbook of Rural Studies*, London: Sage.

Conlogue, W. (2001) *Working the Garden: American writers and the industrialization of agriculture*, Chapel Hill: University of North Carolina Press.

Coupe, L. (ed.) (2000) *The Green Studies Reader*, London: Routledge.

Donaldson, S.V. (2006) "Introduction: the southern agrarians and their cultural wars," in Twelve Southerners, 2006, pp. ix–xl.

During, S. (1993) *The Cultural Studies Reader*, 2nd edn, London: Routledge.

Fiedler, L. (1960) *Love and Death in the American Novel*, New York: Anchor Books, 1992.

Franklin, H.B. (1982) "America as science fiction: 1939," *Science Fiction Studies*, 9(1): 38–50.

Franklin, S. (2007) *Dolly Mixtures: the remaking of genealogy*, Durham, N.C.: Duke University Press.

Franklin, S., Lury, C. and Stacey, J. (2000) *Global Nature, Global Culture*, London: Sage.

Gifford, T. (2000) "Pastoral, anti-pastoral, post-pastoral," in L. Coupe (ed.) 2000, pp. 219–22.

Haraway, D.J. (2008) *When Species Meet*, Minneapolis: University of Minnesota Press.

Hart, J.F. (1998) *The Rural Landscape*, Baltimore: Johns Hopkins University Press.

Hinrichs, C. (2009) Personal communication.

Hochman, J. (2000) "Green cultural studies," in Coupe 2000, pp. 187–92.

Hoggart, R. (1958) *The Uses of Literacy*, Harmondsworth: Penguin.

Jellison, K. (1993) *Entitled to Power: farm women and technology 1913–1965*, Chapel Hill: University of North Carolina Press.

Kennedy, T.A. (2005) "The secret properties of southern regionalism: gender and agrarianism in Glasgow's barren ground," *Southern Literary Journal*, 38: 40–63.

Kolodny, A. (1975) *The Lay of the Land: metaphor as experience and history in American life and letters*, Chapel Hill: University of North Carolina Press.

Lauretis, T. de (1987) *Technologies of Gender: essays on theory, film, and fiction*, Bloomington: Indiana University Press.

Lawrence, D.H. (1923) *Studies in Classic American Literature*, London: Heinemann, 1964.

Le Guin, U. (1996) "The carrier bag theory of fiction," in C. Glotfelty and H. Fromm (eds) *The Ecocriticism Reader: landmarks in literary ecology*, Athens: University of Georgia Press, pp. 149–54.

Levidow, L. (1996) "Simulating mother nature, industrializing agriculture," in Robertson et al. 1996, pp. 55–71.

Lincoln, J.E. (1918) *The Festival Book: May-Day pastime and the May-pole*, New York: A.S. Barnes Company.

Locke, J. (1689) *Two Treatises of Government*, ed. P. Laslett, 2nd edn, Cambridge: Cambridge University Press, 1987.

Lyon, J. (1999) *Manifestoes: provocations of the modern*, Ithaca, N.Y.: Cornell University Press.

Marvell, A. (1938) "The garden," in E. Matthew and W. Black, *Elizabethan and Seventeenth-Century Lyrics*, Philadelphia: J.B. Lippincott, pp. 373–75.

Marx, L. (1964) *The Machine in the Garden: technology and the pastoral ideal in America*, Oxford: Oxford University Press, 1974.

Robertson, G., Mash, M., Tickner, L., Bird, J., Curtis, B. and Putnam, T. (eds) (1996) *Future-Natural: nature, science, culture*, London: Routledge.

Sachs, C. (1996) *Gendered Fields: rural women, agriculture, and environment*, Boulder, CO: Westview Press.

Smith, H.N. (1950) *Virgin Land*, Cambridge, Mass.: Harvard University Press, 1970.

Soper, K. (1996) "Nature/'nature'," in Robinson et al. 1996, pp. 22–34.

Squier, S. (2004) *Liminal Lives: imagining the human at the frontiers of biomedicine*, Durham, N.C.: Duke University Press.

Tennyson, Alfred, Baron (1847) "The Princess: A Medley," ed. Henry Alsopp, Oxford, 1910.

Thompson, P.B. (2007) "Agriculture and working-class political culture: a lesson from *The Grapes of Wrath*," *Agriculture and Human Values*, 24: 165–77.

Thomson, R.G. (1997) *Extraordinary Bodies: figuring physical disability in American culture and literature*, New York: Columbia University Press.

Thurtle, P. (2007) *The Emergence of Genetic Rationality: space, time, and information in American biological science, 1870–1920*, Seattle: University of Washington Press.

Twelve Southerners (1930) "Introduction: a statement of principles," in *I'll Take My Stand: the south and the agrarian tradition*, Baton Rouge: Louisiana State University Press, 2006. Online. Available HTTP: <http://xroads.virginia.edu/~ma01/White/anthology/agrarian.html> (accessed 2 July 2009).

Weinbaum, A.E. (2004) *Wayward Reproductions: genealogies of race and nation in transatlantic modern thought*, Durham, N.C.: Duke University Press.

Western Folklife Center (2008) "Our mission and vision." Online. Available HTTP: <http://www.westernfolklife.org/site1/index.php/About-Us/Our-Mission.html> (accessed 30 June 2009).

Williams, R. (1958) *Culture and Society: 1780–1950*, Harmondsworth: Penguin, 1960.

——(1973) *The Country and the City*, Oxford: Oxford University Press.

Youngquist, P. (2003) *Monstrosities: bodies and British romanticism*, Minneapolis: University of Minnesota Press.

22
ANIMAL STUDIES

Richard Nash

Two skunks, one day, by the roadside stood,
As an old Chevrolet passed by;
And the smell that it left was far from good,
And a tear stood in one skunk's eye.

"Oh, why do you weep?" the other skunk cried;
"Oh, why do you shiver and shake?"
"Because that smell," the first replied,
"Is like mother used to make."
G. Zabriskie, "Two Skunks"

My credit card called me today. It wanted to remind me – in that annoyingly impersonal, unflappable, slightly condescending human voice it has – that I needed to pay it. It gave me precise instructions, which in order to placate it, I dutifully followed to the best of my ability, pushing the button required at the moment indicated, through three or four levels, before it gave up on me and abruptly terminated the conversation by instructing me to call it back at a given number and then hanging up. When I returned its call, I eventually worked my way out of the automated maze, and after a short wait was put through to a courteous operator who spoke clear and articulate English with an inflection that struck my untrained ear as vaguely Pakistani. We conducted our transaction, with him pleasantly (but insistently) offering me products and services; and I, straining to match his courtesy, just as insistently declining these offers. Throughout the transaction, my refusals were strengthened by my irritated awareness that anything purchased would not be purchased from the kindly, precise, efficient fellow now making the offer, but from the hypocritical, overly pleasant machine who had first called me. I tend to be slow to anger when speaking with people, but I notice that I get irritated much more rapidly when conversing with machines.

That last sentence I wrote is the kind I grew up reading in sci-fi narratives of fifty years ago, but today it pops up on my monitor as a straightforward narrative of a widely held, non-idiosyncratic observation of affect in contemporary culture. In fact, if one Googles "anger automated voice," one will get not only the expected news stories documenting how widespread this new source of irritation is, one will also get citations to the burgeoning literature on how to build anger-detection protocols into the automated voice caller, to make it more responsive to the anger being generated.

I begin this chapter with this moment of machine-provoked affective response to underline what was intended to be my opening comment: N. Katherine Hayles's influential text, *How We Became Posthuman*, is already a decade old. When it first appeared, that title seasoned its implicit argument with a dash of audacity: posthumanism was not the brave new territory to be explored by the coming generation, it was the *fait accompli* whose history now demanded to be written. And the ubiquity of the term in literary-critical studies during the past decade, as well as our increasingly techno-mediated culture, testify to the accuracy of that title choice. (As I write this, the online *MLA International Bibliography* lists 170 publications that include the word "posthuman" in the title, none published before 1991, and all but a dozen published in the past decade. However, using the hyphenated "post-human," the *MLA International Bibliography* generates fewer than twenty-five titles. I also note in passing that while "posthuman" proliferates in titles all around me, when I attempt to use the word in this text, my word processor silently separates it into two words – "post human" – and I have to take care to override manually my cyber-supplemented lexicographic superego.) In a world where "social networking" is more likely to refer to an activity conducted alone in a room with a computer than at a cocktail party or some other collective gathering; where "friending" is a verb form that requires a specific software application; and where twitterers tweet quotidian events like unreflective Prufrocks, our posthuman condition seems clearly established, and its currency in the fields of literary and cultural criticism fully comprehensible.

An important corollary question – particularly important for the next generation of literary critics – is demanded by that reconfiguration: what will be the new role of literary criticism in particular and cultural criticism more generally in the redefined academy? Literary studies developed into a core discipline of the humanities, but do universities need a posthumanities, and if so, what role does literary study play within such a reconfigured academy? That is no idle question, as liberal arts universities increasingly tilt their budgets and their priorities away from a traditional balance of "arts and sciences" and toward a new partnership of science and business. As the "new corporate university" expands away from the traditional humanities, it may be adapting to a new posthuman condition, but it will therefore become all the more important for literary studies to articulate its relevance to a posthumanities university, and to defend against the counterclaim that as we continue becoming posthuman, the discipline that long defined itself as central to the humanities now continues in becoming more peripheral.

For such a long time, a strong feature of disciplinary self-definition was inevitably to some degree traditional, preserving in a curatorial fashion a body of texts that expressed traits and doctrines that were deemed to have particular cultural value in establishing "what oft was thought, but ne'er so well expressed," particularly with respect to those features of the human condition that were deemed to be essential. The last half-century (that period during which Hayles notes we became posthuman) has witnessed a dramatic change in disciplinary self-definition, moving away from the preservation of a narrowly defined core set of canonical texts that express an essential humanity to emphasize instead a set of interpretive practices and theoretical commitments, a critical toolkit that can be used productively to examine a range of texts and their constitutive role in cultural formations. What has, I believe, been rather slower in development – but will ultimately be of even greater significance to the fundamental reorganization of humanities within the academy – is the development of a revised attention to ecological criticism. Where traditional humanism defined culture around the privileged category of the human, the era of the posthuman coincides with an intellectual reorientation to a world in which we are responsive agents within nature-culture networks. The paradigm of dominion, in which the world was a resource at the disposal of the human, is giving way to a paradigm of responsive interaction and mutual interdependencies; and our critical practices need to reflect and respond to that altered orientation. It is in this context that recent attention to animality and animal studies offers dramatic potential for expanding and altering critical practice.

The title figure in the most canonical novel in American literature is a whale. That is a simple statement, almost ludicrous in its naïveté, which makes it all the more marvelous to consider the critical history of *Moby Dick*, which managed so successfully, for so long, to develop complex valuable interpretive arguments in which the non-human animal at the center of that narrative was read as so many things *other* than a whale. That the author went out of his way to intrude on conventional fictional narrative in order to educate his reader about whales and whaling has long been a subject of critical interest, much of it not terribly concerned with cetology itself. My point here is not to digress into the critical history of Melville's major novel, but to point out that a simple alteration in focus can produce dramatically revisionist accounts of familiar texts, even when remaining within familiar methodological paradigms (the MLA informs me that two recently defended dissertations appear to take up this particular challenge). That whales mattered to Melville, and that, therefore, how whales mattered to Melville can matter significantly to his readers, is a simple, straightforward, but not necessarily simplistic work of critical revision.

This is the indirect impact of how a more ecologically alert revision of a humanist tradition requires us to revise our framing of questions in literary and cultural history. Opportunities here abound, and can lead in a variety of rewarding directions. For a generation, historians have been influenced by the important work of Harriet Ritvo, Joan Thirsk, and by Keith Thomas's ambitious *Man and the Natural World*. In books like his influential *Horse and Man in Early Modern England* and more recent *The Horse Trade of Tudor and Stuart England*, Peter Edwards has broken important new ground in economic history by recovering a fuller appreciation for the role companion species play in human historical development. Lisa Jardine and Jerry Brotton's discussion of the traffic in horses and equestrian art in *Global Interests: Renaissance art between East and West* locates the same species in the context of a revisionist art history that expands consideration of cross-species interactions to their commercial and diplomatic engagement with international traffic, a theme that receives considerably fuller treatment in Donna Landry's *Noble Brutes: how eastern horses transformed English culture*.

My momentary focus on the horse (which could be extended to include a significant body of recent critical literature) is not simply a function of my own current research agenda, but a choice intended to highlight how recent critical work has begun two important moves. The first is to differentiate meaningfully between different disparate manifestations of non-human animal life (rather than simply speaking of "the animal" as an undifferentiated "other" to the human). The second is to illustrate how, as this work develops, it expands both our awareness of the long-standing web of cross-species relating that has constituted an important, largely ignored (and often only sparsely recorded) component of a historical development explicitly tagged as "human" history, and at the same time how this work is distributed over a range of sub-disciplinary interests that coalesce in cultural studies: literary, economic, diplomatic, aesthetic, transnational, etc. With her contribution to the important collection edited by Nigel Rothfels, *Representing Animals*, and in her own *Perceiving Animals: humans and beasts in early modern English culture*, Erica Fudge offers an engaging and accessible modeling of the case for a cultural history that considers seriously the transspecies nature of cultural formation. Within the history of science, Anita Guerrini's *Experimenting with Humans and Animals* pursues a similar vein by examining how the human–animal barrier (a special case of species boundary) constitutes a special frontier in the history of experimental medicine, and its historical reliance on human and animal experimentation. Her work is explicitly historical, choosing to articulate what has been the history of a fraught aspect of human–animal relations that inform current ethical debates, rather than enter into those debates directly. But these ethical debates do, of course, constitute a significant component of recent work in animal studies.

As fields or areas of inquiry emerge as a meeting ground for common academic study, there is often a period during which nomenclature and terminology sorts itself out somewhat unevenly, and debate, division, and discord frequently accompany the process, quite often productively. Such a moment seems now to be in play around the question of whether one identifies one's intellectual work as better labeled as "animal studies" or "animality." In a rough-and-ready parsing of these terms, the former is more typically claimed by those whose interest in the topic is grounded squarely in animal-rights discourse and activism, while the latter term is more typically invoked by those who identify their interests with posthumanist efforts to theorize the non-human subject. Clearly, those are not so much opposing positions as overlapping commitments with differing emphases. One of the most rigorously sustained and influential discussions of the relation between these different emphases in addressing the ethical dimension of the theoretical problems posed by "the question of the animal" has been Cary Wolfe's *Animal Rites*. While clearly sympathetic to the aims and methods of such projects as the Great Ape Project, or revisions of the U.S. Animal Welfare Act, or a variety of arguments that seek to extend rights to animals by expanding the notion of personhood on which rights discourse depends, Wolfe is at the same time acutely aware of the degree to which such efforts remain grounded in the same ideological bedrock that was the foundation for the centuries of humanist philosophy that denied those rights on the basis of an unquestioned articulation of human exceptionalism:

> What this means, then, is that such projects which strategically invoke ethical models and theories that are rhetorically very powerful precisely *because* they are relics, because they are "residual" (to use Raymond Williams's well-worn term), are in fact, in intellectual terms, the *easy* part. What is harder, I think, is the project I have tried to make a start on in this book: to address, squarely within the purview of postmodern theory, the theoretical and ethical complexities that attend the question of the animal in several registers. This means considering not only that we share our world with non-human others who inhabited this planet before we arrived on the scene and will in all likelihood far outlast the tenure of *Homo sapiens* but also that *we* – whoever "we" are – are in a profound sense constituted as human subjects within and atop a non-human otherness that postmodern theory has worked hard to release from the bad-faith repressions and disavowals of humanism – whether in Deleuze and Guattari's invocation of the multiplicity of the subject "becoming-animal" in their critique of psychoanalysis, in Derrida's insistence on the fundamentally "inhuman" quality of language itself and the subjection of "the living" in general to the force of the trace, in Donna Haraway's focus on the multiplicity and situatedness of the subject and in myriad other ways.
>
> (Wolfe 2003: 192–93)

Perhaps the most ambitious of recent efforts in contemporary philosophy to confront "the question of the animal" in ways that re-engage the problem of ethical relating across species boundaries without resorting to a reassertion of an ideology that presumes human exceptionalism is Jacques Derrida's final essay, *The Animal That Therefore I Am*. In this deeply influential and wide-ranging essay, ostensibly on "the autobiographical animal," Derrida tracks himself as he follows the philosophical tradition of confronting the animal other from Plato to Levinas. It is a typically labyrinthine and dizzying text, one that recurs repeatedly to the trope of tracking, following, hunting, and hunted; and it is animated by a persistent return to Bentham's revision of the familiar separation of human and animal by the boundary of reason and speech, a revision that asked, instead, "Can the animal suffer?" That question – what the capacity for suffering means to thought – marks an important conjunction where the ethical demands of animal studies meet the boundary-defining work of posthuman animality studies.

One of the more compelling confrontations staged in *The Animal That Therefore I Am* comes when Derrida faces off (as it were) with Levinas over the latter's contention that ethical relations depend on the notion of a face-to-face encounter in which one is able to recognize the difference of the other without reducing to a version of sameness. Such a notion of ethical relations is one that could readily be extended to relations across the species boundary, and in a particularly moving account of his time in a Nazi prison camp, Levinas seems to make such an extension; yet in interviews, he chose to back away from extending the notion of an ethical "face" to non-human animals:

> I cannot say at what moment you have the right to be called "face." The human face is completely different and only afterwards do we discover the face of an animal. I don't know if a snake has a face. I can't answer that question. A more specific analysis is needed.
>
> (cited in Atterton and Calarco 2004: 49)

This disavowal of Levinas's, his refusal to part entirely with human exceptionalism, forms the central feature of Derrida's specific analysis of Levinas's ambivalence on the question of the animal (Derrida 2008: 106ff.), but it is also difficult not to see the entirety of *The Animal That Therefore I Am* as responding directly to Levinas. For Levinas opens the door that he refuses to cross with his episode of the dog, Bobby, who, in effect, by recognizing their humanity, saved Levinas and his fellow prisoners of war from dehumanizing treatment. It is specifically the dog's response to brutalized humans that protects those humans' humanity from being erased by their brutalizing human captors. Such a response across species lines would seem to require a reciprocal acknowledgment, but Levinas betrays Bobby in the end by withholding a recognition of an animal face. Derrida's essay, in pointed opposition, is initiated by his encounter with his cat in the bathroom. Naked before his cat, and contending with his own feeling of shame, he contemplates, "What if the animal responded?" And in that gap that opens up around the distinction between "response" and "reaction," Derrida begins working away from a Cartesian mechanistic account of animal being, through Bentham's consideration of "can the animal suffer," that will lead to his explicit analysis of Levinas. Derrida contemplating his cat – and acknowledging the cat's response – stands as the stark (naked) counter-narrative to Levinas disavowing the face of the dog whose response to his humanity had helped him hold on to it.

Bentham's question that means so much to Derrida – "Can animals suffer?" – is an important one. But perhaps it is also worth reflecting on how Derrida works his way there through his shame at his nakedness before the animal:

> War is waged over the matter of pity. This war is probably not ageless but, and here is my hypothesis, it is passing through a critical phase. We are passing through that phase, and it passes through us. To think the war we find ourselves waging is not only a duty, a responsibility, an obligation, it is also a necessity, a constraint that, like it or not, directly or indirectly, no one can escape. Henceforth more than ever. And I say "to think" this war, because I believe it concerns what we call "thinking." The animal looks at us, and we are naked before it. Thinking perhaps begins there.
>
> (Derrida 2008: 29)

The path that leads from shame to pity is both interesting and important. At the same time it is important to recognize that it is not only not the only path, but also not one that should be followed blindly. As valuable as pity can be, it can also be pernicious; and certainly at times, some skepticism may be warranted as to the ego that authorizes it. Donna Haraway, while recognizing many virtues in Derrida's analysis, may be described as wryly amused by his certainty that the little female cat who contemplates him in the bathroom shares the fascination that is voiced as shame. One must, I think, agree with Haraway when she writes that "whatever else the cat might have been doing, Derrida's full male frontal, human nudity before an Other, which was of such interest in his philosophical tradition, was of no consequence to her" (Haraway 2007: 23).

As important as the question of pity is, I believe Haraway is right in pressing us to move beyond it (and the self-involved projections that it will always encourage) to other equally challenging and complicated questions:

> The question of suffering led Derrida to the virtue of pity, and that is not a small thing; but how much more promise is in the question, Can animals play? Or work? And even, can I learn to play with this cat? Can I, the philosopher, respond to an invitation or recognize one when it is offered? What if work and play, and not just pity, open up when the possibility of mutual response, without names, is taken seriously as an everyday practice available to philosophy and to science? What if a usable word for this is joy?
>
> (Haraway 2007: 105)

Haraway's attention to companion-species relating is productively insistent in acknowledging the ecological stakes in choosing between Darwinian evolution and Judeo-Christian myth: the logic of dominion that has for so long governed human–animal relations derives its force from that old Adamic myth. When one prefers as a better story the narrative of evolution, one is confronted with the evidence that animals and humans are not mutually independent entities, but that evolution operates at a level of systemic interaction in which changes in one organism trigger changes in other organisms within the habitat. That world of mutual interdependence and interrelation will require us to acknowledge that thinking about humans is a form of, and requires more from, thinking about animals.

Derrida dates the war being waged over pity to the past two centuries, when doctrines of sentiment at the end of the eighteenth century mounted a serious challenge to Cartesian notions of the beast-machine, presenting the case for cross-species sympathy, advocating the view that animals responded as well as reacted, and ushering in the first public policies and legislations protecting animals from human cruelty. David Perkins has sought to contextualize Romantic literature within this change in attitude toward animals and the ideologies of sentiment that produced it. More recently, Tobias Menely, in a dissertation now being revised as a monograph, "historicizes the logic of feeling that characterizes sympathy as disturbingly sentimental when its recipient is an animal" (Menely 2006). These are important contributions to what I believe Derrida is right to characterize as a two-century struggle over the limits of compassionate sympathetic identification, and the perceived differences between reaction and response.

I grew up in a household that valued poetry and animals, and the doggerel verse that serves as an epigraph to this chapter is an extemporaneous composition of the minor American poet and advertising executive George Zabriskie. To the best of my knowledge, it was never published, but in my family it was recited on more than one occasion with some pleasure. As I have grown and the culture has aged, my pleasure in that poem has only grown alongside us. The beast-fable dialogue stages wittily an opposition between those twin "others" of the human (machine and animal) who have emerged as our constituent companions in a postmodern era that was only faintly anticipated by my parents' generation. And the sly mixture of (olfactory) sense and (mawkish) sentiment still satisfies with its ironic double articulation that offers a link to a larger community even as it undercuts our pretension to access that community. As we seek a more democratic, more ecologically responsible framing of the world than the ideology of human dominion that we inherited, we find ourselves checking those impulses against a skeptical concern neither to anthropomorphize the animal nor to bestialize the human. In his elegant attempt to wrestle directly with concerns toward which Zabriskie's doggerel verse was only willing to gesture playfully, Giorgio Agamben articulates the space of "bare life":

Both machines are able to function only by establishing a zone of indifference at their centers, within which – like a "missing link" which is always lacking because it is already virtually present – the articulation between human and animal, man and non-man, speaking being and living being, must take place. Like every space of exception, this zone is, in truth, perfectly empty, and the truly human being who should occur there is only the place of a ceaselessly updated decision in which the caesurae and their re-articulating are always dislocated and displaced anew. What would thus be obtained, however, is neither an animal life nor a human life, but only a life that is separated and excluded from itself – only a *bare life*.

(Agamben 2004: 37–38)

What follows in Agamben's text is a distillation of the important work of the early twentieth-century ethologist Jakob von Uexkull and his notion of *umwelt*. The simple insight of the *umwelt* is that one only has access to the world through one's sensorium; and therefore, since different organisms have different sensory apparatuses, we occupy different, overlapping *umwelts* in the same world. I am returned to the question of what a Chevrolet smells like to a skunk, every bit as important as the question of how trans-specific maternal attachment is. We are members of a community larger than our politics, entangled in a world that exceeds the reach of our senses. This may make the task of re-articulating our sense of who we are impossibly difficult, but that should not keep us from the attempt.

How much larger is that community? How far beyond our senses does it reach? Let's keep in mind that when Derrida stands naked before his cat, the philosophical reflections that follow may not be triggered simply by the human–feline dyad. Each of those organisms is itself a carrier of multiple parasitic organisms. One of the more prevalent parasites in the world's cat population is *Toxoplasma gondii*, a parasite whose natural host is the cat, but who parasite ecologists have found is particularly adept at migrating to other organisms and affecting their behavior. In rodents, for instance, studies show that the parasite triggers more risk-taking behavior, thereby feeding the cat population. Projections indicate that the incidence of *Toxoplasma gondii* in the human population may reach as high as half the world's population. And Kevin Lafferty, a parasite ecologist at UC-Santa Barbara, has published research showing a statistically significant correlation between regions of high parasite infestation and what appear to be cultural behavioral traits. The large possibility suggested Lafferty's research is that some aspects of what we identify as cultural behavior may be triggered by other organisms in the environment. The specific case of *Toxoplasma gondii* and its influence suggests that the parasite affects men and women differently: "Research has shown that women who are infected with the parasite tend to be warm, outgoing and attentive to others, while infected men tend to be less intelligent and probably a bit boring" ("Cat parasite" 2009).

What Lafferty's research opens up as an avenue for exploration in cultural studies is every bit as exciting as what it may offer to respondents to Derrida. Perhaps it is the stultifying influence of *Toxoplasma gondii* – I do share a residence with three cats – but I can't help thinking that: for all the ways in which the mechanical and the technological prompt us to reimagine our borders and boundaries; for all the ways that the feedback loop between my internal affect and the triggering mechanism of the automated voice that called me (and even more dizzying to contemplate, the next generation of those automated dialers who will have their own feedback mechanism to "respond" to the affect my voice communicates to my machine caller) implicates me in a more complex apparatus than the one contained by my body's boundaries; for all these ways that we are becoming posthuman; for all that, the most mysterious, the most compelling, and ecologically the most important for all of us to participate in understanding is the complex web of animate – including, but not limited to, animal – life that includes us and exceeds us.

Bibliography

Agamben, G. (2004) *The Open: man and animal*, trans. K. Attrell, Stanford: Stanford University Press.

Armstrong, P. (2008) *What Animals Mean in the Fictions of Modernity*, New York: Routledge.

Atterton, P. and Calarco, M. (eds) (2004) *Animal Philosophy: essential readings in continental thought*, New York: Continuum.

Baker, S. (2001) *Picturing the Beast: animals, identity, and representation*, Urbana: University of Illinois Press.

"Cat parasite affects everything we feel and do" (2009) Online. Available HTTP: <http://a. abcnews.com/Technology/DyeHard/Story?id=2288095& page = 1> (accessed 17 July 2009).

Daston, L. and Mittman, G. (eds) (2005) *Thinking with Animals: new perspectives on anthropomorphism*, New York: Columbia University Press.

Derrida, J. (2008) *The Animal That Therefore I Am*, ed. M.-L. Mallet, trans. D. Wills, New York: Fordham.

Edwards, P. (2004) *The Horse Trade of Tudor and Stuart England*, Cambridge: Cambridge University Press.

——(2007) *Horse and Man in Early Modern England*, London: Hambledon Continuum.

Fudge, E. (2000) *Perceiving Animals: humans and beasts in early modern English culture*, New York: St. Martin's Press.

Guerrini, A. (2003) *Experimenting with Humans and Animals: from Galen to animal rights*, Baltimore: Johns Hopkins University Press.

Ham, J. and Senior, M. (eds) (1997) *Animal Acts: configuring the human in western history*, New York and London: Routledge.

Haraway, D. (2007) *When Species Meet*, Minneapolis: University of Minnesota Press.

Hayles, N.K. (1999) *How We Became Posthuman*, Chicago: University of Chicago Press.

Hearne, V. (1987) *Adam's Task: calling animals by name*, New York: Random House.

Jardine, L. and Brotton, J. (2005) *Global Interests: Renaissance art between East and West*, Chicago: University of Chicago Press.

Kalof, L. and Fitzgerald, A. (eds) (2007) *The Animals Reader: the essential classic and contemporary writings*, New York: Berg.

Landry, D. (2009) *Noble Brutes: how eastern horses transformed English culture*, Baltimore: Johns Hopkins University Press.

Menely, T. (2006) "Cultivated sympathies: human sentiments and animal subjects in the long eighteenth century," dissertation, Indiana University.

Nash, R. and Broglio, R. (eds) (2006) "Thinking with animals," *Configurations*, 14(1–2): 1–192.

Perkins, D. (2003) *Romanticism and Animal Rights*, Cambridge: Cambridge University Press.

Ritvo, H. (1990) *The Animal Estate: the English and other creatures of the Victorian age*, New York: Penguin.

——(1998) *The Platypus and the Mermaid: and other figments of the classifying imagination*, Cambridge, Mass.: Harvard University Press.

Rothfels, N. (2002) *Representing Animals*, Bloomington: Indiana University Press.

Thirsk, J. (1978) *Horses in Early Modern England: for service, for pleasure, for power*, Reading: University of Reading Press.

Thomas, K. (1983) *Man and the Natural World*, New York: Pantheon.

Wolfe, C. (2003) *Animal Rites: American culture, the discourse of species, and posthumanist theory*, Chicago: University of Chicago Press.

——(ed.) (2003) *Zoontologies: the question of the animal*, Minneapolis: University of Minnesota Press.

23
ART CONNECTIONS
Robert Pepperell

In art there is only one thing that counts: the thing you can't explain.

Georges Braque

Too precise a meaning erases your mysterious literature.

Stéphane Mallarmé

The most beautiful emotion we can experience is the mysterious.

Albert Einstein

Introduction

We live in a time when dialogue between the arts, sciences, and humanities is widely encouraged. Funding agencies offer incentives for scientists to work with artists; books are being written that seek to span C.P. Snow's "gulf of mutual incomprehension" between scholarly cultures (see Wilson 1998); inter-disciplinary conferences are being convened that support cross-area dialogue and report the findings of collaborative projects. There is a sense that previously disconnected fields of study are actively converging.

All this is welcome, given the fractured state of contemporary knowledge. Born just over 400 years ago, the poet John Milton is reputed to be the last person who would have been able to read every book then in print. Certainly the well-educated person of his time would have understood a wide range of subjects. The subsequent tendency towards micro-specialism in academia has brought breadth and depth at the price of fragmentation and isolation; no longer could any individual hope to absorb more than a tiny fraction of published information, and most disciplines work in ignorance of each other. Ulrich's directory of periodicals (*Ulrich's* 2009), which lists most of the world's scholarly journals, boasts over 300,000 titles, each representing the tip of an iceberg of accumulated knowledge. And a report in 2002 by the Association of American Colleges and Universities identified the "atomization of the curriculum," caused by artificially dividing knowledge into distinct fields, as a significant barrier to the future of education (AACU 2002).

But a note of caution: if we embrace interdisciplinarity as an antidote to over-specialization we should be wary of negating the foundational and historical differences among disciplines. In the introduction to his lucid and comprehensive survey of human thought, *The Story of Philosophy*, Bryan Magee divides the great span of human knowledge into four major areas: religion, which relies on faith; art, which relies on intuition; science, which operates through experiment; and philosophy, which proceeds through argument (Magee 2001: 8). Although not exhaustive, these groupings can guide us in understanding the overall organization of human knowledge, as well as in capturing the distinct approaches to understanding that each area offers. Putting religion aside as beyond the scope of the current volume, this chapter considers the ways in which art, literature, and science might be connected, and to some extent unified in a wider interdisciplinary project. As I hope will become clear, however, being connected or even unified does not necessarily mean surrendering disciplinary differences.

Interdisciplinarity: homogeneity or plurality?

Anxiety about the fragmentation of knowledge dates back at least to the late nineteenth century. The great anatomist and advocate of Darwinian evolution Thomas Henry Huxley was deeply committed to science, yet argued publicly that art and literature (what we would now call the humanities) are not only equal to science in importance but basically identical in purpose and process. In one of several addresses he made to the Royal Academy, then the foremost artistic institution in Britain, he warned of the dangers of excessive specialization in science and bid for recognition of "the great truth that art and literature and science are one, and that the foundation of every sound education and preparation for active life in which a special education is necessary should be some efficient training in all three" (Huxley 1887). Huxley was a keen draughtsman and produced many of the scientific illustrations for his own publications and lectures, as well as numerous cartoons and caricatures of contemporary figures. He was an autodidact and something of a polymath for whom the beauty of nature revealed through the scientific method was no different in essence from that revealed by art or philosophy: each seeks to penetrate "the mystery and wonder which are around us" (Huxley 1887).

The publications on meteorology and geology of Huxley's learned contemporary John Ruskin are less well known than his still widely read works on art and aesthetics. Like Huxley, he was to a large extent self-taught, published voluminously, and engaged in many of the social and intellectual issues of his day. Ruskin, however, would lay greater stress on the intrinsic differences between science, art, and literature, noting in one of his Oxford lectures that "In science, you must not talk before you know. In art, you must not talk before you do. In literature, you must not talk before you think" (Ruskin 1872: 4). For Ruskin, the proper places for the study of science (in Victorian England at least) were the institutions regulated by the Royal Society, where factual knowledge about nature was generated and deposited. The "fine and mechanical" arts, meanwhile, were the province of the Royal Academy and its schools, which cultivated skills proper to the artist or architect. Ruskin counted within literature intellectual or philosophical ideas, which were to be nurtured by the universities.

Ruskin's concept of "literature" is akin to what C.P. Snow conceived as one half of the "two cultures" in his famous characterization of the intellectual landscape of the mid-twentieth century, the opposing other being science, and in particular the hard sciences of physics and chemistry. Trained as a physicist and later becoming a distinguished novelist, Snow was well placed to assess the academic milieu of his day. This led him in his 1959 Rede lecture to bemoan the "sheer loss to us all" of the polarization between, on the one hand, the "traditional" culture of the humanities (philosophers, intellectuals, writers) and the highly specialized domains of the physical sciences, on the other hand (Snow 1993: 11). The inability of both to speak a common language had damaging consequences for our culture as a whole. Like Huxley, Snow advocated reform of the educational system in order to repair the damage at its root. Such pronouncements on the relationship between science, art, and the world of letters reveal not just the conventional tension between disciplinary cultures but between different ways of conceiving how interdisciplinarity might be made to work in practice: either we try to unify the various strands of knowledge by eliminating their distinctions on the basis that, as Huxley would have it, they are essentially homogeneous, or we maintain the plurality of distinctions (as Ruskin would do), albeit encouraging informed reflection or Snow's educational reforms to keep them in balance.

If we think interdisciplinarity is worthwhile – perhaps even essential to the development of knowledge – then we must decide whether we are seeking a kind of integration that is homogeneous or pluralistic. Do we focus only on the common ground between historically distinct areas, or do we embrace these distinctions and try to reconcile them without compromising their integrity? In either case, in order to achieve a fully interdisciplinary form of inquiry we should expect that each area be given equal standing, and for each to contribute to the advancement of the other.

A recent case of interdisciplinarity

The interaction of the artistic imagination and scientific inquiry is enjoying unprecedented attention.

(Warner 2000)

As novelist Marina Warner noted, the beginning of the twenty-first century has seen a conspicuous convergence of art, science, and humanities, nowhere more evident than in the avowedly interdisciplinary field of consciousness studies. In the early 1990s philosophers, neuroscientists, psychologists, and cognitive scientists had recognized that the problem of explaining human consciousness was too deep and far-reaching to be accounted for by any single discipline, and so began formally discussing common approaches and sharing knowledge. An example of such cooperation is the biennial "Towards a Science of Consciousness" series of conferences organized since 1994 by the University of Arizona, Tucson.

One publication that has reflected this convergence is the *Journal of Consciousness Studies*, which, unusually for specialist journals, solicited contributions from a range of disciplines, even encouraging debate on the neural basis of art. It published three special issues on "Art and the Brain" (1999, 2000, 2004) and a more recent special edition devoted to Velazquez's *Las Meninas* (2008). These issues have featured contributions from eminent scientists and philosophers, including Bernard Baars, Richard Gregory, Nicholas Humphrey, Alva Noë, and V.S. Ramachandran, each addressing what the study of art could reveal about the workings of the human mind.

The same decade saw the publication of a number of books that further suggested a rapprochement between art and science (Zeki 1999; Livingstone 2002; Solso 2003; Zangemeister and Stark 2007). Semir Zeki's original work on the neuroscientific processes involved in the perception of art has spawned a nascent hybrid discipline – neuroaesthetics – that seeks to give an account of aesthetic perception on the basis of what is known about the biology of the brain. This new field is attracting investigators and a growing literature, with a substantial volume of related texts being published (Martindale 2006), and at least two international conferences being convened in 2009. All this demonstrates the considerable level of interest in art from scientists and philosophers of mind, and indicates a growing climate of cross-disciplinary inquiry. At the same time, we've seen a growth in creative art–science collaborations, where artists and scientists have sought to share knowledge and methods in making works of art, as well as many cases where artists have embraced technologies like genetic manipulation, digital media, and robotics because of their potential as new artistic mediums.

Does all this activity represent a genuine convergence of knowledge, of a kind perhaps not seen since the Renaissance, in which artists, technologists, scientists, and philosophers are starting to establish common grounds of inquiry? Could this even represent the beginning of the end for disciplinary boundaries between art, science, and the humanities as we have known them? Much as this might be welcomed, I doubt it is yet so. It turns out that the recent interest in art by science and philosophy consists for the most part in scientists and philosophers using their specialist knowledge to make low-level interventions in art theory. What is less evident – indeed almost entirely absent – among the recent literature and conferences on the relationship between art, brain, and mind is the voice or presence of the artists themselves. Only one of the many contributors to the special issues of *Journal of Consciousness Studies* has an art-making background, while none of the contributors to Martindale's volume on neuroaesthetics does. With a background as an art historian, John Onians (2008) at least starts to reverse this trend by assimilating his art-historical knowledge with recent findings in neuroscience. And even though Semir Zeki can claim "artists are neurologists" (Zeki 1999: 80) because they have intuitively understood the organizing principles of the visual brain, it is unlikely that any artists will be invited to expound their theories on the basic principles of neuroscience in the way neuroscientists have on the basic principles of art. To date, artists are, by and large, subjects of rather than participants in this discussion.

Meanwhile, the commercial art world remains to be convinced about the long-term merit of much of the "art-science" work being made, with few resulting pieces making it beyond the realms specifically created to fund them. And the extent to which these ventures have contributed to the real advancement of science and technology is even less certain. The science director of the British Council raised serious doubts about the value to either community of the projects funded by the Sciart initiative operated by the Wellcome Trust, saying little good work had resulted (*Times Higher Education Supplement* 2005). Despite all the recent enthusiasm for integration between the arts, sciences, and humanities, it is hard to point to examples of genuinely equitable collaboration resulting in significant contributions to knowledge, understanding, and methods in *all* areas concerned. True interdisciplinary integration, where parity and mutual advancement are evident, still seems some way off.

The methods of science, philosophy, and art

If we compare the methods of science and philosophy to those of art we are struck by some important differences. In the scientific method investigators are subject to a number of tight constraints on how they can maneuver: the hypothesis must be testable; phenomena under investigation must be measurable; errors, ambiguities, and subjective bias must be eliminated; interpretations must strictly adhere to the data; the principles of reason must be adhered to. These constraints are essential if the integrity and universality of scientific findings are to be upheld. In philosophy similar though arguably less severe constraints apply: subjectivity is discouraged and rigorous rules of argument must be followed in which logical consistency is considered essential. Philosophy differs most substantially from science in that its propositions are generally tested through argument instead of experiments, and this allows philosophy to interrogate the kinds of conceptual problems that would be beyond the means of science to investigate.

Professional artistic activity is also constrained by numerous codes of conduct, but their purpose and outcome can be very different·than those of science and philosophy. While in science it is perfectly acceptable to repeat the experimental procedures of another scientist, in art one should avoid repeating the work of another artist. Likewise, where scientists and philosophers are expected to explain their deliberations and findings as explicitly as possible, artists prefer to avoid explanations of their work, which, as Magee pointed out, is often arrived at intuitively. And where the work of scientists and philosophers should ideally remain clear and logically coherent, it is often desirable for artists that their work remains ambiguous, enigmatic, and even provocatively irrational. Artists work within rules, but ones that are different, and in many cases entirely contradictory to those of professional science and philosophy. The fact that the methods of science and philosophy have far more in common with each other than either do with art may start to account for the lack of parity so far evident in recent interdisciplinary activity.

A function of art

What I am trying to convey to you is more mysterious; it is bound up with the very roots of being, in the intangible source of sensation.
(Paul Cézanne, cited in Kendall 2001: 303)

There is a further difference between art compared to science and the humanities. All major areas of human inquiry ultimately seek to understand the mysterious aspects of existence and reality. The essence of any kind of inquiry is to delve into what is not already known. But (with the possible exception of religion) art is the only one that approaches this task by becoming mysterious itself. The philosopher Schopenhauer refers to the boundless and inaccessible essence of nature when invoking his concept of the *Will*, just as Einstein reaches into the cosmological unknown he called the "most beautiful emotion" through theoretical physics. But the works produced in response to these investigations are not in themselves mysterious, they are *about* mysteries. Velazquez's *Las Meninas* (1656, Museo del Prado, Madrid), on the other hand, is a riddle wrapped in an enigma, a painting that presents the facts of daily existence as at the same time quotidian and inexhaustibly perplexing. Science and philosophy are well equipped to investigate the unknown, but are professionally bound to produce outcomes that are conceptually transparent – at least to those in the relevant communities. After all, if objectivity is a major criterion of validity, then wide consensus and understanding is desirable. Artists, meanwhile, may be concerned with similar questions about the nature of perception, mind, and reality as scientists and philosophers, but are apt to produce outcomes that, at their best, are far more open to subjective interpretation, even to the point of indecipherability.

I briefly offer as an example a Cubist painting produced by Braque in the period leading up to World War I Figure 23.1). During this so-called "analytic"

Figure 23.1 Georges Braque. *Fruit Dish, Bottle, and Glass: "Sorgues"*, 1912. Oil and sand on canvas, 60 x 73 cm. Musée National d'Art Moderne, Centre Georges Pompidou, Paris. Gift of Louise and Michel Leiris. © ADAGP, Paris and DACS, London 2009.

period of Cubism the artist presented scenes of ordinary domestic objects – bottles, glasses, bowls, fruit, a table – in a way that is utterly extraordinary. Everything is present, everything is represented, but in a way that defies recognition (certainly for the untrained viewer). The painting, in this sense, is highly *indeterminate*. For Braque, the Cubist collaboration with Picasso was nothing less than a refashioning of the very act of pictorial representation. A painting need no longer "look like" what it represented in order to be a veridical depiction. Instead, abrupt, truncated, and fragmented iconic signs could stand in for objects to which they bore little physical resemblance.

Moreover, Cubism can be seen as a refashioning of the idea that perception gives us direct knowledge of the world as it is "out there." For although we *imagine* we see a world of complete objects, in fact what we really see is hesitant, fleeting, partial, fractured, and often uncertain. We know from work in vision science that our rich picture of the world is actually built up from momentary fixations in our visual field captured by the tiny *fovea centralis* (Palmer 1999: 528).

From a young age we have to learn to scan and "read" the world, just as we have to learn to read a book or a Cubist painting, in order to extract comprehensible information from the fragmented images we apprehend. Until we can do this, the world remains indeterminate and essentially mysterious, much as in the Cubist work considered here.

For many artists, art is a method by which we explore the extreme reaches of what we know, but in a way quite different from philosophy and science. Rather than trying to solve mysteries, artists are more frequently trying to create them, using the everyday materials of reality to offer signposts into the unknown.

> My aim is always to get hold of the magic reality and to transfer this reality into painting – to make the invisible visible through reality. It may sound paradoxical, but it is, in fact, reality which forms the mystery of our existence.
>
> (Max Beckmann, cited in Protter 1997: 211)

This impulse is most apparent in the tradition of religious art in which artistic objects come to represent, or stand in for, invisible spirits or deities. Modern art at its best trades on that same tradition in which the object is venerated not because of its intrinsic material value but for what it offers beyond itself in terms of transcendent experience. A review of the Mark Rothko show in London in 2008 talked of "intimations of something beyond the material," so attesting to the continuing potency of this belief:

> Sitting among the paintings for the Four Seasons restaurant, engulfed by the brooding ox-bloods and burgundies of those enormous canvases you do feel a sense of awe appropriate to a place of worship. The fact that this sense of reverence is almost impossible to quite define is the essence of Rothko's appeal.
>
> (Hudson 2008)

Art is often spoken of in such reverential and indefinable terms, as though it takes over where language gets off, drawing up to the edge of the known and leading us beyond – into something indeterminate. Hence art's reputation for difficulty, willful abstruseness, and yet also profundity, a profundity that is of a different order than that produced by works of science or philosophy. Writing of Paul Cézanne, Maurice Merleau-Ponty contends that art avoids imposing on primordial experience both the rational coding or operationalism of science and the linguistic determinism of philosophy:

> Now art, especially painting, draws upon this fabric of brute meaning which operationalism would prefer to ignore. Art and only art does so in full innocence. From the writer and the philosopher, in contrast, we

want opinions and advice. We will not allow them to hold the world suspended. We want them to take a stand; they cannot waive the responsibilities of humans who speak.

(Merleau-Ponty, cited in Johnson 1996: 123)

Indeterminacy in literary theory

Writers who have attempted to capture the essence of our relationship to art (both visual and literary) have often made reference to the indeterminacy of perception in which the familiar world is momentarily disturbed by the effect of a work of art. The critic Victor Shklovsky developed an aesthetic theory in which art's function is to resist what he calls our perceptual habitualization, whereby we become unconsciously accustomed to the world as it appears to us and therefore oblivious to the world "as it is" prior to our acquired perception of it. The purpose of art, according to Shklovsky, writing in 1917, is to defamiliarize our perceptions of the world: "The technique of art is to make objects 'unfamiliar,' to make forms difficult, to increase the difficulty and length of perception because the process of perception is an aesthetic end in itself and must be prolonged" (Shklovsky 1965: 12).

Although Shklovsky is primarily referring to literature, the aesthetic function he describes could just as well be applied in the case of the visual arts, and in particular the kind of painting considered here. Similar sentiments had been proposed in the previous century in relation to Symbolist theories of poetry. Speaking in 1891, when the impact of Impressionist methods had contributed to reshaping the intellectual and artistic climate of France, the poet Stéphane Mallarmé asserted:

> To name an object is to suppress three-quarters of the enjoyment of the poem, which derives from the pleasure of step-by-step discovery; to suggest, that is the dream. It is the perfect use of this mystery that constitutes the symbol: to evoke an object little by little.
>
> (cited in Dorra 1995: 141)

Mallarmé and Shklovsky both stress a criterion for aesthetic efficacy in which art is enigmatic and evocative to the imagination and at the same time difficult to decipher, so problematizing the processes of perception and cognition. They call for a suspension of those customary or facile modes of attention where we are either oblivious to the raw perceptual qualities of the world or offered representations that leave no room for imaginative interpretation. Instead, they each urge that the habitual link between seeing and knowing be loosened or broken in order to raise the aesthetic value of our experience.

More recently, the author A.S. Byatt has ambitiously linked the theories of neuroscientist Jean-Pierre Changeux to the poetic effects of John Donne's poetry.

In doing so, she accounts for the neural impact of Donne's poetry through the imaginative struggle required to grasp its meaning, arguing that "some of Donne's most beautiful effects are derived from the foregrounding of the difficulty and complexity – and density – of grammatical constructions" (Byatt 2006). Clearly, critics and writers remain interested in the perceptual and cognitive processes through which art is appreciated, and are perhaps intuitively aware of why certain works have the psychological impact they do. Combining the insights of creative thinkers with the investigative techniques of modern neuroscience, in the way suggested by Byatt, may offer genuinely new avenues of interdisciplinary knowledge, providing that all contributors can find common ground that does not require them to relinquish their disciplinary integrity.

The potential for interdisciplinary knowledge

Art (including literary art), science, and the humanities can justly claim common ground: they share an aspiration to bring us into closer contact with the unknown aspects of existence. But they also have different histories, trajectories, and methods that cannot be lightly overwritten. Most importantly, art stands aside from philosophy and science insofar as artworks are made less to explain the mysteries of existence than to invoke them; something often achieved by presenting the world as difficult, unfamiliar, or indeterminate. Science and the humanities, on the other hand, are more strongly compelled to explain these mysteries, and present their findings in ways that are coherent and transparent. This may go some way in accounting for the disparities that occur when art, science, and philosophy are brought together, and for why artists are inclined to let the artworks carry their voice instead of engaging more directly in the debates themselves.

Looking broadly across Western culture, we see that the impulse to explain, which science and philosophy share through their deep roots in Greek thinking and common heritage in natural philosophy, has never driven art in the same way. Instead, art had an artisan heritage that the Church put to the task of manifesting the invisible, thus bringing it into direct contact with the divine. A painting or a musical composition alone can explain nothing (even a diagram needs annotation), precisely as Merleau-Ponty says, because neither speaks. The fact that Leonardo da Vinci artfully creates Mona Lisa's indeterminate smile while Margaret Livingstone seeks to explain it by reference to analysis of spatial frequencies (Livingstone 2002) encapsulates the fundamental difference between art and science.

And even to the extent that literary art and poetry speak, they often do so, as Mallarmé would have it, only enough to push the mind of the reader beyond what the words say. It is apt that the physicist Werner Heisenberg's realization of the limits of what can be known about reality at the quantum level should be named the "Indeterminacy Principle." We delude ourselves if we think that science, philosophy, or any other method of inquiry can transport us beyond the essential indeterminacy that inhabits all perception of reality. And so it is even more apt that in Balzac's *The Unknown Masterpiece* of 1832, the canvas upon which the fictional artist Frenhofer labors for years to produce the perfect image of a woman should appear to the characters Porbus and Poussin as a "chaos of colors, of tones, of uncertain shades, that sort of shapeless mist" (Balzac 1899: 42). Balzac's tale is an allegorical reminder that our most exhaustive attempts to penetrate reality, whether through art, science, or philosophy, will always lead us eventually into this same ungraspable indeterminacy.

So finally, it seems there is no simple choice between homogenizing disciplines or retaining their distinctions; the commonalities are as fundamental as the differences. Rather than this being grounds for confusion or despair, though, I would suggest this is an optimistic sign of our maturing capacity for understanding at this time in human history. The fact that there is a growing appetite for interdisciplinary inquiry – albeit one that is not yet symmetrical between the areas – offers us the chance to affirm the plurality of our methods while at the same time fostering their underlying convergence, without one approach effacing another. Problems like the nature of consciousness or art are clearly too vast to be any longer the province of a single discipline; they can only be tackled through the subtle cooperation of all areas concerned, the precise terms of which we are perhaps yet to define. It's timely to be reminded that, however diverse human knowledge may be, the unknown is the same for us all.

Bibliography

AACU (2002) *Greater Expectations*. Online. Available HTTP: <http://greaterexpectations.org/> (accessed 8 May 2009).

Balzac, H. (1899) *The Unknown Masterpiece*, London: Caxton Press.

Braque, G. (1971) *Notebooks 1917–1947*, New York: Dover Press.

Byatt, A. (2006) "Observe the neurones: between, above and below John Donne," *Times Literary Supplement* (22 September).

Dorra, H. (1995) *Symbolist Art Theories*, California: University of California Press.

Frank, P. (1947) *Einstein: his life and times*, New York: Alfred A. Knopf.

Hudson, M. (2008) "Rothko exhibition: art replaces religious faith," *Telegraph* (26 September).

Huxley, T.H. (1887) Report in the London *Times*, 2 May 1887; cited in *Nature*, 36 (914): 13–16.

Johnson, G. (1996) *The Merleau-Ponty Aesthetics Reader: philosophy and painting*, Evanston: Northwestern University Press.

Journal of Consciousness Studies (1999) "Art and the brain," 6(6–7).

——(2000) "Art and the brain, part II," 7(8–9).

——(2004) "Art and the brain, part III," 11(3–4).

——(2008) "*Las Meninas* and self-representation," 15(9).

Kendall, R. (2001) *Cézanne by Himself*, London: Macdonald and Co.

Livingstone, M. (2002) *Vision and Art: the biology of seeing*, New York: Abrams.

Magee, B. (2001) *The Story of Philosophy*, London: Dorling Kindersley.

Martindale, C. (ed.) (2006) *Evolutionary and Neurocognitive Approaches to Aesthetics, Creativity and the Arts*, London: Baywood.

Onians, J. (2008) *Neuroarthistory: from Aristotle and Pliny to Baxandall and Zeki*, New Haven: Yale University Press.

Palmer, S. (1999) *Vision Science: photons to phenomenology*, Cambridge, Mass.: MIT Press.

Protter, E. (1997) *Painters on Painting*, New York: Dover Press.

Ruskin, J. (1872) *The Eagle's Nest: ten lectures on the relation of natural science to art*, London: Smith, Elder and Co. and G. Allen.

Shklovsky, V. (1965) "Art as technique," in L. Lemon and M. Reis (eds) *Russian Formalist Criticism*, Nebraska: University of Nebraska Press.

Snow, C.P. (1993) *The Two Cultures*, Cambridge: Cambridge University Press.

Solso, R. (2003) *The Psychology of Art and the Evolution of the Conscious Brain*, London: MIT Press.

Times Higher Education Supplement (2005) 16 September.

Ulrich's Periodicals Directory (2009) Online. Available HTTP: <http://ulrichsweb.com/ulrichsweb/> (accessed 8 May 2009).

Warner, M. (2000) "The inner eye of two cultures," *Times Higher Education* (17 March): 34.

Wilson, E.O. (1998) *Consilience: the unity of knowledge*, London: Little, Brown.

Zangemeister, W. and Stark, L. (2007) *The Artistic Brain Beyond the Eye*, London: AuthorHouse.

Zeki, S. (1999) *Inner Vision: an exploration of art and the brain*, Oxford: Oxford University Press.

24
CULTURAL SCIENCE STUDIES

Maureen McNeil

What are cultural studies of science?

While the term "cultural studies of science" designates a stream of research within the broader field of social studies of science, there is no clear consensus about what work is associated with this term. Joseph Rouse has defined "the term broadly," suggesting that it includes "various investigations of the practices through which scientific knowledge is articulated and maintained in specific cultural contexts, and translated and extended into new contexts" (Rouse 1992: 2). In 1994 Susan Squier identified "cultural studies of science" as "extending from the early work of Thomas Kuhn to more recent work by Latour and Woolgar, Keller, Rouse, Schiebinger, Haraway and others"; for Squier, Kuhn's "new understanding of how science produces knowledge launched by ... [his] *Structure of Scientific Revolutions*, with its two crucial notions, the *scientific paradigm* and the *paradigm shift*" (Squier 1994: 11) opened up this new trajectory within social studies of science. In 1996, Michael Menser and Stanley Aronowitz issued their "Manifesto" for cultural studies of science, declaring that cultural studies was "the name we give to the transformation of social and cultural knowledge in the wake of an epochal shift in the character of life and thought whose origins and contours we only dimly perceive" (Menser and Aronowitz 1996: 16). For Menser and Aronowitz, Kuhn was not the founding father of cultural studies of science. Rather, they regarded cultural studies as ushering in a new radical epistemology which highlighted and explored the contextuality of all knowledge claims (Aronowitz 1993: ch.7) and which was generated and sustained by poststructuralism, postmodernism, and cyberculture. They deemed this new epistemology as having the potential to transform the study of science and technology.

Although these commentators propose rather different visions of cultural studies of science, they come together in foregrounding contextualization as one of its key features. Squier pinpointed what she regarded as distinctive about cultural studies of science research when she observed:

> These scholars have illuminated the processes by which scientific fields as diverse as cell biology, primatology, and physics have constructed both the questions they ask and the artifacts they accept as facts in relation to the cultural and historical milieu.
>
> (Squier 1994: 115)

"Context" and/or "milieu" are key words for cultural studies of science, which revolves around the notion that scientific knowledge emerges from specific historical contexts and takes the historical embeddedness of science more seriously than some other forms of social studies of science. Hence, it is not surprising that cultural anthropology has also provided inspiration for cultural studies approaches to science. Its insights and methods have been employed in the study of Western culture and adapted to render aspects of that culture – including science – "strange" and "other" (McNeil 2007: 14–16).

This strand of social studies of science has been characterized as a reorientation of the field, beginning in the last decades of the twentieth century, involving methodological borrowings, adaptations, and extensions from the humanities. Dorothy Nelkin, an influential analyst of science in the media, noted in 1996 that some humanities researchers and social scientists were "defining their work as cultural studies of science and bringing to bear their skills in interpreting narratives and discourses" (Nelkin 1996: 34). Squier offers a more elaborated account of the methodological features of the cultural turn within science studies: "science is thus opened up to the wide range of analytic and investigative practices appropriate to cultural studies, ranging from context, content, and discourse analysis to analyses of processes of production, dissemination, and consumption of scientific knowledge" (Squier 1994: 11).

Another related way of characterizing cultural studies of science is to see these as deriving from the recognition that science constitutes or generates a set of identifiable cultural forms (including, for example, texts and images) that can be subjected to cultural analysis. Cultural studies of science may undertake investigations of these phenomena, borrowing from conceptual and methodological repertoires developed in various fields of the humanities. For example, as I shall discuss in more detail below, scrutinizing key scientific texts by applying established forms of textual analysis has proved fruitful in some cultural studies of science. Likewise, the conceptual and methodological repertoires provided by art history and film studies have been used to challenge and stretch the parameters of science studies by scholars such as Ludmilla Jordanova (1989), Giuliana Bruno (1992, 1993), and Lisa Cartwright (1995) (McNeil 2007: 17).

The foregoing account of diverse routes into cultural studies of science (see also McNeil 2007, 2008; Lykke 2002, 2008) provides some background to the rest of this chapter, which considers ways in which, beginning in the last decades of the twentieth century, encounters between literary studies and science studies have been staged within and helped to forge cultural studies of science as a distinctive strand of science studies. However, it may be useful at this point to draw out crucial features of cultural studies of science which are important in considering the dialogues between literary and science studies that I will explore below. First, the insistence on the cultural specificity of science and the alignment of science with other cultural forms undermines assumptions about the transcendental and universal nature of scientific knowledge. For many, this is the most challenging aspect of cultural studies of science. Second, cultural studies of science are oriented around the investigation of science in its context, although the form of such investigations has varied greatly.

The following sections review three key contributions in the development of cultural studies of science. These works are highlighted because they have been highly influential, and also because each of the researchers considered below has realized distinctive enactments of cultural studies of science which probe the relationship between literature and science.

Gillian Beer: Darwin's plots, narrative, and argument

Although there had been studies of Darwin's influence on literature and even studies of the literary influences on Darwin previous to the appearance of *Darwin's Plots* in 1983, Gillian Beer's book exceeded these in offering a complex exploration both of the literary embeddedness of Darwin's theories and of the impact of those theories on the late nineteenth-century English novel. As Beer herself emphasizes and as George Levine has noted, *Darwin's Plots* demonstrated that "the cultural traffic ran both ways" (Beer 2009: 5; Levine 2009: xii) between Darwin and English literature. Beer made a strong claim: she contended that Darwin's theories could not be understood without reference to the literary culture in which he was immersed and from which he drew in formulating his theories in *On the Origin of Species* of 1859. Offering much more than a study of influences, it is Beer's full engagement with the textuality of *The Origin of Species* and her comprehensive tracing of its relationship to literary context that makes her book a landmark in the cultural studies of science. Three important aspects of her treatment of *The Origin* are her detailed studies of its language, readership, and narrative form.

Beer contends that "how Darwin said things was a crucial part of his struggle to think things, not a layer that can be skimmed off without loss" (Beer 2009: xxv), and she devotes Part I of her study to Darwin's language. Her rich array of observations includes comments on "the element of address" and the conversational mode of Darwin's text, which conveyed "the work's imaginative history" (61). Her careful reading across the various editions of *The Origin* enables her to speculate suggestively about the "struggles" (62) Darwin encountered in "precipitating his theory as language" (47). For example, she considers difficulties linked to the anthropomorphism of language and his attempts to disentangle his theories from the dominant framework of natural theology. Beer provides much more than a gloss on Darwin's linguistic style; she regards Darwin's language as integral to his evolutionary theory: "it was essential to his project that it should be accepted not as invention, but description. His work is, therefore, conditional upon the means of description: that is upon language" (46). Beer's rigorous study of Darwin's language thereby became a powerful form of cultural studies of science.

Another dimension of Beer's engagement with the textuality of *The Origin* is her attention to issues of readership. She acknowledges that Darwin wrote "to the confraternity of scientists but with the assumption that his work would be readable by any educated reader" (41). She notes that, in opting for accessible language, Darwin secured a wide readership while precipitating disparate appropriations of his terms. She later labels this "multivocality" and traces the revisions from the first edition, in which his language was "expressive rather than rigorous" (32–33), suggesting that Darwin tried to rein in interpretations of his text. Nevertheless, the "need to please his readers as well as unsettle and disturb them" was as important to Darwin as it was to Dickens (35). Aware that Darwin was an "omnivorous reader," Beer shows that he considered himself to be "reading" the physical world, and that such reading becomes not just a matter of language and syntax, but of narrative (27, 39): "Reading *The Origin* ... involves you in a narrative experience" (3). In fact, it is Beer's adept exploration of Darwin's narrative modes which yields a rich picture of the "two-way traffic" between literature and his writing. She detects the influence of Carlyle and Dickens in Darwin's striking mode of narration, characterized by its capacity to bring his readers to the "brink of finding out" (43) the mechanisms by which the natural world evolves.

Through detailed study of Darwin's text, Beer demonstrates "the degree to which narrative and argument share methods" (xx, 34). This constitutes an important insight for cultural studies of science, which renders narrative analysis a valuable resource for science studies. But she carries this further in showing the affinities between literary fiction and Darwin's mode of theorizing. She points out that Darwin "displays, categorises, and argues, but does not expect to contain the working of the world in his mind, or ever fully to understand them," then observes that "It took a hundred years for Darwin's projections, his 'fictions' or theories, to be thoroughly authenticated empirically"; *The Origin* is "a polemical book, a work which drives *through* fiction and observation to achieve a condition beyond fiction" (46). While Beer is adamant in the Preface to the second edition of her book that she is not claiming Darwin's theory *is fiction*, she has shown that Darwin's narrative form *operates as fiction* and that appreciating this is crucial for understanding his text, his theories, and the response to them.

Beer then turns her analytical tables to show that Darwin's theory transformed the design of narratives and the activity of narrating within British fiction of the late nineteenth century. The preoccupation with time and change which were at the heart of evolutionary theory, she contends, was also integral to the problems and, indeed, the form of narratives in novels. In Part III of *Darwin's Plots* she explores how late nineteenth-century English novelists (especially Eliot and Hardy) "tested the extent to which" evolutionary theory could "provide a determining fiction by which to read the world" (2). George Levine praises Beer's accomplishment in demonstrating "through both argument and enactment that the recognition of the creative and imaginative aspects of science does not in any way diminish the importance or distinctiveness of scientific work" (Levine 2009: xii). In insisting that Darwin's language, his orientation towards his readership, and his narrative form were intrinsic to his evolutionary theory, Beer realized a powerful version of cultural studies of science. She shows, in Darwin's case at least, that there is much to be gained by looking at scientific writing through the lens of literature, particularly fiction.

Donna Haraway: science fiction and/as cultural studies of technoscience

From *Frankenstein* through to cyberfiction and beyond, science fiction has been the quintessential literary genre staging encounters between technoscience and literature. It has proved to be a powerful arena for writers' and readers' imaginative explorations of hopes, fears, and visions linked to technoscience. However, it is only recently that researchers have begun to explore its potential as a resource for science and technology studies. An avid fan of science fiction (particularly feminist science fiction), Donna Haraway has been an influential exponent of this trajectory within the field, forging her own version of cultural studies of technoscience which draws extensively on science fiction.

Haraway's most widely circulated text is her "Cyborg Manifesto" of 1985. Although presented as a manifesto, in its writing and presentational style it borrows heavily from science fiction. Haraway welcomed the new feminist science fiction which proliferated in the 1970s and 1980s and hailed its authors as "our story-tellers exploring what it means to be embodied in high-tech worlds" (Haraway 1991: 173). Acknowledging their influence as "theorists for cyborgs" (173), she provides her readers with "an abbreviated list" of feminist science fiction books informing her essay. In the last section of the "Cyborg Manifesto," Haraway turns to science fiction to conjure the cyborg as a challenge to late twentieth-century "myths of political identity." Beginning with Anne McCaffery's "pre-feminist" text, *The Ship Who Sang* (1969), she presents a brief review of "the cyborgs populating" the fiction of Joanna Russ, Samuel R. Delany, James Tiptree, Jr., John Varley, Octavia Butler, and Vonda McIntyre. For Haraway, science fiction is not only a powerful source of personal inspiration in her own writing, it also demonstrates the inadequacies of "universal, totalizing theory" (Haraway 1991: 179). Beyond this, she relishes it as comprising a rich vein of reimaginings of life with(in) technoscience, beyond and outside of the stifling dualisms of human/machine, nature/culture, animal/human, etc.

Having recommended science fiction as a valuable resource for critical cultural studies of science, Haraway draws on it extensively in her major study of the making of the twentieth-century science of primatology, *Primate Visions* (1989): "Both science and popular culture are intricately woven of fact and fiction" (Haraway 1989: 3), so she will "treat science as narrative" (5). This brings her to science fiction (which she designates "SF") as "a territory of contested cultural reproduction in high-technology worlds"; it is this genre's capacity for contestation in a high-technology context that appeals to her: "Placing the narratives of scientific fact within the heterogeneous space of SF produces a transformed field ... so, in part, *Primate Visions* reads the primate text as science fiction" (5).

In turning to SF, Haraway invokes not only its modes of writing and conceptualizing the technoscientific world, but also its relationship to reading: "Conventions within the narrative field of SF seem to require readers radically to rewrite stories in the act of reading them"; she sees her "placing this account of primatology within SF" as an "invitation" to her readers to re-vision "the traffic between what we have come to know historically as nature and culture" (Haraway 1989: 15). More generally, Haraway frames her investigation of a specific "scientific discourse" as the analysis of "story telling within several contested narrative fields" (6). Her research entails pursuing and parsing diverse stories in and around primatology: the stories primatology has generated about the natural world, the life stories of those who have worked in this field, the stories told about the emergence and consolidation of this field of science, as well as the stories of primatology conveyed in museums and popular films.

Science fiction quite literally frames *Primate Visions*, since this long text not only begins with an introduction in which Haraway proposes to place her account of primatology "within SF," but, as its title suggests, the conclusion – "Reprise: science fiction, fictions of science, and primatology" – rounds off the project through further engagement with science fiction. Haraway opens the chapter by deploying Isaac Asimov's imaginary construct of the *Second Foundation* of 1953 to review the main themes of her study. She regards Asimov's story as providing a particularly illuminating lens through which to read the activities of an important institution and phase in the evolution of primatology – the Center for Advanced Study in the Behavioral Sciences' second Primate Project of 1983–84 (Haraway 1989: 370). However, in the final section of this chapter Haraway undertakes her most daring use of science fiction. Reversing her strategy of reading primatology as science fiction, she proposes instead to read science fiction as primatology. The last few pages of *Primate Visions* thereby become a kind of "what if" speculation, as Haraway presents a reading of the African-American Octavia Butler's novel *Dawn* as if it were the "the first chapter for the text that might issue from the next primate year, The Third

Foundation for the third planet from the sun at the Center for Advanced Study in the Behavioral Sciences" (376).

Haraway's extensive study of primatology, then, revolved around her tracing and interrogation of the multiple storytelling practices generated in and around it. In employing the literary trope of storytelling and unpacking narratives as they emerged not only on the field site, but also in textbooks, conference reports, autobiographies, museum panoramas, advertising, and films, Haraway challenged the conventions of the disciplines of history and social studies of science. Her foregrounding of science's own practices of storytelling was itself an unconventional, if not irreverent, gesture within social studies of science. Moreover, her laborious analyses demonstrated not only that primatology was made on field sites, in textbooks, or by designated primate scientists, but that its making also required the exploration of diverse sites and disparate narratives. Simple origins stories were not adequate to the diffused making of this science.

Haraway's turn to science fiction as the genre that inspired and shaped her project gave *Primate Visions* its radical edge. She challenged commonplace assumptions about the sharp divisions between science and fiction and demonstrated with rich empirical detail that "both science and popular culture" were "intricately woven of fact and fiction." This not only justified her license in reading primatology as science fiction, but gave her the courage to read science fiction as primatology. Her use of literary, particularly science fiction, tropes enabled her to probe the assumptions and the imaginaries of an important twentieth-century science, but also to explore with her readers how it might be constructed otherwise.

Katherine Hayles: the encounter between cybernetics and cyberliterature

Katherine Hayles concludes the first chapter of her important cultural study of the emergence of information science by expressing her hope "that this book will demonstrate, once again, how crucial it is to recognize the interrelations between different kinds of cultural productions, specifically literature and science" (Hayles 1999: 24). *How We Became Posthuman* (1999) presents her analysis of three "waves of changes in cybernetics" – from 1945 to 1960, 1960 to 1980, and 1980 to 1999. Three chapters are devoted to each of these phases, and each phase is covered through another tripart structure, with an "anchoring chapter discussing the scientific theories," followed by one tracing the applications of the theories, and a third considering literary texts "contemporaneous with" and "influenced by the development of cybernetics" (20–21). Although Hayles uses the language of "influence" in sketching the structure of her book, she is adamant that the "cross-currents are considerably more complex than a one-way model of influence would allow," citing a now familiar illustration of that claim: William Gibson's *Neuromancer*'s vision of cyberspace anticipated the development of virtual reality (Hayles 1999: 21; see also 296, fn.39). She contends that literary texts "actively shape what technologies mean and what scientific theories signify in cultural contexts" (21). Moreover, at crucial junctures, the assumptions which inform scientific theories can be detected in related literary texts.

Hayles's approach to science and literature underscores their cultural symmetry: "culture circulates through science no less than science circulates through culture" (21). She rejects any notion that literature simply reflects, illustrates, or explores the social and cultural implications of scientific theories and technological developments. This symmetrical framing enables her to juxtapose her own narratives about the key assumptions informing the three phases in the development of cybernetics with her readings of literary texts which explore these assumptions. Narrative is the critical linch-pin of Hayles's project. Her tracing of specific phases of cybernetics and systems theory becomes an elaborate account of personalities, events, clashes, contestations, with diverse tracks and trails. Her analysis offers "complex interplays" (7) rather than a history, and she highlights moments when key assumptions of the field are contested. She offers a detailed, web-like narrative that clashes with the dominant, monolithic metanarrative "about the transformation of the human into a disembodied posthuman," which she abhors.

She opens the field to scrutiny by fleshing out the linear story of progress and abstraction, drawing on a selected set of literary narratives that offer diverse textual enactments of issues in each of the phases of cybernetics. Hayles presents this double employment of narrative as a critical strategy: "shifting the emphasis from technological determinism to competing, contingent, embodied narratives about scientific developments is one way to liberate the resources of narrative so that they work against the grain of abstraction running through the teleology of disembodiment." Foregrounding the "situated specificities of narratives" (22), through her dual strategy Hayles hopes both to unsettle technological determinism and to demonstrate the mixing of matter and information – "their inextricably complex compounding and entwinings" (22–23).

The literary texts Hayles considers are all "alternative" fictions. These include Bernard Wolf's *Limbo*, which conjures a post-war society with reference to, but not restricted by, early cybernetic theory. For the second phase of cybernetics, Hayles turns to the now popular but previously marginal author Philip K. Dick, demonstrating that he was caught up with the questions posed by "second-wave" cybernetics, delivering visions of the shaky distinctions between humans and androids and problematic scenarios revolving around the politics of race, gender, and sexuality. In considering the most recent phase of cybernetics, Hayles selects Greg Bear's *Blood Music*, Cole Perriman's *Terminal Games*, Richard Power's *Galatea 2.2*, and Neal Stephenson's *Snow Crash*. Reading these texts as generating visions of the posthuman, she also sees them as reinstantiating forms of liberal humanism.

Hayles's study of cybernetics constitutes a distinctive cultural studies of science project with a powerful assemblage of science studies and literary studies. Literary texts are particularly important in "displaying the passageways that enable stories coming out of narrowly focused scientific theories to circulate more widely through the body politic" (Hayles 1999: 21). Her employment of narrative as a critical conceptual and methodological pivot enables her to revision the history of the development of cybernetic science, to draw on entangled, embodied enactments of its key issues in exemplary literary texts, and thereby to expose and critique the dream of disembodied information which, she contends, had come to dominate and orient cybernetic science.

Hayles's explorations of the interrelationship between literature and information technoscience have continued. In the Preface to *Writing Machines* (Hayles 2002: 7), she refers to her "journey" from "traditional literary criticism" to the investigation of "technology from a literary point of view," leading to the investigation of the materiality of literature. As part of this trajectory, *Writing Machines* is an experimental text probing the materiality of texts, a "robust and nuanced account of how literature is changing under the impact of information technologies" (19). A main thread of this experiment entails the analyses of exemplar texts representing three kinds of literature: an electronic "coterie" text (her term), a specialized art book, and a best-selling, printed novel. With her next book, *My Mother Was a Computer* (2005), Hayles retrospectively presents it, *Writing Machines*, and *How We Became Posthuman* as constituting a trilogy, which

> arcs from mid-twentieth century to the present, a trajectory that moves from a binary opposition between embodiment and information through an engagement with the materiality of literary texts to a broadening and deepening of these ideas into computation and textuality.
>
> (Hayles 2005: 2–3)

In *My Mother Was a Computer* Hayles confronts the extension of computational technologies realized in the early twenty-first century and the related "claim that the universe is generated through computational processes running on a vast computational mechanism underlying all of physical reality," which she calls the concept of "the Computational Universe." She investigates the changes in subjectivity and reading practices linked to this pervasive computational turn, the "dialectical positioning of humans and artificial creatures" (Hayles 2005: 4–5). She proposes the term "intermediation" as a way of conceptualizing the "complex transactions between bodies and texts" and she identifies "different forms of media" with the penetration of computational technologies within developed countries (7).

Hayles's trilogy comprises a fascinating exploration of the development of information technoscience. Particularly in the last two books, the project becomes a study of the changing nature of texts and literature as computational technologies have become increasingly pervasive. She extends literary studies beyond modern "classics" to include genre texts. However, her deployment of literature is ambivalent. As she pursues its material transformations in and through its interactions with computation technology, Hayles treats literature as a changing phenomenon. Nevertheless, this dynamic view of literature is somewhat in tension with her employment of it as a methodological touchstone in her investigations. She repeatedly uses her readings of key literary texts – drawing on what she sees as their capacity to generate "vividly imagined worlds" (Hayles 2005: 6) – to explicate assumptions, features, and problems of computational technoscience.

Conclusion

This chapter began by considering a selection of views on cultural studies of science as a relatively recent form of social studies of science emerging at the end of the twentieth century. While I did not offer any resolution to debates about this label, I did nominate some salient features of this strand of science studies, most notably its preoccupation with cultural specificity, the alignment of science with other cultural phenomena, the questioning of assumptions about the transcendental nature of scientific knowledge, and the orientation around the investigation of science in its context. I then offered brief reviews of recent influential cultural studies of technoscience executed through explorations of science and literature. These reviews have indicated some of the ways in which Gillian Beer, Donna Haraway, and Katherine Hayles have each forged distinctive ways of doing cultural studies of science. Their practices have challenged the conventions of social studies of technoscience and brought science studies and literary studies into dialogue in exciting, if sometimes controversial, ways. While not resolving the questions around what cultural studies of science are, these and other projects have expanded the domains of both science studies and literary studies.

Bibliography

Aronowitz, S. (1993) *Roll Over Beethoven: cultural strife*, London: Routledge.

Aronowitz, S., Martinsons, B. and Menser, B. (eds) (1996) *Technoscience and Cyberculture*, New York and London: Routledge.

Beer, G. (2009) *Darwin's Plots: evolutionary narrative in Darwin, George Eliot and nineteenth-century fiction*, 3rd edn, Cambridge: Cambridge University Press.

Bruno, G. (1992) "Spectorial embodiments: anatomies of the visible and the female bodyscape," *camera obscura*, 28: 239–61.

——(1993) *Streetwalking on a Ruined Map: cultural theory and the city films of Elivira Notari*, Princeton: Princeton University Press.

Cartwright, L. (1995) *Screening the Body: tracing medicine's visual culture*, Minneapolis: University of Minnesota Press.

Haraway, D. (1989) *Primate Visions: gender, race and nature in the world of modern science*, New York and London: Routledge.

——(1991) "A cyborg manifesto: science, technology, and socialist-feminism in the late twentieth century," in *Simians, Cyborgs, and Women: the reinvention of nature*, London: Free Association Books, pp. 149–81.

Hayles, N.K. (1999) *How We Became Posthuman: virtual bodies in cybernetics, literature, and informatics*, Chicago: University of Chicago Press.

——(2002) *Writing Machines*, Cambridge, Mass.: MIT Press.

——(2005) *My Mother Was a Computer: digital subjects and literary texts*, Chicago: University of Chicago Press.

Jordanova, L. (1989) *Sexual Visions: images of gender in science and medicine between the eighteenth and twentieth centuries*, Hemel Hempstead: Harvester Wheatsheaf.

Kuhn, T.S. (1962) *The Structure of Scientific Revolutions*, 3rd edn, Chicago: University of Chicago Press, 1996.

Latour, B. (1987) *Science in Action: how to follow scientists and engineers through society*, Cambridge, Mass.: Harvard University Press.

Levine, G. (2009) "Foreword" to the 2nd edn, in Beer 2009.

Lykke, N. (2002) "Feminist cultural studies of technoscience and other cyborg studies: a cartography," in R. Braidotti, J. Nieboer and S. Hirs (eds) *The Making of European Women's Studies*, IV (November): 133–43.

——(2008) "Feminist cultural studies of technoscience: portrait of an implosion," in Smelik and Lykke 2008, pp. 3–15.

McNeil, M. (2007) *Feminist Cultural Studies of Science and Technology*, London: Routledge.

——(2008) "Roots and routes: the making of feminist cultural studies of technoscience," in Smelik and Lykke 2008, pp. 16–31.

Menser, M. and Aronowitz, S. (1996) "On cultural studies, science, and technology," in Aronowitz, Martinsons and Menser 1996, pp. 7–30.

Nelkin, D. (1996) "Perspectives on the evolution of science studies," in Aronowitz, Martinsons and Menser 1996, pp. 31–36.

Rouse, J. (1992) "What are cultural studies of scientific knowledge?", *Configurations*, 1: 1–22.

Smelik, A. and Lykke, N. (eds) (2008) *Bits of Life: feminist studies of media, bioculture and technoscience*, Seattle: University of Washington Press.

Squier, S.M. (1994) *Babies in Bottles: twentieth-century visions of reproductive technology*, New Brunswick: Rutgers University Press.

25

DECONSTRUCTION

Vicki Kirby

Deconstruction's disciplinary home is conventionally found in those disciplines that profess special expertise in studying the complex structures of rhetoric, logic, discourse, and representation – in sum, language itself. Such approaches in the humanities are conventionally defined *against* the sciences, inasmuch as they question objectivity, emphasize the subjective dimension of interpretation, and turn the object under investigation into a textual or discursive artifact. Given this emphasis on the vagaries of interpretation, it is not surprising that deconstruction's relationship with science has been an uneasy and even notorious one. In the myriad publications that came to be known as the "Science Wars" and then the "Sokal hoax," Jacques Derrida's name and references to deconstruction were routinely associated with scientific ignorance and rhetorical obfuscation. As Arkady Plotnitsky describes the denigration of deconstruction at this time, Derrida's thought "figures most prominently and, again, nearly uniquely throughout these discussions" (Plotnitsky 1997).[1]

In sum, as the de facto exemplar of postmodernism's inability to engage a substantive and enduring facticity, the real world no less, deconstruction came to represent the impasse of the "two cultures." This involves the perceived incommensurability between the aims and methods of the humanities and those practiced in the sciences. In the former, the meaning of the referent changes because it is deemed a cultural product, an ideational or socially inflected entity that, inasmuch as it mediates reality, is constructed or *invented*. In the latter, the pragmatism of scientific research demands the referent's relative stability, concrete endurance, and accessibility, and to this end, proof of the referent is thought to be *discovered*. What is important here is that the humanities tend to circumscribe knowledge, emphasize its contingency, and define the human condition in terms of hermeneutic enclosure. In the main, the project of the sciences is very different: science strives for access to a universal truth that, inasmuch as it pre-exists interpretation, cannot be constituted by it.

As the blurring of deconstruction with a battery of postmodern theories has become routine, it is not surprising that the anti-science aspects of such representations have provoked few scholars. There are two notable exceptions.

In *Complementarity* (1994) and *The Knowable and the Unknowable* (2002), Plotnitsky explores deconstruction's resonance with arguments in physics and quantum mechanics, especially with the work of Niels Bohr. This detailed reading is matched by Christopher Johnson's remarkable analysis of the history of structuralism and deconstruction in *System and Writing in the Philosophy of Jacques Derrida* (1993).[2] Although working with quite different material and intellectual purpose, both writers shift our understanding of deconstruction as an intricate analysis of representation in its myriad forms, namely a cultural enterprise, to something that is not easily defined against, or separate from, scientific practice.

The importance of Johnson's contribution is that he reminds us of the shared historical and intellectual milieu that links models and approaches in the life sciences with the inauguration of deconstruction and the shift from "language" in the restricted or conventional sense to a "generalized language" or "writing" that carries very different implications. The importance of this move from language to "writing" is anticipated in structuralism's aspiration to a scientific status that would exceed, or certainly complicate, philosophical and ideological concerns. Johnson reminds us that structuralism not only promised "a methodological efficacy in the study of man comparable to that of the exact sciences" (Johnson 1993: 2), but also and more importantly, it linked the sciences with the humanities by confounding the defining difference between their respective objects.

Consequently, at the end of the nineteenth century there is a paradigm shift in the way the object of investigation is perceived, and this culminated in the confluence of cybernetics and molecular biology during and after World War II. If the exact nature and truth of the scientific object is subject to permutation and combination, in other words, if it is a code or language of some sort whose comparative complexity resonates with the abstract cipherings of human language, then this is more than an extension of language into what were previously alien fields. It is the *question* of language – what makes it work as a self-referential "organism" with an apparent substantive leverage, and how, or if, we can circumscribe its constitutive efficacy, that becomes the focus of investigation. How can the language of human culture and ideas connect and merge with the deep communicative structures of the animal, the vegetable, indeed, even the inorganic? The provocation that attends this "expanded" sense of language that Derrida brings under the banner of "writing" was registered in the original dissemination of poststructural arguments in both the humanities and human sciences. In the words of Michel Serres we hear something of the wonder that made this contemporary moment so extraordinary:

> The sciences of today are formalistic, analytical, grammatical, semiological, each of them based on an alphabet of elements. ... Their affinities are so apparent that we are once again beginning to dream of the possibility of a *mathesis universalis*. ... What biochemistry has

discovered is not the mysterious noumenon, but quite simply a *universal science of the character*. Like the other sciences, it points towards a general philosophy of marked elements.

(cited in Johnson 1993: 3)

It is important to appreciate that Derrida's project was actively inspired by this broad interdisciplinary context that included the discoveries and also the challenges of scientific investigation. Clearly, Derrida's attempt to generalize language could not be contained within philosophy proper, for as Johnson notes, Derrida's use of the term "writing" to capture this generality "is as much a symptom as it is a cause" (Johnson 1993: 4). In other words, this sense that the life of language and information is as much a bio-gram as a grapheme "is not the initiative or inspiration of one individual thinker (Derrida), but the effect of a more general transformation of the modern episteme" (5). Indeed, in the introduction to *Of Grammatology* Derrida acknowledges how the peculiar pro-liferation of "writing" has become the analytical term that binds quite disparate intellectual endeavors:

> For some time now, as a matter of fact, here and there, by a gesture and for motives that are profoundly necessary ... one says "language" for action, movement, thought, reflection, consciousness, unconsciousness, experience, affectivity, etc. Now we tend to say "writing" for all that and more. ... The contemporary biologist speaks of writing and *pro-gram* in relation to the most elementary processes of information within the living cell. And finally, whether it has essential limits or not, the entire field covered by the cybernetic *program* will be the field of writing.
>
> (Derrida 1984: 9)

The chatter of myriad informational ciphers, feedback loops, language codes, and algorithms is now so ubiquitous in the representation of knowledges that we are desensitized to the wonder of its very possibility. Put simply, how can a language be specific and local, yet at the same time universally comprehensible? An illustration will prove helpful here. It will explain why Derrida's attentions were thoroughly captured by the puzzle of a "generalized language," and it will also suggest why this language does not conform to the tripartite structure of communication (sender, message, and receiver). More provocatively, it will trouble Johnson's description of this moment as a "general transformation of the modern episteme," a notion echoed in the title of Plotnitsky's *The Knowable and the Unknowable*, because although true, there is even more to this story.

The disciplinary cross-talk of forensic crime-scene investigation provides us with an exemplary instance of the riddle of language. It also allows us to dilate on the implications of Derrida's assertion, elaborated in *Writing and Difference* (1978) and *Of Grammatology* (1984; both books originally appeared in 1967), that "there is nothing outside of the text [there is no outside-the-text; *il n'y a pas de hors-texte*]" (Derrida 1984: 158). For our purposes, we can think of the crime scene as a text of sorts, its meaning brought into focus through the lens of different practices and representational models. These might include geology, geography, climatology, genetics, hematology, dentistry, psychology, entomology, veterinary studies, botany, orthography, sociology, historical expertise – the list is endless. Importantly, these diverse methods of isolating and understanding data illustrate two paradoxical insights. First, it is the act of circumscribing a crime scene that provides the necessary focus and access to its internal logic – that special signature of self-referential relationships that carry revelatory promise. Indeed, in the search for a culprit, it is as if the unknown figure is virtually present in the weave of different methodologies and apparently random signs. The logic of the scene resides in its peculiar ability to endure, or hold, despite this dynamic cacophony of internal cross-referencing, for it is *through* these chattering patterns of data alignments that the actual integrity of the scene emerges. Importantly, then, the scene should not be understood as a collection, or accumulation, of different items of evidence – an aggregation of significance – for it is the entire scene that actively identifies and informs each item with special meaning. In other words, the *context* that appears to surround an object will also come to situate and explain it, as if the entirety of the crime scene inheres within any one aspect.

And so we come to the second paradox, or more accurately, another perspective on the first. If each item of evidence is informed by its context, its particular significance determined by what appears to be exterior and separate from it, then this same logic can be applied to the very notion of an individual crime scene, indeed, an individual anything. To explain this, we know that the framing of a scene, its isolation from the rest of life, will invest that scene with special meaning and indicative relevance. In other words, its predictive truth function rests upon, and is relative to, a very particular frame of reference. Nevertheless, it is also the case that in order to read an item of evidence, for example, a blood-spatter pattern, a catalogue of alternative patterns from outside the boundary of investigation will inform and explain its special significance. A puzzle of quantum proportion emerges in this apparent contradiction, where the differences that are relative to a specific context – a determined or local "event" – are also dispersed and informed by a wider field of informational possibilities that appear utterly different. Perhaps we can risk calling this wider field a unified or universal field of reference (which clearly doesn't imply homogeneity). If the difference between *context*, *pre*-text and *text* seems to collapse and yet endure in this example, then we are faced with a real conundrum.

The individual departure points that conventionally provide us with analytical security; the anchors for what are spatially external or temporally prior, the divisions that underpin simple causality, the oppositional valuations that allow us to navigate conceptual, ethical and political discriminations, as well as

the most basic difference between subject and object, observer and observed –
all these coordinates that presume separation are now in question. The reason
for this merger, or contagion between entities, is that the border that allows us
to define and differentiate one thing from another is also subject to the systemic
entanglement that Derrida calls "language in the general sense." As Derrida
explains it, if "there is no-thing outside the text, this implies, with the transformation of the concept of text in general, that the text is no longer the snug
airtight inside of an interiority or an identity-to-itself ... but rather a different
placement of the effects of opening and closing" (Derrida 1981a: 35–36).
Commenting on this passage, André Brink is acutely aware of its transgressive
implications for the way we segregate the practice and purpose of the humanities
from those of the sciences. He notes:

> [Derrida] introduces a new awareness of permeability, of interpenetr-
> ability, of osmosis through a membrane, a *hymen* (Derrida 1981a: 209).
> This in itself suggests a transgression as an elemental act of language,
> of experience, of "writing": transgressions of limits between wave and
> particle, energy and mass, time and space; between word and thing, word
> and thought, thing and thought.
>
> (Brink 1985: 21–22)

The real provocation that attends this sense of the system (this field of
interconnectivity from which nothing is excluded) is that it precludes the possibility of a truly independent, homogeneous and autonomous entity, whether that
entity is the field or system itself, or the identity of what appear to be its internal
components. In other words, any entity is not so much an element *among* others,
an element whose existence is locatable *within* the field or among other fields, but
rather, an element whose identity is an expression *of* the field's interactivity with
itself. In a very real sense, the field individuates itself, "writes" and articulates
itself in quite specific ways: the particular is not the opposite of the general
or universal in this understanding. A helpful illustration can be drawn from
Saussurean linguistics and the difference between the notion of *langue*, the
natural language or tongue that all members of a community share, versus *parole*,
or individual speech. We tend to regard the individual as the author of their
particular speech behavior because *parole* captures a unique and inventive signature. In a Derridean reading, however, and one that Saussure anticipates when
he insists that the individual is never the origin of change, the unique pattern-
ment of *parole* is exemplary of the infinite permutations and combinations of
langue. The general "quickens," or generates the particular: it is not external or
alien to it. This means that even if, contra Saussure, we could attribute the origin
of a language shift or neologism to a particular individual – say, a literary author,
or even to the muddled error of someone's mispronunciation or grammatical
blunderings – the very workability of that shift, the reasons that explain its

genesis and endurance, will rest on the fact that *parole* is a specific instantiation of more general forces. *Parole* presumes a communication model, namely intercourse between independent individuals. However, within a common field of writing, or *langue* in this case, *parole* marks the *internal* cross-talk, or reproductive genesis, of *langue* itself.

As this last point is a difficult one to grasp, a further clarification will underline its broader importance. Derrida uses what he calls the non-concept "*différance*" to mark a process that individuates and separates ("writes") entities into recognizable "units" (whether by this we mean signs, subjects, objects, intentions, events). And yet what enables this process of discrimination, this cutting up and dividing, actually arises from the internal dynamics of intertextuality – entanglement and inseparability. I mention this here because it provides some insight into why the communication model based on information theory cannot accommodate the layered complexity of this involvement. Derrida problematizes the space of separation that the word difference implies, as well as its corollary, the assumption of identifiable entities that both pre-exist and initiate communication. By changing the spelling of difference (*différence*) through a silent marker that is not registered in the French pronunciation (*différance*), identity becomes a dynamic and contingent phenomenon. Karen Barad's neologism, "intra-activity," is perhaps a more accessible or suggestive illustration of this same process. Referring to the dynamic of quantum involvement, Barad notes that this is not an *interaction*, an effect caused by one entity upon another, separated in space and time:

> Crucially, *agency is a matter of intra-acting; it is an enactment, not something that someone or something has.* It cannot be designated as an attribute of subjects or objects (as they do not preexist as such). It is not an attribute whatsoever. *Agency is "doing" or "being" in its intra-activity. It is the enactment of iterative changes to particular practices – iterative reconfigurings of topological manifolds of spacetime–matter relations – through the dynamics of intra-activity.*
>
> (Barad 2007: 178)

This process of tautological intricacy, an "always/already" that is never simple repetition, has significantly stretched the conventional meaning of "text" and allowed us to appreciate why scientific goals and practices cannot be excluded from this comprehensive text, this field of language (intra-activity, *différance*).

Further insight into how deconstruction might reconfigure our understanding of the sciences, as well as the more general question of knowledge formation, is heralded in Derrida's insistence that deconstruction is not a methodology: it is not a procedural set of maneuvers, an application or template of inquiry through which an alien object might be ciphered. But what are the implications of such a comment for the sciences? To open this question, Rodolphe Gasché makes the unusual claim that deconstruction "is never the effect of a subjective act of desire or will or wishing. What provokes a deconstruction is rather of an 'objective' nature. It is a 'must' so to speak" (Gasché 1986: 123). The comment seems to contradict what many have understood as the anarchic essence of deconstruction, the sense of untrammeled freedom or "play" where "anything goes." However, "play" actually carries a sense of determination for Derrida, as we see when he likens it to the internal movement of a machine (Derrida 1970: 268). It is something that is quite circumscribed, something that the machine generates from the particular rhythms that arise from its own workings. And yet, despite this sense of the objective, and even the pull of determinism, Gasché does not attribute deconstruction with scientific instrumentalism, noting that deconstruction, "as a methodical principle, cannot be mistaken for anything resembling scientific procedural rules" (Gasché 1986: 123). Nevertheless, his comments remind us that deconstruction is difficult to place.

Deconstruction can certainly appear to adopt a meta-position in relation to its object, a gesture that seems compatible with scientific methodologies and claims to objectivity. Indeed, we might remember that Derrida's earliest attempts to explicate the difficulty of his project acknowledge certain affinities between deconstruction and science. In the chapter "Of Grammatology as a Positive Science," which explores this question, Derrida concludes, the "constitution of a science or a philosophy of writing is a necessary and difficult task" (Derrida 1984: 93). And in answer to Julia Kristeva's question in *Positions*, "to what extent is or is not grammatology a 'science,'" Derrida refuses to reject the term. "Grammatology must pursue and consolidate whatever, in scientific practice, has always already begun to exceed the logocentric closure. This is why there is no simple answer to the question of whether grammatology is a 'science'" (Derrida 1981b: 35–36).

If Derrida's "double-science" encourages us to "understand this *incompetence* of science which is also the incompetence of philosophy" (Derrida 1984: 93), then perhaps deconstruction's home is as uncomfortable yet essential to our understanding of the sciences as it is to the humanities. Certainly, its *"point de méthode"* (point/lack of method) is not a distinct analytical approach with a definite object and limited disciplinary application. However, the awkward question that arises if we forfeit method, or put the notion of mediation into question, is how we might hope to interrogate the process of understanding if its most routine discriminations are contestable. For example, what happens if the technology or apparatus that separates observer from observed, reader from object, interpreter from interpreted, cannot be secured? Whereas Brink's earlier description of this blurring of identities likened the process to the permeability and interpenetration of osmosis, the "transgressions of limits," the question gathers quantum complexity if we concede that these "entities" do not pre-exist their interpenetration. If what appears outside and therefore different from the inside is always/already the involved inside of an event that differentiates *itself*, that instantiates the oppositional logic of identification/separation even as it exceeds this restricted comprehension, then there is no originary integrity to be transgressed.

What can it mean to suggest that the observer, the locus of intention, agency, and intellectual calculation, the origin of the desire to comprehend and decipher, to read or experiment, is non-local? In this counter-intuitive review of the notion of intent and calculation, the very identity of the human as the unique repository of agential capacities is curiously destabilized and strangely dispersed. If the absolute break between natural objects and cultural methods of understanding them is fraught, as suggested by Serres's allusion to a *mathesis universalis*, and again, in the predictive or agential capacity of forensic informatics, then what or where is the human subject? "Who" speaks this "general language" if its author is dispersed? One possible way to catch at the marvel of this question is to find in the *system* of differentiation a field of self-expression, a subject writ large – subject to the reflex of its own curiosity and self-involvement. Importantly, if the world of natural objects and processes already articulates the will to know, the will to be otherwise, then this intimate reflex/reflection, this "transformation of the modern episteme," has an ontological dimension. To decenter the human as the origin of language, the one, indeed, the only one, who writes and reads, doesn't obliterate the identity of the human; rather, it opens it to question. To practice deconstruction as a positive science, to interrogate the notion of "textuality" *within which* the human is "written," is to appreciate that an epistemological transformation is, at the same time, an ontological one.[3]

We can re-enter this conundrum by returning to Johnson. Commenting on the shock wave that was to redefine disciplinary formations and generate deconstruction in the process, Johnson underlines that life could not be reduced to a static, irreducible essence if its iterations involve decipherment: "the logic of life is scriptural" (Johnson 1993: 3). Johnson's statement draws energy from François Jacob's *The Logic of Life* (1993). Winner of the Nobel Prize for his work on RNA information transfer, Jacob wrote at length about the way memory and design in the study of heredity could be compared with the structure of natural languages. It is the detail of Jacob's discussion, elaborated in the book's introduction, "The Programme," that exercises Derrida's close attention in a series of unpublished seminars entitled "La Vie La Mort" (1975). Here, Derrida addresses this question of the bio-gram more closely, asking what Jacob and Georges Canguilhem[4] actually "mean by this semiotic or rather by this graphic of life, of this non-phonetic writing that they call 'without writing'" (Derrida 1975, Seminar 1: 22). Derrida's purpose is twofold. First, he wants to acknowledge the evidence of a generality of language that encompasses what Jacob describes as "the cerebral-institutional," or what Derrida will gloss as "psychic, social, cultural, institutional, politico-economic etc" (Derrida 1975, Seminar 1: 19), *as well as* the genetic. Derrida will insist that Jacob's representation of the difference that separates these apparently discrete systems of nature and culture is misguided, because what Jacob reserves for the genetic program is also apparent in the "cerebral-institutional." And here we arrive at the nub of Derrida's intervention.

We can read Derrida's impatience with Jacob as a bid to remind the geneticist that he is really a philosopher of sorts, caught in the metaphysical commitments of cultural representations. In other words, the presumptive explanations of the behavior and literacy of genes are an inevitable reflection of the language Jacob must use to (mis)represent them: the tool constitutes and contaminates the object. However, given Derrida's acknowledgment of the cybernetic turn and his rejection of classical understandings of mediation, it would make little sense to conflate such textual enclosure with human language and interpretation, as if the presumptive language of genes is an error – a projected (and therefore misplaced) anthropocentrism. The purchase of Derrida's argument is that it simply won't work as an epistemological corrective if the logic of life is, indeed, scriptural, and science can take pragmatic leverage from this insight.

Derrida's second point is to remind us of what he said in *Of Grammatology* – "the biologist speaks today of writing and of pro-gram with respect to the most elementary information processes in the living cell." However and importantly, he goes on to emphasize that these comments were not made

> in order to reinvest into the notion or the word *program* all of the conceptual machine that is the *logos* and its semantic, but rather in order to attempt to show that the call to a non-phonetic writing in genetics should implicate and provoke a whole deconstruction of the logocentric machine.
>
> (Derrida 1975, Seminar 1: 22)

We need to take stock at this juncture and reassess what it might mean to evoke a starting point for deconstruction where the system – "textuality," "writing," or "language in the general sense" – already, and at once, articulates the heterogeneity of biological algorithms, cybernetic communication, the discriminating grammars of molecular and atomic parsing, and the puzzles of quantum space/time configurations. What could exceed the system's comprehension (of itself) if, as Derrida insists, "there is no outside-the-text"?

Derrida animates the subject Life with critical capacity, noting how life "divides itself originarily (*urteilen*) in order to produce itself and reproduce itself" (Derrida 1975, Seminar 1: 3). This suggestion complicates the accepted division between the letter of life, its genetic and reproductive programs, and the life of the letter in literature and representation, because reproduction/re-presentation *is* discrimination/judgment. If, as biologists insist, the constant of life is reproducibility, then from a deconstructive point of view, even literature in the conventional sense is alive to such iterative processes.

When we consider the relationship between deconstruction and science, the conjunction "and" segregates the difference between these endeavors. This is a conversation that has yet to take place, a conversation whose outcome has yet to be registered/written. However, the deconstructive legacy challenges us to consider these projects as already entangled, already in conversation/conversion. Whether scientific modeling, natural languages, computational algorithms, or hormonal chatter, it is from within this grammatological textile,[5] or universal *langue*, that the pragmatics of referential being materialize. How can modes of knowing – apparently second-order cultural models and representations – already animate the natural order? By interrogating the divisions that identify the human as inherently *un*natural, a positive science of grammatology might be appreciated. Indeed, inasmuch as certain aspects of science have always been in the process of discovering human complexity in alien (natural) literacies and numeracies, it seems that a positive science of grammatology is already underway.

Notes

1 The specific focus of Derrida's critics concerned the notion of "the Einsteinian constant," a phrase initially coined by the philosopher Jean Hyppolite when questioning the detail of one of Derrida's earliest papers. For an informed analysis of this specific point, as well as the broader intellectual context of the "Science Wars," see Plotnitsky 1997, 2002. Other examples where Derrida's work makes mention of scientific concerns include Gödel's Incompleteness Theorem (Derrida 1981a: 219; Plotnitsky 1994: 196–202; Taylor 2001: 93–98), his earliest work on Husserl and the question of geometry (Derrida 1989), and his discussion of François Jacob's understanding of the language of genes (Derrida 1975).

2 Among a handful of publications that do explore the relationship between science and deconstruction, albeit to different effects, see Brink 1985; Norris 1997; Johnson 2001; Malabou 2007; Staten 2008.

3 As this is a brief summation, I refer the reader to Derrida's dilation on evolution as "writing." See his response to Jean Hyppolite in the "Discussion" following "Structure, Sign, and Play in the Discourses of the Human Sciences" (Derrida 1970). Here, Derrida refuses the suggestion that if evolution is a form of writing then humankind arrives as an aberration in these scribblings, an aberration because the complexities of intention and calculation belong to the writing of humanity alone and could not precede this arrival.

4 Derrida's interest in Georges Canguilhem mainly concerns *La Connaissance de la Vie* (1952) and *Etudes d'histoires et de philosophie des sciences* (1968).

5 The sense that "elements" do not pre-exist their involvement, indeed, that they express what I prefer to gloss as a hyper-presence of involvement, is evident in Derrida's explanation of "textile":

> no element can function as a sign without referring to another element which itself is not simply present. This interweaving results in each "element" – phoneme or grapheme – being constituted on the basis of the trace within it of the other elements of the chain or system. This interweaving, this textile, is the *text* produced only in the transformation of another text. ... There are only, everywhere, differences and traces of traces.

> (Derrida 1981b: 26)

Bibliography

Barad, K. (2007) *Meeting the Universe Halfway: quantum physics and the entanglement of matter and meaning*, Durham, N.C.: Duke University Press.

Brink, A. (1985) "Transgressions: a quantum approach to literary deconstruction," *Journal of Literary Studies*, 1(3): 10–26.

Canguilhem, G. (1952) *La Connaissance de la Vie*, Paris: Hachette.

——(1968) *Etudes d'histoires et de philosophie des sciences*, Paris: Vrin.

Derrida, J. (1970) "Structure, sign, and play in the discourses of the human sciences" and "Discussion," in R. Macksey and E. Donato (eds) *The Languages of Criticism and the Sciences of Man: the structuralist controversy*, Baltimore: Johns Hopkins University Press, pp. 247–72.

——(1975) *La Vie La Mort* (Jacques Derrida Papers MS-CO1 Special Collections and Archives, The UC Irvine Libraries, Irvine, CA), trans. A. Pont (private copy).

——(1978) *Writing and Difference*, trans. A. Bass, London: Routledge & Kegan Paul.

——(1981a) *Dissemination*, trans. B. Johnson, Chicago: University of Chicago Press.

——(1981b) *Positions*, trans. A. Bass, Chicago: University of Chicago Press.

——(1984) *Of Grammatology*, trans. G. Chakravorty Spivak, Baltimore, MD, and London: Johns Hopkins University Press.

——(1989) *Edmund Husserl's Origin of Geometry: an introduction*, trans. J.P. Leavey Jr., Lincoln: University of Nebraska Press.

Gasché, R. (1986) *The Tain of the Mirror: Derrida and the philosophy of reflection*, Cambridge, Mass.: Harvard University Press.

Jacob, F. (1993) *The Logic of Life: a history of heredity*, trans. B.E. Spillman, Princeton: Princeton University Press.

Johnson, C. (1993) *System and Writing in the Philosophy of Jacques Derrida*, Cambridge: Cambridge University Press.

——(2001) "Derrida and science," in M. Meyer (ed.) *Questioning Derrida: with his replies on philosophy*, Aldershot: Ashgate.

Malabou, C. (2007) "The end of writing?: grammatology and plasticity," trans. A. Wiese, *The European Legacy*, 12(4): 431–41.

Norris, C. (1997) "Deconstructing Anti-Realism: quantum mechanics and interpretation theory," *Substance: A Review of Theory and Literary Criticism*, 26(3): 3–37.

Plotnitsky, A. (1994) *Complementarity: anti-epistemology after Bohr and Derrida*, Durham, N.C.: Duke University Press.

——(1997) "'But it is above all not true': Derrida, relativity, and the 'science wars,'" *Postmodern Culture*, 7(2). Online. Available HTTP: <http://muse.jhu.edu/login?uri=/journals/pmc/v007/7.2plotnitsky.html> (accessed 15 July 2009).

——(2002) *The Knowable and the Unknowable: modern science, nonclassical thought, and the "two cultures"*, Ann Arbor: University of Michigan Press.

Staten, H. (2008) "Derrida, Dennett, and the ethico-political project of naturalism," *Derrida Today*, 1(1): 19–41.

Taylor, M.C., (2001) *The Moment of Complexity: emerging network culture*, Chicago: University of Chicago Press.

26
E-LITERATURE

Joseph Tabbi

Despite a landmark essay by the novelist Robert Coover, the emergence of literary writing in new media does not signal an "end of books." Conceivably, there could be an end to literary studies as an autonomous discipline and a cessation of literary reading as a significant cultural practice. However, what new media enact is a more direct engagement of the literary arts with the arts of image, sound, and computation, and hence a renewed appreciation of a long-standing insight, available in the writings of Walter Ong, Elizabeth Eisenstein, and Marshall McLuhan but only now reaching general consciousness: the idea that print literature has long been part of a fragile "media ecology" (Tabbi and Wutz 1997). The representational requirements of literary narrative, for example, change radically after film takes up the burden of depicting realistic settings, and the placement of words in proximity to filmic, video, and sound elements continues that relocation of the literary in new media. With the redrawing of narrative and visual boundaries comes the emergence and continued differentiation of modern literary forms (whose reflexivity foregrounds verbal inventions that were always present in earlier writing, especially in *sui generis* narratives such as *Tristram Shandy*).

The continuation of the print legacy itself remains as uncertain as the fate of globalization and modernity (see Cochran 2001). For reading to re-emerge as a consequential activity in the new media ecology, more is required than the scanning, storage, and promotion of our classics. As books cease to be the primary storage vehicle for recording, preserving, and disseminating thought, our legacy texts need to be engaged actively in "born-digital" writing – which is to say, in works that are designed for the media where the current generation does its reading. We should not look to the internet for forms and genres that emerged in print and continue to thrive there. Rather, the task of defining electronic literature is an ongoing process of differentiation, not the least of which is the distinction between how we read books and how these practices circulate in current reading and writing spaces.

The literary prefiguration of the internet

Electronic literature is not just a "thing" or a "medium" or even a body of "works" in various "genres." It is not poetry, fiction, hypertext, gaming, code-work, or some new admixture of all these practices. Electronic literature is, arguably, an emerging cultural form, as much a collective creation of terms, keywords, genres, structures, and institutions as it is the production of new literary objects. The ideas of cybervisionaries Paul Otlet, Vannevar Bush, and Ted Nelson, foundational to the electronic storage, recovery, and processing of texts, go beyond practical insights and can be seen to participate in a long-standing ambition to construct a world literature in the sense put forward by David Damrosh: "not an infinite ungraspable canon of works but rather a mode of circulation and of reading ... that is applicable to individual works as to bodies of material" (Damrosh 2003: 5).

The failure of print scholars to create a space for traditional literature in new media is evident, however, even among those with an avowed interest in the "global" circulation of discourse. For example, the postcolonial scholar Arjun Appadurai (2000: 22) writes that "public spheres" are "increasingly dominated by electronic media (and thus delinked from the capacity to read and write)" (cited in Prendergast 2004). That "thus" can rankle. Obviously, Appadurai is not thinking of the internet, which is still (and likely always will be) overwhelmingly textual, despite an insistently instrumental visual presence. The assumption that reading and writing are of course "delinked" from electronic media shows just how deep the separation of spheres has become for scholars like Appadurai, who continue to evaluate globalization primarily through the reading and writing of printed materials. Appadurai and most of the contributors to *Debating World Literature* (Prendergast 2004) want to locate a literary practice commensurate with processes of globalization. But by dissociating reading and writing from electronic media, these scholars fail to entertain the idea that writing produced in new media might in fact *be* an emerging world literature.

It was not supposed to be like this. Appadurai's casual dismissal of reading and writing as active elements in "electronic media" should seem strange if one recalls how cyberculture visionaries advanced the idea of a universally accessible, open-ended archive that primarily stores *texts*. That was the idea behind Vannevar Bush's (1945) "Memex" and Ted Nelson's (1974) "hypertext" – not the current expanse of decontextualized hot links that take readers serially away from the text they are reading at any given time, but rather, a means of bringing documents, in part or in their entirety, to a single writing space for further commentary and the development of conceptual connections. The worldwide collaborative potential of collecting documents, not lost on these American information specialists after World War II, had already been expressed by the Belgian Paul Otlet in his *Traité de documentation* (1934). There the thought of connecting people to the libraries of the world via telephone and electronic screens led to his vision of a technological encyclopedia. In Otlet's "conceptual prefiguration of the Internet" (*préfiguration conceptuelle d'Internet*), every extant work in print would be but chapters and paragraphs in a single "universal book" (*unique livre universel*) (Levie 2007).

Of course, Otlet, Bush, and Nelson understood that electronic media might include works of all countries, cultures, and languages. But inclusiveness alone did not make their vision universal. Rather, the operative feature everywhere in early cyber-literary thought – what would make the technologically enhanced book more than the sum total of books in print and in manuscript everywhere – was its promise of reshaping boundaries. National and cultural divisions would thereby shift toward more conceptual discriminations: the kind of distinction that does not separate people categorically but is capable of connecting them in discourse. Concepts and connections that had remained potential (because of the book's physical separation from other books) could now be activated in the mind of a reader. The technological excitement lay, that is, precisely in its promise to renew the "capacity to read and write" (Appadurai), with the added value (so necessary to universalist thought) that the results of one's reading could be conveyed to others, debated, and revised. In every case, the knowledge transfer would occur not through interpretive activity or through description or summary alone but because every user would be similarly free, in Nelson's words, to "list, sketch, link, and annotate the complexities we seek to understand, then present 'views' of the complexities in many different forms" (Nelson 1974: 332).

Reconsidered in the context of computational and communications media, the universality of literature would not lie in attaining a single common language or in the expression of an essential human spirit but rather in inhabiting a common workspace. A word Nelson coined for this process was "transclusion" – an inclusion through site transfers of separate texts that could be full or partial, depending on one's requirements: in every case, the "original" document or set of documents remains at its home address while being reproduced at the target address (not just referenced or linked sequentially). The achievement of this capacity, which can make reading and researching also a kind of worldwide consortium building, could potentially bring to the public a literary project that had earlier been considered private and secluded.

In *If on a Winter's Night a Traveler*, Italo Calvino implies the threat posed by entertainment media to literary privacy when he has his narrator advise the reader to shut the door and "let the world around you fade. ... Tell the others right away, 'No, I don't want to watch TV!' Raise your voice – they won't hear you otherwise – 'I'm reading, I don't want to be disturbed!' ... Speak louder, yell: 'I'm beginning to read Italo Calvino's new novel!' Or if you prefer, don't say anything; just hope they'll leave you alone" (Calvino 1979: 1). The situation is different in the collaborative, receptive media that, like the internet and unlike television, include text as a primary component – although here, too, demands are made on a reader's time and attention. In new media, readers can risk becoming like Calvino's harried publisher later in the novel, whose room is full of books that are never read, only circulated and recirculated, their authors too well known to us as personalities and occasional celebrities for their works to hold any fascination.

In *Industrial Poetics* (2005), the poet and literary scholar Joe Amato questions whether even the authors of most blogs ever go back and read what they have written, for an audience that is for the most part never even hinted at in the writing. A literary text contains, traditionally and of necessity, an "implied reader" within its rhetorical structuring. Premature announcements of hypertext's "interactivity" notwithstanding, a close reading of random unsponsored web writing reveals a deep inability of many would-be authors to imagine that someone actually could be reading or responding. Those sites that do attract readers, generally (still) attract *authors* – but web authorship may differ from print in that authors do not speak while readers listen: this is to say, print remains a *broadcast* media, directing communications from one to many – even though, unlike radio, television, and other broadcast media, the sense of *one-to-one* communication is achievable in print through the aforementioned creation of an "implied reader," a role which any individual can, through attentive reading, apply to oneself. The internet, by contrast, is a *reception* medium, from many to many and without the narrative continuity or sustained rhetorical address needed to single out individuals.

In reception media such as Otlet's universal book and the internet, documents and imaginative discourses are not given as ends in themselves but as material to be reworked, relocated, and remixed (to use an anachronistic formulation that came into vogue after the digitization of music). The idea that this potential needed to be liberated, implicit in Otlet and Bush, is made explicit in Nelson's titular concept of "computer lib." Nelson's program for the freeing of mental capacities through human/machine interaction, consistent in so many ways with contemporary programs of racial, sexual, and lifestyle liberation (and often exceeding these in rhetorical fervor), to a degree brought technological transformations into the realm of worldwide social and cultural transformations.

Three decades into the computer revolution, the conceptual freedom celebrated by Nelson is no longer so convincing, and the open-source, do-it-yourself culture of file sharing is no longer so fluid when the interfaces encountered by most readers have been largely pre-formatted to serve commercial and instrumental ends. In the time of Nelson and Bush and during the rise of the IBM mainframe, computers were still largely available only to big business and a cohort of researchers. The personal computer came later, and no one predicted its transformation of the writing space essentially into an office and entertainment center. Under such conditions, the liberation of "minds" from the constraints of new media now requires a more active, oppositional role available not to the mass of computer users but only to a subgroup of "hackers" who are capable (often by breaking copyright laws and proprietary protections that did not exist in Nelson's heyday) of penetrating and changing configurations at the level of source code. That kind of competence remains the domain of only a few.

"To hack," writes the literary critic Adelaide Morris, "is to work within a set of constraints – linguistic rules, programmatic structures, protocols that organize data exchange and enable telecommunication connections – to keep possibilities in circulation. In this sense, the purpose of a hack is to interrupt inevitability, to put ghostly alternatives back into motion, to engender fresh abstractions, to find a way, like Emily Dickinson, to 'Dwell in Possibility'" (Morris 2007). Only by keeping these constraints in view and at the same time "engendering fresh abstractions," posing alternative source codes as well as experimental textual formations against the achieved configurations of worldwide commerce and communication, is it possible to maintain literature in its potential state – not as a revolutionary program to be realized (Nelson's "computer lib"), but rather, as a condition for creativity.

The dream life of literal letters

First-generation electronic literature, contemporary with Ted Nelson at the dawn of the brief age of the "personal computer," tended to explore the openness and freedom of linkages and modes of circulation that were available to authors having some programming knowledge and working with a range of often unreliable, but largely open-source, software. That may have helped reinforce Nelson's libertarian pose, and proponents still speak of the "affordances" of ever new, mostly obsolescent technologies. Generally, however, the born-digital works that have lasted tend to gain creative traction not from exploiting ready-made affordances but from revealing and writing against the *constraints* inherent in additional levels of mediation (beyond the comparatively direct linkage from mind to hand to pen and paper). It is no accident, for example, that games – concerned with rules of operation and conduct – were among the first achieved examples of electronic literature and they remain the only commercially viable practice for the literary arts.

With the publication in 1984 of *Mindwheel*, Robert Pinsky contributed not only a pioneering work of electronic literature but also a rare crossing over from the literary world, where he was a recognized poet teaching English at Berkeley. Pinsky brought his abilities to interactive fiction, which many people at the time saw as "just games." Thomas Disch, a novelist and poet, did something similar with his game *Amnesia*, but Disch was frustrated that no one would recognize and review *Amnesia* as literature and he denounced interactive fiction afterwards. Pinsky didn't do this, but neither did he remain active as an author of electronic literature. The same can be said of Robert Coover, who introduced a generation of graduate students at Brown University to the practice of electronic literature but himself continued to write print novels.

The same can be said of each author who has achieved a reputation in the field of electronic literature: the poet Stefanie Strickland presents online and print versions of her major work, *V: Wave.Son.Nets/Losing L'Una* (2002); Michael Joyce (who according to his Vassar University web page is "no longer maintaining a public web presence") has moved from his landmark hypertext, *Afternoon: A Story* of 1987–91, to a print novel, *Liam's Going*, published in 2002; and Shelley Jackson has achieved a successful transition from her debut e-literary work, *Patchwork Girl*, a cyber-feminist hypertext revision of Mary Shelley's *Frankenstein*, to a career of cross-genre (and cross-gendered) experimentation in print (2002's *The Melancholy of Anatomy* and 2006's *Half Life*) and in performance art – notably her *Skin Project*, a network narrative in which each word is tattooed on the skin of a volunteer. In such work, electronic literature emerges as a realization of literary qualities that might reference, but rarely tries to reproduce, the narrativity and lyrical flow that remain the province of print. Jackson herself sees her work as continuous with the very literary goal of producing a world apart from our conventional narratives. But Jackson's hybrid literary "world" is "full of things that you can wander around in, rather than a record or memory of those wanderings" (Jackson 1998). Electronic literature, then, to a degree, represents a move from the literary to the literal – a presentation not of stories but of words themselves as they are transformed by multiple media.

In second-generation electronic literature, not infrequently, not even the word but the letter becomes the unit of operation, as in Brian Kim Stefans's "Star Wars: One Letter at a Time" (2006). There, for example, Stefans might present, flashing on the screen and accompanied by the sound of a clicking typewriter, the letters purportedly typed by *Star Wars* creator George Lucas, one letter at a time. Typically for works of electronic literature, Stefans presented the work in the context of an art exhibition. Significantly, he presented the work along with a generic tag: "lettrism." Playfully, since the ring of the typewriter can be heard at the end of each typed line, the author further locates the work under the category of "bell letters."

The invention of terms and creation of new categories on the page or in linked documents, if conducted collaboratively in a networked environment of metatags, keywords, and coded reference, could give the literary community control over language's current development and its materiality in letters. The metatag offers a literary specificity and materiality not achievable in print. Through tags and glosses that attach to the text and reappear in other similarly tagged texts, readers everywhere can indicate types and genres that will be searchable, so long as they are recognized by other readers and other taggers. The terms attach directly to a range of texts, unlike a literary index that requires the turning of pages, or notes that require access to a book or article in some other physical location. As electronic literature develops, new genres will need to emerge (different from, say, "novels," "poems," and "narratives," whose conceptual work evolved with print and can best be experienced there). The development of a metatag vocabulary, continuous with the development of electronic literature itself, is unique in that each stage in this development, determined by crowd consciousness more than by critical fiat, can be recorded and traced by readers and researchers (see Heckman and Tabbi 2010).

Authors of born-digital work (notably Mez [Mary-Anne Breeze], who has invented a literary language, Mezangel, mixing coded symbols and English) extend this control to computer code, which is sometimes written to be read as text, though this practice is surely exceptional. As John Cayley (2002) puts it in the title to his contribution to the "cyberdebates" at www.electronicbookreview. com, "The Code Is Not the Text (Unless It Is the Text)." When code operates at speed, it is not being read by humans, and besides, those literary authors who create code will always be a minority, a professional cadre or community of hackers whose specialized and often proprietary knowledge is less and less likely to reach the universality (among educated classes) of print literacy. Even if widespread code literacy were achieved, it is unlikely that people would think in code, the way everybody thinks (and communicates) in language. Information might be lost in translation from one linguistic language to another, and this is not a hindrance but rather a *condition* of literariness – as David Damrosh recognizes when he makes the capacity to "gain in translation" one of his criteria for world literature (Damrosh 2003: 281). Code, by contrast, is not enriched by being brought into written language – it simply becomes inoperable.

What the creation of terms in print and metatags in electronic networks can accomplish is a positioning of the imagination at the place where language is generated. Hence the creativity of Ben Marcus, whose aesthetic emerges from the intersection of mathematics and semantics, is a mode of invention wholly consistent with an electronic environment where letters, words, and sentences themselves are capable of becoming elements of a network (in this case, the specifically verbal network of definitions and cross-references in a glossary):

SHIRT OF NOISE Garment, fabric, or residue that absorbs and holds sound, storing messages for journeys. Its loudness cannot be soothed. It can destroy the member which inhabits it. ...

CARL Name applied to food built from textiles, sticks, and rags. Implements used to aid ingestion are termed, respectively, the lens, the dial, the knob. ...

SPEED-FASTING EXPERIMENTS Activity or practice of accelerated food abstention. It was first conducted in Buffalo. The record death by fasting occurred in two days, through motor-starving and exhaustion, verbal.

(Marcus 1995: 14, 41, 44)

Marcus's writing is not born digital. Published in 1995, *The Age of Wire and String* could have accounted for the internet only in its infancy, when it was still used mostly by scientists, small working groups, and niche social networks. If Marcus's work is "experimental," it is so in the best sense of trying out concepts and carrying a certain hypothesis through to the end (however counter-intuitive or defamiliarizing the conclusion might be). *Wire and String*, a network of short experimental fictions in print, has the feel of electronic literature. It has the capacity to conceive of language in some primordial state of semantic mutability where each word can first take on meanings arbitrarily, based on how we happen to hear of a term or where we look it up, and then can build new meanings in use, as one term comes into contact with other terms. Meanings accrue not primarily by narrative means alone but rather by glossary-like definitions and cross-references, a "dreamlife of letters" that Stefans would literalize in his "Internet text" but which has haunted print culture for a long time.

Constrained writing

By contrast to the early, "computer-liberated" writing of first-generation electronic literature, the work of Cayley, Stefans, Strickland, and others develops in the contexts of the internet and database technology and so tends to be more aware of the limitations of proprietary technologies. Second-generation electronic literature is often more consciously about writing under constraint. While embracing expressive freedoms in their vocabulary and syntax, second-generation electronic literary works formally reflect a growing sense that limits have been reached, materially and ecologically, in the rationalist technological project. Aware of the contingency of technology (and the more likely universality of abstract mathematics and language, which are of course embodied in but not tied to some specific technology or software), electronic literature can develop differently, more universally. Electronic literature can achieve universality by placing greater importance precisely on words whose presence is not platform-specific, or at least by striving for platform independence in a Semantic Web (Web 2.0) environment of shared keywords and metatags. The renewal of semantic diversity could be as important to "ecological" literature as any topical engagement with questions of biodiversity and declining resources. The "exhaustion, verbal" cited by Marcus compels a renewed verbal invention as well as a backward-looking, etymological, and (in Stefans) typographical exploration.

This displacement of writing from formal to semantic constraints is already recognizable in the work of several precursors of constrained writing, notably the Oulipo group (*ouvroir de littérature potentielle*) whose members self-consciously have submitted their verbal productions to mathematical rigor. The reasons for shifting to semantic constraints were set out, for example, by

Harry Mathews, who (consistent with Marcus) defines literary potential as a question of new words, "beyond the words being read," lying "in wait to subvert and perhaps surpass them" (cited in Motte 1986: 126). With computers as one – but not an exclusive – context for renewed literary creation, Mathews approaches the problem of writing in constrained environments through a straightforward and familiar distinction, between syntax (how a phrase, sentence, or work is structured) and semantics (what a site or work is about conceptually and not only in terms of information). The distinction has been important in the development of the Oulipo away from mainly structural, combinatorial, and material experimentation (where the mathematical structure is outside the process of creation) toward a concern with the ends of narrative, content, and creativity. "Mathews's Algorithm," an essay in Warren F. Motte's *Oulipo: A Primer of Potential Literature* (1986), is remarkable precisely in its concern with gathering and recombining semantic elements from past literatures – as, on the one hand, a mode of literary commentary and, on the other hand, a stimulation to the creation of new stories, potential stories that haunt those we know from the literary canon.

Mathews's concern with semantic innovation (rather than narrative or generic continuity) hints at the kinds of continuities that are enabled in our move from predominantly print to electronic environments. Not least, the Oulipian project of recovering not masterworks but productive *constraints* from prior eras (even prior to print) offers an excellent precursor to the current project of carrying literary qualities from the past into new media environments. "Mathews's Algorithm," instead of proposing numerical constraints exclusively, would enable authors to identify and select "semantic elements" from (for example) a play by Shakespeare so as to mark phrases, words, and episodes and then to reconfigure the events and outcomes, producing alternative plays. But Mathews does not stop there. He extends his tabulation to include elements in *Hamlet* of "love," "possession," and "victory" and how these terms course through moments of "consummation," "danger," "war," and so forth. Here, "the elements are far more abstract" than the numerical constraints on plot and structure, though still the "abstractions fall short of a concept" (Mathews 1986). That prospect, using words to generate conceptual configurations, while still to be realized, is now actively being pursued by many, among them several literary writers, in the (as yet speculative) construction of a worldwide Semantic Web (Web 2.0).

Toward a semantic literary web

The reason authors would want to interest themselves in a Semantic Web is straightforward. This network promises to establish within electronic environments a place where connections have to do with semantics, involving conceptual linkages among documents, not the decontextualized hot links of the internet as we have known it (namely, Web 1.0). Semantic Web database technology allows not only the tracking of keywords and concepts but also an awareness of their evolution in time. If works are identified and tagged not just according to bibliographical criteria (author, title, and publication date) but also according to literary values (for example, representations of the "actual structures and modes of functioning of literary genres" cited in Prendergast 2004: x), then the opportunity emerges for the creation of a "living" archive (where past works are, in Nelson's terms, "transcluded" into the writing space of new works). To be sure, the living archive is highly presentist: past works that are *not* tagged and transcluded will be lost and forgotten or, given the inevitability of technical obsolesence, they will be accessible only to forensic recovery, which means they're as good as gone (see Kirshenbaum 2008).

"Leaves and writings fade, but words remain," as Jean Lescure noted in "A Brief History of Oulipo" (cited in Motte 1986: 32). A literary deployment of database technology has to be, like literature itself, reflexive and flexible, capable of looking forward to corresponding works by others as well as backward to discovered precedents, able to reference print and born-digital works with equal ease. A viable electronic literary practice also needs to persist and continually reproduce itself in a shifting "now" that changes each time a work is brought in touch with another work, past or future. Indeed, "publication" itself needs to evolve so that a work's significance is accounted for, not by the number of hits or number of objects distributed and sold, but by the density of connections.

The Semantic Web project (Web 2.0), to realize itself, depends on the adoption of Web standards and a certain a priori agreement in principle by practitioners in numerous fields, among which literature is unlikely to take the lead (although one hopes the literary won't be left behind, its critics debating technoculture while the work of material creation is left to others). What is found during electronic searches would depend, in principle, not on a matching of character strings but on the identification of metadata and the development of a terminological vocabulary shared among numerous content providers, creators of literary works among them. Not all texts on the internet would be so marked, but those that did conform to a developing conceptual vocabulary would be available to searches and (proponents argue) would reinforce and be reinforced by other texts using a conforming vocabulary. This conformity at the level of the database, however, should not produce conceptual uniformity: new names, hybrids, and descriptors can be created continually. The development of the field would in some sense *be* the change in the frequency with which certain names are used and others drift into disuse.

This is a viable use of the Semantic Web. It differs from the utopian promise, roundly critiqued by Florian Cramer (2007), that "semantic technology" can "allow people to phrase search terms as normal questions, thus giving computer illiterates easier access to the Internet." The quest for natural language intelligence using computers, a grail of AI research for the past thirty years, had best be set aside – just as the pursuit of narrative can be safely left to its continued development in print. Not all literary qualities need to migrate into electronic environments, but some qualities, semantic descriptors, for example, can be put to literary use. In this more limited version, enacted by humans in collaboration with machine intelligences, the Semantic Web would appear to be consistent with the cultural traffic that in past centuries generated the idea of a world literature, though it differs from past exchanges in that literary genres are not just discussable but capable of being identified and tracked during the time of their development: persistence, in such a practice, would be given not by critical canon formations but rather by an emerging crowd consciousness, enacted by anyone and all who take an active interest in tagging the texts they find valuable.

A coalescence of theory and fiction

A critical practice equipped to engage the world-building potential of electronic literature will emerge only when such syntactic/materialist awareness is also informed by a semantic approach, one that can trace *what* works are about – what genres they employ and deform, and how concepts circulate within individual works and in networks too. Indications of such a critical approach turn up not frequently but often enough to give a sense of what is at stake. When Jaishree Odin (2007) describes a prominent e-lit production by Talan Memmot as being about "the coming into being of words and sentences as codework," and when Odin notes, moreover, that such a development reflects "a coalescence of theory and fiction," this literary critic is finding in Memmot's work a promise held by the Semantic Web itself. When Lori Emerson (2008) describes an "emergent, flexible poetics" that embraces avant-garde traditions in both bookbound and digital poetries, she indicates how poetry always tends to "move toward abstraction," using formal invention not as an end in itself but as a way to convey meanings beyond the materiality of sense and syntax and (on screens especially) to enact spatial relations beyond measure and number. Eric Rasmussen (2008) in his turn has usefully proposed the term "senseless resistance" for describing how affective elements of aesthetic objects resist being encoded into the symbolic mode.

Once we leave aside the sense-making and narrative satisfactions of print literature, we might learn to admire the computer-aided virtuosity of a work of electronic literature such as *2002: A Palindrome Story*, 2002 words in length, by electronic literary artist Nick Montfort and Spineless Books publisher William Gillespie. Beating a record set precisely by an Oulipo member, *2002* establishes a direct line from the Oulipo to electronic literary practice. But the primary continuity – what counts as a world literary practice – is more a matter of Montfort's and Gillespie's perpetuating a literary network of collaborative text production. In this case, with the passing of print into one tradition among many emergent practices, the constraint "discovered" in past literature is the Oulipo program itself.

Montfort/Gillespie and Queneau certainly share a willingness to subject themselves to arbitrary rules: that a "story" must read the same going forward as going backward or that a line in a Queneau poem (or, rather, his *100 Trillion Poems*) must make sense when read with previous or subsequent lines in another poem from the same ten-page collection. But Oulipian and electronic literary practice do not aim at the creation of compelling narratives or absorbing poetic meditations. Those will continue to be produced in print, a medium we can now appreciate as uniquely suited to narrative demands for the creation over time of beginnings, middles, and ends (a working out of information through sequence and duration that more often than not is frustrated in electronic environments). Even a subversion of closure or a nonchronological narrative, to be meaningful, needs to happen against prose structures that reasonably extend over a period of time. Indeed, one signal accomplishment of electronic literature may have been to help locate narrativity not as a literary universal but as one of many literary qualities best realized in particular media such as print and film.

"O readers, meet Bob. (Elapse, year! Be glass! Arc!) Bob's a gem" (Montfort and Gillespie 2002). Indeed, he is. At any rate, Bob's as good a protagonist as Anna or Inna, Kiki or Abba, or for that matter Bob's babe, Babs. Individual preference is beside the point when it comes to the production and reception of Oulipian works and works of electronic literature. What the Oulipo offered instead of isolated, subjectively rich poems, stories, and critical prose was an alternative way of looking at literary practice, a new formulation of its problems and its potential. This alternative, in turn, would be as much a project of rereading and reformatting achieved work as of creating new works.

What the Oulipo was doing, not coincidentally during the same early years of cybernetic exploration that produced the visions of Bush (1945) and Nelson (1974), the mathematics of Norbert Wiener and the sociology of Gregory Bateson, is caught up in the unprecedented proximity of literature to computers, the coexistence in the same writing space of code and text, perceptual image and temporal narrative. The literary precedence of Oulipo, of Otlet's 1934 prefiguration of the internet, of postmodern literature, and of other past programs to be rediscovered (and whose potential may be recognized and realized for the first time in new media environments), constitutes the promise of electronic literature.

Bibliography

Amato, J. (2006) *Industrial Poetics*, Iowa City: University of Iowa Press.
Appadurai, A. (2000) *Modernity at Large: cultural dimensions of globalization*, Minneapolis: University of Minnesota Press.

Bush, V. (1945) "As we may think," *Atlantic Monthly* (July). Online. Available HTTP: <http://www.theatlantic.com/doc/194507/bush> (accessed 28 December 2009).

Calvino, I. (1979) *If on a Winter's Night a Traveler*, trans. W. Weaver, New York: Harcourt Brace Jovanovich, 1981.

Cayley, J. (2002) "The code is not the text (unless it is the text)", Online. Available HTTP: <www.electronicbookreview.com/thread/electropoetics/literal> (accessed 10 November 2009).

Cochran, T. (2001) *The Twilight of the Literary: figures of thought in the age of print*, Cambridge, Mass.: Harvard University Press.

Coover, R. (1992) "The end of books," *The New York Times Review of Books* (21 June).

Cramer, F. (2007) "Critique of the 'semantic web,'" *Nettime*. Online. Available HTTP: <http://www.vknn.at/texte/cramer_semantic_critique.html > (accessed 4 January 2010).

Damrosh, D. (2003) *What Is World Literature?*, Princeton: Princeton University Press.

Emerson, L. (2008) "The rematerialization of poetry: from the bookbound to the digital," PhD diss., University of Buffalo.

Heckman, D. and Tabbi, J. (2010) "Electronic literature directory working group handbook." Online. Available HTTP: <http://www.directory.eliterature.org> (accessed 1 January 2010).

Jackson, S. (1998) "Stitch bitch: the hypertext author as cyborg-femme narrator," interview with Mark Amerika. Online. Available HTTP: <http://www.heise.de/tp/r4/artikel/3/3193/1.html> (accessed 20 November 2009).

Joyce, M. Online. Available HTTP: <http://faculty.vassar.edu/mijoyce/> (accessed 4 May 2009).

Kirschenbaum, M.G. (2008) *Mechanisms: new media and the forensic imagination*, Cambridge, Mass.: MIT Press.

Levie, F. (2007) Excerpts on Paul Otlet from her book *L'homme qui voulait classifier le monde*, in *Les impressions novelles*. Online. Available HTTP: <http://www.lesimpressionsnouvelles.com/l%27homme_qui_voulait_classer_le_monde.htm > (accessed 14 November 2009).

Liu, A. (2004) *The Laws of Cool: knowledge, work, and the culture of information*, Chicago: University of Chicago Press.

Marcus, B. (1995) *The Age of Wire and String*, New York: Knopf.

Mathews, H. (1986) "Mathews's Algorithm," in Motte 1986.

Montfort, N. and Gillespie, W. (2002) "2002: a palindrome story." Online. Available HTTP: <http://www.spinelessbooks.com/2002/palindrome> (accessed 10 November 2009).

Morris, A. (2007) "How to think (with) thinkertoys," *Electronic Book Review* (posted October 10). Online. Available HTTP: <http://www.electronicbookreview.com/thread/electropoetics/distributed> (accessed 28 December 2007).

Motte, W.F. (ed.) (1986) *Oulipo: a primer of potential literature*, Normal, Ill.: Dalkey Archive, 1998.

Nelson, T. (1974) "Computer lib/dream machines," in Wardrip-Fruin and Montfort 2003, pp. 303–38.

Odin, J. (2007) "The database, the interface, and the hypertext: a reading of Strickland's *V*," *Electronic Book Review*. Online. Available HTTP: <http://www.electronicbookreview.com/thread/electropoetics/isomorphic> (accessed 4 May 2009).

Otlet, P. (1934) *Traité de Documentation: le livre sur le livre, theorie et pratique*, Brussels: Mundanaem.

Pinsky, R., Hales, S., Mataga, W. and Sanford, R. (1984) *Mindwheel*, Synapse Software.

Prendergast, C. (ed.) (2004) *Debating World Literature*, London: Verso.

Rasmussen, E. (2008) "Senseless resistances: affect and materiality in postmodern american fiction," PhD diss., University of Illinois at Chicago.

Stefans, B.K. (2006) "Star wars: one letter at a time," Electronic Literature Collection, Vol. 1. Online. Available HTTP: <http://collection.eliterature.org/1/works/stefans_star_wars_one_letter_at_a_time.html> (accessed 2 January 2010).

Strickland, S. (2002) *V: Wave.Son.Nets/Losing L'Una*, New York: Penguin. Online. Available HTTP: <http://vniverse.com> (accessed 2 January 2010).

Tabbi, J. (2007) "Toward a semantic literary web: setting a direction for the electronic literature organization directory," Electronic Literature Organization, Vol. 1.0. Online. Available HTTP: <http://eliterature.org/pad/slw.html> (accessed 15 August 2009).

——and Wutz, M. (eds) (1997) *Reading Matters: narrative in the new media ecology*, Ithaca, N.Y.: Cornell University Press.

Wardrip-Fruin, N. and Montfort, N. (eds) (2003)*The New Media Reader*, Cambridge, Mass.: MIT Press.

27
FEMINIST SCIENCE STUDIES

Susan M. Squier and Melissa M. Littlefield

Feminist science studies emerged in the mid-1980s as a response to the masculinist paradigms of participation and epistemology in the natural sciences. A survey of initial efforts in the area reveals a schism between the women-in-science movement and feminist critiques of science (Hammonds and Subramaniam 2003). The former was predominantly focused on gender equity in science, reflecting the shared awareness that science was dominated by men in terms of membership, status, and access. Participants in women-in-science projects – frequently themselves scientists – worked collaboratively at raising the numbers, improving the conditions, increasing the retention, and strengthening the status of female scientists. Scholarship in the latter area – the feminist critiques of science – tended to be more disciplinarily diverse and driven by the work of individual scholars. There, researchers in a variety of humanities and social science fields took a critical perspective on science itself, arguing that limited definitions of objectivity, sex/gender, nature, and classification restricted the kinds of questions that scientists could and would ask, and thus the validity and worth of the research results.

"Science" is an abstraction, of course; the feminist critique of science focused initially on physics, and later on biology, as the target scientific discipline, with other disciplines soon taking their turn in the spotlight (Hammonds and Subramaniam 2003: 925). At conferences, academic meetings, and in academic journals, these two realms of feminist research celebrated their shared commitment to feminist intervention into scientific practice, hoping to produce what Sandra Harding called a "successor science" (Harding 1986: 197). Yet they struggled to find common ground in their formulation of the appropriate goals, strategies, and methods for making that intervention. The challenge facing feminist science studies was captured by Donna Haraway's formulation of "my problem and *our* problem,"

> how to have *simultaneously* an account of radical historical contingency
> for all knowledge claims and knowing subjects, a critical practice

for recognizing our own "semiotic technologies" for making meanings, *and* a no-nonsense commitment to faithful accounts of a *real* world, one that can be partially shared and friendly to earth-wide projects of finite freedom, adequate material abundance, modest meaning in suffering, and limited happiness.

(Haraway 1991a: 187)

Or as Evelyn Fox Keller would explain a decade later: "clearly, we have gotten hold of a gargantuan entity – not only huge but amorphous and ever changing" (Keller 2001: 98).

Despite this ongoing struggle to forge workable common ground and despite the fact that science remains stubbornly resistant to feminist interventions and men still dominate many of its individual fields, feminist science studies has successfully challenged many of the assumptions and traditions that have informed scientific research for over a century and a half. From affirming the privilege of marginal perspectives, to a reconceptualization of objectivity as something necessarily situated and partial, feminist science studies has gone on to carry out fine-grained explorations of the role of gender in scientific disciplines ranging from archaeology to biology, information technology, physics, and primatology (Longino 1987; Haraway 1989; Traweek 1992; Spanier 1995; Turkle 1995; Strum and Fedigan 2002; Wylie 2002).

One useful example of feminist science studies' developmental trajectory can be found in feminist theory and philosophy publications such as *Feminist Theory* (which produced a special issue on "Feminism and/of Science" in 2004) and *Hypatia*, which published two special issues on feminist science studies. The first, a two-volume set, appeared in 1987–88; the second, a single volume, was published in 2004. While the initial special issues dealt primarily with skeptical audiences in feminist theory and philosophy as well as skepticism from scientists (Tuana 1987, 1988), the more recent special issue assumes an audience of supporters in "a vibrant field of scholarship that has matured and diversified ... and that presupposes a number of hard-won insights that were just beginning to emerge in the mid-1980s" (Nelson and Wylie 2004: vii). Over the past decade, a plethora of anthologies on the subject have also helped to sharpen and hone the field's foci into discrete scholarly areas (Tuana 1989; Marchessault and Sawchuck 2000; Creager, Lunback, and Schiebinger 2001; Lederman and Bartsch 2001).

If we explore the difference that a feminist perspective makes in the questions researchers ask, we can map more precisely the relation between feminist science studies and the broader field of science studies. While science studies research asks questions about the cultural networks of knowledge production, feminist science studies focuses on the gendered nature of inclusion and access. How many female scientists exist? What positions do they hold relative to their male peers? What kinds of obstacles did they face in their education or employment? Additionally, feminist science studies researchers focus on recovering the work of forgotten or overlooked female scientists. To the science studies focus on the contextual nature of scientific facts and the value-laden nature of scientific procedures, in the late 1980s and early 1990s feminist science studies added explorations of the systematic exclusion of women and the feminine through language (including metaphor), epistemology (ways of knowing), and the hegemony of classificatory schemas. Finally, to the general exploration of the social construction of scientific facts as well as the scientific construction of social facts, feminist science studies added attention to the role of science in the construction of gender, sexuality, and women's material bodies.

As women's studies scholars and feminist theory scholars more generally have already suggested, the adoption of a "textbook" or "disciplinary" scheme for feminist science studies has its drawbacks. For example, institutionalization can lead to decreased flexibility in terms of scope for the field; and yet, what we have witnessed over the past twenty-five years is not the hardening of boundaries, but their continual breaching. Contemporary feminist science studies sustains its commitment to the pragmatic improvement of the position of women in science and maintains the work of the feminist critique of science, while drawing on the analytic perspectives of a range of disciplines to illuminate an ever-increasing variety of scientific practices and fields, and to engage in pioneering collaborations with scientists – projects characterized by critical reflexivity and a mutual commitment to an emancipatory science (Brown, Lemons, and Tuana 2006).

Despite its revolutionary vision, at least two areas remain in which the field of feminist science studies has yet to reach its full potential. First, except for the work of a few scholars, feminist science studies has an inadequate account of the central importance of race and ethnicity in the scientific project (Harding 1993; Schiebinger 1989). Just as in the 1980s and 1990s scholars in feminist theory and women's studies were forced to acknowledge the field's inadequate attention to race and ethnicity as categories of analysis, so too, by the turn of the twenty-first century, a number of feminist science studies scholars pointed to a similar gap in their theory (Hammonds and Subramaniam 2003; Roberts 1998). Indeed, Hammonds and Subramaniam argue that, due to the lack of adequate historical or statistical data on women of color in the sciences, as well as the small numbers of women of color currently active as scientists and/or feminist science studies researchers, even as feminist science studies scholarship advances into new scientific fields, "structures of invisibility" are "proliferating across feminist studies of science" (Hammonds and Subramaniam 2003: 931). And the challenge of coalition building within feminist science studies remains: "There are no linkages drawn between the status of women of color in 'women in science' efforts to the projects on 'gender and science' and 'feminist science studies'" (2003: 932).

Given the breadth and depth of feminist science studies, it is also somewhat surprising that the field has forged few connections with literary scholarship, a discipline that supplies many of its analytic tools. We believe that this is the second area of unrealized potential for feminist science studies. From the outset, the fields of feminist science studies and literature and science share a commitment to reinterpreting the foundational premises of scientific theory and practice. Much feminist science studies work relies on the significance of language, metaphor, image, representation, and translation, matters that are central to but, within feminist science studies, often unrecognized as, literary scholarship (Hesse 1963; Keller 1996; Martin 1987, 1995). While feminist science studies research makes frequent use of literary examples to introduce or exemplify scientific developments, few non-literary practitioners consider the importance of literary discourse as an alternative critical and epistemological perspective on science. Despite the work of literary scholars to map the co-creative relations between literature and science in Victorian, postmodern, and most recently modern literary texts (Beer 1983; Levine 1988; Gates 1988; Jordanova 1989; Shteir 1996; Hayles 1991, 1999; B. Clarke 1996, 2001), the full potential of literature as a powerful technology of subject production remains to be tapped by feminist science studies. An improved relationship between the two fields would enable feminist science studies to appreciate the ways that fiction (broadly defined to include canonical and non-canonical literatures, poetry, theater, and cinema) and science are networked phenomena indebted to their mutual cultural production. Through the inclusion of fiction, feminist science studies analyses can and should be broadened to include the reflexive relationship between cultural artifacts and scientific theories.

Given its diverse and interdisciplinary heritage, clearly no exhaustive description of the research findings of feminist science studies is possible, but we want to highlight one dominant theme: the management and control of life. From reproductive technologies; to images of the cell, the fetus, and the body; to the environment and the microbes, plants, and animal beings that dwell within it, feminist science studies has explored the emergence, definition, and utility of "life" (Cartwright 1995; Franklin, Stacey, and Lury 2000). Here, we will discuss two examples of this phenomenon: reproduction and the interactions between gender and technology. Reproduction has long been an important topic for feminist literary scholars, who investigated the metaphor of "literary paternity," explored Mary Shelley's *Frankenstein* as a portrait of the scientific usurpation of maternal agency, and considered the impact on Victorian women of a corporeal economy that consigned women to the bodily work of procreation and men to the brain work of cultural creation (Gilbert and Gubar 1979; Russett 1991). Yet with the birth in 1978 of Louise Brown, the world's first "test-tube baby," feminist science studies began to address reproduction as an emergent and highly contested arena of technoscience.

Early studies by members of FINNRAGE, the Feminist International Network of Resistance to Reproductive and Genetic Engineering, were highly critical of reproductive technology (as it was then called). Scholars compared the procedures of *in vitro* fertilization and prenatal sex selection to eugenic breeding practices and to agricultural practices of reproductive management; argued that surrogate motherhood, extra-uterine gestation and cloning would lead to women being treated as machines; warned that reproductive technology usurped the role of mother (or transferred it to male doctors); and cautioned that it could lead to the alarming prospect of human breeding farms and a complete loss of women's biological autonomy – a speculative world that was also imagined in fictional narratives such as Kate Wilhelm's *Where Late the Sweet Birds Sang* (1976) (Corea 1985; Arditti, Duelli-Klein, and Minden 1984).

This wholly critical position shifted in the late 1980s and 1990s with the publication of a number of studies that took a more nuanced view of what was by then referred to as "assisted reproduction." These studies situated the technologies in the legal, political, and economic context of their development and use; analyzed the changes they produced in the institutions of mothering and kinship; and assessed their impact on notions of female bodily privacy and autonomy (Stanworth 1987; Strathern 1992; Farquhar 1996). As the reproductive sciences were increasingly deployed to manage the entire course of a woman's life, scholars began to analyze the historical origins of this apparatus of control in the agricultural sciences, to explore its roots in the popular science writing and fiction of the early twentieth century, and to consider how the metaphors that were applied to conception, gestation, and menopause (even in medical practice) subordinated women and consolidated male cultural power (Martin 1987; Squier 1994, 2005; A. Clarke 1998). Studies at the intersection of literature and science, cultural studies, and literature and medicine explored the disciplines and practices that contributed to the development of the new reproductive technologies: gynecology, endocrinology, contraceptive production and dissemination, technologies of literary representation (the novel, poetry), technologies of visual representation (microscopy, X-ray, the camera, cinema), technologies of the gendered body (body building and cosmetic surgery), maternal/fetal surveillance technologies (the fetal monitor and the ultrasound machine as well as community prenatal health programs), and practices of gynecological education from the gynecological manikin to the gynecology teaching associate (Oudshoorn 1994; Adams 1994; Rapp 2000; Cartwright 1995; Balsamo 1996; Kapsalis 1997; Roberts 1998; Kaplan and Squier 1999).

Another parallel strand of research extended this analysis of sexed and gendered embodiment, fertility, procreation, and reproductive technologies to men as well as people of intermediate sex and gender. Beginning with the analysis of the constructed nature of human morphology, as sexuality shifted from the one-sex model of ancient Greece and Rome to the modern two-sex model, scholars went on to explore the medicalized imposition of gender upon ambiguously sexed bodies and the function of the concept of deviance to monitor and channel human bodies away from homosexuality, disability, illness, and other socially stigmatized categories into various versions of normativity (Laqueur 1992; Terry and Urla 1995; Terry 1999; Fausto-Sterling 2000). The male body in science and medicine has also come under the purview of feminist science studies scholars interested in finding connections to the relatively new field of masculinity studies (Daniels 1997; Moore 2002; Serlin 2003). Just as feminist science studies joined feminism in broadening its focus in response to critiques that it excessively reflected the position of white, middle-class women from the global North, and as female scientists of color began to play a major role in theory building, so the study of reproduction, and specifically, of technologies ranging from assisted reproductive technology (ART) to contraception and surrogacy, has gradually come to focus on the central role played by race and ethnicity in shaping practices and outcomes (Ginzberg and Rapp 1995; Roberts 1998; Briggs and Kelber-Kaye 2000).

Although feminist science studies scholarship necessarily encountered technologies throughout its development and growth, including the test tubes and techniques of ART, the speculum, and the X-ray, scholars did not begin critically to engage issues of gender and technology until the early 1990s. One of the foundational texts for such work is Teresa De Lauretis's *Technologies of Gender: essays on theory, film, and fiction* (1987). Drawing on the work of Michel Foucault, De Lauretis proposed that gender "both as representation and as self-representation, is the product of various social technologies, such as cinema, and of institutionalized discourses, epistemologies, and critical practices, as well as practices of daily life" (De Lauretis 1987: 2). Her theory, which imbricates gender and technology by definition, and her method, which turns to fiction and film, is a model for much of the scholarship that has followed. Indeed, later work on gender and technology has turned to film, fiction, and the media as important counterparts and equal players in the history and development of various bio-medical technologies (Landecker 2007).

From redefining gender as a technology to understanding technology as gendered (Wajcman 1991, 2004; Terry and Calvert 1997), feminist science studies has addressed issues such as technological determinism, technophilia, and technophobia; discrepancies between designers and users, including the fluidity between a "brown good" (read masculine) and a "white good" (read feminine); the multiplicity of identities (race, class, sexuality, disability, gender, sex) in spaces such as the World Wide Web (Kolko, Nakamura, and Rodman 2000; Nakamura 2002, 2007); the larger economic and political systems in which technology is embedded; the merger of organic and inorganic material in/as cyborg theory (Haraway 1991b); and the visualization and construction of bodies via imaging technologies (Cartwright 1995; Waldby 2000; van Dijck 2004).

If literature is largely absent from feminist science studies, it is more firmly entrenched in this subsidiary field of gender and technology. For Haraway, science fiction is often a key component of situating technologies in their larger systems. From Joanna Russ (1978), Haraway (1997) borrows and reconstructs the figure of the FemaleMan. While Haraway may not have been aware of C.L. Moore's "No Woman Born" (1944), in which a dancer's brain is granted a second life in a robotic body, her later interlocutors have firmly connected Haraway's cyborg with this 1940s narrative. Other critics, including Catherine Waldby (2000), find connections between biblical imagery and the references to Adam and Eve that surround the male and female bodies preserved through the Visible Human Project. For José van Dijck (2004), science fiction films, as well as art exhibits such as Body Worlds, serve as a centerpiece to theories about nature, culture, and gender.

And yet, even discussions of gender and technology could benefit from a more sustained engagement with fiction, as can be seen in a survey of scholarship on the sphere of the domestic space and its technologies (Wajcman 1991, 2004; Green and Adam 2001; Bell, Blythe, and Sengers 2005). These discussions trace the history and dynamic adaptations of technologies such as the microwave – a military technology that was initially introduced to the domestic sphere as a "brown good" marketed to men and stocked alongside electronics and other leisure technologies, and later changed to a "white good" marketed to modern housewives (Wajcman 2004: 37). However, the scope of analysis can be broadened to include a consideration of the role of gender and technology in the construction of domestic space by turning to an analysis of literary texts, such as Ray Bradbury's "There Will Come Soft Rains" (1945), which portrays the home against the backdrop of World War II, the rise of the 1950s housewife, and the military technologies that decimated the domestic spaces of Hiroshima and Nagasaki, and which concerns the only "smart" house left standing in a post-apocalyptic America of 2023. The family of four who once populated this domestic space are mere imprints – shadows of frozen motion caught forever on an external wall, while inside, the house continues to function according to all the modern routines that manage and control life: timetables, automatically pre-pared food, robot cleaners, measured leisure (Bradbury 1945). The ultimate irony is that the domestic technologies expected to manage life inside the home manage only to consume themselves and the house in a final cannibalistic blaze.

In recent feminist science studies scholarship, the smart technologies of the post-WWII era have been replaced by smart technologies of the digital age and repurposed for a feminist agenda. Take, for example, Anne Balsamo's "Teaching in the belly of the beast" (2000: 187), a riff on Neal Stephenson's cyberpunk-inflected "A Young Lady's Illustrated Primer" in *The Diamond Age* (1996). Balsamo's multimodal primer is a "thought experiment" in which she tries to imagine "what a feminist primer would look like that took as its focus the edu-cation of women in science and technology" (187). As she conceptualizes and describes her primer, Balsamo covers much the same territories we have laid out in this introductory chapter: women's participation in science, what Sandra Harding terms "the science question in feminism," the rhetoric of science (language, discourse, representation), and the influence of popular media on science. She comes away from her musing to assert that because feminist science studies has no such primer, its success and its successful challenge of the masculinist paradigms depend on educators in myriad fields willing to test assumptions about women's participation in and feminists' impact on science and technology studies.

As we have explained in this brief overview, feminist science studies has made strides in the past quarter century to take up the diverse set of questions and challenges posed by feminist theorists. While feminist science studies, and its sister-field of gender and technology studies, must become more inclusive and aware of issues of intersectionality (including especially race, ethnicity, class, and disability), the field is ready and able to incorporate the fruits of these labors. So, too, is feminist science studies ready not only to recognize the contributions of scholars working in mixed media – including literature and science – but also to acknowledge the field's historical and continuing tradition of using the tools of literary analysis.

Bibliography

Adams, A.E. (1994) *Reproducing the Womb: images of childbirth in science, feminist theory, and literature*, Ithaca, N.Y.: Cornell University Press.

Arditti, R., Duelli-Klein, R., and Minden, S. (1984) *Test-Tube Women: what future for motherhood*, New York: HarperCollins.

Atwood, M. (2004) *Oryx and Crake*, New York: Anchor.

Balsamo, A. (1996) *Technologies of the Gendered Body: reading cyborg women*, Durham, N.C.: Duke University Press.

——(2000) "Teaching in the belly of the beast: feminism in the best of all places," in J. Marchessault and K. Sawchuck (eds) *Wild Science: reading feminism, medicine and the media*, New York: Routledge, pp. 185–214.

Beer, G. (1983) *Darwin's Plots: evolutionary narrative in Darwin, George Eliot, and nineteenth century fiction*, Cambridge: Cambridge University Press.

Bell, G., Blythe, M., and Sengers, P. (2005) "Making by making strange: defamiliarization and the design of domestic technologies," *CM Transactions on Computer–Human Interaction (TOCHI)*, 12(2): 149–73.

Bradbury, R. (1945) "There will come soft rains," in P. Warrick (ed.) *Science Fiction: the SFRA anthology*, New York: Harper Collins, 1988, pp. 230–34.

Briggs, L. and Kelber-Kaye, J. (2000) "There is no unauthorized breeding in Jurassic Park: gender and the uses of genetics," *NWSA Journal*, 12(3): 92–113.

Brown, D., Lemons, J., and Tuana, N. (2006) "The importance of expressly integrating ethnical analyses into climate change policy formation," *Climate Policy*, 5: 549–52.

Cartwright, L. (1995) *Screening the Body: tracing medicine's visual culture*, Minneapolis: University of Minnesota Press.

Clarke, A. (1998) *Disciplining Reproduction: modernity, American life sciences, and the problems of sex*, Berkeley: University of California Press.

Clarke, B. (1996) *Dora Marsden and Early Modernism: gender, individualism, science*, Ann Arbor: University of Michigan Press.

——(2001) *Energy Forms: allegory and science in the era of classical thermodynamics*, Ann Arbor: University of Michigan Press.

Corea, G. (1985) *The Mother Machine*, New York: Harper and Row, Inc.

Creager, A., Lunback, E., and Schiebinger, L. (eds) (2001) *Feminism in Twentieth-Century Science, Technology and Medicine*, Chicago: University of Chicago Press.

Daniels, C. (1997) "Between fathers and fetuses: the social construction of male reproduction and the politics of fetal harm," *Signs*, 22(3): 579–616.

De Lauretis, T. (1987) *Technologies of Gender: essays on theory, film, and fiction*, Bloomington: Indiana University Press.

Farquhar, D. (1996) *The Other Machine: discourse and reproductive technologies*, New York: Routledge.

Fausto-Sterling, A. (2000) *Sexing the Body: gender politics and the construction of sexuality*, New York: Basic Books.

Franklin, S., Stacey, J., and Lury, C. (2000) *Global Nature, Global Culture*, London: Sage.

Gates, B. (1988) *Kindred Nature: Victorian and Edwardian women embrace the natural world*, Chicago: University of Chicago Press.

Gilbert, S. and Gubar, S. (1979) *The Madwoman in the Attic: the woman writer and the nineteenth-century literary imagination*, New Haven, Conn.: Yale University Press.

Ginsberg, F. and Rapp, R. (1995) *Conceiving the New World Order: the global politics of reproduction*, Berkeley: University of California Press.

Green, E. and Adam, A. (2001) *Virtual Gender: technology, consumption and identity*, New York and London: Routledge.

Hammonds, E. and Subramaniam, B. (2003) "A conversation on feminist science studies," *Signs*, 28(3): 923–44.

Haraway, D.J. (1989) *Primate Visions: gender, race, and nature in the world of modern science*, New York: Routledge.

——(1991a) "Situated knowledges: the science question in feminism and the privilege of partial perspective," in D.J. Haraway, *Simians, Cyborgs, and Women: the reinvention of nature*, New York: Routledge, pp. 183–201.

——(1991b) "A cyborg manifesto: science, technology, and socialist-feminism in the late twentieth century," in D.J. Haraway, *Simians, Cyborgs, and Women: the reinvention of nature*, New York: Routledge, pp. 149–81.

——(1997) *Modest_Witness@Second_ Millennium. FemaleMan©_ Meets_OncoMouse^{TM}: feminism and technoscience*, New York: Routledge.

Harding, S. (1986) *The Science Question in Feminism*, Ithaca, N.Y.: Cornell University Press.

——(1993) *The "Racial" Economy of Science: toward a democratic future*, Bloomington: Indiana University Press.

Hayles, N.K. (1991) *Chaos and Order: complex dynamics in literature and science*, Chicago: University of Chicago Press.

——(1999) *How We Became Posthuman: virtual bodies in cybernetics, literature, and informatics*, Chicago: University of Chicago Press.

Hesse, M. (1963) *Models and Analogies in Science*, London: Sheed and Ward.

Hubbard, R. (1990) *The Politics of Women's Biology*, New Brunswick: Rutgers University Press.

Jacobus, M., Keller, E.F., and Shuttleworth, S. (1990) *Body Politics: women and the discourses of science*, London: Routledge.

Jordanova, L. (1989) *Sexual Visions: images of gender in science and medicine between the eighteenth and twentieth centuries*, London: Harvester Wheatsheaf.

Kaplan, E.A. and Squier, S.M. (1999) *Playing Dolly: technocultural formations, fantasies, and fictions of assisted reproduction*, New Brunswick: Rutgers University Press.

Kapsalis, T. (1997) *Public Privates: performing gynecology from both ends of the speculum*, Durham, N.C.: Duke University Press.

Keller, E.F. (1996) *Refiguring Life*, New York: Columbia University Press.

——(2001) "Making a difference: feminist movement and feminist critiques of science," in A. Creager, E. Lunback, and L. Schiebinger (eds) *Feminism in Twentieth-Century Science, Technology and Medicine*, Chicago: University of Chicago Press, pp. 98–109.

Kolko, B., Nakamura, L., and Rodman, G. (2000) *Race in Cyberspace*, New York: Routledge.

Landecker, H. (2007) *Culturing Life: how cells became technologies*, Cambridge, Mass.: Harvard University Press.

Laquer, T. (1992) *Making Sex: body and gender from the Greeks to Freud*, Cambridge, Mass.: Harvard University Press.

Lederman, M. and Bartsch, I. (eds) (2001) *The Gender and Science Reader*, New York: Routledge.

Levine, G. (1988) *One Culture: essays in science and literature*, Madison: University of Wisconsin Press.

Longino, H. (1987) "Can there be a feminist science?," *Hypatia*, 2(3): 51–64.

Marchessault, J. and Sawchuck, K. (2000) *Wild Science: reading feminism, medicine and the media*, New York: Routledge.

Martin, E. (1987) *The Woman in the Body: a cultural analysis of reproduction*, Boston, Mass.: Beacon Press.

——(1995) *Flexible Bodies*, Boston, Mass.: Beacon Press.

Moore, C.L. (1944) "No woman born," in P. Sargent (ed.) *Women of Wonder: the classic years*, Orlando: Harcourt Brace, 1995, pp. 21–64.

Moore, L.J. (2002) "Extracting men from semen: masculinity in scientific representations of sperm," *Social Text*, 20(4): 91–119.

Nakamura, L. (2002) *Cybertypes: race, ethnicity, and identity on the internet*, New York: Routledge.

——(2007) *Digitizing Race: visual cultures of the internet*, Minneapolis: University of Minnesota Press.

Nelson, L. and Wylie, A. (eds) (2004) "Introduction, special issue on feminist science studies," *Hypatia*, 19(1): vii–xiii.

Oudshoorn, N. (1994) *Beyond the Natural Body: an archaeology of sex hormones*, London: Routledge.

Rapp, R. (2000). *Testing Women, Testing the Fetus: the social impact of amniocentesis in America*, New York: Routledge.

Roberts, D. (1998) *Killing the Black Body: race, reproduction, and the meaning of liberty*, New York: Vintage.

Russ, J. (1978) *The Female Man*, New York: Bantam Books.

Russett, C. (1991) *Sexual Science: the Victorian construction of womanhood*, Cambridge, Mass.: Harvard University Press.

Schiebinger, L. (1989) *The Mind Has No Sex? Women in the origins of modern science*, Cambridge, Mass.: Harvard University Press.

Serlin, D. (2003) "Crippling masculinity: queerness and disability in U.S. military culture, 1800–1945," *GLQ: A Journal of Gay and Lesbian Studies*, 9(1–2): 149–79.

Shteir, A.B. (1996) *Cultivating Women, Cultivating Science: Flora's daughters and botany in England, 1760–1860*, Baltimore: Johns Hopkins University Press.

Spanier, B. (1995) *Impartial Science: gender ideology in molecular biology*, Bloomington: Indiana University Press.

Squier, S. (1994) *Babies in Bottles: twentieth-century visions of reproductive technology*, New Brunswick: Rutgers University Press.

——(2005) *Liminal Lives: imagining the human at the frontiers of biomedicine*, Durham, N.C.: Duke University Press.

——and Littlefield, M. (eds) (2004) "Introduction: feminism and/of science," *Feminist Theory*, 5(2): 123–26.

Stanworth, M. (1987) *Reproductive Technologies: gender, motherhood, and medicine*, London: Polity Press.

Stephenson, N. (1996) *The Diamond Age*, New York: Random House, 2000.

Strathern, M. (1992) *Reproducing the Future: essays on anthropology, kinship, and the new reproductive technologies*, Manchester: Manchester University Press.

Strum, S. and Fedigan, L.M. (2002) *Primate Encounters: models of science, gender, and society*, Chicago: University of Chicago Press.

Terry, J. (1999) *An American Obsession: science, medicine, and homosexuality in modern society*, Chicago: University of Chicago Press.

——and Calvert, M. (1997) *Processed Lives: gender and technology in everyday life*, New York: Routledge.

——and Urla, J.L. (1995) *Deviant Bodies: critical perspectives on difference in science and popular culture*, Bloomington: Indiana University Press.

Traweek, S. (1992) *Beamtimes and Lifetimes: the world of high energy physicists*, Cambridge, Mass.: Harvard University Press.

Tuana, N. (ed.) (1987) "Special issue: feminism and science," *Hypatia*, 2(3).

——(ed.) (1988) "Special issue: feminism and science," *Hypatia*, 2(4).

——(ed.) (1989) *Feminism and Science*, Bloomington: Indiana University Press.

Turkle, S. (1995) *Life on the Screen: identity in the age of the internet*, New York: Simon & Schuster.

van Dijck, J. (2004) *Transparent Bodies: a cultural analysis of medical imaging*, Seattle: University of Washington Press.

Wajcman, J. (1991) *Feminism Confronts Technology*, University Park: Pennsylvania State University Press.

——(2004) *Technofeminism*, Cambridge: Polity Press.

Waldby, C. (1996) *AIDS and the Body Politic: biomedicine and sexual difference*, London: Routledge.

——(2000) *The Visible Human Project: informatic bodies and posthuman medicine*, New York and London: Routledge.

Wilhelm, K. (1976) *Where Late the Sweet Birds Sang*, New York: Orb Books, 1998.

Wilson, E. (1998) *Neural Geographies: feminism and the microstructure of cognition*, New York: Routledge.

——(2004) *Psychosomatic: feminism and the neurological body*, Durham, N.C.: Duke University Press.

Wylie, A. (2002) *Thinking from Things: essays in the philosophy of archaeology*, Berkeley: University of California Press.

28
GAME STUDIES
Gordon Calleja and Ivan Callus

Digital games may have been considered cultish or adolescent two decades ago, but interest in them is now mainstream and ranges across diverse social and cultural groupings. Their appeal is now so broad and pervasive, and their inventiveness and their claim on a distinct aesthetic so compelling, that they demand attention from across the academic spectrum, prompting the rise of the multidisciplinary field of game studies.

Approaches to studying games

The first volume of the journal *Games and Culture* (2006) offered a number of perspectives on the question "Why Game Studies now?" The contributors' academic backgrounds reflected the variety of disciplinary perspectives that can – perhaps *should* – be applied to games. Certainly the last five years have seen an unprecedented expansion in research on games (Bryce and Rutter 2006), characterized by a multidisciplinary dynamic that reflects games' centrality to distinct and novel departures in studies of media theory, mind, cognition, aesthetics, and the socio-cultural. This diversity of approaches has led to theoretical differences over the analysis of games.

There is fundamental and significant disagreement even when determining what kinds of activities can be classified as games, and what disciplines and methods are appropriate to their study. For while common usage applies the term "game" to a wide range of activities, more precise conceptualization is essential. It is common, for example, to call virtual worlds like *Second Life* (Linden Lab 2003) "games," even if it is clear to the casual visitor that they bear few, if any, specific game objectives. Thus various games can be accommodated within *Second Life*, which is not in itself a game – just as a *piazza* is not a game, though games might be played there. This distinction is quite sharp in the case of virtual social worlds like *Second Life*, but also in other virtual worlds that contain more evidently constraining rule-based structures, like *EVE Online* (CCP Games 2003) or any other Massively Multiplayer Online Game (MMOG), where the slippage between what we generally call games and what it is exactly that certain contemporary digital artifacts have developed into is more fraught. If we take a stricter analytical view on what constitutes a game, this slippage occurs also in single-player games like *Half-Life 2* (Valve Software 2004b) or *Grand Theft Auto IV* (Rockstar North 2008), where the nature of the interaction with projected worlds problematizes comparisons with non-digital games. Indeed, are these games in the same way as contests in tiddlywinks or chess, table-tennis or baseball? Do analytical frameworks established for the study of games apply to digital as well as non-digital examples?

These are just some of the fundamental questions that game studies has addressed, at least since the founding editorial of the first academic journal on digital games, *Game Studies*. Espen Aarseth there proclaimed 2001 as the first year of "Computer Game Studies as an emerging, viable, academic field" (Aarseth 2001). His claim rests on three noteworthy events of that year: the first conference dedicated to the study of digital games, the first related postgraduate programs, and the first issue of a peer-reviewed online journal dedicated to games. Aarseth's assertion that game studies needs to be established as a discipline related to, but independent of, other disciplines like media studies, literary studies, sociology, or computer science, among others, is a proclamation of academic independence, based on the conviction that theories developed in other disciplines cannot be applied unproblematically to digital games. That is because, as Aarseth had already argued in *Cybertext* (1997), digital games have characteristics intrinsically different from media texts studied in other disciplines. Gonzalo Frasca's (1999) application of a key term, "ludology," to define a "discipline that studies game and play activities" did not dispel the need for game definitions that distinguish the factors that constitute the crucial difference between digital games and other media forms, or for engaging with what Juul (2003) called the "heart of gameness." Comprehensive reviews of histories of game definitions have in fact been made by Juul himself (2005), and by Salen and Zimmerman (2003). Their conclusions are worth summarizing.

For Salen and Zimmerman, "A *game* is a system in which players engage in an artificial conflict, defined by rules, that results in a quantifiable outcome" (Salen and Zimmerman 2003: 80). They isolate six critical elements: system, players, artificiality, conflict, rules, and quantifiable outcomes, and suggest that all games are intrinsically systems. A *system* is "a set of things that affect one another within an environment to form a larger pattern that is different from any of the individual parts" (50). *Players* are indispensable to the game, which is experienced by interacting with its system. The third element, the *artificial* aspect of games, envisages a mode of experience different from everyday life. This is related to the concept of the "magic circle" coined by Huizinga (1955) in *Homo Ludens*. The fourth element, *conflict* – "all games embody a contest of powers" (80) – encompasses both competition and collaboration with other players, as well as with a game system (as in solo games). *Rules* enable play through defining what players can and cannot do, while *quantifiable outcomes* or goals mean that in the end a player has won, lost, or at least received some sort of numerical score or assessment. This element distinguishes games from generalized play, which may not have a quantifiable outcome.

Meanwhile, in his "classic game model" (Juul 2005: 22) Juul proposes a definition applicable to digital *and* analogue games:

> A game is a rule-based system with a variable and quantifiable outcome, where different outcomes are assigned different values, the player exerts effort in order to influence the outcome, the player feels emotionally attached to the outcome, and the consequences of the activity are negotiable.
>
> (Juul 2005: 36)

Again, the definition is built on six elements: rules, variable and quantifiable outcome, valorization of outcome, player effort, player attachment to outcome, and negotiable consequences. Juul argues that because *rules* can be computed by a machine or enforced by human participants, they are the common factor linking digital and non-digital games. Games are therefore "transmedial," as confirmed by the ability of certain games to migrate across media. Chess can be played with classic pieces, marked bottle tops on improvised boards, or on a computer. In Juul's account, the rules constitute the system of relations which is the game, and these rules are independent of the media instantiating them. They also create the possibility of a *variable and quantifiable outcome* – a state of affairs that is objectively final at the end of the game and *valorized* by the players involved. Some of the possible outcomes are objectively better than others and harder to obtain, and are valued for their emergence from *player effort*. This effort will tend to result in an *attachment to the outcome* of the game – winning, for instance, can be savored – although this element is less determining than the others and depends on players' attitudes. Finally the *consequences* of the game are *negotiable*: games can be assigned consequences reaching beyond their domains, and the consequences can be modified across sessions.

Juul provides a diagram that maps a number of activities in three concentric circles: games, borderline cases, and "not games." Traffic, hypertext fiction, and free-form play are examples of non-game activities. Pen and paper role-playing games, games of pure chance, and open-ended simulations like *Simcity* (Maxis Software 1989) are borderline cases because they do not satisfy all six categories of the classic game model. Juul's discussion does not clarify what the difference between the status of borderline games and non-games implies for game analysis, since both are considered activities that fall outside the classic game model. However, Juul is clear that the latter is no longer adequate:

> The classic game model is no longer all there is to games. With the appearance of role-playing games, where a game can have rules

interpreted by a game master, and with the appearance of video games, the game model is being modified in many ways.

(Juul 2005: 52)

The usefulness of this model is therefore not in creating a strict taxonomy of what constitutes a game and what does not; rather, "it provides a bare-bones description of the field of games; it explains why computers and games work well together; it explains why games are trans-medial and it points to some recent developments in games" (Juul 2005: 54). Juul's work lays the foundation for a formalist perspective on traditional games while highlighting how digital media challenge this conception. By admitting that this model has its limitations in the context of contemporary developments in digital games, Juul implies that game researchers need to ask how video games deviate from this model. Indeed, what aspects of games like *Half-Life 2* (Valve Software 2004b), *The Elder Scrolls IV: Oblivion* (Bethesda Softworks LLC 2006) or *World of Warcraft* (Blizzard Entertainment 2004) are omitted when the classic games model is applied to their analysis?

Ludology and its discontents

In its attempt to respond to such questions, game studies has sometimes been riven by the so-called "narratology versus ludology" debate. Ludologists argue that although narrative is an important aspect of games, it is not their principal quality. Consequently, a direct application of narrative theory to the analysis of games cannot yield a sufficiently well-rounded account. The opposing camp argues for a more central role for narrative in the analysis of games. As the question of narrative – once one has dug beneath the surface claims made in the "tired debate," as it has been often called (Steinkuehler 2006; Tosca 2003) – detracts attention from the more considerable epistemological and methodological conflicts between ludologists and various other clusters of interest, it might be helpful to see this debate as a clash between formalist approaches to the study of games and the variety of other theoretical paradigms that might be brought to bear.

Other underlying tensions remain. The view that game studies is a separate discipline, or the perception that games require specific analytical theories that take into account their game structure, or "gameness," has been resisted by some media studies theorists. A reviewer of Juul's book states:

Designers, gamers and writers have gotten along without the crystalline purity of an idea of gameness or a neo-structural account of the relation between rules and fiction; perhaps the job of the academic aesthetician is to generate informed, sensitive evaluations of particular games on their own terms rather than abstract prescriptions. Apart from delaying the advent of an academic criticism that might be useful to those designing games, or learning how to, one is left wondering what precisely is at stake in this late bloom of ludology.

(Wilson 2006)

Wilson summarizes the tension on the two axes of difference referred to earlier: diversity among the games being discussed and disciplinary methodologies used to study them. If the breadth of variety in the artifacts that are called games is unquestionable, attempts at defining common characteristics by Juul and by Salen and Zimmerman are an important step in the development of a theoretical framework for the study of games. However, a critical issue remains. Can digital and non-digital games be fully accommodated within any one analytical framework?

The specific characteristics of digital games

If all games share a set of common characteristics, then theories created for the analysis of non-digital games such as board games, card games, and sports should be applicable to digital games such as console, computer, and mobile games. But there is considerable disagreement on that. For example, Bryce and Rutter direct harsh criticism at game studies theorists seeking to found a distinct discipline, noting that qualities described as unique are not in fact specific to games at all:

> Wolf stresses the aesthetic content of digital games to suggest that research into digital games "adds new concepts to existing ideas in moving image theory, such as those concerning the game's interface, player action, interactivity, navigation, and algorithmic structures" (2001: 3). However, this emphasis on discontinuity prevents any significant comparison with other new technologies. Digital games (or rather their design and play) may well draw on the issues Wolf highlights but are they really unique in doing so? Do many of these issues have equal relevance to other forms of multimedia design, head-up display in fighter planes (or racing driver's [sic] helmets) and programming structures in general?
>
> (Bryce and Rutter 2006: 7–8)

A head-up display (HUD), it should be explained here, is an interface designed to aid processing of information in the context of a very immediate material environment with terminal consequences, while digital games *are* virtual environments that include the interface but are not reducible to it. Making a case for the analytical equivalence between fighter-plane HUDs and digital game interfaces confuses two categorically different objects: the game's interface is only one component of the media object in question, while the HUD fully constitutes the object studied.

Meanwhile, Bogost makes it clear from the outset that he does not feel it is appropriate to create a methodology for game analysis without separating digital from non-digital games:

> When I speak of videogames, I refer to all the varieties of digital artefacts created and played on arcade machines, personal computers, and home consoles. Although videogames follow in the long tradition of parlour games, table games, pub games, and the many varieties of board games evolving from classic games like chess and Go, their necessary relation ends at this bit of common history.
>
> (Bogost 2006: xiii)

Following Bogost, we agree that digital games require specific theoretical models that account for their digitally mediated nature. This becomes particularly important when considering issues relating to the textuality of digital games. Bryce and Rutter sideline media specificity when they argue that this mediation can take forms other than digital:

> As a games-related example, think of a simple shooting gallery game, such as one of the numerous Flash and shareware games that can be found on the Internet. As a game, this could be compared and contrasted with a game in which rocks are thrown at cans staked along the top of the fence. It may be clear that the digital game is a technological simulation of the low technology version of the game. In the digital game, technology replaces the physical action of throwing. However, by replacing the rocks with the shooting of an air rifle, we can mediate the throwing action with technology without going digital.
>
> (Bryce and Rutter 2006: 8)

Equating shooting of an air rifle with moving cross-hairs on a screen and pressing mouse buttons to "shoot" targets made entirely of "flickering signifiers" (Hayles 1999: 30) ignores the crucial fact that one is an activity in the material world, while the other is a simulation of such an activity engaged through a representational medium. The shooter of an air-rifle and the mouse clicker are fully aware of the different contexts of their actions, making the two activities of a completely different experiential order. Applying the term "mediation" to digital game-play or rifle shooting ignores the crucial differences between a mediated activity in a wholly designed, representational space and a mediated activity in the material domain. It does therefore seem, on balance, that games, or virtual designed environments, can support orders of experience and interaction that are not quite prefigured or configurable in non-digital contexts, where apparent analogies to what might be replicable when "going digital" underplay understanding of the specificities of the affordances and challenges, not to say the phenomenology, of the remediation possible in games and virtual environments.

Finding a middle ground in game studies

Like Bogost, Crogan advocates an approach that treats digital games as distinctively different from non-digital games. He proposes a middle-ground method that brings together theories that treat game aspects of digital games in conjunction with work done in related fields:

> I nevertheless believe that the ludological insistence on the game as game points to something very significant about the specificity of games in comparison to narrative-based media works. ... I propose to pursue a line of inquiry that departs from an acceptance in broad terms of the ludological approach, namely that narrative is insignificant to understanding what is of most concern for analysing a computer game as a game, that is, as a work that is played.
>
> (Crogan 2004: 14)

Although Crogan states that in the ludological approach "narrative is insignificant," it is worth noting that when Frasca proposed the term "ludology," in the context of discussion of digital games (not games in general), he intended it to be used in conjunction with other theories, not in rejection of them: "Our main goal was to show how basic concepts of ludology could be used along with narratology to better understand videogames" (Frasca 1999). Correspondingly, Juul's work has addressed narrative structures in games, even in a book like *Half-Real*, which is often cited as a bulwark of "reductionist" ludology. As Juul asserts, his title refers to digital games as a hybrid of the game structures embodied in the rules and the fictional elements associated with textual elements:

> In the title, *Half-Real* refers to the fact that video games are two different things at the same time: video games are *real* in that they consist of real rules with which players actually interact, and in that winning or losing a game is a real event. However, when winning a game by slaying a dragon, the dragon is not a real dragon but a fictional one. To play a video game is therefore to interact with real rules while imagining a fictional world, and a video game is a set of rules as well as a fictional world.
>
> (Juul 2005: 1)

Like Crogan, Juul is here attempting to bridge the divide between the textual/ representational and the "essentialist" notion of "gameness." This move is also related to exploring the divergence of digital games from the classic game model, discussed earlier. When he states that digital games problematize the classic game model, he is foregrounding the need to weave the textual and representational aspects of games with their rule-based, coded structures. That is a crucial assertion of the nature of digital games as more complex media artifacts that can be partly described, but not wholly subsumed, under a game definition – precisely because they afford a wider potential for action and expression than is possible in the more traditional games that provide the basis for the classical game model.

One way of overcoming the limitations of formal definitions of games is proposed by Malaby, who argues that the analysis of games demands a processual perspective: "One of the first things we must recognize is that *games are processual*. Each game is an ongoing process. As it is played it always contains the potential for generating new practices and new meanings, possibly refiguring the game itself" (Malaby 2007: 8). The term "processual" refers to the potential of change in every engagement and favors a dynamic and recursive view of games. Malaby stresses the importance of replacing rules as a starting point for game analysis. He points out the different nature of game rules from social or bureaucratic rules. The latter are "intended to reduce unpredictability across cases" (8), while game rules "are about contriving and calibrating multiple contingencies to produce a mix of predictable and unpredictable outcomes (which are then interpreted)" (9). Malaby formulates games as processes that create carefully designed unpredictable circumstances that have meaningful, culturally shared, yet open-ended interpretations. Therefore both the game practice and the meaning it generates are subject to change.

Malaby goes on to define games in terms of four types of "contrived contingency": stochastic, social, performative, and semiotic. *Stochastic contingency* refers to the random elements in games. This ranges from dice rolling to the weather at a football game. Thus stochastic contingency can be designed into a game, such as the rolling of dice in board games, or be extraneous to the designed intent of the game, such as the weather in an open-air game. *Social contingency* refers to the unpredictability of the choices and decisions made by other players, whether in collaboration or opposition. Making informed deductions about the actions of other players is a key element in most games. *Performative contingency* refers to the execution of actions by game participants, and is thus related to the ability to carry out intended actions. This can cover anything from the gaming ability of a *Counter-Strike Source* (Valve Software 2004a) player, to the simple act of counting the right number of spaces in a game of *Monopoly* (Darrow 1935). Finally, *semiotic contingency* refers to the unpredictability of meaning that is involved in interpreting the game's outcomes.

As Taylor (2006) and Malaby (2007) have noted, recent developments in networked gaming, particularly in the case of MMOGs, raise further issues on contingency in game studies. The kind of flexibility built into Malaby's model therefore becomes both useful and necessary for media artifacts that evolve so rapidly and change not only in the style of representation but also in the scope of activities they afford. And therein lies the biggest challenge in devising methodologies for game analysis. The difference between a game like *Pong* (Atari Inc. 1972) and *Grand Theft Auto IV* (Rockstar North 2008) can scarcely be traced on a single continuum of evolution. The latter transcends conventional understanding of games to deliver, instead, an intricately detailed simulated city, inhabited by thousands of individually designed inhabitants and supporting a span of activities ranging from adrenaline-pumping car chases and fire-fights to casual clothes shopping, flirtation, and a series of embedded mini-games. An environment like *Grand Theft Auto*'s Liberty City has several self-contained games within it that are only one feature of the whole package one gets when inserting the "game" into the console. Reading the future of game studies, then, becomes a real challenge, not least because the very notion of "gameness" is processual, contingent on the development of new platforms and their multiple affordances.

The future of game studies

To conclude, the future of game studies must be intimately linked to three considerations. The first is the evolution of games themselves, as their creators continue to make ever more cutting-edge use of new affordances in technology and design. Consequently, the critical work occasioned, say, in New Media Studies necessarily finds itself both catalyzed and exceeded by those developments, even as the specificity of games, their particular challenges to the protocols of critical discourse and of established conceptualities become more evident to commentators. One might then expect the timeliness and integrity of game studies, as a discipline, to be vindicated. However, that vindication will not be straightforward. This cues the second consideration. As game studies acquires greater penetration in institutional settings, the field can expect to find itself experiencing the same kinds of polemics about its own disciplinary status and its place in academia that were once instigated by literary theory or cultural studies and – lest we forget – by sociology or even English, none of which encountered, in the different eras of their coming to acceptance, unopposed recognition within the academy.

In all this, game studies is potentially undermined by what may well be most compelling about it: its apparent freshness but also its comparative innocence. Game studies seems to mediate an uncomplicated vista on the very possibility of the "new" that had been almost entirely discredited, within various perspectives in the humanities, by those positions that held that ours is a time of ultimately quite sterile "postality." A dependence on ironic revisitation, jadedness in regard to art and culture, cynicism about the possibility of the avant-garde: these are some of the familiar attributes of the postmodern, almost all of which have been predicated on critiques of familiar art forms and cultural practices and on a stance towards cyberculture that remains largely disengaged from and sometimes oblivious to its modalities. Games, however, tend to problematize all that. They do so not through some pointed deployment of their thematic or formal texture, but quite often by nothing more than the uncomplicatedness of their appeal, the beguilements of their own surface textures, their invitation to an unreflected engaging experience that is bigger on goals and mechanics than on "meaning" or adherence to an "aesthetic." Undoubtedly, they can be breezier about their own attunement to the digital age and their place in it than many of the forms they coexist alongside in the twenty-first century.

Additionally, games posit different ways and tempos and communities of seeing, reading, and interacting – and, indeed, of play itself. They thereby enable a quite novel focus for conventions of critique and analysis, suggesting that distinct critical idioms and protocols more directly appropriate to games ought to be devised. That is because games subvert too many aspects and preconceptions of originality, intertextuality and intermediality, virtuality, authorship, aesthetics, reader/audience-response, and the phenomenology of fiction to make the claims of postmodernism or the procedures of traditional criticism quite adequate or viable in their regard. Quite fundamentally, they also collapse the work–play distinction (see Taylor 2006). Commentary on games' diverse emphases on collective authorship, on networked engagement involving potentially innumerable concurrent players, on multisensory stimuli and multimediatic dimensions, to name but a few characteristics, are not straightforwardly containable or articulable within the discourse of those claims or procedures. Therefore games might well compel a distinct kind of critique whose formulation and development would be one of the primary objectives of game studies.

The problem for games studies is that games do suffer from an image problem. This goes beyond routine debates on games' encouragement of violence and dissociation. Certainly within academia, the values of scholarship and the rewards of a certain kind of disciplinary cachet are not intuitively associable with the field. Nor is it immediately clear, to those who have never played them, that games might mediate some kind of technological sublime. To such an uninitiated perception, games rather exemplify the depthlessness and waning of affect that Fredric Jameson famously identified in the postmodern. This view is not helped by characteristic game storylines and iconography being overinvested in cultures and subcultures that might come across as adolescent. It is true that some virtual environments that are coextensive with games are overdetermined by the fantastical topographies and demographics of Middle Earth-like landscapes, or, alternatively, by the trigger-happy immediacy of first-person shooters or the occasional vapidity of *Sims*-like scenarios.

That impression, however, is likely to be quickly allayed by any initial encounter with games. In any case, there are games that look set to richly exploit

the logic and frameworks uniquely afforded and pioneered in this most contemporary of media. *Portal* (Valve Corporation 2007) is, famously, one such
game. Its gameplay makes the most of a counter-intuitive physics to which only
the virtual worlds configurable in games could give instantiation, while nobody
who has even sampled user-created content in *LittleBigPlanet* (Media Molecule
2008) is likely to be condescending in regard to the potential of games. Any such
stance is allayed further by the encounter with games (or environments) created
by independent producers, like *Dear Esther* (The Chinese Room 2008), or others
that appear to privilege the paidic over the ludic (Caillois 1962), like *Flower*
(ThatGameCompany 2009).

In this respect, the third consideration becomes irresistible. Quite simply,
games are too important to be left to luminaries and practitioners within game
studies. That might sound like a provocation to the purists within game studies
who would advocate that only commentators with clear affiliations to the field,
or aficionados of games and their parallel and fictional worlds, can meaningfully
and informedly pronounce upon it. But the gradual coming to canonicity of
game studies will mean that the other disciplines will draw themselves to it,
collaborating with it or appropriating aspects of it. That cannot be bad, especially since games offer such intriguing vistas to narratology, anthropology, critical and cultural theory, psychology, media studies, philosophy, and sociology.
This, then, will have been yet another episode in the familiar, timeless tale of the
recuperation of the marginal or the popular. Indeed, the recuperation looks to
be already in place, as indicated by many of the studies quoted here, or by the
monographs on games published by some of the more prestigious academic
publishers – or by this very entry in a *Routledge Companion*, especially if it does
not appear incongruous in the company of the other articles.

Bibliography

Aarseth, E. (1997) *Cybertext: perspectives on ergodic literature*, Baltimore: Johns Hopkins
  University Press.
——(2001) "Computer game studies: Year one," *Game Studies*, 1(1). Online. Available HTTP
  <http://www.gamestudies.org/0101/editorial.html> (accessed 24 February 2010).
——(2003) "Playing research: methodological approaches to game analysis," *Digital Arts and
  Culture Conference*, 19–23 May 2003, School of Applied Communication, RMIT,
  Melbourne.
Atari Inc. (1972) *Pong*, Arcade: Atari Inc.
Bethesda Softworks LLC (2006) *The Elder Scrolls IV: Oblivion*, PC: 2K Games.
Blizzard Entertainment (2004) *World of Warcraft*, PC: Vivendi Universal.
Bogost, I. (2006) *Unit Operations: an approach to videogame criticism*, Cambridge, Mass.: MIT
  Press.
Bryce, J. and Rutter, J. (2006) *Understanding Digital Games*, London: Sage.
Caillois, R. (1962) *Man, Play, and Games*, London: Thames and Hudson.
CCP Games (2003) *EVE Online*, PC: CCP Games.

Crogan, P. (2004) "The game thing: ludology and other theory games," *Media International Australia, Incorporating Culture & Policy*, 110: 10–18.

Darrow, C. (1935) *Monopoly*, Parker Brothers.

Frasca, G. (1999) "Narratology meets ludology: similitude and differences between (video) games and narrative." Online. Available HTTP: <http://www.ludology.org/articles/ludology. htm> (accessed 13 October 2009).

Hayles, N.K. (1999) *How We Became Posthuman: virtual bodies in cybernetics, literature, and informatics*, Chicago: University of Chicago Press.

Huizinga, J. (1955) *Homo Ludens: a study of the play-element in culture*, Boston, Mass.: Beacon Press.

Juul, J. (2003) "The game, the player, the world: looking for a heart of gameness," *Level Up*: Digital Games Research Conference, 4–6 November, 2003, Utrecht, Netherlands.

——(2005) *Half-Real: video games between real rules and fictional worlds*, Cambridge, Mass.: MIT Press.

Linden Lab (2003) *Second Life*, PC: Linden Lab.

Malaby, T. (2007) "Beyond play: a new approach to games," *Games and Culture*, 2(2): 95–113.

Maxis Software (1989) *Simcity*, PC: Electronic Arts.

Media Molecule (2008) *Little Big Planet*, PS3: Sony Computer Entertainment Europe.

Rockstar North (2008) *Grand Theft Auto IV*, Xbox 360: Rockstar Games.

Salen, K. and Zimmerman, E. (2003) *Rules of Play: game design fundamentals*, Cambridge, Mass.: MIT Press.

Steinkuehler, C. (2006) "Why game studies now?", *Games and Culture*, 1: 97–101.

Taylor, T.L. (2006) *Play between Worlds: exploring online game culture*, Cambridge, Mass.: MIT Press.

ThatGameCompany (2009) *Flower*, PS3: Sony Computer Entertainment.

The Chinese Room (2008) *Dear Esther*, PC: www.moddb.com.

Tosca, S. (2003) "Melbourne dac weblog." Online. Available HTTP: <http://hypertext.rmit. edu.au/dac/blog_archive/cat_oddments.html > (accessed 7 October 2009).

Valve Corporation (2007) *Portal*, PC.

Valve Software (2004a) *Counter-Strike Source*, PC: Vivendi Universal Games.

——(2004b) *Half-Life 2*, PC: Vivendi Universal.

Wilson, J. (2006) "*Half-Real: video games between real rules and fictional worlds*, the handbook of computer game studies," *Convergence*, 12(4): 471–74.

Wolf, M.J.P. (ed.) (2001) *The Medium of the Video Game*, Austin: University of Texas Press.

29
HISTORY OF SCIENCE

Henning Schmidgen

The history of science comes from the Middle Kingdom. That is, it stems from the interstices, the spaces between science and literature, science and philosophy, and science and science. At the same time, it studies interstices: the changing interfaces and relays that connect experimental set-ups, laboratory desks as well as published texts, but that also divide those from one another. In other words, historians of science investigate the development of heterogeneous couplings that exist or are created between instruments and organisms, numbers and curves, images and concepts, in order to construct new knowledge and deconstruct the old – and vice versa. Interstices in this sense can always be found where the production of scientific knowledge is tied to specific material cultures: to the laboratory, the observatory, the museum, or the archive. However, they also exist in discursive formations and metaphorical tropes that facilitate but some-times also complicate exchanges between one scientific discipline and another, between science and the broader public, as well as between contemporary science and its past. The history of science, then, works on, at, and with these interstices. It is a discipline from the Middle Kingdom, an interdiscipline, and arguably the interdiscipline par excellence.

The interstice as leitmotiv for this historiography is not radically new. Since the beginning of the twentieth century, the "in-between" separating and binding You and I, perception and movement, cause and effect, has been a focus of theo-retical attention, in authors as diverse as Martin Buber, Eugène Dupréel, Erwin Straus, and Hannah Arendt (see Theunissen 2004). "Life lurks in the interstices of each living cell, and in the interstices of the brain," notes Alfred North Whitehead (1960: 161) in *Process and Reality*, while Maurice Merleau-Ponty observes in his phenomenology of speech that "the sense appears only at the intersection of and as it were in the interval between words" (Merleau-Ponty 2007: 243–44).

In similar ways, traditional science studies, historical as well as sociological, have used the concept of the interstice and/or the interval, even if they did not apply the exact term. The most famous example of this is the idea that, under the conditions of a scientific crisis, "Gestalt switches," akin to radical shifts in the interpretation of an ambiguous visual perception, lead from one paradigm of scientific practice to another (Hanson 1958; Kuhn 1962). But the same holds true for the notion that epistemological "ruptures" (*coupures*) separate sensorial knowledge from scientific knowledge, as well as today's science from its non-scientific past (Bachelard 1940). In both cases, in Thomas Kuhn just as in Gaston Bachelard, gaps and pauses appear as essential elements marking the collective process of acquiring scientific knowledge.

Recent studies in the history of science have rephrased this leitmotiv in forceful ways. Focusing on single laboratories and experiments, historians of science have filled the empty time between the paradigms and epistemes. They have replaced the relatively closed world of Gestalt-switches and epistemological ruptures with an open universe of micro-fissures residing in the space between diverse laboratories and their local milieus, between experimental things and experimental texts, between measuring instruments and model organisms, even between single scientific statements and images. One of the results of this remarkable change has been that historians no longer characterize the progressions of science as revolutions, but as gradual displacements that occur within circumscribed constellations of scientific practice, leading from states of productive precariousness to states of reproductive stability, and vice versa (see, e.g., Pickering 1995; Rabinow 1996; Rheinberger 1997; Stengers 2000).

At the same time, the image of science that has emerged from this shift emphasizes materiality and chance as key elements of scientific practice. It thereby contradicts the classical view of science as based on strictly organized and clearly programmed practices. Instead, recent studies in the history of science highlight the fundamental role of encounters, appropriations, and deviations as epistemologically relevant events. But where does this new image of science stem from? What are the encounters and events that have produced these novel approaches to writing the history of science? There is no comprehensive history of science history that would provide an answer to this question. Given the proliferation of methods and topics in recent times, it has even become difficult to survey the entire field (however, see Kragh 1994; Golinski 1998; Daston 2001; Kelley 2002; Biagioli 2009). All one can say is that, besides traditional philosophical and structural accounts, there are now social and cultural histories of science, and that besides general or encyclopedic investigations, there is a rapidly increasing number of micro-histories and case studies, i.e. historical accounts of science focusing on specific discourses and disciplines, individuals and instruments, images and inscriptions.

In this proliferating situation, a short sequence of exemplary observations concerning the genesis and structure of history-of-science discourses should help us glimpse some of the reasons why the contemporary state of this kind of inquiry is characterized by productive diversity and even disunity, and why this heterogeneity is the perhaps paradoxical but certainly stimulating basis for its constantly changing identity. Eventually, I suggest, it is science itself that is speaking to us here.

Post-positivism in the historical study of science

At first sight, the new history of science seems to have emerged from recent developments at the intersections between history, philosophy, and sociology of science. As Peter Galison has put it, these developments amount to a turn away from orientations that are usually identified as "positivism" and "anti-positivism" (Galison 1997: 781–844), as exemplified respectively by Rudolf Carnap's *Aufbau der logischen Welt* (1928) and Thomas Kuhn's *Structure of Scientific Revolutions* (1962). It is true that Carnap and Kuhn disagreed in fundamental respects: the first conceived of science as a project based on observations and protocols that lead to general theories, the latter saw it as an activity firmly grounded in conceptual schemes and theories that result in facts which, in turn, correspond to the adapted schemes and theories used to comprehend them. Still, both started from the assumption that science is a unified and, in this sense, also universal endeavor. Whether it be the grand story of single observations resulting in theories or, instead, a macro-history of paradigms that successively break down, only to yield new ones, Carnap as well as Kuhn were convinced that the existence and development of science can be depicted by master narratives, or *grands récits*.

The "post-positivism" of recent history and sociology of science has proposed an image of science that is considerably less abstract (Zammito 2004). Here, scientific activities no longer resemble a painting by Mondrian where orderly ways lead from observation to theory and vice versa. Instead they come close to an assemblage, say a box by Joseph Cornell, where multifarious, network-like connections between diverse objects exist: both artificial and natural, found and made, flat and deep. In other words, historians of science no longer deal with the sensorial and concrete on the one side and the cognitive and abstract on the other. What they mainly investigate are the spaces "in between," i.e., transitional zones populated with numerous actors: scientists and technicians, instruments and organisms, but also and above all, inscription devices of all kinds. As a consequence, laboratory notes, databases, photographs, movies, simulations, and other media technologies have become crucial objects and means for historical research concerning the sciences (see Lenoir 1998; Berthelot 2003; Holmes, Renn, and Rheinberger 2003; Dotzler and Schmidgen 2008).

Towards a genealogy of "history *and* science"

However, the new look of science history also pays tribute to long-lasting trends in modern science itself. As is well known, the emergence and development of discourses about the history of science is not at all limited to the twentieth century. As Wolf Lepenies (1976) has pointed out, historical discourses on the sciences are profoundly tied to the temporalization processes that have characterized modern science since at least 1800. According to Lepenies, these processes can be detected on the level of scientific objects, the form of scientific theories, and the organizational structure of science. In fact, since the late eighteenth century, scientists have been increasingly interested in time measurements, case histories, and traditions of all kinds – from printed texts to social rules and geological strata. The developing interest in time as an object of scientific study went hand in hand with the emergence of theories of science that emphasized active experience and inductive reasoning over contemplation and ideas. This development was paralleled by the founding of a growing number of scientific institutions that functioned according to principles of divided labor. With the rise of new institutions, the time of scientific operation became detached from the careers and life-spans of individual scholars. Furthermore, as Lepenies has argued, from the late eighteenth century onward, physics, chemistry, and the emerging life sciences met the growing "empirical imperative" (*Empirisierungszwang*) by making new kinds of observations and experiments, but also by developing discursive and non-discursive historical practices, e.g., by collecting data and things, by ranging innovative facts into an order of scientific advancement, and by situating individuals vis-à-vis increasingly established research practices and projects.

Some authors claim that the beginnings of the history of science can be traced back to antiquity, in particular to Aristotelian philosopher Eudemus of Rhodes (Zhmud' 2006). However, peripatetic histories of mathematics and astronomy failed to establish themselves as a successful genre of philosophical and scientific writing, and only a restricted number of fragments from the original texts have survived. In the late Renaissance, scientists such as Johannes Kepler may have been inspired by these ancient models. However, Kepler and others used historical arguments and narrations mainly to justify the study of topics that were otherwise considered to be useless and undignified. More generally, historical representations of sciences such as mathematics and astronomy served as a means to reflect upon such disciplines and science in general, to articulate their content and to organize their teaching in the fifteenth and sixteenth centuries (Grafton 1997; Goulding 2006). Only in the late seventeenth century did depictors of science draw things together in ways that started to resonate with our contemporary understanding of history-of-science discourses. In the *Éloges* that literary writer Bernard le Bovier de Fontenelle presented to the Academy of Science in Paris, starting in the 1690s, he insisted for the first time that the contradictory connections between science, life, and time were a crucial topic for the history of science. In 1731, Fontenelle published a two-volume collection of his *Éloges*, including a sketch of the history of the Parisian Academy of Science. According to Georges Canguilhem (1968), these volumes significantly prefigured the history of science in today's sense. On the one hand, Fontenelle complained about the huge number of repeated and varied experiments that can hardly have been accounted for. On the other hand, his eulogies focused on the relation between knowledge and life. In other words, the discourse of science history here manifested itself under the specifically modern sign of individuality, finitude, and the lack of time. It is remarkable that this did not result in a discourse that spoke against the ideal of leading a scientific life. To the contrary, Fontenelle connected his historical accounts to the "popularization" of science. While historicizing science he also wrote literary works on scientific problems, e.g., *Entretiens sur la pluralité des mondes* (1686).

Progressions and projections

Between 1750 and 1840, numerous studies were published that presented the historical development of the sciences (mostly mathematics and astronomy, but also physics, alchemy, chemistry, and medicine) as continuously gaining better approximations to truth. This approximation was often seen as valuable in itself. At the same time, Enlightenment philosophers attributed positive ethical and political value to scientific achievements (Laudan 1993). Working along these lines were authors such as Jean-Baptiste de La Chapelle in his *Traité des sections coniques, et autres courbes anciennes* of 1750, or Alexandre Savérien in his *Histoire des progrès de l'esprit humain dans les sciences exactes et dans les arts qui en dépendent* of 1766. From today's standpoint, much of these progressive histories appear to be epistemologically rather shallow. By and large they were based on the assumption that scientific knowledge resulted from a growing number of observations of nature, observations that were implicitly passive. This epistemological stance was shaken, however, in the wake of the "revolution" in philosophy usually associated with Immanuel Kant.

In 1837, William Whewell, in his extensive *History of the Inductive Sciences from the Earliest to the Present Times*, underscored again the empirical nature of science. Simultaneously, however, Whewell emphasized the active role of the human mind: the mind applied its theories to nature and, if necessary, subjected nature to thought. A similar view characterizes Johann Wolfgang von Goethe's contributions to the theory of color published in 1810. Against the background of his own experiments concerning color production and perception, Goethe insisted on a specific, anti-Newtonian "view" or "visual perception [*Anschauung*] of Nature." Less well known is the fact that, in this context, he also developed an elaborate discourse on the history of science centered on the "brave individual" and took into account the individual's conflicted position between experimentation and tradition: "The conflict of the individual with immediate experience and mediated tradition is the proper history of science" (Goethe 1991: 611). Goethe further developed this notion of conflict in another contribution to his theory of colors in which he described trials, or experiments, as "mediators between object and subject." The relation between literature and (the history of) science that had been emphasized in Fontenelle was re-accentuated here in instructive and important ways.

The list as a historical account

In the 1830s and 1840s, philosopher, mathematician, and science popularizer Auguste Comte produced comprehensive progressive histories of science and advocated a largely empiricist epistemology in his "Positivism" (Braunstein 2009). At about the same time, the perspectives embodied in discourses of science history underwent significant changes in other areas, in particular insofar as a growing number of laboratory scientists began to act as historians (Engelhardt 1979). One of the results was that, in the course of the nineteenth century, science history itself was subjected to the empirical imperative that regulated science in general. Laboratory historians emphasized the collection and processing of raw data and presented these in forms as practicable and instructive as possible. The work of the German physicist Johann Christian Poggendorff is a case in point.

From 1824 to 1876, Poggendorff was editor of one of the most important science journals of the nineteenth century, the *Annalen der Physik und Chemie*. In 1853, he published a remarkable book on *Life Lines in the History of the Exact Sciences*, in which he attempted to apply new techniques of "graphic representation" to the history of science. Inspired by Joseph Priestley's "charts of biography," he represented geographical and biographical data from the history of science in curves and diagrams. Poggendorff complemented these visual elements with tables in which he listed scientific "discoveries" in alphabetical order. A decade later he started to publish his *Biographisch-literarisches Handwörterbuch zur Geschichte der exacten Wissenschaften* (1863). Besides short biographies of mathematicians, astronomers, physicists, chemists, geologists, etc., this handbook contained extensive bibliographical information concerning individual scientific authors for the period until 1858.

After Poggendorff's death in 1877, the *Handwörterbuch* was continued by other authors, and was eventually adopted, as a permanent project, by the Saxon Academy of Science. A long-term effort of data collection, it resembles the *Catalogue of Scientific Papers* compiled by the Royal Society of London in nineteen volumes between 1867 and 1925. Similar bibliographical and biographical reference works are the backbone for much of the encyclopedic histories of science written in the nineteenth and twentieth centuries. Prominent models for such reference works range from Ludwig Darmstaedter's chronological list of the "path breaking actions and fundamental events" in the history of science over the past 4,000 years (1904) to the *Dictionary of Scientific Biography*, edited by Charles Gillispie between 1970 and 1980, and today's online databases on Galileo, Newton, Darwin, etc. Given the ongoing importance of such reference works and resources, one might argue that chronological and alphabetical lists are one of the crucial genres of science-history writing.

Polemical use of the history of science

As scientists started systematically to collect raw data from and for the history of science, they also began to use historical discourses for specific purposes. In particular, they historicized science to meet the challenge of the growing competition among researchers and to promote increasingly nationalized cultures of science. The consequence was that, in addition to the role of "popularization," the history of science started to function as a medium for carrying out conflicts and debates. In other words, science history became polemic. As prototypical in this regard, one could choose the work of nineteenth-century German electrophysiologist Emil du Bois-Reymond (perhaps not by coincidence a friend of Poggendorff's). His pioneering contributions to the history of the life sciences have been critically discussed by historians such as Canguilhem (1955), Jardine (1997), and Rheinberger (2010).

Despite the fact that du Bois-Reymond sometimes used the classical form of the eulogy, or *Gedächtnisrede*, his main genre was the extensive historical presentation and discussion of previous research directly within his own scientific publications – today an almost forgotten model. His main motivation for including historical sections in his scientific writings, in particular the *Untersuchungen zur thierischen Elektricität* (1848–84), was to decide the issue of temporal priority and thus gain appropriate recognition, estimation, and reward among the scientific community. As early as 1845, du Bois-Reymond argued against what he considered to be an "excess" of scientific journal publications. In a letter to Alexander von Humboldt, he explained that he "despises of these kinds of premature publications," which "are so common in our days that the journals are flooded with single facts and observations without common connection that come along with hasty claims of authorship" (du Bois-Reymond 1997: 77). As for himself, du Bois-Reymond claimed not to publish the findings of his experimental work until he would be capable "of producing a substantial whole" that would leave "a mark" and help advance his discipline – "because of the number of new facts that would be accumulated there, because of the internal relation that would connect them with one another, and because of the conclusion that could be derived from their hanging together" (77).

What du Bois-Reymond alluded to was the ongoing work at his later famous *Untersuchungen* in electrophysiology. At the same time, he referred to a larger problem that he was also confronted with as a founding member of the German Society for Physics. In the eyes of du Bois-Reymond, it was not the "vanity of the authors" or their "desire for fame" that were the principal reasons for a lack of appropriate references to his work, and hence a lack of recognition of authorship and priority. The main problem was the separation of scientific practice from its history, in particular the "tendency of some physicists to completely neglect the study of writings that preceded their own investigations and never to mention the names of those from whom they have received the fundamental ideas for their work" (du Bois-Reymond 1997: 77). Given this state of things, one of the explicit goals of the German Society of Physics was to act against the "lack of a literary history in physics," mostly by publishing a yearbook on the advances in physics (Karsten 1847: viii). In a sense, history here took on an explicit role in contributing to the progression of science (Maienschein, Laubichler and Loettgers 2008). And this role tends to be overshadowed when the sciences develop in increasingly dynamic ways and the history of science starts looking at itself as a largely autonomous discipline of the humanities.

History as interpretation and diagnostics

With the advent of Darwinism, discourses about the history of science underwent another remarkable shift. In the 1870s and 1880s they found a new basis and resource in science itself. In other words, historians of science did not any longer just refer to an object, i.e., "science," but also began to use science, and in particular the life sciences, as a reference frame for discussing what science *and* history were all about. In this sense, Alphonse de Candolle, in his *Histoire des sciences et des savants depuis deux siècles* (1873), invoked the model of botany. Shortly later, Francis Galton referred to contemporary research on heredity in his *English Men of Science* (1874). In the following years, authors such as Ernst Mach, Friedrich Nietzsche, and Georg Simmel, who placed more emphasis on scientific processes, referred to and relied on evolutionary theory in their historical and philosophical writings (Richards 1989).

While this relating of science to science may be considered as circular, it has proven extremely productive. It is precisely this circle that enabled the history of science to become an activity of interpretation and diagnosis that, in its approaches and perspectives, could profoundly engage with the sciences it investigated. The recurring starting point for this self-referential project was the language of science, in particular of scientific concepts. Already for Nietzsche and Simmel, language constituted the indivisible medium of scientific knowledge, the interstice that connected science and non-science, while at the same time separating them from one another. Almost all of the big figures in twentieth-century history of science subscribed to this view – from Gaston Bachelard and Alexandre Koyré to Michel Foucault and Hans Blumenberg. Although there are significant differences in their broader concerns, these authors held true to language as the decisive level of historical analysis, despite the increasingly important status assumed by the mathematization and visualization of scientific knowledge.

Against the background of evolutionary theory, however, "language" did not remain a purely linguistic category. In his studies of biological concepts, Canguilhem, for example, did not just focus on the meaning and use of single entries from the historical vocabulary of science. Often referring to Darwin and Nietzsche, he emphasized the theoretical and practical orientations, the vital postures and gestures, the attitudes and allures that were connected to concepts such as "reflex" or "*Umwelt*." Canguilhem even went so far as to deduce such concepts from the forms that individuated life produces out of itself or brings about, with the help of human beings, in technology and the arts. Moving away from concepts, history thus started to concentrate on images and the machine – topics that, in recent science history, have gained great significance. In fact, historians of science who are focusing on "forms of knowledge" in this sense are able to demonstrate that these forms are deeply entrenched in life as such. At the same time, they can show that in the ongoing conflict between human beings and their surroundings, these preconceptual forms of knowing often enter into unexpected relations of correspondence, for example, when the "reflex" is compared to an explosion of canon powder or the "cell" to a honeycomb.

Such analogies are not purely formal. From the perspective of evolutionary theory, they can be viewed as referring back to the process of assimilation that is a basic feature of life in all its individuated forms. In other words, the initial forms of concepts are related to the general biological problem of the inside and the outside, of expulsion and assimilation (Johns Schloegel and Schmidgen 2002). Consequently, the sense or meaning of a scientific concept never explains itself horizontally, simply with respect to other words and texts. Only by having recourse to the vertical forces that, historically or currently, "take possession of a thing," e.g., health, heredity, or thinking, can the sense of a concept be grasped and investigated (see Latour 1988: 153). Interpretation, then, turns into a special kind of diagnostics, a search for signs of "taking possession of something." Conversely, the same approach opens the possibility of connecting literature and science (and the history thereof) in novel ways. A passage from the physics of Pierre Gassendi can now become translated by a poem by La Fontaine, a philosophical attitude towards the machine can be explained by a quote from a novel by Villiers de L'Isle-Adam, and a problem of epistemology becomes illustrated by a sentence from Paul Valéry (see, e.g., Canguilhem 1955).

Discipline or interdiscipline?

In parallel and contrast to these critical developments in the interstices between history and science, the late nineteenth and twentieth century saw increasing attempts to establish the history of science as an autonomous humanities discipline within the existing academic landscape, similar to the history of art and/or religion (Corsi 1983). In 1892, the first chair devoted to the history of science was created at the Collège de France in Paris. In 1901, the German physician Karl Sudhoff created the first national society for the history of science and medicine, the *Deutsche Gesellschaft für Geschichte der Medizin und der Naturwissenschaften*. In 1912, the Belgian mathematician and chemist George Sarton founded the journal *Isis: Revue consacrée à l'historie de la science*, the first issue of which appeared in 1913, mostly containing publications in French, Italian, and German. In 1924, together with Lawrence Joseph Henderson, Sarton founded the History of Science Society in Boston. The first international congress for the history of science took place in Paris in 1929, under the presidency of the Italian mathematician and historian of mathematics Gino Loria. In the following years and decades an uncounted number of national and international meetings of general and discipline-specific societies for the history of science took place (Sarton 1952: 48).

There is no doubt that these institutions and events served an important social role. They fostered the exchanges among their members and contributed to the professional identity of historians of science. However, whether or not the pursuit of disciplinary autonomy was and is a productive strategy with respect to the topics, problems, and methods of the history of science remains doubtful. In his programmatic article concerning "An Institute for the History of Science and Civilization" (1917), Sarton argued that the history of science could only be done in creative and convincing ways if it was constantly inspired by a close coordination of three points of view: the points of view of the historian, the philosopher, and the scientist. This interdisciplinary perspective tends to be lost when the history of science defines itself as a discipline exclusively expressing the point of view of the historian (Daston 2009).

In the recent history of science, the translation of Gestalt-switches and epistemological ruptures into a multiplicity of gaps and interfaces in scientific practice has been a more successful strategy, resulting in numerous innovative studies of the structure and evolution of laboratory instruments, images, and inscriptions. But acknowledging this success does not always go hand in hand with seeing what that change has neglected. When explaining the discontinuities in the process of science, Kuhn as well as Bachelard referred the history of science back to science. Kuhn used experimental investigations concerning ambiguous perceptions of visual patterns (e.g., the duck-rabbit diagram) as a "model" for the explanation of paradigm shifts in the history of scientific knowledge (Kuhn 1962). Similarly, Bachelard referred to the laboratory technology of stroboscopy to bolster his argument that even the process of sensory knowledge "is clearly marked by novelties, surprises, ruptures" and "by blanks cut into pieces" (Bachelard 1950: 29). That is, Bachelard extended an analogy from psychological experience into the realm of history, which is itself slowed down and externalized, as it were, by the discontinuous development of scientific knowledge. Similar operations of relating science to science itself (e.g., the history of physics to Gestalt psychology, or the history of biology to cybernetics) seem desirable and even necessary if the production of new knowledge is to remain a crucial topic for historical science studies. From where, if not from science, can we derive categories that will allow us to grasp the new *as the new?*

In his study on bacteriology in the nineteenth century, Bruno Latour has argued that the conceptual framework of history and the social sciences (e.g., notions such as "society," "modernization," or "interest") is, by and large, inappropriate for tackling this task (Latour 1988: 9). As Latour explains, this framework was developed at about the same time as bacteriology. As a result, it biases our perspective on the object under investigation. Latour's answer to this problem consisted in choosing a quasi-literary approach. He adopted Tolstoy's novel *War and Peace* as a narrative framework for posing general questions concerning the agency of scientific practice. Although this strategy proved to be successful in his study of Pasteur, Latour's proclaimed "agnosticism" with respect to science seems contradictory. In a culture saturated with science, it is highly questionable whether historical studies of science can situate themselves "outside" of science, in a purified realm of the non-scientific. The real challenge for historical accounts of scientific practice seems to be to engage with contemporary science and its fundamental concepts – if necessary by a detour through philosophies that have met scientific knowledge with exemplary openness. It is precisely this detour that has proven highly productive for recent studies in the history of science. With Derrida's *Grammatology*, historians of science such as Hans-Jörg Rheinberger have rephrased issues of communication and tradition in terms of cybernetics and bioinformatics. Deleuze, with his references to Charles M. Child, Albert Dalcq and other embryologists, has inspired Stengers, Pickering, and other science historians and drawn general attention to developmental biology as an important resource for reconceiving historical processes.

Conclusion

The history of science comes from the interstices, from the changing spaces between science and literature, science and philosophy, and science and science. At the same time, historians of science study interstices. Instead of focusing on the knowing subject and their capacities, on the one side, and the knowable objects, on the other, they investigate the technological and cultural conditions under which and within which the processes of acquiring scientific knowledge go on. In other words, the history of science is not primarily interested in the question "how knowing subjects might attain an undisguised view of their objects." Instead it investigates "what conditions had to be created for objects to be made into objects of empirical knowledge under variable conditions" (Rheinberger 2010: 3). In short, the history of science is the investigation of *means* and *methods* of the production of knowledge.

Situated between history, philosophy, and science, it finds itself in a rather unique position. As interdiscipline par excellence, it can act as a driving force for innovation in the humanities. At the same time, it may contribute to what Stengers, following Whitehead, has called a "culture of interstices" (Stengers 2002: 367) – a culture that refrains from exacerbating impatience with scientific institutions and social organisms and instead decelerates and percolates, in other words, historicizes.

Acknowledgments

Thanks to Ed Jurkowitz, Jeffrey Schwegman, and Bruce Clarke for their suggestions and corrections. Unless otherwise stated, all translations from French and German are my own.

Bibliography

Bachelard, G. (1940) *La philosophie du non: essai d'une philosophie du nouvel esprit scientifique*, Paris: P.U.F.

——(1950) *Dialectique de la durée*, 2nd edn, Paris: P.U.F.

Berthelot, J.-M. (ed.) (2003) *Figures du texte scientifique*, Paris: P.U.F.

Biagioli, M. (2009) "Postdisciplinary liaisons: science studies and the humanities," *Critical Inquiry*, 35: 816–33.

Braunstein, J.-F. (2009) *La philosophie de la médecine d'Auguste Comte: vaches carnivores, Vierge Mère et morts vivants*, Paris: P.U.F.

Candolle, A. de (1873) *Histoire des sciences et des savants depuis deux siècles, d'après l'opinion des principales académies ou sociétés scientifiques*, Geneva: Georg.

Canguilhem, G. (1955) *La formation du concept de réflexe aux XVIIe et XVIIIe siècles*, Paris: P.U.F.

——(1968) "Fontenelle, philosophe et historien des sciences" (1957), in *Etudes d'histoire et de philosophie des sciences*, Paris: Vrin, pp. 51–58.

Carnap, R. (1928) *Der logische Aufbau der Welt*, Berlin-Schlachtensee: Weltkreis-Verlag.

Corsi, P. (1983) "History of science, history of philosophy and history of theology," in P. Corsi and P. Weindling (eds) *Information Sources in the History of Science and Medicine*, London: Butterworth Scientific, pp. 3–26.

Darmstaedter, L. (1908) *Handbuch zur Geschichte der Naturwissenschaften und der Technik: in chronologischer Darstellung*, 2nd edn, Berlin: Springer.

Daston, L. (2001) "The historicity of science," in G. Most (ed.) *Historicization – Historisierung*, Göttingen: Vandenhoeck and Ruprecht, pp. 201–21.

——(2009) "Science studies and the history of science," *Critical Inquiry*, 35: 798–813.

Dotzler, B.J. and Schmidgen, H. (eds) (2008) *Parasiten und Sirenen: Zwischenräume als Orte der materiellen Wissensproduktion*, Bielefeld: Transcript Verlag.

Du Bois-Reymond, E. (1848–84) *Untersuchungen zur thierischen Elektricität*, 2 vols in 4 parts, Berlin: Reimer.

——(1997) "[Letter to Alexander von Humboldt, May 20, 1845]," in I. Schwarz and K. Wenig (eds) *Briefwechsel zwischen Alexander von Humboldt und Emil du Bois-Reymond*, Berlin: Akademie-Verlag, pp. 75–78.

Engelhardt, D. v. (1979) *Historisches Bewußtsein in der Naturwissenschaft von der Aufklärung bis zum Positivismus*, Freiburg/München: Karl Alber.

Fontenelle, B.L.B. d. (1686) *Entretiens sur la pluralité des mondes*, Paris.

——(1731) *Éloges des académiciens de l'académie royale des sciences*, 2 vols, LaHaye: VanDerKloot.

Galison, P. (1997) *Image and Logic: a material culture of microphysics*, Chicago: University of Chicago Press.

Galton, F. (1874) *English Men of Science: their nature and nurture*, London: Macmillan.

Gillispie, C. (ed.) (1970–80) *Dictionary of Scientific Biography*, 10 vols, New York: Scribner.

Goethe, J.W. v. (1991) *Zur Farbenlehre*, ed. M. Wenzel, Frankfurt am Main: Dt. Klassiker-Verlag.

Golinski, J. (1998) *Making Natural Knowledge: constructivism and the history of science*, Cambridge: Cambridge University Press.

Goulding, R. (2006) "Histories of science in early modern Europe: introduction," *Journal of the History of Ideas*, 67(1): 33–40.

Grafton, A. (1997) "From apotheosis to analysis: some late Renaissance histories of classical astronomy," in Kelley 1997: 261–76.

Hanson, N.R. (1958) *Patterns of Discovery: an inquiry into the conceptual foundations of science*, Cambridge: Cambridge University Press.

Holmes, F.L., Renn, J. and Rheinberger, H.-J. (eds) (2003) *Reworking the Bench: research notebooks in the history of science*, Dordrecht: Kluwer.

Jardine, N. (1997) "The mantle of Müller and the ghost of Goethe: interactions between the sciences and their histories," in Kelley 1997: 297–317.

Johns Schloegel, J. and Schmidgen, H. (2002) "General physiology, experimental psychology, and evolutionism: unicellular organisms as objects of psychophysiological research, 1877–1918," *Isis*, 93(4): 614–45.

Karsten, G. (1847) "Vorbericht," *Fortschritte der Physik im Jahre 1845*, Berlin: Veit, pp. iii–x.

Kelley, D.R. (ed.) (1997) *History and the Disciplines: the reclassification of knowledge in early modern Europe*, Rochester: University of Rochester Press.

——(2002) "The History of Science," in *The Descent of Ideas: the history of intellectual history*, Burlington: Ashgate, pp. 205–30.

Kragh, H.S. (1994) *An Introduction to the Historiography of Science*, Cambridge: Cambridge University Press.

Kuhn, T.S. (1962) *Structure of Scientific Revolutions*, Chicago: University of Chicago Press.

La Chapelle, J.-B. d. (1750) *Traité des sections coniques, et autres courbes anciennes*, Paris: Quillau.

Latour, B. (1988) *The Pasteurization of France*, trans. A. Sheridan and J. Law, Cambridge, Mass.: Harvard University Press.

Laudan, R. (1993) "Histories of science and their uses: a review to 1913," *History of Science*, 31: 1–34.

Lenoir, T. (ed.) (1998) *Inscribing Science: scientific texts and the materialities of communication*, Stanford: Stanford University Press.

Lepenies, W. (1976) *Das Ende der Naturgeschichte: Wandel kultureller Selbstverständlichkeiten in den Wissenschaften des 18. und 19. Jahrhunderts*, München: Carl Hanser Verlag.

Maienschein, J., Laubichler, M. and Loettgers, A. (2008) "How can history of science matter to scientists?," *Isis*, 99: 341–49.

Merleau-Ponty, M. (2007) "Indirect language and the voices of silence" (1960), in T. Toadvine and L. Lawlor (eds) *The Merleau-Ponty Reader*, Evanston: Northwestern University Press, pp. 241–82.

Pickering, A. (1995) *The Mangle of Practice. Time, agency and science*, Chicago: University of Chicago Press.

Poggendorff, J.C. (1853) *Lebenslinien zur Geschichte der exacten Wissenschaften seit Wiederherstellung derselben*, Berlin: Duncker.

——(1863) *Biographisch-literarisches Handwörterbuch zur Geschichte der exacten Wissenschaften*, 2 vols, Leipzig: Barth.

Rabinow, P. (1996) *Making PCR: a story of biotechnology*, Chicago: Chicago University Press.

Rheinberger, H.-J. (1997) *Toward a History of Epistemic Things: synthesizing proteins in the test tube*, Stanford: Stanford University Press.

——(2010) *On Historicizing Epistemology*, Stanford: Stanford University Press.

Richards, R.J. (1989) "The natural-selection model and other models in the historiography of science," in *Darwin and the Emergence of Evolutionary Theories of Mind and Behavior*, Chicago: University of Chicago Press, pp. 559–93.

Royal Society of London (1867–1925) *Catalogue of Scientific Papers*, 19 vols, London: Royal Society.

Sarton, G. (1917) "An institute for the history of science and civilization," *Science*, new series, 46(1191): 399–402.

——(1952) *A Guide to the History of Science: a first guide for the study of the history of science, with introductory essays on science and tradition*, New York: Ronald.

Savérien, A. (1766) *Histoire des progrès de l'esprit humain dans les sciences et dans les arts qui en dépendent*, Paris: Lacombe.

Stengers, I. (2000) *The Invention of Modern Science*, trans. D.W. Smith, Minneapolis: University of Minnesota Press.

——(2002) *Penser avec Whitehead: une libre et sauvage création de concepts*, Paris: Éditions du Seuil.

Theunissen, M. (2004) "Zwischen," in J. Ritter, K. Gründer, and G. Gabriel (eds) *Historisches Wörterbuch der Philosophie*, vol. 12, Darmstadt: Wissenschaftliche Buchgesellschaft, pp. 1543–49.

Whewell, W. (1837) *History of the Inductive Sciences: from the earliest to the present times*, 3 vols, London: J.W. Parker.

Whitehead, A.N. (1960) *Process and Reality: an essay in cosmology*, New York: Harper & Row.

Zammito, J.H. (2004) *A Nice Derangement of Epistemes: post-positivism in the study of science from Quine to Latour*, Chicago: University of Chicago Press.

Zhmud', L.J. (2006) *The Origin of the History of Science in Classical Antiquity*, trans. A. Chernoglazov, Berlin: de Gruyter.

30
MEDIA STUDIES
Mark B.N. Hansen

Media innovation

To the extent that each new medium of communication operates through a technology for exteriorizing some function of human cognition and memory, it involves both gain and loss. This fundamental duality of media innovation has often taken the form of myth. In the *Protagoras*, Plato himself deploys the Hesiodic myth of Prometheus and Epimetheus as a means of characterizing the singularity of the human, but also of grasping our fundamental dependence on technology. Let us recall the salient details of Plato's account: charged with the task of equipping mortal creatures with suitable powers, Epimetheus makes his distribution following the principle of compensation, giving to each creature those capacities that will insure their survival. Not being particularly clever, Epimetheus used all of his available powers on the brute beasts, leaving the human race unprovided for, and so compelling the theft of fire by his more famous brother, Prometheus. Because of our Promethean legacy, so Plato's myth recounts, we humans have had a share in the portion of the gods and have distinguished ourselves from all other animals through our use of the arts of fire, which is to say, of technologies. This use has resulted in the development of articulate speech and names, the invention of houses and clothes and shoes and bedding, and the introduction of agriculture.

By changing the conditions for the production of experience, all media technologies, when they are new, destabilize existing patterns of biological, psychical, and collective life at the same time as they furnish new facilities. This convergence of privation and supplementation already informs what many critics hold to be the primal scene of media innovation in Western thought: Plato's meditation in the *Phaedrus* on the new medium of *writing*. There the issue is developed metaphorically through writing's status as a *pharmakon*, at once a poison and its antidote, a threat to memory and its extension. The profound ambivalence of writing is clearly expressed in the myth that Socrates recounts to Phaedrus of Theuth, the Egyptian God who invented writing:

> But when it came to writing Theuth said [to the Egyptian king, Thamus], "Here, O king, is a branch of learning that will make the people of Egypt wiser and improve their memories; my discovery provides a recipe for memory and wisdom." But the king answered and said, "O man full of arts, to one it is given to create the things of art, and to another to judge what measure of harm and of profit they have for those that shall employ them. And so it is that you, by reason of your tender regard for the writing that is your offspring, have declared the very opposite of its true effect. If men learn this, it will implant forgetfulness in their souls; they will cease to exercise memory because they rely on that which is written, calling things to remembrance no longer from within themselves, but by means of external marks. What you have discovered is a recipe not for memory, but for reminder. And it is no true wisdom that you offer your disciples, but only its semblance."
>
> (Plato 1995)

Thamus's well-reasoned reservations notwithstanding, this myth recaptures the fundamental duality that will drive media innovation onward. In this case, even if writing results in a waning of memory, it furnishes an external supplement to internal memory that will become ever more necessary as information proliferates and social life complexifies.

That Prometheus suffered unending punishment for his theft from the gods should not be forgotten. Indeed, it is this aspect of the myth that reappears throughout our history, at moments of large-scale technological change. To cite one particularly forceful example, Mary Shelley's *Frankenstein, or the Modern Prometheus* casts Victor Frankenstein in the role of a latter-day Prometheus, whose theft of the spark of life leads to disastrous consequences all too familiar to us. What Shelley's deployment of the figure of Prometheus exemplifies is the cultural anxiety that surrounds moments of technological newness: any Promethean step forward is, so it seems, necessarily accompanied by fears that we have overstepped, that we have introduced something detrimental to our "natural" life. One need only recall the anxieties that welled up around cinema at its origin (and that ranged from the physiological, namely that it would hurt our eyesight, to the moral, that it would cater to the lowest impulses). Or, still more unequivocally, think of the myriad anxieties that today surround genetic engineering and stem-cell research. What the longevity of this mythic kernel would seem to point toward is the dialectic that surrounds adaptation to the new: to the extent that new media introduce modes of experience that challenge the familiar, they are bound to occasion anxiety, resistance, even hostility, as they make their way toward cultural acceptance or "naturalization."

The Promethean dimension in this dialectic underscores the fact that such anxiety is not trivial or misguided, but is a constitutive dimension of the human experience of cultural change.

The medial turn

"Media determine our situation." With this opening to *Gramophone Film Typewriter* (1999), German "media scientist" Friedrich Kittler issued a challenge that has profoundly impacted research in literary and cultural studies, including work in science and technology studies. Put succinctly, Kittler's challenge runs something like this: pursue a form of analysis that, while methodologically prohibited from accounting for its material conditions, nevertheless acknowledges such conditions and brings these to bear on the outcome of analysis.

Kittler's work, more than anyone else's, serves to set out the stakes of what we might call the "medial turn" in research in the humanities. Specifically, his work is attuned both to the constraints that media places on hermeneutics, that is, on the claims we can make in the name of meaning and the signified, and also to the new potentialities for exploration that media makes possible, as, for example, when informatic noise in a given domain of material inscription becomes generative of meanings, new effects of sense. Kittler's paradigmatic status as the inaugurator of the "medial turn" lies at the heart of David Wellbery's characterization of the contribution made by his seminal text, *Discourse Networks 1800/1900* (Kittler 1990). In his helpful introduction to the 1990 translation of that text (originally published in 1985), Wellbery compellingly demonstrates how Kittler's particular remix of the poststructuralism of Derrida, Lacan, and Foucault managed to transform what, in the Anglo-American context, had become a predominately negative-critical methodology into a "positive research program for a post-hermeneutic criticism" (Wellbery 1990: xii). Wellbery enumerates three components of this program – the presuppositions of "exteriority," "mediality," and "corporeality" – which together displace the question of subjective agency in favor of the cultural inscription ("training") of bodies.

At the very core of the medial turn exemplified by Kittler's *Discourse Networks* project is a more general positive research program that would open the post-hermeneutic focus on materiality to effects far distant from the kinds of meaning effects most commonly associated with literary study and analysis (whether traditional or deconstructive). What characterizes this general program is the interference of the materiality of media not simply with hermeneutics and meaning effects, but also with the functioning of media systems themselves. That is, in the wake of the generalized medial turn, the cultural critic knows that the basis of her knowledge – a given, concretely material media system – is beyond the grasp of that knowledge. In this sense, the generalized medial turn marks a certain critical inversion of what might well be taken as its proximate source – namely Foucault's archaeology of knowledge, and its notion that what can be said at any moment in history (the "sayable") is relative to an archived set of potential statements (Foucault 1972).

In supplementing Foucault's historical archive with a concrete exploration of mediatic materiality, Kittler radicalizes the pre-hermeneutic dimensions of Foucault's work in a way that bears decisive significance for contemporary media theory. In effect, Kittler's intervention institutes a fundamental division between two types of approach to media: one that explores the experiential dimension of media, which remains keyed to the ratios of human perception and sensation, and another that excavates the technical logics of media, logics which – for Kittler at least – are only contingently and impermanently synchronized with those subjective ratios. What results from this division is a permanent oscillation between the materiality and the phenomenality of media. While the poles of this oscillation are not necessarily incompatible, the recognition of that constitutive difference does seem to impose the necessity for a perspectival shift, such that the media critic must choose whether to foreground the infrastructure con-ditioning experience (media materiality) or the experience thereby realized.

This oscillation comprises the fundamental theoretical challenge that media poses to the cultural theorist. The challenge is more than simply an updating for our media age of literary deconstruction – which, with *its* many oscillations, troubled the possibility for any simple meaning claims and identity formations. This mediatic oscillation comprises something of a new transcendental structure of experience, although one that – anchored as it is in concrete technologies – disturbs the traditional division between transcendental and empirical. On this score it resembles both Foucault's historical a priori and Deleuze's "transcendental empiricism" (Foucault 1972; Deleuze 1995). Like them, it prof-fers the conditions for real experience without exceeding the domain of experi-ence, without being, properly speaking, transcendental at all (in the Kantian sense of being rooted in pure reason rather than in phenomenal perception). As the accomplishment of the generalized medial turn, media theory marks the chance for us to overcome the empirical–transcendental divide that has structured Western thought about technics.

It is precisely because media contaminates thinking at the same time as it makes thinking possible that we can affirm (with, but also perhaps against, Kittler) that media determines our situation: by giving the empirical–technical infrastructure for thought, by specifying a certain technical materiality for the possibility of thinking, media remains an ineliminable, if unthematizable, aspect of the experience that gives rise to thought. This revelation of media's funda-mental irreducibility underscores the insufficiency of any theoretical stance that fails to interrogate the oscillation itself, that remains content to treat it solely and simply as a radical challenge to hermeneutics and not as the very configuration of the admittedly complex condition for whatever hermeneutics might be in our world today. In seeking to interrogate this oscillation here, I shall make an effort to address both the theoretical and the historical dimensions of media, even though, in the end, these will prove inseparable, if not in fact indistinguishable, from one another. For if, in one sense, the particular opportunity just outlined for contemporary theory stems from the specific state of media today, it also marks an "originary" correlation of technics and thought, one that comes "before" history and that is, for this very reason, necessarily expressed by history, by the history of technics as much as that of thinking.

The discipline of media studies

Media studies emerges as a distinct academic and cultural enterprise at or around the moment when it becomes possible to speak of media in the collective singular, which is equally to say, as something other and indeed more than a simple accumulation of individual mediums, of divergent media contents. If we rely on the *Oxford English Dictionary*, this moment can be pinpointed to the mid-1960s and is exemplified by writer Kingsley Amis's observation that "the treatment of *media* as a singular noun … is spreading into the upper cultural strata" (Amis 1966). Amis's observation serves perfectly to invoke Canadian media theorist Marshall McLuhan. For at the very heart of McLuhan's project – arguably the first and still most influential effort to articulate a comprehensive theory of media – is a displacement of media-in-the-plural with a concept of media as a singular collective: the passage from content to medium, from a plurality of media contents to a quasi-autonomous concept of media. In his *Understanding Media* (1964), McLuhan famously equated the medium and the message; he defined the message (or "meaning") *as* the medium itself. In this way, McLuhan meant to catalyze a conceptual shift from the content of a message to its technical form.

From McLuhan's standpoint, a medium impacts on human experience and society not primarily through the content that it mediates, but rather through its formal, i.e., technical, properties as a medium. McLuhan's preferred example, in a central section of *Understanding Media*, is the light bulb, which, despite having no content of its own aside from the light it sheds, profoundly impacts on social life by literally bringing light to the darkness and so extending the time of human social interaction. With his phrase "understanding media," then, McLuhan does not mean just (or primarily) understanding different individual mediums, like electricity, the automobile, the typewriter, or clothing; rather, he means something like understanding *from the perspective of media*, where media forms an abstraction (a collective singular) denoting an attentiveness to the agency of the medium in the analysis of social change.

Though some practitioners of media studies find McLuhan's marginalization of content problematic, his redirection of the study of media was foundational for media studies. McLuhan urges us to focus on media independently of any ties with content and in the process redefines media itself as content, and not just a vehicle or channel for the transmission of content. For this reason, McLuhan's approach to media has a capaciousness that can encompass the multiple and historically disjunctive origins of the term "media" as well as related terms like "medium" and "mediation."

Not surprisingly, this generalized sense of media is very much at the heart of McLuhan's conceptualization of media as "extensions of man." Indeed, by linking media – and the operation of mediation as such – to the historically changing, sensory, and perceptual "ratios" of human experience, McLuhan underscored the fundamental correlation of the human and the technical. McLuhan is the recognized source for Friedrich Kittler's media science, which, as its author suggests, can be understood as a working out of the *impossibility* of understanding media, where media (as we noted above) form the infrastructural condition of possibility for understanding itself. Indeed, for McLuhan it is the coupling of the human and the technological that holds primacy; while imbricated in myriad, complex ways, embodied human enaction and technological materiality remain two distinct forms of informatic embodiment, two distinct processes of materialization that, no matter how much they may converge, retain their respective autonomy. For McLuhan, the human body simply cannot be understood as a first or primary medium, as some posthumanist critics and artists currently propose to understand it (for example, the Australian body artist Stelarc [2010]); nor can it be relegated to the status of merely optional receiver of technically mediated information, as Kittler proposes. Rather, the body for McLuhan comprises the non-self-sufficient "ground" for all acts of mediation, including those (that is to say, the vast majority of mediations) which expand its agency beyond the "skin"; the body, in sum, is a capacity for relationality that literally requires mediation, and that, in a sense, cannot be conceptualized without it.

Media apparatuses

Prior to the invention of writing, what media scholar Walter Ong calls "primary orality" comprised the media system of culture (Ong 1982). Central to this media system was the technology of the word itself. Expressing inner thoughts and feelings in words allowed for the exteriorization of symbolic knowledge and social obligations and, as evolutionary anthropologist Terrence Deacon (1998) has convincingly demonstrated, made possible the practices of hunting and marriage. In his understanding of orality, Ong drew on the work of classicist Milman Parry, who had demonstrated how the poetic schemas of the *Iliad* and the *Odyssey* were constructed to manage the informational needs of oral Greek society: oral epic foregrounded poetic patterns in ways that made recall easier and the memorization of long passages possible (Parry 1971).

The invention of writing did not eliminate orality in one blow, however, and the history of literacy in Western culture is an object lesson in how technical innovation depends upon complex social factors. In his study of writing in the Greek period, classicist Eric Havelock (1982) showed how the passage from an oral to a literate culture was mediated by a scribal culture in which only an elite subgroup of society either considered it necessary or had the opportunity to learn to read and write. And the persistence of scribal cultures beyond the Greek period – one finds such cultures in medieval Europe as well as in ancient Egypt – attests to the ubiquity of this social logic and its predominance over simple technological change. In order to conceptualize the complex social logic that characterizes the passage from oral to literate society, Ong invents the category of "residual orality" for the persistence of an "oral residue" in cultures that have been exposed to writing but that have not fully interiorized its use. Both Ong and McLuhan theorize the re-emergence of a form of orality in the electronic age – what Ong calls "secondary orality" – that by displacing the predominance of the written word partially return us to conditions of immediacy and presence that are characteristic of oral communication.

Beyond the print revolution

In *The Gutenberg Galaxy* (1962), his study immediately preceding *Understanding Media*, McLuhan focused on the transformational impact of the invention of moveable type and the print revolution it catalyzed. While McLuhan analyzed the expansion of knowledge afforded by the printed book, his central focus was on the altered form of consciousness that emerged in the wake of the printing press. According to McLuhan, the shift from manuscript culture to print culture witnessed the dissolution of sensorily distributed and integrated experience in favor of the tyranny of the visual. Other scholars, however, have eschewed McLuhan's subjective emphasis on the alienation of individual experience in order to concentrate on the profound material effects of the new medium of print. Elizabeth Eisenstein (1979) analyzed the social and political impact of the printing press as a form of standardization that afforded unprecedented capacities for storage and dissemination of information. Moving beyond McLuhan's focus on individual experience, Eisenstein convincingly demonstrated the important role that the invention of moveable type and the print revolution played in the Renaissance, the Protestant revolution, and the rise of modern science.

Eisenstein's stress on the standardization of linguistic marks that lies at the heart of the printing press anticipates the media revolution of the nineteenth century as analyzed by Kittler. For Kittler (1999), the triad of gramophone, film, and typewriter differentiated the inscription, storage, and dissemination of the various sensory fluxes – aural, visual, and linguistic – in a way that expands the standardization of print to other experiential registers. Interestingly enough, for all of these scholars, who are otherwise so different in their methodologies and commitments, the advent of digital technology promises some form of experiential reunification ranging from the utopian (McLuhan) to the dystopian (Kittler).

In *Technics and Time, 1: the fault of Epimetheus* (1998), French philosopher Bernard Stiegler transforms McLuhan's vision of media into a full-fledged philosophy of technical evolution. At the heart of Stiegler's thought is the understanding that human beings, from the very proto-origin of the human as a distinct species, have always been technically mediated. Stiegler's effort to overturn the repression of technics in Western philosophy follows in the wake of the efforts of his teacher and mentor, Jacques Derrida, to deconstruct the metaphysics of presence by way of the *essential* technicity of writing and other technologies of *différance*. As he has shown in a range of studies spanning the Platonic myth of writing discussed above (Derrida 1983) to his seminal discussion of the grammatological logic of the supplement in Jean-Jacques Rousseau (Derrida 1976), the antecedence of writing (here understood as the iterability of the mark or *grammé*) in relation to speech and concrete writing systems means that the origin of meaning is always given through *différance*, which is to say, given as a meaning effect both differing and deferred from its origin.

In his own take on Derrida's crucial concept of *arche*-writing, Stiegler insists on the necessity of thinking a history of the (technical) supplement, such that the operation of *différance* is put into a functional relation with concrete technologies of storage and transmission (see Stiegler 2002). With this move, Stiegler relativizes what he calls the "quasi-transcendental" field of *différance* or *arche*-writing in relation to the material infrastructure of its appearance and efficacy in the world at any given moment in time. Thus the paradoxical anteriority or withdrawal of any moment of origin (presence) becomes tightly bound up with the technical conditions of its belated appearance.

As the sub-title of *Technics and Time, 1* indicates, Stiegler routes his own negotiation with the figure of paradoxical origin through the crucial but neglected figure of Epimetheus in the Hesiodic myth and its legacy. In a compelling argument, he insists that the figure of Prometheus, and the dialectic of technological change it expresses, would have no meaning without the "fault" of Epimetheus, without the originary act of forgetting that left the "natural" human being naked and unprotected, in need of technical supplementation. In Stiegler's reading, what the myth expresses is the "originary technicity" of the human, the fact that human beings have always depended on and co-evolved with technologies. Drawing on paleontological studies of early flint tools, Stiegler foregrounds the fundamental correlation of the *cortex* with the *silex* (flint) as the basic characteristic of the human: from their very onset, human beings have evolved not simply genetically but culturally, which is to say, by exteriorizing their know-how and collective memory in the form of cultural artifacts and objective memory supports. This would mean, of course, that the evolution of the human can be characterized in terms of a long series of "new media revolutions": what our material history teaches us is that human beings co-evolve in correlation with the evolution of technics; the long line of once-new "new media" would simply be the index of this coevolution. In light of the complex form of human evolution ensuing from our coupling to technics (a form Stiegler dubs "epiphylogenesis," meaning evolution by other than biological means), it follows – and this is Stiegler's thesis – that human beings, in their developmental and genetic evolution, are "essentially" correlated with technical media.

Lest this account sound overly anthropocentric, as if media existed exclusively to support human evolutionary and developmental processes, it should be pointed out that media have increasingly come to converge with technical forms of inscription of experience and, ultimately, of time. As a result, they now participate in processes of technological evolution and development that, at least since the Industrial Revolution, can lay claim to some sort of qualified autonomy. More than any other critical corpus, the work of Kittler (1990, 1999) has drawn attention to this sobering reality. Kittler has articulated a history of media that moves from the monopoly on information storage long exercised by alphabetical coding to the media differentiations of the nineteenth century (photography, phonography, typewriting, cinema) and finally to the contemporary convergence of media in the form of digital code and computer processing. At the core of Kittler's media history is an appreciation for technics as a material production (a production of the real) that is *not* pre-adapted to or constrained by the sensory and perceptual thresholds of human experience.

Media and technics

A glimpse of this qualified autonomy of technics can be found in techniques for sound analysis that developed out of the phonographical revolution, which is to say, in the wake of the new medium of the gramophone. While the dominant uses of the gramophone from its invention until its recent obsolescence (and now, of course, in its afterlife) invest almost wholly in the synchrony of technical recording and human sense perception (meaning that they involve the recording and replaying of sound for human consumption), the capacity of technical sound recording to inscribe frequencies outside the range of human hearing allows for an inscription (or "symbolization") of the flux of the real that is not narrowly bound to human modes of experience. Sound inscription thus instances the break with natural language and alphabetic writing that characterizes technical recording as such: whereas the inscription of natural language operates on the discrete ordering of the alphabet, the inscription of sound operates on a far more fine-grained discretization of the sonic flux.

One technique for such discretization, Fourier analysis, symbolizes the raw flux of sound by means of intervals (so-called Fourier intervals) which periodize or code for non-periodic, innumerable frequency series. According to Kittler, what is most important about Fourier intervals – and what makes them exemplary of digital signal processing per se – is the recourse to real-number analysis (a mathematical technique encompassing the continua between whole numbers) they make necessary. Generalizing from the technicalities of Kittler's discussion, we can say that high-frequency analysis "symbolizes" the flux of the real (in the Lacanian sense) on the matrix of real numbers (whereas the alphabet does it on the matrix of natural language). To say this is to suggest that the technical inscription of sound symbolizes the real for systems other than human sense perception, and indeed this is what, for Kittler, makes it exemplary of the operation of the computer as such.

As the generalization of an operation (machinic symbolization) that could (and did) remain marginal until its widespread social proliferation, the computer marks a certain dissociation of media from technics. Arguably for the first time in history, the technical infrastructure of media is no longer homologous with its surface appearance. As distinct from phonography, where the grooves of a record graphically reproduce the frequency ranges of humanly perceivable sound, and from film, where the inscription of light on a sensitive surface reproduces what is visible to the human eye, properly computational media involve no direct correlation between technical storage and human sense perception. What we see on the computer screen (or any other interface) and what we hear on the digital player (or other interface) is not related by visible or sonic analogy to the data that is processed in the computer or digital device. Indeed, as the work of some digital media artists has shown, the very same digital data can be output in different registers, thus yielding very different media experiences. Pioneering new media theorist Lev Manovich (2001) has described this unique situation in terms of a divide between the media surface and the underlying code:

> New media in general can be thought of as consisting of two distinct layers – the "cultural layer" and the "computer layer." ... Because new media is created on computers, distributed via computers, and stored and archived on computers, the logic of a computer can be expected to significantly influence the traditional cultural logic of media; that is, we may expect that the computer layer will affect the cultural layer. The ways in which the computer models the world, represents data, and allows us to operate on it; the key operations behind all computer programs (such as search, match, sort, and filter); the conventions of HCI – in short, what can be called the computer's ontology,

epistemology, and pragmatics – influence the cultural layer of new media, its organization, its emerging genres, its contents.

(Manovich 2001: 46)

Manovich situates the conjunction in computational media of surface and code as the legacy of two converging, yet hitherto distinct cultural traditions, of media and of computation. According to Manovich, these two traditions are held together by the cultural dominance of the cinematic metaphor, which has largely dictated how digital data has been transposed into readily consumable media forms.

While this may be (or may have been) an appropriate analysis of the empirical deployment of computational media, it doesn't begin to tap the potential that the computer holds for fundamentally remapping our experience of space and time (see Hansen 2004). Taking stock of the massive role played by computational processes in creating the infrastructure for experience today, it becomes difficult to ignore the reality that we depend on regimes of technical mediation, what geographer Nigel Thrift (2004) has called the "technological unconscious," that not only exceed our attention but that remain fundamentally unfathomable by us. Put another way, the forms of media – visual, aural, tactile – through which we construct information about our universe are no longer homologous with the actual materialities, the temporal fluxes, that they mediate. While these media forms may still adequately capture the flux of our experience (although recent studies in the fine-scale temporal processes of cognition suggest that in fact this may not be the case), they – like the experiences they inscribe – are only indirectly coupled to the underlying computational processes supporting them. In light of this computational disjunction of technics and media, we must differentiate and hold separate two distinct functions of media: on the one hand, to exteriorize human experience in durable, repeatable, and hence transmissible form (the traditional function of media); and on the other, to mediate for human experience the non- (or proto-)phenomenological, fine-scale temporal computational processes that increasingly make up the infrastructure conditioning all experience in our world today. What is mediated in both cases is, to be sure, human experience, but according to two distinct programs: for whereas media in the first, traditional sense mediates human experience itself (its content is that experience), media in the second sense mediates the technical conditions that make possible such experience – the "transcendental technicity" underlying real experience in our world today.

With this observation, we return to our point of theoretical departure, namely the certain radicalization that I located in Kittler's work once it is generalized as the basis for a "medial turn" in cultural studies. In concluding this brief overview, let me propose that media studies rehabilitates understanding from Kittler's anti-hermeneutical critique precisely by resituating it: what is to be understood is not media in the plural, but media in the singular; and it is by understanding media in the singular – which is to say, by reconceptualizing understanding from the perspective of media – that we will discover ways to characterize the impact of media in the plural. Whether they can be considered to be modes of understanding in themselves, such characterizations will involve much more than a unidimensional account of the technics of a given medium. Indeed, precisely by pursuing a generalization of technics along the lines suggested by Stiegler (as the correlate of human life), such characterizations necessarily involve mediations among domains that are all too often and all too artificially dissociated. That these mediations themselves require yet another kind of mediation – critical mediation – is the very burden of McLuhan's abiding injunction to understand from the perspective of media. From this perspective, media do not so much *determine* our situation: they *are* our situation.

Bibliography

Amis, K. (1996), cited in *OED* entry on "media."

Deacon, T. (1998) *The Symbolic Species; the co-evolution of language and the brain*, New York: W.W. Norton.

Deleuze, G. (1995) *Difference and Repetition*, trans. P. Patton, New York: Columbia University Press.

Derrida, J. (1976) *Of Grammatology*, trans. G. Spivak, Baltimore: Johns Hopkins University Press.

——(1983) "Plato's pharmacy," in *Dissemination*, trans. B. Johnson, Chicago: University of Chicago Press, pp. 66–171.

Eisenstein, E. (1979) *The Printing Press as an Agent of Change*, Cambridge: Cambridge University Press.

Foucault, M. (1972) *The Archaeology of Knowledge and the Discourse on Language*, trans. A. Sheridan, New York: Pantheon Books.

Hansen, M.B.N. (2004) *New Philosophy for New Media*, Cambridge, Mass.: MIT Press.

Havelock, E. (1982) *Preface to Plato*, Cambridge, Mass.: Harvard University Press.

Kittler, F. (1990) *Discourse Networks 1880/1900*, trans. M. Metteer, Stanford: Stanford University Press.

——(1999) *Gramophone Film Typewriter*, trans. G. Winthrop-Young and M. Wutz, Stanford: Stanford University Press.

Manovich, Lev (2001) *The Language of New Media*, Cambridge, Mass.: MIT Press.

McLuhan, M. (1962) *The Gutenberg Galaxy: the making of typographic man*, Toronto: University of Toronto Press.

——(1964) *Understanding Media: the extensions of man*, New York: New American Library.

Ong, W.J. (1982) *Orality and Literacy: the technologizing of the word*, New York: Routledge.

Parry, M. (1971) *The Making of Homeric Verse: the collected papers of Milman Parry*, ed. A. Parry, Oxford: Oxford University Press.

Plato (1995) *Phaedrus*, trans. A. Nehamas and P. Woodruff, Indianapolis: Hackett.

Stelarc (2010). "Stelarc." Online. Available HTTP: <http://www.stelarc.va.com.au> (accessed 12 January 2010).

Stiegler, B. (1998) *Technics and Time, 1: the fault of Epimetheus*, trans. R. Beardsworth and G. Collins, Stanford: Stanford University Press.

——(2002) "Derrida and technology: fidelity at the limits of deconstruction and the prosthesis of faith," in T. Cohen (ed.) *Jacques Derrida and the Humanities: a critical reader*, Cambridge: Cambridge University Press, pp. 238–70.

Thrift, N. (2004) "Remembering the technological unconscious by foregrounding knowledges of position," *Environment and Planning D: Society and Space*, 22(1): 175–90.

Wellbery, D. (1990) "Foreword," in Kittler 1990: pp. vii–xxxiii.

31
PHILOSOPHY OF SCIENCE

Alfred Nordmann

Handbooks and companions are literary genres of their own and usually pretend to provide a review of theory or a survey of a field of inquiry. One should expect, therefore, that a community of scholars has taken an interest in the relation of philosophy of science to literature, or at least in the contributions by philosophers of science to an understanding of the relation of literature and science. Interestingly, this is not the case. The present chapter thus takes poetic license to imagine a field of inquiry that is not entirely unpopulated but wide open and that offers room for various kinds of inquiry. Rather than collect together isolated contributions to this field of inquiry, it picks some of them in a rather eclectic manner and only to hint at further work that could be done along these lines. And instead of giving a complete account of the sparse activities in the open field, it issues an invitation for others to enter, and it does this by highlighting some of the more general research projects that might be pursued there.

Philosophy of science

This is not the place to define "philosophy of science." Not even philosophers of science try to do this, let alone the society for the History of the Philosophy of Science (HOPOS). This society considers all reflections on the principles and methods, teachings and practices of science as a kind of philosophy of science, especially if these reflections are performed by certified scientists or philosophers. Accordingly, one might talk about Aristotle's or Descartes's, Lavoisier's or Newton's philosophy of science; or what the Ptolemeans meant by "saving the phenomena" as a question about their largely implicit philosophy of science. On this approach, the relation of philosophy of science to literature becomes indistinguishable from "philosophy and literature" more generally, including the many ways in which conceptions of nature are engaged by literary practice.

"Philosophy of science" is also the name for a branch of philosophy, however, and this branch of philosophy originated under rather specific conditions towards the end of the nineteenth century. At that time, the claims of philosophy to offer a scientific or absolute grounding of the sciences came apart at the seams. First, scientists were put off by such claims, especially those associated with the powerful philosophy of Hegel. Second, within the most advanced philosophical and scientific traditions of the nineteenth century there came the realization that a science of metaphysics is not possible. After Immanuel Kant had proposed that Newton's laws articulated the basic and necessary suppositions that make any knowledge of nature or scientific experience possible, and after the physiology of the senses looked at such necessary conditions from an empirical point of view, scientists and philosophers recognized that the formulation and adoption of any theory involved acts of judgment that could not be eliminated from accounts of science. This recognition came under the name of "conventionalism" or "under-determination of theories by evidence": scientists must choose a geometry within which to represent the facts, they can choose a formulation of mechanics that does not include "force" or "energy," and they routinely choose conventions that guide their work in the name of simplicity, descriptive faithfulness, or consistency. Third, these acts of judgment or elements of choice foreground that scientists are not solitary thinkers who produce evidence and then draw logical conclusions, but that there is a scientific community. Hence, the methods of science are no longer just methods of doing and thinking, they are methods for securing agreement, and thereby for an "intersubjective" kind of objectivity. And thus arose among philosopher-scientists like Hermann von Helmholtz, William Whewell, Heinrich Hertz, Ernst Mach, Henri Poincaré, Pierre Duhem, Emile Meyerson, Karl Pearson, or Charles Sanders Peirce a philosophy of science that is distinct from theory of knowledge, philosophy of nature, ontology, or logic. It is concerned with a peculiar form of public reasoning and the rationality of scientific procedure. It is for this philosophy of science – the highly disciplined investigation mostly of the natural sciences – that we now ask about its relation to literature.

Resonance

The most straightforward question always appears to be the one concerning influence: Where did philosophy of science leave its imprint on the manner of writing? On the face of it, this question invites only anecdotal answers and no sustained program of research. One might look for the occasional novel that features a philosopher of science. In a similar spirit of eclecticism, one might wish to reconstruct from portraits of science and of scientists how images of science are shaped by philosophies of science. Do we see scientists in the image of an inductivist philosophy of science, as tireless collectors of evidence? Do we see them along the lines of Karl Popper's falsificationism, as acerbic critical minds who question all human belief? Or do we see unglamorous "normal scientists" who seek to find just another small piece of the puzzle in the course of articulating a Kuhnian paradigm?

Beyond the question of influence as the reappearance of people and ideas in another setting, there is the question of how literary productions and images of objectivity rely on a methodology that is informed by philosophical views of scientific method. Thomas Bernhard's novel *Wittgenstein's Nephew*, for example, is all Thomas Bernhard and very little Ludwig Wittgenstein. To be sure, Bernhard evokes the eccentric life of Wittgenstein and the culture that produced not only Wittgenstein and the Vienna circle of philosophers of science but also himself, a writer presumably of equal stature (Bernhard 1989). In contrast, David Markson's *Wittgenstein's Mistress* does not explain the curious title of the book at all – it features neither Wittgenstein nor the mistress he never had – and yet there is an uncanny presence of Wittgenstein in the sequence of remarks that consider in their obliquely factual barrenness a world that signifies its own limits and its own end (Markson 1990). Only the latter novel thus invites the challenge to characterize the influence of a philosophy of science on its literary method.[1]

Such questions about the indebtedness of literary method to philosophical accounts of scientific method have been brought to the work of Robert Musil and Bertolt Brecht.[2] Musil is a particularly obvious case in that he wrote a dissertation on Ernst Mach and thus was himself a certified philosopher of science at least for a period in his life (Musil 1982). Much of the *Man without Qualities* revolves around Mach's proposal that science produces a representation of the facts by constructions of analogy. This "picturing without resemblance" amalgamates truth and untruth and produces accurate determinations of reality by means of the imagination (Schelling 1970; Moser 1984; Frank 1988). The famous opening lines of the book as well as the intellectual regime of *Young Törless* announce this probing of a kind of positivism (Arvon 1970; Luserke 1987; Musil 1982, 1995; Mehigan 1997; Smith 2000; also Barnouw 1978).

Brecht constantly took up and reworked philosophical ideas to bolster his theatrical method and he therefore took a considerable interest in the new, anti-Aristotelian logic that developed just prior to his own anti-Aristotelian poetics (Danneberg 1996; Danneberg and Müller 1990; Sautter 1995; Giles 1997). Years later, he turned to the philosopher of science Hans Reichenbach for advice about *Galileo Galilei*, a play which probably informed a radical revisioning of science in Paul Feyerabend's *Against Method* (Feyerabend 1988; but see Jungius 2000).[3] Indeed, Feyerabend's philosophy of science may be the one place where the direction of influence has been reversed and where a literary strategy informed notions of scientific rationality. Feyerabend's "anarchist" or "Dadaist" theory of knowledge proposes anti-methodical methods such as the principle of counter-induction, and these methods may well have drawn inspiration from Brecht's "Five Difficulties of Writing Down the Truth" which prepared the ground for the Galileo play (Brecht 1966; cf. Dusek 1998; Feyerabend 1967).

Difference

"All that philosophy can hope to accomplish is to make poetry and science complementary, to unite them as two well-defined opposites." These words summarize Gaston Bachelard's work on the scientific spirit and the poetic imagination (Bachelard 1987: 2; see also Gaudin 1971). They also offer a different perspective on the relation of philosophy of science and literature – different philosophies of science construe the difference between science and literature differently. And surprisingly, perhaps, few philosophies of science fortify the boundary between them as well as does Bachelard's: beholden to first impressions, to principles of sympathy and analogy, the work of the imagination needs to be denied by a scientific spirit that inexorably drives a wedge between rationality and intuition (Tiles 1984; McAllester 1989; Chimisso 2001).

The boundary between poetic imagination and scientific rationalization proves far more porous than first meets the eye, especially in the accounts offered by the logical empiricists of the Vienna Circle. Rudolf Carnap's 1932 essay "The Elimination of Metaphysics through Logical Analysis of Language" is known for drawing a sharp divide between the language of science, with its clarity of meaning, and all other forms of expression that are lumped together as metaphysics, poetry, music, and art. It sounds like an ultimate denigration, then, when in this essay Carnap likens Heidegger's metaphysics to poetry (Carnap 1959).[4] Yet this is the same Rudolf Carnap who was read and to some extent appropriated by Brecht, and the same Rudolf Carnap who was influenced by Ludwig Wittgenstein and who admired Friedrich Nietzsche's critique of metaphysics – two authors who adopted literary strategies to expose the meaninglessness of certain uses of language.

Wittgenstein's, Nietzsche's, and perhaps also Carnap's critiques of language may well be compatible with a certain respect for the ineffable, and the association of metaphysics with poetry may therefore amount to a necessary division of labor (Friedman 2000; Gabriel 2003). According to logical empiricism and in contrast to Bachelard, science in the sphere of empirical meaningfulness and the so-called context of justification cannot say "no" to the imagination, quite simply because science and imagination don't speak the same language. Moreover, the scientifically undisciplined and ungrammatical language of metaphysics, speculation, and imagination may well play a significant role in the context of discovery. This division of labor between "context of discovery" and "context of justification" is most pronounced in the works of Hans Reichenbach and Karl Popper (Reichenbach 1938; Popper 1959). It does not coincide with Bachelard's distinction between poetry and science but differentiates a hedonistic sphere in which everything is permitted from a highly disciplined sphere that is governed by criteria of meaningfulness and in which science becomes scientific. By speaking about science, then, these philosophers of science also invoke the unspeakable context in which scientific ideas originate.[5]

The examples of Bachelard and Carnap suggest that philosophy of science is engaged in "boundary work" not just in respect to science and non-science in general, but on behalf of science and literature in particular (Gieryn 1983).[6] This becomes even more evident in recent decades, though the boundary work is still performed mostly implicitly. The notion of "style" is one arena where this work takes place, the notion of "objectivity" is another, and the topic of "fiction" is a third.

With Thomas Kuhn's philosophy of science and its proliferation of paradigms, the question arose whether there is a close affinity between literary styles and scientific paradigms as schemes of thought and practice that organize phenomena and orient perception. Kuhn himself raised the question, and since then it more or less silently accompanied discussions of styles of scientific reasoning (Kuhn 1977; Hacking 1992; Crombie 1995; Kwa 2005). Similarly, a historical understanding of "objectivity" weakened its ties to representational truth. The trained eye of scientific genius, impersonal and mechanical procedures, and the achievement literally of phenomena, capabilities, and artifacts at various times represent the accomplishment of objectivity – and science shares this accomplishment with literature and the arts (Galison 1999; Daston and Galison 2007). Finally, recent discussions of scientific modeling foreground the role of fictions in science. Inspired in part by Hans Vaihinger's *Philosophy of 'As If'*, this discussion revolves around the idea that scientific models are not so much true isomorphic representations, but serve rather as substitutes of reality that are fictitiously taken for the real thing in order to allow for some useful conceptual and exploratory work (Vaihinger 1924; Fine 1993; French 2003; Nordmann 2006; Suárez 2008). Just as a literary character like Hamlet serves inquiries into questions of knowledge and action, so a fictional molecule like "siligen" might enable the construction of a predictively successful multi-scale model (Winsberg 2006).

Valorization

None of this boundary work on the difference between science and literature establishes any categorical distinction between the two, and if philosophers of science have been diffident about openly engaging in this boundary work, this is probably because they do not wish to be caught assuming a categorical distinction that essentializes science and literature and that merely needs to be articulated. By attempting to distinguish, instead, between science and pseudo-science, meaningful and meaningless language, public and private ways of knowing, the philosophy of science does not delimit the scientific in contrast to the literary. It valorizes a certain mode of speaking and writing or of representing the world, and leaves it up to literature and the arts as to what extent they appropriate these modes for their own purposes. Philosophy of science has thus propagated at various times models of proper prose, and with these norms of representation it intervenes in the domain of the literary.

Such interventions and the responsiveness to them in the literary world cannot be detailed here. One or two suggestions or reminders must suffice. "What can be said at all, can be said clearly" is a stylistic injunction by Wittgenstein that has guided the philosophy of science in two ways: it set an ambitious goal, namely to clearly specify criteria of clarity, and it shaped philosophy of science as an academic field by producing patterns of exclusion and inclusion (Wittgenstein 1922: Preface).[7] Initially, this ambitious goal was to be met by constructing or reconstructing a language of science in which all sentences are either logical or empirical and in which it is possible to specify for every empirical sentence the exact conditions under which it is true or false. A related approach consisted in building up the language of scientific theory from a language of sense data which objectifies perceptions and subjects them to collective scrutiny: "Otto's protocol at 3:17 o'clock [Otto's speech-thinking at 3:16 o'clock was: (at 3:15 o'clock there was a table in the room perceived by Otto)]" (Neurath 1983). When Otto Neurath called in 1932 for the formulation of such protocol statements, the stylistic injunction by philosophers of science proved linguistically innovative – it is a far cry from reconstructing merely the bland impersonal language of the average scientific research publication.

Starting with Heinrich Hertz's rigorous elimination from language of the metaphysically obscure conceptions of "force" and "cause and effect" (Hertz 1895) and with Ernst Mach's *Analysis of Sensations* (1916), philosophers of science sought to explicate what remains implicit in conventional discourse and to impersonalize as much as possible perception and processes of reasoning. Although this radical program of a metaphysical cleansing of language came to an end along with the rise of a more historicist philosophy of science in the 1960s, it reverberates in the still-prevailing idea that a shared paradigm affords literalness and that scientists always need to interpret data but never need to interpret words (Nordmann 2008). It would be to short-change philosophy of science if one took this idea as a sign of naïveté. It is at this point where even the most descriptive and historicist philosopher advocates a linguistic norm, namely that a genuine community of speakers can be created as one joins a language game that constitutes shared meanings through shared practices. This is a norm that is sometimes taken up and sometimes undermined by literary strategies.

A genre of its own

Though few philosophers of science – Bachelard being the most notable exception – propose theories about the relation of literature and science or theories about literary aspects of science, they are not neutral toward questions of language. In the name of science, they intervene in the literary sphere with a critique of language and with more or less explicit norms of representation.

Writers who undertake a critique of language are bound to be highly self-conscious about their own use of language. When Wittgenstein found that only the language of science and other descriptive sentences are meaningful, he drew the conclusion that this excludes his own philosophical writing: "My sentences elucidate through this: who understands me recognizes them in the end as nonsensical" (Wittgenstein 1922: 6.54). Wittgenstein remains an exception, of course, and while many philosophers of science follow the genre conventions enforced by *Philosophy of Science* and other journals, they don't appear to be terribly self-conscious about their own use of language. And yet, it may well be worthwhile to look at this mainstreamed and canonical philosophy of science as a genre of its own which emerged from the struggle to reflect science in a scientific idiom.

There are three literary forms, in particular, which may have shaped this genre: the formal system, the dialogue, and the aphorism. The formal system is an inheritance of rationalism and aims to display an architectonic of concepts or hierarchy of principles – in rational reconstructions of bodies of theory or of the choices made by scientists. In contrast, the genealogy of the aphorism refers in a twofold manner to empiricism. First, it can be traced from Francis Bacon via the eighteenth-century physicist Georg Christoph Lichtenberg, romanticist *Naturphilosophie*, the philosophers Arthur Schopenhauer and Friedrich Nietzsche at least to Ludwig Wittgenstein. Second, the poignant brevity of the aphorism corresponds to the poignant saliency of the scientific fact. The dramatic appearance of a fact on the stage of an experiment is supposed to have the rhetorical force of dispelling the doubt of skeptics. The aphorism works in a similar way in that it presents a thought solely for its power to unsettle belief or to suggest a possibility of reasoning (Baird and Nordmann 1994; Daston 2001). The aphoristic mode survives only as a rhetorical gesture in mainstream philosophy of science and often enough in close association with the dialogue and the trading back and forth of striking examples and counterexamples. The implicit and explicit dialogue becomes the preferred mode of writing for the later Wittgenstein (but see Wittgenstein 1922: 6.53); it is taken up, for example, by Imre Lakatos (1976) and Paul Feyerabend (1991). Since these dialogues are not designed to elicit truth but, rather, to explore an impasse between equally plausible, perhaps undecidable positions, it may be difficult to construct a simple genealogy all the way back to Galileo, or even to Socrates.

What the formal system, the dialogue, and the aphorism have in common is that they are self-limiting: they constrain linguistic expressions in such a way that they cannot silently advance a substantive metaphysical view. They permit unselfconscious formulations that are put forward as objectified linguistic artifacts that stand ready to be countered and qualified, and which therefore do not require a reflective stance or a meta-language in which the philosophy of science might critique itself.[8] This, then, might be a very tentative character-ization of philosophy of science as a literary genre of its own: the scientific possibility of writing unselfconsciously and yet not dogmatically is taken up at least by that philosophy of science which aims to reflect science without disrupting it or making it self-conscious. A literary analysis of styles of writing by such philosophers of science will therefore have to contend with this semblance of transparency as their inconspicuous beginning (Gabriel 2001; Schildknecht 2002).

Imagining philosophies of science

After asking whether philosophy of science might represent a literary genre in its own right, we can finally turn the tables and ask whether writers who imagine a literary methodology for producing knowledge or who imagine fictitious sciences and scientists are thereby also imagining alternative philosophies of science. The challenge to reflect the relation of philosophy of science and literature is thereby returned to those who draw on the literary imagination to question the hege-mony of the sciences. As one might imagine, the philosophy of science itself has been rather oblivious to the construction of alternative sciences and alternate philosophies of science. Thus, philosophers of science did not respond to the brilliant and elaborate presentation by Alfred Jarry and his followers of 'pataphysics as the science that searches the laws that govern the exceptions (Shattuck and Taylor 1960; Bök 2002; Ferentschik 2006). The most notable exception to this is the persistent challenge to the laboratory sciences and their mode of causal analysis by an alternative conception of science that remains associated with Johann Wolfgang von Goethe. To be sure, his morphological method of revealing organizing principles by arranging series of phenomena failed to displace Newtonian physics, especially his *Optics*. Most philosophers of science consider this failure of Goethe's theory of colors reason enough not to take it seriously. However, to the extent that German scientists in the nineteenth and twentieth centuries remained deeply attached to Goethe as a literary figure and cultural icon, his views on science lived on and surfaced especially in the so-called life sciences. They have experienced a renaissance of sorts in the recent morphological turn of evolutionary theorists (Richards 2002).

Goethe, of course, was dead serious about his claim to be a natural scientist as well as a literary giant. At the intersection of philosophy of science and literature, what should be taken seriously instead is the dead-pan seriousness of the 'pataphysicians and of other quasi-scientific methods claiming alternative forms of objective knowledge.[9] This can bring to light the madness in the method of science and perhaps the madness in the particular way in which philosophers of science are taking science seriously. It can also bring to light, however, the peculiarly illuminating delight of scientific rigor as it extends out from the sciences via philosophy of science to philosophy and a certain disciplined manner of writing and thinking.

Notes

1 While it is a bit of a stretch to consider Ludwig Wittgenstein a philosopher of science, his early *Tractatus Logico-Philosophicus* was enormously influential on philosophy of science, and Wittgenstein engaged in the 1920s in a series of conversations with members of the Vienna Circle (Waismann 1979). As such, literary treatments of Ludwig Wittgenstein might serve as a good point of comparison – the biographical novel by Bruce Duffy (1987), the crime novels by Philip Kerr (1993) and Heinrich Steinfest (2004), the biographical and philosophical works by Iris Murdoch (1954) and W.G. Sebald (2001), and various other literary works. Beyond that, of course, there are the films by Peter Forgács (1992) and Derek Jarman (Eagleton and Jarman 1993), and the essays, exhibitions, and installations by conceptual artist Joseph Kosuth (1989).

2 Many other authors deserve to be considered in this light, for example, Hermann Broch, Alain Robbe-Grillet, Max Frisch, Hans Magnus Enzensberger, William Vollmann, or Michel Houllebecq. If it appears that German-speaking authors are featured very prominently in this text, this is largely due to the fact that the most influential group of philosophers of science were deeply entrenched in Viennese and German culture until their emigration to the United States (compare Reisch 2005).

3 In his autobiography, Feyerabend reflects his ambiguous relation to Brecht (Feyerabend 1995: 18, 73, and 180).

4 Like Wittgenstein, Martin Heidegger can hardly be considered a philosopher of science in the narrow sense of the term, though he offers a rather fully developed theory of modern science. Ironically, perhaps, it also considers modern science in contrast to poetry – like poetry, science is a bringing forth and revealing of truth, but unlike poetry it considers nature a calculable system of forces that are standing in reserve to be commandeered in experimentation and technological application (Heidegger 1977).

5 A less generous and less differentiated charge against "nonsense" was raised in the context of the so-called "Science Wars." These began with a literary intervention by a physicist, namely a clever parody of a particular style of writing about physics. This approach to physics was to be exposed as obscurantist, metaphysical, and nonsensical. Here, no accommodations were made for the rightful place of this kind of writing, even though the hoax worked only because the initial parody was intelligible on its own terms (Sokal 1996; Sokal and Bricmont 1999).

6 A term with considerable currency in contemporary science studies and cultural studies, "boundary work" was coined to describe one of the central concerns of the philosophy of science, namely to offer a demarcation criterion to distinguish science from pseudoscience. Karl Popper famously suggested that the falsifiability of genuinely scientific hypotheses affords such a criterion (Popper 1959).

7 Paradoxically, perhaps, these patterns led to the virtual exclusion of Wittgenstein as a philosopher of science. The flagship journal *Philosophy of Science* demonstrates the desired clarity of prose in the most exemplary and exclusive fashion (even today, for example, its readers might get the impression that scientists produce text only and hardly rely on visualizations). In more than sixty years, only one contribution (on the philosophy of mathematics) featured Wittgenstein in the title and as an authoritative reference. Despite his vigorous celebration of scientific rationality, Gaston Bachelard has also been excluded from a philosophy of science that rallies around clarity as a stylistic norm.

8 Within the philosophy of science, reflection on its own language came to the fore, especially with the question whether it speaks in a meta-language about the language of science or whether as a science of science it must reject the very idea of a meta-language. This debate has never been settled nor does it continue today – it withered away with the aspirations of logical empiricism.

9 Gustave Flaubert's *Bouvard and Pecuchet* comes to mind, the work of Jorge Luis Borges, Alain Robbes-Grillet, Alexander Kluge, or William Vollmann – to name but a few.

Bibliography

Arvon, H. (1970) "Robert Musil und der Positivismus," in K. Dinklage (ed.) *Robert Musil: Studien zu seinem Werk*, Reinbek: Rowohlt Verlag, pp. 200–13.

Bachelard, G. (1987) *The Psychoanalysis of Fire*, Boston, Mass.: Beacon Press.

Baird, D. and Nordmann, A. (1994) "Facts-well-put," *British Journal for the Philosophy of Science*, 45: 37–77.

Barnouw, D. (1978) "Skepticism as a literary mode: David Hume and Robert Musil," *Modern Language Notes*, 93(5): 852–70.

Bernhard, T. (1989) *Wittgenstein's Nephew*, New York: Knopf.

Bök, C. (2002) '*Pataphysics: the poetics of an imaginary science*, Evanston: Northwestern University Press.

Brecht, B. (1966) "Writing the truth: five difficulties," in E. Bentley (ed.) *Bertolt Brecht: Galileo*, New York: Grove, pp. 133–50.

Carnap, R. (1959) "The elimination of metaphysics through analysis of language," in A.J. Ayer (ed.) *Logical Positivism*, New York: Free Press, pp. 60–81.

Chimisso, C. (2001) *Gastomn Bachelard: critic of science and the imagination*, New York: Routledge.

Crombie, A. (1995) *Styles of Scientific Thinking in the European Tradition: the history of argument and explanation especially in the mathematical and biomedical sciences and arts*, London: Gerald Duckworth.

Danneberg, L. (1996) "Brecht's reception of locigal empiricism," *Deutsche Zeitschrift für Philosophie*, 44(3): 363–87.

——and Müller, H. (1990) "Brecht and logical positivism," in M. Silberman (ed.) *Essays on Brecht (Brecht Yearbook 15)*, Madison: University of Wisconsin, pp. 151–63.

Daston, L. (2001) "Perché i fatti sono brevi? [Why are facts short?]," *Quaderni storici*, 108: 745–70.

——and Galison, P. (2007) *Objectivity*, Boston, Mass.: Zone Books.

Duffy, B. (1987) *The World as I Found It*, New York: Ticknor and Fields.

Dusek, V. (1998) "Brecht and Lukács as teachers of Feyerabend and Lakatos: the Feyerabend–Lakatos debate as scientific recapitulation of the Brecht-Lukács debate," *History of the Human Sciences*, 11(2): 25–44.

Eagleton, T. and Jarman, D. (1993) *Wittgenstein: the Terry Eagleton script, the Derek Jarman film*, London: British Film Institute.

Ferentschik, K. (2006) '*Pataphysik: Versuchung des Geistes*, Berlin: Matthes & Seitz.

Feyerabend, P. (1967) "The theater as an instrument of criticism of ideologies," *Inquiry*, 10: 298–312.

——(1988) *Against Method*, London: Verso.

——(1991) *Three Dialogues on Knowledge*, Oxford: Blackwell.

——(1995) *Killing Time: the autobiography of Paul Feyerabend*, Chicago: University of Chicago Press.

Fine, A. (1993) "Fictionalism," *Midwest Studies in Philosophy*, 18: 1–18.

Forgács, P. (1992) *Wittgenstein Tractatus*, seven short films, Hungary, 52min. Online. Available HTTP: <http://www.forgacspeter.hu/english/films/Wittgeinstein+Tractatus/28> (accessed 12 October 2009).

Frank, M. (1988) "Remythisierte Erkenntniskritik (Robert Musil)," in M. Frank, *Gott im Exil: Vorlesungen über die Neue Mythologie*, Frankfurt am Main: Suhrkamp, pp. 315–32.

French, S. (2003) "A model-theoretic account of representation (or, I don't know much about art … but I know it involves isomorphism)," *Philosophy of Science*, 70: 1472–83.

Friedman, M. (2000) *A Parting of the Ways: Carnap, Cassirer, and Heidegger*, Chicago: Open Court.

Gabriel, G. (2001) *Zwischen Logik und Literatur*, Stuttgart: Metzler.

——(2003) "Carnap's 'elimination of metaphysics through logical analysis of language': a retrospective consideration of the relationship between continental and analytic philosophy," in P. Parrini, W.C. Salmon and M.H. Salmon (eds) *Logical Empiricism: historical and contemporary perspectives*, Pittsburgh: University of Pittsburgh Press.

Galison, P. (1999) "Objectivity is romantic," American Council of Learned Societies Occasional Paper No. 47: *The Humanities and the Sciences*, pp. 15–43.

Gaudin, C. (1971) *On Poetic Imagination and Reverie: selections from the works of Gaston Bachelard*, New York: The Bobbs-Merrill Company.

Gieryn, T. (1983) "Boundary-work and the demarcation of science from non-science: strains and interests in professional ideologies of scientists," *American Sociological Review*, 48: 781–95.

Giles, S. (1997) *Bertolt Brecht and Critical Theory: Marxism, modernity and the Threepenny lawsuit*, Bern: Peter Lang.

Hacking, I. (1992). "'Style' for historians and philosophers," *Studies in History and Philosophy of Science*, 23:1–20.

Heidegger, M. (1977) *The Question Concerning Technology*, New York: Harper & Row.

Hertz, H. (1895) *The Principles of Mechanics*, New York: Dover Press (1956).

Jungius, B. (2000) "Wahrnehmung und Naturerkenntnis: zur Darstellung des Galilei bei Brecht und Feyerabend," *Leviathan*, 28(1): 69–86.

Kerr, P. (1993) *A Philosophical Investigation*, New York: Farrar, Straus Giroux.

Kosuth, J. (1989) *Wittgenstein: the play of the unsayable*, Vienna: Wiener Secession.

Kuhn, T. (1977) "Comment on the relations of science and art," in *The Essential Tension*, Chicago: University of Chicago Press, pp. 340–51.

Kwa, Chunglin (2005) *De ontdekking van het weten: Een andere geschiedenis van de wetenschap*, Amsterdam: Boom [forthcoming as: *Styles of Knowing: a new history of science from ancient times to the present*, Penn State University Press].

Lakatos, I. (1976) *Proofs and Refutations*, Cambridge: Cambridge University Press.

Luserke, M. (1987) *Wirklichkeit und Möglichkeit: modaltheoretische Untersuchung zum Werk Robert Musils*, Frankfurt am Main: Peter Lang.

Mach, E. (1916) *The Analysis of Sensations, and the Relation of the Physical to the Psychical*, Chicago: Open Court.

Markson, D. (1990) *Wittgenstein's Mistress*, Elmwood Park: Dalkey Archive Press.

McAllester, M. (ed.) (1989) *The Philosophy and Poetics of Gaston Bachelard*, Washington, D.C.: University Press of America.

Mehigan, T. (1997) "Robert Musil, Ernst Mach und das Problem der Kausalität," *Deutsche Vierteljahrsschrift für Literaturwissenschaft und Geistesgeschichte*, 71: 264–88.

Moser, W. (1984) "The factual in fiction: the case of Robert Musil," *Poetics Today*, 5(2): 411–28.

Murdoch, I. (1954) *Under the Net*, New York: Viking.

Musil, R. (1982) *On Mach's Theory*, Washington, D.C.: Catholic University of America Press.

——(1982) *Young Törless*, New York: Pantheon.

——(1995) *The Man without Qualities*, New York: Knopf.

Neurath, O. (1983) "Protocol statements," in R.S. Cohen and M. Neurath (eds) *Otto Neurath: philosophical papers*, Dordrecht: Reidel, pp. 91–98.

Nordmann, A. (2006) "Collapse of distance: epistemic strategies of science and technoscience," *Danish Yearbook of Philosophy*, 41: 7–34.

——(2008) "'Getting the causal story right': hermeneutic moments in Nancy Cartwright's philosophy of science," in S. Hartmann, C. Hoefer, and L. Bovens (eds) *Nancy Cartwright's Philosophy of Science*, New York: Routledge, pp. 369–88.

Pieper, H. (2002) *Musils Philosophie: Essayismus und Dichtung im Spannungsfeld der Theorien Nietzsches und Machs*, Würzburg: Königshausen and Neumann.

Popper, K. (1959) *The Logic of Scientific Discovery*, New York: Basic Books.

Reichenbach, H. (1938) *Experience and Prediction*, Chicago: University of Chicago Press.

Reisch, G. (2005) *How the Cold War Transformed Philosophy of Science: to the icy slopes of logic*, New York: Cambridge University Press.

Richards, R. (2002) *The Romantic Conception of Life: science and philosophy in the age of Goethe*, Chicago: University of Chicago Press.

Sautter, U. (1995) "'Ich selber nehme kaum noch an einer Diskussion teil, die ich nicht sogleich in eine Diskussion über Logik verwandeln möchte': der logische Empirismus Bertolt Brechts," *Deutsche Zeitschrift für Philosophie*, 4: 687–709.

Schelling, U. (1970) "Das analogische Denken bei Robert Musil," in K. Dinklage (ed.) *Robert Musil: Studien zu seinem Werk*, Reinbek: Rowohlt Verlag, pp. 170–99.

Schildknecht, C. (2002) *Sense and Self: perspectives on nonpropositionality*, Paderborn: Mentis.

Sebald, W.G. (2001) *Austerlitz*, New York: Random House.

Shattuck, R. and Taylor, S.W. (eds) (1960) *What is 'pataphysics?*, New York: Grove Press.

Smith, P.D. (2000) "The scientist as spectator: Musil's *Törleß* and the challenge to Mach's neo-positivism," *The Germanic Review*, 75(1): 37–51.

Sokal, A. (1996) "A physicist experiments with cultural studies," *Lingua Franca*, 6(4): 62–64.

——and Bricmont, J. (1999) *Fashionable Nonsense: postmodern intellectuals' abuse of science*, New York: Picador.

Steinfest, H. (2004) *Nervöse Fische*, München: Piper.

Suárez, M. (2008) "Scientific fictions as rules of inference," in *Fictions in Science: philosophical essays on modeling and idealization*, New York: Routledge, pp. 153–78.

Tiles, M. (1984) *Bachelard: science and objectivity*, Cambridge: Cambridge University Press.

Vaihinger, H. (1924) *The Philosophy of 'As If'*, London: Kegan Paul.

Waismann, F. (1979) *Wittgenstein and the Vienna Circle: conversations recorded by Friedrich Waismann*, New York: Barnes and Noble.

Winsberg, E. (2006) "Handshaking your way to the top: inconsistency and falsification in intertheoretic reduction," *Philosophy of Science*, 73: 582–94.

Wittgenstein, L. (1922) *Tractatus Logico-Philosophicus*, London: Kegan Paul.

32

POSTHUMANISM

Neil Badmington

Posthumanism marks a careful, ongoing, overdue rethinking of the dominant humanist (or anthropocentric) account of who "we" are as human beings. In the light of posthumanist theory and culture, "we" are not who "we" once believed ourselves to be. And neither are "our" others.

According to humanism – a clear and influential example of which can be found in René Descartes's *Discourse on the Method* (1637) – the human being occupies a natural and eternal place at the very center of things, where it is distinguished absolutely from machines, animals, and other inhuman entities; where it shares with all other human beings a unique essence; where it is the origin of meaning and the sovereign subject of history; and where it behaves and believes according to something called "human nature." In the humanist account, human beings are exceptional, autonomous, and set above the world that lies at their feet. "Man," to use the profoundly problematic signifier conventionally found in descriptions of "the human condition," is the hegemonic measure of all things.[1]

Posthumanism, by way of contrast, emerges from a recognition that "Man" is not the privileged and protected center, because humans are no longer – and perhaps never were – utterly distinct from animals, machines, and other forms of the "inhuman"; are the products of historical and cultural differences that invalidate any appeal to a universal, transhistorical human essence; are constituted as subjects by a linguistic system that pre-exists and transcends them; and are unable to direct the course of world history towards a uniquely human goal. In short, posthumanism arises from the theoretical and practical inadequacy – or even impossibility – of humanism, from the relativization of the human that follows from its "coupling ... to some other order of being" (Clarke 2008: 3).

Posthumanist criticism has certain things in common with the "antihumanism" commonly associated with the work of theorists such as Louis Althusser, Michel Foucault, and Jacques Lacan, but tends to depart from antihumanist discourse when it comes to the matter of approaching the figure of "Man."[2] Antihumanists regularly set out actively to shatter the hegemony of humanism by making a radical, sometimes avowedly scientific, break from the legacy of the human.

Althusser, for instance, wrote in *For Marx* of how "the myth of Man is reduced to ashes" by the mature science of historical materialism (Althusser 1965: 229), while Foucault set out in his *History of Madness* to tell the tale of insanity *itself* in order to correct the rational, anthropocentric accounts habitually offered by psychiatry, "which is a monologue by reason *about* madness" (Foucault 1961: xxviii). And, although he confessed to appreciating humanism when "it at least has a certain candor about it," Lacan also admitted that he was "flattered" to find the term "a-human" used to describe his work in psychoanalysis (Lacan 1966: 701). Posthumanism, however, often takes as its starting point not the illegitimacy but the inherent instability of humanism. "Man" does not necessarily need to be toppled or left behind with a giant leap, because "he" is already a fallen or falling figure, and the task of the critic or artist committed to posthumanism therefore becomes one of mapping and encouraging this fading.

Much scholarship has explicitly and extensively addressed different aspects of posthumanism in recent times; indeed, as Bruce Clarke has acutely observed, in "the last two decades the theoretical trope of the posthuman has upped the ante on the notion of the postmodern" (Clarke 2008: 2). In fact, in 2002 the Modern Language Association of America (MLA) announced in one of its newsletters that it was, given the growing interest, considering adding the subject term "the posthuman" to its influential *MLA International Bibliography* (Grazevich 2002: 6). The recent statistical information from the online *MLA Bibliography* provided by Richard Nash in his chapter on Animal Studies in this volume would appear to confirm that the MLA was unable to resist the rise of "the posthuman." And the sheer range of academic disciplines in which posthumanist concerns have been addressed – literary studies, cultural studies, philosophy, film studies, theology, geography, animal studies, architecture, politics, law, sociology, anthropology, science and technology studies, education, gender studies, and psychoanalysis, for example – testifies to the ways in which posthumanism cuts across conventional disciplinary boundaries. Posthumanism belongs nowhere in particular in the modern university, in that it has no fixed abode, but its presence is everywhere felt.

But posthumanism is not merely an abstract academic affair, for popular culture has been crucial in the examination and expansion of posthumanist existence. Works of fiction such as William Gibson's *Neuromancer* (1984), Bruce Sterling's *Crystal Express* (1989), Richard Powers's *Galatea 2.2* (1995), and China Miéville's *Perdido Street Station* (2000) have – along with television series such as *Star Trek: The Next Generation* and films such as *Blade Runner* (dir. Ridley Scott, 1982), *Tetsuo: The Iron Man* (dir. Shinya Tsukamoto, 1989), *Ghost in the Shell* (dir. Mamoru Oshii, 1995), and *eXistenZ* (dir. David Cronenberg, 1999) – depicted humans and machines interfacing with and transforming each other in new, complex, provocative, pleasurable, and sometimes highly eroticized ways. To encounter such narratives is to see the certainties of humanism fade and to find bodies, minds, desires, limits, knowledge, and being itself reimagined in ways for which traditional anthropocentrism cannot possibly account. For instance, *Galatea 2.2* refers at one point to "the crumbling bastions of the spent, pre-posthumanist tradition" (Powers 1995: 193). Upon these ruins dances post-humanism. That is to say, posthumanism is as much a matter of theory as it is a question of fiction. In fact, one of the recognitions of posthumanist culture has been that "the boundary between science fiction and social reality is an optical illusion" (Haraway 1985: 66), for with the deconstruction of the opposition between the human and the inhuman also comes a waning of the conventional distinction between fact and fiction.

The timing of this flourishing has meant that the term "posthuman" often feels like a fairly recent invention, as if it were perhaps coined with the rise of online existence or the creation of the microchip. But *"post-Human"* (with the hyphen, subsequent capital letter, and italics) can actually be traced back as far as 1888, when it was briefly used in H.P. Blavatsky's *The Secret Doctrine*, a strange and dense theosophical treatise (Blavatsky 1888: 2: 684).[3] Blavatsky did not develop a detailed theory of the posthuman, however, and neither did the handful of writers – Jack Kerouac among them (Kerouac 1995: 81) – who used the term in passing at various points in the first half of the twentieth century. The signifier seems to have been born too soon and to have waited patiently for its moment to come.

That moment was almost certainly the publication of Donna J. Haraway's "A manifesto for cyborgs" (1985). Although she did not actually use the terms "posthumanism," "posthumanist," or "posthuman" anywhere in her essay, Haraway proposed that a series of three interrelated "boundary breakdowns" (Haraway 1985: 68) have transformed the long-established and long-dominant figure of the human into a hybrid cyborg.[4] Humanism, Haraway noted, has always relied upon firm and fierce distinctions between human and animal, organism and machine, and physical and non-physical, but a host of dramatic modern developments (in science, science fiction, technology, capitalism, race and ethnicity studies, militarism, animal studies, and feminism, for example) had made such rigid, absolutist thinking unsustainable and politically dubious. "By the late twentieth century," she wrote, "our time, a mythic time, we are all chimeras, theorized and fabricated hybrids of machine and organism; in short, we are cyborgs. The cyborg is our ontology; it gives us our politics" (66). The human has become obsolete; the figure of "Man" has been replaced, and we "cannot go back ideologically or materially" (81).

Although Haraway notes that the cyborg has troubled and troubling roots in "militarism and patriarchal capitalism" (68), and although from "one perspective, a cyborg world is about the final imposition of a grid of control on the planet, about the final abstraction embodied in a Star Wars apocalypse waged in the name of defense, about the final appropriation of women's bodies in a mascu-linist orgy of war" (72), her essay argues powerfully for seeing hope and promise in a different reading of the cyborg. "From another perspective," she continues, "a cyborg world might be about lived social and bodily realities in which people are not afraid of their joint kinship with animals and machines, not afraid of permanently partial identities and contradictory standpoints" (72). A certain incarnation of the cyborg is to be embraced and celebrated, in other words, for its ability to expose the problems of thinking in essences and universals, and for the way in which it can "suggest a way out of the maze of dualisms in which we have explained our bodies and our tools to ourselves" (100–101). The passage from humanism to a posthumanist cyborg condition need not alarm those whom Haraway calls "progressive people" (71), for it is in the pollution of the "last beachheads of [human] uniqueness" (68) that enchanting new possibilities for being and becoming, for ethics and politics, sparkle.

In the wake of Haraway's intoxicating and widely reproduced manifesto, many accounts of posthumanism have addressed how modern technoscientific culture has radically undermined the hegemony of anthropocentrism. In N. Katherine Hayles's *How We Became Posthuman* (1999), Chris Hables Gray's *Cyborg Citizen* (2001), Elaine L. Graham's *Representations of the Post/human* (2002), and Thomas Foster's *The Souls of Cyberfolk* (2005), for instance, the posthumanist implications of cybernetics and cyberspace, informatics, artificial intelligence, genetics, and medicine have been examined in detail (often with reference to Donna Haraway's groundbreaking manifesto). When computers can beat humans at chess, when life is understood as a readable code, when death can be deferred or redefined by radical medical intervention, when the Genome Project has revealed that humans share 98 percent of their genetic composition with chimpanzees, when artificial limbs outperform and blend seamlessly with their organic counterparts, and when some experts in the field of artificial intelligence believe that it will soon be possible for humans to achieve immortality by transferring themselves into a computer, the old humanist model seems desperately incapable of speaking to the present order of things. The rigid and absolutist position developed in Descartes's *Discourse on Method* loses its persuasiveness, and only a thoroughly revised account – a posthumanist account – can make sense of such shifted scenes.

Posthumanism is not purely a question of high technology, however, and not merely because, as Hayles points out in *How We Became Posthuman*, technological rapture can all too easily shore up some of the most fundamental assumptions of humanist discourse.[5] While it is true that a great deal of criticism and fiction has imagined the posthuman as a technological figure, other strands of scholarship have examined posthumanism in terms of architecture (Hays 1992), mathematics (Baofu 2008), intersex (Morland 2007), geography (Castree and Nash 2006), education (Spanos 1993), paleoanthropology (Mordsley 2007), sensation and cognition (Merrell 2003), rights (Baxi 2009), fetishism (Fernbach 2002), complexity theory (Smith and Jenks 2006), extraterrestrials (Badmington 2004a), botany (Didur 2008), autopoietic systems theory (Clarke 2008), and postcolonialism (Lin 1997).

One of the most striking and persuasive texts to argue in recent years for a posthumanism not reliant upon technology is Cary Wolfe's *Animal Rites*, where the focus falls upon the "unexamined framework of *speciesism*" (Wolfe 2003a: 1) that underlies anthropocentric discourse.[6] Wolfe begins by noting how literary and cultural studies are still dominated by speciesist assumptions, even though everyday American culture – in the form of articles in popular publications such as *Time* and *Newsweek*, for instance – has at least started to recognize that "the humanist habit of making even the *possibility* of subjectivity coterminous with the species barrier is deeply problematic, if not clearly untenable" (1–2; emphasis in original). Western humanism, Wolfe proposes, is founded and fed upon the hierarchical binary opposition between "human" and "animal," and "the aspiration of *human* freedom, extended to all, regardless of race or class or gender, has as its material condition of possibility absolute control over the lives of *nonhuman* others" (7; emphases in original).

Drawing notably upon the work of Jacques Derrida, *Animal Rites* proceeds to offer productive ways to unsettle the sway of the discourse of species and to recognize that "the 'human' ... is not now, and never was, itself" (Wolfe 2003a: 9).[7] Humanism is a myth – a remarkably powerful myth, certainly, but an untenable and dubious myth nonetheless. As long as "this humanist and specie-sist *structure* of subjectivization remains intact," Wolfe concludes, in a powerful and convincing challenge to those who believe that politics and ethics cannot continue without humanism,

> and as long as it is institutionally taken for granted that it is all right to systematically exploit and kill nonhuman animals simply because of their species, then the humanist discourse of species will always be available for use by some humans against other humans as well, to countenance violence against the social other of *whatever* species – or gender, or race, or class, or sexual difference.
>
> (Wolfe 2003a: 8; emphases in original)

In the same year that Wolfe's book shifted the terms of posthumanist debates, Donna Haraway published *The Companion Species Manifesto*, the title of which clearly echoes that of her earlier cyborg manifesto.[8] But the book soon signals a certain unease with the cyborg, that figure which had, by 2003, so often been associated with Haraway's name. "I appointed cyborgs," she writes, "to do feminist work in Reagan's Star Wars times of the mid-1980s. By the end of the millennium, cyborgs could no longer do the work of a proper herding dog to gather up the threads for critical inquiry" (Haraway 2003: 4). The reference to a herding dog gives a clue about Haraway's shift of emphasis, for she continues:

> So I go happily to the dogs to explore the birth of the kennel to help craft tools for science studies and feminist theory in the present time,

when secondary Bushes threaten to replace the old growth of more livable naturecultures in the carbon budget politics of all water-based life on earth. Having worn the scarlet letters, "Cyborgs for earthly survival!" long enough, I now brand myself with a slogan only Schutzhund women from dog sports could have come up with, when even a first nip can result in a death sentence: "Run fast; bite hard!"

(Haraway 2003: 4–5)

The reason for this move away from the cyborg and toward animals is pencilled lightly between the lines of the slender *Companion Species Manifesto*, but two texts published since 2003 make matters absolutely clear. First, in an interview published in *Theory, Culture and Society* in 2006, Haraway responds to a question about the term "posthuman," about what the signifier means to her, about whether or not she finds it productive and enabling:

I've stopped using it. I did use it for a while, including in the "Manifesto." I think it's a bit impossible not to use it sometimes, but I'm trying not to use it. Kate Hayles writes this smart, wonderful book *How We Became Posthuman*. She locates herself in that book at the right interface – the place where people meet IT apparatuses, where worlds get reconstructed as information. I am in strong alliance with her insistence in that book, namely getting at the materialities of information. Not letting anyone think for a minute that this is immateriality rather than getting at its specific materialities. That I'm with, that sense of "how we became posthumanist." Still, human/posthuman is much too easily appropriated by the blissed-out, "Let's all be posthumanists and find our next teleological evolutionary stage in some kind of transhumanist tech-noenhancement." Posthumanism is too easily appropriated to those kinds of projects for my taste. Lots of people doing posthumanist thinking, though, don't do it that way. The reason I go to companion species is to get away from posthumanism.

Companion species is my effort to be in alliance and in tension with posthumanist projects because I think species is in question. In that way I'm with Derrida more than others, and with Cary Wolfe's reading of Derrida.[9]

(Haraway 2006: 140)

Second, two years later, Haraway's *When Species Meet* appeared as the third volume in the "Posthumanities" series edited by Cary Wolfe for the University of Minnesota Press. The opening chapter of the book, which builds as a whole upon the concerns of *The Companion Species Manifesto*, contains a striking statement about posthumanism:

I find [the notion of "companion species"], which is less a category than a pointer to an ongoing "becoming with," to be a much richer web to inhabit than any of the posthumanisms on display after (or in reference to) the ever-deferred demise of man. I never wanted to be posthuman, or posthumanist, any more than I wanted to be postfeminist. For one thing, urgent work still remains to be done in reference to those who must inhabit the troubled categories of woman and human, properly pluralized, reformulated, and brought into constitutive intersection with other asymmetrical differences. ... I am not a posthumanist; I am who I become with companion species, who and which make a mess out of categories in the making of kin and kind.

(Haraway 2008: 17–19)

Haraway's recent work, in other words, has been marked by a notable anxiety concerning the term "posthumanism." But her turn to companion species nonetheless retains the powerful resistance to humanism that informed her "Manifesto for cyborgs." "Human exceptionalism," she proposes at one point in *When Species Meet*, "is what companion species cannot abide" (Haraway 2008: 165), and in the ordinary, everyday relationships between humans and animals dwell the seeds for radically rethinking the anthropocentric discourse of species.

Cary Wolfe and Donna Haraway evidently disagree at the level of the signifier "posthumanism," but their work nonetheless shares an insistence that the problematic reign of "Man" will continue until the familiar binary opposition between "the human" and "the animal" (the singular in each case is significant) is called into question. And texts such as *Animal Rites*, *The Companion Species Manifesto*, and *When Species Meet* have potent companions in scholarship by critics such Erica Fudge (2002, 2008) and Julie Ann Smith (2003, 2005) that examines how humanist speciesism fades in the face of ordinary encounters between humans and other animals. But there are also anxious voices. While a great deal of scholarship devoted to posthumanism celebrates the waning of humanist discourse – Donna Haraway, for instance, famously ends her "Manifesto for cyborgs" by declaring that she would "rather be a cyborg than a goddess" (Haraway 1985: 101) – it would be a mistake to conclude that everyone who writes about the subject is in favor of posthumanist existence.

For instance, the political theorist Francis Fukuyama published a widely discussed book entitled *Our Posthuman Future* (2002), in which he proposed that the contemporary drift away from the principles of humanism was a dangerous development in need of urgent correction. Modern biotechnology, for Fukuyama, is a "threat" because it will possibly "alter human nature and thereby move us into a 'posthuman' stage of history. This is important ... because human nature exists, is a meaningful concept, and has provided a stable continuity to our experience as a species" (Fukuyama 2002: 7). As humanism threatens to slide into the "potential moral chasm" (17) of posthumanism, Fukuyama calls for a defense of human nature, the transcultural "common humanity that allows every human being to potentially communicate with and enter into a moral relationship with every other human being on the planet" (9), and the "natural differences" between men and women (217). The final section of *Our Posthuman Future*, meanwhile, is entitled "What to do" and advocates strict regulation of biotechnology and an outright ban on the "unnatural" practice of reproductive cloning (207). Posthumanism, Fukuyama concludes, offers a "false banner of liberty," and "[t]rue freedom" can only be achieved if humanism is preserved (218). In other words, while writers such as Donna Haraway and Cary Wolfe have stressed the promising ethical and political possibilities that open up with the shift from humanism to posthumanism, Fukuyama sees only terrible loss in the fading of "Man"; the posthuman future identified in the title of his book is to be resisted at all costs, and politics, *pace* Haraway and Wolfe, cannot exist without recourse to "Man."[10]

There is, in conclusion, no convenient consensus when it comes to questions of posthumanism: different critics have approached the term in different ways and have drawn different conclusions. And posthumanism is not the property or progeny of any particular academic discipline; on the contrary, it touches and troubles across the lines that conventionally separate field from field, mode from mode. One thing, however, is certain: posthumanism has become a major site of debate in recent years because anthropocentrism, with its assured insistence upon human exceptionalism, is no longer an adequate or convincing account of the way of the world. As N. Katherine Hayles reflected in 2005:

> [T]he interplay between the liberal humanist subject and the posthuman that I used to launch my analysis in *How We Became Posthuman* [in 1999] has already begun to fade into the history of the twentieth century. In the twenty-first century, the debates are likely to center not so much on the tension between the liberal humanist tradition and the posthuman but on different versions of the posthuman as they continue to evolve in conjunction with intelligent machines.
>
> (Hayles 2005: 2)

And other others.

Notes

1 For a concise, nuanced, and accessible overview of humanism, see Davies 2008.
2 An excellent account of the relationship between humanism and antihumanism can be found in Soper 1986. For a discussion of the relationship between humanism, antihumanism, and posthumanism, see Chapters 2 and 4 of Badmington 2004a.
3 I am not interested in establishing an absolute origin of the term "posthuman"; there may be uses that predate that of Blavatsky (although I have yet to find them). In the name of historical accuracy, however, it should be noted that Oliver Krueger (2005: 78) is

completely wrong to claim that "posthuman" is present in Thomas Blount's *Glossographia* of 1656. Blount refers in his dictionary only to "posthumian," a now-obsolete word which is taken simply to mean "following," "to come," or "that shall be" (Blount 1656: n.p.; spelling modernized).

4 Although cyborgs are often associated with the realm of science fiction (see Caidin 1972, for instance), the term itself was actually coined in 1960 by two scientists, Manfred E. Clynes and Nathan S. Kline, to describe the technologically enhanced human being – the cybernetic organism – that they imagined safely exploring the dangerous depths of outer space. For more on the history of the cyborg, including a reprint of Clynes and Kline's original article, see Gray et al. 1995.

5 The reading of Hans Moravec's *Mind Children* (1988) with which Hayles's book begins is particularly insightful in this respect. Hayles points out that Moravec's apparently post-humanist drive to see human consciousness transferred into a computer relies entirely upon the classical humanist division between mind and body, in which the former is the immaterial, disembodied essence of the individual, while the latter is ultimately insignificant matter (Hayles 1999: 1–6).

6 For an excellent collection that acts as some kind of companion volume to *Animal Rites*, see *Zoontologies* (Wolfe 2003b). For an imagining of "a posthumanism without technology," see Callus and Herbrechter 2007.

7 For Derrida's most sustained engagement with the question of "the animal," see Derrida 2006; related material is to be found in Derrida 2009. Although *Animal Rites* was published several years before the appearance of *The Animal That Therefore I Am* in either French or English, Wolfe regularly quotes from the unpublished typescript of David Wills's translation.

8 Haraway acknowledges this connection in the first few pages of *The Companion Species Manifesto*, in fact, when she writes: "This is not my first manifesto; in 1985, I published 'The Cyborg Manifesto' to try to make feminist sense of the implosions of contemporary life in technoscience" (Haraway 2003: 4).

9 Haraway is wrong to claim here that she uses the term "posthuman" in the "Manifesto for cyborgs"; perhaps she is thinking of a related text published several years later (Haraway 1992).

10 I have discussed at length what I see as the fundamental flaws in Fukuyama's book in "Mapping posthumanism" (Badmington 2004b).

Bibliography

Althusser, L. (1965) *For Marx*, trans. B. Brewster, London: Verso, 1996.
Badmington, N. (2004a) *Alien Chic: posthumanism and the other within*, New York: Routledge.
——(2004b) "Mapping posthumanism," *Environment and Planning A*, 36(8): 1344–51.
Baofu, P. (2008) *The Future of Post-human Mathematical Logic*, Newcastle: Cambridge Scholars Publishing.
Baxi, U. (2009) *Human Rights in a Posthuman World*, Oxford: Oxford University Press.
Blavatsky, H.P. (1888) *The Secret Doctrine: the synthesis of science, religion, and philosophy*, 2 vols, Pasadena, CA: Theosophical University Press, 1952.
Blount, T. (1656) *Glossographia*, Menston: Scolar Press, 1969.
Caidin, M. (1972) *Cyborg*, London: W.H. Allen, 1973.
Callus, I. and Herbrechter, S. (2007) "Critical posthumanism or, the invention of a posthumanism without technology," *Subject Matters*, 3(2)–4(1): 15–29.

Castree, N. and Nash, C. (eds) (2006) *Posthuman Geographies*, special issue of *Social and Cultural Geography*, 7(4).

Clarke, B. (2008) *Posthuman Metamorphosis: narrative and systems*, New York: Fordham University Press.

Davies, T. (2008) *Humanism*, 2nd edn, New York: Routledge.

Derrida, J. (2006) *The Animal That Therefore I Am*, ed. M.-L. Mallet, trans. D. Wills, New York: Fordham University Press, 2008.

——(2009) *The Beast and the Sovereign*, vol. 1, trans. G. Bennington, Chicago: University of Chicago Press.

Descartes, R. (1637) *Discourse on Method and Related Writings*, trans. D.M. Clarke, London: Penguin, 1999.

Didur, J. (2008) "Postcolonial posthumanism in Kincaid's *Among Flowers*: 'sniffing at the last post'?," unpublished paper delivered at the Critical Posthumanism conference, 27–29 March, Concordia University, Montreal.

Fernbach, A. (2002) *Fantasies of Fetishism: from decadence to the post-human*, Edinburgh: Edinburgh University Press.

Foster, T. (2005) *The Souls of Cyberfolk: posthumanism as vernacular theory*, Minneapolis: University of Minnesota Press.

Foucault, M. (1961) *History of Madness*, ed. J. Khalfa, trans. J. Murphy and J. Khalfa, New York: Routledge, 2006.

Fudge, E. (2002) *Animal*, London: Reaktion.

——(2008) *Pets*, Stocksfield: Acumen.

Fukuyama, F. (2002) *Our Posthuman Future: consequences of the biotechnology revolution*, London: Profile.

Gibson, W. (1984) *Neuromancer*, New York: Ace.

Graham, E.L. (2002) *Representations of the Post/human: monsters, aliens and others in popular culture*, Manchester: Manchester University Press.

Gray, C.H. (2001) *Cyborg Citizen: politics in the posthuman age*, New York and London: Routledge.

——et al. (eds) (1995) *The Cyborg Handbook*, New York: Routledge.

Grazevich, G.M. (2002) "Emerging terminology in the MLA International Bibliography," *MLA Newsletter*, 34(1): 6.

Haraway, D.J. (1985) "A manifesto for cyborgs: science, technology, and socialist feminism in the 1980s," *Socialist Review*, 80: 65–107.

——(1992) "Ecce Homo, ain't (ar'n't) I a woman, and inappropriate/d others: the human in a posthumanist landscape," in J. Scott and J. Butler (eds) *Feminists Theorize the Political*, New York: Routledge, pp. 87–101.

——(2003) *The Companion Species Manifesto: dogs, people, and significant otherness*, Chicago: Prickly Paradigm Press.

——(2006) "When we have never been human, what is to be done?: Interview with Donna Haraway," interview by N. Gane, *Theory, Culture and Society*, 23(7–8): 135–58.

——(2008) *When Species Meet*, Minneapolis: University of Minnesota Press.

Hayles, N.K. (1999) *How We Became Posthuman: virtual bodies in cybernetics, literature and informatics*, Chicago: University of Chicago Press.

——(2005) *My Mother Was a Computer: digital subjects and literary texts*, Chicago: University of Chicago Press.

Hays, K.M. (1992) *Modernism and the Posthumanist Subject: the architecture of Hannes Meyer and Ludwig Hilberseimer*, Cambridge, Mass.: MIT Press.

Kerouac, J. (1995) *Selected Letters: 1940–1956*, ed. A. Charters, New York: Viking Penguin.

Krueger, O. (2005) "Gnosis in cyberspace?: body, mind and progress in posthumanism," *Journal of Evolution and Technology*, 14(2): 77–89.

Lacan, J. (1966) *Écrits*, trans. B. Fink et al., New York and London: W.W. Norton, 2006.

Lin, L. (1997) "The irony of colonial humanism: *A Passage to India* and the politics of posthumanism," *Ariel*, 28(4): 133–53.

Merrell, F. (2003) *Sensing Corporeally: toward a posthuman understanding*, Toronto: University of Toronto Press.

Miéville, C. (2000) *Perdido Street Station*, London: Macmillan.

Moravec, H. (1988) *Mind Children: the future of robot and human intelligence*, Cambridge, Mass.: Harvard University Press.

Mordsley, J. (2007) "Tracing origins in paleoanthropology," *Oxford Literary Review*, 29: 77–101.

Morland, I. (2007) "Plastic man: intersex, humanism and the Reimer case," *Subject Matters*, 3(2)–4(1): 81–98.

Powers, R. (1995) *Galatea 2.2*, New York: Farrar, Straus and Giroux.

Smith, J. and Jenks C. (2006) *Qualitative Complexity: ecology, cognitive processes and the re-emergence of structures in post-humanist social theory*, New York: Routledge.

Smith, J.A. (2003) "Beyond dominance and affection: living with rabbits in post-humanist households," *Society and Animals*, 11(2): 181–97.

——(2005) "'Viewing' the body: towards a discourse of animal death," *Worldviews: Environment, Culture, Religion*, 9(2): 184–202.

Soper, K. (1986) *Humanism and Anti-humanism*, London: Hutchinson.

Spanos, W. (1993) *The End of Education: toward posthumanism*, Minneapolis: University of Minnesota Press.

Sterling, B. (1989) *Crystal Express*, Sauk City, WI: Arkham House.

Wolfe, C. (2003a) *Animal Rites: American culture, the discourse of species, and posthumanist theory*, Chicago: University of Chicago Press.

——(ed.) (2003b) *Zoontologies: the question of the animal*, Minneapolis: University of Minnesota Press.

33

SCIENCE FICTION

Lisa Yaszek

Literary and cultural historians describe science fiction (SF) as the premiere narrative form of modernity because authors working in this genre extrapolate from Enlightenment ideals and industrial practices to imagine how educated people using machines and other technologies might radically change the material world. This kind of future-oriented technoscientific speculation lends itself to social and political speculation as well. While authors working in other literary modes can represent the past and present from new perspectives, only those allied with speculative fiction show us how intervening into the material world can change human relations and generate new futures as well. Thus SF enables authors to dramatize widespread cultural hopes and fears about new technoscientific formations as they emerge at specific historical moments.

The history of SF is very much bound up with the history of modern technoscientific development and the proliferation of writing that accompanied it. By means of the first scientific journals, scholars associated with the scientific academies of seventeenth-century France and Great Britain disseminated new ideas about the quantifiable nature of the material world and the importance of human agents within that world. By the eighteenth century such ideas had become central to the philosophical writings of Immanuel Kant and David Hume and the socio-political treatises of Adam Smith and Voltaire. These ideas inspired the public imagination as well. This was particularly apparent in books such as Charles Leadbetter's *Astronomy* (1727), periodicals such as Eliza Haywood's *The Female Spectator* (1744–46), and natural histories such as René-Antoine Ferchault de Réaumur's *Histoire Naturelle des Insects* (1734–42). While books and periodicals introduced scientific ideas to the newly literate middle class, natural histories inspired readers to become amateur scientists themselves by applying close observation skills to the world around them.

The late eighteenth and early nineteenth centuries also saw the publication of the first proto-science fiction stories. The authors of these stories were often science enthusiasts who engaged new scientific ideas in their fiction. For example, Voltaire's passion for physics led to the creation of a fully functional laboratory at Château de Cirey and the 1752 publication of *Micromégas*, a fantastic voyage story in which human scientist-explorers learn about galactic physics from a Jovian space traveler whom they encounter at the North Pole. In 1818 British author Mary Shelley drew upon her reading in pre-Darwinian evolutionary theory and her experience with public demonstrations of galvanism to create *Frankenstein*, which follows the tragic adventures of an isolated young scientist who uses electricity in a misguided attempt to create a new race of beings that will worship him. Despite their apparent differences, Voltaire and Shelley's stories both insist that science can yield great rewards as long as it is practiced according to the established methods of the scientific community. They also mark the emergence of SF's two oldest archetypes: the heroic scientist-explorer who shares knowledge with his intellectual brethren and the mad scientist who makes disastrous decisions that wreak havoc.

The next generation of speculative fiction writers turned their attention to what would become the central interest of SF: the creation of machines that could transform both the material and social worlds. This new interest emerged at the height of the Industrial Revolution, when steam-powered technologies enabled new modes of locomotion and new methods of production. These developments fostered the proliferation of new trade routes, factories, and urban spaces. They also fostered the rise of a new professional: the engineer. Engineering schools, including the National School of Bridges and Highways in France and Rennselaer Polytechnic Institute in the U.S., first opened their doors at the turn of the nineteenth century; by the mid-nineteenth century graduates of these schools could join specialized organizations dedicated to civil, mechanical, and mining engineering. While engineering was an overwhelmingly masculine profession, in the late nineteenth century technical institutes began granting degrees to the female students who would go on to create the discipline of scientific home management, or domestic engineering.

New technologies and professions were central to the speculative stories that authors on both sides of the Atlantic published in the nineteenth century. These authors conveyed their ideas about the future of industrial society by updating older fantastic narrative traditions. The European leaders of this experiment were Jules Verne and H.G. Wells. Like Voltaire before him, Verne used the extraordinary voyage to spark a sense of wonder in readers regarding the marvels of the physical universe. However, he updated this story type in 1867's *From the Earth to the Moon*, 1871's *A Journey to the Center of the Earth*, and 1872's *Twenty Thousand Leagues Under the Sea* by extrapolating from contemporary transportation technologies to show how humans (rather than aliens) might travel to exotic locales on the Earth and amongst the stars. In Great Britain, Wells used the future war story – a narrative form often employed by government officials to argue for increased spending on war technologies – to show how submarines, airplanes, and bombs might herald the end of war altogether. This is particularly evident in 1903's "The Last Ironclads," 1908's *The War in the Air*, and 1914's *The World Set Free*, where warring nation-states destroy themselves by underestimating new military technologies, thereby paving the way for the emergence of peaceful, scientifically managed global civilizations. In the stories of both Verne and Wells, the success of new technocultural endeavors depends on the action of a new technocultural hero: the creative engineer who works for the good of all people, rather than the benefit of any individual person, business, or nation.

The principles of creative engineering were even more central to the technological utopias of American authors Edward Bellamy and Charlotte Perkins Gilman. Bellamy's 1888 novel *Looking Backward 2000–1887* depicts a future America reorganized along lines later associated with the Fordist factory, with all work parceled out amongst specially trained individuals. In contrast to the often overworked and underpaid factory workers of his own day, however, Bellamy imagined that the citizens of America 2000 who volunteered for menial labor would be rewarded with drastically reduced hours and that all workers would enjoy high pay, abundant goods, and early retirement at the age of 45. In a similar vein, the female citizens of Gilman's 1915 *Herland* enjoy unprecedented living standards because their wide-scale application of the principles of domestic engineering transform their hostile tropical land into a fertile paradise. They also extend the scientific management of the home to the scientific management of people, combining eugenics with education to create perfectly adjusted children. Thus Bellamy and Gilman built upon the utopian tradition extending back to Sir Thomas More by demonstrating how new and better societies might be created not just by the application of rational thought, but also by the application of rational industrial processes.

The first four decades of the twentieth century marked the consolidation of engineering as the premiere profession of the modern era. They also marked the height of excitement about engineering in the public imagination, especially as it was expressed in the philosophy of technocracy, a pseudo-populist movement that emerged in reaction to the Great Depression and that, at its height, boasted over half a million followers. Led by engineer Howard Scott and the professors of Columbia University's Industrial Engineering department, technocrats advocated the creation of a scientifically educated and technically skilled populace whose best and brightest would naturally rise to the top. This technoscientific elite would apply scientific and engineering principles to political and economic problems, thereby mitigating the woes of the Great Depression and laying the foundation for a utopian, post-scarcity society.

This period also saw the consolidation of SF as a distinct genre complete with its own literary community, publishing outlets, and stylistic conventions. The birth of genre SF is associated with the founding of *Amazing Stories* in 1926 and *Astounding Stories* in 1930. These two magazines – printed on the cheap wood-pulp paper that would give this period of SF history its name – were the first dedicated solely to speculative fiction. While authors, editors, and fans worked collaboratively to establish SF, one man is generally recognized as the father of the genre: Luxembourg-American author, inventor, and technocrat

Hugo Gernsback. As the first editor of *Amazing Stories*, Gernsback developed three rules to ensure that speculative fiction would get readers excited about science and technology: "good" SF would be organized around a prophetic vision of the technoscientific future; it would didactically explain how that future came to be; and it would do so in an entertaining way, with approximately 25 percent of each SF narrative dedicated to science and technology and 75 percent dedicated to adventure. These rules inform Gernsback's own writing, most notably in 1911's *Ralph 124C 41+: A Romance of the Year 2660*. Like other utopias, Gernsback's is comprised of dialog between a native of the utopia in question (here, the world-famous superscientist Ralph 124C) and a naïve visitor who stands in for the reader (Ralph's love interest, Alice 212B). But Gernsback departed from the staid utopian tradition by framing his characters' conversations about the marvels of New York City 2660 with action sequences featuring avalanches, invisible assailants, and battles in outer space.

The elements that Gernsback added to the utopian narrative tradition – depictions of scientists and engineers as action heroes, the celebration of fantastic gadgets, and planet-spanning adventures – became central to the pulp-era space opera. The two authors who perfected this sub-genre were Edmund Hamilton and E.E. "Doc" Smith. In the linked *Interstellar Patrol* stories which ran from 1928 to 1930 and stand-alone tales such as 1934's "Thundering Worlds," Hamilton imagines far-off futures where humans create intergalactic technocracies while battling with rogue stars, invading aliens, and even the death of their own sun. Meanwhile, Smith's 1928–63 *Skylark* and 1934–48 *Lensman* series follow the adventures of a human technoscientific elite who ventures into space only to learn that they are key to the outcome of billion-year-old battles between good and evil. Unlike Gernsback before them, neither Hamilton nor Smith spent much time explaining how their characters created their technocivilizations. However, what science they did include tended to be relatively accurate. Most importantly, the triumphant tone of much space opera neatly conveyed the technoscientific optimism central to early SF.

Technocratic ideals also permeated pulp-era thought-variant stories, which were driven by speculative ideas rather than gadgets. This is particularly apparent in Stanley G. Weinbaum's "The Adaptive Ultimate," which updated the Frankenstein narrative for the modern scientific era. Weinbaum's 1935 story follows the adventures of two scientists who develop a serum based on insect hormones that enables wounded organisms to heal themselves. After serious ethical debate, the overly enthusiastic scientists decide to skip standard testing protocols and inject the serum into a dying young woman. When she turns into an amoral creature bent on conquering the world, Weinbaum's scientists recognize that they cannot simply, as Victor Frankenstein did, reject their creation. Instead, they take responsibility for their actions and contain the threat of the young woman, thereby transforming themselves from mad to heroic scientists. The principles of technocracy were also fundamental to John W. Campbell's 1939

"Forgetfulness," which takes place on a far-future Earth where humans live in modest glass domes situated on the outskirts of ruined megacities. At the end of the story readers learn that these humans have not lost control of science and technology, but have actively chosen telepathic over technoscientific ways of being to avoid repeating their war-torn history. Thus Campbell's protagonists apply engineering techniques to the problem of human history and gain control over evolution itself.

The middle decades of the twentieth century seemed to epitomize the technocratic ideals of the pulp-era SF community. The new connections forged with industry and government during World War II led to a period of record growth for American science in the Cold War era. Much of this growth occurred in the two areas of research seen as key to national defense: atomic energy and space exploration. The expansion of defense spending, combined with the consumer demands of a newly affluent public, spurred the rapid development of American technology as well, especially as it pertained to the creation of automated machines designed to run complex industrial operations. Indeed, while atomic energy and space exploration research promised to transform the American future, automation seemed poised to transform America in the present as factory workers began working with robots and computer experts swelled the ranks of the technoscientific elite. The technocratic transformation of labor extended to women's work as well. During World War II women were encouraged to express their patriotism by working in laboratories and factories while men went overseas to fight. Afterward, they were encouraged to continue serving their country by applying their technoscientific expertise to life in the suburbs. In particular, women were expected to prepare their homes for the possibility of nuclear attack and foster family togetherness through the judicious consumption of domestic goods. Thus men and women alike were figured as essential to the United States's development as a technocultural world leader.

Much like science, SF experienced a Golden Age in the 1940s and 1950s. Prior to World War II, SF authors were often dismissed for writing about impossible sciences and technologies. Afterward, they were hailed as visionary prophets and invited to consult with entertainment, industry, and government leaders alike. This period also marked the appearance of the first SF anthologies, the beginning of the SF paperback novel trade, and the explosion of SF storytelling across radio, film, and television. Even with all these changes, magazines remained the heart of the SF community. The most important magazine editor of this period was physicist-turned-pulp SF author John W. Campbell, who took over *Astounding Science Fiction* (formerly *Astounding Stories*) in 1939. Campbell believed that SF was an important part of the larger scientific discourse already changing history. As such, he insisted that authors write stories that were logically extrapolated from current knowledge about the physical world and that they carefully consider the impact of new sciences and technologies on society. While Campbell's editorial vision dominated SF for years to come, two other editors made equally lasting contributions to the development of the genre: Anthony Boucher, who co-founded the *Magazine of Fantasy and Science Fiction* in 1949, and H.L. Gold, who launched *Galaxy Science Fiction* in 1950. Boucher was a respected mystery writer and translator who published experimental stories of high literary quality, while Gold was a fantasy and comic book writer who excelled at fostering socially satiric SF. Taken together, these three editors shaped SF as a modern genre.

The new story types that proliferated throughout this period underscore the literary and cultural maturity of Golden Age SF. This is particularly evident in the future histories of Robert Heinlein and Isaac Asimov. Heinlein's future history stories (originally published in *Astounding* between 1930 and 1960, then reprinted in *The Past Through Tomorrow* in 1967) tell the tale of a determined humanity that automates travel on Earth and then, over the course of the next three millennia, goes on to colonize the stars. Meanwhile, Asimov's future history sequence (including the stories collected in 1950's *I, Robot*, the *Robot* novels published between 1947 and 1958) predicts that humans' robotic creations will eventually become their caretakers, fostering the flame of civilization in even the darkest of times. With their emphasis on galaxy-spanning futures populated by sleek space ships and autonomous robots, such Golden Age stories were clear successors to their pulp-era counterparts. However, both Heinlein and Asimov dramatized technoscientific change in ways that spoke to the lived experience of mid-century readers, treating it as something that comes from the collaborative effort of scientists, soldiers, businesspeople, and government officials and that provokes both hope and fear in the individuals living through ages of wonder that are not necessarily of their own making.

While Heinlein and Asimov used future histories to celebrate technocratic ideals, other Golden Age authors used other SF story forms to critically assess the relations of science, technology, and society. The most significant of these was the nuclear-war narrative. In Judith Merril's 1950 novel *Shadow on the Hearth*, Walter Miller's 1960 novel *A Canticle for Leibowitz*, and Nevil Shute's 1957 novel *On the Beach*, nuclear war is not – as popular thinking then held – something that can be either limited or won. Instead, even the most minor atomic explosions reverberate through space and time, destroying families, plunging nations into savagery, and wiping out humanity altogether. Meanwhile, the media landscape story – which explored worlds dominated by images of advertising and the popular arts – seemed to be a relative lighthearted mockery of American consumerism. And yet short stories such as Fritz Leiber's 1949 "The Girl with the Hungry Eyes" and Ann Warren Griffith's 1953 "Captive Audience," as well as Frederik Pohl and C.M. Kornbluth's 1953 novel *The Space Merchants*, turn out to be almost as frightening as their atomic-themed counterparts. As media landscape authors insisted time and time again, the mid-century tendency to protect corporations at the expense of consumers might well lead to the rise of a surveillance state where individuals would be stripped of their civil rights and required to purchase indiscriminately in the name of national security.

Both science and SF developed in new directions in the 1960s and 1970s. One of the most important events influencing the former was the institutional ascendancy of the social sciences. Throughout this period sociologists, psychologists, and anthropologists sought to legitimate their work by emphasizing the scientific nature of their subject matter (the quantifiable world of social relations) and methodologies (including the techniques of statistical inquiry and group research). These efforts were so successful – and so popular with students looking for socially relevant classes – that even the most conservative technical institutes made room for social science courses in their curricula. But social scientists were not the only new players in the technoscientific arena. Supported by Cold War legislation that guaranteed educational funds for talented youth, women flooded science, math, and engineering departments in record numbers. When these women found themselves blocked from graduate school and the best professional careers, they took action. Leading scientists joined the National Organization for Women and led the first class-action lawsuits against sexual discrimination in public university hiring practices. Such efforts led to the ratification of the 1972 Educational Amendment Acts, whose Title IX guaranteed equal pay for men and women working in higher education, while banning sex discrimination in all federally funded educational programs.

The initial challenge to speculative writing in this period came from a group of transatlantic authors and editors associated with what would eventually be called New Wave SF. The New Wave movement coalesced around Michael Moorcock's *New Worlds* magazine in Great Britain in the mid-1960s and debuted in the U.S. with the publication of Harlan Ellison's *Dangerous Visions* anthology in 1967 and Judith Merril's *England Swings SF* anthology in 1968. New Wave authors maintained that the characters, story types, and technocratic ideals of earlier SF were no longer adequate for dramatizing life in the modern world. As such, it was necessary to make SF new by turning from the hard to the soft sciences and exchanging stories about outer space for those focusing on the inner spaces of individuals and their societies. Other challenges came from the scores of new women writers who joined SF during this period. Feminist author-critics Joanna Russ, Pamela Sargent, and Samuel R. Delany all readily acknowledged that women had always written speculative fiction. But they also maintained that even the best SF remained trapped in "galactic suburbia": an imaginary space of dazzling technoscientific extrapolation where, oddly enough, social relations still looked like those of 1950s middle-class America. Accordingly, feminist writers called for their comrades to rethink their aesthetic practices and fulfill the Campbellian ideals of good SF by writing fiction that complicated mainstream notions about the future of scientific, social, and sexual relations.

Although they sometimes differed in their ideas about the relations of modern SF to its generic traditions, both New Wave and feminist SF authors used their chosen genre to explore how humans might grapple with alienation from them-selves and their worlds. This is particularly apparent in the natural and urban disaster novels of British New Wave author J.G. Ballard. Ballard's 1962 novel *The Drowned World* imagines that humans might greet apocalypse (caused, in this case, by solar radiation that transforms Europe and North America into boiling lagoons) as an opportunity to give up technoscientific mastery and embrace devolution. Meanwhile, his 1973 *Crash* explores a near future where people come to terms with their media-saturated world by restaging and starring in famous car accidents. Much like Ballard, American author Harlan Ellison used the setting of a radically transformed world to explore the inner space of indivi-duals and their societies. This is particularly apparent in Ellison's infamous 1967 short story "A Boy and His Dog," which explores the impact of nuclear war on the nuclear family. In its broad outline, Ellison's story seems much like the conventional Golden Age nuclear-war narrative, but Ellison takes his critique in surprising new directions, insisting that the instigators of war are not impersonal bureaucrats, but hypocritical fathers whose adherence to Cold War socio-political ideals decimates the land and drives their children to rape, murder, and cannibalism.

Feminist SF authors of the 1960s and 1970s tended to be more optimistic about the future than their New Wave counterparts. This is apparent in Ursula K. Le Guin's 1969 novel *The Left Hand of Darkness*, which uses anthropology, sociology, and psychology to demonstrate how androgynous cultures might distribute childbearing responsibilities and thus power relations more equitably than cultures grounded in sexual division. It is even more evident in Marge Piercy's 1976 *Woman on the Edge of Time* and Joanna Russ's 1975 *The Female Man*, which illustrate how reproductive technosciences might reform social relations among men and women. In Piercy's mixed-sex utopia, babies are gestated in mechanical wombs while both men and women use hormone therapy to produce breast milk and enjoy the experience of mothering. Meanwhile, technologically enabled reproduction in Russ's single-sex utopia liberates women to engage in everything from romance to dueling. Like Bellamy and Gilman before them, feminist SF authors celebrated the possibility of creative social engineering. Drawing inspiration from their politically charged counterparts in the technoscientific professions, however, they insisted that such engineering would be not just a natural side effect of industrial production, but the deliberate achievement of men and women striving to change science and society alike.

New Wave and feminist ideas are still central to SF, but in recent decades the genre has evolved in response to two new technocultural events: the massive expansion of information technologies and the emergence of a transnational economic system supported by these technologies. In the early 1980s home video games and personal computers encouraged users to combine work and leisure in new ways within the privacy of their own homes; the development of the World Wide Web a decade later enabled users to reach out from those homes and forge new kinds of community based on affinity rather than biology or geography. Modern people have been further encouraged to rethink their relations to the larger world by virtue of their position within increasingly global networks of industrial production. The advent of such networks requires people – especially Western people – to reconsider who and what counts within the practice of science and technology. On the one hand, the dominance of industrial production suggests that Western ways of knowing the world are highly successful ones. But gaining access to a global stage allows people to share other technoscientific traditions with one another and even experiment with using those traditions (alone or in tandem with their Western counterparts) as templates for building new and truly more equitable global futures as well.

The premiere narrative form of the information age has no doubt been cyberpunk, the stylish mode of SF storytelling that merges strong interest in cybernetics and biotechnology with generally left-wing or libertarian politics and the do-it-yourself attitude of the early punk rock scene. The term "cyberpunk" was coined by SF author Bruce Bethke in his 1983 story of the same name, but was immediately taken up by editor Gardner Dozois to describe much of the fiction he was publishing in *Isaac Asimov's SF Magazine* at that time. First-generation cyberpunk fiction, including William Gibson's celebrated 1984 novel *Neuromancer* and the short stories collected in Bruce Sterling's 1986 *Mirrorshades* anthology, drew energy from the technocultural events of its time, providing SF with new character types and settings. In cyberpunk, creative engineers and faithful robots give way to amoral but usually good-hearted hackers and willful but usually benign artificial intelligences, all of whom struggle to survive and even transcend the conditions of their existence as tools of a transnational economy. Much of this drama takes place in cyberspace, a sphere of artificial or virtual reality where human and machine intelligences can interact with one another and with the flows of information that comprise modern capitalist practice itself. In the 1990s a new generation of SF novels – including Pat Cadigan's 1991 *Synners*, Neal Stephenson's 1992 *Snow Crash*, and Melissa Scott's 1996 *Trouble and Her Friends* – built upon the cyberpunk tradition by exploring how people (and machines) who recognize the value of raced and gendered bodies within the abstract world of computation might exchange the old dream of transcendence for the new one of material engagement, thereby transforming bad corporate futures into new and more egalitarian ones.

The technoscientific and social ideals endemic to cyberpunk have inspired the development of other SF sub-genres. The artificial intelligences of cyberpunk are predicated on what computer scientist and SF author Vernor Vinge has described as the technological singularity: a near-future moment when computational power enables the creation of superhumanly intelligent machines that change the world in ways that pre-singularity humans cannot even begin to imagine. This has not stopped Vinge trying to imagine such worlds in the 1981 novella *True Names* and the 1984 and 1986 novels *The Peace War* and *Marooned in Real Time*, all of which are told from the perspective of pre-singularity humans who survive the transition to a post-singularity society. Other notable books to explore this theme include Cory Doctorow's 1996 *Down and Out in the Magic Kingdom* and Charles Stross's 2005 *Accelerando*. Still other SF authors have seized upon the tension between cybernetic and biological enhancement, driving cyberpunk to imagine startling new "wet" futures. Key works in this vein include Kathleen Ann Goonan's 1994–2000 *Nanotech Quartet*, Paul Di Filippo's 1996 *Ribofunk*, and Margaret Atwood's 2003 *Oryx and Crake*. Although these works are very different in tone (Goonan's books are cautiously utopic, Atwood's novel is largely dystopic, and Di Filippo makes a playful end run around the whole issue), all three authors are, like their post-singularity counterparts, profoundly interested in the fate of human values, emotions, and aesthetic productions in a posthuman world.

The development of global socioeconomic networks has drawn attention to the fact that SF is no longer the exclusive province of white, Western people. Indeed, it turns out that this has never been the case. Over the course of the twentieth century that other great industrial nation, the Soviet Union, developed an SF tradition parallel to its anglophone counterpart. As early as 1970 English-speaking readers could learn about that tradition in Isaac Asimov's *Soviet Science Fiction* anthology; today, new anthologies such as Alexander Levitsky's 2008 *Worlds Apart: An Anthology of Russian Science Fiction and Fantasy* attest to the continued evolution of Russian SF. The SF community has also recently become aware of an alternate speculative fiction within the transatlantic region itself: Afrofuturism. Early Afrofuturist works include Edward Johnson's 1904 utopia *Light Ahead for the Negro*, W.E.B. Du Bois's 1920 disaster story "The Comet," and George Schuyler's 1936–38 serialized future war stories *Black Internationale* and *Black Empire*. Since the 1960s Afrodiasporic authors including Samuel R. Delany, Octavia E. Butler, Nalo Hopkinson, and Minister Faust have become luminaries within the SF community; stories by these and other notable Afrofuturists are collected in Sherree R. Tepper's 2000 and 2004 *Dark Matter* anthologies and Hopkinson and Uppinder Mehan's 2004 *So Long Been Dreaming: postcolonial science fiction and fantasy* collection.

SF has flourished in countries as diverse as China, Japan, and Brazil since the late nineteenth century as well. Perhaps not surprisingly, authors from these countries began writing speculative fiction at the same time that merchants began using industrial technologies. The earliest of these publications include Huang Jiang Diao Sou's 1904 "Lunar Colony," Oshikawa Shunro's 1900 *Undersea Warship*, and Joachim Felício dos Santos' 1868–72 *Pages from the History of Brazil Written in the Year 2000*. Anglo-American readers can learn about contemporary Chinese, Japanese, and Latin American SF in Dingbo Wu and Patrick D. Murphy's 1989 *Science Fiction from China*, Gene van Troyer and Grania Davis's 2007 *Speculative Japan: outstanding tales of Japanese science fiction and fantasy*, and Andrea L. Bell and Yolanda Molina-Gavilan's 2003 *Cosmos Latinos: an anthology of science fiction from latin America and Spain*. Like their Russian and Afrodiasporic counterparts, Chinese, Japanese, and Brazilian SF authors have both revised Western genre conventions and developed new ones in light of their own fantastic literary traditions to better dramatize the processes of industrialization and globalization in their own societies. Taken together, these speculative writing traditions demonstrate that SF is the literature not just of engineers, but of all people living in the modern world.

Bibliography

Alkon, P.K. (1994) *Science Fiction Before 1900: imagination discovers technology*, New York and London: Routledge.

Barron, N. (ed.) (2004) *Anatomy of Wonder: a critical guide to science fiction*, 5th edn, Westport, CT: Libraries Unlimited.

Bould, M., Butler, A.M., Roberts, A. and Vint, S. (eds) (2009) *The Routledge Companion to Science Fiction*, New York and London: Routledge.

Csicsery-Ronay Jr., I. (2008) *The Seven Beauties of Science Fiction*, Middletown, CT: Wesleyan University Press.

Donawerth, J.L. (1997) *Frankenstein's Daughters: women writing science fiction*, Syracuse: Syracuse University Press.

Luckhurst, R. (2005) *Science Fiction*, Cambridge: Polity Press.

Melzer, P. (2006) *Alien Constructions: science fiction and feminist thought*, Austin: University of Texas Press.

Roberts, R. (1993) *A New Species: gender and science in science fiction*, Urbana: University of Illinois Press.

Seed, D. (1999) *American Science Fiction and the Cold War: literature and film*, Chicago: Fitzroy Dearborn.

Stableford, B. (2006) *Science Fact and Science Fiction: an encyclopedia*, New York and London: Routledge.

Vint, S. (2007) *Bodies of Tomorrow: technology, subjectivity, science fiction*, Toronto: University of Toronto Press.

Wolmark, J. (2000) *Cybersexualities*, Edinburgh: Edinburgh University Press.

Yaszek, L. (2008) *Galactic Suburbia: recovering women's science fiction*, Columbus: Ohio State University Press.

34
SEMIOTICS
Paul Cobley

The relation between semiotics, science, and literature is, like the history of semiotics, two-sided, with either side almost – but not quite – a mirror of the other. In fact, one could argue that the relation of semiotics to the fields of science and literature is actually a key constituent of the definition of semiotics itself. Semiotics is not yet an institutionalized discipline like, say, linguistics or biology. Nor is it viewed in the same way by different groups: those who write for semiotics journals and publish books in the field and participate in semiotics conferences, and those who are aware of semiotics' existence but have no commitment to semiotics except insofar as it can be used as a tool or a straw man for other pursuits.

Semiology, structuralism, literature, and scientificity

As is well known, semiotics is defined as "the study of the sign," a problematic definition because much of semiotics' project and analysis is concerned with entities larger than the sign (for example, the "text") and because the concept of "sign" often seems to bracket out the nature of the consciousness that apprehends or constitutes that sign. Semiotics is also associated with a number of proper names: Charles Sanders Peirce, the American logician, scientist, and philosopher; Ferdinand de Saussure, the Swiss linguist; and Thomas A. Sebeok, the Hungarian-American linguist and "biologist *manqué*."

Since Saussure's impact on the study of literature has been held by many to be profound (e.g., Culler 1975) and to be so by virtue of his sign theory, it is necessary to mention some technicalities. The theory is principally to be found in his *Cours de linguistique générale* (1916; translated into English in 1959 and 1983). Saussure's *Cours* has been taken as projecting "a science *which studies the role of signs as part of social life*" (Saussure 1983: 15). Saussure makes it clear that a linguistic sign is not "a link between a thing and a name, but between a concept [*signifié*, signified] and a sound pattern [*signifiant*, signifier]" (66). Moreover, "the sound pattern is not actually a sound; for a sound is something physical" (66).

The linguistic sign is thus a "two-sided psychological entity" (67), not a relation between a thing in the world and the way that it is designated.

A *signifié* is bound to each *signifiant* but their binding is not natural or pre-ordained. For example, the connection between a *signifiant* "duck" and the concept of "duckness" is specific only to the development of a particular national language. Put another way, there is an arbitrary relation in the linguistic sign; thus, "when semiology is established ... the main object of study in semiology will ... be the class of systems based upon the arbitrary nature of the sign" (Saussure 1983: 68). For Saussure, the object of linguistics (and, by extension, sign study) is the collective phenomenon, the system that allows signifying: *langue*. *Langue* is the set of multifarious and interconnected differences between all signs (with their arbitrary relations). Available to, and stemming from, all speakers, *langue* enables *parole* – speech – "the sum total of what people say" (19).

As Harris (2001) argues rather persuasively, Saussure's version of linguistics aspired to some of the criteria of "science" that various fringe subjects of the late nineteenth century were queuing up to acquire, particularly that it has an "object" (*langue*) that can be systematically broken down into smaller elements. The *Cours* does discuss entities larger than the sign, such as *syntagma* (the sentence, phrase or clause); but it holds back from suggesting that such "texts" are beyond the determinations of the system and cannot be broken down into smaller components for the purpose of analysis.

Despite – or because of – its systematic take on linguistic signs, many of the *Cours'* champions were contributors to major currents in twentieth-century literary analysis (Harris 2001: 118; 2003). Saussurean sign theory was conveyed to the Moscow Linguistic Circle, including the young Roman Jakobson, the Russian Formalists, and Mikhail Bakhtin (Todorov 1984: 6–13). Possibly the most influential receptions of Saussure were the closely argued essays on linguistics by Emile Benveniste, the father of poststructuralism, and by the high structuralist "glossematics" of Louis Hjelmslev, who sought to extend the system concept of *langue*. The theoretical heir to Hjelmslev was the early work of Roland Barthes; yet Barthes, like Jakobson and the anthropologist Claude Lévi-Strauss, was now promoting structuralism through the study of literature. His first book, *Le Degré zéro de l'écriture* (1953), discussed literary writing in terms of Saussurean "arbitrariness," a theme that he was to continue a decade later in his polemical volume *Sur Racine* (1963). Like his other writings of the period, these viewed cultural artifacts as dependent not on transcendent factors such as beauty or truth but on the nature of the system – *langue* – that generated or facilitated them.

Lévi-Strauss effectively considered mythic narratives in a manner similar to Barthes's literary criticism, as revealing the *langue* behind copious examples of *parole* (e.g. Lévi-Strauss 1977), thus providing the impetus for a major research project in literature and beyond. Another influential Saussurean, A.J. Greimas, in a fashion which, from a distance at least, is akin to that of Lévi-Strauss, gave priority to structural relations between narrative entities rather than to their intrinsic qualities. Along with the recovered work of Vladimir Propp, Greimas effectively gave birth to the discipline known as "narratology," a specific way of understanding narrative – not just "literary writing" – relying on a systematic, thorough, and disinterested approach to narrative's mechanics. Unsurprisingly, this approach provided a stark contrast to those which observe or seek out "value" in some narratives (and not others) or which provide hierarchies of narratives based on spurious categories such as the "genius" of an author or artiste.

Given this systematic approach to literature, coupled with the heritage of Saussurean linguistics' attempt at scientific status (Parisian intellectuals were making similar claims for psychoanalysis and Marxism), there was excitement about semiology's claim to knowledge. In issue 47 (1971) of *Tel Quel*, the literary organ edited by novelist Philippe Sollers and house journal of early Parisian poststructuralism, Barthes revealed a "euphoric dream of scientificity" arising from semiology's influence on literary criticism (cited in Coward and Ellis 1977: 25).

In his 1970 book *S/Z*, Barthes attempted to implement a "scientific" analysis of literature. *S/Z* dissects a Balzac short story, "Sarrasine," dividing it up into very brief segments and by elaborating five codes through whose matrix the text passes. The idea of a "code" has a scientistic bearing here, since it suggests the stability of the *signifiant/signifié* relationship that structuralism purported to reveal as the central conceit of traditional "realist" texts. Yet, the final implication of *S/Z* – that this relationship is inherently unstable in literature – is ambiguous in relation to the project of literature's "scientificity," since it suggests a high degree of subjectivity on the part of the reader is responsible for enacting any relationship between *signifiant* and *signifié*.

Irrespective of such ambiguity, semiology, structuralism, and post-structuralism have, through their co-opting of literature and science, assisted in producing a "discursive imagination," a perspective in which human affairs and the effecting of change in human affairs are determined by the vicissitudes of signs and collections of signs in discourse. Assisted by the much-vaunted "linguistic turn" in social thought (Rorty 1967), this perspective has persisted until recently, not just in the study of literature but also in the study of culture in general. Although claiming to avoid ahistoricism (for example, Barthes's position from *Mythologues* [1957] onwards was that he was exposing, by reference to history [or "culture"], the "naturalization" of artifacts), the post-semiological perspective has increasingly relied on the almost Berkeleyan idea that the world is "constructed in discourse." As such, science as advocated by, say, Darwin, was to be bracketed or supplanted by a "science" of culture represented in the nexus of Marx–Freud–Saussure (refracted, arguably, through the prism of Althusser–Lacan–Derrida). In philosophical terms, there is something obvious to be gained from this perspective: the rejection of a naïve one-to-one relationship between the world and its representations. In political terms, there is something equally obvious to be gained: constant suspicion of social-scientific engineering, such as eugenics, social Darwinism, or Lysenkoism, as well as an awareness of the way that so-called "pure science" serves power interests. Yet, in the philosophical case, semiology did not establish a new terrain: the grounds upon which it conducted its arguments have a long, albeit largely forgotten, history in scholastic debates about nominalism and realism (Deely 2008: 29–46). In the political case, semiology's attempt to forge a new "science" of literature (and culture) threatened to bracket scientific research into nature altogether and create not just a "prison-house of language" that it was the task of critique to analyse, but a real "prison-house" in which either nothing existed beyond the system of *langue* or what did exist there was unknowable.

Contemporary semiotics, science, and the literary view

Semiotics, as opposed to semiology, is the study of *all* signs, not just linguistic ones. Historically, semiotics *precedes* semiology. Both terms are derived from a Greek root, *seme*, but "semiotics" was taken up by the American philosopher, Charles Sanders Peirce, who sought to classify all types of signs in the universe. In this way, semiotics constitutes the major tradition of sign study derived from the ancient semioticians – medics such as Hippocrates of Cos and Galen of Pergamon who developed a science of symptomatology (see Sebeok 2001a; Staiano-Ross 2009a, 2009b, 2009c) and were concerned with natural signs – and, later, from Augustine, who proposed a sign theory applicable to language and culture (see Deely 2009a). If semiology created the impression that the whole of sign study was human discourse and the human sign, semiotics demonstrated something very different. The localized study of the *linguistic* sign, a sign type used by humans alone, is only one component of the study of the sign in general. The human phenomenon of language is just one minuscule aspect of a broader *semiosis*, the action of signs throughout the universe no matter how they might be embodied. Put this way, language looks tiny compared to the array of signs engendered by, say, interactions between living cells.

Semiotics, even in comprising some aspects of semiology, is very much a pre-Socratic project. The recognition of bodies as containers of signs, humans' repertoire of verbal and non-verbal communication, the systematicity of signs, and the dissemination of signs throughout nature that informed the construction of the Hippocratic Corpus are instances of this. The ancient medics' concern with *projecting* the course of an illness was also a prefiguration of modern science and an anticipation of semiotics after Peirce. Yet, the major tradition of semiotics also pre-Socratically unifies science and philosophy by its concern with how the entire cosmos operates – the Earth, its inhabitants, and the elements – rather than just the interactions that constitute the polis. Both Peirce and Sebeok, out of step with the intellectual fashions of their times, shared this outlook. For the later Peirce, especially, the entirety of logic, philosophy, and science was only approachable through an expansive sign theory. Peirce himself was a scientist in his post at the U.S. Coast and Geodetic Survey (see Brent 1998), but was so also in the way his "semeiotic" was totally interwoven with the "assertion and interpretation" that are the hallmark of science (see Hookway 1985: 118–44).

For Peirce, the sign was crucial: he wrote to Lady Welby late in life, revealing that he had recognized ten basic types of signs and 59,049 different classes of signs in all (Peirce 1966: 407). The roots of Peirce's triadic sign can be discovered in his profound knowledge of not just classical logic but the Latin scholastic tradition. The Latins took as part of their task the exegesis of the perspective on signs emanating from the teachings of St. Thomas Aquinas. The most important of these exegetes was John (sometimes "Jean" or "Joao") Poinsot: his *Tractatus de Signis* (1632), nearly sixty years before Locke coined the term "semiotics," offers a realist foregrounding of the sign as the object of study to illuminate two key states: mind-dependent being and mind-independent being. The Kantian idealist notion of the *Ding an sich*, the thing-in-itself, so important for modern thought and, putatively, for science, posits an entity that is unknowable (i.e., mind-independent being). Before Kant, however, Poinsot's semiotic offered the means to overcome the impasse of the knowable and the unknowable by demonstrating how cultural reality in the human species is where the differences between mind-independent and mind-dependent being become knowable and distinguishable (see Deely 2005: 76).

Deely, the scholar who rescued Poinsot from mere footnote status, demonstrates how Poinsot defined an *object* as always an *object* signified (involving, though not necessarily reducible to, mind-dependent status), definitionally distinct from a *thing* (a mind-independent entity). The latter may be made an *object* by the *thing* being experienced; but, even then, through the sensations it provokes, the feelings about them and their consequences, that *thing* is never available "in full" – it is available only through a *sign* (Deely 1994: 11–22; cf. 2009b). The *sign* is simultaneously of the order of mind-independent *and* mind-dependent being, no matter what futile attempts to bracket off one or the other form of being might be made in an attempt to render the sign as either solely *object* or *thing*. As Peirce noted, "Reals *are* signs. To try to peel off signs & get down to the real thing is like trying to peel an onion and get down to the onion itself" (Peirce 1905: L 387).

These arguments about the nature of signs have been suspended by much of modern thought, including semiology, structuralism, and poststructuralism. This suspending of the consideration of signs' purchase on the real takes place in spite of the fact that such a consideration is central to what constitutes *scientific* knowledge, precisely the reason in the Latin arguments reviewed and expanded by Peirce (shifting the focus from the being to the action of signs and introducing the "interpretant" as the "third term" of the sign relation). One way in which the suspension has been achieved is through historiography: that is, the convenient reiteration that between 1350 and 1650 – effectively between William of Ockham and Descartes – nothing happened in the history of Western thought (see Cobley 2009). Arguably the most important living American philosopher, John Deely, has stressed that the Latin thinkers cannot be disregarded: as with semiotics, their project was not fixated on twentieth-century preoccupations such as power and the polis but, like the pre-Socratics, considered "psychology" and the investigation of living things. Modern thought (roughly from the Enlightenment to ultra-modern poststructuralism), epitomized on the one hand by literature that eschews the unified version of the world in literary "realism" and, on the other, by philosophy that sees reality constructed in the vagaries of "language," has bequeathed a view of the world in which a one-to-one relationship of the world and its representation, and even of a signifier and a signified, is irredeemably faulty.

The Latin thought that informs contemporary semiotics was well apprised of the faults of representation, as evident in the concept of mind-dependent being (*ens rationis*); but more importantly, it recognized, unlike semiology and much modern thought, that representation is not the whole of the sign. For Poinsot and, later, for Peirce, the sign needs to be understood as the entire relation of elements that constitute it rather than just the representational "relation" between some vehicle and some terminus. The real relation that constitutes the sign is precisely the relation that unites vehicle with terminus: a triad comprising vehicle, terminus, and the relation between them (representamen-object-interpretant). The "relation of representation" must be distinct from that of "signification by a sign in general," must be merely *a part* of sign action, simply because a sign's object or terminus can represent another and also represent itself, whereas it would be a contradiction for a sign to be a sign of itself. A sign – even if referring to itself – must have some level of difference from its object in order to function as a sign. This is not to say that a sign *cannot* refer to itself, but that a sign's object – when that object is itself – is characterized by a different order of experience than that for the object alone. Poinsot emphasized that the relation in a sign is not so much suprasubjective as contextual: in one set of circumstances the relation in a sign could be of the order of mind-independent being (known as *ens reale* by the Latins), in another set it could be of mind-dependent being (*ens rationis*) (Deely 2001: 729).

The Latin heritage of sign study was relatively vaguely known by Peirce scholars, including Jakobson, the ex-Russian Formalist, and Charles Morris, both of whom were teachers and friends of Sebeok. The latter encouraged Deely's recovery of the scholastics from the late 1960s to the twenty-first century, but it was Sebeok himself who was to demonstrate at length the broad importance for science of semiotics' figuring of relations in the triadic sign across different domains and for different species. Although a prolific linguist, Sebeok was also a polymath maintaining a "biological outlook" (cf. Sebeok 2010). This is worth mentioning in light of the breadth of semiotics on which Sebeok insisted; but it also demonstrates that, unlike semiology, Sebeok's semiotics would be sympathetic to research into the natural world without being naïve about the relation of the sign and world and without proposing itself as an alternative or true "science" (Sebeok always referred to the *doctrine* of signs). Emphatically, Sebeok inaugurated zoosemiotics in 1963, but it was his development of biosemiotics which was to prove most consequential for the relation of semiotics to science.

From linguistics, cybernetics, and communication science, Sebeok began to develop semiotics in the direction of Jakob von Uexküll (see Sebeok 2001b: 34). The notion of *Umwelt*, from von Uexküll, central now to contemporary semiotics, suggests that all species live in a "world" that is constructed out of their own signs, the latter being the result of their own sign-making and receiving capacities. There are signs which function as signs for *us* (or for others) and, as has been noted, *things* beyond signs. Yet, whereas the nominalist tradition of semiology would pronounce the world of things to be unknowable – or, in more cunning versions, "abject," "a semiotic chora" (Kristeva 1982), "undecidable" (Derrida 1981) – the *realist* tradition of contemporary semiotics seeks further. The world of the thing is apprehended only by the sign, to be sure – that is, any organism's *Umwelt* is constituted by its own sign-making capacity, its own semiosis facilitated by the sensory apparatus it possesses, whether it is a human or a mere tick. Yet, signs in an *Umwelt* have considerable richness. A dog's hearing, for example, has advantages specific to that species; a fly's antennae and visual organs, to take another example, invariably enable it to swiftly avoid even the most deadly of rolled-up newspapers. In sum, an *Umwelt* offers an indispensable guide to reality which, while not comprehensive, is sufficient to maintain the continued existence of specific species. Contemporary semiotics thus employs a realist understanding of the sign which recognizes that species cannot "see" everything, yet that the relationality beheld through semiosis is not just rich but imperative for survival.

Uexküll's concept of *Umwelt* provided the basis for Sebeok's acceleration of semiotics' consideration of its natural and biological foundations. As early as 1975, he had already named the project in print in an essay on the way that zoosemiotics stands at the intersection of nature and culture. In the next two and a half decades, Sebeok sought to bring together the leading thinkers in biosemiotics from the sciences: Giorgio Prodi (oncology), Heini Hediger (zoology), Thure von Uexküll (medicine), Jesper Hoffmeyer (molecular biology), and Kalevi Kull (botany) among others. In addition to zoosemiotics, sign study now would involve a semiotics of plants ("phytosemiotics"), of fungi ("mycosemiotics"), and of the 3.5-billion-year-old global prokaryotic communication network within and between different bacterial cells ("microsemiotics, cytosemiotics").

Semiotics (the major tradition) has demonstrated a commitment to knowledge in a number of ways, then: through a sophisticated sign theory that is aware of the lure of nominalism and versions of constructionism but is geared towards realism; through a holistic grasp of the myriad domains across nature where sign action takes place; and, at a time when modern thought in its death throes is fixated on the *polis* and shifts of power relations as the limit point of reality, through an embrace of the possibilities of science, particularly biology, rather than an outright rejection of it. All this is clear from the recent development of biosemiotics alone (see, for example, Barbieri 2007; cf. Deely 2009c). Yet, interesting in the context of this chapter is the role of literature or literary modes of thought. In one sense, semiology imploded because its quasi-scientistic insistence on the singularized sign tended to go against the text- or discourse-orientated study of literature that had so fueled sign study in the second half of the twentieth century. Nowhere was this more the case than in the so-called Tartu-Moscow school which, in the circumstances of a large part of its existence, was compelled to concern itself with Russian classics. Yet, partly out of Lotman's work in that school (see, for example, Lotman 1977) there arose new possibilities as a result of the study of literary forms of "knowing" or, more specifically in contemporary semiotic terms, "modeling."

For Sebeok, embracing the work of both Lotman and von Uexküll, the most apt English translation of *Umwelt* was "model." The human *Umwelt* – "language" understood as an innate capacity for verbal differentiation *plus* non-verbal communication – evinced three kinds of modeling: Primary (the world as derived from the innate capacity for differentiation); Secondary (the world constructed in verbal expression); Tertiary (the world growing out of sophisticated cultural forms with a basis in Primary and Secondary modeling) (Sebeok 1988). In terms of literature, writing occupies an interesting space in this formulation because it is clearly a kind of Tertiary modeling while also being Primary because it "organizes experience and surrounding reality both spatially and temporally, conferring sense upon them and constructing whole new worlds" (Ponzio 2003: 7). It is no coincidence that Sebeok's final original monograph (with Danesi), *The Forms of Meaning* (2000), while seeking principally to institute a new, post-biosemiotic terminology for sign study, did so by way of the concept of modeling. Moreover, it focused on "forms" rather than singularized signs. In addition to Sebeok's not inconsiderable literary and cultural analysis (see, for example, Sebeok 2000), his project of biosemiotics arguably rests on the reconceptualization of science – biology in particular – in terms of how organisms "know" the world. It might be more contentious to suggest that this interest in "knowing" has a literary basis; however, if one considers Sebeok's early career alone – in anthropology, linguistics, and biology, convening the major conferences such as those on Myth (1955), Style in Language (1958) and Approaches to Semiotics (1962) – literature, as a putatively dominant form of culture allied to linguistics, would have been high on the agenda. Biosemiotics is, in some measure, a critique of science's failure to acknowledge agency and "knowing" (see Hoffmeyer 1996, 2008; see also Brier 2008). Its alliance with approaches to cultural – or literary – forms of knowing (sometimes called "sociosemiotics" or "cultural semiotics") is inevitable, because biosemiotics has predominantly arisen from them.

Plain semiotics

The development of semiotics is clearly instructive for understanding the relation of approaches to science and literature. In the case of semiology, "science" has been a rhetorical battering ram employed to break into the financially and technologically bolstered citadel of science (without inverted commas). In short, semiology and its mode of studying literature tended to present itself as a new, all-knowing "science." As a constituent of the lesser partner in the binary of the two cultures, it had good reason to be both suspicious and arrogant in the face of perceived oppression. Yet, unlike semiotics, it did not have the benefit of the distinction, introduced by Peirce from Jeremy Bentham, of "ideoscopic" and "cenoscopic" sciences (see Deely 2008: 3–9). The Enlightenment perspective, with the invention of scientific technologies after Galileo, was dominated by the search for new phenomena – ideoscopy; before the Enlightenment, however, there was much to gain from the scrutiny of common experience – cenoscopy. The major tradition of semiotics (stemming from Peirce and Sebeok) did not simply take a different tack to semiology; rather, it had an almost completely distinct lineage, partly based on cenoscopic science. Rather than straightforwardly provoking conflict within the binary, or even projecting three cultures (cf. Kagan 2009), semiotics' theory of semiosis – signs, texts, discourse, relation, context, and *Umwelt* – has presented a path to knowledge that serves as a bridge between the humanities and the sciences (see Perron et al. 2000; see also Brier 2008: esp. 82–83, 266–68; and, above all, the "manifesto" of Anderson et al. 1984). Although the following statement seems to force the tentative mirror image announced at the outset, the most direct way to sum up is to say that sign study in the guise of semiology attempted to give "scientific" status to the analysis and practice of literature; semiotics, on the other hand, has pursued a project of "literarizing" science. The major tradition has taken a concept previously associated with the world of trivial or rarefied cultural artifacts – signification – and attempted to demonstrate the benefits of recognizing its guiding role in cultural and natural phenomena, both of which, in the end, are natural.

Bibliography

Anderson, M., Deely, J., Krampen, M., Ransdell, J., Sebeok, T. and von Uexküll, T. (1984) "A semiotic perspective on the sciences: steps toward a new paradigm," *Semiotica*, 52: 7–47.

Barbieri, M. (ed.) (2007) *Introduction to Biosemiotics: the new biological synthesis*, Dordrecht: Springer.

Barthes, R. (1953) *Le Degré zéro de l'écriture*, Paris: Seuil.

——(1957) *Mythologiques*, Paris: Seuil.

——(1963) *Sur Racine*, Paris: Seuil.

——(1970) *S/Z*, Paris: Seuil.

Brent, J. (1998) *Charles Sanders Peirce: a life*, 2nd edn, Bloomington: Indiana University Press.

Brier, S. (2008) *Cybersemiotics: why information is not enough*, Toronto: University of Toronto Press.

Cobley, P. (2009) (ed.) *Realism for the 21st Century: a John Deely reader*, Scranton and London: University of Scranton Press.

Coward, R. and Ellis, J. (1977) *Language and Materialism: developments in semiology and the theory of the subject*, London: Routledge & Kegan Paul.

Culler, J. (1975) *Structuralist Poetics: structuralism, linguistics and the study of literature*, London: Routledge & Kegan Paul.

Deely, J. (1994) *The Human Use of Signs; or elements of anthroposemiosis*, Lanham, MD: Rowman & Littlefield.

——(2001) "A Sign is What?" *Sign Systems Studies*, 29(2): 705–43.

——(2005) *Defining the Semiotic Animal*, Sofia: New Bulgarian University.

——(2008) *Descartes and Poinsot: the crossroad of signs and ideas*, Scranton and London: Scranton University Press.

——(2009a) *Augustine and Poinsot: the protosemiotic development*, Scranton and London: Scranton University Press.

——(2009b) *Purely Objective Reality*, Berlin: Mouton de Gruyter.

——(2009c) "Pars pro toto from culture to nature: an overview of semiotics as a postmodern development, with an anticipation of developments to come," *American Journal of Semiotics*, 15(1–2): 167–92.

Derrida, J. (1981) *Dissemination*, trans. A. Bass, London: Athlone.

Harris, R. (2001) "Linguistics after Saussure," in P. Cobley (ed.) *The Routledge Companion to Semiotics and Linguistics*, London: Routledge.

——(2003) *Saussure and His Interpreters*, 2nd edn, Edinburgh: Edinburgh University Press.

Hoffmeyer, J. (1996) *Signs of Meaning in the Universe*, Bloomington: Indiana University Press.

——(2008) *Biosemiotics: an examination into the signs of life and the life of signs*, Scranton and London: University of Scranton Press.

Hookway, C. (1985) *Peirce*, London: Routledge & Kegan Paul.

Kagan, J. (2009) *The Three Cultures: natural sciences, social sciences and the humanities in the 21st century*, Cambridge: Cambridge University Press.

Kristeva, J. (1982) *Powers of Horror*, trans. L. Roudiez, New York: Columbia University Press.

Lévi-Strauss, C. (1977) "The structural study of myth," in *Structural Anthropology*, Vol. 1, trans. C. Jacobson and B.G. Schoepf, Harmondsworth: Penguin.

Lotman, J. (1977) "Primary and secondary communication-modeling systems," in D.P. Lucid (ed.) *Soviet Semiotics: an anthology*, Baltimore: Johns Hopkins University Press.

Peirce, C.S. (1905) "Letter to Francis C. Russell, 3 July," L 387, The Charles S. Peirce Papers. Manuscript Collection in the Houghton Library, Cambridge, Mass.: Harvard University Press. (Number of letter [L] given according to numbering in R.S. Robin, *Annotated Catalogue of the Papers of Charles S. Peirce*, Amherst: University of Massachusetts.)

——(1966) "Letters to Lady Welby," in P.P. Wiener (ed.) *Charles S. Peirce: Selected Writings*, New York: Dover Press.

Perron, P., Sbrocchi, L.G., Colilli, P. and Danesi, M. (eds) (2000) *Semiotics as a Bridge between the Humanities and the Sciences*, Toronto: Legas.

Ponzio, A. (2003) "By way of introduction: report on the status of writing in today's world of communication," in S. Petrilli and A. Ponzio, *Views in Literary Semiotics*, trans. S. Petrilli, Toronto: Legas.

Rorty, R. (ed.) (1967) *The Linguistic Turn: essays in philosophical method with two retrospective essays*, Chicago: University of Chicago Press.

Saussure, F. de (1983) *Course in General Linguistics*, trans. R. Harris, London: Duckworth.

Sebeok, T.A. (1975) "Zoosemiotics: at the intersection of nature and culture," in T.A. Sebeok (ed.) *The Tell-Tale Sign: a survey of semiotics*, Lisse: Peter de Ridder.

——(1988) "In what sense is language a 'primary modeling system'?," in H. Broms and R. Kaufmann (eds) *Semiotics of Culture*, Helsinki: Arator.

——(2000) *Essays in Semiotics II: culture signs*, Ottawa: Legas Press.

——(2001a) "Galen in medical semiotics," in *Global Semiotics*, Bloomington: Indiana University Press.

——(2001b) "Biosemiotics: its roots and proliferation," in *Global Semiotics*, Bloomington: Indiana University Press.

——(2010) "Summing up: in lieu of an introduction," in P. Cobley, J. Deely, K. Kull and S. Petrilli (eds) *Semiotics Continues to Astonish: the intellectual heritage of Thomas A. Sebeok*, Berlin: Mouton de Gruyter.

——and Danesi, M. (2000) *Forms of Meaning: modeling systems theory and semiotic analysis*, Berlin: Mouton de Gruyter.

Staiano-Ross, K. (2009a) "Galen," in P. Cobley (ed.) *The Routledge Companion to Semiotics*, London: Routledge.

——(2009b) "Hippocrates," in P. Cobley (ed.) *The Routledge Companion to Semiotics*, London: Routledge.

——(2009c) "Medical semiotics," in P. Cobley (ed.) *The Routledge Companion to Semiotics*, London: Routledge.

Todorov, T. (1984) *Mikhail Bakhtin: the dialogic principle*, trans. W. Godzich, Minneapolis: University of Minnesota Press.

Part III

PERIODS AND CULTURES

Some scholars of literature and science repaired from training in the sciences to graduate programs in literature. Their work thus rests on especially strong preparation in science and familiarity with its institutions. But most academics who would approach scientific matters for purposes of literary scholarship and its related disciplines do not have advanced scientific training. Parts I and II of this *Companion* are designed to provide advanced introductions to the range of scientific disciplines and multiple points of entrance of the interdisciplinary specializations in literature and science. Part III reflects the circumstance that many current practitioners in these specializations initially came up to speed on their sciences of interest through the rigorous tutorials provided by modern scholarship in the history of science. As Henning Schmidgen argued in Part II (Chapter 29), the history of science is "an interdiscipline, and arguably the interdiscipline par excellence." Works such as *Energy and Empire*, Norton Wise and Crosbie Smith's cultural biography of Lord Kelvin, and Lily Kay's history of modern genetics, *Who Wrote the Book of Life?*, ease the details of scientific and technological developments toward the cultural chronologies of the humanities. Solid historical platforms such as these help prepare one to do literature and science with the requisite empirical as well as critical purchase.

A longer historical view attunes us to the multiple anachronisms we commit when reading our modern ideas of "science" back into any number of earlier historical periods. Emma Gee's article on Greece and Rome, for instance, notes that during the classical period, "Areas which we might call 'scientific' were covered by a range of terms, often more different from one another in nuance than in meaning. These terms include *sophia* (wisdom) and *philosophia*, *logos* (reason, often opposed to *mythos*), *techne* (art, skill), and *episteme* (knowledge or understanding)." And Arielle Saiber reminds us that, during the Middle Ages and early Renaissance, while both "*scientia* and *ars* were part of 'natural philosophy,'" debates over the sense of *scientia* revolved "around the Aristotelian distinction between *scientia quia* (knowledge of the fact) and *scientia propter quid* (knowledge through the cause)" – that is, between bodies of knowledge we now distinguish as scientific, on the one hand, and philosophical, on the other.

Both institutionally and with regard to the practical overlap of scholarly activities, the history of science is the prior disciplinary specialization closest to literature and science. Acknowledging the more recent imperative to relativize and complicate the Western Eurocentrism endemic to the standard chronicling of scientific thought and practice, Part III also pairs Western historical periods with non-European cultures. In his chapter on Russia, Kenneth Knoespel studies how "Russian natural history involves the continuous rehearsal of the place and exploratory capacity of the Russian language," in a dialectic both of openness and of resistance to Western European developments. And as Thomas Lamarre remarks (Chapter 42), the case of Japan highlights the limitations of both unitary and binary models of world and scientific culture: "Japan's technoscientific modernization has frequently been presented not only as the exception among non-Western nations but also as a model for them." These historical constructions presume "a unitary Eastern or Oriental worldview or cultural paradigm." However, all "such unities are metaphysical, as are the binary oppositions of East and West, and tradition and modernity." Historical periodizations and cultural comparisons remain indispensable, if always debatable, organizational principles for the scholarly work of literature and science.

In earlier accounts of post-Renaissance culture, the sense of "science" became attached to the notion of a "revolution," which notion has itself come under recent historical critique. Alvin Snider (Chapter 37) affirms that "Historians of science now generally doubt the existence of a revolutionary moment of origin in the seventeenth century, of a fixed method for the production of new knowledge, of a cultural totality captured by the anachronistic word 'science.'" These properly revisionist accounts of early modern science are matched by a similar tendency in the discussion of postmodernism. In his chapter concluding this volume, Stefan Herbrechter comments on "the effect of a new permeability between science and culture – a certain 'culturalization' of science as a practice combined with an increased 'presence' of science within culture."

Even while one still marks a distinction between "science" and "culture," this is now done in the cognizance of their mutual "permeability." The work in literature and science gathered here overcomes the "two-cultures" dilemma not by forcing a one-culture solution from either direction, but by intellectual acclimation to a world of many intersecting cultures, their myriad specificities as complexly coupled as the life-forms of an ecosystem. Going forward, as Richard Nash affirms (Chapter 22, this volume), we confront "an intellectual reorientation to a world in which we are responsive agents within nature-culture networks." One will do best to model their scholarly mediations, it would seem, on complex ecologies, within which multiple systems are always enmeshed with coevolving and unpredictable environments.

35

GREECE AND ROME

Emma Gee

Literary intellectuals at one pole – at the other scientists, and as the most representative, the physical scientists. Between the two a gulf of mutual incomprehension.

C.P. Snow

Snow's opposition between literature and science may seem more naive to us
than to his audience of 1959; to the Greeks and Romans it would have been
incomprehensible. The concept of antipathy between representatives of the two
poles, as it operates today, was unavailable to ancient thinkers. There was, in
antiquity, no one word equivalent to "science." Areas which we might call
"scientific" were covered by a range of terms, often more different from one
another in nuance than in meaning. These terms include *sophia* (wisdom) and
philosophia; *logos* (reason, often opposed to *muthos*); *techne* (art, skill), and *episteme*
(knowledge or understanding).

One can see immediately from Plato (often the source of such definitions in
modern literature) the slipperiness of some of these terms in their original
context. Consider, for instance, the discussion of *techne* and *episteme* at Plato,
Gorgias 449–52. *Techne*, which is said by Rihll (1999: 2) to be the Greek term
usually translated as "science," cannot be limited in this ancient text either
to scientific practice as opposed to theory, or even to the sciences per se.
At *Gorgias* 449c9 the orator Gorgias is described by Socrates as *rhetorikes ...
epistemon technes*, "being skilled (*epistemon*) in the science of rhetoric." Here *epistemon* denotes theoretical knowledge, *techne* the thing practiced (here rhetoric).
But the noun *episteme* can also be used of practical knowledge, as it is
shortly afterwards, at 449d9–10, *episteme peri logous*, "the science of speaking."
Moreover, in another Platonic dialogue, *Phaedrus* 260d, *techne* is used as
episteme was in the *Gorgias*, to mean "the science of speaking," *ten ton logon
technen*. Thus there is no straightforward theoretical/practical antithesis between
episteme and *techne*. Not only that, but Plato's Socrates casts the net very wide in
terms of the activities covered by *techne*. At *Gorgias* 452a1–d5, the doctor, fitness
trainer, and entrepreneur could all say the same – *techne* refers to all of their
activities.[1]

Similar problems exist in connection with the other terms used to describe
ancient science. For instance, as Geoffrey Lloyd has shown (1987: 83–102),

sophia could often refer to poets and poetry. *Sophia* cannot be confined to science, but is an area in which knowledge of the natural world competes with knowledge expressed in poetry, the first referent of the term. Nor are *philosophia* and its cognate verb, *philosophein*, confined to areas of activity we recognize as science, although they may *include* the natural sciences (Lloyd 1987: 94 n153). *Logos*, too: sometimes *logos* could mean "science" or "reason";[2] at other times, its distinction from *muthos* could be blurred.[3] We need not even expect a one-word designation for "science": Socrates, for instance, calls his youthful devotion to "natural science" an enthusiasm for "that [sort of] wisdom which they call 'the investigation of nature,'" *tautes tes sophias hen de kalousi peri phuseos historian* (*Phaedo* 96a7–8). Kahn (1991: 2) uses *peri phuseos historia*, unreferenced, as if that were the standard Greek designation for "science." However, in the context in which it appears, Plato's Socrates describes his disillusionment with that type of wisdom because the material causes it offers are insufficient to explain the underlying principles of the cosmos.

Moving from terminology to concepts and practices, the idea of a scientific "revolution" was not defined before the twentieth century. There was no thoroughgoing scientific "revolution" in antiquity and no way of thinking about technological progress in these terms. True, war machines, aqueducts, and concrete represent substantial innovations (and – in the case of the latter two at least – improvements in quality of life); but something as fundamental as accurate time-keeping devices had to wait until much later. The Greeks, in particular, appear not to have made the fullest use of technologies available to them: instruments such as the Antikythera mechanism, the earliest sophisticated scientific calculator known (150–100 BC?), while possible in terms of manufacture, seem to have been the exception rather than the rule.[4] Accuracy in measurement was possible but often subordinated to metaphysics, perhaps (in part) under the influence of a Platonic mistrust of sense-perception.[5] Even the "big ideas" of ancient science, such as calculation of the size of the Earth, or the estimation of the extent of the universe, arguably had little impact, in that scientific activity and readership were confined to a tiny elite.[6]

It is debated how far ancient science can be differentiated from what went before. Most scholars would agree that, while "science" and "literature" are grown together at the roots, there is at the same time no small degree of discontinuity between them, even initially.[7] I want to begin by focusing on some of the evidence adduced in support of a head-to-head battle between "literature" and "science" in the fifth century BC. Secondly, I shall call on another fifth-century text, Aristophanes' *Clouds*, to demonstrate how the "science"–"literature" debate could be theorized by one ancient author. Finally, I shall look at Roman permutations of the "literature"–"science" dichotomy, and show how the latter was effectively assimilated to the former to form a literary-scientific vision of Roman space. This chapter will range selectively from the fifth century BC to the first century AD, using examples to construct an argument both for the complexity of the relationship between "literature" and "science" in antiquity, and for the increasing interconnectedness of the two polarities, resulting in a process of give and take rather than an antithesis.

An "ancient quarrel"?

What was the state of play between "literature" and "science" in the fifth century BC, the formative period of Greek "science"? Many would like to see a clean break. Glen Most states, "The quarrel of the early Greek philosophers with the traditional poets begins with Xenophanes, who asserts that 'both Homer and Hesiod attributed to the gods all things that are blameworthy and a reproach among men: stealing, committing adultery, and deceiving one another'" (Most 1999: 337).[8] Using this fragment to show a break between early Greek poetry and philosophy, Most asserts that in Xenophanes' successor Heraclitus "this quarrel" (between poetry and philosophy) "reaches its bitterest extreme" (338), referring to Heraclitus' *dictum*, "Learning of many things does not teach intelligence: if so it would have taught Hesiod and Pythagoras, and again Xenophanes and Hecataeus" (KRS 190). We cannot assume, however, that poetry is in the firing line; nor can we uncritically align the exchange between Heraclitus and Xenophanes with a later idea of an "ancient quarrel between philosophy and poetry." On the first issue, Most is not alone in asserting that Xenophanes represents a break with tradition;[9] but it is too easy a dichotomy to say that he marks a discontinuity between the new (pre-Socratic) "science" and the older poetry. The view that the Xenophanes fragment is part of a debate between philosophy and poetry cannot be sustained in the light of Heraclitus' response. Xenophanes is not hammered for being a poet – although he was one, since his "cosmology" was in verse – nor is he grouped explicitly with other poets. Of those in Heraclitus' line of fire, only Hesiod can *prima facie* be considered a "literary" figure: Pythagoras was a philosopher and mystic, Hecataeus, a contemporary of Xenophanes, a historian and geographer. If Heraclitus is "interpreting" Xenophanes' statement, he is not doing so in the light of a science-versus-literature debate recognizable in our terms. Rather, he does it in a spirit of intellectual pugilism, whereby he takes issue with all those with some claim to inspired knowledge, and marks out a territory for himself. Heraclitus' statement cannot, therefore, be read, in succession with Xenophanes', as an effort to ditch poetry in favor of the new science.

Most assumes that poetry is the wrong medium for natural philosophy and had to be replaced, in the natural order of things, by prose: "One of the most grievous scandals of early Greek philosophy is the fact that, even after the invention of philosophical prose, some of the greatest thinkers returned to poetry as the medium in which to publicize their philosophical message" (Most 1999: 350). But while *we* might think of prose as a suitable medium for scientific discourse, there is no reason for this view to be ascribed to the ancients. The very persistence of that medium testifies to its value. Empedocles' *On Nature* (fifth century BC) and Lucretius' *De rerum natura* (first century BC) are in verse. We should not downgrade the serious contribution of these works – the four-element theory, atomism – on the grounds of their literary form.

Moreover, for the pre-Socratics there is no pre-existing dichotomy between poetry and prose as philosophical media. It might be argued that this dichotomy was never in operation in any straightforward form in antiquity. As Most himself acknowledges (Most 1999: 332–33), Aristotle is the first to articulate a polarity between "science" and "poetry": "But Homer and Empedocles have nothing in common *except* their meter; so one should call the former a poet, the other a natural scientist" (*Poetics* 1447b17–20, trans. Halliwell 1995). Even in this famous passage the distinction between "science" and "literature" is not a distinction between verse and prose: note that the authors on each side of Aristotle's divide both wrote in *verse*. Poetry per se, then, is not one of Aristotle's criteria in marking a literature–science divide.[10]

Secondly, the "ancient quarrel between philosophy and poetry" is a Platonic phrase, taken from *Republic* 607b5–6. In context, it does not refer to a quarrel between poetry and natural philosophy; rather, it is the poets' inability to justify their truth-claims in a rational manner that renders poetry a candidate for banishment from the ideal republic – *if* indeed we take it that poetry is to be banished at all.[11] And we must remember that Plato's Socrates can be equally trenchant in his criticisms of the material explanations offered by the natural scientists, as he is at *Phaedo* 96a5–99d4. Tempting as it may be to see it as such, what we are witnessing is not a debate in the early stages of Western thought between "literature" and "science." The debate is not even necessarily between mythical and rational ways of looking at the world, but rather, between intellectuals arguing in favor of the truth-status of their own utterances. Nonetheless, it is possible to see such debate as representing in itself a substantially new development, and one still with us in the area of scientific discourse, where problems are put forward, tested, and argued about.[12] In the process of debate, cosmologies do emerge, to be subsumed by other cosmologies, vindicated, built upon, or discarded.

Science and pretentiousness in Aristophanes' *Clouds*

Our first example has taken the form of a snapshot of the debate about tradition and authority among the pre-Socratic philosophers. Our next example shows how such debate could be theorized in fifth-century drama. As construed by Aristophanes in his comedy of 423 BC, the figure of Socrates is a composite of various pre-Socratics. Scholars with an interest in "science" have tended to approach the *Clouds* as if it can be used to make certain claims for fifth-century Greek thought about the natural world (see Althoff 2007). Used with caution, the play can act as a sort of index to topics which interested "scientists" in the fifth century BC: the "experiment" with the flea at 144–53 (a problem of spatial measurement in empirical science),[13] speculation about the gnat's humming at 154–68 (acoustic theory and zoology),[14] and – of course – astronomy, as at 171–72, where Socrates is seen investigating "the moon's paths and revolutions." At 177–79 there is a reference to the demonstration of a geometrical proof, undercut by a joke about passive homosexuality (Althoff 2007: 109). The "scientific" instruments described in 200–17 presumably reflect to some extent a "real" fifth-century concern with measurement, although the joke is in Strepsiades' grindingly utilitarian interpretation of them (as in line 203).[15] The existence of the map of the world described in 206 can be corroborated by other evidence of a fifth-century interest in cartography.[16]

One result of this approach to the text is an appreciation of Aristophanes' remarkable familiarity with the ideas of the pre-Socratics. This is especially evident in Strepsiades' and Socrates' question-and-answer session about the causes of thunder and lightning (374–407). The question under scrutiny is one which intrigued the pre-Socratics, and many of the ideas bandied around in Aristophanes' text can be paralleled from Heraclitus, Anaximander, Parmenides, Empedocles, and the early atomists.[17] Socrates' use of analogies from everyday life (sometimes *too* everyday, as at 385–93) may reflect the pre-Socratic use of such analogies, as, for example, when Anaximander says that the sphere of flame around the air surrounding the earth is "like bark around a tree."[18]

More fruitful, however, than the selective, often too straight-faced use of the play as evidence for fifth-century "science," is to see how it characterizes Socrates. The Socrates whom Aristophanes paints as "scientist" is an uneasy conglomerate of rationalist views and poetically elevated language. When Socrates is introduced at 223, his first words can be taken as a parody of high poetic style: "Why do you summon me, O creature of a day?"[19] This is in line with how he will be characterized later in the play as a fellow-devotee of the Clouds, along with seers, doctors, and *poets*. At 225 he describes himself in a ridiculously grandiose metaphorical way resonant of poetry: "I tread the air (*aerobato*) and scrutinize the sun."[20]

Poetic language is married with "scientific" discourse. Socrates' first extended speech, at 228–34, is a pastiche of "scientific" gobbledegook: "To make accurate discoveries about heavenly phenomena (*ta meteora pragmata*) I had to suspend my mind, to commingle my rarefied thought (*noema*) with its kindred air." "*Meteora pragmata*" are fundamental to Aristophanes' portrait of Socrates (cf. 333, 360, 1284), as well as being a key area of pre-Socratic speculation (see, for instance, Anaximander, *KRS* 121). "*Noema*" (229) is a term favored by the early philosophers, notably Empedocles (*KRS* 394). Likewise, Socrates' "theory" about thought and air reflects the ideas of his contemporary, Diogenes of Apollonia, who held that perception is the movement of air within the body (see *KRS* 603; Dover 1968: nn. ad 230–33). Later, the idea of lightning as a result of the compression of wind (404–7) is probably Anaxagorean (*KRS* 130, 131).

We can see how this double portrait of Socrates as natural philosopher and poet reflects some of the characteristics of the pre-Socratics seen above: the cut-and-thrust of debate, the nuanced interaction of different media – prose, poetry – and the struggle for authority in the realm of *sophia*. We can also see how language is used as a battle-ground for different types of wisdom. In his opening speech, as well as elsewhere in the play, Socrates lays himself open to the charge of appropriating poetic discourse to lend greater authority to his "scientific" utterances. Moreover, Aristophanes is trying to win the space back for poetry, his type of discourse, as much as for Athenian values, when he refers to himself in *Clouds* 520 as *sophos* (and elsewhere to Socrates and others – possibly including Empedocles – dismissively as *sophistes*).[21] The poet of *Clouds* wins out over the natural philosophers – verse and prose – whose ideas are held up for scrutiny in the play.

Roman reconciliation?

So far I have been engaged in cautious exploration of a divide between "literature" and "science" in fifth-century Greece. But there are also many areas where, instead, the intersection of the two might be demonstrated. Although it could be argued that discontinuity between the sciences and literature grew greater as the more "technical" or "specialized" sciences developed, especially in the Hellensitic period (after the death of Alexander, 323 BC),[22] it is possible at the same time to see how, in certain ways, science and literature became more enmeshed. The work of Hellenistic intellectuals often embraced both spheres. Eratosthenes, for instance, not only measured the circumference of the earth accurately, but had literary interests which were more than just side projects or *parerga*.[23]

The fruitful interaction of science and literature is easiest to see in the genre of poetry we call didactic, thus designated because of its ostensible aim of teaching the reader (although this aim is often window-dressing for learned literary play). In the Hellenistic period, didactic poetry self-consciously took upon itself the task of converting abstruse technical matter into readable verse. The best example of this is the *Phaenomena* of Aratus, an astronomical poem which rendered into verse two treatises of Plato's pupil Eudoxus.[24] The didactic tradition flourished in Rome: in the first century BC, Cicero "translated" Aratus into Latin hexameters, forging in the process an unprecedented vocabulary of Roman star-names (see Gee 2001, 2007). Cicero's translation of Aratus was followed by others, including a partial one by Virgil in Book 1 of his agricultural didactic poem, the *Georgics*;[25] a more complete, even augmented, one by Germanicus, writing in the early years of the first century AD;[26] and finally the verbose rendition of Avienus in the fourth century AD (Soubiran 1981).

Didactic poetry, while concerned with technical minutiae, also had the power to take on entire world-systems. In the first century BC, Lucretius composed his extraordinary poem the *De rerum natura*, on the physical and ethical system of the atomist philosopher Epicurus.[27] The Lucretian style of didactic, although not Lucretius' Epicurean substance, is most clearly taken up in another extraordinary poem, the *Astronomica*, written by Manilius in the first century AD (see, most recently, Volk 2009). In the Renaissance, didactic becomes a signature genre of humanistic activity; its long life continued at least into the seventeenth century.[28] In the Renaissance, the arsenal of Classical "science" could be used, through the medium of didactic poetry, in the battles waged around the "new science" of the Copernican system (Gee 2008).

The presence of science in literature is not, however, confined to didactic, or even to poetry. Rome developed its own special genre of technical and encyclopaedic literature. This includes the agricultural works of Cato, Varro, and Columella.[29] Agriculture was a particularly Roman concern, and none of these works is "purely" technical: all of them, even Cato, the earliest surviving Roman prose author (c.160 BC), espouse a conscious ideal of "Roman-ness" in style and substance. The "technical" genre also includes Vitruvius' *De Architectura*, dedicated to the emperor Augustus (on Vitruvius, see McEwan 2003). Again, this is by no means only a technical treatise: its scientific ambit outlines the knowledge strictly necessary for architecture, mapping the Roman project onto the wider world, particularly in Book 9, which is concerned with the principles of astronomy. Roman building, therefore, took place against the canvas of the cosmos and atop the underpinning of Greek philosophy and science. Likewise, the geographical treatise of Pomponius Mela, writing c.43 AD, can be read against the background of Roman expansion, most notably the Emperor Claudius' British expedition.[30] The encyclopaedic treatise of Pliny the Elder, the *Natural History*, composed c.77–79 AD, is a fascinating compendium of scientific knowledge in all fields, including astronomical, meteorological, ethnographic, and geographical; arguably such a project was a product of the ability of Rome to view the wider world in catalog form, facilitated both by Hellenistic science and by imperial expansion.[31] Pliny's style is not as flamboyant as his predecessor Seneca's, whose *Quaestiones Naturales*, written under Nero, are a model of Roman rhetorical style, as well as a Stoic account of natural phenomena.

Overall, technical literature in Rome ran the gamut of subjects and styles, from Cato to the military and veterinary works of Vegetius (fourth century AD), and is too rich an area to cover here.[32] It could be in Greek as well as Latin: the medical treatises of Galen (second century AD), written in Greek, but in a

Roman context, are a particular area of interest in present scholarship (see Hankinson 2007; Gill, Whitmarsh, and Wilkins 2009).

It is probably partly due to the prominence of technical writing from the earliest period of Roman literature that catalogs form a particular feature of Roman epic poetry. Thus, in Lucan's Neronian epic on the Roman civil war, the *De bello cilivi*, we are presented with long catalogues in the first two books, 1.396–465 (ethnography), and 2.396–438 (geography). These function to orient the Roman reader in the wider world. Moreover, a scientific view of the world becomes characteristic of representations of the state in Roman literature. Cosmological order can represent the proper functioning of the Roman empire in accordance with the laws governing the universe; cosmological dissolution – anti-cosmogony – the disintegration of the state; the principles of the divinely governed cosmos could be invoked in contexts of Roman imperialism. I should like to end with an illustration of this phenomenon, which amounts in some sense to a collapse of the divide between "science" and "literature."

The speech of Aeneas' father, Anchises, in the underworld in Virgil, *Aeneid* 6 (lines 724–886) demonstrates the reconciliation of natural-philosophical thought with a Roman vision.[33] Anchises begins by recounting the shape of the universe. This account is influenced by the Hellenistic philosophical school of Stoicism, which held the pantheistic view that the universe is shot through by the ordering principle of Mind, also called Spirit, god or Zeus:[34] "First of all, Spirit nourishes from within the earth and the watery levels, the phosphorescent globe of the moon and the Titan star (the Sun); and Mind, spread throughout its limbs, animates the whole mass and mingles itself with the great body." Anchises goes on (728–32) to assimilate the soul of the universe just described with the nature of the human soul. A differentiated afterlife is then constructed, with purifications according to the sins of each, and rewards for some (lines 735–51). The reader is then presented with a vision of proto-Roman souls arrayed on the transmigratory production line, ready to leave the underworld for their incarnate state as the Roman heroes of the future (756–86).

The speech's slide from cosmology to eschatology is a mark of a certain type of "scientific" literature, bizarre to us but familiar in antiquity, which united a "scientific" vision of the world with mythic or poetic features. This scheme is found as early as Empedocles (see Sedley 1998: 2–8); Virgil probably owes his progression more immediately to the Myth of Er in Book 10 of Plato's *Republic*, where a cosmological vision, the "Spindle of Necessity," is united with an account of reincarnation.[35] Virgil combines the idea of reincarnation with a vision of Roman history, as Cicero had also done in his *Somnium Scipionis*, one of Virgil's key Roman models (see Hardie 1986: 66–83). In terms of diction, the speech has touches of the Epicurean poet Lucretius (see Austin 1977: ad *Aeneid* 6.724); its cosmology, however, shows the influence of Cicero's Stoic contemporary, Posidonius.[36]

Philosophically, Virgil unites old schools (Empedocles, Pythagoreanism, Platonism) with newer, even conflicting, schools (Stoicism and Epicureanism), and combines Greek with Roman traditions. Yet, although it shares features with some of its Roman antecedents, the speech surpasses them all in the degree to which it is scientifically, historically, and eschatologically totalizing, as befits a vision of the new Roman age under Augustus. Virgil's knowledge of philosophy in this passage gives the lie to the "scientific" part of Anchises' famous disclaimer: "*Others* (I truly believe it) will hammer out more sensuously bronze figures that look as if they're breathing, and carve living faces out of marble, plead cases better, mark out with a pointer the paths of the heaven and describe the risings of the stars: remember, Roman, it's your place to rule peoples under your empire" (*Aeneid* 6.847–51). That Virgil felt it necessary, through the person of Anchises, to apologize for the scientific part of his endeavor, should not blind us to its actuality. It is up to each generation of readers to decide whether Virgil's harnessing of science to a literary vision of empire, which set a pattern followed for many hundreds of years, represents the best use and culmination of scientific knowledge in antiquity.

Abbreviations

EANS = Keyser and Irby-Massey (2008)
KE = Kidd and Edelstein (1972–99)
KRS = Kirk, Raven, and Schofield (1983)
NP = Cancik and Schneider (1996–2003)

Notes

1 "In the broadest terms … a *techne* is the capacity to produce the right results in a given sphere, based on a knowledge of the relevant principles" (Rowe 1986 ad *Phdr.* 260d3–9). On *techne* as "art," see Halliwell 1998: 44–51.
2 Lloyd 1987: 4–6 seems to take it thus, referring to "*logos*-unacceptable" (6) answers given by myth.
3 The account of the universe in Plato's *Timaeus* is famously called an *eikos muthos* (29d2), a "likely *story.*" On *muthos* and *logos* in Plato, see Morgan 2000: 271–89.
4 The Antikythera mechanism has undergone intensive study in recent years: see Marchant 2008 and Lehoux 2007; further bibliography at www.antikythera-mechanism.gr/bibliography, the website of the Antikythera Mechanism Research Project.
5 "When there was sufficient motivation, the ancient Greeks could develop some quite sophisticated instruments, but in general the improvements made in measuring instruments were modest" (Lloyd 1987: 281).
6 See Lloyd 1987: 331. Perhaps this is less true in the Roman period: for example, Cicero's *Dream of Scipio* (*Somnium Scipionis*) sets human endeavor against the great size of the universe, marrying Hellenistic science with a Roman vision designed for a more "general" leadership. See introduction and notes in Powell 1990.

7 A good discussion is Lloyd 1970: 1–15. For the two ends of the debate, still in operation, see Kahn 1991, who in my view over-argues the case for discontinuity in an effort to make Greek science more "modern," as opposed to Sedley 2007: 1–8, who demonstrates that similar approaches to cosmology were shared by the early Greek poets and the first "natural scientists."

8 The fragment of Xenophanes is KRS 166 (references to the pre-Socratics in this article are numbered as in KRS).

9 For instance, Xenophanes is described as "an apostle of enlightenment" by Fränkel 1975: 325.

10 On the fundamental criterion of mimesis at work in this passage of Aristotle, see Halliwell 1998: 127–28.

11 In fact, Plato may not even be whole-hearted in his proposal to banish poetry, as Halliwell (forthcoming) shows. (Thanks are due to Stephen Halliwell for letting me see his chapter in manuscript.)

12 Lloyd 1987: 85–102 shows how an agonistic culture may have dictated to some extent the path of development in early Greek "science." The Hippocratic writings are most distinctive in this regard. Although these works present a spectrum of different ideologies and approaches, there is in some of these texts a self-conscious rationalism, and an advocacy of observation as a tool for prediction.

13 Dover 1968: xl–xli and nn. ad lines 148–52; I recommend his note ad 150 as an instance of (possibly) unconscious mimicry of his comic subject matter. See also Althoff 2007: 105–6.

14 Dover 1968: ad 163 speaks of "the study of sound in the fifth century," deflating the comic force of Aristophanes' fart-joke; see also Althoff 2007: 106–7.

15 Dover 1968: ad 201; see also Althoff 2007: 110–13.

16 Althoff 2007: 111 n.30. The earliest map was supposedly that of Anaximander (also fifth century), on which see Fränkel 1975: 264–65.

17 See Dover 1968: nn. ad 374–407. Particularly interesting is Aristophanes' provocative use of pre-Socratic buzzwords. One instance is "necessity" (*anagke*) at 376 and 405. For *anagke* as a key term in determining value of evidence/proof in early "science" (particularly medicine), see Lloyd 1987: 119–23.

18 KRS 121. See Most 1999: 351 on this and similar pre-Socratic analogies, which in his view reflect Homeric technique.

19 See Dover 1968 ad loc. for poetic parallels.

20 Aristophanes' hyperbolic characterization must have hit home: Plato picks up on this verb in his answer to Aristophanes at *Apology* 19c2–6: "For you yourselves saw these things in Aristophanes's comedy, a Socrates being carried about there, proclaiming he was treading on air (*aerobatein*) and uttering a vast deal of other nonsense."

21 On the distinction between Socrates and the "Sophists," later constructed by Plato, see Wallace 2007.

22 On Hellenistic "science," cf. Lloyd 1973; Sharples 1996; Irby-Massey and Keyser 2002; Lang 2005.

23 Lloyd 1973: 4. His work on the circumference of the earth is one of the success stories of the exact sciences in antiquity (see also Lloyd 1987: 231–34); at the same time, he is credited with a work on the mythical origins of the constellations, the *Catasterismoi* (*Turning-into-stars*).

24 Kidd 1997: 14–18. The fragments of Eudoxus (Lasserre 1966) come to us largely through the commentary on Aratus' text by the astronomer Hipparchus: this is indicative of serious readership of Aratus' poem.

25 See the introduction and notes of Thomas 1988.

26 The English edition is Gain 1976; interpretative issues in Possanza 2004.

27 The literature on Lucretius, even in English, is too extensive to cite at length: one could start with Gale 1994; Sedley 1998; Volk 2002.

28 See Haskell 1998 on Renaissance astronomical didactic, Haskell 2003 on seventeenth-century didactic.

29 On the agricultural writers, see Pagan 2006; on the agricultural writers and the calendar, particularly Ovid's calendar poem, the *Fasti*, see Gee 2000: 9–20.

30 See *EANS*, pp. 685–86, with bibliography there cited.

31 On Pliny, see French and Greenaway 1986; Beagon 1992.

32 On later technical literature, see Formisano 2001.

33 The bibliography on this passage is extensive; see, for example, Wright 1963–64; Clark 1979; Tarrant 1982; Hardie 1986: 66–83; Feeney 1986; Habinek 1989; Solmsen 1990; Goold 1992; Jönsson and Roos 1996; Braund 1997.

34 On Stoicism in general, see, for instance, Sharples 1996. On the Stoicism of the passage under consideration, see Austin 1977: nn. ad *Aeneid* 6.724–51.

35 On the Platonic passage, see Halliwell 1988: nn. ad 614c4–621c5. Halliwell is particularly helpful on the "serious" astronomical background to the metaphor of the spindle of Necessity, while remaining cautious about its over-literal interpretation: "It is important to understand that Plato is offering an image of a metaphysical order, not a strictly astronomical hypothesis" (n. ad 616d6–7).

36 For instance, compare to *Aeneid* 6.726–27 Posidonius fr.21 *KE* – "Stoics say that the universe is governed according to intelligence ['mind'] and providence (*kata noun kai pronoian*), as Chrysippus says in Book V of *On Providence*, and Posidonius in Book III of *On Gods*, since intelligence pervades every part of it like soul in us." On the fiery soul (*Aeneid* 6.730–32) compare fr.101: "Posidonius said that god is intelligent and fiery *pneuma* ['spirit' or 'breath'] (*pneuma* = Virgil's *spiritus*) running through all being."

Bibliography

Allan, W. (2005) "Tragedy and the early Greek philosophical tradition," in J. Gregory (ed.) *A Companion to Greek Tragedy*, Oxford: Blackwell, pp. 71–82.

Althoff, J. (2007) "Sokrates als Naturphilosoph in Aristophanes *Wolken*," in J. Althoff (ed.) *Philosophie und Dichtung in antiken Griechenland*, Stuttgart: Steiner, pp. 103–20.

Austin, R. (1977) *P. Vergili Maronis Aeneidos Liber Sextus*, Oxford: Oxford University Press.

Beagon, M. (1992) *Roman Nature: the thought of Pliny the Elder*, Oxford: Clarendon Press.

Braund, S. (1997) "Virgil and the cosmos: religious and philosophical ideas," in C. Martindale (ed.) *The Cambridge Companion to Virgil*, Cambridge: Cambridge University Press, pp. 204–21.

Buxton, R. (1999) *From Myth to Reason: studies in the development of Greek thought*, Oxford: Oxford University Press.

Cancik, H. and Schneider, H. (eds) (1996–2003) *Der Neue Pauly: Enzyklopädie der Antike*, Stuttgart: J.B. Metzler.

Clark, R.J. (1979) *Catabasis : Vergil and the wisdom-tradition*, Amsterdam: Grüner.

Cohen, M. and Drabkin, I. (1948) *A Source Book in Greek Science*, 2nd edn, New York: McGraw-Hill, 2008.

Cornford, F.M. (1937) *Plato's Cosmology*, London: Routledge.

De Vries, G.J. (1969) *A Commentary on the Phaedrus of Plato*, Amsterdam: Hakkert.

Dodds, E.R. (1951) *The Greeks and the Irrational*, Berkeley: University of California Press.

Dover, K., (ed.) (1968) *Aristophanes*: Clouds, Oxford: Clarendon Press.

Feeney, D. (1986) "History and revelation in Virgil's underworld," *Proceedings of the Cambridge Philological Society*, 32: 1–24.

——(2007) *Caesar's Calendar: ancient time and the beginnings of history*, Berkeley: University of California Press.

Formisano, M. (2001) *Tecnica e scrittura: le letterature tecnico-scientifiche nello spazio letterario tardolatino*, Rome: Carocci.

Fränkel, H. (1975) *Early Greek Poetry and Philosophy*, trans. M. Hadas and J. Willis, Oxford: Blackwell.

French, R. and Greenaway, F. (eds) (1986) *Science in the Early Roman Empire: Pliny the Elder, his sources and influence*, London: Croom Helm.

Gain, D. (1976) *The Aratus Ascribed to Germanicus Caesar*, London: Athlone Press.

Gale, M. (1994) *Myth and Poetry in Lucretius*, Cambridge; New York: Cambridge University Press.

Gee, E. (2000) *Ovid, Aratus and Augustus*, Cambridge: Cambridge University Press.

——(2001) "Cicero's astronomy," *Classical Quarterly*, 51: 520–36.

——(2002) "*Vaga signa*: Orion and Sirius in Ovid's *Fasti*," in G. Herbert-Brown (ed.) *Ovid's* Fasti: *historical readings at its bimillennium*, Oxford: Oxford University Press, pp. 47–70.

——(2007) "Quintus Cicero's astronomy?," *Classical Quarterly*, 57: 565–85.

——(2008) "Astronomy and philosophical orientation in classical and renaissance didactic poetry," in J. Feros Ruys (ed.) *What Nature Does Not Teach: didactic literature in the medieval and early modern period*, Turnhout: Brepols, pp. 43–96.

Goold, G.P. (1992) "The Voice of Virgil: the pageant of Rome in *Aeneid* 6," in T. Woodman and J. Powell (eds) *Author and Audience in Latin Literature*, Cambridge: Cambridge University Press, pp. 110–23.

Gill, C.J., Whitmarsh, J.M., and Wilkins, T. (eds) (2009) *Galen and the World of Knowledge*, Cambridge: Cambridge University Press.

Habinek, T. (1989) "Science and tradition in *Aeneid* 6," *Harvard Studies in Classical Philology*, 92: 223–55.

Halliwell, S. (ed.) (1988) *Plato, Republic 10*, Warminster: Aris and Phillips.

——(ed.) (1995) *Aristotle: Poetics*, Cambridge, Mass: Harvard University Press.

——(1998), *Aristotle's Poetics*, London: Duckworth.

——(forthcoming) "To banish or not to banish? the dilemma of Plato's relationship to poetry," in S. Halliwell *Between Ecstasy and Truth: problems and values in Greek poetics from Homer to Longinus*, Oxford: Oxford University Press (2011).

Hankinson, R.J. (ed.) (2007) *The Cambridge Companion to Galen*, Cambridge: Cambridge University Press.

Hardie, P. (1986) *Virgil's* Aeneid: *cosmos and imperium*, Oxford: Oxford University Press.

Haskell, Y. (1998) "Renaissance Latin didactic poetry on the stars: wonder, myth and science," *Renaissance Studies*, 12: 495–522.

——(2003) *Loyola's Bees: ideology and industry in Jesuit Latin didactic poetry*, Oxford: Oxford University Press.

Henderson, J. (1998) *Aristophanes: Clouds, Wasps, Peace*, Cambridge, Mass.: Harvard University Press.

Irby-Massey, G.L. and Keyser, P.T. (2002) *Greek Science of the Hellenistic Era: a sourcebook*, London and New York: Routledge.

Jönsson, A. and Roos, B.-A. (1996) "A note on *Aeneid* 6.893–98," *Eranos*, 94: 21–28.

Kahn, C. (1979) *The Art and Thought of Heraclitus*, Cambridge: Cambridge University Press.

——(1991) "Some remarks on the origins of Greek science and philosophy," in A.C. Bowen (ed.) *Science and Philosophy in Classical Greece*, New York and London: Garland, pp. 1–10.

Kennedy, D. (2002) *Rethinking Reality: Lucretius and the textualization of nature*, Ann Arbor: University of Michigan Press.

Keyser, P. and Irby-Massie, G. (2002) *Greek Science of the Hellenistic Era: a sourcebook*, London: Routledge.

——(eds) (2008) *The Encyclopedia of Ancient Natural Scientists: the Greek tradition and its many heirs*, London: Routledge.

Kidd, D. (1997) *Aratus, Phaenomena*, Cambridge: Cambridge University Press.

Kidd, I. and Edelstein, L. (1972–99) *Posidonius*, 4 vols, Cambridge: Cambridge University Press.

Kirk, G., Raven, J.E. and Schofield, M. (1983) *The Presocratic Philosophers*, Cambridge: Cambridge University Press.

Lang, P. (ed.) (2005) *Re-inventions: essays on Hellenistic and early Roman science*, Kelowna, B.C.: Academic Printing and Publishing.

Lasserre, F. (ed.) (1966) *Die Fragmente des Eudoxos von Knidos*, Berlin: de Gruyter.

Lehoux, D. (2007) *Astronomy, Weather, and Calendars in the Ancient World: Parapegmata and related texts in classical and near-eastern societies*, Cambridge: Cambridge University Press.

Lloyd, G.E.R. (1970) *Early Greek Science: Thales to Aristotle*, New York: Norton.

——(1973) *Greek Science After Aristotle*, London: Chatto & Windus.

——(1979) *Magic, Reason and Experience*, Cambridge: Cambridge University Press.

——(1987) *The Revolutions of Wisdom: studies in the claims and practices of ancient Greek science*, Berkeley: University of California Press.

Long, A.A. (ed.) (1999) *The Cambridge Companion to Early Greek Philosophy*, Cambridge: Cambridge University Press.

Marchant, J. (2008), *Decoding the Heavens: solving the mystery of the world's first computer*, London: Heinemann.

McEwan, I.K. (2003), *Vitruvius: writing the body of architecture*, Cambridge, Mass.; London: MIT Press.

Morgan, K. (2000) *Myth and Philosophy from the Presocratics to Plato*, Cambridge: Cambridge University Press.

Most, G. (1999) "The poetics of early Greek philosophy," in A.A. Long (ed.) *The Cambridge Companion to Early Greek Philosophy*, Cambridge: Cambridge University Press, pp. 332–62.

Mourelatos, A. (1991) "Plato's science: his view and ours of his," in A.C. Bowen (ed.) *Science and Philosophy in Classical Greece*, New York: Garland, pp. 11–30.

Norden, E. (1916) *P. Vergilius Maro Aeneis Buch VI*, Leipzig: Teubner.

Pagan, V. (2006), *Rome and the Literature of Gardens*, London: Duckworth.

Possanza, D.M. (2004) *Translating the Heavens: Aratus, Germanicus, and the poetics of Latin translation*, New York: Peter Lang.

Powell, J. (1990) *Cicero: On Friendship and the Somnium Scipionis*, Warminster: Aris and Phillips.

Rihll, T.E. (1999) *Greek Science*, Greece and Rome New Surveys in the Classics, no. 29, Oxford: Oxford University Press.

Rosenmeyer, T. (1989) *Senecan Drama and Stoic Cosmology*, Berkeley: University of California Press.

Rowe, C. (1986) *Plato: Phaedrus*, Warminster: Aris and Phillips.

——(1993) *Plato: Phaedo*, Cambridge: Cambridge University Press.

Samons, L.J. (ed.) (2007) *The Cambridge Companion to the Age of Pericles*, Cambridge: Cambridge University Press.

Sedley, D.N. (1998) *Lucretius and the Transformation of Greek Wisdom*, Cambridge: Cambridge University Press.

——(2007) *Creationism and its Critics in Antiquity*, Berkeley: University of California Press.

Sharples, R. (1996) *Stoics, Epicureans and Sceptics: an introduction to Hellenistic philosophy*, London: Routledge.

Snow, C.P. (1959/1964) *The Two Cultures*, Cambridge: Cambridge University Press, repr. 1993.

Solmsen, F. (1990) "The World of the Dead in Book 6 of the *Aeneid*," in S. Harrison (ed.) *Oxford Readings in Virgil's* Aeneid, Oxford: Oxford University Press, pp. 208–23.

Soubiran, J. (1972) *Cicéron*: Aratea, *fragments poétiques*, Paris: Les Belles Lettres.

——(ed.) (1981) *Aviénus: Les* Phénomènes *d'Aratos*, Paris: Les Belles Lettres.

Tarrant, R. (1982) "Aeneas and the gates of sleep," *Classical Philology*, 77: 51–55.

Thomas, R.F. (1988), *Virgil*: Georgics, vol. 1, Books 1–2, Cambridge: Cambridge University Press.

Vernant, J.-P. (1983) *Myth and Thought Among the Greeks*, London: Routledge.

Vlastos, G. (1975) *Plato's Universe*, Oxford.

Volk, K. (2002) *The Poetics of Latin Didactic: Lucretius, Vergil, Ovid, Manilius*, Oxford: Oxford University Press.

——(2009) *Manilius and his Intellectual Bcakground*, Oxford: Oxford University Press.

——and Williams, G. (eds) (2006) *Seeing Seneca Whole: perspectives on philosophy, poetry, and politics*, Leiden: Brill.

Wallace, R.W. (2007) "Plato's sophists, intellectual history after 450, and Sokrates," in Samons 2007: 215–37.

Warren, J. (2004) *Facing Death: Epicurus and his critics*, Oxford: Clarendon Press.

——(2007) *Presocratics*, Stocksfield: Acumen.

Wright, M.R. (1963–64) "*Principio caelum* (Aeneid 6.724–53)," *Proceedings of the Virgil Society*, 3: 27–34.

36
MIDDLE AGES AND EARLY RENAISSANCE

Arielle Saiber

In this period in the Western world, literature and science were aligned in many questions and struggles. How do I disseminate my work (or keep it secret, as the case may be)? Should I write in Latin or the vernacular; should I follow the style and content of the "ancients" or the "moderns"? Does my work teach properly? How do I reconcile what I observe in the natural world and in human nature with Church doctrine? Is my "new" idea a discovery of what was already there/ known, or an invention? If I can invent, is the "new" a good thing, or dangerous? Is the contemplative life of scholarship (*vita contemplativa*) as important to society as the active life (*vita activa*) of civic duty? Does my work reflect the ideal proportions and harmonies – a Pythagorean/Platonic *harmonia mundi* – I see (or wish to see) around me? How do I present my work such that it pleases a patron and garners support? Why *not* say what I want to, how I want to?

When thinking about the links between literature and science in these centuries, a good place to start is with Martianus Capella's fifth-century treatise on the liberal arts, *De Nuptiis Philologiae et Mercurii*. A reasonable place to end is with the first decades of the 1500s, before Copernicus literally turns the world on its head with his *De revolutionibus orbium coelestium* in 1543 and Vesalius revolutionizes anatomical study with his *De humani corporis fabrica* in that same year. This is the period in which the arts and sciences began to become the disciplines we know today, developing subfields, new literary genres, and countless new technologies; when (beginning in the eighth century) Islamic learning migrated to Europe and contributed significantly to scientific and literary thought; when schools moved out of the Church and into *studia*, universities, as well as court workshops (even though the Church's hand in controlling the production and dissemination of knowledge continued to be fierce); when transmission of information took a revolutionary leap with the advent of the printing press; when the "new world" was discovered and ignited literary and scientific imaginations and study; and when new technologies led to increased global trade and enlarged markets, the development of banking, a growing merchant class, an augmented pool of educated people, and men (and a few women) of learning being celebrated for their genius and virtuosity. The sciences and the arts were building their identities, and, to a great extent, they did so in step and in dialogue with one another. The very richness of their conversation marks this period of Western history as remarkable.

The trajectory of science from the Middle Ages through the Renaissance can be – and nowadays is, more frequently than not – seen as a continuity and precursor to later scientific developments. A similar trajectory can be traced in the history of literature. The energy devoted to the recovery, assimilation, commentary, translation, and promulgation of earlier authorities in both literature and science was accompanied by empirical and experimental work in the sciences, and active re-examination and reinterpretation of established sources in both science and literature. What is more, as we shall see, both fields had major shifts in thinking about the world and the self.

"Science," *scientia*, in this period generally referred to "theoretical knowledge" of the physical world (*sapientia* was knowledge of the metaphysical, divine world). Debates around the Aristotelian distinction between *scientia quia* (knowledge of the fact) and *scientia propter quid* (knowledge through the cause) characterized *scientia* throughout the Middle Ages and early Renaissance. It even questioned its ultimate purpose as ancillary to theology, how much God wished to reveal to our minds, and when to use faith instead of Aristotelian syllogistic reasoning in thinking about the natural and divine worlds. "Art," *ars*, on the other hand, was practiced or applied (and more refined than the craftsman's *techné*). Both *scientia* and *ars* were part of "natural philosophy." Medicine, for example, would have been considered a science and an art, because it required both theoretical knowledge and skill (surgery, on the other hand, was considered primarily a trade). Other fields of inquiry, such as mnemonics, alchemy, astrology, and magic were most often called arts, but in many contexts they were also thought of as sciences (not, as has been ascribed to them by some, as pseudo-sciences), and as part of natural philosophy.

"Literature" comprised not only epic, romance, love lyric, comic verse, short prose works, drama, and the like, but much religious, political, and philosophical writing. Generally, a work of "high" literature would have been penned for the educated elite, and often in Latin; "low" would have been designated for the masses, often in the vernacular, and often recited or performed, especially in the Middle Ages. Dante Alighieri (1265–1321) and other authors began to challenge these norms with new ideas about the nature and purpose of literature. However, the general acceptance of the vernacular in works of high literature as well as science happened slowly. The reasons for this are many, such as low literacy rates; feudal culture's lack of a merchant middle class (although by the fifteenth century this class begins to emerge with court culture) educated and rich enough to afford hand-copied books; the elite's desire to keep learning for the educated few; and an innumerable number of regional dialects that made

Latin – the *lingua franca* – a much more sensible choice for communicating to an audience beyond one's province. What is more, the writer of any text – literary or scientific, in Latin or in the vernacular – was informed, and often constrained, by other factors, such as the Church's tight control of all circulating information through censorship and various edits, and the scholastic interpretations of Aristotle and a select group of ancient sources that dominated the day.

Let us turn to some examples of the conversations between literature and science, noting the strikingly similar issues with which both grappled in this 1,000-year period. We will look at the following major categories: liberal arts and the encyclopedia; mathematics; astrology/astronomy; physics and technology; medicine; and natural history. The sciences/arts of magic, alchemy, and music will be referred to only in passing. Readers will note a majority of Italian sources referenced. This is due to the extraordinary amount of production from the Italian peninsula in these centuries, but also to the author's area of expertise.

Liberal arts and the encyclopedia

As we know from a liberal arts education today, in the ideal curriculum courses are balanced between the arts and sciences. Scholars since antiquity have been in favor of this. Martianus Capella's fifth-century *De Nuptiis Philologiae et Mercurii* shows us the dominant disciplinary categories in the Middle Ages and early Renaissance. The text itself is written like an allegory, recounting the courtship and betrothal of Mercury, the fleet-footed god of commerce, eloquence, literature (and other things), to Philology, the studious lover of words. At the wedding, Philology's seven handmaidens – Grammar, Rhetoric, Logic, Geometry, Arithmetic, Astronomy, and Music – each give a long monologue on the nature of their art. Capella uses beautiful and complex language for these descriptions, as well as revealing some misunderstandings of the workings of the arts. Flourishes and flaws aside, for centuries the text was the primary source for structuring curricula, with the first three "verbal" disciplines of the *trivium* and the following four "quantitative" ones of the *quadrivium*, comprising the seven liberal arts.

Capella did not invent this categorization. The Pythagoreans are thought to have been the first to have designated the four quantitative arts of the *quadrivium* (see Proclus's commentary on Euclid's *Elements*, Bk. I), although the term "quadrivium" arose much later, in Boethius (see *De arithmetica* I.i). The *trivium* would be given its name a few centuries later. Before one could go on to study higher disciplines – such as medicine, law, philosophy, or (especially) theology – he had to be trained in the arts of a "free" (*liber*) man. And whether he was studying in a monastery, cathedral school, or university, these arts were the building blocks. Many were the debates, however, about which of the arts should be studied first (especially intense were discussions over whether logic or geometry should come first), but most agreed that all seven served one another. Learning grammar, for example, would help one to learn arithmetic, and vice versa. Medieval study of the arts was known, in fact, as the *circulares disciplina* or the *encyclius*, implying a united "circle of disciplines."

The belief that intellectual knowledge reflected divine knowledge and that it should (and could) be catalogued was the foundation of the encyclopedia. Massive tomes by thinkers such as Isidore of Seville, Brunetto Latini, and Vincent of Beauvais included entries on topics ranging from rainbows to rhetorical tropes. Isidore (c. 560–636), archbishop of Seville and prolific writer of theological and natural philosophy treatises, is considered the first of the great medieval encyclopedists. His *Etymologies*, a twenty-book text that endured for centuries, served as a source of great knowledge and authority, even if many of the etymological glosses – while often suggestive and fascinating – were fanciful and false. The chapters expounded on topics ranging from the liberal arts, medicine, Roman law, and the calendar, to elements of Christian doctrine, kinds of heresy, the Roman and Greek gods, languages, family, mythological monsters, animals, weather, architecture, mineralogy, agriculture, weaponry, military strategies, sports, food, and crafts. Isidore (and other classical, medieval, and Renaissance thinkers) believed that understanding the root of a word would help one understand the essence of the thing to which the word referred.

The three books of Latini's *Li livres dou Trésor* (mid-1260s) comprised nearly 500 chapters. Book I covers the greatest number of topics, and it is this book that makes the *Trésor* one of the first scientific works in any vernacular. Similar to medieval bestiaries are descriptions such as the one for the basilisk, "so full of venom that it gleams on the outside; but its sight and its smell carry the venom far and near, and through this it spoils the air and destroys the trees. With its odor it kills birds in flight; and with its sight it kills men when it sees them" (I.140: 109). More lengthy and didactic are entries such as "How the world is round, and how the four elements are established" (I.104: 64–66) and "How one should choose land for cultivation" (I.125: 98–101). Many entries include stories or legends, such as the one in which "a child from Campania raised a dolphin on bread for a long time, and made him so tame that he could ride on his back, and finally the dolphin carried him out to sea, and there the child drowned, and finally the dolphin let itself die when it saw that the child was dead" (I.134: 106–7).

Vincent's *Speculum Maius* is a mammoth thirteenth-century summa numbering eighty books and nearly 10,000 chapters. It was considered the greatest (and largest) encyclopedia until the eighteenth century. The *Speculum* was originally divided into two parts, one on the natural world and one on history since Creation (later Vincent added one on the arts and sciences, and later still, a fourth volume was added by an unknown author). The *Naturale* covered all matter of natural philosophy known in Europe at the time. The *Doctrinale* discussed philosophy, all the liberal arts, medicine, rhetoric and poetics, economics (in the sense of maintaining one's estate), and more. Vincent, like Isidore and Latini, mixed verifiable information with superstitious tales, legends, and myths, and this is what makes medieval encyclopedias so fascinating for discussions of literature and science. Modern scientific method had yet to be outlined, and understanding the natural world happened through weaving observed data and experiment with earlier authorities, Church doctrine, hearsay, aesthetic ideals, and the imagination.

The universe itself was thought to be an encyclopedic book, "bound by love into a single volume," as Dante would say in the *Commedia* (*Par.* XXXIII, 86), with God as the author, the bookbinder, and the glue. Dante's fourteenth-century *Commedia*, too, is often considered a work of encyclopedia scope, filled with medieval science and arts. Encyclopedia building continued through the Renaissance, aided by philology. Giorgio Valla, who was the first to translate Aristotle's *Poetics* into Latin, produced the forty-nine-book *De expetendis et fugiendis rebus* of 1501, which included the first printed translations of fragments from Apollonius, Archimedes, Hero, and many other classical mathematicians.

The question of how to have all knowledge, both knowable and known, was linked to other metaphysical questions, such as that of seeing the macrocosm in the microcosm (and vice versa). These were not only theological and philosophical musings, but concerns for natural philosophers and writers of literature who described the natural world. Words were thought to hold great power, and had to be utilized with care. Nominalists such as William of Ockham contemplated the problem of how words "mean" and denote entities in the real world. Others, such as Erasmus, were more interested in questions of *copia* and *varietas*, that is, how to enrich one's language and modes of describing the world and ideas. A fascination with Hebrew, hieroglyphics, and kabbalist theories about language also spread throughout Christian Europe, interesting great minds such as Marsilio Ficino, Pico della Mirandola, Johann Reuchlin, and Cornelius Agrippa. In these centuries, the many powers within and endowed by language led readers to study closely classical treatises on rhetoric (Cicero and Quintilian). They wove them tightly with theories of dialectic, and used them for exegeses not only of *the* text (the Bible), but of all texts, as well as of the natural world. The personification of dialectic, interestingly, was often depicted with a scorpion in one hand and a frond in the other, showing language's ability to sting or to yield blossoms; or alternately, the ability to yield blossoms *through* the use of a pointed sting.

Mathematics

Of all the liberal arts, Capella gives geometry the honor of being the "most learned and generous," and the mistress of the other six (vol. II: 272). Onto her robe are woven numbers and measurements, outlines of the planetary orbits, and the dark purplish hue of the earth's shadow upon the golden orb of the sun. In singing the praises of Lady Geometry, Capella calls her the offspring of mythological architect Daedalus, and superior to Apelles and Polyclitus in their respective arts of painting and sculpture. Plato, it has been said, had an inscription over the doorway to his Academy stating that anyone ignorant of geometry should not enter. In Plato's *Timaeus*, geometric forms were the fundamental building blocks of the universe (53c–55c). With Capella, geometry's image as architect, artist, geographer, and guide-extraordinaire of the other arts is established for the Middle Ages. God himself comes to be portrayed as holding a compass or calipers: a *fabrica mundi* "disposing all things," as described in the Bible, "according to measure and number and weight" (Song of Sol. 11:21; Prov. 8:27–28).

A few centuries after Capella, Dante fuses geometry with poetry in his *Vita Nuova* (1292). Here, Love says to the bleary-eyed, long-suffering Dante that He (that is, Love) is the "center of a circle to which all points of the circumference are equidistant, and you [Dante] are not." This idea may have been seeded in Dante's mind from an earlier geometric definition of God, perhaps of ancient origin (Empedocles is often cited as a possible source) and in the air at the time; or from Alain de Lille in his *Regulae theologicae* (see the sermon *De sphaera intelligibili*); or perhaps from a twelfth-century pseudo-hermetic manuscript, *Liber viginti quattuor philosophorum*, as "God is a sphere of which the center is everywhere and the circumference is nowhere" (Def. II). For the medieval mind, God was seen as an eternity and the origin point of space and time; the point from which "all the heavens hang" (Dante, *Commedia*, *Par*. 28, 41–42).

Geometry, for the Middle Ages and the early Renaissance, is emblematic of the interconnectedness between the arts and sciences – its debt to logic, which all proofs use, is evident – as well as central to philosophical and theological reasoning and imagery. A mere glance at both medieval gothic and Renaissance neo-classical architecture, with their strict proportions and symmetries – rose windows and spires in the Middle Ages and parallel lines and domes (elliptical and spherical) in the Renaissance – makes this clear. The presence of religious poetry reflecting geometric shapes, *technopaegnia* (see, for example, Hrabanus Maurus's poems), further reinforces this connection.

At the end of the fourteenth century and throughout the fifteenth century, the Italian humanists brought previously lost or unknown ancient mathematical works to the fore, treatises by Archimedes, Pappus, Apollonius, Hero, and Diophantus, as well as Euclid's books on number theory (VII–IX) and solid geometry (X–XIII) – treatises which became part of both the humanist library and the mathematician's repertoire. Powerful patrons like Cardinal Bessarion and the Farnese in Rome, the Medici in Florence, the Dukes of Urbino, and popes Pius II, Nicholas V, and Marcellus II encouraged the seeking out, translating, and printing of ancient works. Humanists Coluccio Salutati, Pier Paolo Vergerio, and Angelo Poliziano believed mathematics (especially geometry) crucial for training orators, writers, and philosophers. The overlapping use of terms such as *permutatio, conversio, disjunctio* in both geometric proofs and rhetorical figures was not lost on these scholars.

While mathematicians across medieval and early Renaissance Europe used some forms of abbreviation and notation for mathematical operations, symbolic conventions did not formally develop until the end of the sixteenth century. Most problems and solutions were written in words, and read, in a certain sense, like word problems. Occasionally, one even finds them written in verse. Mathematician Niccolò Tartaglia (1499–1557), for example, wrote the solution to an equation for the cubic as a poem. Tartaglia says that the fourteen lines in *terza rima* served to help him remember the steps in solving cubics; it also made it difficult for fellow mathematician and competitor Girolamo Cardano – who desperately wanted the solution – to extract it without Tartaglia's aid.

Similar to encoding mathematics into words was the reverse, as can be seen in Leon Battista Alberti's *De cifris*. Alberti's 1466 treatise, written for a papal secretary, is considered the first-known on cryptography in the Western world, as well as offering the most advanced system for the next four centuries. Alberti opens the treatise with a discussion of grammar, spelling, and letter frequency in both Latin and Italian, outlining the relationship between the verbal and the combinatoric. Alberti was well equipped to do so, having written the first known grammar textbook for Tuscan Italian (the *Grammatichetta*), poetry, plays, fables, literary dialogues, as well as important mathematical and technical treatises, such as the mathematically focused *De pictura* (1435), which explained how to employ perspective into painting, enhancing its rhetoric of *istoria*, the tale it tells to move the viewer.

The language of algebra and *abaco* (accounting) were evolving in the Middle Ages and Renaissance. Mathematician Leonardo Pisano (a.k.a. Fibonacci, c.1170–c.1250) – who was exposed to the Hindu–Arabic number system, the number/concept of zero, and much advanced mathematics during his childhood in North Africa and on many travels – was the main force in introducing the new way of writing numbers and the beginnings of algebra to Europe. His work moved European theoretical mathematics and accounting forward, as well as encouraged the Western imagination to explore a particular numeric series named after him, and what we now call the Golden Ratio. Approximately 1.618, the ratio (known now as *phi*) has been noted in the natural world, such as in the cells of a nautilus shell and the seed packing of sunflowers. Art, architecutre, music, philosophy, literature, and even theology reveal this period's intense fascination with ratios.

Mathematician Luca Pacioli (c.1445–1517) continued the discussion of these and other "divine" ratios in his *De divina proportione* (1509), a book that had great success in the arts and sciences throughout Italy and was illustrated by

Paciolo's friend, Leonardo da Vinci. Pacioli also moved the practical mathematics of accounting even further with the *Summa de arithmetica, geometria, proportioni et proportionalita* (1494), which offered the first description of double-entry book-keeping in the vernacular. While not a visionary mathematician, Pacioli was an important compiler of mathematical thought; this skill, along with his use of the vernacular and newly born printing technologies, made his methods widely accessible and valuable. Mathematics was now becoming available not only to mathematicians and those who needed it for their trade, but also to the arts.

Astronomy

Astronomy (a.k.a. astrology) in this period came in two basic flavors: natural and judicial. The former was a mathematical art/science used to describe the move-ment of the stars and the heavens, and had practical application for agriculture, calendar making, navigation, cartography, and medicine. The latter, which made predictions about individuals' lives, was considered by the Church to be dangerous and potentially linked to magic (of the demonic kind).

The interaction between literature and astronomical and cosmological science is among the most fertile not just in the Middle Ages and the Renaissance, but before and after. The sparkly things that move (or rather, seem to) above our heads and seem to affect our planet (tides, crops, etc.) have always been the subject of philosophical and poetic musing. The very word "consideration" contains stars – *sidera* – in it, and to consider is to "be with the stars." Authors (literary and scientific alike) in the Middle Ages and early Renaissance wrote extensively about the beauties and powers of the heavens, often in verse (see, for example, Alain de Lille's *Rhythmus de Incarnatione* and Cecco d'Ascoli's *L'acerba*); and some through liturgical songs (see Hildegard of Bingen's *Symphonia armoniae celestium revelationum*). Geoffrey Chaucer wrote a treatise on the astrolabe; and Ludovico Ariosto (1474–1533) depicted space travel when the knight Astolfo voyages to the moon astride a hippogriff in search of Orlando's lost wits (*Orlando furioso*, Canto XXXIV).

The medieval and early Renaissance universe was "closed" and finite. Only God could be infinite. The physical cosmos was generally imagined as unboun-ded, but finite – a difficult space to imagine, but one depicted by the hyper-sphere-like architecture in Dante's *Commedia*. The Ptolomaic cosmos located the earth (thought to be round, not flat) at the center and made it immobile. God in the heavenly Empyrean surrounded the earth, and the angels circled Him, and in their circling they moved the planetary spheres, which in turn influenced the earthly realm. The angelology of Pseudo-Dionysius, in particular, became the basis for numerous celestial systems of theologians and natural philosophers alike. Man was thought, in fact, to be a microcosmic version of the macroscopic universe. His body parts were associated with constellations; the movements of the planets and stars (angelic forces) could affect his physical and mental health. He could not control the universe, but he could adjust his behaviors to better his chances at well-being.

With the Renaissance, and the translation of Plato and hermetic texts, there came a greater focus on the notion of "man as a measure of all things." While present in antiquity and the Middle Ages (see Vitruvius's *De architectura*, and Hildegard of Bingen's *Liber divinorum operum*, for example), the idea became increasingly popular, as did the focus on the beauty and perfection of man's proportions, famously depicted in Leonardo's Virtuvian Man. Natural astronomy helped man figure out his place in the world and how to live in and with it; judicial astrology helped him anticipate events (like conflict) and prepare himself, as well as make myriad decisions. The studies of astronomy/astrology, along with cosmology and cartography, offered narratives about the genesis of the cosmos, the shape and contents of the globe, and one's place within the universe. It could also help guide people in the writing, or narrating, of their own lives. Even in the seventeenth century, judicial astrology's influence and Ptolomaic ideas of the universe's architecture would still be present, and figures such as Kepler would not have an easy time convincing others – and even themselves, at times – what their observations were telling them.

Physics and technology

The debates around *imitatio* (stylistic and thematic imitation of classical writers), *mimesis* (copying or imitating nature), and human artifice – in both literature and science – involved questions as to whether something made by man could ever be anything other than artificial, and thus inferior to what God made. Subsequently, scholars explored whether or not it was even licit to make new things, since they were not naturally occurring, and not, it would seem, ordained by God. Were the mechanical arts simply imitators of nature, or could they actually be something more sinister, or merely a form of trickery? Interestingly, Hugh of Saint Victor divides mechanical arts into seven: fabric making, armament, commerce, agriculture, hunting, medicine, and theatrics. Theatrics? He, like William of Conches in *De philosophia mundi*, explains that entertainment is a technology essential to human life, keeping man's mind sharp and allowing his body to rest (*Didascalicon*, Bk. II, Ch. 20; Ch. 27). And like theater, poetry was of human making, an inferior version to that of God's making. The word "poetry" comes from the Greek *poiesis* meaning "to make," and poets knew themselves to be artificers. Not only could it be flawed, but it could be dangerous – it could seduce one to distraction and/or to commit sin (see the famous Paolo and Francesca episode in Dante's *Inferno*, Canto V). And what is more, the Muses were known to be capricious – able and willing to lie.

Yet even with all the anxiety around the making of new things, human invention would not stand still. Machines, chemical compounds, tools, and literary forms continued to proliferate, and the artisan and the scholar often collaborated (see, especially, Alberti). The magnifying lens, for example, had been known since the early eleventh century (see Alhazen and Roger Bacon), but in the 1280s it began to be used for correcting vision. Italy, a center for commerce in the Middle Ages, was also a center for the study of optics (and later for the art of linear perspective; see Alberti here, too). With increasing literacy came an increasing need for lenses that could aid in reading. Francesco Petrarca (1304–74), Europe's first poet laureate and arguably the first humanist scholar, in his famous *Letter to Posterity* mentions his need for such a device.

The printing press – preceded, importantly, by the introduction of the bound volume and paper making – was perhaps the most glorious technological achievement of the early Renaissance. In the 1470s, the German mathematician Regiomontanus would begin his printing program for a long list of treatises on mathematics and natural philosophy. The humanists helped Regiomontanus's project with their recent recoveries, commentaries, and Latin translations of ancient mathematical texts. They also contributed to printing technology in suggesting moveable type font designs, based on the proportions of classical lettering (Aldo Manuzio's italic font and Roman capital letters, used for the famed, erotic dream narrative *Hypnerotomachia Poliphilii* of 1499, is an example of precisely this).

Equally revolutionary in their impact were the inventions of gunpowder and automata. Roger Bacon was among the first to note the former in writing. The development of weapons that used gunpowder changed the way battles were waged, and those who followed the chivalric code did not approve. Soldiers would attack each other from a distance, which seemed cowardly and even déclassé. Writers of chivalric epic, such as Ariosto, whose own patron, Alfonso d'Este, was a famous cannon enthusiast, expressed their disdain. In his *Orlando furioso* he calls the cannon a "cursed, abominable device, cast ... by the hand of evil Beelzebub" (IX.xci). Like gunpowder, self-moving mechanisms or automata were celebrated, disdained, and feared as some sort of magic. Items such as flying machines can be traced back to the Greeks (and elsewhere), and seen equally in scientific writing (see Leonardo's notebooks) and in literature (see Chaucer's "The Franklin's Tale"). No doubt, myths, fairy tales, and many early thought experiments hold within them seeds of the extraordinary mechanisms that exist today.

Medicine

In a period remembered often for its spate of plagues, its struggle to achieve an effective *regimen sanitatis*, its restrictions on human dissection, and its frightening remedies, the medical profession certainly had its challenges. Medical writing of this time was closely linked with herbology, astrology, alchemy, natural magic (as opposed to demonic), and theology, as well as with literature. The *consilium*, for example, was a common written means to respond to a medical question, such as a given plague. It consisted of advice from different authors and sources, bound in a collection. *Consilia* were used for both the teaching and practice of medicine, and they show how much medicine then, as it does still today, relied on reportage, anecdote, and storytelling for the transmission of information.

Among the dominant ways of thinking about health in this period was humoral theory, as outlined by Galen and in Avicenna's *Canon of Medicine* and *Book of Healing*, which transmitted the Hippocratic corpus of learning, as well as theories from Asia and the Middle East, and was a mainstay in the teaching and practice of medicine through the seventeenth century. Sanguine, choleric, phlegmatic, or melancholic: these were the four basic categories of a human's physical and mental state. An illness came from an imbalance of these influences (which could be due to the planets' alignment, intake of certain foods, weather conditions, etc.) and all manner of remedies were devised to reset the balance. Depressed people (often writers) were believed to have an excess of black bile, the invisible substance for which melancholy is named. Medici physician and renowned philosopher and translator of Plato (among other Greek authors), Marsilio Ficino, recommended, for example, that these saturnine people avoid foods which were "hard, dry, salted, bitter, sharp, stale, burnt, roasted, or fried; beef and the meat of the hare, old cheese ... anything that is black," as well as "darkness ... and strenuous exercise" (*De vita* I.x: 133).

While medicine could aid the writer, the writer could also provide means for healing. Some viewed poetry as a narrative prophylaxis. The frame of Giovanni Boccaccio's fourteenth-century *Decamerone* is ten noblemen and noblewomen taking to the hills outside Florence to escape the plague and distract themselves by telling stories. Literature was thought to have twin purposes: delight and education. Petrarca defended poetry's social utility in an invective against doctors who thought otherwise (see the *Invectiva contra medicum*, 1357). In 1530 renowned physician Girolamo Fracastoro published his long epic poem on syphilis: the "French disease" (known as the "Italian disease" in France, the "Spanish disease" in Holland, etc.). He sets his description of the disease's origin, symptoms, and cures within two myths, the second about a shepherd named Syphilus, who apparently offended Apollo and was the first to be punished with the disease (Bk. III). Yet Fracastoro, even in pointing out that "Since Nature's then so lyable to change, / Why should we think this late Contagion strange; / Or that the Planets where such mischiefs grow, / Should shed their poison on the Earth below?" (Book I: 13), recognizes how the disease is transmitted, although he does not state its venereal nature in the poem, as he would in 1546 in his influential *De contagione*.

Speaking of Venus, the *ars amandi*, art of courtly love (first formally articulated in the twelfth-century work of Andreas Capellanus), and its accompanying lyric – both amorous verse (see provençal, troubador, Minnesänger, and Sicilian lyric, for example) and chivalric epic (see the *Roman de la rose*, for example) – were also tied to medical theories. Pursuing a love interest could easily tip one into an unbalanced humoral state. Reason (the highest faculty of the human soul) and restraint were needed to control and guide love's flames. Love was thought to be experienced by the "sensitive" part of the soul (more precisely, the "bodily spirit," as "soul" usually designated the immaterial, eternal something that gave life), which dwelled between the "vegetative" (physical) and "rational" (intellective) parts, often serving as a bridge between them. Medieval psychology, based firmly in Aristotelian and Galenic tradition (although variations of the Stoic and Epicurean sort were certainly discussed), studied the movement of the bodily spirits that composed the "psyche." Love physically heated up and expanded the heart, and could be ignited when *spiritelli*, little spirits, escaped from the eyes of the beloved, entering the eyes and then the heart of the lover. Guido Cavalcanti, *stil novo* poet, for example, often discussed the entrance and exit of spirits. In his sonnet "Pegli occhi fere un spirito sottile" every verse has the word "spirit" in it, a means to tracing the many ways spirit is shared between people's hearts and minds.

Related to questions of the physics and psychology of amorous love was the metaphysical discussion of *coincidentia oppositorum* (the coincidence of opposites). Perhaps Pythagorean in origin, this idea fueled work in medicine (for example, Johannes Peyligk, *Compendium philosophiae naturalis*, 1499) and many arts and sciences, as it did literature. Opposite entities, be they physical elements, emotional states (or many other things) were thought to seek harmony – *concordia discors* and reconciliation. In the natural world, this harmony was a desired and good thing. The coinciding of opposites in such literature as the amorous poetry of the Middle Ages and Renaissance, however, was often a fraught one. The lover was frequently described as suspended in the liminal space between life and death, burning and freezing, ecstasy and rage. Petrarca's Sonnet 134 of the *Canzoniere* offers a good example: "I find no peace, and yet I make no war: / and fear, and hope: and burn, and I am ice: / ... I see without eyes, and have no tongue, but cry: / and long to perish, yet I beg for aid: / and hold myself in hate, and love another. / I feed on sadness, laughing weep: / death and life displease me equally: / and I am in this state, lady, because of you."

Natural history: animals, plants, minerals

Medieval bestiaries, herbals, and lapidaries – like medieval tapestries adorned with unicorns and fruit tree topiaries – delight with all manner of flora and fauna, aquatic and geological substances, real and imagined. These, along with genres/modes such as travel writing, hunting manuals, and heraldic catalogues, are some of the ways in which the natural world came into print. Hugely popular throughout the Middle Ages and early Renaissance, the bestiary was at its height in thirteenth- and fourteenth-century England and France, increasingly written in vernacular verse and prose. Among the early sources for these bestiaries are Aristotle, Galen, Pliny, the anonymous *Physiologus*, Albertus Magnus's *De animalibus*, the encyclopedias of Isidore of Seville and Vincent of Beauvais, and to some degree travel logs – food for the imagination that they were – like those of Marco Polo, Cristoforo Colombo, and missionaries to faraway places.

While presenting common, exotic (or simply less known), or magical-mythical creatures to their readers, bestiaries were also intent on conveying wisdom or morals. Like classical fables and medieval fabliaux (see Marie de France), bestiaries used the device of allegory to entertain and edify. Some, like Richard of Fournival's thirteenth-century *Le Bestiaire d'amour*, turn their attention to a specific topic, such as courtly love. Leonardo da Vinci himself – excellent observer of nature that he was and *omo sanza lettere* [man without letters] that he claimed to be – wrote a series of fables in his notebooks that read like bestiaries. In one he writes, "When an ant found a grain of millet and picked it up, it cried out: 'If you do me a great favor and let me achieve my desire to sprout, I shall give you a hundred of me.' And that's what happened" (11: 283).

One can similarly find scores of plants and minerals, not to mention exquisite menageries or gardens (formal, or secret; filled with topiaries and/or mathematical in design; a safe place for amorous encounters or a place for evil to insinuate itself) decorating chivalric poetry, love lyric, and novellas, as well as pharmacological herbals (interestingly, the ancient way of identifying plants that resemble the part of the body they can be used to cure was called the "doctrine of signatures," as if the plants were "signed" by the hand of nature for specific medicinal purposes). In Wolfram von Eschenbach's thirteenth-century epic *Parzival*, descriptions of the many herbal, animal, and mineral remedies employed to extract venom from the Fisher King's wound are recounted in striking detail (Bk. IX). None succeeds, and supernatural aid (such as effluvia from paradise, and the garnet/ruby "carbuncle" under a unicorn horn) is sought. In Guido Guinizzelli's thirteenth-century "Al cor gentil" love and a noble heart are like magnets and iron. And crusade knights Astolfo and Ruggiero are lulled into letting their guard down in Alcina's garden in Ariosto's *Furioso* (Cantos VI–VII), only to be subsequently seduced by her magic.

As with biblical stories, classical myths, legends, and fairy tales, medieval and early Renaissance literature (bestiaries included) was rich with curious creatures and monstrous generations. John Mandeville's fourteenth-century *Travels* depict marvelous, invented animals and curiously formed people (see Ch. XXII), as do many of the Alexander legends. These creatures, like the gargoyles decorating European buildings, reveal a fascination with hybridity and metamorphosis (Ovid's popularity in these centuries cannot be overemphasized). Italian "macaronic" poetry (in Germany they called it *Nudelverse*, and Johann Fischart's *Die Geschichstklitterung* of 1575 is a good example) formalized this interest, including not only weird creatures and foodstuffs, but a raucous, clever language fusing Latin and Italian vernacular (syntax and semantics), dialect, and a cornucopia of neologisms. What exactly these humorous, hybrid texts are satirizing ("satire" originating from the word for "medley") is not the right question: what they are *not* would be a better one. Teofilo Folengo's *Baldus* (1521) is the most renowned example of the *ars macaronica*. The tale of Baldus, the ever-famished hero of the mock epic (Carolingian, given Baldus's supposed relation to Charlemagne himself), begins not with an appeal to the Olympian muses, but to the chubby *macaronaeam musae*, who "ladle out" their arts via platters of pasta and polenta (Bk.I: 1–16).

The desire to master a comprehensive knowledge of the workings and order of the natural world so as to better understand its beauties, its monsters, wonders, and powers, and what they teach us or give us; the dance between elite knowledge and vernacularization, popularization, and dissemination; the increasing confidence in the empirical and the positive value of the man-made – these are what characterize the literature and science of the Middle Ages and early Renaissance.

Bibliography

Translations of primary sources cited

Capella, M. (5th century) *De Nuptiis Philologiae et Mercurii*, trans. W.H. Stahl, R. Johnson, and E.L. Burge, 2 vols, New York: Columbia University Press, 1977.
Da Vinci, L. (late 15–16th centuries) "Fables," in *Renaissance Fables: Aesopic prose by L.B. Alberti, Bartolomeo Scala, Leonardo da Vinci, Bernardino Baldi*, trans. D. Marsh, Tempe: Arizona Center for Medieval and Renaissance Studies, 2004.
Ficino, M. (1489) *De vita libri tres*, trans. and ed. C. Kaske and J.R. Clark, Binghamton: MRTS, 1989.
Fracastoro, G. (1530) *Syphilidis, sive Morbi Gallici*, trans. N. Tate, London: J. Tonson, 1686.
Hugh of St. Victor, *Didascalicon*, trans. J. Taylor, New York: Columbia University Press, 1961.
Latini, B. (13th century) *Li Livres dou Trésor*, trans. P. Barrette and S. Baldwin, New York: Garland, 1993.
Liber viginti quattuor philosophorum (12th century?) trans. F. Hudry, Turnhout: Brepols,1997.

Suggested secondary readings

Bono, J. (1995) *The Word of God and the Languages of Man: interpreting nature in early modern science and medicine*, Madison: University of Wisconsin Press.
Colish, M. (1997) *Medieval Foundations of the Western Intellectual Tradition, 400–1400*, New Haven: Yale University Press.
Copenhaver, B. (1990) *Natural Magic, Hermeticism, and Occultism in Early Modern Science*, Cambridge: Cambridge University Press.

Crombie, A.C. (1952) *Augustine to Galileo: the history of science A.D. 400 to 1650*, London: Falcon Press.

Daston, L. and Park, K. (eds) (1998) *Wonders and the Order of Nature, 1150–1750*, New York: Zone Books.

Denery, D. (2005). *Seeing and Being in the Late Medieval World: optics, theology and religious life*, Cambridge: Cambridge University Press.

Eamon, W. (1994) *Science and the Secrets of Nature: books of secrets in medieval and early modern culture*, Princeton: Princeton University Press.

Eisenstein, E. (1979) *The Printing Press as an Agent of Change*, Cambridge: Cambridge University Press.

Frasca-Spada, M. and Jardine, N. (eds) (2000) *Books and the Sciences in History*, Cambridge: Cambridge University Press.

French, R. et al. (eds) (1998) *Medicine from the Black Death to the French Disease*, Aldershot: Ashgate.

Funkenstein, A. (1986) *Theology and the Scientific Imagination from the Middle Ages to the Sixteenth Century*, Princeton: Princeton University Press.

Grafton, A. (1991) *Defenders of the Text: the traditions of scholarship in an age of science 1450–1800*, Cambridge, Mass.: Harvard University Press.

——and N. Siraisi (eds) (1999) *Natural Particulars: nature and the disciplines in Renaissance Europe*, Cambridge, Mass.: MIT Press.

Grendler, P. (1989) *Schooling in Renaissance Italy: literacy and learning 1300–1600*, Baltimore: Johns Hopkins University Press.

Heninger, Jr., S.K. (1974) *Touches of Sweet Harmony: Pythagorean cosmology and Renaissance poetics*, San Marino: The Huntington Library.

Koyré, A. (1957) *From the Closed World to the Infinite Universe*, Baltimore: Johns Hopkins University Press.

Lindberg, D. (1992) *The Beginnings of Western Science: the European scientific tradition in philosophical, religious, and institutional context, 600 B.C. to A.D. 1450*, Chicago: University of Chicago Press.

Long, P. (2001) *Openness, Secrecy, Authorship: technical arts and the culture of knowledge from antiquity to the Renaissance*, Baltimore: Johns Hopkins University Press.

Ogilvie, B. (2006) *The Science of Describing: natural history in Renaissance Europe*, Chicago: University of Chicago Press.

Rose, P.L. (1975) *The Italian Renaissance of Mathematics: studies on humanists and mathematicians from Petrarch to Galileo*, Geneva: Droz.

Saliba, G. (2007) *Islamic Science and the Making of the European Renaissance*, Cambridge, Mass.: Harvard University Press.

Siraisi, N. (2007) *History, Medicine, and the Traditions of Renaissance Learning*, Ann Arbor: University of Michigan Press.

Smith, P. (2009) "Science on the move: recent trends in the history of early modern science," *Renaissance Quarterly*, 62: 345–75.

37
SCIENTIFIC "REVOLUTION" I
Copernicus to Boyle

Alvin Snider

In the second half of the twentieth century, the study of the scientific revolution itself underwent a revolution. As early as the eighteenth century, European thinkers decided that something crucial emerged in the period stretching between Copernicus and Newton, but had trouble describing exactly what. Few now share the Enlightenment's confidence in "an unambiguous triumph of rationality over obfuscation," or regard our own scientific knowledge as "a neutral and inevitable product of progress" (Dear 2001: 2). We can still find a hardy perennial version of the tradition in a body of contemporary fiction that narrates stories about the triumphant defeat of medieval superstition and scholastic inertia. Nicolaus Copernicus remains a canonical figure in this saga, and does duty as the hero of John Banville's prize-winning *Doctor Copernicus*, published in 1976, the first in a trilogy of novels, with additional volumes on Johannes Kepler and Isaac Newton. Banville draws on conventional historiography when he invokes two well-worn metaphors (fortifications and tides) to describe the young Copernicus's first glimpse of the Cracow Academy at the end of the fifteenth century: the college "had reminded him of nothing so much as a fortress, for it was, despite its pretentions, the main link in the defences thrown up by scholasticism against the tide of new ideas sweeping in from Italy, from England, and from Rotterdam" (Banville 2000: 35).

Copernicus not only sets his face against the medieval past, but must also stave off the grubby reality of the present, which threatens to contaminate the purity of his vision and disembodied fixation on the heavens. Specialists tell us that the Copernican system, when it did not meet with condemnation on religious grounds, became subject to various attempts to reconcile it with Aristotelian physical theories and reintegrate it into a Christianized natural philosophy (Gaukroger 2006: 125–26). Followers of Copernicus had little trouble blunting the edge of his theories, accommodating heliocentrism and descriptions of planetary motion with religious belief, because his ideas emerged from the matrix of late scholasticism and spoke its language. Banville nevertheless prefers to give us a quasi-mythic portrait of an aloof, transcendent genius instead of the versatile public figure recorded in the historical archive, diligently engaged in economic, legal, medical, and ecclesiastical pursuits.

With *Quicksilver* (2003), the first volume of Neal Stephenson's Baroque Cycle, another novel trilogy, a writer best known for cyberpunk shoulders the burden of fictionalizing the scientific revolution. *Quicksilver* includes among its sprawling cast of characters notables such as Robert Boyle, Robert Hooke, Christiaan Huygens, and Newton. When one character advises another to "consider the future of the revolution," by which he means an epistemological insurrection or uprising ("You speak and think in a language that did not exist when you and Sir Isaac entered Trinity"), he pronounces as a traditional historian of science *avant la lettre* (Stephenson 2003: 46). Stephenson's protagonists float above their societies, behaving as our postmodern contemporaries do and participating in a celebrity culture that reduces the novel of ideas to chat-show banter. The revolution he invokes admittedly entails no "single dramatic moment of apocalypse," since one cannot point to "the Moment It All Happened" (864). Yet this historical novel very much depends on the narrative constructed by two of the distinguished historians Stephenson acknowledges as his sources, A. Rupert Hall and Richard S. Westfall, who published scholarship after World War II that sealed the significance and singular identity of the scientific revolution for decades.

In a bibliographical essay annexed to his revisionist *The Scientific Revolution*, Steven Shapin describes the "Great Tradition" in historiography, exemplified by Hall and Westfall, as marked by

> robust confidence that there was a coherent and specifiable body of early modern culture rightly called revolutionary ... that it had an 'essence,' and that this essence could be captured through accounts of the rise of mechanism and materialism, the mathematization of natural philosophy, the emergence of full-blooded experimentalism, and for many, though not all, traditional writers, the identification of an effective 'method' for producing authentic science.
>
> (Shapin 1996: 168)

Historians of science now generally doubt the existence of a revolutionary moment of origin in the seventeenth century, of a fixed method for the production of new knowledge, of a cultural totality captured by the anachronistic word "science." At the same time, they have not discarded the use of the problematic term altogether, and few would doubt its utility in designating a significant historical transformation in thought and practice. If literary scholars continue to use the phrase for want of a better, in the recent historical studies surveyed below the concept barely registers.

We would expect any alteration in the Western understanding of nature, not to say a tectonic realignment in the forces of disciplinary knowledge, to encroach well beyond fields such as celestial dynamics, and certainly as far as the elite literary culture of the period. To sound the depths of this rethinking of nature and language, readers can turn to writers of poetry and other literary genres who tuned in to these developments. In them we find more subtle and searching critiques than in fictionalized accounts of the scientific revolution produced in our own day. Without attempting to distill any "scientific" essence from literary works, the following pages sample texts that explicitly draw on controversies involving astronomy, and also discuss how literature could serve an agenda linked to the theory and practice of natural philosophy. Neither literature nor science functions as an autonomous domain in this period, and sometimes one can work to catalyze the other.

In standard accounts of the "construction of modern science," mathematics, astronomy, physics, and chemistry tend to win pride of place, while anatomy, physiology, and other fields get relegated to secondary status or snipped to a mechanistic pattern (Westfall 1971). What made the Copernican revolution especially significant for Thomas Kuhn involved not only its eventual culmination in Newtonian dynamics and classical mechanics but also its consequences in disciplines external to astronomy and physics. According to Kuhn, a wider crisis of modernity prepared the way for innovation in astronomy because decisive change in one field typically has a domino effect on other modes of inquiry (Kuhn 1957: 124). The general upheaval of the age – and Kuhn takes into account European exploration, the expansion of the Ottoman empire, the revival of classical learning, the Reformation, and many other factors, large and small – provides the backdrop to his study of astronomy.

Kuhn's study brings to center stage an exposition of the shift from two-sphere cosmology to a new understanding of planetary motion, which abolished concepts such as epicycles and eccentrics and promoted an entirely new view of the universe. Nevertheless, in Copernicus's major work, *De revolutionibus orbium Coelestium* of 1543, Kuhn discovers a text closer in spirit to ancient and medieval cosmology than to the science that later became synonymous with the author's name (Kuhn 1957: 135). Copernican astronomy, which relocated the earth from the center and assigned it to a place among the planets, retained many of the features of an orderly, hierarchical, and finite system. Trained as a physicist, Kuhn treats the science of motion as integral to a wider intellectual history, breaking down artificial boundaries and reading planetary astronomy back into the culture from which it emerged. His methodology allows him to unravel the tangled skein of high culture and canonical texts, from which he extricates scientific theories that warrant much closer attention than (say) the poetic passages from Dante, Du Bartas, and John Donne he sometimes quotes.

One can compare Kuhn's strategy of disentangling various cultural strands – even while he eventually and famously disallowed any distinction between the context of discovery and the context of justification – to a more recent study, Harold J. Cook's *Matters of Exchange: Commerce, Medicine, and Science in the Dutch Golden Age*. Cook brings into close conjunction the rise of early modern natural history and medicine, the expansion of Dutch commerce, developments in epistemology, the circulation of trade and information, studying the interplay between the emergence of global trade and the concerns of the new science. He embeds the production of knowledge in systems of accumulation and networks of exchange (Cook 2007: 411), taking the Dutch case to exemplify developments elsewhere in Europe. In this book the commanding figure of Copernicus gives way to scientists and physicians of decidedly smaller reputations (the botanist Georg Eberhard Rumphius, the physician Herman Boerhaave, the anatomist Nicolaes Tulp, among many others); today only the names of the philosophers whom Cook treats at length (René Descartes and Benedict Spinoza) have wide currency outside of the Netherlands. Cook's analysis of the scientific revolution at once keeps close to the ground in its focus on medicine, natural history, and technology, even while it emphasizes how the enterprise of collecting and exchanging information involved people from all over the world, of varying social and educational backgrounds (414). The book's global scope and interdisciplinary method counterbalance its materialist and microanalytical approach to the scientific revolution, making the study at once compendious and highly specialized in ways altogether typical of the best current work.

Despite its broad outlook on early modern culture, Cook's substantial volume has nothing to say about literature as a form of knowledge, apart from some stray comments about Dutch writers and Tulp's efforts to ban Joost van Vondel's play *Lucifer* ("a model for John Milton's *Paradise Lost*") (159). Post-war writers on the history of science, such as Kuhn or Alexandre Koyré, enjoyed quoting lines from Lucretius, Donne, and Milton, but did so in an off-hand way. More recent studies, such as Cook's, routinely take note of the participation of humanists in social networks built by scientists, and relations between the scientific community and traditional centers of authority and expertise, religion in particular. But they have relatively little to say about literature. Literary scholars, too, have not always exercised whatever disciplinary prerogatives remain to them. In the 1980s, structuralism and semiotics, mythology and "poetics" (understood as the analysis of tropes, submerged metaphors, analogy, and commonplaces) provided impetus for work on cosmology by scholars such as Fernand Hallyn (1993). Yet all the texts Hallyn subjected to analysis have either a philosophical or an astronomical orientation; his poetics proceeds without reference to poetry or poets.

Closer in methodology to what we now might think of as a characteristically "literary" (or book-centered) project on early modern science is Adrian Johns's *The Nature of the Book* (1998). Johns includes a chapter on what he calls "Literary Life," drawing simultaneously on the title of Bruno Latour and Steve Woolgar's classic study, *Laboratory Life*, which turns to literary criticism and anthropology for its analysis of the social construction of scientific knowledge, and on a neologism applied disparagingly to the bookseller Edmund Curll's workshop for textual production. Johns's contribution lies within the parameters of science studies, but also the history of the book, since the processes that produced early modern print culture also produced the cultural construction that goes by the name of "science." The chapter on literary life looks to various overlapping "domains" in early modern London to consider how "the 'social geography' of the printing house and bookshop meshed with that of the wider urban environment, and how together they conditioned the knowledge that could be produced and encountered in early modern London" (Johns 1998: 62). Johns writes a version of cultural history that integrates scientific research into a very specific framework: the networks of trust and authority that produced and disseminated knowledge about nature. Grand narratives about the emergence of scientific method or biographies of great scientists play no part in his project.

In tying the success of experimental philosophy to the processes of textual production and distribution, Johns relies on anecdote and *récit*, or narrative reconstruction, somewhat in the manner of new historicism or of cultural anthropology. Milton figures for Johns (if only tangentially) much in the same way he figures in book studies, as a writer enmeshed in an interlocking network of stationers, licensers, censors, authors, printers, and readers. In other words, the interdisciplinary method of Johns's book draws literary authorship and literary property into the orbit of the history of science, all under the auspices of print culture and questions of "credit" or intellectual authority. Such an approach has little in common with the "rhetoric of science," a field that parses particular styles of persuasive argumentation in order to determine how they induce agreement by mobilizing distinctive modes of reasoning, but rather, shares powerful affinities with literary criticism that takes a sociohistorical bent.

We can say, then, that the varied enterprises bundled under the heading of "science" – according to a later convention where the term marks the site of a universal and timeless rationality – had no revolutionary significance for those who undertook them before 1700. The general absence of clear lines of demarcation between scientific and non-scientific knowledge had another effect. Just as humanist textualism suffuses the discourses of medicine and astronomy, natural philosophy seeped into the sanctum of high literary culture. Intellectual traffic flowed in both directions. Christiaan Huygens, son of a poet and composer, wrote a treatise (posthumously published) on the plurality of worlds, which included fictional elements. Huygens notes the blurring of the boundaries when he points to modern experts, the great astronomer Kepler among them, who "have coined some pretty Fairy Stories of the Men in the Moon, just as probable as *Lucian*'s true History" (Huygens 1698: 3).

A much more famous astronomical text, Galileo's 1632 *Dialogue on the Two Chief World Systems, Ptolemaic and Copernican*, takes the form of a colloquy that embraces both performative and dialectical precedents. (Philip Glass's 2002 opera, *Galileo Galilei*, restores the physicist to the theater, treating the contribution to early opera of Galileo's father, Vincenzio, as key to unlocking the physicist's later career.) Part humanist symposium and part theatrical entertainment, Galileo's *Dialogue* conjures the presence of Giovanfrancesco Sagredo and Filippo Salviati, together with the sharply satirized Aristotelian philosopher Simplicio, and rescues his friends from oblivion "by reviving them in these pages of mine and using them as interlocutors in the present controversy" (Galilei 1997: 82). Thus, the Venetian diplomat Sagredo and the Florentine virtuoso Salviati emerge as characters in search of an author, and Copernican theories find expression in persons whose standpoints are grounded in their historical moments. Galileo had employed dialogue form in his earliest publication in 1605, and returned to it towards the end of his career with renewed assurance about its persuasive power. The literary, theological, and philosophical sophistication on display in the *Dialogue*, not to mention the skillful use of vernacular Italian, obviously failed to impress the authorities, and Galileo's attempt to make Copernican theories accessible to a lay audience attracted the unwelcome attention of the Inquisition in 1633 and the book's prohibition.

Unique among Milton's contemporaries, Galileo makes an appearance by name in *Paradise Lost*, in a passage that describes the angel Raphael's first glimpse of earth: "As when by night the Glass / Of Galileo, less assur'd, observes / Imagin'd Lands and Regions in the Moon" (5.261–63). Despite the note of skepticism sounded with the phrases "less assur'd" and "imagin'd," the simile records an extraordinary moment of recognition. Milton's selection of Galileo owes to several factors: in 1638 he had met, still under house arrest, "the famous Galileo, grown old, a prisner to the Inquisition, for thinking in Astronomy otherwise then the Franciscan and Dominican licencers thought" (cited in Campbell and Corns 2008: 112; in fact, Galileo had obtained a license to print the *Dialogue*); the astronomer's persecution served zealous Protestants such as Milton as shorthand for the repressive forces of Catholicism and censorship; and Galileo's observations of the lunar surface, reported in *Sidereus Nuncius* of 1610, challenged the dominant lunar theory derived from Aristotle in ways that served Milton's larger purpose in the epic. This last discovery belongs together with two other iconic moments in empirical research: Galileo's experiment with falling objects and the experiment with rolling balls down inclined planes.

Gazing through a telescope – "an apparatus that signifies the 'New Science' of the seventeenth century, and a technology that makes 'new worlds' available for inspection" (Albanese 1996: 122) – Galileo observed changing dark and light patches on the moon's surface. Where Aristotle considered the moon perfectly spherical and smooth, Galileo observed that the moon's surface, like that of the Earth, has an irregular topography, with mountains and valleys visible in shadows that swell and shrink relative to the position of the sun. Milton, however, deprives the reader of certainty, or even any sense of human agency, since, in the passage quoted above, the "Glass" carries out the observation, not the star gazer. The syntax of the simile refuses to attach the point of view to the blind Galileo, the blind poet, or the disoriented reader. On some level, the perception of a world in the moon could appear the product of analogy itself, of an assumption, by no means self-evident, that a single principle obtains in all bodies of a similar type.

With this loaded simile, Milton opens to further investigation questions about knowledge, certainty, and intellectual authority. Galileo and Milton lived in a period when Aristotelian and scholastic explanations had stopped making sense for many of those acquainted with them, but the intelligibility of Copernican theories (and the mechanistic worldview in general) remained subject to fierce debate. An older generation of Miltonists, who pondered the question of whose astronomical theory Milton adopts in *Paradise Lost* (Ptolemy's? Copernicus's? Tycho Brahe's?), of whether he posits a closed or infinite universe, labeled Milton's astronomical views as basically Ptolemaic. Yet Milton would hardly endorse the outcome of Galileo's trial for heresy, and well understood that the new cosmological models faced much less resistance in Protestant England (and Lutheran Germany) than in Catholic countries.

Convinced that Galileo's *Dialogue* can function as "a shadowy intertext for Milton's universalizing epic" (Albanese 1996: 149), and treating the telescope as a token of epistemological innovation, literary scholars have sought out additional points of convergence between Milton and science. Recently some have directed attention to environmental issues, giving new attention to herbals, bestiaries, manuals of animal husbandry, and so forth, and launching an early modern ecocriticism in which Milton occupies a central role (e.g. Hiltner 2008). Such an approach may in the long run prove more fruitful than looking for extensive evidence of Milton's direct engagement with the new science (Poole 2004). Scholars nevertheless have recognized that from his youth Milton traveled in circles that included contemporaries we might describe as polymathic humanists with strong scientific interests (Joseph Mede, Carlo Dati), and that he corresponded with two notable figures closely associated with the Royal Society of London, Samuel Hartlib and Henry Oldenburg (Campbell and Corns 2008: 28, 113–14, 180, 267; Duran 2007). Within the last two decades, Miltonists have begun seriously to investigate the significance of such cross-currents. John Rogers's work on convergences among science, poetry, and politics in the period focuses on theories of animist materialism, and casts Milton and Margaret Cavendish as "notable participants in the seventeenth-century literary practice of scientific speculation," who both struggled in their writings "to accommodate divergent and contradictory forms of sanctioned truth" (Rogers 1996: 180–81).

The traditional view of Milton's cosmology, that he reverts to a Ptolemaic model of the universe and a "medieval" idea of Nature, often serves a program of reclaiming the poet for Christian humanism and literary value. More recently,

Stephen M. Fallon (1991) has put Milton in dialog with his contemporaries, sharply distinguishing his animist materialism from the mechanical philosophy of Descartes and Thomas Hobbes, finding an analog to Milton's monistic ontology in the monism of Anne Conway, a neo-Platonist metaphysician. Fallon contends that, despite resemblances between Miltonic and Hobbesian views, the poet sees all matter as basically alive, while the philosopher sees only particles in motion. Mechanists considered it an Aristotelian error to talk about the natural world as something imbued with life or goal directed, while Milton has Raphael speak of "one first matter all, / Indu'd with various forms, various degrees / Of substance, and in things that live, of life" (5.472–74).

Karen Edwards (1999) points out that when the old science resurfaces in *Paradise Lost*, Milton's tone tends to grow satirical and dismissive, whereas the poem "consistently makes available new representational possibilities suggested by the experimental philosophy, and it does so with excitement, wit, and creative relish" (Edwards 1999: 10). Milton swam in the same current that set in motion the processes and discoveries that gave seventeenth-century English science a central place in European intellectual life, and in the writings of Hooke and Boyle we can find many of the ideas and concerns that animate Milton's attitudes towards experience, the human body, and the phenomenal world. Milton's representation of the natural world in *Paradise Lost* grows out of the same doubts and possibilities that provided the impulse for the founding of the Royal Society in 1661. We can also detect the influence of Francis Bacon and the legacy of Baconianism in his thought. Catherine Gimelli Martin (2007), for example, detects the presence of Bacon shining through Milton's work, linking the poet to the Royal Society virtuosi whose politics and religion he held in anathema. We find such inconsistencies and apparent contradictions everywhere in the intellectual life of the age. For example, Kepler and Bacon hoped to reform astrology, not to drive it underground, and John Flamsteed, the Astronomer Royal whose residence at the Royal Greenwich Observatory remains a popular site of science tourism, both dabbled in and disputed astrology.

Before the seventeenth century, a "revolution" signified something cyclical, not a violent upheaval that produces an irreversible new social, political, or intellectual order. Many writers associated with the coming of modernity "saw themselves not as bringing about totally new states of affairs but as restoring or purifying old ones" (Shapin 1996: 3). Margaret Cavendish, Duchess of Newcastle, shared few political or religious opinions with her compatriot John Milton, yet, like him, she took an active interest in the intellectual currents of the day, especially natural philosophy. Driven by the civil wars to join the court of Queen Henrietta Maria in France, in 1645 Cavendish married William Cavendish, a dilettantish nobleman friendly with some of the leading lights of the age, including John Dryden, Hobbes, Anthony van Dyck, and Descartes. In 1660 Margaret returned to England and published, among many works in different forms, her *Observations upon Experimental Philosophy* in 1666. To this text, contemporaneous with the first edition of *Paradise Lost*, she appended *The Blazing World*, a prose narrative sometimes regarded as an early work of science fiction. Cavendish was not alone in thinking that natural philosophy might don the guise of fable (see, e.g., Huygens 1698: 1–11), but few launched themselves into philosophical debates with such daring and originality.

The antithesis of a radical in any political sense, Cavendish outlined a critique of the new science in the *Observations* and *The Description of a New World, Called The Blazing World* that has only recently received the careful attention it deserves. The story of *The Blazing World* involves the making and dissolving of mental worlds, the creation of an infinitely recursive set of imaginative constructs. It tells the story of a lady abducted and taken aboard a ship driven northward by a storm toward the Pole and into the Blazing World, located beyond "another Pole of another world, which joined close to it" (Cavendish 2003: 8). Once married to the Emperor of that world, as an Empress she assembles an academy of savants to instruct her and whom she engages in a freewheeling seminar on scientific, religious, and political subjects. Cavendish adopted a philosophy of vitalist materialism, which subordinates empiricism to "Rational Contemplation" and valorizes observation by the naked eye. She lays out a critique of telescopes for their distortion of the visible world and for only representing surfaces of things, for causing differences among astronomers rather than producing consensus.

Impatient with the results of a series of unsuccessful experiments using telescopes, the Empress labels the instruments "false informers" and denounces them for deluding the sight (Cavendish 2003: 27). Glasses, she argues, cannot compete with "sense and reason," and a proper empirical method must not depend on artifice for assistance, or escape the limitations of ordinary perception. Some liberal feminist critics (e.g., John Rogers) conclude that Cavendish's treatment of nature as autonomous, self-knowing, and self-moving strikes a telling blow against mechanism and patriarchalist logic. Other readers of Cavendish have situated the text between the emergent discourses of British colonialism and the new science. Mary Baine Campbell finds multiple connections among early modern utopianism, scientific experiment, exploration, and colonialism, joining Hooke's *Micrographia* with *The Blazing World* to show how both works encourage Europeans to define themselves through the exclusion or domination of others (Campbell 1999: 204–5). Whether or not Cavendish succeeded in devising a feminist epistemology, her skeptical assessments of Cartesian dualism, Royal Society experimentalism, and mechanist notions of matter (as inert, lifeless particles moved by external forces) offered a radical critique of the new science. In *The Blazing World* she installs herself at the helm of an institution that captures the Royal Society in a mirror image, faithful to the original but simultaneously inverted, and a challenge to many of its basic assumptions, not least of all the exclusion of women from its ranks.

The Royal Society found its exemplar, the highest expression of the Baconian principles it espoused, in another aristocrat, Robert Boyle, who combined the skills of a chemist, theologian, and accomplished writer of English prose. A seminal study of debates between Boyle and Hobbes, *Leviathan and the Air-Pump*, identifies "the technical, literary, and social practices" deployed in the creation and validation of "experimental matters of fact" (Shapin and Schaffer 1985: 18). Shapin and Schaffer argue, if you will, the importance of language and representation in the production of knowledge. They devote considerable energy to studying Boyle's technique of "virtual witnessing," by which they mean the creation of an aura of reliability through the use of pictorial representations of the air pump in pneumatic experiments, and a particular discourse of scientific discovery, heavy on circumstantial detail and dedicated to rendering the scene of experiment in vivid colors. Boyle wields a highly wrought yet unbuttoned English prose, carefully designed to present the author as disinterested, innocent of theory, and modest (Shapin and Schaffer 1985: 60–69). At times he adopts a convoluted periodic style, characterized by intricate clausal structures and other formal devices intended to simulate an effect of the mind in motion. More often he lays aside any hint of rhetoricity or learned citation in order to achieve an effect of selfless dedication to matters of fact (67). Such techniques strive to preserve the experimental community from splintering into factions and offer a simulacrum of eye-witnessing for second-hand observers, for consumers of the printed text.

The scare quotes encasing the word "revolution" in the title of this chapter could expand to engulf the entire phrase and every other keyword we have discussed. The idea behind the term, however, retains its hold on the cultural imagination of the West because it encapsulates notions about modernity and the autonomy of science that we surrender with reluctance. A radical disjunction of science from other realms of knowledge underwrites many of the tales we tell about the origin of the modern world. If we cannot shake off the term altogether, the study of early modern literature and science provides one approach for breaking through the wall that separates laboratory and literary life.

Bibliography

Albanese, D. (1996) *New Science, New World*, Durham, N.C.: Duke University Press.

Banville, J. (2000) *The Revolutions Trilogy: Doctor Copernicus, Kepler, the Newton letters*, London: Picador.

Campbell, G. and Corns, T.N. (2008) *John Milton: life, work, and thought*, Oxford: Oxford University Press.

Campbell, M.B. (1999) *Wonder and Science: imagining worlds in early modern Europe*, Ithaca, N.Y.: Cornell University Press.

Cavendish, M. (2003) *Political Writings*, ed. S. James, Cambridge: Cambridge University Press.

Cook, H.J. (2007) *Matters of Exchange: commerce, medicine, and science in the Dutch golden age*, New Haven: Yale University Press.

Dear, P. (2001) *Revolutionizing the Sciences: European knowledge and its ambitions, 1500–1700*, Princeton: Princeton University Press.

Duran, A. (2007) *The Age of Milton and the Scientific Revolution*, Pittsburgh: Duquesne University Press.

Edwards, K.L. (1999) *Milton and the Natural World: science and poetry in "Paradise Lost"*, Cambridge: Cambridge University Press.

Fallon, S.M. (1991) *Milton among the Philosophers: poetry and materialism in seventeenth-century England*, Ithaca, N.Y.: Cornell University Press.

Galilei, G. (1997) *Galileo on the World Systems: a new abridged translation and guide*, trans. M.A. Finocchiaro, Berkeley: University of California Press.

Gaukroger, S. (2006) *The Emergence of a Scientific Culture: science and the shaping of modernity, 1210–1685*, Oxford: Clarendon Press.

Hallyn, F. (1993) *The Poetic Structure of the World: Copernicus and Kepler*, D.M. Leslie (trans.), New York: Zone Books.

Hiltner, K. (ed.) (2008) *Renaissance Ecology: imagining Eden in Milton's England*, Pittsburg: Duquesne University Press.

Huygens, C. (1698) *The Celestial Worlds Discover'd: or, conjectures concerning the inhabitants, plants and productions of the worlds in the planets*, London: Timothy Childe.

Johns, A. (1998) *The Nature of the Book: print and knowledge in the making*, Chicago: University of Chicago Press.

Kuhn, T.S. (1957) *The Copernican Revolution: planetary astronomy in the development of Western thought*, Cambridge, Mass.: Harvard University Press.

Martin, C.G. (2007) "Rewriting the revolution: Milton, Bacon, and the Royal Society rhetoricians," in J. Cummins and D. Burchell (eds) *Science, Literature and Rhetoric in Early Modern England*, Aldershot: Ashgate, pp. 96–123.

Poole, W. (2004) "Milton and science: a caveat," *Milton Quarterly*, 38(1): 18–34.

Rogers, J. (1996) *The Matter of Revolution: science, poetry, and politics in the age of Milton*, Ithaca, N.Y.: Cornell University Press.

Shapin, S. (1996) *The Scientific Revolution*, Chicago: University of Chicago Press.

——and Schaffer, S. (1985) *Leviathan and the Air-Pump: Hobbes, Boyle, and the experimental life*, Princeton: Princeton University Press.

Stephenson, N. (2003) *Quicksilver*, New York: HarperCollins.

Westfall, R.S. (1971) *The Construction of Modern Science: mechanisms and mechanics*, New York: John Wiley.

38
SCIENTIFIC "REVOLUTION" II
Newton to Laplace

Lucinda Cole

The history of early modern science has sometimes been represented by a straightforward narrative of displacement: "occult" knowledges were replaced by the mechanical, mathematical, and empirically grounded models of Nature, culminating in the science of Isaac Newton (Vickers 1986: 3–44). But theology played a more significant role for Bacon, Boyle, Newton, and others than such a progressivist description allows (Markley 1993; Bono 1999). Newton's writings on alchemy, religion, polytheistic theologies, and other so-called "unscientific" topics surfaced in an auction in 1936 and were sold to various libraries, thereby creating a schism in Newton studies between those who dismissed these writings as a product of senility or mercury poisoning and those who saw them as integral to Newton's scientific theories (Westfall 1980; Castillejo 1989; Force and Popkin 1999). It is essential to recognize that neither Boyle nor Newton, nor any of their followers, claims that science is an independent means to truth, but only what Boyle calls a "handmaid to divinity" (Hellegers 2000). In his letter to Richard Bentley, Newton says of his *Principia*, "When I wrote my Treatise about our System, I had an Eye upon such Principles as might work with considering Men, for the Belief of a Deity" (Turnball et al. 1959–77: 3, 233). While the Royal Society banned debates about politics and religion, both discourses helped structure the work of British natural philosophers who, rather than rejecting a hermetic tradition and the religiosity underwriting it, often debated in their letters and papers the ways in which their empirical experiments and mathematical advances could be assimilated to – and reinforce – the theological metanarratives of Protestant voluntarism: the belief in God's unlimited power and unpredictable, mysterious intervention in nature, in a world that, through His will, can be redeemed or destroyed.

Late seventeenth-century British natural philosophers like Boyle and Newton lived in and studied what they regarded as a post-lapsarian world in which nature, humans, language, and even knowledge itself had been corrupted by original sin. For these men, human sin was both cause and effect of a fallen but temporary state of Nature. "The present course of nature," Boyle writes, "shall not last always, but that one Day *this World* ... shall be either Abolished by Annihilation, or (which seems far more probable) be Innovated, and, as it were, Transfigur'd" by "Fire" which "shall dissolve and destroy the present frame of Nature" (Boyle 1674: 22). The idea of the clockwork universe where, in Bruno Latour's words, a "crossed-out God was 'relegated to the sidelines'" (Latour 1993: 13) was really the byproduct of a different historical period. Some hundred years later, in Revolutionary France after the Catholic Church had been banned and its houses of worship desecrated, Pierre Simon de Laplace, not Newton, proposed an entirely orderly and mechanistic universe based upon a rigorous mathematical determinism (Numbers 1977). To associate the "rise" of early modern science with a vision of mathematical determinism, then, depends on suppressing any number of political and religious discourses promoted by writers in both the English and Continental traditions, and on the occlusion of a complex historical context and its obsessions with order and origin (Hall 1980).

Boyle, Noah, and the book of nature

One of the dominant structuring metaphors in early modern science is the idea of the "two books": the belief that one must read nature, as one reads the word of God, because both are paths to ultimate salvation for the soul and redemption for a fallen world. "The Book of Grace," writes Robert Boyle, "doth resemble the Book of Nature; wherein the Stars ... are not more Nicely nor Methodically plac'd than the Passages of Scripture" (Boyle 1674: a1r). But often early modern scientists had very different ideas from their predecessors about how "Nature" could be defined. Boyle addresses this problem in his *Free Inquiry Into the Vulgar Notion of Nature*, which is primarily directed against two interrelated notions that he believes have had "an ill effect upon religion": treating merely "corporeal" things as though they had "life, sense, and understanding," which is the basis of pantheism, and ascribing to Nature "things that belong to God alone," which is the basis of idolatry (Boyle 1686: 113). Boyle inveighs here and elsewhere against the neo-Pythagorean tradition of *anima mundi*, or world soul. Implicit in Virgil, revised in certain neo-Stoic sects, and popularized through successive translations of Ovid's *Metamorphoses*, the idea of *anima mundi* – literally, the breath of life – played an important part in physiognomy and Galenic approaches to the world, such as Giambattista della Porta's immensely popular *Natural Magick* (1558). Sometimes called plastic nature, the Pythagorean idea of the world soul implied an idea of kinship among all animate creatures or, in some Stoic versions, the idea of an immanent, living, natural force which was often at odds with both voluntarist and, later, agnostic notions of the universe (Jacob 1977).

Debates about the nature of matter and the question of an animate soul had profound effects on a range of scientific discourses, from alchemy to physiology to physics, where it was often subject to charges of atheism and impiety. At stake in *anima mundi* was a host of issues: whether the transmigration of souls is a possibility; whether the universe could tolerate a vacuum; whether humans are a microcosm of a larger macrocosm; whether humans are alone in possessing a soul; the nature of God; whether or not the Deity can be said to be "in" the world; the truth of scripture; and the distinction between modern and "pagan" or "heretical" thought. Writing in 1741, the encyclopedist Ephraim Chambers offers a succinct, but bloodless, description of the issue many seventeenth-century natural philosophers faced: "the principle thing objected ... against [the ancient] doctrine of the *anima mundi*," he writes, "is that it mingles the deity too much with the creatures, confounds in some measure, the workman with his work, making this, as it were, a part of that, the several portions of the universe as so many parts of the Godhead" (Chambers 1741: sig 1Bb). Underwriting the relationship between the creator and his creatures is an equally fundamental question about the beginning and the ending of the world. Charles Blount (1679), citing Lucretius, polemically contrasts the assumptions about pagan and Christian ideas. Of the former, he writes, since no egg could be without a bird, and no bird without an egg, "superstitious" ancient philosophers "conceiv'd that the World, and the beginning of every begotten thing, together with the end thereof, must be by perpetual revolution semipiternal." From this "semipiternal" perspective, God may be Nature, Nature may be God, and both must be regarded as "eternal, and void of all corruption" (Blount 1679: 11–12).

Boyle addresses the chicken-and-egg problem first by coming down on the side of the producer rather than the product. More precisely, for the self-creating nature of the ancients – the *Natura naturans* – he substitutes "the word God" (Boyle 1686: 14). In his voluntarist view, the coherence of Nature is the effect of God's will: "*Nature is the Aggregate of the Bodies, that make up the World, framed as it is, considered as a principle, by virtue whereof, they Act and Suffer according to Laws of Motion, prescribed by the Author of Things*" (Boyle 1686: 71). God, not Nature, is therefore the universal force that directs and orders the universe, now conceived as fallen. Second, however, Boyle uses the fact of a post-lapsarian world to justify the project of experimental philosophy. "For Boyle, scientific experimentation is to nature what exegesis is to the Bible" (Markley 1993: 41). The proper study of both ultimately leads to "an Endlesse Progress" (Boyle 1674: 63) in natural and scriptural knowledge – that is, in the unending, asymptotic efforts to redeem science, Nature, and the scientist from irrevocable sin.

One byproduct of Boyle's rejection of *anima mundi* is the elevation of humans at the expense of the animals upon which they feed and experiment: "It is an act of piety to offer up for the creatures the sacrifice of praise to the creator" (Boyle 1762: 8). Boyle's insistence on human dominance of a fallen nature closely follows the argument made in *The Novum Organon* by Francis Bacon, who flatly asserts that he does "not approve" of the "confused and promiscuous philosophers" who would treat the human soul as though it differed "*in degree rather than species from the soul of the brutes*" (Bacon 1899: 125). One consequence of this argument for Bacon is that animals can be dissected in order to "answer the design" of experimental philosophy (Bacon 1899: 116). Boyle's *Of the Usefulness of Experimental Philosophy* similarly opens with an extended defense of "skillful dissection" against those "dis-approving the study of physiology" (Boyle 1762: 8) and articulates a Christian justification for distinguishing radically between humans and the other animals by using the story of Noah to justify man's dominance. Boyle explicitly connects scientific practice to a Noachian history and its sacrificial economy:

> So when in Noah's time, a deluge of impiety called for a deluge of waters, God, looking upon the living creatures, as made for the use of man, stuck not to destroy them with him, and for him; but involved in his ruin all those animals, that were not necessary to the perpetuation of the species, and the sacrifice due for Noah's preservation.
>
> (Boyle 1762: 17)

In rejecting *anima mundi* and in linking experimental science to Noachian history, Boyle promotes a view that makes all of creation a laboratory for human beings for the sake of their individual and collective redemption. In his words, Noah's "noble sacrifice" of different species of animals constituted a "thank-you offering for the reprieve of the world" (Boyle 1762: 18). To the extent that science, for Boyle, is a form of prayer, his devotion demands a sacrifice – animal experimentation – that becomes a measure of his faith. In Boyle's sacrificial and voluntarist world, there is no messy "mingling" between the deity and his creatures, no conflation between Nature and God, and no confusion about the differences between humans and the organic "texts" which constituted their proper objects of study.

Boyle's sacrificial justification occurred during a period when markers of the difference between human and animal – based on anatomy, intelligence, and emotions – were being challenged by the new empiricism (Fudge 1999; Guerrini 2003). Ultimately, man's claim to religion was the only difference left standing, making the question of animal immortality one of the most hotly debated issues of the late seventeenth and early eighteenth centuries. When situated within this volatile context, the doctrine of *anima mundi* is not simply an archaism of pre-scientific thought, but part of the deep history by which the tensions that characterize early modern science and its relationship to the natural world were articulated. Latour argues that modernity set itself the task of carving two realms, one characterized by a free-thinking subject – the realm of humans and politics – and one inhabited by mute objects – the realm of "Nature" – that, through scientific representatives, are thought to "speak the truth." These "nonhumans," writes Latour, "lacking souls but endowed with meaning, are even more reliable than mortals, to whom will is attributed but who lack the capacity to indicate phenomena in a reliable way" (Latour 1993: 23–24). Cast with new semantic powers, experimental animals contribute to a new kind of text, the experimental science article, "a hybrid between the age-old style of biblical exegesis ... and the new instrument that produces new inscriptions" (23–24). By virtue of experiments – the most famous being those of the air pump to demonstrate the properties of a vacuum – animals were re-constituted as what Latour calls hybrids or quasi-objects, products of the laboratory. In a very real sense, the cultural history of early modern science is an effort to negotiate between the proliferation of hybrids in the laboratory and the ideology of purification that strives to distinguish humans from animal, spirit from Nature, theory from practice.

Newton's fire

Keith Thomas writes that Boyle had no patience for the "veneration" of an uncorrupted Nature explicit in many ancient and Eastern religions, which he recognized as "a discouraging impediment to the empire of man over the inferior creatures" (Thomas 1983: 22). This sensibility he shared with Newton, although Newton's relationship to religious history was more complicated. Boyle was a faithful member of the Anglican Church, a low-church latitudinarian; Newton, in contrast, was an anti-Trinitarian who perceived himself as outside established church doctrine and as entertaining the kinds of heretical beliefs that got his successor as the Lucasian Professor of Mathematics at Cambridge, William Whiston, fired from his post (Force 1985). For Boyle, both the Bible and nature are perfectly ordered; for Newton, the bulk of the Bible "is a flawed, imperfect text that had been corrupted by poor translations and the willing deceit of Trinitarians" (Markley 1993: 144–45). In Newton's view, the metaphor of the two books had been called into question, if not undermined, by a Roman Catholic and then Anglican institutionalizing of Trinitarian corruption of the Bible. In search of a more reliable grounding for the argument from design, Newton embarks upon a multifaceted research program, developing two interrelated strategies for dealing with a post-lapsarian world: he makes the study of Nature, rather than the Bible, the basis of religious faith; and he attempts to recover a true history of an uncorrupted monotheism characterized by a pristine knowledge of the heliocentric universe, a history corrupted by the arch-villain of Trinitarianism, Athanasius. In pursuit of this project, Newton returns to and revitalizes a hermetic tradition.

In his 1687 *Principia Mathematica* Newton introduced gravitation and the three laws of universal motion that, for two hundred years, were foundational to explaining everything from the movement of planets to the behavior of sub-atomic particles. But this masterwork of mathematical theory was, for

Newton, only part of a larger project that took him, for the final four decades of his life, into sustained investigations of alchemy, religious history, and mythography. The way in which science continues to serve as a "handmaid to divinity" for Newton can be found in his treatment of the prytanea (Westfall 1982; Markley 1999). After writing the *Principia*, Newton returned to his obsessive study of ancient religions, arguing in an English précis of his Latin treatise *Origines*, "The Original of Religions," that the "most ancient" and "most generally received" religion after the Flood was that of "Prytanea or Vestal Temples" (cited in Markley 1999: 135). For Newton, these temples, built around a sacrificial altar, recall Noah's sacrifice of clean animals after the Flood; they thereby provide evidence that a primitive monotheism antedates subsequent religious and philosophical corruption: "I gather that the sacrificing of clean birds and beasts by a consecrated fire in a consecrated place was the true religion until the nations corrupted it. For it was the religion of Noah, ... the religion which Noah propagated down to his prosperity was the true religion" in which the father of the family "did the office of the Priest" (cited in Markley 1999: 136). In this respect, the prytanea stands for Newton as the ur-model of the heliocentric universe; the existence of a primitive scientific knowledge is embodied in the very "frame" – that is, the proportions of the prytanea – with its sacred fire at the center. "So then was one design of ye first institution of ye true religion to propose to mankind by ye frame of ye ancient Temples, the study of the frame of the world as the true Temple of ye great God they worshipped" (cited in Markley 1999: 136). Newton deliberately conflates Temple and world, architectural design and a pristine mathematical knowledge of the order of the universe, and like Boyle, albeit in different ways, locates his natural philosophy within a sacrificial economy that divides a heterogeneous world into the human and "the animal": the sacrifice of the animal – the bodily, the material, the contingent – becomes the structural necessity for the realization and transcendence of the human.

Conceived both as a form of consumption and a means of regeneration, fire is the purifying agent that stands in for the unrepresentable evidence of the true religion and the millenarian renovation of a fallen world. Like Pythagoras, Newton considered fire as an "active principle" set against a physical world in which motion is "always decreasing" (Newton 1718: 375). As he writes in the *Opticks*, an active principle is the

> cause of Fermentation, by which the Heart and Blood of Animals are kept in perpetual Motion and Heat; the inward Parts of the Earth are constantly warm'd, and in some places grow very hot; Bodies burn and shine, Mountains take Fire, the Caverns of the Earth are Blown up, and the Sun continues violently hot and lucid, and warms all things by his Light.
> (Newton 1718: 375)

Comets are a special case of this active principle.

Provoked, as were many others, by a comet that appeared over Cambridge in 1680, Newton began thinking about the forces that could determine the comet's elliptical orbit – a line of thought which led to his theories on gravity – but his investigations of the comet's path were always at least partially informed by hermetic and scriptural invocations of fire. Preceding the formulation of principles of gravity, in other words, was a long-standing interest in the relationship between decay, or destruction, and creation, or growth, from both an alchemical perspective and a scriptural one. His undergraduate notebook contains an extended reference to II Peter 3: "the heavens that now are, and the earth, by the same word have been stored up for fire, being reserved against the day of judgment and destruction of ungodly men." Towards the end of his life, as Dobbs points out, Newton explained to John Conduitt that comets are probably the mechanism by which the sun, which is subject to "waste by the constant heat and light it emitted" could be replenished "as a faggot would this fire" (cited in Dobbs 1991: 235). With Newton's work, she continues, "comets were promoted in status" from "signs," or portents of disaster, to "agents of destruction" (236). Destruction by fire, however, allowed for and even made necessary the creative capacity of what Newton elsewhere calls a "powerful ever-living Agent" who can move through divine will "the Bodies within his boundless uniform Sensorium" (Newton 1718: 379) and who, in the face of always-decreasing natural energies could periodically destroy and repeople the earth.

A Newtonian view of comets as a providential principle of regeneration is apparent in Richard Glover's poem that prefaces Henry Pemberton's *A View of Sir Isaac Newton's Philosophy* (1728). Calling upon "the great dispenser of the world" to inspire his song, Glover recounts how the "still indulgent parent of mankind" has provided comets as a counteragent to "the vital principle decay/ By which air supplies the springs of life":

> Thou hast the fiery visag'd comets form'd
> With vivifying spirits all replete,
> Which they abundant breathe about the void,
> Renewing the prolifick soul of things.
> (Glover 1728)

Comets, once sources of trembling and terror, have now been recognized, thanks to Newton, in their true role as "vivifying spirits," as principles of regeneration. Rather than signs of impending doom, Newtonian comets become compatible with the laws of gravitation "around the sun mov[ing] regularly on":

> And with the planets in harmonious orbs,
> And mystick periods their obeisance pay

To him majestick ruler of the skies
Upon his throne of circled glory fixed.
                        (Glover 1728)

In this extended metaphor, comets – Newton's life-bearing seeds – function like
the prytanea in demonstrating fundamental physico-theological principles to
those who know how to read them. Both the prytanea and the comet have a
double life as images of decay, or consumption, and regeneration; the prytanea
consumes life for the sake of spiritual renewal; the sun, in Newton's mythos, will
eventually consume the earth and the beings on it for the sake of regeneration on
a cosmic scale. Without the active principle represented by gravity and fire,
planets like Earth are prey to the corruptions of a sinful humankind and a fallen
nature.

From the Newtonian sublime to a clockwork universe

By the middle of the eighteenth century, the very real threats to Baconian
physico-theology once offered by the ancient doctrine of *anima mundi* seem to
have been resolved, or least minimized. Thus, in his entry on *anima mundi*,
Chambers (1741) draws a direct line between Pythagoras and Newton, between
the ancient and modern. While "most ... modern philosophers reject the doctrine of *anima mundi*," the "generality of them admit something very much
like it." The Cartesians, he points out, have their doctrine of "subtile matter,"
while some others "substitute fire," and still others a "subtle elastic spirit or
medium diffused through all of space" (Chambers 1741). In relation to the latter,
he cross-references "Newtonian," thereby making Newton, in a kind of mutually
reinforcing back formation, a modern Pythagorean, or Pythagoras, an ancient
Newton. In a rhetorical strategy that minimizes religious and theological
differences central to eighteenth-century natural philosophy, Chambers even
goes so far as to claim that the Aristotelians had simply "misunderstood"
the Pythagorean doctrine of *anima mundi*, interpreting it in ways that, prior to
Newton's clarifications, had created "confusion" (Chambers 1741).

   How had Newton's concept of gravity "clarified" the question of immanentism that had troubled Western philosophy since its inception? Newton claims
that God created and controlled the related principles of heat, fire, and light,
"And yet we are not to consider the World as the Body of God," Newton
insists, but as a "uniform Being, void of Organs, Members, or Parts," who
created all creatures but is in no way identical with them: "and are his Creatures
subordinate to him, and subservient to his Will; and he is no more the Soul of
them, than the Soul of the Man is the Soul of the Species of Things carried
through the Organs of Sense into the place of its Sensation. ... God has no
need of such Organs, he being everywhere present to the Things themselves"

(Newton 1718: 379). While Newton is not the first to make an argument against immanentism, what he demonstrated were the laws – although not the cause – of universal forces, and this, he claimed, was enough. "These principles I consider not as occult Qualities ... but as general Laws of Nature, by which the Things themselves are form'd: their Truth appearing to us by Phaenomena, though their Causes be not yet discover'd" (Newton 1718: 376–77). Newton writes in the *Opticks* that he is willing to "propose" principles of motion "and leave their Causes to be found out" (377). In truth, however, Chambers correctly implies that Newton complicates rather than rejects the idea of causation: reworking older notions of animal spirits, Newton is impelled by some vitalist assumptions, but these are subordinated – perhaps even sacrificed – to an emerging scientific method.

The hallmark of Newton's commitment is the inductive study of phenomena rather than deductive assertion. By transposing metaphysical questions into physical and phenomenological ones, by focusing upon effects rather than first principles, Newton's writings offered a more systematic understanding of once-mysterious universal laws that struck many of his contemporaries as being God given, and whole. "O wisdom truly perfect!" writes James Thomson (1727): "Thus to call / From a few causes such a scheme of things, / Effects so various, beautiful, and great, / A universe compleat!" The *Principia* and *The Opticks* – or at least a popularized understanding of them – found their way into literature through such works as Glover's "Poem on Sir Isaac Newton" of 1728, Elizabeth Tollet's *Hypatia* of 1724, James Thomson's *The Seasons* of 1727–30, Pope's *Essay on Man* of 1732–34, and a host of other writings about Nature, reason, and the limits of understanding that have come to be associated with an "Enlightenment" sensibility. Tollet, for example, extols the predictive qualities of Newton's universe, in which comets follow regular motions through the skies, as "Real Stars, which unextinguish'd burn / Thro' larger periods of a just Return" (Tollet 1755). Once again, an image of fire validates the movement of an orderly cosmos in a mode of writing that has been termed the Newtonian sublime, both for its ability to inspire awe, the attitude most characteristic of the sublime from Longinus to Edmund Burke, and for its mimicry of alchemical sublimation. In this respect, the creation and coherence of the Newtonian system requires the transformation, through fire, of concepts once regarded as "occult."

Along with the celebration of Newton's regular and harmonious universe was his deification within an emerging history of science. Casting Newton as the endpoint in a developmental and progressivist history, didactic poets, elegists, and a new breed of universal historians helped create Newtonianism, sometimes by covering over the religiosity underwriting his science, and sometimes by exploiting it. "Snatches from the dark abyss," writes Thomson (1727), "at [Newton's] approach / Blaz'd into suns, / the living centre each / Of an harmonious system ... rul'd unerring by that single power, / Which draws the stone projected to the ground" (ll. 61–67). In these lines, as elsewhere,

Thomson conflates religious and scientific history – like a cosmic light, Newton illuminated the laws of "that single power" (gravity or God) manifest in a heliocentric universe.

The best extended example of such reconciliation is Glover's "Poem on Sir Isaac Newton." Representing Newton as a kind of divine authority in a chain of natural philosophers that includes Pythagoras, Plato, Aristotle, Copernicus, Bacon, and Boyle, Glover poetically outlines a progressivist history of science, then reinforced by Pemberton's essay on Newton's ideas. Evoking the divine origins of Newton's science, Glover writes: "Newton demands the muse ... his sacred hand / Shall guide her infant steps; his sacred hand / Shall raise her to the Heliconian height, / Where, on its lofty top inthron'd, her head / Shall mingle with the Stars" (Glover 1728). This coupling – or even tripling – of the natural philosopher, poetic inspiration, and God is reinforced through an extended Miltonic simile in which Newton becomes yoked with Noah. Glover compares the state of knowledge before Newton to the Earth submerged by the Flood: "The Deity's omnipotence, the cause, / Th' original of things long lay unknown":

> As when the deluge overspread the earth,
> Whilst yet the mountains only rear'd their heads
> Above the surface of the wild expanse,
> Whelm'd deep below the great foundations lay,
> Till some kind angel at heav'n's high command
> Repul'd back the rising tides, and haughty floods,
> And to the ocean thunder'd out his voice:
> Quick all the swelling and imperious waves,
> The foaming billows and obscuring surge,
> Back to the channels and their ancient seats
> Recoil affrighted: from the darksome main
> Earth raises smiling, as new-born, her head,
> And with fresh charms her lovely face arrays.
>   (Glover 1728)

Newton's science is simultaneously illuminative (exposing the "originals" of things) and regenerative ("Earth raises smiling"). Much like Newton's own theological writings on the prytanea, Glover's poem yokes a Judeo-Christian tradition of symbology with the notion of *prisca scientia*, the ancient pristine knowledge of a heliocentric, sacrificial universe. This time, however, Newton occupies the place of redeeming angel in a fallen world. Redemption for Newton, as Markley argues, is "based not upon an idealized vision of an uncorrupted nature but on an idealization of an uncorrupted *knowledge* of nature" (Markley 1993: 147). In the Noachian mythos as represented by both Newton and Glover, knowledge of the universe is regenerative but always brief, partial, and – the ubiquitous eighteenth-century's metaphors of light notwithstanding – viewed through a glass, darkly.

Their shared sense of impaired vision contrasts sharply to those who believe in the perfectibility of knowledge. James Fortescue (1750) envisions a progressive future history that will pass by Newton: "The time will come when such shall know / Much more than Newton ever knew, / Than fancy e'er conceiv'd" (ll. 154–56). This point seems worth making in the face of a still widespread assumption that Newton and Newtonians promoted a mechanistic, "clockwork" universe. In fact, mechanistic views of the universe are more accurately associated with the late eighteenth century and the work of Laplace. Laplace first articulated the nebular hypothesis in his *Exposition du systeme du monde* of 1796, positing a completely natural, rather than divine, origin of the world. After meeting William Herschel in 1802, Laplace borrowed Herschel's claim to have discovered a "nebulous" fluid around distant stars and used that observation to support an account of the origin and order of the universe, which by the mid-nineteenth century was "widely accepted by scientists of opposing philosophical and theological views" (Markley 2005: 55–56). The eighteenth century, in contrast, was a time when wildly heterogeneous theories about the beginning of the world, and the stuff of which it was made, were part of theologically weighted arguments that had not only personal but also political and economic implications for Newton and his contemporaries. Alexander Pope's famous epitaph – "Nature, and Nature's Laws, were all hid in Night / God said 'Let Newton Be!' and all was light" – simultaneously reveals the importance of Newton as a scientist to the eighteenth century and obscures the complex negotiations required of Newton and Newtonians in their shared desire to reconcile religious and natural history.

In the work of the Newtonians, the religious threats and philosophical indeterminacies represented by the doctrine of "the world soul" that partially compelled the work of Boyle and Newton become the basis of a constitutive aestheticism. "Our creator," Pemberton explains, has "adapted" the minds of humans so that before fully understanding nature, his visible works "strike us with the most lively ideas of beauty and magnificence" (Pemberton 1728: 4). It is "desire after knowledge," he continues, "this taste for the sublime and the beautiful in things, which chiefly constitutes the difference between the human life, and the life of brutes":

> The thoughts of the human mind are too extensive to be confined only to the providing and enjoying of what is necessary for the support of our being. It is this taste, which has given rise to poetry, oratory, and every branch of literature and science. ... Perspicuous reasoning appears not only beautiful; but, when set forth in its full strength and dignity, it partakes of the sublime, and not only pleases, but warms and elevates the soul.
>
> (Pemberton 1728: 3–4)

In what Latour identifies as an "act of purification" characteristic of science, aesthetic discourse is deployed to create "two entirely distinct ontological zones: that of human beings on the one hand; that of nonhumans on the other" (Latour 1993: 11). According to Pemberton's tautological logic, the ability to appreciate the "perspicuous reasoning" characterized by Newton's philosophy serves as proof of, and justification for, a nature made for humans alone simply because only humans are capable of appreciating the nature of the universe's systemic beauty. The Newtonian sublime, with its enthusiastic, collective emphasis upon universal laws and cosmic harmony, in this regard, helped create the conditions that led later to British Romanticism and its celebration of a human mind that can reflect and appreciate the perfection of a divinely created blade of grass. A related inheritance from the Newtonians, however, is the one rendered by William Blake in his etching *Newton*. Looking down at his paper and instruments, Newton, the divine geometer, appears tragically (and anachronistically) as father of a mechanistic system in which the mind was elevated over body, science over the imagination, religious orthodoxies over the natural world.

Bibliography

Bacon, F. (1899) *The Advancement of Learning and Novum Organon*, London: James Edward Creighton.

Blount, C. (1679) *Anima Mundi; or, an historical narration of the opinions of the Ancients concerning Man's soul after this life*, London.

Bono, J. (1999) "From Paracelsus to Newton: the word of God, the book of nature, and the eclipse of the emblematic world view," in Force and Popkin 1999, pp. 45–76.

Boyle, R. (1661) *Some Considerations Touching the Style of the Holy Scriptures*, London.

——(1686) *Free Inquiry Into the Vulgar Notion of Nature*, London.

——(1674) *The Excellency of Theology, as Compar'd with Natural Philosophy*, London.

——(1762) *The Usefulness of Experimental Philosophy in The Works of Robert Boyle*, Vol. 2, London.

Castillejo, D. (1989) *The Expanding Force in Newton's Cosmos and Shown in his Unpublished Papers*, Madrid: Ediciones de Arte y Bibliofilia.

Chambers, E. (1741) *Cyclopaedia: or, an universal dictionary of arts and sciences*, London.

Cohen, I.B. (1980) *The Newtonian Revolution*, Cambridge: Cambridge University Press.

Dobbs, B.J.T. (1991) *The Janus Faces of Genius: the role of alchemy in Newton's thought*, Cambridge: Cambridge University Press.

Figala, K. (1977) "Newton as alchemist," *History of Science*, 15: 102–37.

Force, J. (1985) *William Whiston: honest Newtonian*, Cambridge: Cambridge University Press.

——and Popkin, R.H. (1999) *Newton and Religion: context, nature, and influence*, Dordrecht: Kluwer.

Fortescue, J. (1750) *Science: an epistle on its decline and revival*, London.

Fudge, E. (1999) *Perceiving Animals: humans and beasts in early modern culture*, New York: St. Martin's Press.

Glover, R. (1728) in Pemberton 1728.

Guerrini, A. (2003) *Experimenting with Humans and Animals: from Galen to animal rights*, Baltimore: Johns Hopkins University Press.

Hall, A.R. (1980) *Philosophers at War: the quarrel between Newton and Leibnitz*, Cambridge: Cambridge University Press.

Hellegers, D. (2000) *Natural Philosophy, Poetry, and Gender in Seventeenth-Century England*, Norman: University of Oklahoma Press.

Jacob, J.R. (1977) *Robert Boyle and the English Revolution: a study in social and intellectual change*, New York: Burt Franklin.

Latour, B. (1993). *We Have Never Been Modern*, trans. C. Porter, Cambridge, Mass.: Harvard University Press.

Markley, R. (1993) *Fallen Languages: crises of representation in Newtonian England, 1660–1740*, Ithaca, N.Y.: Cornell University Press.

——(1999) "Newton, corruption, and the tradition of universal history," in Force and Popkin 1999, pp. 121–43.

——(2005) *Dying Planet: Mars in science and the imagination*, Durham, N.C.: Duke University Press.

Newton, I. (1713) *The General Scholium to Isaac Newton's Principia mathematica*. Online. Available HTTP: <http://www.isaacnewton.ca/gen_scholium/scholium.htm > (accessed 4 January 2010).

——(1718) *The Opticks: or, a treatise of the reflections, refractions, inflections, and colours of light*, Book Three. Online. Available HTTP: <http://www.newtonproject.sussex.ac.uk/view/texts/normalized> (accessed 5 January 2010).

Numbers, R. (1977) *Creation by Natural Law: Laplace's nebular hypothesis in American thought*, Seattle: University of Washington Press.

Pemberton, H. (1728) *A View of Sir Isaac Newton's Philosophy*, London.

Porta, G. della (1558) *Natural Magick*, Naples.

Stanley, T. (1655) *The History of Philosophy*, London.

Thomas, K. (1983) *Man and the Natural World: changing attitudes in England 1500-1800*, London: Allen Lane (Penguin).

Thomson, J. (1727) *A Poem Sacred to the Memory of Sir Isaac Newton*, London: J. Millan.

Tollet, E. (1755) *Poems on Several Occasions*, London.

Turnball, H.W. et al. (eds) (1959–77) *The Correspondence of Isaac Newton* (7 vols), Cambridge: Cambridge University Press.

Vickers, B. (1986) *Occult and Scientific Mentalities*, Cambridge: Cambridge University Press.

Westfall, R.S. (1980) *Never at Rest: a biography of Isaac Newton*, Cambridge: Cambridge University Press.

——(1982) "Isaac Newton's *Theologiae Gentillis Origines Philsophicae*," in W.W. Wagar (ed.) *The Secular Mind: Transformations of Faith in Modern Europe*, New York: Holmes and Meier.

39
ROMANTICISM
Noah Heringman

I

The most famous Romantic scientist, Victor Frankenstein, set out to reject the old practice of natural philosophy for the new practice of chemistry. In Mary Shelley's *Frankenstein* (1818), Victor refers to each of these practices as a "science," but the meaning of that word changed radically during what is now called the Romantic period (roughly 1780–1830). Young Victor's fascination with sixteenth-century works on alchemy, cosmology, and medicine merely increases when his father rejects these antiquated writings as "sad trash" (Shelley 1818: 67). Only his professor, M. Waldman, manages to persuade Victor that "modern chemistry" is more powerful than the occult science of the Renaissance (76). Equipped with Waldman's inspiring lectures and two years of intensive training, Frankenstein embarks on a project that nevertheless harks back to the pagan and magical elements of early modern natural philosophy: creating human life. Percy Bysshe Shelley's preface to his wife's novel already registers what has proved to be a long-standing concern with the plausibility of Victor's undertaking in the context of modern science. The preface cites Erasmus Darwin and other authorities to support the idea that Victor's discovery of a means of "bestowing animation upon lifeless matter" (80) could be an "event … not of impossible occurrence" (47).

The practice of galvanism, as Shelley suggests in her own introduction to the novel in 1831, might also be seen as corroborating Frankenstein's ability to endow his Creature with the "spark of being" (84) – memorably imagined as a jolt of electricity in various film adaptations. The popularizer of galvanism, Giovanni Aldini, made a murderer's corpse twitch violently by subjecting it to electrical shocks in a celebrated public experiment in London in 1802, when Shelley was five. Despite these and many other traces of the novel's engagement with issues belonging to the history of modern science, the fact remains that Shelley provocatively collapses the boundary between pre-modern and modern science. Professor Waldman and his real-life counterpart, the chemist Humphry Davy, distinguish carefully between modern chemistry and the mystical practices of the alchemists who came before them. Nonetheless, Frankenstein fails to make that distinction, or loses sight of it, when he conceives his overweening, metaphysically tinged experiment.

Frankenstein remained a powerful figure in the Hollywood era because the novel and the Romantic literary culture associated with it were recognizably poised on the brink of an understanding of science that remained familiar to twentieth-century readers. Romantic science was pre-disciplinary. By the time James Whale made *Frankenstein* in 1931, Davy had been firmly canonized as one of the "distinguished discoverers" (76) who founded modern chemistry. Natural philosophy had been largely consigned to a prescientific past. But Waldman still refers to chemistry as only the most developed "branch of natural philosophy" (77), and Davy, known by chemists today for his pioneering discovery of sodium and potassium, presented himself as a philosopher in his writings and his popular public lectures.

Though later used to describe him, the word "scientist" was coined only in 1833, four years after Davy's death. On one hand, then, the self-understanding of modern science was underway by the time the novel was written; two prominent historians have argued that that self-understanding was consolidated by the "second scientific revolution," occurring around 1800, in which Davy played an important role (Cunningham and Jardine 1990: xix–xx). On the other hand, Romanticism – not just in Great Britain, but in Germany and other countries – was still a culture of science (meaning simply "knowledge") that was driven by competing literary and philosophical models of nature. Mary Shelley questioned the narrative of revolutionary progress by pointing out that modern chemists, like the alchemists, still pursued knowledge as power. For Davy, even though he was a champion of scientific progress, the continuity between natural philosophy and chemistry was just as important as the rupture between modern and pre-modern practices.

Davy's philosophical chemistry, Shelley's imagined laboratory, the evolution of the encyclopedia, German *Naturphilosophie*, geological explanations of the sublime, the advent of scientific voyaging, the craze for natural history – all these Romantic-era developments can be fruitfully understood in terms of pre-disciplinarity. This is not to dismiss the period's burgeoning network of methods for producing natural knowledge as crude or incomplete by comparison to our current, seemingly orderly, landscape of university disciplines. Though the case can be made for their objects of study, there is nothing natural or inevitable about biology, anthropology, and the other disciplines themselves. Unlike the term "chemistry," the term "biology" was not yet in general use when Mary Shelley was writing her novel (Lawrence 1819: 42), "geology" was still controversial (Rudwick 2005: 448), and "sociology" would not appear in English until 1842 (*OED*). The disciplines that preceded them understood themselves equally as disciplines: the precursor disciplines still active in the Romantic period, such as natural history and anti-quarianism, were all the more complex and diverse because they operated outside the university, through informal networks and learned societies.

The pre-disciplinarity of Romanticism as a culture of science is a vital context for the formation of current (twenty-first-century) disciplines. The critic Clifford

Siskin has described a movement of "dedisciplinarity," "a shift in the ways of knowing from the older organization, in which every kind was a branch of philosophy, into our present system [of] narrow but deep disciplines" (Siskin 1998: 20). By attending to *pre*-disciplinarity we can see that there were in fact multiple "ways of knowing" and that the shift to modern disciplinarity was neither sudden nor uniform, nor (even now) complete. "Natural philosophy" as used by Shelley and Davy remained a valid synonym for the physical sciences through 1900, but most of those who practiced natural history and antiquarian research in the field recognized no affiliation with philosophy, following instead the seventeenth-century empirical tradition of Francis Bacon.

II

The relationship between Romanticism and science has gained renewed visibility from the cultural turn in the history of science. As historians develop narratives of science pursued in "particular social locations" (Secord 1986: 318), their work becomes increasingly valuable for students of literature seeking to understand cultural production in broad terms. Inspired by theorists including Bruno Latour and Lorraine Daston, literary scholars have increasingly contributed to the cultural history of science as well. Historians began rejecting "Whiggish" histories of science – that is, histories favoring the theories or methods that most closely resemble current scientific practice, while discounting others – as early as the 1960s (Jardine 2003), but the flourishing interdisciplinary scholarship of recent years has shown even more decisively that no modern discipline can dictate the terms for understanding the discipline that preceded it.

Romanticism has a long history as an "extrascientific" term (Kuhn 1970: 4) used to describe a culture of science. Recently there has been more consensus that Romanticism is not "extrascientific" at all, but rather designates cultural and political inspirations that acted on all aspects of intellectual life. In Germany, where the term "Romanticism" was current from the late 1790s, and motivated new philosophies of nature (e.g., Schelling 1797) that set out to unify the arts and sciences, the "Romantic" and "scientific" ideas of nature were linked from the start. In the anglophone context, where "Romanticism" was only applied retrospectively to poets of the French Revolutionary era, the presupposition of a conflict between Romanticism and science was much stronger. The distinguished literary critic and historian of ideas Marjorie Hope Nicolson challenged this presupposition and spent her career arguing that scientific discovery inspired many of the poems of Wordsworth, Byron, Keats, and their predecessors. Nonetheless, the many studies of these poets (along with Blake, Coleridge, and Shelley) that defined the field of British Romanticism until the 1990s rarely touched on science, and this omission was reflected as well in classroom anthologies and syllabi.

Recent contributions to Romantic studies have directed attention back to the other forms of natural knowledge – including those now understood as scientific – that coexisted with Romantic poetry and fiction. The competition over nature has been situated more firmly in its broad European and colonial context (Bewell 2004) as well as in a social framework that understood "literature" as referring to *all* forms of writing (Siskin 1998). This picture is emerging in studies of the encyclopedia and encyclopedism; in the recovery of neglected writers such as Jane Marcet and Charlotte Smith, and of boundary-crossing figures such as Darwin and Davy; and in studies of colonialism and exploration. The rich multidisciplinary scholarship on exploration, especially on the perennially fascinating career of Captain Cook, has created a new focus for the study of Romantic subjectivity.

George Forster and Alexander von Humboldt were two of several naturalist-explorers who achieved scientific fame by means of Romantic first-person voyage narratives. The new global natural history cultivated by these explorers has been of particular interest for students of Romanticism, who have traditionally focused on representations of nature associated with the cosmopolitan and increasingly secular literary culture of the period. Jean-Jacques Rousseau, long considered the "father of Romanticism" (Barzun 1975: 18), promoted the practice of botany along with the interrelated ideas of the "noble savage" and a return to nature in the setting of a sublime, untainted natural landscape. Forster, Humboldt, and the others who cultivated botany, zoology, and mineralogy (the three traditional branches of natural history), had Rousseau's ideas among their equipment; they integrated a colonial ethnography of noble and ignoble savages into the practice of natural history.

The large body of writers and readers who voyaged with them in reading their narratives helped fuel the popularity that led Robert Ramsay to exclaim: "Natural History is, at present, the favourite science over all Europe, and the progress which has been made in it will distinguish and characterise the 18th century in the annals of literature" (Ramsay 1772: 174). Natural history belonged equally to literature and to science: some readers might have seen a contradiction here by the end of the Romantic period, if only because the sheer volume of data gathered in the intervening decades by collectors worldwide had forced the kinds of specialization that led to such distinctions and, eventually, to the formation of new disciplines. Many of the collectors, including Thomas Pennant, of whom Ramsay is speaking here, were followers of Carolus Linnaeus, whose *System of Nature* (1735) introduced the system of classification that motivated the collecting enterprise. A century later, on the *Beagle*, Charles Darwin was still collecting distant fauna, flora, and minerals in the Linnaean tradition; and though his *Origin of Species* (1859) is a theoretical work drawing its examples mainly from zoology, he refers to his scientific practice as "natural history" throughout that work.

Darwin's "romantic materialism" (Beer 1983: 42) is the legacy of the global zoology of Pennant and Johann Reinhold Forster; the botany of Sir Joseph Banks and Daniel Solander; and the earth science contributions of collectors ranging from Banks to Mary Anning. According to Foucault's influential history of ideas (1970), the dynamic study of organisms – biology – began to supersede the taxonomic enterprise of natural history when Georges Cuvier systematically compared fossilized skeletons, supplied by collectors like Mary Anning, with the skeletons of living animals. Cuvier, the celebrated genius of Revolutionary and Napoleonic Paris, gave a course of public lectures on "geology" in 1805, using his knowledge of fossils to fuel controversy about this newly named and still contested science (Rudwick 2005: 447). Humphry Davy also gave a course of public lectures on geology in London the same year. It was the first such course in English.

The resurgence of interest in natural history among students of Romanticism, solidified by an important classroom anthology (Nichols 2004), makes it tempting to think of natural history as the quintessential Romantic science. However, chemistry may have an equally strong claim. Humphry Davy appears in retrospect as the quintessential Romantic scientist – or philosopher, as he would have said – an appearance surely reinforced by his association with Frankenstein's professor, M. Waldman. Like Cuvier, he was a lionized celebrity as well as an official in institutions closely linked to the power of the state, such as the Royal Society, of which he became president in 1820. Davy's name was always known to students of Romantic poetry because of his friendship with Wordsworth, Coleridge, and Robert Southey: the latter two participated in his experiments with nitrous oxide at the utopian Pneumatic Institution run by Dr. Thomas Beddoes, where he began his laboratory career. He proofread *Lyrical Ballads* (1800) for Wordsworth and Coleridge, as he remained in Bristol (where the book was published) after they moved north to the Lake District.

Davy also wrote poems on such Romantic themes as "The Sons of Genius," and later, Mont Blanc; at one point he planned to publish a volume of these poems, and Southey included a selection in the *Annual Anthology* for 1799. Some of Davy's writing in his lectures, given when he was Professor of Chemistry at the Royal Institution (1801–12), is even more vivid and powerful than these early poems. In one lecture that (in published form) attracted the ambivalent fascination of Mary Shelley, he wrote of his ambition to "interrogate nature with power, not simply as a scholar … but rather as a master, active with his own instruments" (Davy 1839: 2.319). Jan Golinski's *Science as Public Culture* illuminates the political currents of revolution and reaction at work as Davy's interests shifted from ameliorating social conditions through medical chemistry, to consolidating the influence and prestige of science as a profession (Golinski 1992: 176–203).

Davy was a standard-bearer for the new chemistry, for genius and the sublime in nature, and for the reaction that swept up many intellectuals formerly caught up in the utopian energy surrounding the French Revolution. He was also a natural philosopher for whom the history and methodology of a science were crucial to its practice; his ten lectures on geology, for example, include three that trace the history of the science from Pythagoras through James Hutton (Davy 1805: 24–57). This emphasis on auto-historiography, sometimes called "Romantic reflexivity," has long been noticed by students of Romanticism, and links Davy more strongly with the German *Naturphilosophen* (such as Schelling and Lorenz Oken) than is generally recognized. At the same time, Davy's strong and continuing identification with chemistry illustrates the break-up of natural philosophy into specialized modern disciplines. Davy's science, then, like Cuvier's, is recognizably pre-disciplinary, and the comparison illustrates the way in which the conflict between natural history and natural philosophy was gradually resolved.

Sir Joseph Banks, who collected with Cook in the South Pacific, was also the president of the Royal Society whom Davy succeeded in 1820. Banks's celebrated achievements in the field of natural history, as well as his social position, accounted for his early rise to power in the Royal Society and, eventually, within the government of George III as well. In the early years of his presidency he had many detractors who charged him with ignorance of natural philosophy, in their view a more rigorous discipline that conserved the legacy of Sir Isaac Newton, who had also been president of the Royal Society (Heringman 2009). Outside the walls of the learned society, natural history was a truly popular practice by this time, for reasons ranging from the economic motives of self-taught rural fossil hunters to the sociality of "artisan botanists" (A. Secord 1996) and to the lavish display cultivated by the Duchess of Portland, whose famous collection included some of Banks's South Pacific specimens. Charlotte Smith defended natural history, as a literary and socially inclusive practice, against the encroachment of new "theories" in her long "local poem" *Beachy Head* (1807). Nature poets, including Smith and John Clare (proponents of natural history), Erasmus Darwin (a natural philosopher), and Wordsworth (who claimed neither affiliation), all participated in the pre-disciplinary ferment surrounding the project of natural knowledge.

III

Though Davy and Banks now appear as Romantic scientists, public response at the time, before the word "scientist" was available, was varied and complex. Davy, Banks, and many other public intellectuals were polymaths who made substantial contributions across the arts and sciences, extending the old network of European learning known as the "republic of letters." To look for a quintessential Romantic science is thus to miss the point: Romanticism, in the process of re-emerging as a culture of science, has been associated with a wide variety of disciplines and disciplinary changes, including emerging disciplines such as ethnography and meteorology, disciplines in flux such as medicine and natural history, and disciplines that have since disappeared, such as physiognomy and phrenology. The period's polymathic intellectuals were understood and claimed in different ways by different constituencies.

The poetry of Anna Letitia Barbauld (1743–1825), always attuned to scientific questions because of her upbringing at the Warrington Academy, provides a valuable record of imaginative engagement with figures and issues now absorbed into the history of science. A closer look at works from two different phases of her career will help establish the contours of one broad constituency within the public culture of Romantic science. Surveying the intellectual scene in 1811, Barbauld cited Davy for eloquence first and discovery second. In the future, she imagined, the Royal Institution would be remembered as a "site" of "glory," "where mute crowds on Davy's lips reposed, / And Nature's coyest secrets were disclosed" (Barbauld 1994: 157–58). She takes the same occasion to redeem Joseph "Priestley's injured name," a name that would have been familiar to some of her readers from her own much earlier poetry, published in 1773, in which she celebrated Priestley's genius (now primarily associated, like Davy's, with chemistry).

Priestley was, like Barbauld's father, John Aikin, a tutor at Warrington Academy, and by 1773 was well on his way to becoming one of the most distinguished experimental natural philosophers of the generation that preceded Davy's. He was also, like Barbauld's father, a dissenting minister (that is, of a sect that did not conform to the Church of England). Aikin was Presbyterian, Priestley a Unitarian, and the academy or college where they taught, located between Liverpool and Manchester, provided an advanced secondary education to young men who were barred from attending Oxford or Cambridge because they too were Presbyterians, Unitarians, or Quakers. The institution prided itself on emphasizing "the most useful branches of Science and Literature" in its curriculum (Enfield 1774: iii), which covered not only ancient Greek and Latin literature, the staple of public school education, but also chemistry, anatomy, and English literature. *The Speaker* (1774), an elocution textbook written for the students at Warrington by William Enfield, another one of the tutors, went on to become a classroom standard and stayed in print for the better part of a century. *The Speaker* sets out to teach "reading and speaking" by substituting "classics" of English literature for the ornamental knowledge of classical antiquity often associated with upper-class education. By including Barbauld's poem "The Invitation" (retitled "Warrington Academy"), Enfield's anthology also gave readers an overview of the other forms of useful knowledge that defined the academy's middle-class curriculum.

"The Invitation" (1773) is one of several early poems by Barbauld to insist on the proximity of arts and sciences, an association developed in several of her prose works and echoed in her later reference to Davy's eloquence. These poems regularly refer to Priestley, who joined the Warrington faculty in 1761 as a lecturer in languages and belles-lettres. In her serio-comic "Inventory of the Furniture in Dr. Priestley's Study," Barbauld describes the many manuscripts that testify to Priestley's prolific writing career, as well as the instruments he used in his experiments on electricity, published in 1767 as *The History and Present State of Electricity*. Priestley's own teaching was mainly literary, but in 1767 the Academy appointed a new tutor in modern languages and natural history: Johann Reinhold Forster, who later sailed with Captain Cook. "The Invitation," which apostrophizes the academy as a "nursery of men for future years" (Barbauld 1994: 11, l.82), places significant emphasis on natural history and natural philosophy as part of the curriculum.

Barbauld depicts Warrington students who "rove" among the willows by the river Mersey, unfolding the secrets of nature, and with them the "eagle wings" of "science," "too long" restrained by the "bigot rage" of conservative institutions (ll. 95–100). Here Barbauld allies exploration and discovery with poetry and literature against superstition: "Where science smiles, the Muses join the train" (108–9). The poem joins an Enlightenment view of scientific progress with the academy's educational program, which empowers middle-class students as it symbolically elevates the humble Mersey, which now "dares to emulate a classic tide" (90). Barbauld ends her catalogue of the students' future careers (133–82) with the conventional choices of politics, poetry, and divinity, but first dwells, significantly, on exploration and discovery. In the nationalist and masculinist context of the poem, the specimens and commodities gathered by voyagers appear as colonial "spoil" (150), while the study of botany, entomology, and nature's "various laws" is figured as a predatory pursuit in which naturalists "disrobe" and "hunt" a feminized nature (155–62). This early poem articulates the social importance gradually assumed by scientific education, distinct but not divorced from literature, during the Romantic period. It also betrays the strong association between scientific progress and the exploitation of nature, an association closely linked to the ideology that Mary Shelley critiques in *Frankenstein*.

Barbauld's numerous poems addressed to Priestley and natural philosophy cultivate a different set of associations, a connection between experimentation and liberty – both intellectual and political – that also belonged to the Enlightenment and was reinforced by Romantic enthusiasm for the French Revolution. In this light, the pursuit of natural knowledge appears progressive and undercuts the dualistic construction of exploitative vs. holistic views of nature. In "The Mouse's Petition," she speaks for an animal she "found in a trap where he had been confined all night by Dr. Priestley, for the sake of making experiments with different kinds of air [gas]." The mouse presents his petition as one of "nature's commoners" resisting "oppressive force," suggesting in mock-heroic terms the progressive politics she sees as an obligation of experimental research. A related poem replaces feudal "arms and conquest" with "Liberty" as a more appropriate symbol for "the sons of science and the Muse" (Barbauld 1994: 36).

Barbauld anticipates the connection between electric "lightning" and liberty that became associated with the career of Benjamin Franklin, who provided valuable encouragement when Priestley met him in London in 1766. By 1791, when the government was encouraging patriotic protests against the French Revolution, liberty had become so dangerous that this association nearly cost Priestley his life. Barbauld stood by him, however, in a new poem advising him that the "hooting crowds" that burned his house in Birmingham were not worthy even of his scorn (Barbauld 1994: 125). Barbauld's continued defiance of the government's war on France and repressive measures at home in *Eighteen Hundred and Eleven* (which again redeems "Priestley's injured name") provoked savage and insulting reviews. Barbauld's participation in the culture of science was by no means limited to her association with Priestley, though these poems provide a convenient index to the changing political status of natural philosophy. "A Summer Evening's Meditation," for example, develops an independent and challenging vocabulary concerning the "embryo systems and unkindled suns" of astronomy (Barbauld 1994: 83).

IV

Barbauld's poetry, as well as her prose, helped to refocus the term "science" and thus contributed to a major shift in its meaning. As a woman writer participating in the culture of science – albeit in specific ways defined more or less by her gender – Barbauld also contributed to the expanding field of possibility for women writers, occupied by Mary Shelley later in the period. In her prose, Barbauld helped establish didactic science writing as a scientific practice that was permissible for women, a larger development explained by Barbara Gates and Ann Shteir (1997: 7). Her influential essays of this kind include "The Hill of Science" (1773) and a number of pieces on natural history in the collection *Evenings at Home* (1792), which she co-authored with her brother, John Aikin, "for the instruction and amusement of young persons."

Since the 1980s, literary history has increasingly been reorganized around the "domestic ideology" of separate spheres for men and women, and many critics have grappled with the implications of what seem at times to be two distinct, gendered literary cultures. Two cultures separated in a different way are the subject of C.P. Snow's *The Two Cultures* of 1959, which describes a deep rift between science and literature as they were practiced in academic circles in the mid-twentieth century. Gates and Shteir's historical model dovetails these two cultures with two cultures of gender, aligning nineteenth-century scientific women with natural history and didactic writing, and male "scientists," as they came to be called, with modern science. Barbauld and Charlotte Smith are among the Romantic poets who anticipate this division; Smith wrote didactic works on natural history but also asserted herself, in *Beachy Head*, as a serious practitioner of that discipline. In her poetry, Barbauld depicts herself as a commentator rather than a practitioner. In "A Summer Evening's Meditation," in particular, she embarks on an imaginary cosmic voyage of the kind made popular by early eighteenth-century poets such as James Thomson, who launched his career with "A Poem Sacred to the Memory of Sir Isaac Newton" (1727).

Mark Greenberg (1990) has cited the example of Thomson to argue that the "two-cultures" model of literature and science was well established long before the Romantic period. The opposing "one-culture" model promoted by scholars such as Gillian Beer (1983) and George Levine (1987) designates, in part, the survival of a common humanistic culture that defines the work and the reception of Romantic natural history and natural philosophy. There is also a sense, however, in which the "one-culture" concept was reformulated, if not constructed, during the Romantic period. The professional expertise that seemed to define the "emerging institution" of science (Greenberg) in Newton's time became a contested commodity, as we have seen, during Banks's and Davy's terms as presidents of the Royal Society. The pre-disciplinary organ-ization of natural history and natural philosophy collapsed under this pressure, and the terms "science" (redefined) and "scientist" (new) gradually came into play as the terrain of natural knowledge was reconfigured. Barbauld's rea-lignment of "science" with the Muses and with liberty constitutes a significant early intervention in this process; Charlotte Smith's declaration, "very vain is Science's proudest boast," marks another, later kind of intervention (Smith 1807: 233). Greenberg, in an earlier essay on the poetry of William Blake, observed that "'Science' becomes for Blake a kind of demonic synecdoche – the whole word symbolizing only a part of its former meaning" (Greenberg 1983: 125).

Blake had fewer readers at the time than either Barbauld or Smith, but his massive influence in the twentieth century may well have contributed to the impasse described by Snow's The Two Cultures. The hostility to science that, according to Snow, characterizes modern "literary intellectuals" is often linked with Romanticism by way of a famous line from Wordsworth's poem "The Tables Turned": "we murder to dissect." Those using the line in this way tend to forget that this poem also declares, "Enough of science and of art," a sentiment that captures something of our post-disciplinary discourse concern-ing a "third culture." Snow's paradigm of two cultures has long been superseded by more complex ideas in science studies, but its specter continues to haunt the antinomian controversy often referred to as the "science wars." Neither Wordsworth nor any other Romantic went so far as to deny the transhistorical validity of scientific knowledge, nor did any apologist at that time propose to absorb the humanities into science. These two extreme views are both end-products of the pre-disciplinary flux that flourished as Romanticism, in which the concepts of science and the scientist were the subjects of a generative public discussion that was in some ways both more subtle and more accessible than our own.

Bibliography

Barbauld, A.L. (1994) *The Poems of Anna Letitia Barbauld*, ed. E. Kraft and W. McCarthy, Athens: University of Georgia Press.

Barzun, J. (1975) *Classic, Romantic and Modern*, rev. edn, Chicago: University of Chicago Press.

Beer, G. (1983) *Darwin's Plots: evolutionary narrative in Darwin, George Eliot, and nineteenth-century fiction*, London: Routledge.

Bewell, A. (2004) "Romanticism and colonial natural history," *Studies in Romanticism*, 43: 5–34.

Cunningham, A. and Jardine, N. (eds) (1990) *Romanticism and the Sciences*, Cambridge: Cambridge University Press.

Davy, H. (1805) *Humphry Davy on Geology: the 1805 lectures for the general audience*, ed. R. Siegfried and R. Dott, Madison: University of Wisconsin Press, 1980.

——(1839) *The Collected Works of Sir Humphry Davy*, ed. J. Davy, 9 vols, London: Smith, Elder, & Co.

Enfield, W. (1774) *The Speaker: or, miscellaneous pieces*, London: Joseph Johnson.

Foucault, M. (1970) *The Order of Things. an archaeology of the human sciences*, New York: Random House.

Gates, B. and Shteir, A. (eds) (1997) *Natural Eloquence: women reinscribe science*, Madison: University of Wisconsin Press.

Golinski, J. (1992) *Science as Public Culture: chemistry and enlightenment in Britain, 1760–1820*, Cambridge: Cambridge University Press.

Greenberg, M. (1983) "Blake's 'science,'" *Studies in Eighteenth-Century Culture*, 12: 115–30.

——(1990) "Eighteenth-century poetry represents moments of scientific discovery," in S. Peterfreund (ed.) *Literature and Science: theory and practice*, Boston, Mass.: Northeastern University Press, pp. 115–37.

Heringman, N. (2009) "Natural history in the romantic period," in J. Klancher (ed.) *A Concise Companion to the Romantic Age*, Oxford: Blackwell, pp. 141–67.

Jardine, N. (2003) "Whigs and stories: Herbert Butterfield and the historiography of science," *History of Science*, 41: 125–40.

Kuhn, T. (1970) *The Structure of Scientific Revolutions*, rev. edn, Chicago: University of Chicago Press.

Lawrence, W. (1819) *Lectures on Comparative Anatomy, Physiology, Zoology and the Natural History of Man*, London: Henry G. Bohn, 1848.

Levine, G. (ed.) (1987) *One Culture: essays in science and literature*, Madison: University of Wisconsin Press.

Nichols, A. (ed.) (2004) *Romantic Natural Histories: selected texts with introduction*, Boston, Mass.: Houghton Mifflin.

Ramsay, R. (1772) "To the lovers of natural history," *Scots Magazine*, 34: 174–75.

Rudwick, M.J.S. (2005) *Bursting the Limits of Time: the reconstruction of geohistory in the age of revolution*, Chicago: University of Chicago Press.

Schelling, F.W.J. von (1797) *Ideas for a Philosophy of Nature as Introduction to the Study of this Science*, trans. E. Harris and P. Heath, Cambridge: Cambridge University Press, 1988.

Secord, A. (1996) "Artisan Botany," in N. Jardine, J.A. Secord, and E.C. Spary (eds) *Cultures of Natural History*, Cambridge: Cambridge University Press, pp. 387–93.

Secord, J. (1986) *Controversy in Victorian Geology: the Cambrian-Silurian dispute*, Princeton: Princeton University Press.

Shelley, M. (1818) *Frankenstein; or, the modern Prometheus*, ed. D.L. McDonald and K. Scherf, 2nd edn, Peterborough, Ont.: Broadview, 1999.

Siskin, C. (1998) *The Work of Writing: literature and social change in Britain, 1700–1830*, Baltimore: Johns Hopkins University Press.

Smith, C. (1807) *Beachy Head*, in S. Curran (ed.) *The Poems of Charlotte Smith*, Oxford: Oxford University Press, 1993, pp. 217–47.

40
INDUSTRIALISM
Virginia Richter

I

According to his biographer, Charles Darwin "was born into Jane Austen's England" (Browne 1995: 3). While the Industrial Revolution, of which his grandfather Josiah Wedgwood was one of the main protagonists, had been in full swing for several decades by the beginning of the nineteenth century, life in small rural towns such as Darwin's native Shrewsbury was largely unaffected by industrial development. By the end of Darwin's life, however, English society as a whole, as well as the daily life of individuals, had been drastically changed by the impact of industrialization. By then,

> Britain possessed two-thirds of the world's capacity for cotton factory production and accounted for half the world's output of coal and iron, an unmatched degree of industrial pre-eminence. The length of railway track snaking across the countryside doubled from 1850 to 1868. Lawnmowers, water-closets, gas lights, iron girders, encaustic tiles, and much, much more were available to those who could afford them.
>
> (Browne 2002: 3)

From home-based craft to large factories, from water mills to steam engines, from horses and carriages to the railway: no area of life, including domestic arrangements, fashion, and leisure as well as production, trade, and transport, remained untouched by the dramatic technological changes introduced between 1712 – the first steam engine built by Thomas Newton – and, say, the switch from gaslight to electric light around 1900.

Another development during Charles Darwin's lifetime concerned his own profession. Whereas Darwin started out as, and in many respects remained, a gentleman who pursued "natural history" for the sake of his own gratification, without ever being affiliated with a research institution, by the end of the century not only had his field become "science," subdivided into separate disciplines such as biology, botany, geology, and so on, but it had also become nearly impossible to work as a scientist without being appointed to a position at a university, laboratory, or other institution recognized by the scientific community. This institutional reconfiguration of science went hand in hand with a shift within its epistemological framework, in the terms of Lorraine Daston and Peter Galison, from "truth to nature" to "mechanical objectivity." The individual personality of the researcher was henceforth to be separated from the object of science, a divide best ensured by the use of mechanical devices of observation and recording: "To be objective is to aspire to knowledge that bears no trace of the knower – knowledge unmarked by prejudice or skill, fantasy or judgement, wishing or striving. Objectivity is blind sight, seeing without inference, interpretation, or intelligence" (Daston and Galison 2007: 17). How incompletely this ideal was realized is shown best by Darwin's own example. Although the success of his *On the Origin of Species* of 1859 depended in part on "his earlier work [that] had confirmed his status as a trustworthy 'gentleman of science' capable of treating even his own ideas and hypotheses with scepticism, detachment, and critical distance" (Smith 2006: 17), in other words, on a form of scientific objectivity, it was also helped by Darwin's strikingly idiosyncratic voice, his "presence" in the text.

Besides the pure science pursued at research institutions, there is another branch of science which is often overlooked, perhaps because it precisely does not confirm to the ideals of a pursuit of knowledge for its own sake, mechanical objectivity, and intellectual (and economic) independence. This is the applied science carried out in the workshops and laboratories of privately owned factories. Its goals are pragmatic, and result in the discovery, and finally mass production, of technological innovations such as James Watt's improved steam engine (1763–75), James Hargreaves's spinning jenny (1764), and the steam locomotive built by George Stephenson (1829). While industrial experimentation followed the usual precepts of good scientific practice (such as recording every step of an experiment), and, in the early stages, the dividing line between manufacturer and scientist was far from clear, it is distinguished by the fact that personal "wishing or striving" – for gain, success, or simply for getting working results – was an openly acknowledged part of the process.

II

Since so many of these innovations originated on British soil and, even more importantly, their large-scale industrial production and modern marketing were most vigorously introduced in Great Britain, the Industrial Revolution is widely perceived as an *English* phenomenon, and perhaps it is not by chance that the great critiques of industrial capitalism and its consequences – Friedrich Engels's 1845 *The Condition of the Working Class in England in 1844* (translated in 1887), Henry Mayhew's 1851 *London Labour and the London Poor*, Karl Marx's theoretical writings – were written in England. However, in the present age of globalization it is useful to remind ourselves that the wave of innovations associated with this period is neither the first nor the last one in human history, nor can it be seen in national isolation. The entrenchment of agriculture between 12,000 and 2000 BCE, and the invention of fired pottery and of technologies for working metal around 6000 BCE, were, in their way, similarly "dramatic," resulting in an explosion in food production and population that was of at least equal importance in human history as the bio-political changes wrought by nineteenth-century industrialism. But obviously, there are crucial differences between earlier technological upheavals and the one taking place in the nineteenth century, not least the acceleration of information transmission which gave modern industrialism indeed the urgency of a revolution (see Keep 2002).

Several factors contributed to the rapid implementation of industrialism: the increased supply of raw materials (coke, replacing charcoal; iron; cotton), the mass production of goods and machinery, better transport, ready access to capital and labor, modern marketing, and the opening up of new markets. Britain's rise to the world's leading industrial nation would not have been pos-sible without access to global trade routes developed during the colonial expan-sion, and without the colonies as suppliers of cheap raw materials and as outlet markets. However, technological innovation too was a constitutive feature of modern industrialism; not only better machinery as such, but the "improving mindset" of manufacturers, which led to a constant striving for innovation through experiments, and the corresponding willingness to invest – and take risks – in industrial production. The places of production were often places of experimentation; the pioneers of industrialism and their skilled workmen usually had some scientific training, and a wider interest in questions of science. Candice Goucher and Linda Walton stress the close connection between the scientific and the industrial revolutions: "the scientific revolution of the sixteenth and seventeenth centuries led to a new habit of mind: a new way of analyzing prac-tical problems to solve them. Technological innovations took place in spheres far removed from the rarefied and well-educated arenas of abstract scientific philosophy and theory, but they also relied on the research and reasoning skills of science" (Goucher and Walton 2008: 37). In fact, not a few practical inventors – potters, machinists, engineers – were members of scientific societies, as well as employees or owners of factories.

A prime example for the combination of the scientific "habit of mind" with business acumen is Josiah Wedgwood, who was not only the founder of the most successful English pottery works – supplying a clientele from Queen Charlotte to Catherine the Great – but also a member of the Lunar Society, an informal learned society meeting regularly in Birmingham and including Joseph Priestley, Erasmus Darwin, Benjamin Franklin, and James Watt among its members. Wedgwood was thus part of an intellectual network in which Enlightenment philosophers, poets, scientists, manufacturers, and practical inventors exchanged ideas and prepared the ground for the industrial and social transformation of Britain.

Not a university-trained scientist, but a skilled craftsman, Wedgwood conducted the development of new products along the lines of controlled experimentation, close observation, and careful recording, forming the basis of good scientific practice. His most important innovation, the invention of jasper – the durable, colored stoneware the classicist design of which is to this day associated with Wedgwood – was the result of infinite labor and patience: "He spent month after month systematically experimenting with new kinds and proportions of clay, mixing them with chemicals, and test-firing the materials at different temperatures, using small, swatchlike samples. As always, he meticulously recorded each step in secret code in his experiment books" (Dolan 2004: 246). Where the procedure is concerned, this practice is indistinguishable from the search for basic principles conducted, for example, in chemistry at that period, but it is coupled with the desire for practical implementation, reliable production, and, obviously, commercial success. In moments such as this, science, industrialism, and capitalism form an intricately linked trinity.

This close connection with scientific practice apart, Wedgwood's pottery works at Etruria, Staffordshire (founded in 1769), marked the transition from a traditional, pre-industrial family business to a modern industrial enterprise in other ways as well. Josiah Wedgwood's partnership with a man outside his own family, Thomas Bentley, their incessant introduction of new designs and products, their attention to marketing and branding – a circle mark bearing the names "Wedgwood & Bentley" was one of the first industrial logos, stamped on each piece leaving the works at Etruria – and their search for new, middle-class and international, markets constituted hallmarks of industrialism, together with the "distinctive institution of the capitalist Industrial Revolution," namely "the factory system of production, whereby workers were herded together in buildings for fixed hours of labour at power-driven machines" (Goucher and Walton 2008: 156). Sociologically speaking, the separation between a domestic sphere (of family life and leisure) and a public sphere (of productive work) was the most important change wrought by industrialism, with far-reaching consequences for gendered and generational practices. Women's labor and child labor, for example, a matter of course on farms and in small family workshops, were perceived as increasingly problematic after the productive sphere had been designated as "male."

Although the transition from a pre-industrial economy, where the weaver sat at his handloom in his own cottage, to the industrial factory system was much less homogeneous and teleological than has been suggested in this short sketch, and in some areas pre-industrial practices continued well into the nineteenth century, the Industrial Revolution was widely perceived precisely as such: as a social upheaval affecting not only the world of commerce, but the whole of British society. The problems resulting from this revolution, often connected to the fact that a corresponding political change was slow to materialize, offered rich food for literary engagements with industrialism.

III

As Igor Webb has claimed, "*any* novel written between, say, 1780 and the 1850s bears the impress of and is at its core a response to that transformation of society somewhat inaccurately called the Industrial Revolution" (Webb 1981: 16). He goes on to prove his point by including as avowedly "non-industrial" novels as Jane Austen's in his study. In a general way, it is of course true that fiction as a cultural practice cannot remain isolated from social processes; therefore, novels written in the industrial age cannot fail to reflect its social impact, and be it by denial – such as Austen's critical but oblique view of "unrest" disrupting the life of the landed gentry, resolved at the end of her novels in favor of an uneasy social harmony. However, if one looks more specifically at the thematic representation of industrialism in connection with science, it is striking how selective this representation turns out to be, and into what kinds of generic divisions it falls. Industrialism and science are, as I have argued above, closely linked. But in nineteenth-century fiction the two are represented as completely separate entities, and neatly distributed into two different, not to say antagonistic, genres. By and large, industrialism constitutes the setting, and sometimes the explicit main theme, of realist fiction, including the "industrial novel" written by Harriet Martineau, Benjamin Disraeli, Elizabeth Gaskell, Charles Dickens, George Eliot, and other authors interested in social and political reform (see Childers 2000; Gallagher 1985; Simmons 2002). Science, on the other hand, belongs to the more spectacular and fantastic realm of Gothic novels and scientific romances, genres characterized precisely by their repudiation of realist aesthetics. The heroics of invention and investment, intimately connected in the social practices of industrialism, apparently could not be represented as a unity in fiction.

The epitome of science in early nineteenth-century fiction, Victor Frankenstein, does not differ so much in his practice from a scientist like Charles Darwin or an inventor like Josiah Wedgwood: he also gathers material, tries it out, varies the components, observes, and records the results. However, the embodiment of this practice by the Gothic scientist is dramatically different, changing the whole epistemological foundation of his endeavors:

> I collected bones from charnel-houses; and disturbed, with profane fingers, the tremendous secrets of the human frame. In a solitary chamber, or rather cell, at the top of the house, and separated from all the other apartments by a gallery and staircase, I kept my workshop of filthy creation: my eye-balls were starting from their sockets in attending to the details of my employment. The dissecting room and the slaughter-house furnished many of my materials; and often did my human nature turn with loathing from my occupation, whilst, still urged on by an eagerness which perpetually increased, I brought my work near to a conclusion.
>
> (Shelley 1992: 54f.)

Frankenstein represents a perversion of "normal science" in several respects. In the first place, he fails to maintain the objective detachment from the object of his research which is established as one of the prerequisites of science in the course of the nineteenth century. While he isolates himself not only from his fellows, but also from the institution in which scientific experimentation should legitimately be carried out – the University of Ingolstadt, to which he belongs – the description of his bodily reactions shows his too close, too personal involvement with his research. Obviously, his aspiration, the desire to overcome the boundary between life and death and become a "new Prometheus," producing a "new species [who] would bless me as its creator and source" (Shelley 1992: 54), contravenes the modesty and self-effacement expected from the scientist, in real life ideally represented by Darwin – who depicts himself in his *Autobiography* as "a very ordinary boy, rather below the common standard of intellect" (Darwin 2005: 27), before circumstances and systematic application rather than "genius" transform him into an eminent scientist – but rarely found in fiction. From the point of view of industrialism, possibly the most interesting aspect of Shelley's novel is the sterility of Frankenstein's experiment. His creature is a one-off, never-to-be-repeated invention. Even at the creature's insistent pleading, Frankenstein refuses to create a mate allowing reproduction; in other words, he rejects the "distribution" of his new "product" that would be the rationale of scientific practice within industrialism.

The features found in *Frankenstein* – the scientist's self-aggrandizement, his lack of detachment, the ultimate sterility of his experiments, and the anti-social, individualist stance of his undertaking which necessitates secrecy and a withdrawal from society – are typical of representations of science in nineteenth-century fiction, such as Robert Louis Stevenson's *The Strange Case of Dr Jekyll and Mr Hyde* of 1886 and H.G. Wells's *The Island of Doctor Moreau* of 1896. Perhaps it is this romantic view – carried over into Victorian literature – of the scientist as a heroic overreacher, pursuing his thirst for knowledge outside of if not against society, that has called forth the generic separation between novels about science and novels about industrialism. The latter are precisely constituted by their commitment to social questions; they are almost by definition condition-of-England novels observing, and experimenting upon, the collective social body (Simmons 2002). However, science does play a crucial role in realist narratives, even if it does not constitute a text's explicit theme:

> Victorian realism was the first aesthetic form in literary history to have systematically incorporated the methods, procedures, and analytical goals of science. It was also the first literary aesthetic to make epistemological methods drawn from science the basis for the formal principle of order within literary works.
>
> (Kucich 2002: 123)

In other words, scientific principles appear on the level of discourse and determine a text's narrative structure (cf. Levine 2002).

IV

How science affects narrative is best exemplified by a brief look at three realist texts dealing more or less explicitly with industrialism, and featuring the scientific practices of observation and experiment, albeit in widely different ways: Charles Dickens's *Hard Times* of 1854, Elizabeth Gaskell's *North and South* of 1854–55, and George Eliot's *Middlemarch* of 1871–72. In Dickens's novel about the fictional industrial town of Coketown, these features are deployed on the level of characters and events. The chief experiment in the story is Mr. Gradgrind's new method of education, famously based on positive factual knowledge to the detriment of emotional and ethical qualities. The primary objects of his didactic experiment are the pupils at his model school as well as his own children, while the ultimate goal is a transformation of society in the service of industrial production. His experiment is bound to fail because it is deficient in the primary virtue that should accompany it, detached accurate observation. Despite his commitment to a fact-based utilitarianism, Mr. Gradgrind is not objective enough. He is so wrapped up in his "principle" – "Facts alone are wanted in life. [...] This is the principle on which I bring up my own children, and this is the principle on which I bring up these children" (Dickens 2003: 9), i.e., the pupils at his school – that he quite overlooks the growing misery of his eldest children, Louisa and Tom, resulting in the son's utter and the daughter's near ruin.

In the crucial scene in which Louisa has to decide whether to marry the execrable Mr. Bounderby, her father "might have seen one wavering moment in her" (99), but he is blinded by his preconceived theory: "to see it, he must have overleaped at a bound the artificial barriers he had for many years been erecting, between himself and all those subtle essences of humanity which will elude the utmost cunning of algebra" (99). This social experimenter is a bad empiricist: because his concept of life is too mechanical and mathematical, he fails to see the more "subtle essences" detectable only through an organic approach to the living social body. In consequence, the process of discovery is flawed as well: all the disclosures made in the course of the narrative – Louisa's wretchedness, almost pushing her into adultery, Bounderby's fraud, Tom's criminality – come to light not as the results of regulated observation, but through contingent external events. While Mr. Gradgrind is stupefied by the various revelations, they are rather predictable for the reader, in consequence of the narrator's overt dissociation from Gradgrind's educational experiment. The narrative voice does not participate in the scientific stance which is confined to the characters' limited perception of the world, and in fact is a cause of their limitation.

By contrast, the social experiment in Gaskell's *North and South* is located in the story as well as in the organization of its narrative structure. On the structural level, the opposition between the industrial North and the agricultural South is seemingly clear cut at the beginning, but, as in a chemical experiment in which two elements are brought together and begin not only to amalgamate but to be transformed in their very substance, binary oppositions – between North and South, but also between factory hands and manufacturers – disintegrate and are replaced by a new state of aggregation. While this structural shift occurs on the level of the narration, within the story it is manifested in a transformation of the characters' worldview and even their language (Margaret picks up some technical terms, much to the disgust of her London friends, who find industrial vocabulary "vulgar"). The two main characters, Margaret Hale (South) and John Thornton (North), begin by staunchly clinging to their respective semantic poles but soon learn to perceive society as less fixed, as something that can be forged into a holistic organism through growing mutual knowledge. While Dickens's Gradgrind is cured of his aspirations to experiment with the social body, the manufacturer Thornton, by contrast, progressively adopts the stance of an experimental scientist, careful not to theorize before he has his data.

Following his bankruptcy, caused by strikes, lack of capital, but also his insufficient understanding of the "human factor," Thornton determines to seek employment as a factory manager, while pursuing a social experiment which is based not on an abstract "principle" and on deduction – "I can depend upon myself for having no go-ahead theories that I would rashly bring into practice" (Gaskell 2008: 431) – but on observation and induction, namely on "cultivating some intercourse with the hands" (431). In contrast to the methods employed by fictional scientists such as Frankenstein and Dr. Moreau, Thornton's practice is diffident, fumbling, collective, and driven by modest goals:

> I am not sure of the consequences that may result from [these experiments]. But I am sure they ought to be tried. I have arrived at the conviction that no mere institutions, however wise, and however much thought may have been required to organise and arrange them, can attach class to class as they should be attached, unless the working out of such institutions bring the individuals of the different classes into personal contact. ... A complete plan emerges like a piece of machinery, apparently fitted for every emergency. But the hands accept it as they do machinery, without understanding the intense mental labour and forethought required to bring it to such perfection. But I would take an idea, the working out of which would necessitate personal intercourse; it might not go well at first, but at every hitch interest would be felt by an increasing number of men, and at last its success in working come to be desired by all, as all had borne a part in the formation of the plan.
>
> (Gaskell 2008: 431f.)

The result is not an efficient social machine in the service of industrialism, as in Gradgrind's vision. Rather, industrialism is harnessed to social welfare, and the intercourse between manufacturers and workers is transformed from the impersonal to the personal. Thornton no longer perceives society as "machinery," but as an organism whose living parts have to "grow" together.

The concerns of George Eliot's *Middlemarch* are not far removed from Gaskell's, but the scientific disposition – embodied in the story by Lydgate – is deployed even more strongly on the level of narration. While industrialism is not the central theme of *Middlemarch*, the action unfolds against the backdrop of industrial change and social unrest. The provincial town of Middlemarch, with its textile industry and its agricultural hinterland, constitutes a microcosm closely observed by the narrator:

> Even with a microscope directed on a water-drop we find ourselves making interpretations which turn out to be rather coarse; for whereas under a weak lens you may seem to see a creature exhibiting an active voracity into which other smaller creatures actively play as if they were so many animated tax-pennies, a stronger lens reveals to you certain tiniest hairlets which make vortices for these victims while the swallower waits passively at his receipt of custom.

(Eliot 1987: 83)

The narrator appears here as a detached observer, seemingly fulfilling the requirements of "mechanical objectivity" posited by Daston and Galison: it is the quality of the apparatus rather than the scientist's personality that yields accurate results. However, objectivity understood as "blind sight, seeing without inference, interpretation, or intelligence" (Daston and Galison 2007: 17) would, according to Eliot's narrator, "be rather coarse" – inference, interpretation, and intelligence are precisely what is needed to make sense of the "vortices" animating, and disrupting, the biotope under observation. As Sally Shuttleworth has argued, in Eliot's mature works the scientifically minded narrator is more than a passive transcriber of an objectively perceived reality: "The scientist does not merely record; he actively constructs a schema within which his observations are placed. Such an act of 'make-believe,' or heuristic construction, threatens the comforting conception of science as the unquestionable transcription of the unchanging external world" (Shuttleworth 1984: 1). The complex narrative of *Middlemarch* thus functions as a vast experiment in which the focus does not lie, as in *Hard Times* and *North and South*, on the development of individual characters, but on their interconnectedness, on the social structure as such – to the point where individual autonomy, a concept otherwise dear to nineteenth-century fiction, is challenged and the individual strands of the story are totally subordinated to the narrative experiment: "each part of Middlemarch life is related to every other part; individual identity is not only influenced by the larger social organism, it is actively defined by it" (Shuttleworth 1984: 143).

In Eliot's description of the animated water-drop, society is imagined not as *one* organism – implying a hierarchical albeit malleable structure – but as a fluid medium in which tiny paramecia move and interact without a predetermined direction. In contrast to Dickens's and Gaskell's view, Eliot's metaphor suggests that the social "body" is not a unified – or potentially unifiable – organism but an unsettled biotope, churned up by the contingent movement of its inhabitants. In fact, this image is close to Darwin's view of a population modified by the collective and relational effects of natural selection, not necessarily resulting in perfect adaptation and stability:

> As natural selection acts by competition, it adapts the inhabitants of each country only in relation to the degree of perfection of their associates; so that we need feel no surprise at the inhabitants of any one country, although on the ordinary view supposed to have been specially created and adapted for that country, being beaten and supplanted by the naturalised productions from another land.
>
> (Darwin 1859: 472)

This phrase is strikingly echoed in the narrator's comment on the gradual transformation of Middlemarch under the auspices of industrialism:

> Old provincial society had its share of this subtle movement: had not only its striking downfalls ... but also those less marked vicissitudes which are constantly shifting the boundaries of social intercourse, and begetting new consciousness of interdependence. Some slipped a little downward, some got higher footing: people denied aspirates, gained wealth, and fastidious gentlemen stood for boroughs; some were caught in political currents, some in ecclesiastical, and perhaps found themselves surprisingly grouped in consequence; while a few personages or families stood with rock firmness amid all this fluctuation, were slowly presenting new aspects in spite of solidity, and altering with the double change of self and beholder. ... Settlers, too, came from distant counties, some with an alarming novelty of skill, others with an offensive advantage in cunning.
>
> (Eliot 1987: 122)

While some of the old inhabitants are "beaten and supplanted by the naturalized productions from another land," others, such as Dorothea Brooke, find that their personal development has limits imposed by "the degree of perfection of their associates," that is, by collective imperfection. A specifically Darwinian outlook thus constitutes the matrix for the novel's action, while the narrator,

in the role of the active but simultaneously detached experimenter and commentator, adheres to a more general scientific epistemology that could be called
"critical objectivity," in modification of Daston and Galison's "mechanical
objectivity." Of the three realist novels discussed here, *Middlemarch* is the one
most deeply steeped in the scientific epistemology of its time, allowing it to
unfold on the levels of characterization, story, and narration (see also Beer 2009).
As a general conclusion, it can be stated that despite the generic partitioning
observed initially, science, industrialism, and narrative forge a close link in
nineteenth-century British literature – put differently, that there is an essential
connection between narration and epistemology even if this is not explicitly
broached on a thematic level.

Bibliography

Beer, G. (2009) *Darwin's Plots: evolutionary narrative in Darwin, George Eliot and nineteenth-century fiction*, 3rd edn, Cambridge: Cambridge University Press.

Brantlinger, P. and Thesing, W.B. (eds) (2002) *A Companion to the Victorian Novel*, Oxford: Blackwell.

Browne, J. (1995) *Charles Darwin: voyaging*, Princeton: Princeton University Press.

——(2002) *Charles Darwin: the power of place*, Princeton: Princeton University Press.

Childers, J.W. (2000) "Industrial culture and the Victorian novel," in D. David (ed.) *The Cambridge Companion to the Victorian Novel*, Cambridge: Cambridge University Press, pp. 77–96.

Darwin, C. (1859) *On the Origin of Species by Means of Natural Selection, or the preservation of favoured races in the struggle for life*, London: John Murray, 1st edn. Online. Available HTTP: <http://darwin-online.org.uk> (accessed 15 September 2009).

——(2005) *The Autobiography of Charles Darwin*, ed. N. Barlow, New York: Norton.

Daston, L. and Galison, P. (2007) *Objectivity*, New York: Zone Books.

Dickens, C. (2003) *Hard Times*, ed. K. Flint, Harmondsworth: Penguin.

Dolan, B. (2004) *Wedgwood. The first tycoon*, New York: Viking/Penguin.

Eliot, G. (1987) *Middlemarch, a study of provincial life*, ed. W.J. Harvey, Harmondsworth: Penguin.

Gallagher, C. (1985) *The Industrial Reformation of English Fiction: social discourse and narrative form 1832–1867*, Chicago: University of Chicago Press.

Gaskell, E. (2008) *North and South*, ed. A. Easson, intro. S. Shuttleworth, Oxford: Oxford University Press.

Goucher, C. and Walton, L. (2008) *World History: journeys from past to present*, London: Routledge.

Keep, C. (2002) "Technology and information: accelerating developments," in Brantlinger and Thesing 2002, pp. 137–54.

Kucich, J. (2002) "Scientific ascendancy," in Brantlinger and Thesing 2002, pp. 119–36.

Levine, G. (2002) *Dying to Know: scientific epistemology and narrative in Victorian England*, Chicago: University of Chicago Press.

Shelley, M. (1992) *Frankenstein or the modern Prometheus*, ed. M.K. Joseph, Oxford: Oxford University Press.

Shuttleworth, S. (1984) *George Eliot and Nineteenth-Century Science: the make-believe of a beginning*, Cambridge: Cambridge University Press.

Simmons, J.R. (2002) "Industrial and 'condition of England' novels," in Brantlinger and Thesing 2002, pp. 336–52.

Smith, J. (2006) *Charles Darwin and Victorian Visual Culture*, Cambridge: Cambridge University Press.

Webb, I. (1981) *From Custom to Capital: the English novel and the Industrial Revolution*, Ithaca, N.Y.: Cornell University Press.

41
RUSSIA

Kenneth J. Knoespel

Although it is possible to identity a rich indigenous Slavic pre-science (Ryan 1999), this chapter directs the reader to a range of sources and themes that apply to Russia's role in the emergence of natural philosophy and in shaping the development of technology closely related to the Russian state. From a Russian vantage point, "literature and science" has a particular Western stamp often associated with C.P. Snow's commentary on the "two cultures." Given the multifaceted force of both literature and science, Russia provides a rich setting from which to approach their conjunction.

The Imperial Academy of Sciences and Peter the Great

From a European perspective, the foundation of the Imperial Academy of Sciences in St. Petersburg often appears as a departure point for "science" in Russia. While the formation of that institution in 1725 by Peter the Great (Pyotr Alexeyevich Romanov) provides a convenient mark, Russians also had a range of contacts with emergent natural philosophy in the fifteenth and sixteenth centuries. During the reign of Ivan the Terrible, for instance, Italians were employed to build the Diamond Palace in the Kremlin. Efforts by English traders, including Richard Chancellor, established contacts in Archangel as early as 1553. Such contacts affirm not only the geographical range but the continuous presence of trade in shaping the exchange of information.

The foundation of the Imperial Academy itself shows the vital importance of expanding communication dealing with natural philosophy and the rapidly expanding interest in natural resources (see Black 1986). While the European, and especially German, origins of the academy are often emphasized, European counsel also provoked a Russian interest in identifying what was unique about Russian "natural philosophy." While Western history of science often gives special weight to "philosophy" in the discussion of "natural philosophy," Russians were inclined to emphasize the "natural," which underscored Russia's geographical breadth and wealth of natural resources. The Siberian Expeditions undertaken in the eighteenth century offer a strong example of Russian interest in identifying their unique flora and fauna (Knoespel 2004). Another example is the translation of Christian Huygens's *Cosmotheoros* of 1698 into Russian in 1717, which Peter the Great used to animate the study of navigation in the naval schools because it provoked students to think about the imagined uses of geometry (Boss 1972).

The work of Mikhail Vasilyevich Lomonosov provides a strong example of an evolving Russian view of natural philosophy that also manifests itself in Russian literature. Lomonosov is recognized for his work in chemistry, but he also participated in translating classical European literary genres into Russian. His poems on the Arctic call attention to Northern phenomena and celebrate the wealth of learning inherent in the Russian landscape.

> In vain does stern Nature
> Hide from us the entrance
> To the shores of the evening in the East.
> I see with wise eyes:
> A Russian Columbus speeding between the ice floes –
> Defying the mystery of the ages.
>
> (McCannon 1998: 93)

Lomonosov also became a leader in the codification of the Russian language and a powerful advocate for the use of Russian (Cracraft 2004: 220). He renounced German participation in the later Siberian Expeditions in order to advocate the Russian language and also to protect information on Russian natural resources from being translated out of Russia. The recognition of his knowledge led him to be ordered to provide information for Voltaire's biography of Peter the Great. An anonymous French poem on Peter the Great is thought to be Lomonosov's own ironic Russian response to the French appropriation of Peter (Cerny 1964).

The eighteenth and nineteenth centuries

Pushkin remains the most recognized name in the formation of Russian culture because of the ways he exemplifies the language's flexibility. While his work registered a range of natural philosophy practiced by the aristocracy, Pushkin participated in creating linguistic links between European and Russian culture (Lachmann 1996, 1997). Pushkin was part of an elite network of young Russian aristocrats developing intellectual exchanges pertaining to literature and science alike (Mikeshin 1997). The continuous celebration of Pushkin in Russian literature has often been compared with the place English literary history gives to Shakespeare. The comparison shows how both national cultures established practical but at the same time ideological measures. Recent work on Pushkin's legacy has emphasized its manipulation for multiple purposes (Sinyavsky 1993). Pushkin could exemplify at the same time the accomplishments of the Soviet school system in Russia and the spirit of liberation for Russians who left after the Revolution.

Russian natural history involves the continuous rehearsal of the place and exploratory capacity of the Russian language. Russian offered an extraordinary means for creating an urban literature of social and psychological transformation (Berlin 1955). Hardly to be enclosed up by so-called literary history, the work of Gogol and Dostoevsky opened up mental landscapes associated with the growth of cities. Nineteenth-century Russian literature was at the intersection between literature and science in shaping the emergence of sociology, psychiatry, and the renewal of philosophy. Gogol and Dostoevsky were not simply authors but also inventors of a language that negotiated the normal and the abnormal. Their creation of case histories of abnormal behavior gave impetus to the development of early twentieth-century psychiatry.

In contrast to the case histories of abnormality found in Dostoevsky, Tolstoy recovered the epic as a counter to history. In their interweaving of minute idio-syncrasies of individual characters, his works comprise a vast symphonic array that falls together over time like a progression of chords. Just as we think of Dostoevsky's abnormal case histories, Tolstoy worked as a moral diagnostician, assisting generations to discover in art and history means for rethinking or reworking social structures. The group of nineteenth-century Russian critics that includes Belinsky, Chernyshevsky, and Dobrolyubov explored the ways litera-ture serves above all as a modeling device. In his reception in Western literary studies, Chernyshevsky in particular has come to represent a poetic modeling (Wellek 1965), and the interest in modeling and remodeling found in nineteenth-century Russian literature also appeared in the work of scientists such as Dmitri Mendeleev, who worked out the periodic table of elements.

The presentation of models as roadmaps for social change and technological development became even more important in the period leading to the Revolution. While such modeling appeared in myriad political pamphlets, it also emerged in the early interest in science fiction. Works by Jules Verne featured prominently in the development of Russian authors who inspired a population to participate in the ongoing industrialization of Russian urban centers. The early work in radio transmission, such as that by Alexander Popov, also resonated with an ongoing attraction to spiritualism. Although not directly linked to Russian orthodoxy, spiritualism, especially when associated with invi-sible physical phenomena, became a vehicle for the popularization of science and technology, as in the representation of radio transmission in Yakov Protazanov's 1924 film *Aelita: Queen of Mars*. Science fiction helped to integrate the multi-faceted experience of Soviet science (McGuire 1977; Howell 1990). Even now, the development of pre-revolution science fiction remains relatively unexamined.

The Soviet era

We are also challenged to rethink the implications of "literature and science" when we turn to the 1917 Revolution and the Soviet era. Especially in the early phases of the Revolution, literature was regarded as an important vehicle for social transformation and for enhancing science and technology. A rich material experimentalism emerged from the symbolist and modernist work of early twentieth-century poets such as Alexander Blok and Osip Mandelstam. The major accomplishments of Russian modernism associated with the Revolution, however, became increasingly thwarted as the state apparatus came to view cultural endeavor narrowly as a tool for promoting advances in Soviet science and technology. Yevgeny Zamyatin's *We* of 1921 and Mikhail Bulgakov's medical fantasy of 1924, *Heart of a Dog*, both deconstruct the concept of engineering the new Soviet citizen. The bureaucratic manipulation of literature resulted in a split between state literature and work regarded as "inappropriate" or subversive. The suppression of literature that challenged the state resulted in the growth of an émigré Russian literature often represented as the voice of humanism and thus in outright opposition to Soviet science. While a Marxist-Leninist view sought harmony between literature and science, Russian émigré work by figures such as Vladimir Nabakov, both as novelist and accomplished lepidopterist, could play with their intersection. Boris Pasternak's *Doctor Zhivago* of 1957 or Solzhenitsyn's *Cancer Ward* of 1967 offer dramatic examples of literature as an ideological weapon during the Cold War. The twentieth-century poetry of Marina Tvestaeva, Anna Akhmatova, and Joseph Brodsky has established itself within the canons of Russian and English literature alike, just as their lives have come to represent the decades of witness and struggle for survival in Soviet darkness.

The vigorous cultural experimentation at the beginning of the last century associated with speed, urbanization, and mechanization continues to be a powerful global resource for early twenty-first-century cultural aspirations. The works of Vladimir Tatlin, Kazimir Malevich, Alexander Rodchenko, Vladimir Maykovsky, and Varvara Stepanova epitomize circles and movements that included many other artists (Lodder 1983). Art and design as a vehicle for cultural experimentation and social transformation contributed to the use of the theater as a micro-environment or laboratory for social experiment (Zhadova 1988). The work of Vsevolod Meyerhold, the visionary of Russian theater, prepared for the revolutionary filmmaker Sergei Eisenstein. The Soviet experimentalism associated with Suprematism and Constructivism, to cite only two examples, cannot be isolated or contained in museums but continues to influence art in many forms.

During the Soviet period a weaving of the natural and human sciences emerged in the work of Vladimir Vernadsky. His extension of the idea of the biosphere, envisioning life as a force that shapes the Earth, belongs to an early Soviet contribution to the history of science. Vernadsky's biosphere influenced

Teilhard de Chardin and contributed to Yuri Lotman's work on what he called the semiosphere. Science fiction also provided a powerful exploration of the natural and human sciences, as in the novels of Arkady and Boris Strugatsky, which were published in Russia and in the West. In many ways science fiction offered a zone in which ideological discussions could be rendered through the proto-allegorical structure of the genre. See, for example, Chingiz Aitmatov's *The Day Lasts Longer than One Hundred Years* of 1980, which brings together space travel, nuclear arms, and the erasure of memory that includes tradition as well as local ethnicities. The race to the moon or, more to the point, the Cold War effort to demonstrate the capacity of long-range missiles, certainly nurtured the dissemination of Soviet science fiction as well as the Russian interest in Western science fiction. For example, when visiting Sergey Korolyov's library in his Moscow home and now museum, I was struck by the number of Ray Bradbury novels.

The matter of Russian literature and science is found repeatedly in the significant work on linguistics and literature. With its roots in the multilingualism of the Continent, well before the Revolution, Russian linguistics sought to develop programs to study the multiple languages of the Empire. During the Soviet period, interest in linguistic study shifted to the means for assuring the unification of the Soviet Union through the use of Russian. Lev Vygotsky, Roman Jakobson, M.M. Bakhtin, Yuri Lotman, and others demonstrate how linguistics could approach literature and science through research in communication. Each of these figures informed and inspired literary and scientific research in linguistics that became highly influential in academic discourse during the latter half of the twentieth century (Jameson 1972). While Soviet interest in cybernetics in the 1950s certainly emerged through a practical interest in relations between human and machine language, it was also shaped by an interest in material accounts found in research on linguistics. Soviet linguists, for instance, debated the work of Norbert Wiener on cybernetics (Gerovitch 2002). Soviet linguistics must also be regarded as part of a national project of language education and communication. While the Russian language went through stages of standardization, beginning in the eighteenth century, the function of Soviet linguistics as an instrument of nationalization and state propaganda substantially contributed to its identification as a cultural science.

While the Soviet era came to an end in 1991, its history and legacy continue to occupy researches in science and literature, for which so much remains to be studied within Russian archives. It will not do to ignore Soviet science and literature before 1991 and to create a Soviet mythology only from the vantage point of émigrés or Western researchers. The frequently cited resurgence of Russian nationalism at least in part comes as a consequence of facile attempts to "read" Russia only from the Western perspective. The essays assembled by Daniel A. Alexandrov (1993) provide an important insight into the reception of Bakhtin by historians of science in the early 1990s (Emerson 1997: 280).

An interview with established philosophers Anatoly Akhutin and Vladimir Bibler focused on the radical implications inherent in dialogic communities such as "backstreet circles" and "kitchen seminars." Is it not the case that what is truly dialogical is our own "inner speech" that we carry with us and that allows us to live in the "the great time of culture" (Alexandrov 1993: 384)? Perhaps "in the solitude and silence of a closed society, one can hear the voices of a universal cultural community better than in the midst of an open society" (Alexandrov 1993: 325). Also in the early 1990s Vladimir Admoni – distinguished Russian linguist, translator of Ibsen, friend of Anna Akhmatovoa, and defender of Joseph Brodsky at his Leningrad trial of 1964 – projected an era of "New Humanism" that would transform the totalitarian era of Soviet techoscience. The transformation of "kitchen seminars" into the fragmentation associated with postmodernism and of "New Humanism" into a new cultural nationalism partly describes the Russian intellectual terrain since 1991.

Post-1991

Russian literature and science since 1991 has shaped a zone of interaction marked by efforts to archive and understand the Soviet era as well as by a strong impulse to cultural experimentalism (I am pleased to acknowledge my use of Epstein, Genis, and Vladiv-Glover (1999) for the following paragraphs; see as well Sinyavsky 1997). The Khrushchev thaw of the mid-1950s resulted in Russian versions of Hemingway found in Aksyonov, Nagibin, Kazakov, and Gladilin. This was the time when Yevtushenko, Voznesensky, and Rozhdestvensky were heavily monitored, and Andrei Sinyavsky attempted to break away from established canons of literary criticism. In the 1970s writers such as Andrei Bitov, Viktor Erofeev, and Evgeny Popov formed what became referred to as a Russian new wave. In the late 1980s and early 1990s, articles in established journals such as *Novy mir* and *Soviet Literature* even referred to these "new wave" writers as the post-avant-garde. The work of Vladimir Sorokin purposely imitated a panoply of different Russian and non-Western styles in order to disfigure and scramble socialist-realistic models.

While Sorokin's work draws on the Futurist notion of *zaum* or trans-meaning, it is even more closely connected to the work the Russian Conceptualists such as Ilya Kabakov. Here the decades-long Soviet effort to shape an aesthetic based on a materialist philosophy, manifest in a controlled social realism, is dismantled in what might be thought of as a new experimental ontology. Rubbish becomes a departure point for an investigation into the juxtaposition of objects that provoke chance meaning, for example, in Ilya Kabakov's artwork, his 16-volume *Rubbish Novel*, or his *Man of Rubbish*. Works by other Russian postmodernists amplify the idea of a junk world through violence and sexual spectacle. Viktor Erofeev, Leonid Gabyshev, and Alexander Kabakov, for example, invite comparisons with Sade. Their work repeatedly explores strategies for breaking apart normative ways of creating meaning and may certainly be viewed as an anti-scientific force, especially if one has in mind the bureaucratic expression of Russian science and engineering.

The experimentalism that appears in what may be regarded as a new ontology of objects is also found in the exploration of new forms of spirituality and religion. While this work may be read as a reaction against the approved atheism of the Soviet era, it is certainly far more complicated than a simple recovery of Orthodox Christianity. While the renewed interest in religion may draw on the cultural resources of Russian orthodoxy, with its deep-set practice of negative theology, its expression also appears in the recovery of a spiritualism that may be experienced in common objects and experience. Simple silence and the epiphanic experience of mystery or the discovery of the divine appears in a kind of experimental spiritual phenomenology. Literary work that gives expression to an experimental religiosity includes writers such as Andrei Bitov, Yuz Alexshkovsky, Yuri Trifonov, Vasily Aksyonov, Bella Akhmadulina, and Venedikt Erofeev.

Mikhail Epstein (in Epstein, Genis, and Vladiv-Glover 1999: 146–49) has compiled a taxonomy of late twentieth-century Russian cultural movements, providing a useful orientation to complex clusters of thinking that cannot be easily translated into movements with origins in Western critical theory of philosophy. Epstein's list includes ten groupings: 1. *Conceptualism* – "a system of linguistic gestures, drawing on the material of Soviet ideology and the mass consciousness of socialist society." 2. *Postconceptualism* – "an experiment in resuscitating 'fallen,' dead languages with a renewed pathos of love, sentimentality, and enthusiasm, as if to overcome alienation." 3. *Zero style* "is the reproduction of ready-made language models, such as, for example, those of the Russian classics of the nineteenth century or the avant-garde of the early twentieth century, through a verbal medium of maximum transparency." 4. *Neoprimitivism* "uses a childish and philistine consciousness of its games with the most stable, familiar, and surface layers of reality." 5. *Ironic and grotesque* – "unlike conceptualism, which works with language models, ironic poetry works with reality itself at the level of concrete utterances and ideolects, not at the more abstract level of their grammatical description. It is designed to provoke laughter rather than the feeling of metaphysical absurdity and emptiness." 6. *Metarealism* "is a poetry embracing the higher levels of reality, the universal images of the European cultural heritage." 7. *Presentism* "is correlated with futurism but without being directed toward the future. Instead, it is a 'technical aesthetics' of objects, focused on the present, on the magic of the object's visual and material *presence* in human life." 8. *Polystylistics* "is a multicoded poetry, uniting various discourses using the principle of collage." 9. *Continualism* "is the poetry of fuzzy semantic fields, voiding the meaning of individual worlds. This poetry is designed to make meaning dissolve and disappear." 10. *The lyrical archive* "is the most traditional of all the new poetries, having retained a psychological center in the form of a lyrical 'I'."

Gennadij Ajgi and Sergei Zavyalov offer important examples of work nurtured by indigenous languages. Born in Chuvasia and encouraged to write in Russian by Pasternak, Ajgi (2004) became a recognized voice before his death in 2006. Zavyalov (2009) has explored his own Mordovian heritage in poems and essays in the past ten years. The rediscovery of landscape as a vehicle for a new anthropology of cultural space serves as another aspect of current research that remains concealed. The emphasis on the Russian city and urban culture often renders invisible a renewed attention to nature and environmentalism, a commitment to nature that extends well beyond the romantic appreciation well documented in Russian literature and painting. This appears in environmental journals and projects that work as an ongoing exploration of the country itself. One recalls that contemporary roadmaps of Russia really were not widely available until the early 1990s. What we may think of as a new spatial anthropology also appears in the detailed studies of urban landscape brought to Western scholars through the research of the German historian Karl Schlögel (1984, 2009). The monumental work of Schlögel draws together the fragmentary archives of local histories that accompanied the development of the innumerable small Soviet museums such as the Korolyov home-museum and the "kitchen discussions" noted above.

Due to the focus of such work on an established idea of science often shaped by Western experience, less attention has been given to questions involving the participation of cultural settings in shaping both the idea and practice of science in Russia. However, the study of contemporary Russian science and literature places special attention on culture (*kul'turologija*) and civilization (*civiliografija*), with a strong interest in affirming the qualities of Russian and Slavic experience (Scherrer 2009). While such research is hardly surprising, given a post-1991 impulse to engage traditions that were often contorted by Soviet institutions, it must also be viewed as an effort to counter the powerful influence of Western cultural identity. An extreme example is the work of Anatoly Fomenko, a mathematician who formed a movement known as the New Chronology, which seeks to situate Slavic Russian culture in the center of civilization (Fomenko 2000, 2005). The celebration of a particular Slavic and Russian identity that can be juxtaposed to the Euro-American Roman-Christian identity manifest in the eclectic titles in Russian bookstores, and even more so in mandatory courses in *kul'turologija* within Russian higher education. After 1991 the new discipline was envisioned to take the place of the obligatory study of Marxism-Leninism and related disciplines within the curriculum. A new Russian dictionary defines *kul'turologija* as a "scientific discipline that studies the spiritual culture of people and nation and the general laws (*zakonomernosti*) of the evolution of culture" (Efremova 2006). Recent national congresses devoted to *kul'turologija* in Petersburg included many papers devoted to a search for identity and meaning in Russian culture.

While I cannot make a detailed comparison of *kul'turologija* with the Euro-American discipline of cultural studies or with German *Kulturwissenschaften* in this chapter, there are significant differences. In contrast to the work of cultural studies on areas of class, race, and gender, Russian practice, directed by the State Ministry of Education, serves to celebrate and shape national identity. The effort to seek out a particular Slavic spiritual identity that also coincides with the resurgence of Russian orthodoxy resonates with the Slavophilism of th e nineteenth century. I have emphasized the scholarly naiveté of a blanket negation of science in the Soviet era. The assumption that the fall of the Soviet Union in 1991 marks the superiority of so-called Western science would also be a mistake. Instead of erasing the Soviet era, it is important to explore the ways in which Soviet science continues to shape the organization of science in Russia today. The extensive work of Loren R. Graham over the past decades serves as an important resource in this work. I would draw special attention to his recent work with Irina Dezhina (Graham and Dezhina 2008), together with Krige (2006). Many have observed how events in Russia and the West – especially the United States – are accompanied by mutual reflection and distortion (Deutscher 1967: 24). The rebuilding of Russian science deserves to be compared as well with the significant reorientation of science in the West, particularly in regard to the biological and medical sciences. As Russia reshapes herself, the human and natural sciences will participate in her transformation.

Dedication

In memory of Frida Avrunina and Vladimir Admoni.

Bibliography

Ajgi, G. (2004) *Fältens ögon: en tjuvasjisk antologi*, ed. Annika Bäckström, Gdynia: Ariel.

Alexandrov, D.A. (ed.) (1993) *Communities of Science and Culture in Russian Science Studies*, *Configurations*, 1:3.

Andreev, A. Iu. (ed.) (2000) *Istoria I antiistoriia. Kritika novoi khronologii akademika A. T. Fomenko*, Moscow: Iazyki russkoi kul'tury; English translation as A. T. Fomenko (2005) *History, fiction or science*, Bellevue, WA: Delamere.

Bakhtin, M.M. (1986) *Speech Genres and Other Late Essays*, ed. C. Emerson and M. Holquist, Austin: University of Texas Press.

——(1996) *Besedy V.D. Duvakina s M.M. Bakhtinym*, Moscow: Progress.

Berlin, I. (1955) *Russian Thinkers*, London: Penguin, 1978.

Black, J.L. (1986) *G.-F. Müller and the Imperial Russian Academy*, Montreal: McGill-Queen's University Press.

Boss, V. (1972) *Newton in Russia*, Cambridge, Mass.: Harvard University Press.

Cerny, V. (ed.) (1964) *L'Apothéose de Pierre le Grand: trois écrits historiques inconnus, présumés de M.V. Lomonosov destinés à Voltaire*, Prague: Éditions de l'Académie Tschécoslovaque des Sciences.

Cracraft, J. (2004) *The Petrine Revolution in Russian Culture*, Cambridge, Mass.: Harvard University Press.

Cross, A. (1971) *Russia under Western Eyes 1517–1825*, New York: St. Martin's Press.

Deutscher, I. (1967) "Myths of the Cold War," in D. Horowitz (ed.) *Containment and Revolution*, Boston, Mass.: Beacon Press, pp. 13–25.

Efremova, T.F. (2006) *Sovremennyj tolkovyj slovar russkogo jazyka*, 3 vols, Moscow: Ast.

Emerson, C. (1997) *The First Hundred Years of Mikhail Bakhtin*, Princeton: Princeton University Press.

Epstein, M.N., Genis, A.A. and Vladiv-Glover, S.M. (1999) *Russian Postmodernism: new perspectives on post-Soviet culture*, New York: Berghahn Books.

Galan, F.W. (1985) *Historic Structures: the Prague school project 1928–1946*, Austin: University of Texas Press.

Gerovitch, S. (2002) *From Newspeak to Cyberspeak: a history of Soviet cybernetics*, Cambridge, Mass.: MIT Press.

Graham, L.R. (1972) *Science and Philosophy in the Soviet Union*, New York: Alfred A. Knopf.

——(1990) *Science and the Soviet Social Order*, Cambridge, Mass.: Harvard University Press.

——(1993) *The Ghost of the Executed Engineer: technology and the fall of the Soviet Union*, Cambridge, Mass.: Harvard University Press.

——(1993) *Science in Russia and the Soviet Union: a short history*, Cambridge: Cambridge University Press.

——and Dezhina, I. (2008) *Science in the New Russia: crisis, aid, reform*, Bloomington: University of Indiana Press.

Holquist, M. (1990) *Dialogism: Bakhtin and his world*, New York: Routledge.

Howell, Y. (1990) *Apocalyptic Realism: the science fiction of Arkady and Boris Strugatsky*, Ann Arbor: University of Michigan Press.

Jakobson, R. (1990) *On Language*, ed. L.R. Waugh and M. Moonville-Burston, Cambridge, Mass.: Harvard University Press.

Jameson, F. (1972) *The Prison-House of Language: a critical account of structuralism and Russian formalism*, Princeton: Princeton University Press.

Karpeev, E.P. (ed.) (1999) *Lomonosov: kratkii en t siklopedicheskii slovar*, St. Petersburg: Nauka.

Knoespel, K. (2004) "The edge of empire: Rudbeck and Lomonosov and the historiography of the north," in U. Birgegård and I. Sandomirskaja (eds) *In Search of an Order: mutual representations in Sweden and Russia during the early age of reason*, Stockholm: Södertörns högskola, pp. 129–54.

Krige, J. (2006) *American Hegemony and the Postwar Reconstruction of Science in Europe*, Cambridge, Mass.: MIT Press.

Lachmann, R. (1996) "Remarks on the foreign (strange) as a figure of cultural ambivalence," in S. Budick and W. Iser (eds) *The Translatability of Cultures: figurations of the space between*, Stanford: Stanford University Press, pp. 282–93.

——(1997) *Memory and Literature: intertextuality in Russian modernism*, Minneapolis: University of Minnesota Press.

Langevin, L. (1967) *Lomonosov 1711–1765: sa vie, son oeuvre*, Paris: Éditions sociales.

Lodder, C. (1983) *Russian Constructivism*, New Haven: Yale University Press.

Lomonosov, M. (2003) *Zapiski po russkoi istorii*, Moscow: Eksmo.

Lotman, Y.M. (1990) *Universe of Mind: a semiotic theory of culture*, Bloomington: Indiana University Press.

Lucid, D.P. (ed.) (1977) *Soviet Semiotics: an anthology*, Baltimore: Johns Hopkins University Press.

McCannon, J. (1998) *Red Arctic: polar exploration and the myth of the North in the Soviet Union, 1932–1939*, New York: Oxford University Press.

McGuire, P.L. (1977) *Red Stars: political aspects of Soviet science fiction*, Ann Arbor: University of Michigan Press.

Mikeshin, M. (1997) "M.S. Vorontsov. A metaphysical portrait in the landscape: a monograph," in *The Enlightened Person in Russian History: problems in historiosophical anthropology*, Almanac 2, St Petersburg: n.p.

Ryan, W.F. (1999) *The Bathhouse at Midnight: magic in Russia*, University Park: Pennsylvania State University Press.

Scherrer, J. (2009) "Culture and civilization as new/old categories in post-communist Russia," presented at the Center for Baltic and Eastern European Studies (CEEBS), Södertörn University, Stockholm, 25 May.

Schlögel, K. (1984) *Moscow*, London: Reaktion Books, 2005.

——(2009) *Petersburg: Das Laboratorium der Moderne 1909–1921*, Frankfort am Main: Fischer Taschenbuch Verlag.

Shklovsky, V. (1990) *Theory of Prose*, Elmwood Park, Ill.: Dalkety Archive Press.

Sinyavsky, A. (1993) *Strolls with Pushkin*, New Haven: Yale University Press.

——(1997) *The Russian Intelligentsia*, New York: Columbia University Press.

Terras, V. (ed.) (1985) *Handbook of Russian Literature*, New Haven: Yale University Press.

Todorov, T. (1989) *Mikhaïl Bakhtine le principe dialogique suive de Écrits du Cercle de Bakhtine*, Paris: Éditions du Seuil.

Vygotsky, L. (1978) *Mind in Society: the development of higher psychological processes*, ed. M. Cole, V. John-Steiner, S. Scribner and E. Souberman, Cambridge, Mass.: Harvard University Press.

——(1986) *Thought and Language*, ed. A. Kazulin, Cambridge, Mass.: MIT Press.

Volkov, S. (1995) *St. Petersburg: a cultural history*, New York: The Free Press.

Wellek, R. (1965) *A History of Modern Criticism: the later nineteenth century*, Vol. 4, New Haven: Yale University Press.

Zavjalov, S. (2009) *Meli and Tal*, ed. M. Nydal, Jelgava: Ariel.

Zhadova, L.A. (ed.) (1988) *Tatlin*, New York: Rizzoli.

42
JAPAN

Thomas Lamarre

Japan is commonly evoked as an example of technoscientific modernization, of a tumultuous yet ultimately successful adoption and adaptation of paradigms originating in the West. One of the enduring images of Japan, among both Japanese and non-Japanese, is that of a land in which ancient traditions coexist harmoniously with highly advanced, sophisticated, even futuristic technologies. Such an imaginary reinforces a fundamental dualism between tradition and modernity, and between East and West, in which Japan succeeds in mixing, fusing, balancing, or mediating (the actual mechanism usually remains unclear) contradictory worldviews, historical experiences, and cultural paradigms. As such, Japan's technoscientific modernization has frequently been presented not only as the exception among non-Western nations but as a model for them.

There are a number of problems with this imaginary. It presumes, in the West, unitary experience and linear development of both science and technology. It also presumes a unitary Eastern or Oriental worldview or cultural paradigm. But such unities are metaphysical, as are the binary oppositions of East and West, and tradition and modernity. They appear ready to crumble at the slightest touch of empiricism or historicism. Yet, if such metaphysical unities and oppositions nevertheless prove exceedingly persistent, even though they seem out of touch with contemporary realities, it is due not only to our psychic, ideological, or subjective investments in them, but also to practices, techniques, institutions, and discourses that ground and perpetuate them. As a consequence, it is not possible or desirable to dismiss this imaginary as sheer fantasy. Rather, we need to scale down the scope of rhetoric and analysis, and explore actual practices, institutions, and discourses.

This is where the study of science and literature in Japan has something to contribute to the understanding of the real experience of science, technology, and modernity, not only in the context of Japan but also in the broader contexts of the non-West and global modernity. As a first step, we need to pluralize the basic terms for discussion: not science but sciences, not technology but technologies, not literature but literatures, and not the nation but nations or peoples. This latter move – discussing Japan in terms of nations or peoples – runs counter to the received and entrenched imaginary of Japan as a mono-ethnic nation, yet we cannot ignore that the modern Japanese nation was from the outset an imperial nation with multi-ethnic aspirations (Sakai 2000), especially since Japan today officially recognizes its multi-ethnicity – in the context of Ainu peoples, although not, unfortunately, vis-à-vis Okinawans, resident Koreans, and other minorities.

Pluralizing these terms, however, is but a first step. We must also consider how unities such as the nation, science, and literature have emerged, and how institutions, practices, and discourses have grounded and sustained them. On the one hand, such an approach demands some manner of historical account of scientific discourses and techniques and of literary institutions and practices. On the other hand, it requires some consideration of how we propose to study the interaction of science and literature.

Of these unities, the unity of science remains the most persistent and problematic today, both in historical accounts of the sciences and scientific discourses in Japan, and in the emerging field of literature and science. Historians and literary scholars have gradually become more accustomed to pluralizing literatures and peoples, even if they are not yet entirely comfortable with them. It has never been uncommon to acknowledge literary movements and schools (naturalism, Romanticism, diabolism, modernism) and varieties of fiction (detective fiction, science fiction, J-lit). And it has become more common to acknowledge peoples in Japan, in the context of minorities, or populations (women, children), or both. But we hesitate to pluralize sciences.

There are good reasons for this hesitation. The history and philosophy of science are heirs to an intellectual movement that began, largely in the mid-nineteenth century, to speak in terms of science rather than sciences. Ian Hacking (1996) gives a persuasive account of the historical emergence of this idea of the underlying unity of the sciences, detailing the theses that have developed in support of it. In addition, in response to this heritage, those who wish to stress the impact of the sciences on the formation of modern societies tend to posit a unified, almost deterministic historical force, whether their intent is to extol science or to rue its excesses. The result is a tendency to think in terms of a monolithic technoscientific modernization, and thus in terms of unified, far-reaching, all-encompassing rationalization, with a relentlessly instrumental relation to nature and social exchanges. Thus the idea of the unity of sciences accords with and reinforces a massive modernity thesis. The desire to acknowledge the efficacy of the sciences tends unwittingly to encourage a lumping together of diverse fields of rationality under the rubric of science, frequently in the guise of a modern technoscientific condition. Whether our aim is to laud or castigate them, we hesitate to speak of plural sciences or of fields of rationality because we fear losing sight of their efficacy.

What proves difficult is retaining a sense of the very real efficacy of the sciences without calling on the metaphysical unity of science or the metaphysical dualisms that often accompany it (West versus East, modernity versus tradition). Yet we get a better sense of the efficacy and impact of the modern sciences when we think in terms of specific fields of rationality rather than a massive over-arching rationalization or modernization. The case of Japan is particularly instructive here, because, even though both literary studies and science studies have tended to rely on and shore up the metaphysical unity of Western scientific modernity (and, by extension, the unity of the Japanese nation), it becomes empirically very difficult to sustain such unities when we take a closer look at science and literature together.

There have long been studies of the impact of science on literature, and Japanese scholars have produced such a prodigious number of studies that it is impossible to cite them here. Such studies have tended, however, to gauge the impact of science on literature largely in terms of a general problem of technoscientific modernity, with an emphasis on how individual writers responded to it. Yet, in a number of recent studies, there is as much emphasis on the analysis of science as on literature, which marks the emergence of a new paradigm of literature and science. Across such studies there is an implicit "disunification" and a localization of the sciences. In the hope of opening up the disunification implicit in this new paradigm of study in which science is taken as seriously as literature, I would here like to offer some general remarks about the relation between science, literature, and Japan. I will focus primarily on the large-scale adoption of Western sciences and technologies in Japan of the Meiji period (1868–1912), for this moment continues to establish the basic paradigms for thinking science in Japan.

Science, Japan

Prior to the revolution of 1868 that laid the foundation for the modern Japanese nation, the Tokugawa shoguns exercised tight control over the flow of knowledge and technologies in the domains unified under their rule, as a measure to maintain the balance of power among and over domains. If one of the semi-autonomous domains should have access to some technology of knowledge that empowered them, the overall balance would have been jeopardized. Nonetheless, for over two hundred years, the shogunate allowed for the study of Dutch sciences, simply called "Dutch studies" (*rangaku*). The impact of Dutch studies was highly localized in terms of scientific efficacy, and the underlying con-ceptualizations of the physical world were largely ignored, while the applications of such sciences were generally perceived as curiosities.

After the "opening" of Japan in 1853 to unequal treaties with the Western powers, the shogunate began to encourage books on Western science, but it was after the revolution of 1868, in which a group of low-ranking samurai abolished the shogunate and legitimated their authority to govern the new nation-state by placing an emperor on the throne as titular head of state, that a coherent set of government policies for "enriching the country and building its defenses" (*fukoku kyōhei*) came into play. The emphasis fell thus on defense, on weapons factories, steamships, and shipyards, and then on industrialization. The government created a number of policies for the development of education in Japan, which entailed, on the one hand, hiring foreign instructors to teach in Japanese institutions of learning, and on the other, sending Japanese abroad to receive sufficient training to replace the foreign experts (Bartholomew 1989: 49–88). The 1870 regulations for study abroad placed emphasis on the general advancement of civilization in Japan, which included knowledge of Western manners, customs, arts, and institutions. But in keeping with the necessity for military and industrial development in order to overturn the unequal treaties, the majority of students went to the United States, Germany, England, or France to pursue natural sciences and engineering.

The necessity of scientific development, and the single-mindedness of purpose needed to achieve it in a relatively short time, encouraged the idea that there existed in the West a unified science, the source of imperial power. Yet, while this concerted effort to master modern sciences and technologies in Western countries and to "catch up" with the imperial powers imparted a sense of a temporal lag between Japan and the West, those who went abroad found their host countries in the process of transformation. It was an era of university reforms, of institutionalization of academic disciplines, with a new emphasis on science-based technologies. Japanese visitors learned that the pursuit of science in France and Britain, for instance, had transformed dramatically in the past forty to fifty years. Rather than construing Japan as lagging hopelessly behind the West, we might, like the first Japanese visitors to the West, conclude that Japan was entering the modern scene of science at roughly the same historical moment. It is even possible to construe Japan's situation as conferring a certain advantage, as Nakayama Shigeru does:

> While science in 19th-century Europe was still in the main a cultural activity, rather than a practical means of achieving economic growth (as is well illustrated by the issue of the theory of evolution), the Japanese in the late 19th century held perhaps the most modern image of science: it was exclusively utilitarian and pragmatic, planned to enhance the national interest if not purely for profit-making, specialized and compartmentalized. (Nakayama 1984: 207)

We see here two factors that contributed to the sense of science as a unity. On the one hand, shifts in Europe and America toward pragmatic applications, institutionalization, and disciplinization reinforced the sense of an underlying unity, in the form of a pragmatically mechanistic stance, in which "the status of any particular discipline was roughly determined by the degree to which the problems it posed were amenable to mechanical solution" (Nakayama 1984: 96).

As Martin Heidegger would later argue, the formulation of knowledge on the basis of problem and solution constitutes a metaphysical position, insofar as everything is evaluated on the basis of optimization. He called this "merely technological behavior" (Heidegger 1954). On the other hand, the drive to construct a modern Japanese nation entailed an imposition of unity upon previously semi-autonomous domains, languages, peoples, and cultural practices, and the frankly utilitarian approach to the sciences in nineteenth-century Japan derived from and contributed to this push for national unity. Consequently, the idea of the unity of the nation found support in the technological behaviors or utilitarian practices that reinforced a sense of the unity of science, and vice versa. In sum, while neither the unity of the West, nor that of the nation-state, nor that of science is empirically given (but must be constantly adjusted and reasserted), the interaction of these three "codes" (their mutual translatability) produces a situation in which the empirical lapses of the one can be compensated for by recourse to the others.

Under such circumstances, the perception that the newly formed Japanese nation lagged behind the West in terms of its technoscientific development neatly dovetailed with Japan's military and industrial ascendancy. After Japan's victories over China (1894–95) and Russia (1904–5), Western nations spoke with a mixture of exaltation and trepidation about Japan's rapid advance. Non-Western nations began to see Japan as a model. Nonetheless, rather than see Japan's rise merely in terms of catching up with the West, we might build on Nakayama's comments and conclude that Japan's success was due not only to institutional factors, prior infrastructures, and canny government, but also to Japan's entry into the modern sciences at the time of the ascendancy of "merely technological behavior." The perception of a temporal lag between Japan and the West contributed to practices and discourses based on the *radical externality* of technologies and applied sciences.

Writing in 1911, one of Japan's most celebrated novelists, Natsume Sôseki, presented two modalities for understanding the dynamics of civilization and progress in the modern world. Sôseki used the term "civilization" to speak of modern progress, because, from the 1870s, the idea of scientific progress had extended to a range of practices, institutions, and domains of knowledge, under the banner of "enlightenment and civilization" (*bunmei kaika*), which became the catch-phrase for the modernization of society. In the West, Sôseki suggested, modern civilization arose internally and spontaneously (*naihatsu*), while in Japan it arose externally (*gaihatsu*) and thus remained artificial and awkward (Natsume 1911: 333–34). He stressed the externality of progress in order to highlight the malaise of Japanese modernity, which he saw deepening in conjunction with Japan's emergence as a military and industrial power. Similarly, Nakayama writes, "Japanese modern science was freed from its European philosophical roots: Japanese accepted the paradigms developed in Europe as self-evident and were concerned only with mastering them technically" (207). Looking at Japanese modernization from very different angles, both writers emphasize the externality of technoscientific paradigms in Japan. Yet it is precisely such externality that translated into an ability to adopt the modern image of science, or technological behavior.

As such, it is really not possible to determine whether Japan is more or less modern than other countries in terms of its technoscientific development in the late nineteenth and early twentieth centuries. The experience of the externality of technoscientific paradigms meant that Japan was, depending on what criteria we accept, at once behind and ahead of Western sciences. While there surely exist indices (however flawed or suspect) for measuring modernization, Sôseki's comments serve to remind us of something immeasurable at work in the modern experience of the radical externality of scientific paradigms and technological applications.

As such examples suggest, the Japanese experience of the radical externality of technoscience resulted in a profound dualism. Alongside the slogan "enlightenment and civilization" appeared another watchword that captures the seemingly inevitable bifurcation of scientific reason, *wakon yôsai* or "Japanese spirit, Western techniques" (coined in the years leading up to the Meiji revolution). This dualism reprises and subsumes other familiar dualisms that inform the modern experience of sciences and technologies, but in Japan it was, above all, the dualism of spirit versus matter (Cartesianism) that proved most amenable in negotiating the radical externality of sciences. Techniques were seen as part of a mechanistic worldview and practices that dealt with what was extensible in space, substantial, and subject to manipulation, while spirit or soul remained inextensible in space and thus belonged to a separable "spiritual" reality. Adding geopolitical categories to the mix – Japan versus the West – made for a situation in which Western modernity itself appears as a form of Cartesianism predicated on dualism (transcendent metaphysical subject or God versus physical world of matter). Once dualism is imputed to the West, Japan appears, in contrast, as a realm of non-dualistic spirit, substantially different from Western materialism, even as Japan adopted those very materialist techniques.

Not surprisingly, a great deal of Japanese thinking about modernity, science, and technology in the twentieth century would build on Nietzsche, Bergson, and Heidegger, and a strong current of vitalism, in the form of a search for non-dualistic understandings of reality, would inform Japanese articulations of modernity, both literary and philosophical (Suzuki 1995). So profound is this current of thought that a contemporary Japanese theorist, Azuma Hiroki, in his conceptualization of manga and anime, characterizes Western modernity as Cartesian (a transcendent subject overseeing the technical manipulation of extensible materials), in contrast to Japan's postmodern rupture with and collapse of that very dualism (Azuma 2000).

For a number of reasons, then, the Japanese experience of modernization became one of the radical externality of sciences and technologies, which was negotiated through recourse to a fundamental dualism. Dualism, however, was frequently disavowed by imputing it to the West, to Cartesianism or a mechanistic worldview, which inspired a search for properly Japanese non-dualistic modes of thought and experience. Thus, at the turn of the century, for instance, writers and philosophers turned to Buddhism (especially Zen), and, stripping it of its rituals and specific systems of practice, reconceptualized it as the site of a uniquely Japanese form of non-dualistic thinking that also promised to ground a new kind of scientific understanding (Sharf 1993). Such instances highlight how the putative unity of the West became inextricable from the unity of the Japanese nation and from practices, discourses, and institutions that at once grounded and were grounded in the unity of science. Today, the study of sciences in Japan needs not only to challenge these received dualisms but also to think non-dualistic approaches differently.

Here it is useful to recall that a number of historians and philosophers have deliberately challenged the characterization of modernity as Cartesian. Foucault (1970), for instance, situates Cartesianism within the classical regime, arguing that it was the breakdown of classical grids of universal knowledge that prepared the way for the emergence of disciplines centered on disciplinization of human bodies as the ground for knowledge. While it is not particularly useful to posit a definitive break between the classical and the modern at the level of Cartesianism versus disciplinization in the manner of early Foucault, the challenge to the characterization of modernity as Cartesian is an important first step in moving beyond the image of modernity as a massive and unitary rationalization, toward an analysis of specific fields of rationality, without dissolving the sciences into social practices in general.

The later Foucault is a good point of reference, in the seminars in which he meticulously differentiates three different modes of exercising power: sovereignty (juridical power acting primarily to assure submission at the level of subjectivity), discipline (disciplinary power exercised on the bodies of individuals, often via segregations), and security (biopower aimed at the governance of populations) (Foucault 2007: 12). While such a schema affords only a tentative point of departure for the analysis of different fields of rationality, it does have the great advantage of delimiting, and of opening possibilities beyond, the analytics of the West versus Japan, which tend to remain focused on questions of sovereignty and subjectivity, on questions of how power acts on the imaginary. Yet, even though the sciences affect and enter into regimes of sovereignty and discipline, the experience of the radical externality of technosciences tends to dovetail with biopolitical and technopolitical regimes of security and population control.

Science, literature

One of the crucial events in the formation of modern Japanese literature was a series of debates about reforming written Japanese called "unification of speech and writing" (*genbun itchi*). Initially the debates addressed general script reforms, but it was in the realm of literature that *genbun itchi* subsequently unfolded into a sort of movement (Twine 1978). While the idea of unifying speech and writing may appear to constitute a call for a phonetic system of writing, phonetic scripts and styles of writing already existed in Tokugawa Japan. As many commentators have pointed out, *genbun itchi* was less about phonetic writing per se, and more about the standardization, simplification, and homogenization of both writing and speech, for the purposes of scientific communication, general literacy linked to newspapers and other modes of mass communication, and standardized education in Japan and in its new colonies. It was a matter of linguistic modernization, comparable to debates and movements in China and Korea as well as those around the vernacular in Europe, North America, and South America.

Linguistic modernization in Japan frequently adopted the language of catching up or being on a par with the West, yet, as with Japan's technoscientific modernization, Japan's reformations were roughly coeval with similar transformations in the Americas and in Western Europe, where the shift from classical languages toward vernacular materials in universities was happening at about the same time. Japan's "unification of speech and writing" is best seen as part of a global movement of linguistic modernization related to the institutionalization of vernacular literary studies and scientific disciplines, in which Japan might be seen as ahead in some respects (literacy rates, respect for education, rapid formation of efficient postal systems and newspapers) and behind in others.

Until Karatani Kôjin's epochal reinterpretation of *genbun itchi* (1980), the movement was largely construed in terms of democratization, because increased access to literacy and new publication venues were integral to the rise of new political and social movements in the Meiji period, as well as to the spread of education. The received view of *genbun itchi* conflated linguistic modernization with democratization. In contrast, Karatani writes of a radical and irrevocable inversion of the (premodern) semiotic constellation that resulted in the "discovery" of interiority, which consisted, in effect, of a naturalization of the ascendancy of subject over object (akin to Cartesianism). At the same time, Karatani demonstrates, this modern interiority made possible an objectification of the subject, in which the subject becomes most remarkable in its anonymity, which is highlighted against the newly invented paradigm of landscape.

The simultaneously subjectified and objectified subject in Karatani's account of modern Japanese literature recalls Foucault's account of Man as combining an empirical and a transcendental side within the human sciences, a double figure that is at once the subject (agent) of history and culture, and its object. Yet where Foucault stresses how this doublet serves to organize disciplinary knowledge of the human in response to the breakdown of the universal grid of the classical era, Karatani places greater emphasis on questions of (national) sovereignty and (Japanese) subjectivity rather than on discipline, even when he explores, for instance, the impact of tuberculosis on literature. Where Foucault shows the disciplinary ground for humanism and the human sciences, Karatani exposes the semiotic ground for Japanese nationalism, thus casting doubt on histories that conflate democratization with modernization. Karatani's approach raises some important questions for the study of Japanese literature and science.

Karatani's account serves as a reminder of the material limits of language, adding a dimension to the analysis of modern literature that often tends to drop out in accounts of European-language literatures. In this respect, his account bears comparison with that of Benedict Anderson, who posits the "fatality of language" as a material limit on the tendency toward the flat spreading of sovereignty characteristic of modernity (Anderson 1983). For Anderson, nation-ness at once discovers this flattening of hierarchies and stops it short at the boundaries of the nation, congealing it in the form of international relations and national identities. Nonetheless, Anderson sees in the emergence of vernacular literature and nation-ness a politically valuable experience of universal equality. In contrast, Karatani's emphasis on the semiotic, linguistic formation of Japanese subjectivity makes any bid for democracy feel impossible, fated in advance to succumb to ultra-nationalism. Such a stance is in keeping with Karatani's general suspicion of the public sphere as invariably yoked to the state.

We might also contrast Karatani's account of modern literature and art with that of Jacques Rancière, who emphasizes the emergence of an aesthetic regime that abolishes the hierarchies of the classical or representative regime by promoting the equality and anonymity of represented subjects and breaking down received connections between style and content (Rancière 2006: 81). While Rancière carefully distinguishes such aesthetic equality from political equality and democracy (53), he nonetheless sees possibilities for thinking and enacting democracy within the modern aesthetic regime. It is significant, however, that Rancière ignores questions about the material limits of language and about (French) nationalism in relation to (French) literature. Where Karatani speaks of the inversion of a semiotic constellation that imprisons the subject within national interiority, Rancière refers to aesthetic *revolution*. And like Anderson, Rancière sees the universal at play in the emergence of modern literature.

Such profoundly different takes on the political possibilities of modern literature derive a very different sense of the West and of modernity. Rather than simply concluding that Karatani is pessimistic about modernity and democracy or that Rancière is blind to nationalism, we might return to the experience of radical externality of the sciences in Japan. This experience is inseparable from a sense of the monolithic unity of the West and the corresponding prison-like unity of the nation. In other words, at stake in thinking about what Hacking (1996) calls the "disunities of the sciences" is the possibility of dissent and of democracy based on a kind of scientific equality, analogous but not identical to aesthetic equality in literature. As Rancière reminds us, such a possibility would also depend on transforming our image of democracy from that of a process of conflict and consensual resolution toward that of dissent. Looking at fields of rationalities rather than the unity of science is thus crucial to thinking about what democracy might mean in the context of scientific modernity. As a first step, we would have to look at *genbun itchi* not in terms of massive rationaliza-tion or unitary modernization but in terms of formation of fields of rationality in the context of democratization and the emergence of anonymity.

Studies of sciences and literatures in Japan have already begun to break the stronghold of the unity of science, the nation, and the West that remains grounded in the unity of science. Studies of literature and of literary theory, for instance, have begun to build strong associations between specific fields of technoscientific rationality and specific writers or literary movements: Shimazaki Toson, naturalism, and regimes of hygiene (Bourdaghs 2003); Mori Ôgai, bacteriology, and historical fiction (Lamarre 1998); literary and evolutionary theories (Ueda 2008); Sôseki and new psychology (Murphy 2004; Lamarre 2008); Miyazaki Kenji, post-Newtonian physics, and ecology (Golley 2009); popular fictions and criminology (Kawana 2005; Seaman 2004); and Abe Kôbô and scientific classification (Bolton 2009), to name some salient instances. But if the "disunification" project remains difficult, it is because the real experience of the externality of sciences in Japan culminated in a technocratic state (Mizuno 2009) whose impact was subsequently disavowed in the post-war era of renewed prosperity by situating it safely in a militaristic past. Moreover, to embark on such a project, we would have to address the ways in which the two modalities that are frequently imagined to counter modern technocracy – the non-Cartesian and the non-Western – are actually coeval and frequently complicit with it. We then begin to see the sciences not exclusively in terms of sovereignty and subjectivity, or of disciplines and disciplinization, but also in terms of the transnational and technopolitical, beyond the comforting frames of Japan versus the West.

Bibliography

Anderson, B. (1983) *Imagined Communities: reflections on the origin and spread of nationalism*, London: Verso.

Azuma, H. (2000) "Suupaafuratto de shiben suru" and "Super flat speculation," in *SUPER FLAT*, Tokyo: Madras, pp. 138–51.

Bartholomew, J. (1989) *The Formation of Science in Japan*, New Haven: Yale University Press.

Bolton, C. (2009) *Sublime Voices: the fictional science and scientific fiction of Abe Kôbô*, Cambridge, Mass.: Harvard University Asia Center.

Bourdaghs, M. (2003) *The Dawn that Never Comes: Shimazaki Tôson and Japanese nationalism*, New York: Columbia University Press.

Foucault, M. (1970) *The Order of Things: an archaeology of the human sciences*, New York: Random House.

——(2007) *Security, Population, Territory: lectures at the Collège de France 1977–78*, New York: Palgrave McMillan.

Golley, G. (2009) *When Eyes No Longer See: realism, science, and ecology in Japanese literary modernism*, Cambridge, Mass.: Harvard University Asia Center.

Hacking, I. (1996) "The disunities of the sciences," in *The Disunity of Science: boundaries, contexts, and power*, ed. P. Galison and D. Stump, Stanford: Stanford University Press, pp. 37–74.

Heidegger, M. (1954) "The question concerning technology," in *The Question Concerning Technology and Other Essays*, trans. W. Lovitt, Harper & Row, 1977, pp. 3–35.

Karatani, K. (1980) *Origins of Modern Japanese Literature*, Durham, N.C.: Duke University Press, 1993.

Kawana, S. (2005) "Mad scientists and their prey: bioethics, murder, and fiction in interwar Japan," *Journal of Japanese Studies*, 31(1): 89–120.

Lamarre, T. (1998) "Bacterial cultures and linguistic colonies: Mori Rintarô's experiments with science, language, and history," *positions*, 6(3): 597–635.

——(2008) "Expanded empiricism: Natsume Sôseki with William James," *Japan Forum*, 21(1): 47–77.

Mizuno, H. (2009) *Science for Empire: scientific nationalism in modern Japan*, Stanford: Stanford University Press.

Murphy, J. (2004) *The Metaphorical Circuit: negotiations between literature and science in 20th century Japan*, Ithaca, N.Y.: Cornell East Asia Series.

Nakayama, S. (1984) *Academic and Scientific Traditions in China, Japan, and the West*, trans. J. Dusenbury, Tokyo: University of Tokyo Press.

Natsume, S. (1911) "Gendai Nihon no kaika," in *Sôseki zenshû*, Tokyo: Iwanami shoten, 1966, Vol. 11, pp. 319–43.

Rancière, J. (2006) *The Politics of Aesthetics*, trans. G. Rockwell, London: Continuum.

Sakai, N. (2000) "Subject and substratum: on Japanese imperial nationalism," *Cultural Studies*, 14(3–4): 432–530.

Seaman, A. (2004) *Bodies of Evidence: women, society, and detective fiction in 1990s Japan*, Honolulu: University of Hawaii Press.

Sharf, R. (1993) "The zen of Japanese nationalism," *History of Religions*, 33(1): 1–43.

Suzuki, S. (1995) *Taishô seimeishugi to gendai*, Tokyo: Kawade shobô shinsha.

Twine, N. (1978) "The Genbunitchi movement: its origin, development, and conclusion," *Monumenta Nipponica*, 33(3): 333–56.

Ueda, A. (2008) "*Bungakuron* and literature in the making," *Japan Forum*, 21(1): 25–46.

43

MODERNISM

T. Hugh Crawford

Although they long predate the official emergence of Modernism proper, two American poems, both written within a few years of each other, in many ways embody the tensions and, ultimately, the direction of the arts and literature in the first part of the twentieth century. In "I like to see it lap the miles," Emily Dickinson attempts to domesticate what was, for her historical moment, the radically transformative technology – the railroad, which brings a change in relation not just to space, but also to nature, and, perhaps most significantly, to time. Dickinson gently raises these questions: her train is obedient, docile, punctual, supercilious, and "licks the valley up" (Dickinson 1976: 286). And her trope is nothing if not inventive; comparing the train to a horse – a new form of transportation to an old, familiar one – is simultaneously absurd and apt. Still, one cannot help but sense that her attempt to clothe such a massive and distributed technological system in a rhetoric of the agrarian familiar is strained, if not a bit desperate. Dickinson's train is completely domesticated, purely docile, and is even sung to a familiar tune: the old and comfortable hymn meter that characterizes her poetic form.

Walt Whitman, on the other hand, presents the reader with a profoundly different train, in part tricked out in operatic finery, but defined primarily by a simple articulation of its parts, perhaps an attempt to depict both its bulk and complexity. His poem, "To a Locomotive in Winter," first published in 1876 (within a few years of the composition of Dickinson's poem), includes the following list:

> Thy black cylindric body, golden brass and silvery steel,
> Thy ponderous side-bars, parallel and connecting rods, gyrating,
>   shuttling at thy sides,
> Thy metrical, now swelling pant and roar, now tapering in the distance,
> Thy great protruding head-light fix'd in front,
> Thy long, pale, floating vapor-pennants, tinged with delicate purple,
> The dense and murky clouds out-belching from thy smoke-stack,

> Thy knitted frame, thy springs and valves, the tremulous twinkle of
>   thy wheels.
>
> (Whitman 1996: 583)

It remains possible to see his approach as, following Dickinson, an attempt to domesticate the train, this time as yet another catalogue, similar to his listing of trees growing on his native continent, but what breaks out of this interpretation and through the poem itself is the sheer *thisness* of the locomotive, which seems to insist that it not be regarded as a horse, or a mythological force, or merely fodder for poetic idealism. Rather it is first and foremost a thing – a massively deployed collection of objects that must be taken on its own terms since there are no poetic resources to capture its modern essence.

From this perspective, Whitman and his locomotive are indeed the "type of the modern": objective, material, productive of its own logic and necessary form, and perhaps above all, an aesthetic object in its own right. For a student of Modernism, it is difficult to read Whitman's poem without calling to mind the industrial landscape paintings of Charles Sheeler or Charles Demuth, the technology photographs of Paul Strand, the industrial design of Raymond Loewy, or Hart Crane's poetic tribute to one of the most massive single technological projects of its era – the Brooklyn Bridge.

Whitman's train poem describes the first of a panoply of technologies that would achieve large-scale deployment in the first years of the twentieth century. Others include air travel (the Wright Flyer – 1903, Bleriot's monoplane – 1907, and Zeppelins), networked communication technologies (telephone and radio), skyscrapers (the 1913 Woolworth Building in New York, 792 feet tall, built with a steel skeleton, and using high-speed elevators), and of course, automobiles (the first Model T rolled off the assembly line in 1908). In many ways the broad disposition of such massive technological systems makes the first decade of the twentieth century one of the most radically transformative periods in the history of the West. In the decade that followed, these very innovations produced the devastation of industrial warfare that was World War I. It is difficult not to see the art and culture that emerged in the West as an almost desperate reaction to these shifts. The chorus of calls for "the new" – for new artistic forms and an aesthetic to accommodate them – was an implicit rejection of an aesthetic based on a rhetoric of familiarity, and instead a recognition that this new disposition would, like Whitman's train, have to be taken on its own terms.

This is not to claim that early twentieth-century technology determined artistic form, but rather to observe that such visible, material transformations, coupled with more broadly theoretical transformations in scientific practices (particularly in physics and the biological sciences) helped prompt a significant re-evaluation of most older cultural forms and helped produce a modern artistic practice and aesthetic sensibility that rooted around in older, often ignored, or forgotten forms (e.g., Ezra Pound and T.S. Eliot) or attempted to forge the radically new (e.g., the music of George Antheil or the poetry of e.e. cummings).

Of increasing significance to poets, novelists, and artists in general were a series of conceptual changes. Crucial changes to cosmology came from the work of theoretical physicists – particularly Albert Einstein, whose *Relativity: The Special and General Theory* was published in 1920. Of equal importance were the transformations of biology, as a result of the adoption of germ theory, originally articulated in the latter part of the nineteenth century by Robert Koch, Louis Pasteur, and Joseph Lister. Medical practices changed along with the rationalizing of medical education on a scientific basis in the early decades of the twentieth century. Add to these the emergence of psychology and psycho-analysis as disciplines in their own right. The influence of William James and Sigmund Freud helped restructure many artists' sense of narrative possibility and symbolic (as well as interpretive) cohesion.

Albert Einstein's popular *Relativity* brought together his own high theoretical concepts with concrete examples that were the preoccupation of many of the denizens of the early twentieth century, combining a relativistic cosmology with careful explanations of the compression and dilation of time and space in the now-famous examples of the man-on-the-bank and the man-on-the-train. His examples served to link his new theoretical understanding of space and time to the equally new sense of space and efficiency permeating industrial life. Through Einstein's metaphors, the labor practices of Henry Ford – along with the innovations promulgated by efficiency expert Fredrick Winslow Taylor as well as by Frank and Lillian Gilbreth (wonderfully lampooned by Charlie Chaplin in *Modern Times*) – were coupled with the more abstract ideas of a space/time continuum.

Among writers and artists, responses to (and theoretical understanding of) the particulars of Einstein's theories were mixed at best (see Friedman and Donley 1989). One of the more sincere efforts was made by the American poet William Carlos Williams who, in response to Einstein's relativity, argued that poetry be written with a variable foot – a relativistic measure that could respond to the compression and dilation of the poet's thought. He describes this idea in "The Poem as a Field of Action": "How can we accept Einstein's theory of relativity, affecting our very conception of the heavens about us of which poets write so much, without incorporating its essential fact – the relativity of mea-surements – into our own category of activity: the poem?" (Williams 1969: 283).

The new physics probably affected art and culture most with the notion of the relativity of time. It is no accident that the two major works of philosophy published in the Modern period – Martin Heidegger's *Being and Time* and Alfred North Whitehead's *Process and Reality* – take time as a significant philosophical question. Stephen Kern titles his study of Modernism *The Culture of Time and Space* (Kern 2003), and time truly became the playground of many writers. While it is difficult to find art that clearly depicted the nuances and implications of the new physics, many modern writers experimented with alternative experiences of time in an attempt to think through the broader implications of Einstein's work, as well as the embodied experience of the multiple temporalities produced by broadly instantiated transportation systems and the complex temporal rhythms of modern industrial culture. Drawing on Einstein and Henri Bergson (as well as on insights derived from the emergence of cinema as a new art form), many novelists both explored and rebelled against the increasing rationalization (if not fetishization) of industrialized time.

For example, John Dos Passos's *USA* trilogy deploys different narrative styles to mark out the different temporal experiences of modern life. Perhaps the classic novel addressing new notions of time remains Virginia Woolf's *Mrs. Dalloway* of 1925, which explores the lives of a number of post-war Londoners across the single day of Mrs. Dalloway's dinner party. Each character experiences their own subjective dureé even as the world of the novel is regularly punctuated by the striking of public clocks, particularly Big Ben as it tolls the hours of Mrs. Dalloway's day. The conceit of the single-day or circadian novel was explored by a number of high modernist writers including James Joyce in *Ulysses* of 1922, and later, in Malcolm Lowry's *Under the Volcano* of 1947. Each writer worked through the experience of time outside the tight regulation of industrial temporality.

Along with the large-scale deployment of new technological systems and the spur to the popular imagination provided by the new physics, shifts in medical practice – both biological and psychological understandings – had a profound impact on the arts and culture more broadly construed. Once again, the nineteenth century provides perhaps the best entry point into this shift, specifically two paintings by the American painter Thomas Eakins, whose studies of the human body in motion would also influence the understanding of human physiology. His 1875 *Gross Clinic* is a brutal depiction of surgery on a young man to clean out a portion of his femur which has deteriorated from osteomyelitis. Dressed in what appears to be street clothing, Dr. Gross stands poised over his incision, looking out at his audience, which is crowding forward to get a clearer view, while a woman in the foreground (presumably the young man's mother) tried to look away in anguish. In 1889 Eakins returned to the subject, this time with *The Agnew Clinic*. There the patient is a woman undergoing thoracic surgery in a room quite different from the harsh contrasts of *The Gross Clinic*. Instead, this space – the audience, the onlooking nurse, and the surgeon himself – is suffused with calm, muted tones. The operating gown, low partition wall separating operation from audience, and the closed instrument case mark the transition to aseptic surgical practice, and, more importantly, the triumph of germ theory.

The understanding of the mechanism of the transmission of infectious diseases brought on by late nineteenth-century microbiology enabled sanitary projects with the potential to vastly expand the size of city populations without significantly raising mortality rates – those very cities that were now expanding as the result of modern transportation technologies and building practices. And, during World War I, sanitary measures enabled large populations of soldiers to live in close proximity with few amenities, and remain at least somewhat healthy. While it is important to note that during World War I disease carried off more soldiers than did combat, and that just after the war an influenza epidemic carried off even more of the population, it remains significant that the improvements made by modern medicine in sanitary science made it possible to mass and sustain populations of soldiers in ways unthinkable in earlier eras.

An ideology of cleanliness and sanitation, militarized by the edict to seek and destroy disease-causing germs, pervaded the modernist sensibility. In architecture, Le Corbusier would advocate building sleek, bare homes, as high-modern but also as sanitary as Agnew's surgical theater – as an antidote to the traditional housing he called "an old coach full of tuberculosis" (Le Corbusier 2008: 277). Although tempered by a more complex presentation, this attitude of literary sanitation recurs in the work of the American physician/poet William Carlos Williams, who reveled in the opportunities afforded him to enter the filthy houses of the urban poor in Paterson, New Jersey, even as he imaginatively purged these very slums in his poems. This sensibility framed his aesthetic position, for example, in the ideal of poetic form he described in a discussion of the work of his good friend, Marianne Moore: "With Miss Moore a word is word most when it is separated out by science, treated with acid to remove the smudges, washed, dried and placed right side up on a clean surface" (Williams 1969: 128).

Perhaps unsurprisingly, physicians and microbiologists of the period also became popular heroes. The leaders of the Pasteur institute – including Pasteur himself, but also Roux, Metchnikoff, and Bordet – as well as others such as Fleming in the United Kingdom, were widely recognized and lauded (they say there are more streets in France named for Pasteur than any other single figure except Bonaparte). Paul de Kruif's *Microbe Hunters* of 1926, offering multiple biographies of illustrious biological scientists, was a remarkably popular work, as was Sinclair Lewis's 1925 *Arrowsmith*, which depicted the exploits of Martin Arrowsmith as country physician, medical-industrial researcher, public-health plague fighter, and, finally, as ascetic pursuer of biological truth. Ultimately, the high-modernist credo articulated early on in Ezra Pound's plea to "make it new" found support through an emerging set of medical practices based on germ theory and the need for hyper-cleanliness, which is then manifested in literature and the arts, all the way to kitchen design and and the emergence of the suburbs.

Medicine, microbiology, and sanitary science were not the only point where biological studies produced transformations in medical practice with broad-reaching cultural implications. Also of significance were developing medical imaging technologies and new models in the emerging behavioral sciences. The technologies developed by Étienne-Jules Marey and the Lumière brothers were originally designed to study bodies in motion – to use photography to break down the movement of human or animal bodies in action into very thin slices of time (Marey) or to reproduce smooth motion via pictures projected at a relatively high frame-rate (the Lumières). Even as they furthered biology's understanding of motion, these physiologists contributed to the emergence of cinema as both a medical and a popular technology. Perhaps the most famous example of such frame principles was deployed in paint in Marcel Duchamp's *Nude Descending a Staircase No. 2* of 1912, a series of angled echo lines following the path of a body moving through space. Of the high-modern painters, Duchamp was perhaps the one who most closely followed emerging science and technology (see Henderson 1998).

Another significant medical imaging technology, this one with its roots in the nineteenth century, was Wilhelm Roentgen's discovery and development of X-rays as a means of seeing inside the human body. This practice was depicted in close detail in one of the great modernist novels, one that also addressed germs, sanitation, medical treatment, and recuperative isolation, Thomas Mann's *Magic Mountain*. Set in the years before World War I, on a visit to his cousin who is resting in a tuberculosis sanitarium, young Hans Castorp discovers that he too is infected with the disease, which affected an inordinately large segment of the population in that era. At the time, rest in a dry climate (a practice generally only available to the wealthy) was the only therapy. Hans spends many years in his alpine retreat, learning about life from the global village of fellow sufferers, but, more important, learning about X-rays, medicine, and, ultimately psychology and psychoanalysis. In effect, Mann brings together each of the biological and medical concerns of the modern period: germ theory and sanitary science, state-of-the-art medical-imaging technologies, and the rapidly developing behavioral sciences.

Regarding the latter, there are many places to begin – the reforms of the nineteenth-century European madhouses (see Foucault 1988), or an entire range of new and novel treatments of the insane deployed in American asylums early in the twentieth century (see Grob 2007). But perhaps the best place to start is William James's research into brain structure and his articulation of what became American psychology. James's brother, Henry, could be regarded as the originator of the complex psychological novel, and his debt to William is evident. Although William James questioned its epistemological status in his justly famous essay "Does Consciousness Exist?," he does begin to provide a concept of human consciousness that had a broad impact, particularly on literary practitioners. His *Principles of Psychology* of 1890 articulated the notion that humans experience the world as a "stream of consciousness," a seemingly dis-jointed but ultimately coherent flow of ideas and images playing out just below a conscious, rational explanation of experience. Such a concept found favor among novelists who were striving for new forms through which to articulate the modern world. Once again, one can find Virginia Woolf at the forefront of formal innovation, whose aforementioned *Mrs. Dalloway* along with *To the*

Lighthouse of 1927 exploited ideas inherent in James's formulation of that mental dynamic. The reader of these novels often gropes through disparate images and impressions. In *Mrs. Dalloway*, Woolf depicted the profoundly disturbed consciousness of Septimus, a veteran of World War I who suffers from what today would be labeled post-traumatic stress disorder. The chaos and the clarity of Septimus's musings and ultimately his suicide show the power and possibility of this narrative technique.

Similarly, the American author William Faulkner refined formal devices derived from his preoccupation with alternative understandings of temporal processes. In order to make narrative sense of the untimeliness of his own post-Civil War American south, he was radically innovative with his narrative technique, particularly in the now-classic *The Sound and the Fury*, where each character has a peculiar relationship to clock time (for instance, Benjy seems to live in some form of perpetual present), while each tells what is essentially the same story. Each chapter is modulated through the peculiar consciousness of a single character, so that only at the end does the story seem to cohere.

Experiments in narrative technique as they relate to a differently articulated notion of human consciousness reached their zenith in the work of James Joyce, whose *Ulysses* and *Finnegans Wake* stand as undisputed classics of high-modernist narrative innovation, and at the same time as brilliant explorations of the complex systems of representation articulated by psychologists and psychoanalysts. Joyce's work also called attention to the complex function of language in mental processes, an area of concern for one of William James's more gifted psychology students, Gertrude Stein. Stein served as hostess for an entire generation of modern artists and writers – Matisse, Picasso, and Hemingway, just to name a few – as mentor to some, as chronicler to the era (Stein 1933), and as brilliant if somewhat opaque experimental writer in her own right. If high modernism is first encountered as high opacity, then Stein is the leading figure of the era, but that opacity is best understood as a continued, imaginative attempt to articulate and explore the psychological insights she first had while working with James.

Stein's formal innovations – verbal portraits, the spare but exquisite *Tender Buttons* of 1914, and the massive, sprawling *Making of Americans* (1925) – all show a thinker struggling with a psychology of character types, framed in a complex understanding of conscious temporal processes. In her attempts to articulate a "perpetual present," Stein imaginatively engaged a range of psychological questions initiated by James, while her later work re-articulated the processual unfolding event that characterized the work of another friend with an influence equal to or complementary with that of James, Alfred North Whitehead. Initially associated with his work with Bertrand Russell, Whitehead then moved on to his own process-oriented metaphysics. A key moment of relationship can be seen in the relation between Stein's research in "automatic writing" with James's and Whitehead's broader interest in non-cognitive perceptions or understandings. Whitehead's *Science and the Modern World* (1925) is in itself a formally innovative text, mixing the history of science and aesthetics with a remarkably complex philosophical argument:

> The word *perceive* is, in our common usage, shot through and through with the notion of cognitive apprehension. So is the word *apprehension*, even with the adjective *cognitive* omitted. I will use the word *prehension* for *uncognitive apprehension*: by this I mean *apprehension* which may or may not be cognitive.
>
> (Whitehead 1925: 69)

Here Whitehead is articulating a key concept that returns magnified in his later *Process and Reality* (1929). But in relation to modernism and psychology, what he helps construct is something deeper than unconscious processes, something which Stein attempted to articulate in different form across much of her work. For Stein, the sound of words, their rhythms in grammatical structures, provided something akin to prehension, what Whitehead would later call "lures for feeling" (Whitehead 1929: 185). The lure tempts or invokes a precognitive understanding, that which underpins the modern search for what goes on in the stream of consciousness or in strangely dilated non-industrialized time structures.

Another key to understanding the impact of psychology on modernism is the emergence of Freudian psychoanalysis as well as the work of his one-time friend and colleague, Carl Jung. While not necessarily a direct influence on major high-modern creative writers, Jung's focus on the importance of mythological archetypes for understanding cultural structures was very much part of the era. Much of the groundwork for such understanding in popular culture in English-speaking cultures was laid by Sir James Fraser and Jesse Weston. In 1922, Eliot reviewed Joyce's *Ulysses* and described what he called Joyce's "mythic method" (Eliot 1975: 175–78). Clearly there was interest among both poets and psychoanalysts in the function of myth to provide coherent symbols or structures to a fragmented or groundless experience. Eliot expressed this sentiment most clearly with his frequent references to mythic archetypes in *The Waste Land*. Near the end of that remarkably fragmented poem Eliot's narrator – the fisher-king – expressed what many post-war moderns were feeling: "these fragments I have shored against my ruins" (Eliot 1991: 69).

Of all the artists and writers of the early twentieth century discussed so far, Freud's articulation of psycho-sexual processes had perhaps the broadest if not the most scandalous impact. In part because Freud's work is malleable – an adaptive explanatory structure for a remarkably broad range of human activities – it is easy to locate Freudian moments in much of the era. But his work was widely read and often consciously deployed. In England, James Strachey did much to promote Freud, particularly among the writers and artists known as the Bloomsbury Group (including Virginia Woolf and E.M. Forster, and masterfully caricatured by Wyndham Lewis in *The Apes of God*). Freudian themes emerge in many central modernist texts – the novels of F. Scott Fitzgerald, Ernest Hemingway, and, perhaps most strikingly, in D.H. Lawrence's *Sons and Lovers*.

Without doubt, Freud's major impact was his clear, if controversial, articulation of the sexually driven manifestations of human behavior – drives that provide explanations for human practice, deviance, and ultimately, for psychic health. However, it is important not to stop with his articulations of human sexuality. In *Civilization and Its Discontents* (1931), he turns toward broader social structures, providing a diagnosis for the angst that had beset humans at least since Whitman and Dickinson imaginatively engaged the locomotive engine:

> Man has, as it were, become a kind of prosthetic God. When he puts on all his auxiliary organs he is truly magnificent; but those organs have not grown on to him and they still give him much trouble at times.
>
> (Freud 1931: 76)

Dickinson's flesh-and-blood iron horse first gave way to Whitman's magnificent object, but it is Freud who put the human uncomfortably back into the formulation. The technological "auxiliary organs" celebrated in much of machine-age art do make mankind magnificent, but also "give him much trouble." No better articulation of high modernism has since been uttered.

Bibliography

De Kruif, P. (2002) *Microbe Hunters*, New York: Harvest.

Dickinson, E. (1976) *The Complete Poems of Emily Dickinson*, New York: Back Bay Books.

Dos Passos, J. (1996) *U.S.A.*, New York: Library of America.

Einstein, A. (2006) *Relativity: the special and the general theory*, New York: Penguin.

Eliot, T.S. (1975) *Selected Prose of T.S. Eliot*, New York: Harvest.

——(1991) *Collected Poems, 1909–1962*, New York: Harcourt Brace Jovanovich.

Faulkner, W. (1990) *The Sound and the Fury*, New York: Vintage.

Foucault, M. (1988) *Madness and Civilization: a history of insanity in the age of reason*, New York: Vintage.

Freud, S. (1931) *Civilization and Its Discontents*, Boston, Mass.: W.W. Norton, 2005.

Friedman, A.J. and Donley C.C. (1989) *Einstein as Myth and Muse*, New York: Cambridge University Press.

Grob, G.N. (2007) *Mental Illness and American Society, 1875–1940*, New York: Princeton University Press.

Heidegger, M. (2008) *Being and Time*, New York: Harper.

Henderson, L.D. (1998) *Duchamp in Context: science and technology in the "Large Glass" and related works*, New York: Princeton University Press.

Joyce, J. (1990) *Ulysses*, New York: Vintage.

——(2000) *Finnegans Wake*, New York: Penguin.

Kern, S. (2003) *The Culture of Time and Space, 1880–1918*, Cambridge, Mass.: Harvard University Press.

Lawrence, D.H. (1999) *Sons and Lovers*, New York: Modern Library.

Le Corbusier (2008) *Towards a New Architecture*, New York: Barnes and Noble.

Lewis, S. (2008) *Arrowsmith*, New York: Signet Classics.

Lewis, W. (1989) *The Apes of God*, New York: Penguin.

Lowry, M. (2000) *Under the Volcano*, New York: Penguin.

Mann, T. (1996) *The Magic Mountain*, New York: Vintage.

Modern Times (1936) dir. C. Chaplin, United Artists.

Stein, G. (1925) *The Making of Americans*, Normal, Ill.: Dalkey Archive, 1995.

——(1933) *The Autobiography of Alice B. Toklas*, New York: Vintage, 1990.

——(1990) *Selected Writings of Gertrude Stein*, New York: Vintage.

Whitehead, A.N. (1925) *Science and the Modern World*, New York: Free Press, 1997.

——(1929) *Process and Reality*, New York: Free Press, 1979.

Whitman, W. (1996) *Poetry and Prose*, New York: Library of America.

Williams, W.C. (1969) *Selected Essays of William Carlos Williams*, Grand Rapids: New Directions.

Woolf, V. (2002) *Mrs. Dalloway*, New York: Harcourt.

44
POSTMODERNISM
Stefan Herbrechter

Postmodern-ism, postmodern-ity, and postmodern-ization

Like any other "ism," postmodernism is first of all a social discourse that manifests itself in "texts," i.e., all practices and statements that are related to the "postmodern," the "postmodernist," "postmodernism," "postmodernity," and "postmodernization." It is therefore important to distinguish, on the one hand, between what these individual terms refer to, and, on the other, between the different pragmatic attitudes towards them, even though secondary literature may not always be consistent in keeping these apart. This is mainly because postmodernism also functions as the generic term for everything related to the postmodern. But the confusion or ambivalence that reigns within the discussion about postmodernism is also the result of the combination of the linguistic components of the term – "post" + "modernism" itself. One of the characteristics of the prefix "post" is that it renders ambiguous the normal idea of temporal succession and thus the standard notion of history. Post- means, of course, "after" – postmodernism in this sense is the period or historically locatable style *after* modernism and is formally distinguishable from the latter. But post- can also be understood as a qualifier of a category, in this case: "modernism" – in this sense, postmodernism would still belong to modernism, or at least to its related terms "modern," or "modernity." In the end, the meaning of post- is a question of emphasis: post*modern* stresses the temporal idea of something after the modern, whereas *post*modern stresses the notion that something has happened to the modern so that it is no longer self-evidently "modern." In short, it is a problematization of the modern from "within" its own definitional boundaries, or, in other words, a "deconstruction" of the naturalized meanings of modern, modernity, modernism, and modernization. This, in fact, applies to any "post-ism," which means that every usage of post- requires clarification as to what might be the relationship between the prefix and that which is prefixed. The pragmatic value of post- might be, for example, that of a critique, a repetition, a pluralization, even an intensification of that which is "post-ed."

In speaking about the "postmodern" in this way, this chapter is already part of "postmodernism" as a theoretical (or "philosophical") and social discourse, as outlined above. It is an example of the kind of "postmodern(ist) theory" that analyzes and submits what is perceived, but also what is often strategically constructed (or "represented"), as a previous philosophical system of thought – grouped under another generic term, namely "modern" or "modernity," which it allegedly and eventually supersedes – to some form of critique. Since there is no agreement about what modernity is or was, neither as a historical period, nor as a social formation, nor as a philosophical system of knowledge, there cannot be just one meaning of the postmodern, postmodernity or postmodernism – there are only postmodernisms.

The relationship between postmodernism and postmodernity is also not clear. If there is synchronicity between the two, then postmodernism is simply the legitimating discourse that either produces or merely reflects (or both) the underlying social, economic, political, or indeed scientific and technological changes which constitute the "end of modernity" and the transition to "post-modernity" (i.e., something "other" than modernity, or at least no longer quite recognizable under the name "modernity"). In sociological circles, however, there is absolutely no agreement about whether to refer to the social transformations occurring in the late twentieth or early twenty-first century as "post-modern," "late modern," or "hypermodern," etc. Marxist critics like Fredric Jameson prefer the term "late modern capitalism"; others who, in the Marxist tradition, see changes to the economic base as the main indicator for historical development (economism) even speak of "hypercapitalism," or "the age of global capital." Others, who see technological development as the driving force behind historical change (technological determinism), speak of the advent of the "(digital) knowledge society," "information society," "network society," or "global media society." Here, as with the emphasis of the post- in general, the question is one of perspective, or, in other words, on stressing continuity or discontinuity between modernity and postmodernity.

The adjective or adjectival noun "postmodern" is also used in a number of ways. Jean-François Lyotard, whose work *The Postmodern Condition* (1992) is arguably responsible for giving the terms postmodern and postmodernism widespread currency in the English-speaking world, uses "postmodern" in a sociological sense as a transition towards a "knowledge society," with knowledge becoming the most precious resource and commodity, which results in what he calls a "legitimation crisis" for traditional "metanarratives" (narrativizations of the kind of belief system that underpins a modern worldview based on the philosophy of the Enlightenment – i.e., liberalism, empiricism, universalism, etc.). On the other hand, in his more philosophical writings and his art criticism, Lyotard also uses the postmodern in opposition to "classic," which means that it might be understood stylistically as a reaction against, for example, the modern canon, academicism, or the institutionalization and commodification of the aesthetic. Finally, in analogy to Kant's, Baudelaire's, and Foucault's understanding of the modern as a "mode," the postmodern could equally be seen, in a transhistorical and transcultural way, as a kind of "attitude" or worldview, seeking an escape from the modern dialectic of progress and nostalgia, and instead opening up the possibility of an entirely "other (than) time" which would not fall into any modern distinction of "new" versus "old."

The most promising reaction towards this irreducible and messy ambivalence is probably not to exclude any of these possible meanings but simply to understand the plurality and uncertainty as the inevitable fallout of an ongoing process and struggle over the historicization of the present. The most neutral term is therefore "postmodernization," as the ongoing transformation of modernity into its as yet unknown "other," with all the epistemological and ontological shifts, erosions, but also confirmations, redrawings, and substitutions of boundaries that this involves. However, what may best characterize postmodernism as a discourse is that it is somehow focused on the idea of otherness. This derives mainly from its historically problematic relation to modernism, modernity, and the modern, as explained above. Due to a certain hermetic structural circularity inscribed into their progressivist and determinist ideology, the modern (and modernity) cannot be "overcome." The modern understands itself as the "latest" development and it therefore always (already) identifies and appropriates the "new" as the latest transformation of modernity. It is governed by an anticipatory and dialectical hermeneutics.

In psychoanalytic terms, the potentially perverse or psychotic effect of this is that modernity craves nothing more than the new, but can deal with newness only as that which can be appropriated and integrated as already recognizable. In fact, modernity at once desires *and* fears radical newness. Radical newness is, strictly speaking, unforeseeable, "risky" in an incalculable sense, or as Derrida would put it, remains "to-come" (*à-venir* understood as radical futurity). If postmodernism is at once the reflection of the contemporary phase of "late modernity" and the announcement of (the coming of a radically other) "postmodernity," it often comes across as the exasperated expression of the interminability of the (eternally) modern. It therefore performs an ongoing critique and a "rewriting" of modernity with an underlying desire for an other (than-the-modern).

In this, the postmodernist critique of modernity coincides with Heidegger's destruction and Derrida's deconstruction of "Western metaphysics" (understood as the tradition of philosophical thinking that privileges an ontology of presence). Since the modern and the metaphysical both include the very principles of their own "overcoming," a simple break or transcendence would be insufficient because any "over-reaching" gesture of this sort would inevitably be reappropriated as a continuation of modernity and Western metaphysics themselves. Postmodernist theory therefore attempts to erode Western metaphysics from "within," while inscribing itself in marginalized counter-traditions and heterology. It is the trust in the other, or the radically heterological – which must remain ineffable in order to escape its appropriation by Western metaphysical thinking – which might eventually lead to a destabilization of Western cultural imperialism and political universalism.

Otherness or "alterity," according to the *Oxford English Dictionary* (OED), is "the state of being other or different; diversity, 'otherness.'" In a postmodernist context, alterity contains the ethical imperative of respecting this otherness *as radical difference*. This attitude is what underpins the postmodernist "ethics of alterity" – informed by the work of both Levinas and Derrida – which aims "to locate an otherness within philosophical or logocentric conceptuality and then to deconstruct this conceptuality from that position of alterity" (Critchley 1989: 94–95; 1992). The other, thus understood in its radically heterological sense, is neither an essence nor a phenomenon; it is "irretrievably plural and cannot be assimilated, digested, represented, or thought as such, and hence put to work by the system of metaphysics" (Gasché 1986: 103). The ethical demand this philosophy of radical heterology presupposes is the inevitable necessity *and* impossibility of doing justice to the (pre-ontological) other as other.

Despite this logical impossibility, because it questions the "discreteness" of the ego, the (pre-)existence of the modern (Cartesian and Enlightenment) subject and the autonomous (liberal, humanist) individual, all of which rely on identification through the reduction of otherness to a paradigm of difference and sameness, an "ethics of alterity" is the only form of ethical thinking available to postmodernism. To experience the exteriority and heterology of the Other can only be achieved through the idea of the infinite, which breaks through the totalitarian aspect of Western metaphysics by questioning the fundamental primacy of the subject, ego, or self. The idea of the infinite gives access to the other as a primordial responsibility.

Postmodernism and literature

Literary postmodernism is first of all a reaction against classical modernism and against its principle of canonization. The modern idea of the canon and its constant revaluation is based on the assumption that a continual renewal and extension of literary experience occurs through a process of canonical "sedimentation." Reception aesthetics, for example, explains the process of canonization according to a dialectic of expectation and appropriation. It is the "aesthetic distance" in relation to the receiver's "horizon of expectation" which, in turn, leads to a negation of and a break with the existing (canonized) literary experience (cf. Jauss 1973: 177ff.). This "change of horizon" is due to a belated understanding of the new, which is gradually appropriated and transferred into the classical or canonized literary experience. The historical dimension of a literary work and thus the task for the literary historian lies in the constant process of measuring the horizon of expectation against the change of expectation in time. The diachronic development within the horizon of expectation leads to a synchronic situating of a work in relation to the canon.

The problem with reception aesthetics, one could say, is that it logically denies the possibility of any true reception taking place. It is impossible to determine a horizon of expectation that a "new" literary work could encounter or change, since this horizon is by definition always receding. How a break with an existing horizon can actually occur must therefore remain inexplicable, because it can only be observed *après coup*, after the fact. The canon can thus never be questioned in its organic continuity. The difference or distance the "new" literary work promises serves only insofar as it affirms a tradition. Its difference is there to be reduced, and its otherness to be appropriated. A text resisting this idea of horizon, or a completely "unexpected" text, would have to remain unreadable and unreceivable. But it is precisely this unreadable text which represents the hope of bringing about a change of horizon. It is the resistance to an aesthetics of reception which makes an unreadable text the most urgent text to be "received." But it can be received only outside the (horizon of the) canon and thus according to an ethics of alterity, which would be an ethics based on a radical idea of the reception of the unclassifiable. It is in following this form of logic that Roland Barthes (1977) called the unclassifiable text (as opposed to the "readerly" or "writerly" text) "receivable."

Strictly speaking, one never really *receives* a text, because one always only *re*-ceives it, one "captures it back/again" (Latin *re-capere*), thus presupposing an object (text), a subject (reader), and a first "capture." To receive the (un)receivable text (in any text) is to receive it as an impossible gift. This is valid for any kind of reading or process of receiving, but in particular it is true for a context that desires itself to be "postmodern(ist)," that is, a discourse that questions the very newness of the new and thus modern. One might argue therefore that to be able to receive postmodernist literature (which is far from being new) and to realize what might be radically other in it – postmodern (as belonging to a "postmodernity" to come, in the strict sense) – a different form of reading is needed, namely a reading that is conscious of its belatedness and bypasses the question of originality and the modernist logic of the avant-garde. This means, of course, reading "outside" of any canon, and ideally even before any canonization sets in – which explains the two main formal characteristics of postmodernist literature and art in general: the frequent use of "pastiche" and the mixing of modern "high" and "low" cultural forms.

Postmodernist literature thus often gives the impression that it is a kind of waiting for an impossible event (the "new" or unexpected other), while writing goes on and endlessly produces fiction, which writes about the (im)possibility of writing the event. There is a kind of performativity and circularity, sometimes even an apocalypticism, which seeks to invoke, conjure up, and express the ineffable. This is also the reason that intertextuality, or the notion of the "intertext," can be seen as one of the central presuppositions of many post-modernist theories. Every text is not only an open system but is also never identical to itself. It is part of a system of textual relations, a form of generalized textuality which alone guarantees the "readability" of our cultural universe. Thus, intertextuality is the very condition of perceiving social reality and has thus quasi-ontological status, which explains the proliferation and *mise-en-abyme* or potentially infinite self-embedding of narratives about narratives and the fragmentation and loss, the dissemination of identities and texts or fictions in postmodernist writing. In a textual world, intertextuality is the only form of social relation with either the present or the past (history as layers of textuality). In a textual world where every fiction is only another text, metafictionality – fiction that narrates its own fictionality – becomes virtually interchangeable with intertextuality.

In postmodernist fiction, both metafictionality and intertextuality are employed to demonstrate the constructed (fictional) nature of human reality. In so doing, postmodernist metafiction serves an important heuristic purpose in helping to understand contemporary ideas about reality – from the idea of general textuality as a "prisonhouse of language" to "new forms of the fantastic, fabulatory extravaganzas, magic realism (Salman Rushdie, Gabriel García Márquez, Clive Sinclair, Graham Swift, D.M. Thomas, John Irving)" (Waugh 1984: 9). The generalized notion of textuality thus often leads to a celebration of the power of fiction and fictionalization seen as equivalent to a reality- and world-building process. Some of the most frequent framing devices to be found in postmodernist metafiction thus include:

> stories within stories, characters reading about their own fictional lives, self-consuming worlds or mutually contradictory situations, Chinese-box structures, which contest the reality of each individual "box" through a nesting of narrators, "fictions of infinity," confusion of ontological levels, through the incorporation of visions, dreams, hallucinatory states and pictorial representations which are finally indistinct from the apparently "real" [thus reaching the conclusion that there] is ultimately no distinction between "framed" and "unframed." There are only levels of form. There is ultimately only content perhaps, but it will never be discovered in a "natural" unframed state.
>
> (Waugh 1984: 31)

Postmodernist metafictional novels usually display a (meta)linguistic awareness and linguistic playfulness. Metafiction draws attention to the process of "recontextualization" that occurs when language is used aesthetically, so that their embraced conception of reality tends towards one of what Waugh calls the two "poles of metafiction" (Waugh 1984: 53). Either they constitute a "parody" (or rather, the whole world is a parody), or they are predominantly "metafictional at the level of the signifier." One could say that it is the importance attributed to language as the only access to reality which assumes a crucial role in the reception of both postmodernist fiction and theory. In the context of a postmodernist ethics of alterity, it is of course important that this alterity be articulated in language. The prospective articulation of otherness, and the fundamental possibility for a dialog with the other, is vital to prevent the foreclosure of otherness and difference. Therefore the underlying assumption is that there must be "something" outside (inter)textuality. Only a problematized notion of referentiality allows at once for the respect of difference, the existence of alterity, and a possibility for an experience of otherness.

Postmodernism and science

The relationship between postmodernism, science, and technology is highly problematic. Modern science, as the product of Enlightenment epistemology, is founded on and inextricably bound up with "Western metaphysics" (realism, empiricism). On the other hand, modern science also contains a critique of some fundamental metaphysical principles, such as "God," and a rejection of all forms of "mysticism" (rationalism). It is therefore no surprise that there are both technophile and technophobic aspects in postmodern thought. Historically, the postmodern period coincides with the rise of a new and intensified scientific and technological age, roughly beginning after World War II, with the rise of nuclear technology, the proliferation of the mass media, new forms of telecommunication, and, eventually, digitalization. Ideologically, postmodernism as a style and mode of thought often expresses skepticism and even resistance to these technological changes, from the beginnings of environmentalism, the Green and anti-nuclear movements, to digital neo-Luddism.

Nevertheless, as already mentioned, Lyotard's *The Postmodern Condition*, the main philosophical manifesto of postmodernism, is a report on the cultural and political changes within the coming "knowledge (or information) society," and its democratizing potential as far as the redistribution of wealth through the accessibility and circulation of knowledge is concerned. In general, where technological change is connected to communication and its extension to virtually all material and cultural aspects, postmodernism tends to be enthusiastic about its pluralizing and networking potential. Wherever technological change means technocracy or the rule of an anonymous technoscientific capitalist apparatus combined with an ideology of technological determinism, postmodernism tends to foreground its skepticism. This is mainly connected to postmodernism's attitude towards plurality and heterology as explained above.

Postmodern techno-skepticism is mainly concerned with the homogenizing power of technoscientific capitalism and bureaucracy, on the one hand, and, on the other, with their connected "derealizing tendencies" – a stance mainly following the writings of Jean Baudrillard. As opposed to the uniformizing potential of new (communicational) technologies and global technoscientific capitalism, postmodernism generally advocates alternative and subjugated forms of knowledge in line with its fundamental value-pluralism, its privileging of difference over sameness, and its openness towards forms of otherness. It opposes the exclusivity of modern, rationalist, instrumental, and empiricist criteria for scientificity and seeks allies in what could be labeled "postmodernizing" tendencies within scientific discourse itself.

Underpinning postmodernism is the critique of the modern Enlightenment tradition, with its underlying rationalism, universalism, and liberalism, a critique to a certain extent also taken up within the philosophy of science itself. Works like Kuhn's *The Structure of Scientific Revolutions* (1962), or Paul Feyerabend's *Against Method* (1979) contributed to an opening up of science towards questions usually asked by the social sciences and the humanities, where science is treated as a historically and culturally specific "practice," and the relationship between science, politics, and economics and their influence on the "production" of knowledge is investigated, and the role of cultural prejudice in scientific institutions is criticized. Other aspects include the representation of science, scientists, and scientific institutions in society, and, generally, the social or cultural "constructedness" of scientific knowledge.

These questions became the starting point for the institutionalization of the so-called (postmodern or critical) science studies, or cultural studies of science, which ultimately provoked the infamous "science wars" and the related "Sokal affair." Alan Sokal placed in *Social Text* an apparently self-evidently "nonsensical" parody article on the alleged postmodern exposure by quantum physics of the constructedness of "gravity," and this can certainly be seen as proof of the fashionable and unreflected character of some postmodernist jargon. On the other hand, however, it can also serve to indicate that a new dialog between certain quarters of the sciences and especially the "new" and digital sciences (bio- , info- , cogno- and nanoscience, for example) and the "new" (digital theoretical and cultural) humanities is all the more desirable.

In general, what might best characterize the coincidence of socio-cultural postmodernization and scientific-technological change in the late twentieth and early twenty-first centuries is the effect of a new permeability between science and culture – a certain "culturalization" of science as a practice, combined with an increased "presence" of science within culture – which can also be seen in the rise of a genre like "science fiction." It is indeed the blurring of the boundary between fact and fiction that erodes modern rationalist scientificity and at the same time allows science to become arguably the most important source of cultural change (as in the notion of "technoculture"). Usually, certain shifts within the sciences, namely towards emphasizing notions like entropy, relativity, complexity, and chaos, are seen as signs of science's own postmodernization. Chaos theory, quantum mechanics, artificial intelligence, or self-organization (emergence) and systems theory have thus become areas in which analogies between the sciences and the humanities have been strongest.

Postmodern – science – fiction

Given the mentioned blurring of the boundaries between culture, science, and technology – which is very much a logical consequence of the blurring of "high" and "low," elite and mass culture in postmodernism – it is in many ways science fiction which can act as a "symptom" of technocultural postmodernization. As the editor of *Liquid Metal* explains, "contemporary science fiction is immersed in the symbols, signs and polymorphous impressions of postmodernity and postmodernism. ... The sense of a postmodern world in a state of flux is replayed again and again in contemporary science fiction" (Redmond 2004: 218). In addition, the blurring of any clear boundaries between science, fiction, and postmodernism cuts both ways, so that, as Andrew Butler explains, "much postmodernism reads like sf" (Redmond 2004: 137).

As in postmodernist writing in general, so also in science fiction in particular, metafictionality, or the awareness of a text's own fictionality or the impossibility of a clear-cut distinction between fact and fiction ("faction") becomes a main aspect of contemporary science fiction. In terms of science fiction, Lyotard's postmodern "incredulity towards metanarratives" involves an ambivalent playfulness towards science and technology. In addition, "if postmodernism [following Fredric Jameson] functions according to or even *is* the logic of late capitalism, then this places cyberpunk as central to the understanding of the period" (Butler 2004: 141). The underlying techno-skepticism of cyberpunk exposes scientific reality as a simulacrum or a special kind of fiction, which nevertheless has "real" (social, economic, political) effects. This explains the prevalence of "schizophrenic" denegation, cynicism, and pastiche, for example, in novels like William Gibson's *Neuromancer* (1984), films like Ridley Scott's *Blade Runner* (1982), and the writings of Philip K. Dick and J.G. Ballard. Science fiction in fact runs parallel to and in some instances even anticipates postmodern theory (cf. Baudrillard's use of science fiction and theory), mainly because literary science fiction itself can be understood as a reaction against "high mod-ernism." Brian McHale even uses science fiction as the paradigmatic postmodern literary genre which is "openly and avowedly ontological ... 'world-building' fiction, laying bare the process of fictional world-making itself" (McHale 1992: 12).

Science fiction has turned "ontological" not just in aesthetic literary terms. In reaching a wide audience, thanks to film, science fiction has entered postmodern everyday life experience with its ubiquitous references to aliens, space, tele-portation, cyborgization, simulation, and virtualization, which has created a kind of sci-fi cultural imaginary, also fueled by the invasion and ubiquity of high-tech appliances in everyday cultural practice. It is, according to Jonathan Benison, precisely as a "mode rather than as a genre that SF speaks to postmodernity," whereby science fiction "emerges through social theory as one way of talking about certain recent developments in advanced industrial society" (Benison 1992: 139). In this sense, science fiction is a cultural "symptom" of late capitalism, an oblique representation of Jameson's understanding of postmodernism as "logic of late capitalism." It is thus possible to analyze science fiction in the light of postmodernist style and technique (metafictionality, self-referentiality, pastiche, etc.), but at the same time it is also a reflection of "social post-modernization" (Benison 1992: 141).

Science fiction as the fictional construction of a simulated world loses its formerly didactic utopian/dystopian intention and instead is accepted as a kind of new (hyper)realism connected with the role of science and technology and as a way of working through the unconscious desires and anxieties of late-capitalist technoscientific society. The main coincidence between postmodernist theory and science fiction lies in a common interest or "specialization" in encountering the other, with all its intended or unintended psychotic-paranoid, ambivalent, derealizing, and reversing side-effects. Undermining the ontological foundations of the "real" world as only one of many "possible" worlds leads to a general fictionalization that can be experienced as both liberating and terrifying. Postmodernism and science fiction play with both freedom and terror: the impression of, on the one hand, increasing control over the world, and, on the other, the world's utter unknowability, a sense of absolute loss of control over both self and world. Through its generalization within the contemporary Western imaginary, science fiction as a separate identifiable literary or filmic genre has ceased to exist as such, but "survives" as arguably the central driving force in contemporary fantasy, fictionality, and simulation in cultural practice.

In conclusion, it may be said that postmodernism as a discourse concerned with the social transformation taking place in the second half of the twentieth and the beginning of the twenty-first centuries is unthinkable without taking into consideration the fundamental transition from an industrial to a post-industrial society, and from a nuclear-energy to a digital-information technology base. On the other hand, postmodernism as formal style and mode of thinking may very well have some lasting effect on the way in which science is perceived and the way it perceives itself, even if this is not (yet) always admitted or admissible in "serious" scientific circles.

Bibliography

Barth, J. (1982) *The Literature of Exhaustion and the Literature of Replenishment*, Northridge, Ca.: Lord John Press.

Barthes, R. (1977) *Roland Barthes*, trans. R. Howard, London: Macmillan.

Baudrillard, J. (1994) *Simulacra and Simulation*, trans. S.F. Glaser, Ann Arbor: University of Michigan Press.

Benison, J. (1992) "Science fiction and postmodernity," in F. Barker, P. Hulme, and M. Iversen (eds) *Postmodernism and the Re-Reading of Modernity*, Manchester: Manchester University Press, pp. 138–58.

Bertens, H. (1995) *The Idea of the Postmodern: a history*, London: Routledge.

Best, S. and Kellner, D. (2001) *The Postmodern Adventure: science, technology, and cultural studies at the third millennium*, London: Routledge.

Butler, A.M. (2004) "Postmodernism and science fiction," in E. James and F. Mendesohn (eds) *The Cambridge Companion to Science Fiction*, Cambridge: Cambridge University Press, pp. 137–48.

Critchley, S. (1989) "The chiasmus: Levinas, Derrida and the ethical demand for deconstruction," *Textual Practice*, 3(1): 91–106.

——(1992) *The Ethics of Deconstruction: Derrida and Levinas*, Oxford: Blackwell.

Deleuze, G. and Guattari, F. (1987) *A Thousand Plateaus: capitalism and schizophrenia 2*, trans. B. Massumi, Minneapolis: University of Minnesota Press.

Derrida, J. (1987) *The Post Card: from Socrates to Freud and beyond*, trans. A. Bass, Chicago: University of Chicago Press.

——(1994) *Specters of Marx: the state of the debt, the work of mourning, and the new international*, trans. P. Kamuf, intro. B. Magnus and S. Cullenberg, New York and London: Routledge.

Ermarth, E.D. (1992) *Sequel to History: postmodernism and the crisis of representational time*, Princeton: Princeton University Press.

Feyerabend, P. (1979) *Against Method: outline of an anarchistic theory of knowledge*, London: Verso.

Gasché, R. (1986) *The Tain of the Mirror: Derrida and the philosophy of reflection*, Cambridge, Mass.: Harvard University Press.

Hayles, N.K. (ed.) (1991) *Chaos and Order: complex dynamics in literature and science*, Chicago: University of Chicago Press.

Heise, U.K. (2004) "Science, technology, and postmodernism," in S. Connor (ed.) *The Cambridge Companion to Postmodernism*, Cambridge: Cambridge University Press, pp. 136–67.

Hutcheon, L. (1988) *A Poetics of Postmodernism: history, theory, fiction*, London: Routledge.

Jameson, F. (1991) *Postmodernism, or, the cultural logic of late capitalism*, London: Verso.

Jauss, H.R. (1973) *Literaturgeschichte als Provokation*, Frankfurt am Main: Suhrkamp.

Kuberski, P. (1994) *Chaosmos: literature, science, and theory*, Albany: State University of New York Press.

Kuhn, T.S. (1962) *The Structure of Scientific Revolutions*, Chicago: University of Chicago Press.

Levinas, E. (1982) *En Découvrant l'existence avec Husserl et Heidegger*, Paris: Vrin.

Lyotard, J.-F. (1991) *The Inhuman: reflections on time*, trans. G. Bennington and R. Bowlby, Cambridge: Polity Press.

——(1992) *The Postmodern Explained to Children: correspondence 1982–1985*, trans. and ed. J. Pefanis and M. Thomas, London: Turnaround.

——(1994) *The Postmodern Condition: a report on knowledge*, trans. G. Bennington and B. Massumi, Manchester: Manchester University Press.

McHale, B. (1987) *Postmodernist Fiction*, New York and London: Methuen.

——(1992) *Constructing Postmodernism*, New York and London: Routledge.

Redmond, S. (ed.) (2004) *Liquid Metal: the science fiction film reader*, London: Wallflower Press.

Rose, M.A. (1991) *The Post-Modern and the Post-Industrial: a critical analysis*, Cambridge: Cambridge University Press.

Waugh, P. (1984) *Metafiction: the theory and practice of self-conscious fiction*, London: Methuen.

INDEX